AF674002

TEASING QUESTIONS

TEASING QUESTIONS

EXPLORING DISCONNECTS IN CONTEMPORARY INDIA

Selected Speeches

2007–2012

of Vice President of India

M. Hamid Ansari

NIYOGI
BOOKS

Published by
NIYOGI BOOKS
D-78, Okhla Industrial Area, Phase-I
New Delhi-110 020, INDIA
Tel: 91-11-26816301, 49327000
Fax: 91-11-26810483, 26813830
email: niyogibooks@gmail.com
website: www.niyogibooksindia.com

Cover Design: Shashi Bhushan Prasad
Layout: Sarojini Gosain

ISBN: 978-93-83098-07-1
Publication: 2014

Printed at: Niyogi Offset Pvt. Ltd., New Delhi, India

To

Salma
Poor compensation for long hours of infuriating silence on my part

THEMES

“We need instrumentalities of communication, education, institutions and policies to help negotiate the country's myriad diversities in the years ahead ... Unchanging and timeless, India is changing and is being born anew, its diversities adding new harmonies, colour and riches to the landscape and mindscape

PREFACE

An occupational hazard associated with the office of the Vice President of India is the demand for a fair amount of public speaking in response to invitations to formal functions.

These include university convocations and inaugural addresses to national and international conferences, seminars, professional gatherings and the like. The themes of the addresses or speeches are sometimes defined by the occasion; at others, chosen by the speaker.

The present volume consists of a selection of these speeches made by me in the five years of my first tenure and the first five months of my second tenure. They cover the period from August 2007 to December 2012.

The rationale for exploring disconnects is to identify the pitfalls and help prepare ourselves for avoiding them. Such an intellectual endeavour, to some extent at least, enlightens and precedes corrective action.

In selecting the theme or subject of a speech, my intention most of the time was to go beyond the obvious, mutely or boldly official, and to focus instead on the challenges that we as a people and a society are facing today or are likely to face in the foreseeable future. I found resonance of my approach in a passage, cited on the preceding page, penned by B.G. Verghese in his book *Rage, Reconciliation and Security: Managing India's Diversities.*

It has been said with much justice that there are times when the present breaks the shackles of the past to create the future, and there are also times when the past creates the future by breaking the shackles of the present. Perhaps we in present-day India need to deal with both imperatives; hence the importance of correct choices. If the perspectives delineated in this volume succeed in some measure in drawing the reader's attention to these, I would consider my effort amply rewarded.

It is always an author's pleasant duty to acknowledge and thank many visible and less visible friends and colleagues whose ideas and help give shape to the end product. Foremost amongst them was Shri P. Harish of the Indian Foreign Service, who, as an Officer on Special Duty in the Vice President's Secretariat, helped me throughout my first term with his unmatched capacity for locating relevant material for many of the subjects covered in these speeches

Finally, I would like to place on record my gratitude to Niyogi Books and the publisher Shri Bikash D. Niyogi and to Smt Mohua Mitra whose diligent efforts were so critical to the publication of this volume.

M. Hamid Ansari
Vice President of India
July 2013

The Selected Speeches
2007-2012

Agriculture and Rural Development

"Everything else can wait but agriculture cannot wait

Fourth Convocation

Sher-e-Kashmir University of Agricultural Sciences and Technology of Kashmir
Srinagar
25 November 2007

Rakht kusha ba-Kashmer, kohe tal-o-daman mee-gar
Sabza jahaan jahaan bibeen, laleh chaman chaman ni-gar

I deem it a privilege to be the Chief Guest at the Fourth Convocation of the Sher-e-Kashmir University of Agricultural Sciences and Technology.

I am not a stranger to Jammu and Kashmir, except in my new responsibility. I consider it a good sign that its focus is on the world of learning. The opportunity to meet the youth of the state, who symbolise the Kashmir of tomorrow, is precious and invaluable.

Graduation is an important aspect of academic life, for the institution and for the students. A university is a place of learning where the students learn to think, acquire knowledge, polish their thought process and learn a thing or two about how the world functions in the diversity of its activities. When they step out of its precincts, they discover that the real world is more complex, somewhat harsher. The training of the mind, however, helps them understand this better and respond appropriately. This is all the more important in a specialised, technical, institution devoted to the most important area of activity, namely, agriculture. The facts speak for themselves:

- The agriculture sector, that includes horticulture, forests, sericulture, fisheries, animal husbandry and allied fields is pivotal to the economy of J&K as it contributes more than 50 per cent to the net domestic product of the State and is the main source of livelihood for around 80 per cent of the population.

- Agriculture in the State is characterised by small peasant holdings and subsistence farming. A heavy dependence on cereals has led to a sub-optimal cycle of low productivity and low investment.
- Productivity of most crops is below the national average and the State suffers a deficit in food crops, oil seeds and vegetables.
- Over 80 per cent of net sown area is of food crops and only 42per cent of the area is under irrigation.
- A large number of people are dependent on cattle rearing and sheep breeding. The productivity in this sector, however, is low and the State depends on imports of animal products.
- Though the state has a high ratio of 900 animals per 1000 persons, only 4 per cent of the gross cropped area is under fodder cultivation.
- Facilities for processing of wool are virtually non-existent.
- Only 25 lakh people are connected directly or indirectly with the horticulture sector in the state. Yet, productivity is low and the sector suffers from low investment, disadvantage of location, poor infrastructure and the presence of many layers of intermediation.

This situation is compounded by literacy levels lower than the national average. In terms of the human development indices, J & K is nearer the bottom than the top. The scars of the recent past are all too evident.

In such a context every graduate of this institution can make a value addition to the socio-economic development of the state, and to the overall well being of the people of Jammu and Kashmir. The potential of this is enormous.

This potential can be harnessed for public good by sound public policy. For a state that has faced the problem of militancy for close to two decades, the path back to normalcy and eventual prosperity goes through the down-to-earth and grass-root sector of agriculture. It is agriculture that has the potential not only to revitalise the economy of the state, but also bring about greater social inclusion and sustainable rehabilitation even while preserving the unique cultural and religious heritage of the state.

My emphasis on the role of the agriculture sector has wider relevance. For the country as a whole, the current share of agriculture in GDP is around

18.5 per cent, that of services is 55 per cent and of industry around 26 per cent. The growth rate in the agriculture sector has been a mere 2.7 per cent in the last financial year. Yet, more than half of the population directly depends on this sector.

The adverse impact of the low growth in agriculture has implications for "the inclusiveness of growth". There is therefore a need to refocus our efforts on the agricultural sector not just in Jammu and Kashmir, but also in the rest of the country. I would even venture to say that the Government of India's proposed push to agriculture through a Second Green Revolution could start from Jammu and Kashmir on a pilot basis.

The low levels of employment opportunities in J&K have been a matter of concern to the public. The need of the hour is to think innovatively and the university has a role to play in this fascinating venture. A few possibilities readily come to mind:

- The university can modulate its syllabus and curriculum to the agro-economic needs of the state. A focus on agro industry would be the most effective way of generating employment in the background of an industrial base that has been eroded by long years of militancy.
- It can take the lead in adult literacy and skills upgradation programmes in employment intensive sectors such as agriculture, horticulture, food processing, and even agro-tourism.
- It could explore the opportunities for imparting entrepreneurial skills to the students so that they can use their energy and enthusiasm to start out on their own, thus creating jobs and prosperity. Agricultural entrepreneurship could be the key to sustainable socio-economic development of the state; the potential for innovation in agriculture is enormous and it has a multiplier payback effect on the society.

I commend the Sher-e-Kashmir University on an aspect of its work that is not appreciated sufficiently. I refer to the extension education in the field of agriculture. The Extension Education Programme of the university has conducted training programmes for a diverse profile of beneficiaries such as students, extension workers, farmers and homemakers. Such efforts to inform and demonstrate to the farmers the findings of research on improved practices are essential to improve rural living and to increase agricultural production.

Globalisation is now a fact of life. In the past the agricultural sector was static and immune to change. The new reality today places a special responsibility on agricultural universities to impart training to students on global factors impacting the agricultural sector in the country. These are climate change, environmentally sustainable development, and multilateral negotiations and agreements on agricultural products and agricultural subsidies. Students and teachers, as much as government officials, must debate these issues that would not only affect our economy and polity but could fundamentally redefine what we eat and how we live.

For the recipients of various degrees and honours, today is a day to celebrate. I wish them success in their careers and happiness in their lives. I am confident that they will carry forward the ideals imbibed during their time spent in this University and continue to work for the development of the state and improving the quality of life of common people, especially in the rural areas.

Inauguration of the South Indian Agricultural Fair

Kerala Agricultural University, Thrissur
27 December 2007

An Agricultural University is a place where theory embraces practice, where the results of learning are presented to the practitioners, to be tested in practice. An agricultural fair in such a university thus becomes a gathering of farmers, entrepreneurs, farm scientists and extension workers from all the southern states of India.

Our agricultural and food processing sectors, and traditional agro-rural industries have tremendous opportunities for growth, especially export-led growth. However, the usage of outdated technology and lack of value addition is preventing the advancement of these sectors. This fair is an important platform to explore the possibility of product diversification and value addition that are critical for strengthening the domestic and export market.

Agricultural fairs constitute a key component of the economic life of rural India. These sustain our rural economy to a significant extent in terms of employment generation and providing livelihood to a multitude of our population. These are an important link between urban and rural India to give new impetus to the agricultural sector for further expansion and promotion. This, I am sure will give new direction to the future of the agricultural sector.

Agricultural researchers in pursuit of professional excellence should not deviate from farmer priorities, which ensure the very survival and progress of our country. Our institutions of governance need to keep in mind the interests of farmers while allocating the budgetary resources and implementing the policies and programmes meant for them. Also the corporate social responsibilities of the industrial sector should be extended to have tie-ups with farmer Self Help Group (SHG) units and other small-scale local ventures. I firmly believe that this important fair will serve these purposes in all its dimensions and act as a launching pad for our farmers to reach global avenues and opportunities offered in the changed economic milieu.

Over a period of time, the agricultural sector has developed deeper interface with market economy through which the growth and development of other sectors of the economy have been facilitated. In India, agricultural GDP comprises about ¼ of total GDP (22 per cent) and generates16 per cent of the value of total exports. My emphasis on the role of the agriculture sector has wider relevance. For the country as a whole, the current share of agriculture in GDP is around 18.5 per cent, that of services is 55 per cent and of industry around 26 per cent. The growth rate in the agriculture sector has been a mere 2.7 per cent in the last financial year. Yet, more than half of the population directly depends on this sector. It also provides livelihood to 58 per cent of the total population especially in the rural areas. However, the agricultural scenario in the country has been witnessing sweeping changes in the last two decades as regards shifting priorities resulting in reduced tariffs, liberalised trade barriers, and dismantled restrictions on domestic and foreign private investment.

Friends, inclusiveness of growth is our national philosophy and the adverse impact of the low growth in agriculture has implications for it. There is therefore a need to refocus our efforts on the agricultural sector in the country. I venture to say that the Government of India's proposed push to agriculture through a Second Green Revolution needs to be considered as thrust area.

Despite some recent signs of a slowdown, the economy is poised to grow at least at a rate of 9 per cent. Services and industry are going to be the main contributors to growth. Agriculture is targeted to grow by 4 per cent. However, even with such growth, the per capita income of people dependent on agriculture will be less than that of those engaged in other sectors. The annual increase in per capita GDP for the agrarian population will be less than 1 per cent, while the rest of the population will be at eight times that rate. This can be attributed to the low per capita output of farms, which needs to be addressed on a priority.

Thus the gains from the economic structural transformation process is yet to materialise for the tilling rural millions of India who are confronted with new challenges such as household nutritional and food insecurity, declining farm profitability and trade competition, global warming and climate change, new pests and diseases, and depletion and degradation of natural resources. Thus, agriculture needs to become more equal in its reach, with enhanced productivity and profitability to accommodate the less privileged who are living on the margins of society.

In different parts of the country there are signs of a looming agrarian crisis caused due to the indebtedness of small and marginal farmers, repeated crop failures, failure of the public sector to cater to the varying needs of the farming community, and the decline of the local economic system that supported production and marketing. The gravity of the crisis has claimed many lives. It shows that the benefit of economic growth has not sufficiently percolated, resulting in widening the gap between the rich and the poor. The interests of the small and marginal farmers and peasants of our country have to be integrated with the greater objective of economic growth of the country through the strengthening of social safety nets for these vulnerable groups.

Globalisation has had a negative impact on the small-scale industries, which are in shambles, and their products are not competitive and are often ignored even in domestic markets. In order to tackle these issues, a paradigm shift is called for to target the post-production scenario through value addition and product diversification by integrating technologies, institutions and markets. The agricultural sector has to be equipped with the capabilities to explore the opportunities thrown open by the globalised economy.

Keeping in view the importance of the agricultural sector in the national economy, it has been given the status of Thrust Area for its overall development. As this sector also contributes significantly towards export earnings, emphasis on training in modern techniques of production, management and marketing plays an important role. This training also helps to improve the techniques, capacities, and strategies to withstand the competition in the present globalised economy. In this regard, the governmental initiatives indeed have a positive impact.

The diversification of Indian agriculture to dairying, poultry, fisheries, meat, vegetables and fruits has an important role to play to give a push to farm growth. Domestic demand, which is the main economic driver of any commodity, is in favour of these products. Agricultural fairs can provide avenues to further the demand for the agro products. Agricultural universities, farm research centres, agro-based industries and development departments are indeed crucial actors in the success of the agricultural fairs.

As the farming systems evolved rapidly, level of commercialisation also increased, giving way to mixed farming systems–which respond rapidly to market forces. In this emerging context the South Indian states with potential for export of cash crops like spices, coffee, tea, rubber, silk, sandalwood, fruits and vegetables have become major economic players. These states are also rich in livestock wealth besides being endowed with immense marine and inland fisheries wealth. There is a great need to integrate the crop, livestock and fisheries sectors to augment value addition and diversification in agriculture. Moreover, it also provides an opportunity for the inclusion of rural women–who play a vital role in all stages of crop production–and harness the new world opportunities. In achieving this we may also consider policy options like changing property rights in favour of women, evolving technologies to suit women farmers, increasing the number of women extension workers, educating and training women farmers.

We need to organise agriculture, animal husbandry and aquaculture activities on modern and scientific lines. Since the area under cultivation has come down, agri-business can be profitable only if there is multi-fold increase in productivity or production through group consortia of farmers at local level. Developing value addition protocols and imparting trainings in field conditions to assure technical expertise would pose a great challenge to be met by the technical experts. Good agricultural practices (GAP) and good manufacturing practices (GMP) have to be ensured from the point of production to the point of product marketing to ensure international standards. The onus for this rests with the researchers, policy makers, entrepreneurs, investors and technology disseminators.

Agricultural fairs need to be fully utilised to tap the agro-economic potential of the southern states. A focus on agro-rural industry would be the most effective way of generating employment. It could explore the opportunities for imparting entrepreneurial skills to the unemployed so that they can use their energy and enthusiasm to start out on their own, thus creating jobs and prosperity. Agricultural entrepreneurship could be the key to sustainable socio-economic development of the state; the potential for innovation in agriculture is enormous and it has a multiplier payback effect on the society.

The Agricultural fairs have a great relevance in the face of increasing competition and provide an opportunity to become global players. Globalisation has given new demand to the agro products because of a shift in the consumer culture. The free movement of goods and capital has provided immense opportunities to our agriculturists to sell their products to the outside world, and also bring in products of other countries. This has opened a new culture of competition, which can only be sustained through protection, and promotion of our agricultural markets. This is possible only when we accord top priority to the agriculture in our policy framework.

National Seminar on Non-Biological Contaminants in Food, Feed and Their Safety Standards

India International Centre, New Delhi

23 September 2008

We live in an age of contamination: of environment, food, water and of most other ingredients essential to human existence. For this reason this seminar, focused on one aspect of it, is of immense relevance to our individual and collective wellbeing. I am therefore happy to be here today to inaugurate it.

There is one other reason evoking our interest in the matter. Tackling non-biological contaminants requires more than an individual effort or attention only to hygiene; instead, it requires awareness and interventions across the food-chain with a focus on the management of food safety and quality.

Food safety goes beyond cheating on ingredients. It endangers life.

It has been a matter of concern in all ages. Kautilya's *Arthashastra* has a section on the control of butchers and prescribes punishment for selling bad meat or fish. Perhaps malpractices with regard to other edibles did not exist. Then and until the advent of the modern age, man-made contaminants were not a serious factor. Today, it is a matter of growing national and global concern.

Laws regulating the quality of food have been in force in India since 1899. The Concurrent List in the Seventh Schedule of the Constitution of India empowers both the central and state governments to legislate on 'adulteration of food stuffs and other goods'.

The Prevention of Food Adulteration Act, 1954 was enacted to ensure pure and wholesome food to consumers and to prevent fraud or deception. The deterrents in it were found to be inadequate. Subsequent amendments have made punishments more stringent and empowered Consumers and Voluntary Organisations to play a more effective role in its implementation.

The government has taken measures to prevent the indiscriminate use of pesticides and fertilisers in agriculture. The use of DDT in agriculture was banned in 1996 and that of Lindane in 1997. Pesticide use has significantly declined from 75,000 tonnes in 1990 to around 40,000 tonnes in 2005. This has meant a corresponding decline in pesticide residues in food items. Dr Hasnain pointed out it is not enough.

In August 2006 Parliament enacted the Food Safety and Standards Act to eventually replace all existing laws on the subject. The Government also proposes to establish a new statutory body-the Food Safety and Standards Authority of India-for laying down standards for articles of food and to regulate their manufacture, storage, distribution, sale and import, to ensure availability of safe food for human consumption. It is the expectation of all stakeholders that this authority will streamline and strengthen activities related to food safety standards and enforcement and ensure that food safety is integrally linked to the health of our people. We have to find out ways to reaching the people.

There is an external dimension to the question. We live in a world where food and agricultural products is an important segment of world trade. Exports of agricultural products every year are around US$ 300 billion, of which 45 per cent originates in developing countries. The WHO recognises food safety as an essential public health function and has devised effective food safety assurance systems. As part of international trading arrangements, the inclusion of international food standards in the WTO's Agreement of Sanitary and Phyto-Sanitary measures (SPS) and the Agreement on Technical Barriers to Trade (TBT) have provided guidelines to ensure food safety and a level playing field for countries involved in food and agricultural trade.

After signing of the SPS and TBT agreements by India and removal of quantitative restrictions on import of food products into India, the government has initiated harmonisation of standards for food products, use of food additives and harmonisation of regulations in line with international standards.

The Ministry of Food Processing Industries has declared the current year as 'Food Safety and Quality Standard Year' with the objective of bringing together the various initiatives of central and state governments, industry associations and civil society organisations. A significant initiative in this regard would be the certification of 10,000 farmers across the country for 'Good Agricultural Practices' and for organic food. This would improve the value accrued from agricultural and horticultural produce from the certified farms.

National seminars on aspect of food safety and food standards play an important role through advocacy, generating debate and coming up with actionable recommendations for all stakeholders, whether in government or in the industry.

In the final analysis, it is important to involve the public through consumer organisations and civil society groups in these discussions. I hope that the deliberations of this seminar would contribute to the ultimate objective of ensuring the food and nutritional security of our citizens.

World Bamboo Day Function

Kohima Naga Heritage Village (Kisama), Nagaland

18 September 2010

I am pleased to be in your midst here in the beautiful Naga Heritage Village, Kisama on the occasion of the World Bamboo Day celebration. I congratulate the government of Nagaland, especially the Chief Minister, and the World Bamboo Organization for taking the initiative to organise this important event. The World Bamboo Day is a day of celebration to increase the global awareness of bamboo and promote its sustainable utilisation. It is also appropriate that the theme chosen for this festival is 'Bamboo for Community and Livelihood'.

I hope that such efforts of the state and central governments, civil society, and the World Bamboo Organization would highlight the potential of bamboo to a wider audience to help protect natural resources and the environment, to ensure sustainable utilisation, to promote new cultivation of bamboo for new industries in India and around the world, and promote traditional and community uses of bamboo.

The North-East region of India, though underdeveloped in economic terms, is extremely rich in natural resources. Bamboo is a prominent natural resource of the region. The North-East, with about 8 per cent of the geographical area of the country, accounts for 66 per cent of the bamboo resources of the country spread over an area of about 3.10 million hectares and housing over 89 species of bamboo.

This precious natural gift has been integral to the life and survival of all the ethnic groups of north eastern India over the centuries. The various uses to which bamboo has been put to, have made it an indispensable resource for rural India and it has been incorporated in their cultural and traditional life. The Nagaland Bamboo Policy of 2004 summarises it well, and I quote:

> 'From the cutting of the umbilical cord to the mats that have wrapped the dead for burial, bamboo has been integral to the life of the Nagas.'

The raw stock of bamboo in the North-East region is conservatively valued at Rs 5,000 crore. Even with a modest target of two-fold value addition to the stock through suitable methodologies, an annual turnover of approximately Rs 10,000 crore can be generated in the region. In the context of India's economy, the market size of bamboo is expected to touch a figure of Rs 42,000 crore in the next fifteen to twenty years. This enormous potential for wealth creation in rural areas, if exploited properly, can truly benefit the people of the region and change their day-to-day lives for the better.

The importance of bamboo is enhanced in the backdrop of global concerns of ecology and environment and the looming threat of global warming and climate change. Bamboo is emerging as the most viable wood substitute. Unlike steel and plastic, it is eco-friendly, being not only biodegradable but also having enormous capacity to sequester carbon. Furthermore, as the fastest growing plant on earth, it is a renewable resource with short gestation. This new perspective of bamboo is indeed a big change from its earlier reference as the "poor man's timber".

We are also witnessing an expansion in the uses to which bamboo is being put to. Apart from its utility as food and medicine, in minor tools, implements and daily utilities, bamboo is extensively used for handicrafts, furniture and even art. Its application has expanded to boards, ply and shuttering materials for use in buildings and construction. It has also been developed as an energy source in the form of charcoal, activated carbon and even to generate electricity through gasification.

Realising the immense socio-economic potential of bamboo, the Government of India has launched the National Bamboo Mission (NBM) and the National Mission on Bamboo Application (NMBA) for its holistic development, cultivation and for developing the technologies and applications for bamboo based products. I am confident that the bamboo scenario in the country will significantly improve in the coming years through these interventions for the benefit of our people.

The state of Nagaland has been a pioneer and had adopted a Bamboo Policy in 2004. The Policy articulates the development of bamboo in Nagaland along two approaches:

1. Development of Bamboo as a Resource, and
2. Development of Bamboo as an Enterprise

Developing bamboo as a resource is focused on optimal cultivation and management of bamboo resources, through development of natural bamboo forests and bamboo plantation development. Development of bamboo as an enterprise is focused on developing bamboo-based industries, service sectors and ancillary activities including tourism. The Nagaland Bamboo Development Agency has a mission to generate new employment opportunities based on bamboo. I congratulate the Chief Minister and the state government for taking such initiatives and call on other bamboo producing states to emulate this example.

In order to realise the full potential of bamboo, various technical, financial and entrepreneurial interventions are needed in the fields of forestry, land use, propagation technology for its cultivation and sustainable use, and in the areas of industry and finance. I am confident that the economic and technological capabilities of our nation can bring about a bamboo revolution in the country.

Convocation Address

Orissa University of Agriculture and Technology, Bhubaneswar

21 October 2010

I am happy to visit Orissa on my first visit, in my current capacity, and take part in the 30th Convocation of Orissa University of Agriculture and Technology.

As the second oldest agricultural university in the country. This university has been a pioneer in educating generations of graduates in agricultural science and technology, animal husbandry and veterinary science, promoting extension programmes and in fostering agricultural research.

Convocation is a special day in the life of every student. For professionals like you, it marks the entry into a select group of those who have made notable contribution to their profession and to the specific requirements of the farmers of Orissa.

I also take this opportunity to heartily congratulate the distinguished scientists who have been conferred with Honoris Causa for their outstanding achievement and services rendered. I also congratulate all the graduating students, especially those who have been awarded medals and prizes for their academic excellence.

The first prime minister of India, Shri Jawaharlal Nehru had said that "Everything else can wait but agriculture cannot wait". Agriculture continues to be the lifeline of the Indian economy and central to our economic development in the long term.

Indeed, the last six decades have seen the dramatic transformation of Indian agriculture from shortages to surpluses. This has happened simultaneously with a decrease in the share of agriculture in the GDP from over 50 per cent at the time of independence to around 15 per cent today.

The nation has achieved food grain self sufficiency by enhancing production from around 50 million tonnes in 1950 to over 230 million tonnes today. This was achieved through the Green Revolution that brought about through strong political will and environment of favourable infrastructure, new technology induction, policy support and energised agricultural extension system.

Yet, recent trends of the last fifteen years are a cause of concern. After improving steadily from 1980 to 1997, the terms of trade turned against agriculture since 1999. The Eleventh Five-Year Plan documents the problems as:

- A deceleration in agricultural growth and widening economic disparities between irrigated and rain-fed areas
- Increased vulnerability to world commodity price volatility following trade liberalisation
- Uneven and slow development of technology, and inefficient use of available technology and inputs
- Lack of adequate incentives and appropriate institutions
- Degradation of available natural resource base, including decline in ground water table with adverse impact on small farmers
- Increased non-agricultural demand for land and water due to urbanisation and economic growth and
- Aggravated social distress due to cumulative impact of all these factors leading to upsurge in farmer suicides

To counter this trend, the Eleventh Five-Year Plan has suggested measures for a 'more efficient, sustainable and inclusive' growth in Indian agriculture that addresses the 'technology fatigue', sustainability question and the 'yield gap'.

The Eleventh Plan had a sharp focus on rain-fed areas and 85 per cent of farmers who are small and marginal farmers, and increasingly, women. It also recommended increasing systems support while rationalising subsidies, encouraging diversification while protecting against food security concerns, and fostering a group approach to ensure that the poor are able to access land, credit, skills and scale. The Plan targeted a 4 per cent growth per annum in GDP from agriculture and its allied sectors, in the knowledge that agriculture-related GDP growth is actually twice as effective in alleviating poverty as compared to GDP growth from other sectors.

The Government of India had also announced a 'New Deal to Rural India' focused on reversing the declining trend in public investment in agriculture with a special emphasis on irrigation, wasteland development, agricultural research and extension.

The Mid-Term Appraisal of the Eleventh Five-Year Plan has some disturbing facts and conclusions:

It notes that 'it would be safer to assume that agricultural growth in the Eleventh Plan may fall short of the 4 per cent per annum target' in view of the severe drought in 2009.

Not all aspects of the Plan strategy are doing well and much more needs to be done on the supply side. The current high GDP growth is increasing demand for agricultural products and putting pressure on food prices, especially in the 'hottest and driest decade'.

Farm income variability rose after agricultural trade was opened up under WTO since this ended the negative correlation between output and prices, and existing price stabilisation measures were inadequate to cope with volatile global prices of agro-commodities.

These results must be seen in a larger socio-economic context that is characterised by the following:

First, according to FAO (Food and Agriculture Organization) over 250 million Indians are chronically undernourished, constituting 22 per cent of our population. This is anomalous looking at record food grain production in recent years. What is becoming clear is that food security and self-sufficiency should be measured not just in terms of production, but in terms of access to, and actual consumption of food grains.

Second, agriculture provides employment to around 52 per cent of our workforce. Around half of all those engaged in agriculture are illiterate and a miniscule 5 per cent of them have completed higher secondary education. It thus has a disproportionately important role in achieving a higher and inclusive GDP growth, food security, employment expansion and poverty alleviation.

Third, it is now well recognised that the Indian growth story is driven by the strong, entrepreneurial and innovative private sector. Private sector investment in agriculture in the last decade in real terms has only increased by 48 per cent, in comparison to public sector investment which has witnessed 180 per cent increase. As the Economic Survey 2009-10 notes: 'Consistent decline in the share of private sector investment in the agriculture sector is a matter of concern.'

The broad policy and implementation challenges that we need to face to transform Indian agriculture are well etched. State agricultural universities have an important role to play in agricultural research. The Eleventh Plan speaks of these state universities as 'the key to regionally relevant research and for generating quality human resources'. It calls upon state governments to substantially fund their research expenses, in addition to salary and establishment costs, to bring their work in line with local agricultural concerns and needs.

Orissa is blessed with a diverse range of agro-climatic conditions, flora and fauna. At the same time, the state is also vulnerable to natural calamities such as drought, floods and cyclones, which have had an adverse impact on agricultural productivity.

The role of this university in developing viable adaptation and mitigation measures to deal with this and to capitalise on the rich bio-diversity is thus of prime importance.

The university's contribution in the areas of crop improvement, crop production, natural resource management, crop protection, post-harvest technology and extension education would always be remembered.

It is particularly notable that this university has developed 127 high yielding crop varieties including fifty rice varieties suitable for different agro-ecological situations of the State. It has also developed technologies related to livestock, fish, mechanised farming and management of land and water.

I am confident that the students graduating today would follow in the footsteps of the distinguished teachers and alumni of the university, and I sincerely hope that at least some of you would choose unconventional paths to become agricultural entrepreneurs and innovators.

I once again congratulate all of you and especially those conferred with Honoris Causa and those who received prizes and medals.

Twenty-eighth Convocation

Gandhigram Rural University, Dindigul

28 October 2010

I am happy to be participating in this convocation as the Chancellor of the University on my first visit to Gandhigram. The place and the university are unique in many ways. Gandhigram, born in 1947, is as old as independent India. The institute, founded in 1956, reflected the undying faith and deep devotion of its founders to Mahatma Gandhi's revolutionary concept of 'Nai Talim' system of education. It has developed its own approach to synergising academic, research and extension programmes in rural development, rural economics and rural oriented sciences, development administration, rural sociology, and English and Indian languages. The university's contribution to rural education is today nationally and internationally recognised.

Gandhigram's experiment to demonstrate the important role of work in education is still a work-in-progress. Speaking at the second National Basic Education Conference in April 1941 in Jamia Nagar, Dr Zakir Hussain had remarked:

> "A work-school is a society working for a common end. In its cooperative pattern of labour the mistake of one may mar the work of the rest.... It teaches its members how to cooperate in spite of their differences of ability and temperament, it teaches them to accept responsibility for their social duties. But the school, like the individual, must work for something more than itself, or it will merely substitute corporate greed for individual greed. The small society of the school must serve the larger society around it."

The Gandhigram Rural University represents the best example of Nai Talim's 'work-school'. Over the decades, it has served the needs of the villagers in its neighbourhood and has addressed their concerns. The university and its students have discharged their social duties with dedication.

As the graduating students today leave the portals of the university, I implore them to continue with the ideals imbibed here and seek to incorporate this philosophy in their professional and personal lives.

Today I would like to address the concerns and problems of agricultural research in India. Agriculture, including crop and animal husbandry, fisheries, forestry and agro-processing, is a critical element towards ensuring food and livelihood security for our citizens. The agricultural sector provides key support for economic development and social transformation, as it accounts for 15.7 per cent of the GDP and provides employment to 52 per cent of our work force. Research has been a prime driver of agricultural growth in India and hence an essential component of our national mission of poverty alleviation and ensuring a decent life to all of our citizens.

Agricultural research and development faces systemic, institutional and financial problems in the country. While agriculture is a state subject, the bulk of agricultural research is carried out in central government organisations and is primarily in the public domain. We spend about 0.6 per cent of our agricultural GDP on agricultural research and development.

The Eleventh Five-Year Plan has noted that 'a major paradigm shift is needed to transform the present commodity-based research to a systems approach ... so as to bring region-specificity in technologies and their time-bound assessment'. It concluded that 'this kind of approach will help in establishing a research-development-technology transfer continuum involving all stakeholders' and in indentifying 'integrated farming systems in different agro-ecological regions ... to enhance resource utilisation, income and livelihood generation and minimise environmental loading".

Beyond a focus on the macro-picture of agricultural research in the country, it would appear that the potential of the agriculture sector to bring about inclusive development and social transformation can only be achieved if public policy directs agricultural research towards poverty alleviation.

The touchstone to assess the impact of agricultural research is to see whether it has benefited poor farmers and poor regions in the country. Two issues come to mind.

One: In the post-Green Revolution period, productivity growth was sustained through increased input use that was not adjusted to availability of resources of poor and marginal farmers. These farmers had limited access to credit, off-farm inputs and to water, and consequently faced higher levels of risk while adopting such technologies.

Two: Adequate research and development has not been done on dry land and rain-fed farming technologies, semi-arid tropics and marginal land farming and low-cost technologies. It needs no reiteration that the poor would immensely benefit with a research focus on farming systems with lower levels of input usage and sustainable resource utilisation. Agricultural research must focus on commodities that are relevant to the rural poor and on the conditions under which they produce these agricultural commodities.

Policy makers, R&D institutions and academia should pay close heed to some of the recommendations made by the Mid-Term Appraisal of the Eleventh Plan to accelerate agricultural growth and revitalise agricultural research.

First, India needs to raise the spending on agricultural research to at least 1 per cent of agricultural GDP, which is the average of developing countries, so as to raise productivity in a sustained manner.

Second, public research institutions, especially state agriculture universities must be re-energised with adequate funding and commensurate institutional reforms to provide autonomy and incentivise the research system.

Third, the private sector in India, with a minor role in technology generation, has been more effective in ensuring commercial success in popularising seeds such as BT cotton, hybrids such as maize, rice and sunflower. This was done, without much support from the public extension system, mainly by responding to the demand of farmers. The public sector technology generation, on the other hand, has become a supply-driven process 'of putting technologies on the shelf of the scientists without adequate regard to farmers' needs and perceptions and with insufficient marketing of the technology'. Greater space must be created for the private sector in technology generation and diffusion so that new technologies, especially bio-technology including transgenics, could be developed and released under our Regulatory Authority System while adhering to bio-safety norms.

The agriculture sector is not immune from the knowledge-centric economy of today. We live in a world where even manual labour is best optimised through knowledge-based processes. Gandhian approaches towards rural development and the agriculture sector would also need to be integrated into our knowledge economy for realising their objectives.

I am glad that Gandhigram Rural University has taken the initiative in transforming itself into a rural knowledge hub to empower farmers and rural citizens to make optimum use of new rural and agricultural technologies. The key to alleviating rural poverty is to ensure access to information and enable seamless communication on a wide range of themes including businesses, farming practices, government policies, health and education issues and the rights and obligations of citizens.

I once again congratulate the awardees of prizes and medals. I wish all graduating students every success in their future professional and personal endeavours.

Thirtieth Convocation

Institute of Rural Management, Anand (IRMA)
26 April 2011

I feel privileged to attend today's convocation function at the premier Rural Management Institute of India. I take this opportunity to congratulate the graduating students who will be moving out of the confines of academia to their chosen professions and careers.

The graduates of this institute are special as they span the inter-section of management, development, social sciences, the rural sector, the cooperative sector and the corporate sector. You and your predecessors, the alumni of this distinguished institution, have over the years made your teachers proud by contributing to various areas of our political economy and through your initiative and expertise contributed to the development process which is focused on improving the quality of life of all citizens.

When the institute was established in 1979, it was indeed a pioneer. The focus was on producing professional managers who could help rural organisations and institutions and empower rural people by building new rural management knowledge and theories through action oriented and problem solving research. It was a period of lower economic growth rates, limited possibilities and lower levels of human development.

Today, we are on the path towards higher growth rates, greater inclusiveness, improved human development indicators and a changed orientation in the role of government to achieve these outcomes. We have created a new tier of government at the local level through constitutional amendments. Our broad national vision brings together several components that include economic development, employment generation, access to health and education for all, skill development, employment guarantees, environmental sustainability, gender equity and improved governance with a focus on accountability and transparency.

The last two decades have changed the ground rules for our economy in a fundamental manner. The total expenditure of the Central Government has gone up ten times from around rupees ninety-five thousand crores in 1989-90 to around rupees ten lakh crores in 2009-10. The most dramatic jump has been in transfer payments by the Central Government to the rest of the economy that has gone up over fifteen times from approximately rupees forty-four thousand seven hundred crores in 1989-90 to rupees six lakh seventy-four thousand crores in 2009-10.

The volume, mix, variety and legal structures employed for undertaking government expenditure have thus undergone a tremendous change. Flagship social sector and infrastructure programmes of the government and provision for subsidies consume the bulk of resources.

There has been a gradual evolution of the role of government from direct provision of economic goods and services and tight control of private enterprise, to broad regulation of economic sectors, promotion and facilitation of private enterprise and fair competition. Government funds are increasingly devolving through urban and rural local bodies, Special Purpose Vehicles, Non-Governmental Organisations and Public-Private Partnerships.

It has to be admitted, however, that outcomes are not yet commensurate with outlays and the objective of inclusive growth through inclusive governance still evades us in some measure. Correctives are thus essential and the role of rural management in all its dimensions becomes fundamental to the process.

The changed landscape of our political economy raises new questions that have particular significance for rural management education. Convocations are ideal occasions to ponder over such issues.

- Should rural management education have a value focus towards the poor and marginalised sections of our society and empathise with the problems of rural India or should such education be value neutral as in the case of conventional management education? In short, do we need a committed academia to deal with rural management?

- The winds of global change have percolated to the rural and village level. Global developments on economic, agricultural and trade issues have a profound impact on the lives and fortunes of rural citizens. To what extent has rural management education kept pace with the changing global and regional context?
- What is the role and extent of influence of the placement market on the curriculum of the institutions, the type of students it attracts, and the type of careers and professions they choose to pursue after they graduate?
- How is the interface between public administration, politics and rural economy functioning? What is the role of professional rural managers in the planning, implementation and monitoring of outcomes of the government's budgets on rural development, poverty alleviation and rural employment?

A good starting point for our discussion is the dairy sector which provided the initial impetus for the establishment of the institution. Rural management initiatives have been successful in spreading the White Revolution across the country. Today India ranks first in world milk production, increasing its production over six times from 17 million tonnes in 1950-51 to 112.5 million tonnes in 2009-10. The per capita availability of milk has also increased from 112 grams per day in 1968-69 to 263 grams per day in 2009-10.

The successes achieved are considerable and are cause for satisfaction. The real benefit of milk cooperatives has been to both the farmers and to the national economy. This is the only sector where the farmer gets around 70 per cent of what the consumer pays for the end product. When compared to other agricultural produce such as vegetables, fruits or even food grain, this represents one of the best ways for promoting inclusive growth. The farmer gets a good price for the milk and this could even account for up to a quarter of overall income at the farm level.

However, the macro picture is not too encouraging. Our per capita availability of milk is still lower than the world average of 279.4 grams. We have been unable to keep pace with the growing domestic demand for milk at about six million tonnes per year whereas annual incremental production over the last ten years has been about 3.5 million tonnes per year. Moreover, 80 per cent of milk produced is still handled in the unorganised sector and only the remaining 20 per cent is equally shared by cooperatives and private dairies.

Rural managers have an important role in expanding the footprint of the organised sector, modernising marketing systems, improving access to formal credit mechanisms and working to improve transport, veterinary and dairy infrastructure. They will have to work alongside the government in ensuring that there is a strong supply side response to the enhanced demand so that the gap is met through domestic supply rather than imports, with all the inclusive growth benefits accruing to rural citizens. Other elements such as low productivity of animals, breeding programmes, feed and fodder, and research should also be addressed.

I believe that what sets the students at IRMA apart from those in other premier management institutes is their desire to be associated with our rural environment and their strong commitment to work for the public good and to serve social objectives. Each of you has spent around eight months doing field work which provides the value context for your education. You connect with the different organisational structures and situations in rural India and it is this experience that enriches your understanding of some of the core problems of our country and our citizens.

Rural managers are one important component of professionals, alongside the civil service and the Gram Panchayat officials, who will increasingly have to work through cooperative partnerships to achieve our developmental vision for rural India. Like the civil service, I believe that rural managers must be committed to our constitutional ideals to achieve inclusive development, social justice, equality and the opportunity for the full development of capacities of all our citizens.

At the same time, in an era of increasing economic globalisation, decisions taken in global and regional fora have important consequences for the rural sector. Rural management curriculum should keep pace with these changes and rural managers should analyse and watch out for emerging threats and opportunities flowing from these developments.

I would, finally, wish to touch on the aspect of placements which have almost become the *raison d'etre* for management institutes. I think it is critical to emphasise that the principle objective of an educational institution is to provide education and not to become a *de facto* placement organisation. While everyone realises that students take education loans to cover the high fees of management institutions, and that a good career is a legitimate expectation of every student, the job market cannot and should not be the sole guiding light.

I am confident that whichever organisation or sector the graduating students today would choose to work in, you will continue to be guided by the knowledge that has been imparted to you here and the rich experience you have gained in your field assignments. The nation is proud of IRMA and its alumni and you should always work to uphold this institutional legacy.

Business and Industry

❝When things are going well, government should interfere as little as possible. When things are going bad, as they seem to be at present, it is the responsibility of the Government to become more pro-active ...

❝I hope industry is thinking seriously of how to become more competitive. It is because we are confident that it can that we have entered into Comprehensive Economic Partnership Agreement with the ASEAN countries as well as the Republic of Korea. We are hoping to conclude a similar agreement with the European Union soon

—Prime Minister Manmohan Singh's Address
at the ASSOCHAM Annual General Meeting,
19 July 2013

Annual Day Celebrations

Shri Ram College of Commerce, New Delhi
8 March 2008

I am happy to be here today at the Annual Day Celebrations of the Shri Ram College of Commerce.

The College has over the past eight decades emerged as the foremost centre of excellence in commerce education in the country. This can be attributed to the vision of its founder, Sir Shri Ram, and the initiative and drive of its faculty, students and alumni over the years. The college has done well in inculcating in students the spirit of entrepreneurship and innovation.

As a citizen only partially initiated in the intricacies and mysteries of the world of business, I hesitated a good deal before accepting the invitation of the college to be here today. I am not an economist but like many others do understand a bit of the wider debate about what used to be known as 'political economy'.

Business is not an exercise in a vacuum. The question, in other words, is of the environment in which business functions, its instruments of governance, and the manner in which it interacts with society.

Some in this audience may have read Kautilya's *Arthashastra* and its chapter on the management of the state's treasury and economy. A great deal of common sense advice is given there about how to achieve and sustain economic prosperity. He makes the interesting observation that "just as elephants are needed to catch elephants, so does one need wealth to capture more wealth". In other words, wealth plays a role in the generation of wealth.

What then is our wealth? In today's world, it is defined in terms of human and material resources. India is well endowed with both and the progress achieved by the country in the six decades of Independence proves it in ample measure. The rate of growth in recent years has been particularly impressive. The momentum is set to continue. The interaction of the economy with the outside world stands enhanced in good measure.

In this new setting, two aspects need particular attention. The first pertains to corporate governance and the second to the meaning and implications of globalisation. Both have a direct impact on all aspects of economic activity and therefore on the lives of all sections of our people. Both need to be carefully and comprehensively debated by the managerial talent set to graduate from this college.

Corporate governance has been transformed in recent years. Institutions like yours have helped the process. There is awareness, as the former president of the World Bank James Wolfensohn put it, that "the proper governance of companies will become as crucial for the world economy as the proper governing of countries".

Ours is a world in which business corporations are increasingly the principal economic agents of the global stage. Their activities impinge on the output and growth rates of economies; their conduct determines in increasing measure the economic well-being and standards of living of peoples and nations. The role of the governments is increasingly regulatory to ensure fairness, transparency and accountability and to protect the interests of all stakeholders. This is also in tune with efforts to achieve global competitiveness.

Here I wish to dwell on two issues.

First: We need to broad-base the definition of stake holders in a corporate enterprise. One notices a trend to consider Corporate Governance and Corporate Social Responsibility as two distinct entities and in watertight compartments. It is argued that corporate governance responsibilities are towards shareholders and hence gets primacy over Corporate Social Responsibility that is seen in a voluntary context. In the rapidly changing social, economic and political context today, both at the national and global level, this distinction is increasingly getting blurred. Indian corporations going global, and global corporations with Indian operations, need to see both the shareholders and the society; the latter includes the consumers of the goods and services produced by them. For this reason, corporations need to prioritise their obligations towards society at the same level as towards their share holders.

There are demands within the polity that the regulatory role of the government over the private sector should include the vision of the role of the State in the economic sphere as articulated in the Constitution. It is important that such demands be addressed in a framework that safeguards the interests of all stakeholders. As a result, Corporate Social Responsibility would increasingly need to be seen in the larger context of corporate governance.

Second: While the extent and complexity of regulation of corporate behaviour have vastly improved in the last decade in our country, it should be remembered that regulation is a blunt instrument. It might lead to marking of checklists instead of a focus on the spirit of good governance. While regulators and the market are imposing their own discipline on corporate behaviour, a significant measure of self-discipline is not only unavoidable but altogether necessary.

We should also keep in mind that of the over 8.78 lakh companies limited by shares at work, around 10 per cent are public limited companies and a very small percentage are listed on the stock exchanges. While listed companies are well regulated by SEBI, the extent of regulation of non-listed companies needs to be improved considerably.

It is heartening that the drive towards corporate governance in India was initiated by the Confederation of Indian Industries (CII) in 1997 and followed up thereafter by SEBI and the Ministry of Corporate Affairs. In the final analysis, to quote the National Foundation for Corporate Governance, "what is needed is small corpus of legally mandated rules, buttressed by a much larger body of self-regulation and voluntary compliance".

In regard to globalisation and despite a great deal of talk about it, a distinction needs to be made between being there and wanting to be there. The A.T. Kearney and Foreign Policy Globalisation Index for 2007 places India at number 71 in a list of 72 countries surveyed. Furthermore, and as the economist Deepak Nayyar has pointed out, 'globalisation has introduced a new dimension to the exclusion of people from development ... (It) inevitably tends to erode social stability'. We therefore need to be careful about the globalisation agenda and must at all times relate it to our ground realities.

The Fourth North-East Business Summit

Guwahati
15 September 2008

This is a conference with a difference and I am delighted to be present here to inaugurate the Fourth North-East Business Summit, to showcase the potential of this region for domestic and foreign investors.

Nowhere else in the country do we have such a geographical agglomeration trying to attract business and investments with a commonality of purpose, and driven by their common strengths, and indeed, their common problems.

This summit is as much about business as it is about politics, both domestic and external. It is about correctives. The effort today is as much to overcome the physical and commercial isolation of this region, as it is to set aside its 'geo-political isolation and put it on the path of accelerated and inclusive growth'.

The humanitarian and political consequences of the events of 1947 have been well documented. Less understood and appreciated are the implications of parcelling economic entities whose functioning and welfare was contingent on their integrity. This regrettably is the case with the north eastern region; it was among the prosperous regions of India at the time of Independence and six decades later is lagging far behind the rest of the country in most parameters of growth.

Let me cite a few indicators:

1. The region accounts for around 8 per cent of the geographical area of the country and around 4 per cent of our population. Yet, its contribution to the Net Domestic Product (NDP) of India has remained at less than 3 per cent.
2. The region as a whole is amongst the poorest regions in the country with per capita income that is roughly 2/3rd of the

national average. Over 35 per cent of the population of this region is below the poverty line as compared to the national average of 26 per cent.

3. It is a paradox that this region has a literacy rate that is higher than the national average, with one of the states having the second highest literacy rate in the country. Yet, agriculture provides livelihood support to 70 per cent of the population of the region, indicating paucity of employment opportunities in the manufacturing and services sectors. The unemployment rate is close to 12 per cent as against the national average of 7.7 per cent.
4. Despite agriculture remaining the main source of income, the region is a net importer of food grains even for its own consumption, as it produces only 1.5 per cent of our total food grain production.
5. The pace of urbanisation is far slower than the rest of the country. Urban population in the region is less than 15 per cent as compared to the national average of around 28 per cent.
6. Per capita resource consumption and output is far lower than the national averages. For instance, domestic electricity consumption in the region is around 1/4th of the national average and the gross per capita industrial output is about 1/3rd of the national average.

The eight states of the north eastern region have different levels of human development, resource endowments, levels of industrialisation and infrastructure facilities. What are common, however, are the existence of immense potential and the lack of its realisation for the benefit of the peoples in the region.

Despite rich natural resources and high literacy levels, what we see is a pattern of low capital formation, poor infrastructure, high levels of poverty and unemployment, poor geographical and physical connectivities and lack of exploitation of inherent strengths of the region.

The gathering today is an affirmation that it should not be so and that the development deficit of the region should be addressed.

The north eastern region vision 2020 document approved by the members of the North Eastern Council and released by the prime minister in July this year is the best testimony of the commitment of the union and various state governments to the comprehensive, inclusive and accelerated development of the region so as to restore it national economic eminence.

What we need today are similar concerted and innovative approaches to fashioning economic and trade arrangements, not only for ensuring closer integration with the national economy but also with the economies of neighbouring countries in the region.

It is here that I come to the very important external dimension to economic development and growth of business and entrepreneurship in the north eastern region.

The vision document has noted that the region should play 'the arrow-head role … in the vanguard of the country's Look-East Policy'. The 'Look-East Policy' was not just a foreign policy initiative. It was an amalgam of a strategic shift in our global perspective, an aspect of our economic reform process focused on enlargement of our external economic engagement accompanied by renewal of civilisational linkages with our neighbours in South East and East Asia.

The Look-East Policy was also complemented with a 'Look Around Policy' of closer economic and political partnership with our neighbours in the SAARC (South Asian Association for Regional Cooperation) region.

The north eastern region is at the focus of all of these multi-faceted initiatives. South East Asia begins where North-East India ends. Within SAARC Bangladesh, Nepal and Bhutan are central to ensuring sustainable regional economic development and prosperity through close cooperation and partnership.

The institutional structures for increasing economic cooperation and trade are being put in place. Let me cite a few:

- All SAARC states are committed to implementing SAFTA (South Asian Free Trade Area) in letter and spirit.
- The Indo-ASEAN (Association of South East Asian Nations) FTA (Free Trade Area) negotiations have been completed and this lies at the core of our engagement with ASEAN.

- During the visit of Vice Senior General Maung Aye of Myanmar in April this year, the Agreement and Protocols for the Kaladan Multi Modal Transit and Transport Project were signed by both countries. This is a milestone in mutually beneficial cross-border cooperation and would considerably enhance connectivity to the north eastern region.
- Besides ASEAN, The Bay of Bengal Initiative for Multi-Sectoral Technical and Economic Cooperation (BIMSTEC) represents the second element of our Look-East Policy architecture. This grouping focuses on trade and investment, technology, transport and communications, energy and tourism, and is mandated to serve as a bridge between South Asia and Southeast Asia.
- The Mekong Ganga Cooperation brings together Cambodia, India, Laos, Myanmar, Thailand and Vietnam and is focused on promotion of tourism and cultural and educational cooperation.
- Finally, the East Asia Summit provides a forum to take forward our vision of an Asian Economic Community, beginning with a Pan-Asian Free Trade Agreement.

Our target is to enhance connectivities of the north eastern region with Thailand and with other ASEAN countries beyond. The existence of land route connectivity was amply demonstrated by the India-ASEAN Car Rally of 2004. The missing links of the road route need to be upgraded.

All these efforts must be seen within the context of the objectives of the vision statement of 'an imaginative leap in the foreign policy, defence policy and internal security policy as much as in investment, infrastructure and commercial policy' to end the geo-political isolation of the north eastern region and launch it on the growth path. I believe that this new development paradigm is firmly ensconced in the approaches and efforts of the government, business and industry and civil society. The various institutional structures put in place must be harnessed to this end. Only then would there be real and tangible dividends for the people of the north eastern region.

The task is gigantic and cannot be achieved without private investment that can infuse capital, modern technology, managerial best practices and generate employment. For investors, the North-East Industrial Investment and Promotion Policy (NEIIPP) 2007 provides liberal concessions and subsidies. I am happy to note that 68 investment proposals worth over US$ 1.5 billion have been received under this policy covering various economic sectors. Private investment has a huge opportunity in sectors such as agriculture, education, healthcare and tourism. I urge businessmen participating in this summit to take full advantage of this Industrial investment and promotion policy.

The interest shown by members of the diplomatic community is heartening. The Government of India is committed to converting diplomatic initiatives into commercial opportunities for the overall development of the north eastern region.

The efforts of the Prime Minister, Minister Mani Shankar Aiyar and various chief ministers and governors of the states of the region have resulted in a plan of action and identification of sectors where private investments have immense opportunity. The central and state governments are fully aware that good governance, adequate physical infrastructure and power supply, skilled manpower and peace and security are as important as concessions and incentives for attracting investments. The experience and example of Public-Private Partnership in other parts of the country must be used for developing the infrastructure in this region.

Corporate Governance Award Function

The Institute of Company Secretaries of India

Vigyan Bhawan, New Delhi

20 December 2008

I am happy to be here today. This is a distinguished audience of professionals mandated to promote excellence and good corporate governance among business organisations in the country.

Lifetime achievement awards seek to recognise hard work, dedication and toil of decades. The kind of leadership and personality characteristics that result in such achievement need to be better understood and disseminated among industry professionals.

I congratulate the awardee companies and their company secretaries for upholding the principles of good corporate citizenship and social responsibility.

Dr Sreedharan is no stranger to us and in the past one year this is probably the third time that I am presenting him an award for his excellence and leadership.

A discussion on corporate governance is timely. The world is in the throes of economic and financial crises of monstrous dimensions. What began in the financial world has now acutely affected the real economy. The reasons are not far to seek–a failure of corporate governance and abdication of key responsibilities by the boards and managements of the companies and even by the rating agencies and regulators.

While the failure of large investment banks in the developed countries continues to convulse the globe, this week we woke up to a $50 billion Ponzi scheme operated by a Wall Street trader that has claimed numerous and prominent institutional and individual victims. The fact that such a fraud could be perpetrated on a gigantic scale involving sophisticated financial institutions and escaping regulator scrutiny speaks volumes of the state of global corporate governance.

It would appear that globalisation also extends to the darker niches of our economy, polity and society. Two days back the nation heard of a textbook case study of corporate governance failure by the promoters and the management of a top IT company that took a decision with huge financial implications that directly benefits the promoter family with no consultation with other share holders. While the decision has been reversed, it highlights the gap between the profession and practice of corporate governance and corporate social responsibility. Matters are made worse by the fact that the company in question was, quite recently, given a Global Award for Excellence in Corporate Governance!

Investor activism in this case bore fruit because it was a high profile company with many FIIs (Foreign Institutional Investor). Such instances, however, routinely happen with smaller companies.

Every economic framework and political system brings with it its own problems and peculiar characteristics that mark the corporate governance debate. The debate on corporate governance in the United States and Europe is primarily focused on the disconnect between the management and the share holders. In India, and in the light of known facts, I would like to draw attention to three aspects of corporate governance.

Firstly: The central problem of corporate governance is the conflict between the dominant share holders and minority share holders. Some argue that this basic problem cuts across all business enterprises, whether in the private or the public sector.

All too often, we see that the concept of share holder democracy is transformed into dictatorship of the majority. The Board of Directors of business organisations which derives its power from the dominant share holders has proven to be weak in protecting the interests of minority shareholders.

Secondly: The range of corporate governance instrumentalities that guide the behaviour of business organisations is usually dependent on whether the organisation is listed on the stock markets, and if so, the location of listing. Listed companies are governed by Securities Law and SEBI Guidelines and Regulations that are far more forward looking in protecting the interests of minority shareholders. The Revised Clause 49 of the Listing Agreement that is in force since 2006 has incorporated the recommendations made by the Narayana Murthy Committee on corporate governance. Indian companies that are listed in Foreign Stock Exchanges (FSE) have also to comply with country specific and global codes including the OECD (Organisation for Economic Cooperation and Development) principles of corporate governance and the UN Global Compact Programme. These substantially widen the ambit of corporate governance in business organisations.

Unlisted companies, on the other hand, are governed by company law and afford minimal protection to minority share holders.

Thirdly: There appears to be a strong correlation, and possibly causation, between corporate governance failures and the grey economy. The efforts of the government to root out black money transactions have lessened the incentive for corporate fraud. Yet, one notices that many of the instances of failure of corporate governance norms are linked to real estate or other transactions where the true value and pricing of assets and services are not transparent and provide opportunities for profiting from market inefficiencies or manipulation.

It is worth recalling that more than any other nation in history, we in India have been at the receiving end of the biggest and most devastating failure of corporate governance in global history. I refer, of course, to the East India Company. It governed in the name of trade. Jawaharlal Nehru called it "pure loot." Robert Clive and Warren Hastings carried it to such levels that British Parliament was compelled, on the initiative of Edmund Burke, to fashion instrumentalities of corporate governance.

Some of you may also recall that Adam Smith used the East India Company as a case study to argue against monopoly capitalism and for controls on corporate power.

Recent happenings the world over have shown that such manifestation of greed are persistent. They highlight the imperative need for higher standards of corporate governance, and closer scrutiny of their implementation.

The Institute of Company Secretaries thus has a tough task ahead of it. I am confident that its members would accomplish it and thereby reiterate their commitment to professional values and excellence.

I once again congratulate the winners of the award today and hope that they would continue to uphold and propagate the virtues of good corporate governance.

Fourth Convocation

The National Insurance Academy School of Management, Pune
18 July 2009

It gives me great pleasure to participate in the Annual Convocation of the Academy today. Let me confess at the outset that despite an ancestral and fraternal association with the calling, my knowledge of insurance does not go very much beyond the paying of premium on policies directed at minimising pain arising out of unanticipated happenings other than Acts of God!

I would, nevertheless, make bold to share with you some thoughts riveted on a citizen's concerns pertaining to the subject.

This is a convocation with a difference. The graduating MBA students are part of a unique institution that views the insurance sector as an important instrumentality to achieve the objectives of an essential social purpose, namely, of spreading risk that does not arise out of speculative ventures.

The National Insurance Academy has as its objectives 'the creation of an insurance order, which is responsible towards society through the inculcation of ethical and moral values'. As you leave the sheltered portals of this institution, you would be confronted with the harsh unforgiving high tides of national and global economic forces. Your commitment to the ethical and moral values inculcated here would also be severely tested in the marketplace of your vocation. I wish you all success in your professional efforts and moral steadfastness.

Since times immemorial, the human race had to deal with uncertainties. Evolution and progress were critically dependent on the ability to understand, analyse and use the uncertainties of life to one's advantage. The establishment and growth of human civilisation has led to a steady growth in various forms and dimensions of insurance to deal with uncertainty. Today, a vibrant insurance industry is critical to any modern economy.

The insurance sector reform undertaken since 2000 has opened up the sector for private participation, provided a developmental and regulatory mechanism for the sector, and led to de-tariffing of general insurance. It has led to an unprecedented growth in the sector. In the seven-year period since 2000, the life insurance sector had a compound annual growth rate of 42 per cent. As a result, Insurance Penetration in the country more than doubled and increased from 1.93 per cent in 1999 to 4.7 per cent in 2007. Yet, it is still far short of the Asian average of 6.2 per cent and the global average of 7.5 per cent.

Likewise, though the Insurance Density has increased more than five times from $8.5 in 1999 to $46.6 in the year 2007, it is still far short of the Asian average of $210.7 and the global average of $607. Although our insurance market grew almost eight times from $8 billion in 2000 to $54.375 billion in 2007, it still represented a mere 1.34 per cent of the global insurance market of US$4061 billion.

The process of reform and liberalisation was intended to benefit the common citizen who, in our society, either has no insurance or is under-insured. In this context, a few aspects of our insurance scene need to be noted; they also pose some questions.

First: The common performance indicators of the industry are focused on premium collected patterns of investment and number of insurance agents employed. One does not readily come across data regarding life insurance coverage, life insurance per capita and life insurance carrying capacity. What is lost sight of is that the insurance industry exists not to collect money for investment but to provide insurance. The nature of commissions and compensation to insurance intermediaries directs a greater proportion of premia away from insurance cover towards investments.

Second: An important outcome expected from the reforms process and the entry of private sector was enhanced availability, quality and quantity of commercial health insurance cover to our citizens. Yet, commercial health insurance covers a mere 25 million persons in a country of over 1.1 billion people. The demand for health insurance has not been innovatively met with supply of products and services and many private insurers merely adopted the Mediclaim policy of public sector insurers. Lack of standardised health insurance data and process for data collation and analysis remains a significant lacuna. Much more needs to done to increase the penetration of health insurance in the country and make available risk protection to our citizens in an affordable and sustainable manner.

The real challenge to the industry is to focus on product development adapted to the heterogeneity of health insurance consumers in India. The methodology for collating data, accessing clients, selling and servicing health insurance products must be in tune with the Indian social context and dynamics, and available infrastructure. The availability of medical insurance should be seen as complementary to, and not as a replacement of, state provision of universal health care that constitutes a long term investment in its citizens and their productive capacities. It is to be hoped that one day the 'Right to Healthcare' would become an enforceable fundamental right.

Third: According to the Census of 2001, the rural sector comprises 72 per cent of the population and contributes 26 per cent of the GDP. Private insurers currently look at rural and social sector business more as an obligation rather than as an opportunity. Despite the numbers and the demand for insurance propelled by growth in income, savings and education in rural areas, rural insurance has remained a small component of the total market. There is a need for robust expansion of branches and recruitment of agents in rural areas to tap the rural potential.

Fourth: Micro Insurance aims at meeting the insurance needs of the rural and targeted section of the population to cover the risk of loss of life, income earning assets, habitat and risks to their health. The efforts of the government to promote micro insurance and integrate it with poverty alleviation programmes are slowly bearing fruit. It is worth noting that over 80 per cent of micro insurance business and agents are accounted for by the public sector LIC. It is another area where the promise of reform and liberalisation concerning private enterprise is yet to percolate to the really needy citizens.

Fifth: An important policy objective for risk mitigation and ensuring the welfare of our farmers is to have an effective agricultural insurance mechanism to counter the frequency and severity of droughts, floods and cyclone, rising temperatures and unpredictable agro-climatic variations including erratic rainfall. At present, the National Agricultural Insurance Scheme covers only 17 per cent of all farmers and 20 per cent of crop area.

The Weather Based Crop Insurance Scheme that has been implemented on a pilot basis has been hampered by poor density of weather stations and lack of weather data on real time basis at village level. The scheme faced a reality test after the recent cyclone Aila that devastated West Bengal. Media reports noted that though the resultant crop damage was estimated at over Rs500 crores, insurers may have to pay a mere Rs 7 lakhs as compensation due to technicalities that bulk of the crop damage was due to winds and tides and not rains, and the fact that rains were lower in many places than the threshold level beyond which payment becomes due.

The current agricultural insurance schemes suffer from low coverage and high claims-to-premium ratio. There is an urgent need to seriously consider some proposals including coverage of pre-sowing and post-harvest risks and effecting a transition to actuarial rates and upfront subsidy payments by the Government which will enable timely claim payments. Sustainable agricultural growth and improvement in agricultural technology and productivity would not be possible without reliable risk cover for our farmers.

The format of development of the insurance industry can neither be standardised nor be prescriptive across national contexts. The ultimate beneficiaries of the reforms process and the resultant competitive insurance market should be the Indian public. Insurance is slowly moving beyond tax incentives and statutory insurance requirements towards becoming an effective risk mitigation instrument.

The success of the transition and reaping of the fruits of insurance depends on the efficacy of regulation and timely innovation to cater to the real needs of our citizens. It is my hope that the students graduating today, and those benefiting by the training provided by the National Insurance Academy, would contribute to the development of a vibrant insurance market in the country.

I wish the graduating students all success in their professional efforts and thank the Academy for inviting me to the convocation.

Corruption, Governance, Social Morality

❛ Wherever law ends tyranny begins

Haksar Memorial Lecture

Centre for Research in Rural and Industrial Development, Chandigarh

30 November 2007

The task is daunting, the capability questionable. To be called upon to deliver the P.N. Haksar Memorial Lecture would be a great honour at any time; it is to me particularly because I belong to a generation of Indians who witnessed Haksar saheb's work in two phases of his life–of action and of introspection. Neither of these, let me add, was totally exclusive. By the time of his death in 1998, some of the major premises of his belief system–democracy, secularism, socialism, nonalignment–had come under pressure and were the cause of disillusionment.

In an editorial in *Man and Development* many years back, Haksar spoke of the need "to hold aloft the banner of the moral universe" and opined that "human passions" and "permanent values"play a role in history. Elsewhere, he expressed surprise over the "symptoms of utter confusion in its value system" displayed by the Indian society in a period of change. "Preserving the moral health of body politic and maintaining the ecological balance", he wrote, "are conditions precedent to survival and growth not only of India, but of this entire earth".

It is my purpose today to probe these concepts and Indian responses to them.

A great revolutionary of the twentieth century, Leon Trotsky, described the role of sentiment in critical moments in human history. "The masses", he wrote in his monumental *History of the Russian Revolution* "go into a revolution not with a prepared plan of social reconstruction, but with a sharp feeling that they cannot endure the old regime". He pointed to the difficulties encountered in studying "the changes in mass consciousness in a revolutionary epoch".

How then do we define the moral universe and the role of passion in it? The challenge for India, said Haksar, is "to use its material, intellectual, cultural and philosophical resources to regenerate itself into a truly free, just and humane society, and simultaneously to strive for a similar world society. The two are different aspects of the same objective, for a humane and peaceable India is not possible if it lives in an aggressive world atmosphere".

The operative words are free, just, and humane. They relate to the domestic and the global scene. India became free in 1947 and gave itself a Constitution in 1950 that spelt out the dimensions of justice. It is to be social, economic and political. The sequence is not alphabetical and its logic is not difficult to comprehend. Distributive justice is writ large and has been so understood. It connotes the removal of injustice resulting from transactions between un-equals in society.

The law does not define 'humane' or humaneness. Its dictionary meaning–benevolent or compassionate–is in the realm of morality, ethics and philosophy. What is not defined in law is amplified in common usage. In America, a humane society is defined as 'as a group that aims to stop animal suffering due to cruelty or other reasons; in fact, an American Humane Association for Protecting Children and Animals came into existence in 1877. From this, one could, in Socratic reasoning, perhaps argue on the one hand that humaneness could include prevention of cruelty to humans as a whole and, on the other, draw attention to the unavoidable link between humaneness and justice. On this logic, therefore, a just society has to be a caring society.

Other questions need to be considered before proceeding further. Is there a linkage between the social realm and the moral one? Is it possible to structure relationships on a political basis? Have societies existed that have defined their structures and relationships principally or exclusively on functional terms devoid of a value judgment? What has been the ambit of such societies in terms of inclusion and exclusion?

The debate goes back a long way in history. In *Mahabharata* the sage Vamadeva stresses the need to act righteously: 'There is nothing superior to righteousness. Those kings that are observant of righteousness succeed ... That king who disregards righteousness and desires to act with brute force, soon falls away from righteousness and loses both Righteousness and Profit'.

The pervasiveness of the concept is evident in all periods and in all societies. Rousseau aptly posed the perennial question: "I wish to enquire whether, taking men as they are and laws as they can be made, it is possible to establish some just and certain rule of administration in civil affairs".

This is evident in our own times in Mahatma Gandhi's teachings and in Ambedkar's definition of Dharma as 'righteousness, which means right relations between man and man in all spheres of life' and is, of necessity, social. It is also the essence of morality.

II

The Raj Ghat at New Delhi is visited reverentially by the public, ritually by public figures and out of curiosity by tourists. A little away from the Samadhi is a stone tablet with the inscription: Seven Social Sins. These are listed on the tablet:

- Politics without principle
- Pleasure without conscience
- Wealth without work
- Knowledge without character
- Commerce without morality
- Science without humanity
- Worship without sacrifice

Each of these is a statement of principle that can be comprehended, interpreted and implemented, individually and collectively. On my part, I would like to discern a pattern in the last words of each dictum: principle, conscience, work, character, morality, humanity and sacrifice. A similar pattern, summing up different forms of human activity, is discernible when the first words of the statements are put together.

In the Gandhian approach, therefore, conscience is motivated by considerations of humanity and sacrifice to develop a moral character that holds aloft in its work the banner of a principled approach. The reverse of it would be selfishness inducing an unprincipled, opportunistic, approach to work. The latter would produce neither justice nor humaneness. On this thesis, the choice would be clear if the human being is a moral creature having a sense of right and wrong in his individual and group conduct.

Here we are confronted by a set of questions. Can the principles of public morality be different from those of private morality? Can a society have one set of ethical norms for governing conduct of public institutions and another set of norms for citizens in their individual capacities? Do these norms govern the conduct of the highest form of public institution – the State (a) in relation to its citizens and (b) in inter-state relations? In other words, is the State required to observe norms of behaviour in its functioning?

For purposes of our discussion, therefore, we end up with four possible categories of conduct norms: for individuals, institutions, the State within its domestic jurisdiction, and the State in its dealings with other states. This raises a fundamental question: Is such categorisation desirable? Can virtue and righteousness be imbibed selectively? Is it not desirable to have a unified theory of morality?

The Gandhian, and the ethical approach would be to insist both on a unified theory and on practice in consonance with it. In actual practice, however, selectivity is the norm. This approach concedes the desirability of morality in personal life but finds reasons for departing from it in public life. The proponents of this approach make a beginning with inter-state relations in the comity of nations. An English statesman made the classic statement on this subject in late nineteenth century. 'I am a great believer', he said, 'in morality, public and private; you must however concede that the conduct of nations cannot be governed by it'. He did not add but undoubtedly implied that the State was above moral norms in its external dealings.

The argument had a limited time span. State misbehaviour contributed to it in good measure. The end of World War I saw the beginning of systematic efforts to circumscribe the unchecked conduct of states. World War II gave it an impetus and led to the Charter of the United Nations. International covenants in the past seven decades have put paid to the doctrine of absolute sovereignty and to the unchecked behaviour of states. Practice, of course, lags behind but is not sought to be justified in principle.

III

A parallel evolution was witnessed in regard to the behaviour of the State within its domestic jurisdiction. The principle of rule of law, and of responsible and responsive governance, is no longer disputed and is being implemented in increasing measure. Before we delve into the particular domain of the current situation of our society and polity, I wish to briefly examine the instrumentalities that societal and political evolution has bestowed upon us for dispelling the darkness of moral ambiguity of states – the moral torch lights of our era. These are: 1. A globalising civil society; 2. Fundamental and universal human rights; 3. A global movement for enhanced transparency in the functioning of state actors.

We have seen periods in history where states have applied different standards or moral criteria (a) in their domestic jurisdiction, and (b) while dealing with states and peoples whom they consider as not deserving of equal treatment.

Yet, the horizon is not all dark. In our country, our region and beyond we witness active civil society movements that have supported common peoples and have sought to bring back State behaviour to the moral realm. Advancement in communication and transportation has facilitated the process of globalisation of this civil society movement. This development has been critical in emphasising the primacy of fundamental and universal human rights, not only as a basic norm of State behaviour but also in the behaviour of individuals towards each other. Human rights, in varying degrees, have been internalised voluntarily or on account of external pressures.

The drive for greater transparency in State behaviour was intended to make State actors accountable. In our own country, the 'Right to Information' movement has had significant success and is seen globally as a pioneering effort. Good governance and transparency are being recognised as imperatives in corporate institutions and will be increasingly so in the future.

It is undisputed today that a free, just and humane society is one that respects fundamental human rights not only of its citizens but of all peoples, has a State structure that is transparent in its functioning and encourages the growth of a healthy civil society.

Step by step, therefore, the circle for unprincipled, immoral and amoral behaviour is being narrowed down to individual behaviour. The challenge lies in addressing it because individuals are the building blocks of societies. They are also the principal actors in political life of societies and determine its character by their principles and conduct.

IV

A transition from the general to the particular is essential to carry the argument forward. The Indian society of today, despite its moorings in religion and tradition, is increasingly prone to be amoral in the behaviour of its individual and group components. A good instance is the case of corruption in public life.

Political corruption is defined as the misuse of public office for private gain. Mahatma Gandhi's outburst in 1939 is indicative of its presence even in the period before Independence.

In 1949 the Urdu poet Josh Malihabadi, in a poem titled *Rishwat,* gave vent to public's perception of the prevalent bribery. A quatrain portrays its extent:

Log ham se roz kahte hain yeh aadat chhore de
Yeh tejarat hai khelaaf-e-aadmiyat chhore de
Is se bad tar lat nehain hai koye, yeh lat chhore de
Roz akhbaroan main chhapta hai ki rishwat chhore de

A couplet, towards the end of the poem, was cynically expressive of disgust:

Illat-e rishwat ko is dunya se rukhsat keejiye
War na rishwat ki dharalle se ijazt deejiye

In 1951 the A.D. Gorwala Report made specific observations on this count. In 1964 the Santhanam Committee noted the 'widespread impression that failure of integrity is not uncommon among ministers and that some ministers, who have held office during the last sixteen years, have enriched themselves illegitimately'. It also talked of nepotism and 'other advantages inconsistent with any notion of purity in public life'. More recently, the published portions of the N.N. Vohra Report of 1995 spoke of 'the nexus between criminal gangs, police, bureaucracy and politicians has come out clearly in various parts of the country. The existing criminal justice system, which was essentially designed to deal with individual offences/crimes, is unable to deal with the activities of the Mafia; the provisions of the law in regard to economic offences are weak'.

An observation by a former Chief Justice of India, in 1997, is telling. "The element of deterrence", he noted, "is almost non-existent. The public perception is that the machinery for enforcement of accountability is itself controlled by those whose accountability needs to be enforced. All institutions of law enforcement lack accountability, the difference between them is only in the degree of culpability". He pleaded for "concerted efforts for infusion of ethics in public life".

An official acknowledgement of the problem of corruption came from Prime Minister Dr Manmohan Singh in August 2004. Addressing a conference of state CBI and Anti-corruption Bureau officials, he said:

"The problem of corruption in public life is a source of great concern for all those who are interested in building a new India, an inclusive society, progressive society and a dynamic economy and a compassionate polity. In my Independence Day Address, I said that while the question of ethics in public life has repeatedly agitated our people, we have tried over a period of time, to find constitutional, legislative and administrative devices to deal with the challenge posed by growth of corruption to our body politic. I said in my address that the time has come for us to evolve consensually a code of conduct for all political parties, a code of ethics for all individuals in public life, and a code of best practices for the Government at all levels."

This statement, from the highest levels of Government, is indicative of the seriousness of the problem. It can be supplemented, in ample measure, by civil society perceptions. The Corruption Perception Index of Transparency International, based on public opinion and business community surveys, gave India in 2007 the score of 3.5 on a scale of 10 (highly clean). The corresponding figures for the preceding years were 3.3, 2.9, and 2.8. India was ranked 72 in a list of 179 countries.

This state of affairs has implications that are wide-ranging and multi-dimensional. The challenge is to comprehend, and confront the question in its totality. Corruption is as much moral as a development issue. It tends to distort the decision-making processes on investment projects and other commercial transactions. It impacts at the foundations of the social and political fabric of society. It increases injustice and disregard for the rule of law. As such, it is to be viewed as a symptom of fundamental weaknesses in the institutions; the correctives, therefore, need to focus on a set of fundamental institutional determinants.

To what extent has the political system reacted to the malaise? A good example is the First Report of the Ethics Committee of the Rajya Sabha, in December 1998. It had this to say in its opening paragraphs:

'Moral and ethical concerns of the society weigh a great deal with those in public life as their behaviour is keenly watched by the people. At concerned quarters views are being expressed over the general decline in moral and ethical standards in public life. The Committee has itself noted the general decline in moral and ethical standards in public life. While the Committee felt that it was a serious trend, it did not, however, fully share the despondency …

'There is a general feeling that all is not right with our political system which is functioning under a great strain. In such a situation, the representatives of the people have to set high standards of behaviour in public life. Members of Parliament have not only to represent the society but have also to lead it. Therefore, they have to function as the role models and this naturally casts on them a heavy responsibility …

'The Committee notes that our freedom fighters and national leaders had set high ethical and moral standards in public life and they followed those principles scrupulously. This tendency, the Committee painfully observes, is now on a decline'.

The Report addressed the question of criminalisation of politics and felt it could only be tackled through self-regulatory mechanisms of political parties. It recommended a model code of conduct, of a general nature, for the members of the Rajya Sabha.

The Third Report of the Ethics Committee, in August 2002, opined that 'ethical questions are mainly matters of one's conscience' and therefore cannot be dealt entirely by legislation.

The argument thus returns to its point of commencement. The imperative of ethics in public life is eventually a matter of conscience, of morality, of a sense of values in relation to right and wrong, good and bad, just and unjust, humane and cruel. The perceived dichotomy between public and the private behaviour of individuals, therefore, does not exist in ethical terms and must not exist in practice. It follows that the individual, in relation to the State in any aspect of its functioning, must act in an ethical manner; it then becomes the duty of the State as well as of the civil society to ensure this through appropriate instrumentalities of law as also of social pressures. Only then would we see the day when the corrupt would not only be punished but also ostracised.

Conscience, in other words, may need to be jostled from time to time. The duty of the State, and of the civil society, is to be proactive in the matter. Only then would the moral realm in public life become meaningful and make India of the future truly free, just and humane.

Ninth D.P. Kohli Memorial Lecture
New Delhi
23 April 2008

It is a privilege to be invited to deliver the ninth D.P. Kohli Memorial Lecture. The founder-director of the Central Bureau of Investigation possessed in ample measure the attributes of professionalism, leadership and integrity and served the Bureau and the country with great distinction.

I happen to come from a background where the assigned responsibility was to determine actual or potential threats to Indian interests emanating from abroad, to consider the possible manner of countering them and, in the process, furthering national interest in its most comprehensive sense. Thus, the focus principally was on external actors, state and non-state.

Interestingly, internal threat assessments rarely mention 'non-militant threats'.

The question I wish to pose is whether we consider challenges to governance to be equally threatening to our chosen way of life, as enunciated in the Constitution?

To consider the matter fully, some definitional clarity would be helpful.

Governance is defined in a UNDP document as the exercise of political, economic and administrative authority to manage a nation's affairs. It is the complex mechanisms, processes and institutions through which citizens and groups articulate their interests, exercise their legal rights and obligations, and mediate their differences.

Good governance is participatory, transparent, inclusive, accountable, and effective. International norms now include in it the rule of law and observance of human rights. It 'has the paradoxical attribute of being visible by its absence rather than its presence.'

II

India, wrote two knowledgeable American scholars before the era of economic reforms, "is a political and economic paradox: a rich-poor nation with a weak-strong state". They set out "to unravel this paradox by examining the interactions between polity and economy".

The interaction between polity and economy reflects on governance in its totality. In six decades of independence, we have travelled a good distance, marked successes, made mistakes, learnt a good deal, experimented and innovated in adequate measure.

Critics have spoken of the crisis of governance and de-institutionalisation; others have dwelt on the resilience and adaptability of the structures. There is an element of truth in both these assertions.

Our functioning is a mix of dynamism and inertia, of social equilibrium punctured by occasional eruptions, of rule of law flawed by practice of flagrant violations. We remain committed to democratic governance, transparency and inclusive development but fail to deliver in sufficient measure.

An assessment on various counts would show the glass as half-full. Today, I intend to dwell on the other half of it since it impedes progress. The challenge is to ascertain the cause of debility, and to rectify it.

It is the public perception that one major factor of debility in governance is corruption, defined as 'behaviour by a public servant, whether elected or appointed, which involves a deviation from his or her formal duties because of reasons of personal gain to himself or herself or to other private persons with whom the public person is associated.' Its original meaning has connotations of evil, malignance, sickness, loss of innocence or purity.

This perception of corruption is supported by independent studies undertaken by Transparency International India and other civil society or professional groups. According to TII's India Corruption Study 2005, '62 per cent of citizens think that corruption is not a heresy, but they in fact had firsthand experience of paying bribes or using a contact to get a job done in a public office'.

The Transparency International's Corruption Perception Index 2007 ranks India at 72, bracketed with China, Brazil, Mexico, Morocco, Peru and Surinam and with a score of 3.5 out of possible 10. The same document indicates that there are twenty-two countries with a score of 7 and above, and forty-eight countries with a score of 5 and above.

Two sets of explanations are given to explain, or explain away, the problem. The first states that it is a universal phenomenon, to be found in all societies and therefore to be endured; the second stresses that it is a consequence of democratic functioning and thus compels co-habitation.

Both seem plausible, both are false.

If corruption is a universal phenomenon, then it should be present in all societies in proximate measure. The CP Index shows that it is not so, and that there are countries that steer clear of it with much greater success. Most of them are also democratic societies. Gandhi*ji* was therefore right when he observed that corruption ought not to be an inevitable product of democracy.

The disease in India, nevertheless, has deep roots. Kautilya in *Arthashastra* noted that public servants could enrich themselves improperly in two ways, either by cheating the government or by exploiting the public. He listed forty methods of stealing; most of these have a contemporary relevance.

Rishwat was the title of a long poem written in 1949 by the Urdu poet Josh Malihabadi. It was reflective of public perception even then. One couplet portrayed the perspective of the salaried class:

Jub talak rishwat na lain hum daal gul sakti nahin
Naon tankhwahoan ke paani main to chal sakti nahin

Corruption is pervasive, cancerous and multi-dimensional. In its moral dimension, it impacts the foundations of the social and political fabric of society and increases injustice; in its legal implications, it results in disregard for the rule of law; in its developmental aspect, it tends to distort the decision-making processes on investment projects and other commercial transactions and is wasteful of resources.

But corruption is much more than an irritant or growth retardant; it has emerged as a significant national security threat. The creeping assault of corruption on the national fabric has shaken the legitimacy of the Indian state. It has eroded state sovereignty and capacity to exercise sovereign functions including ensuring law and order and safeguarding national security for the citizens.

The first, and direct, impact of corruption in its simplest manifestation is on the common man and woman. Corrupt practices relating to the availability of essential commodities or medicines, their scarcity or absence due to hoarding or diversion to the open market, causes acute hardship; it has an overall inflationary impact.

There is sufficient empirical evidence to prompt a typology of corruption: it is individual or institutional, petty or large scale, bureaucratic, political or economic. Each type has its own impulses, symptoms and peculiarities. Each requires a different response within the overarching framework of our democratic system.

Societal perceptions, based on tradition, can and do become an instrument for promoting or tolerating corruption. The Urdu term '*kunbah-parvari*' has its equivalents in all our languages. It means looking after the family or clan based on kinship, ethnic, linguistic or religious ties. Tradition considers it a desirable social virtue; modernity translates it as nepotism and frowns upon it.

In terms of methodological analysis, the relevant questions pertain, firstly, to how opportunity structures are created and secondly, to how processes of corruption operate in practice. The role of intermediaries possessing skills in illegality and networking abilities is of great relevance in this regard.

III

In a democracy, political power resides with the people. By definition, therefore, political corruption becomes the most lethal and damaging form of corruption since its processes undermine the institutions of democracy themselves and thereby affect adversely correctives at other levels of society. The quality and integrity of the political representative, therefore, becomes a matter of critical relevance for the proper functioning of a democracy.

An observation of the sociologist Max Weber has a bearing on the debate. There are, he wrote, two ways of making a vocation of politics: either to live for politics, or live off it. The CBI in its institutional memory, would know more about the latter category than the scholars and commentators who have written on the subject!

Corruption, writes Ramachandra Guha in his tome on the history of contemporary India, is the 'inconvenient fact' of Indian democracy. It obstructs the egalitarian and participatory public agenda that the people of India have given themselves. The data cited by him makes depressing reading. He concludes that:

- "Because being in power is so profitable, there is now increasing trade in politicians";
- "Because politics is such good business, it has also become a dirty business";
- "With corruption and criminalisation, Indian politics has also increasingly fallen victim to nepotism";
- "A survey carried out by Gallup in sixty countries found that the lack of confidence in politicians was highest in India, where 91 per cent of those polled felt that their elected representatives were dishonest";
- "Corruption in contemporary India is widespread not merely in the legislature, but in the executive branch as well";
- "Corruption and negligence are not unknown" in the judiciary though "ordinary people look up to judges in a way in which they no longer look up to legislators, ministers or civil servants";
- "The decline of Parliament, and of reasoned public discourse in general, has meant' that 'India is no longer a constitutional democracy but a populist one".

These judgements can be, and have been, quantified nationally and by international agencies. They should leave us in no doubt that we are confronted by a problem of monstrous dimensions.

It is also squarely in the public domain. The Approach Paper to the 11th Five-Year Plan spelt it out unambiguously: 'Corruption is now seen to be endemic in all spheres and this problem needs to be addressed urgently.'

This statement of policy approach is impeccable. The question is of the will, the instrumentality of implementation and of its efficacy. The three go together and interact on each other. None can be considered in isolation.

Where do we stand today about the will and the instrumentality?

Record bears evidence to shortcomings on both counts. A former director of the Central Bureau of Investigation wrote last week about "the near unanimity among political parties of all hues that the CBI should succeed only against minor players and not against major perpetrators of the crime of bribery".

Other perceptions may be more sanguine. Most agree on the imperative need for correctives. Would the system, and particularly the state governments, respond in adequate measure?

IV

We have a situation in which the politics of corruption and the corruption of politics fuel each other. Both impact adversely on governance and therefore on development. A UNDP report estimated sometime back that if corruption levels are reduced to those of Scandinavian countries, investment in India would increase by 10 per cent and the GDP growth by 1.5 per cent.

The conclusion is unavoidable that corruption hampers governance and development and constrains the progress of the Indian society. Since it impacts on all aspects of state activity, it becomes the most important threat to the state, more so because it is less visible than the external enemy.

How then do we confront and overcome this enemy within?

The situation is perilous but retrievable. A successful campaign against corruption in public life needs to have moral, legal, political, administrative and economic dimensions. The following would be relevant:

First: Individual resolve, group pressure and public commitment can help roll back the threat in good measure.

Second: The moral realm is relevant because it motivates and has an impact on the character of individual citizens. Morality is a social necessity since pervasive immorality cannot but be destructive to social order. It derives its sustenance from tradition and religious or ethical principles.

The impediment at the moment is that corruption is accepted in the social psyche and behaviour as an unavoidable fact of life. Even the tinge of disapproval is missing. We need to bring back the sense of right and wrong, and place corruption squarely in the latter category.

Third: Legal structures are necessary to confront breaches of law. A maze of regulations is already in existence. Observers consider them cumbersome and dilatory. Experience highlights their inadequacy. It has been noted that the conviction rate in our courts is only 6 per cent.

The corrective lies in strict enforcement of the principle of accountability at all levels and in simplifying procedures. Endless enquiries allow the wicked to consolidate their gains; a specified time span for investigation and prosecution of corruption cases is essential.

The Supreme Court in the Vineet Narain case had advocated the need for an impartial prosecution agency on the lines of the Director of Prosecution in the United Kingdom.

To restore and enhance public confidence in the investigation agency, its work in corruption cases should be immunised from political considerations.

Fourth: At the political level, it is not sufficient to endorse ritualistically the advice given by sages on the need for righteousness. The bar of integrity has to be raised higher and defaults dealt with greater rigour.

Agreeing with the charge of a general decline in moral and ethical standards in public life, the Ethics Committee of the Rajya Sabha recommended in 1998 that: 'Members of Parliament have not only to represent the society but have also to lead it. Therefore, they have to function as role models'. A decade later, this lead has not been provided.

The question, in reality, goes beyond the individual legislator and relates to the functioning of the political system, the money flows to political parties and individuals, the funding of elections, the phenomenon of 'vote buying', and the practices through which private and corporate interests extract illicit gains from the system in its totality.

The matter eventually relates to the legitimacy of the political system. This, in a democratic state, must be judged by its citizens and renewed on a continuous basis. Periodic elections are the normal way of doing it. If however the system begins to feast on itself, then external correctives become unavoidable.

Fifth: We must look at countering corruption beyond the framework of law enforcement, and promote the participation of individuals and groups outside the public sector. Civil society, NGOs and community based organisations must be harnessed in raising the awareness about this 'enemy within' and in fighting it.

The Right to Information Act, public interest litigation and some steps taken by the Central Vigilance Commission have helped the process considerably. So has the use of information technology and e-governance. Some correctives suggested by the Fourth Report of the Administrative Reform Commission, headed by Shri Veerappa Moily, appear promising.

Sixth: In the matter of crime detection and prevention, the quest for best practices need not stop at national borders. In today's world, corruption has emerged as a global phenomenon and it is important that all countries support international cooperation in the fight against corruption.

The work undertaken by the UNDP on human development and governance and the Anti-Corruption Toolkit developed by the UN Office on Drugs and Crimes proved useful in applying correctives. India has signed the United Nations Convention against Corruption in December 2005. We are yet to ratify this Convention and must do so at the earliest.

Seventh: As a society and polity, we need to encourage more inclusive and universal affiliations based on commitment to pluralism and secularism, rule of law and constitutionalism. Broadening the base of civic and public participation would build a stake for discouraging nepotism and other corrupt practices.

V

In the final analysis, national institutions for governance and for fighting crimes against it sustain their legitimacy by responding meaningfully to the public's desire for clear, effective, and transparent governance. To do so, and in addition to their professional skills, they have to adhere to the Gandhian model of a moral character and hold aloft the banner of a principled approach.

Failure to do so in adequate measure would corrode public confidence, breed cynicism and would be altogether harmful to the Republic and its democratic principles.

This is the challenge that a premier institution like the CBI has to address. I am confident that it has the will, the resources and the leadership to do it.

Book release: *India Corruption Study 2007* compiled by Transparency International India

The India International Islamic Centre, New Delhi

28 June 2008

There is always an air of expectation about annual reports. Sometimes they add to our knowledge, at others reiterate the evident. The contents, again, may cause delight or dismay, or, occasionally, a bit of both! The India Corruption Study 2007 falls in the latter category.

The good news is that inch by inch, year by year, there is greater transparency about the way we are governed. The bad part is that the level and extent of misgovernance is horrifying in legal and moral terms.

Over the years Transparency International India has done commendable work to quantify corruption, described by the Tenth Plan as the 'most endemic and entrenched manifestation of poor governance'. The focus of this latest report is on analysing the misery caused by corruption to the poorest of the land, for accessing the most basic of services.

What are the findings? They cover five basic services–PDS (Public Distribution System), hospital, school education, electricity, and water supply–and six need-based services–police, land records, forests, housing, banking and NREGS (National Rural Employment Generation Scheme). In specific terms, they reveal:

- About one-third of BPL (Below Poverty Line) households paid bribes to avail one or more of these eleven services.
- The benefits of recent steps taken to improve delivery of public services have not substantially percolated down to the poor as yet.

- Nearly two-third of BPL households could not avail of PDS, school education and electricity as they could not pay the bribe or use contact or influence to avail of the service.
- The situation stands at an alarming level with regard to police and land record/registration.
- It is thus evident that our stated resolve to usher in inclusive growth that covers all the marginalised and vulnerable sections of the society is frustrated by corruption that hinders access to basic services.
- Corruption in our country has become pervasive and cancerous and is multi-dimensional. Today's report highlights this in ample measure. Three broad aspects make this evident:
- In its moral dimension, it cuts at the very roots of the social and political fabric of society and increases injustice.
- In its legal implications, it results in disregard for the rule of law.
- In its developmental aspect, it tends to distort the decision-making processes on investment projects and other commercial transactions and is wasteful of resources.

The victims of corruption transcend all classes or groups. It is therefore important to quantify it as a governance problem and present it in terms that resonate with common citizens.

The report brings out that grievance redressal modes that have made an impact at the level of upper and middle classes have not even tangentially impacted upon BPL households. Thus, computerisation, e-governance, citizen charters, RTI (Right to Information) Act and social audits have minimal resonance for the poor. Entitlement of BPL households to basic services provided by the government is meaningless without knowledge of and unhindered access to such services and universal awareness of grievance redressal mechanisms.

The report brings to light the negative impact of competitive politics on targeted schemes aimed at the poor. It has reported instances of BPL, SC/ST and other vulnerable households of being told by political activists of a linkage between benefits and electoral preferences. This, to the extent it is true, amounts to political corruption in its damaging form since it undermines the very institutions of democracy at all levels. A national consensus at its avoidance is thus imperative.

Delineating a problem is one aspect; finding correctives and outlining an action plan for their implementation is far more difficult. The India Corruption Study 2007 has suggested a four pronged drive focused on:

- Simplification of procedures.
- Streamlining of information flows.
- Reorienting front end staff for service provision to BPL households.
- Activating civil society groups to combat corruption.

I am confident that both the government and civil society would take the study and these suggested correctives seriously.

An old maxim states that eternal vigilance is the price of liberty. In today's world, it is also insurance for proper governance. In the final analysis, good governance involves meaningful response to the public's desire for clear, effective, and transparent governance.

Fourth Civil Services Day

Vigyan Bhawan, New Delhi
21 April 2009

It gives me great pleasure to inaugurate the Fourth Civil Services Day. This annual get together provides an occasion for introspection, self-evaluation and exchange of perspectives, experiences, and best practices. This sets the stage for course correction.

I would like to felicitate all those who have won the Prime Minister's Awards for Excellence in Public Administration for the year 2007-2008 for individual and team initiatives in diverse fields. I do hope they would continue their good work and that their example would be emulated by others in the Civil Service.

The concept of civil service has evolved over time; so have notions of its role and responsibilities. Independent India inherited from the British period a comprehensive civil service structure and established practices. Its utility for ensuring national unity and good administration in the country was recognised by Sardar Patel, accepted by the Constituent Assembly and incorporated in the Constitution. It is relevant today to recall the Sardar's perception and his vision:

"I need hardly emphasise that an efficient, disciplined and contented Service, assured of its prospects as a result of diligent and honest work, is sine qua non of sound administration under a democratic regime even more than under an authoritarian rule. The service must be above party and we should ensure that political considerations either in its recruitment or in its discipline and control are reduced to the minimum, if not eliminated altogether … Constitutional guarantees and safeguards are the best medium of providing for these services and are likely to prove more lasting."

This statement enunciated three principles: (1) the civil service will be above party politics, (2) political considerations would be eschewed in its recruitment, discipline and control, and (3) Constitutional safeguards and guarantees essential for its effective functioning will be provided.

The challenge in the early years of the republic was to reconcile differing perceptions, of the political leadership emerging from the freedom movement on the one hand and the inherited civil service on the other, on two aspects of the functioning of the latter. The first of these related to meaning of civil service 'neutrality'; the second to the question of its 'commitment' to policies. Prime Minister Nehru responded to both unambiguously. The civil service cannot distance itself from the fundamentals of state policy nor can it function effectively without being supportive of the policies developed through due process.

Both these notions resurfaced from time to time either to retard change or to stretch commitment from policies to individuals or political groups. It is to the credit of our polity that the overwhelming majority distanced itself, in principle if not always in practice, from such efforts. It also became clear early enough that in a new India the role of the civil service has to go beyond 'good administration' in the traditional sense to include the requisite skills and motivation for nation building and developmental activities.

The Civil Service is an integral part of our society and its structure of governance. Its DNA is shaped by the imperatives of social mores, political calculus, and economic context of the times. One aspect of this is the emergence of coalition politics and governments constituted pursuant to it. It can be attributed to a deepening of democracy and the emergence of a genuinely federalised multi-party system accompanied by the rise of regional, linguistic, caste-based and other parties promoting such sectional interests.

Unlike popular perceptions coalitions are neither unique to India nor inherently destabilising. In many countries the world over, as also in India itself at the state and federal levels, coalitions on agreed programmes have worked satisfactorily. The difficulty lies in demarcating the fine line between political like-mindedness and political opportunism. It is rarely articulated coherently and inevitably surfaces in the day to day functioning of the administrative structure. The first impact of the mischief is thus experienced by the civil servant.

What then should the role of the civil services be in an era of political coalitions? Our own experience sheds light on two of its aspects.

First, a distinguished former cabinet secretary has noted the tendency by political parties to use the bureaucratic machine as a substitute for the lack of active field cadres and thus becomes an alternate cadre for the parties in power. In this context, he observed, the most important quality for the bureaucracy in the coalition era is to be 'apolitical', adding that 'in the Indian context it means that the bureaucracy is loyal to the Constitution, and though under the party in power, it functions in a way which is fair to all irrespective of their political affiliations'.

Second, an editorial in a business daily observed recently that 'coalitions have taken on the nature of the old mansabdari system–the greater the number of horses you can offer to the king, the greater the size of territory for you to pillage'. It expressed concern at the monetary and economic cost for the nation as a consequence of coalition arrangements in power. One consequence of this, in the words of a distinguished former civil servant and legislator, is the propensity to "follow the policy of least resistance." This "indirect participation in the wrong doings of the politicians" by the civil servants through silence and passive inaction, he notes, has "contributed substantially towards the erosion of people's confidence in the objectivity and impartiality of civil servants." Much the same assessment comes from other eminent former civil servants of yesteryears. The near unanimity of their views cannot be altogether ignored.

The effort to influence the functioning of the professional bureaucracy is not an Indian novelty, though the quantum and frequency does matter. Coalition politics, too, is a fact of life. Nostalgia and lamentation for a lost utopia that never really existed, is not an option. Changes in the ground situation, public expectations and technological innovations, are the ground realities. The challenge for the civil service today is to explore and develop the avenues for proper functioning in the context and the spirit of the responsibility assigned to it by the laws of the land and the policies developed through appropriate legislative processes.

The first of these responsibilities pertains to the dispensation of justice. This, in our vocabulary, means the Rule of Law. It is the foundation of democratic governance and the civil service has a pivotal role in upholding it. Professor Upendra Baxi has sought to read the rule of law as the rule of good law that is reflective of the struggle of a people 'to make power accountable, governance just, and state ethical'. He opines that the Indian constitutional conception of the rule of law links its four core notions: rights, development, governance and justice.

A few years back a senior law officer of the Government wrote that the Rule of Law is under serious threat and that there is widespread popular disillusionment. Civil society groups consider the 'delayed justice dispensation system' responsible for it. Why does this happen?

We know that the legal process of securing justice in our country is time consuming; there is also an acquittal rate of around 90 per cent. The public has thus little option but to resort to administrative facilitation and the procedures of administrative justice. Legislators are commonly assessed by their ability to secure administrative facilitation and justice to their constituents rather than by their efficiency in law making or holding the government to account! Thus the ultimate victim of non-implementation of the Rule of Law and delayed justice dispensation system is the common man and woman who are at the receiving end of non-enforcement of their rights and discriminatory application of the laws, and without the clout to secure either of them. Consequently, every effort by a civil servant towards administrative facilitation and accelerated dispensation of administrative justice to the public goes a long way in ameliorating its material condition and redresses its grievances.

Next in relevance to the dispensation of administrative justice are questions of social development and empowerment. Some civil servants have done exemplary work in these fields. It is, however, a matter of some concern that very few civil servants today feel attracted to it. Their priorities, instead, are on finance, banking, communication and IT, railways, aviation, petroleum and natural gas, shipping, road transport and highways, etc. This is suggestive of social priorities and the choices emanating from it and should be a matter of concern.

Take the question of integrity. We constantly hear, and rightly so, of the need for public figures and civil servants to exhibit the highest standards of personal probity and honesty. While this is an essential condition of good governance, is it sufficient? Is not dishonesty of the mind as dangerous as monetary or pecuniary dishonesty? This lack of intellectual and professional integrity has taken many forms—from introducing a slant in policy notes to an excessive careerism and focus on postings leading to regrettable acts of omission and commission. Nor is there any evidence to suggest that any of the functions listed above would be more adversely affected by the existence of a coalition any more than with a one-party government.

These perceptions can be quantified. More importantly, they impact decisively on public opinion. There is, therefore, a demonstrated need for correctives. A performance survey of half a century shows that in terms of Sardar Patel's parameters, while the polity has delivered by giving constitutional safeguards to civil servants and implementing sound recruitment procedures, the politicians have faltered in varying degrees on discipline and control and the civil servants have often enough succumbed to the temptation of tailoring professionally sound advice to subjective considerations.

The only answer would lie in the principles of the Constitution. Civil servants are the servants of the state and not of the government alone. More than at any time in our history as a republic, the necessity for the civil servant to be guided by the Directive Principles of State Policy is paramount and immediate. Each of you is enjoined to promote the welfare of the people by securing and protecting a social order in which social, economic and political justice shall inform all institutions. You need to work to minimise the inequalities of income, status, facilities and opportunities and to secure a legal system that promotes justice on a basis of equal opportunity. These are not rhetorical assertion and the realisation of these ideals should be fundamental to the governance of the country. Coalition programmes cannot be at variance with these principles.

The examples provided by the winners of the awards today give us hope that an innovative and pro-active civil service can continue to act as an agent of social change as envisaged by the Constitution.

Let me conclude by reminding you that there is nothing novel about sound professionalism; it has been prescribed in all periods of history. I will paraphrase for you the advice given to civil servants in the 8th century:

'The ruler cannot dispense with you. You alone make him a competent ruler. Your position with regard to rulers is that you are the ears through which they hear, the eyes through which they see, the tongues through which they speak, and the hands through which they touch. No craftsman needs more than you to combine all the praiseworthy good traits and all memorable and highly regarded qualities …

'(The civil servant) needs on his own account, and his master who trusts and expects him, to be mild where mildness is needed, to be understanding where judgement is needed, to be enterprising where enterprise is needed, to be hesitant where hesitation is needed. He must profess modesty, justice and fairness. He must keep secrets. He must be faithful in difficult circumstances. By virtue of his natural intelligence, good education, and outstanding experience, he must know what is going to happen to him before it happens, and he must know the results of his action before action starts. He must make proper preparations for everything, and he must set up everything in its proper form …

'Detest prejudices with all your heart. Guard against backbiting and calumny. Beware of haughtiness, foolishness and pride.'

Does any of this not hold good today?

Fourth Annual Convention of the Central Information Commission
DRDO (Defence Research and Development Organisation) Bhavan, New Delhi
13 October 2009

It gives me great pleasure to participate in the Fourth Annual Convention of the Central Information Commission. This annual gathering provides a useful forum to discuss whether the intent of the law that set out to provide 'a practical regime of the right to information to citizens' has been realised. It is important to reiterate the purpose of the Act as set out in its preamble: 'to promote transparency and accountability of every public authority' and also 'to contain corruption'.

This Convention is also a stock-taking occasion where all practitioners gather to exchange best practices and explore ways and means to harmonise various conflicting interests while 'preserving the paramountcy of the democratic ideal' as set out in the preamble of the Right to Information Act.

I start today from a contrarian view point. In any democratic society, a level of dissatisfaction among the citizenry towards their government should be taken as a given. Far from being a nuisance to the process of governance, it is such dissatisfaction that propels government to improve its functioning, be sensitive and empathetic to the problems of citizens and ensures efficient allocation and spending of public resources.

It is no surprise that the Right to Information Act is no exception to this trend. When passed in 2005, it was hailed as a revolutionary step aimed at fundamentally altering the balance of power between the government and citizens. Four years hence, some dissatisfaction is evident and pertains to five major themes.

First, a vast number of organisations that should have been covered under the definition of 'public authority' for being owned, controlled or substantially financed, directly or indirectly, by funds provided by the appropriate government, have not come forward pro-actively to be covered by the Act. They await a case-by-case ruling by the Central or State Information Commissions to be so considered and hence covered by the Act. Currently, neither the information commissions nor the governments have ensured that all bodies that are covered by the definition of 'public authority' undertake action as listed in Chapter II of the Act.

Second, very few public authorities of the central and state governments have followed the provisions of Section 4 of the Act in letter and spirit. It would be useful to review if cataloguing and indexing of records and data-sets have changed during the last four years in a manner that could facilitate the Right to Information under the Act. Section 4 (2) of the Act calls on public authorities to provide as much information to the public at regular intervals, through various means of communication, so that public has minimum resort to the use of the Act.

The actual disclosure of information by the public authorities is marked by inconsistency and unevenness. There has been little innovation and adaptation to capture information in government agencies and thereafter bring about suo moto disclosure. The websites of the central and state governments also lack technical and content standardisation. There is clearly a case for putting in place detailed 'RTI Act friendly' record management practices.

Third, it is important to note that Section 4 of the Act mandates every public authority to publish the manner of execution of subsidy programmes, including the amounts allocated and details of beneficiaries. This is a significant step when one considers that the total quantum of subsidies provided by the central and state governments to the citizens in the country exceeds Rs. 200,000 crores. While such a process has been initiated with respect to NREGA, significant work remains to be done on this issue.

Fourth, currently the central and state information commissioners work in relative isolation, with each of their decisions not being available in a systematic manner or in real time to the general public or even to other commissioners. The decisions of the information commissioners also do not constitute precedence for dealing with similar cases. Further, there are still doubts about the validity of decisions taken by individual Commissioners due to a notion that a full bench of the Information Commission should hear the case that comes before it.

Fifth, an important lacuna has been the lack of a mandatory monitoring mechanism to look at the implementation of the RTI Act and to ensure that the Act is implemented in letter and spirit. Currently, the media and civil society groups are undertaking this task on an ad hoc basis. The Price Waterhouse Cooper's report has recommended periodic Third Party Audit to ensure that public authorities comply with provisions and guidelines of the Act.

The existence of dissatisfaction is by no means a denial of the significant achievements of the RTI Act in bringing about transparency and reducing corruption. The basic tenets have been implemented and the institutional structure is being utilised by citizens. The Right to Information has become an important instrumentality to our media and civil society. What we see is the beginning of decentralisation and participatory governance and a citizen-friendly orientation to government.

The previous conventions of the Central Information Commission, I note, came forth with an exhaustive list of recommendations. I am not aware about the extent of acceptance and implementation of these recommendations by various stake holders. The collective outcome of a convention of Information Commissioners must be subject to serious deliberation and active consideration, with a view to appropriate implementation. I hope the results of this Convention will also be seriously studied and lead to better implementation of the Act.

I would like to conclude with an observation. I have noticed that information on the RTI Act, including the translation of the Act itself, is not available in all the 22 languages mentioned in the Eighth Schedule of our Constitution. The website of the Ministry of Personnel, Public Grievances and Pensions has the RTI Act in only 11 languages. The web sites of most information commissions are not multilingual covering the official languages adopted by the appropriate governments. For example, the Central Information Commission does not have a Hindi website for dissemination of information. Likewise, neither the RTI Act nor data on the web sites of information commissions of states where Urdu is the Second Official Language are available in Urdu.

This issue needs to be addressed at the earliest. Empowerment would be meaningless if it is sought to be achieved through a language that the citizen does not understand. Section 4 (4) of the RTI Act mandates that 'all materials shall be disseminated taking into consideration the cost effectiveness, local language and the most effective method of communication in that local area'. Article 350 of the Constitution also entitles every person 'to submit a representation for the redress of any grievance to any officer or authority of the Union or a State in any of the languages used in the Union or in the State, as the case may be'.

Inaugural Function of the RTI Conference

Public Cause Research Foundation, New Delhi
1 December 2009

It gives me great pleasure to inaugurate this conference. I convey my appreciation to civil society organisations such as Parivartan and the Public Cause Research Foundation for monitoring the implementation of the Right to Information Act. The foundation's work for just, transparent, accountable and participatory governance is yielding results and has contributed in some measure to empowering citizens, especially the underprivileged and the marginalised among them.

I confess I am pleasantly surprised at the manner in which common citizens across the country have taken recourse to the RTI Act to address their unending efforts to secure justice. It is no secret that the legal process of securing justice in our country is time consuming; there is also an acquittal rate of around 90 per cent. The public has thus little option but to resort to administrative facilitation and the procedures of administrative justice. Even legislators are assessed by their ability to secure administrative facilitation and justice to their constituents rather than by their ability in law making or holding the government to account.

The interesting experiences of the citizen nominees for the foundation's RTI Award are proof that the RTI Act has become an instrumentality in the hands of the citizen to secure administrative facilitation and grievance redressal through his/her own effort.

The RTI Act, at the initiative of the National Advisory Council, was the outcome of civil society effort of over a decade. It was a legislative recognition of the view of the Supreme Court that the right to information was a fundamental right under the Constitution. It was also an acceptance by the Executive that it is answerable to the people not just once in five years but every time an RTI application is filed, which is hundreds of times a day. It has given a new meaning to citizen engagement with governance.

The RTI Act imposes new obligations on all stakeholders. The government is called upon to be more transparent and accountable in decision and policy making, and manage its records better. The civil society is expected to be an informal clearing house for information to help common citizens understand and use this new instrumentality. This makes possible the participation of citizens in governance beyond elections.

Yet, the Right to Information also remains a fundamental right with limited means of justiceability in comparison to other fundamental rights. An important lacuna of the Act has been the lack of a mandatory monitoring mechanism to look at the implementation of the RTI Act and to ensure that the Act is implemented in letter and spirit. At present, the media and civil society groups are undertaking this task on an ad hoc basis; today's Conference is part of such an effort. This is in consonance with the Department of Personnel-sponsored report prepared by Price Waterhouse Cooper for assessing and evaluating the level of implementation of the Act. It had recommended periodic Third Party Audit to ensure that public authorities comply with provisions and guidelines of the Act.

My understanding of the implementation of the RTI Act leads me to believe that we need clarity on some issues and action on others.

First, a vast number of organisations including non-government organisations that should have been covered under the definition of 'public authority' for being owned, controlled or substantially financed, directly or indirectly, by funds provided by the appropriate government, have not come forward pro-actively to be covered by the Act. They await a case-by-case ruling by the Central or State Information Commissions to be so considered and hence covered by the Act. Currently, neither the information commissions nor the governments have ensured that all bodies that are covered by the definition of 'public authority' undertake action as listed in Chapter II of the Act.

The Act does not define what is meant by 'substantially financed'. Statutory ambiguity has meant that it was left to the Central Information Commission to define it and delineate the scope of coverage of institutions under 'public authority'. The CIC has relied on the CAG Act of 1971, has held that government funding can be direct or indirect or in kind, and opined that government control need not always be financial but could be administrative and functional control. The CIC has also ruled in some cases of commercial entities where there was substantial share holding by other public authorities such as LIC, UTI and nationalised banks.

The civil society and common citizens have articulated that they look forward to the Act covering all private institutions which exercise public functions or deal with public money. It is to be hoped that the statutory ambiguity would be addressed and that in the interests of their credibility, transparency and accountability, concerned organisations including non-Government organisations would voluntarily agree to be covered by the RTI Act.

Second, two important provisions of the RTI Act that have not received the attention they deserve are Sections 4 (1) [c] and [d]. They call on every public authority to 'publish all relevant facts while formulating important policies or announcing the decisions which affect public' and 'provide reasons for its administrative or quasi-judicial decisions to affected persons'. Contrary to general thinking, the Act calls not just for disclosure of, and access to, information but also the reasons for decisions affecting citizens.

Third, information on the RTI Act, including the translation of the Act itself, is not available in all the 22 languages mentioned in the Eighth Schedule of our Constitution. The website of the Ministry of Personnel, Public Grievances and Pensions has the RTI Act in only eleven languages. The web sites of most Information Commissions are not multilingual covering the official languages adopted by the appropriate governments. This issue needs to be addressed at the earliest. Section 4 (4) of the RTI Act mandates that 'all materials shall be disseminated taking into consideration the cost effectiveness, local language and the most effective method of communication in that local area'. This is an area where the civil society and the media can take a pioneering role in taking the message of RTI to the citizens in their own languages and thus meaningfully empower them.

The RTI Act has ushered in the beginning of participatory governance and a citizen-friendly orientation to government. The movement needs to be strengthened at all levels and support of the government, civil society and citizens is vital for its success.

Diamond Jubilee Celebrations

The Election Commission of India, Vigyan Bhavan, New Delhi

25 January 2010

This is a momentous occasion in the life of the Republic and I deem it a privilege to be participating in it.

The Election Commission of India, tasked by the Constitution to undertake a sacred responsibility, has discharged it fully.

In 1950 it was seen as a unique democratic experiment, an act of faith in the judgement of our citizens; today, the world marvels at the scale of its endeavours, their efficacy and comprehensiveness.

A celebration is a festive occasion. In the affairs of a nation, it is also a time for introspection. Six decades on, a fair verdict would be that the glass is neither empty nor full but well above the half way mark.

We have established and sustained procedural democracy. And yet, Dr Ambedkar's foreboding about the contradiction between political *equality* and social and economic *inequality* remains valid. The realisation of 'one person one vote and one vote one value' continues to be elusive.

To fulfil its mandate the Election Commission has been adapting itself in a remarkable fashion to changes in society, polity and technology. Three challenges, however, remain:

First: While we have traversed a long distance in providing a constitutional basis for local government, real empowerment and participative governance at the third tier of government is still a work-in-progress. It is to be hoped, as recommended by the Second Administrative Reforms Commission, that the electoral process at the local self government level would benefit from coordination and sharing of experiences and resources with the Election Commission of India.

Second: Despite stringent efforts, unaccounted election expenses constitute the major expenditure of political parties and their candidates. These relate to the distribution of freebies, liquor and cash during elections, the phenomenon of surrogate advertisements, and the extensive media-related malpractice of 'paid news' and 'coverage packages'. Each of these is a blot on the democratic process and on the objective of free and fair elections. Corrective action by the Election Commission and our political parties is imperative.

Third: The Election Commission has insisted upon and enforced procedural inner party democracy in recognised political parties. The challenge for the political parties now is to bring about substantive organisational democracy.

It was said in the Constituent Assembly of India that democracy was only a top dressing on an Indian soil that was essentially undemocratic. The Election Commission deserves the nation's appreciation and gratitude for making our soil more fertile for the seed of democracy.

Noronha Memorial Lecture
Noronha Academy of Administration and Management, Bhopal
11 February 2010

I am happy to be in Bhopal today and I deem it a great honour to be invited to deliver the Noronha Memorial Lecture.

The Madhya Pradesh Academy of Administration and Management is named after Ronald Carlton Vivian Piedade Noronha. This is appropriate since he was a visionary who devoted his life to good and proper management of public service in the state.

The erstwhile Central Provinces and Berar, today's Madhya Pradesh, has succeeded in producing generations of distinguished and committed civil servants known for their sensitivity, honesty and rectitude. Mr Noronha was among the best. His administrative abilities were widely recognised. The President of India conferred a Padma Bhushan on him.

Mr Noronha had interests and capabilities that went beyond his official duties. He was a wild life enthusiast who eliminated many man-eating tigers, a keen angler, an excellent photographer, an accomplished cook and a polyglot who spoke seven to eight languages. His interest in the tribals of the state was legendary. I can do no better than to cite what Shri M.N. Buch, another eminent civil servant of Madhya Pradesh, wrote about him:

> "A Goan born and brought up in Visakhapatnam, Ron became an adopted Adivasi of Madhya Pradesh, being counted as one of them by the Gonds of Chindwara, Baigas of Mandla and the Marias and Murias of Bastar. He always held that the finest years of his service were spent as the Deputy Commissioner, Bastar, where his work protecting the tribal lands, safeguarding their forests and fighting for their rights was enshrined in tribal songs and legends."

The charms of office held no lure for Mr Noronha. His years in retirement were well spent. His writings give us insights into his approach to rural, tribal and district governance. They are of abiding relevance and can be used with benefit to address the maladies of public administration today. Allow me to recall some of these:

- Socialising by civil servants is undesirable. "High society crookedness", he said, "always starts with social relations".
- Officers must learn the work of their subordinates thoroughly and inspect their work with a good conscience. This is the critical element to ensure good work at grass roots level.
- Officers must educate themselves about the people they serve because without this they cannot help them in an effective manner. Willingness to meet common citizens remains the single biggest check on corruption and exploitation.
- District Collectors must treat the heads of other offices in a district as equal partners in a common enterprise and ensure that their spouses behave in a similar fashion with other spouses.
- Being a public servant means upholding the rule of law. Officers must not to be afraid to rule in order to serve.

It is widely believed today that we are facing a crisis of governance in the country. The public disenchantment is palpable. I would therefore like to focus on the ethical dimension and framework of governance.

The report of the Second Administrative Reforms Commission begins with a candid acknowledgment that governance is the weak link in our quest for prosperity and equity. It defines integrity as 'much more than financial honesty' and addresses the dual facets of institutional and individual corruption. It notes the 'growing permissiveness in the society to the phenomena of corruption' and calls for addressing 'the perverse system of incentives in public life which makes corruption a high return-low risk activity'.

The ARC has recommended that there be a set of 'Public Service Values' and a 'Code of Ethics' governing public service operations to be stipulated by law. Such values would not merely be statements of intent but would be binding on public servants. In 2007, a Draft Public Services Bill was put in the public domain for comments. It seeks to provide a statutory basis for the regulation of public services, as also a set of basic values, a code of ethics and of management. The Bill is yet to be introduced in Parliament.

It needs no reiteration that an ethical framework for governance must begin with consolidating ethical values in politics. Our political parties and the legislative and executive wings constitute the polity whose standards have a fundamental impact on other spheres of governance. Nevertheless, there are many elements which the civil service can implement to bring about a more humane and ethical governance structure. A few of these come to mind:

First: Despite six decades of Independence and a Constitution that is secular and promotes equality, fraternity and liberty, we remain a feudal society with deep asymmetries of power, wealth and status. For a start, each of us can start downplaying these asymmetries and emphasise our founding Constitutional values in our daily behaviour and practice.

Second: We need to encourage the general direction of the government towards deregulation, decentralisation and grassroots empowerment. Reducing discretion, eliminating monopolies, improving competition, enhancing transparency and transactional facilitation would reduce the public space for breeding of corruption.

Third: The meaning of the concept of integrity of public servants needs to be amplified. While financial integrity is one element of it, functional integrity and a high level of efficiency at work are equally important. Public servants have an obligation to protect and promote our constitutional ideals enshrined in the preamble, to uphold the rule of law, dispense administrative justice and ensure administrative facilitation. Associations of IAS/IPS officers in some states have conducted peer reviews on the issue of corruption; this practice could be extended to cover other areas of work.

Fourth: As an elite segment of society, public servants have an important role in informing and even formulating public opinion and perception on various issues. Civil servants from Madhya Pradesh have been well known for taking a keen interest in tribal affairs, rural development and social-sector issues including education and public health. Against this background, the current tendency of showing a marked preference for assignments in infrastructure, finance and technology sectors is disconcerting. This is suggestive of social priorities and the choices emanating from it and should be a matter of concern.

Fifth: The district magistrates remain to this day the fulcrum of administration in the country. Today, in addition, to their traditional duties of revenue administration and executive magistracy, they handle a number of functions focused on rural and human resource development, economic development and local self government. They have become agents of social and economic change with wide mandates. They can lead by example and even raise the profile and priority of various social themes and economic issues.

There is a need for district magistrates and other public servants in the district to revert to the age old methods that facilitated interaction with common citizens and strengthened institutional memory. I refer here to mandatory tours and inspections undertaken by district officers which have resulted in invaluable district gazetteers that highlighted all aspects of district administration in British India. In the last two or three decades, these traditions have not been followed. The Administrative Reforms Commission has also recommended that every District Collectorate must have a tour inspection cell for the purpose. In the final analysis, and despite modern communication methods, district administration is best run through personal interface and interaction.

We need to learn from the experience of our ancestors. Over two thousand years ago, Kautilya in his *Arthashastra* identified forty ways in which government servants can enrich themselves improperly either by cheating the government or exploiting the public. Kautilya also emphasised the importance of the common citizens: "It is the people who constitute a kingdom; like a barren cow, a kingdom without people yields nothing".

This perspective has not changed. The object of good governance and public services is the public and its welfare. As long as today's public servants and administrators keep this in mind, they would be doing justice to their jobs and to our Constitution. By the same token, failure or insufficient delivery could propel public anger, whose manifestations could be unpredictable.

Late Dr V.N. Tewari Memorial Lecture
Punjab University, Chandigarh
9 April 2010

It gives me a great pleasure to participate in today's function and deliver the Dr V. N. Tewari Memorial Lecture.

Dr Tewari's contribution to literature and to the work of Parliament would always be remembered. As an alumnus of Punjab University and a Member of its Senate, he played an important role in strengthening the academic framework and improving the administrative structures in the University.

Professor Tiwari laid down his life for the cause of the nation and the values reflective of our philosophy of nationhood. This lecture is an appropriate occasion to think aloud about the moral and ethical framework underpinning these values, more so because Article 51 A (b) of the Constitution makes it the duty of every citizen "to cherish and follow the noble ideals which inspired our national struggle for freedom".

The principle is impeccable. The devil, as often, is in the manner it is reflected in the norms and practice of governance in its diverse dimensions—legislative, administrative and judicial. The Constitution embodies a set of affirmations and prohibitions; it puts in place a structure of institutions; it presumes the observance of known norms of ethics and morality on the assumption that the human being, besides being a social creature, is also a moral one, having a sense of right and wrong.

It is here that a set of teasing questions confronts us. Are these norms of ethics and morality clearly identifiable? Are they identical for private and public behaviour? Are they universally applicable?

What is the extent of deviation morally permissible?

The philosopher Bertrand Russell, amongst others, sought to respond to the resulting dilemma: "Without civic morality," he said, "communities perish; without personal morality their survival is of no value. Therefore civic and personal morality are equally necessary to a good world". He said there is a need to distinguish between the authority of custom and the authority of law, and conceded what he termed as "deep duality in ethics which, however perplexing, demands recognition." The duality, I may add, arose from the quest for differing norms.

Nearer home and more specifically, do we as a people subscribe to a set of norms of morality and ethics, and do we draw a distinction between public and private morality? While the answer to the first, to most of us, is clearly in the affirmative, responses to the latter often range from ambiguity to evasion.

A second set of questions of an empirical nature, pertaining to governance, also arise. How can the good rule? How to rule the world as it is? How can the good rule the world as it is?

A practical difficulty confronts us. Governments accord primacy to national security, dispensation of justice, maintenance of law and order, social and economic development and ensuring public welfare. Ethical precepts are rarely mentioned in specific terms. There are nevertheless, as the Fourth Report of the Second Administrative Reforms Commission put it, "a set of standards that society places on itself and which help guide behaviour, choices and actions'. The crux of ethical behaviour, it adds, 'does not lie in bold words and expressions enshrined as standards, but in their adoption in action' leading to the promotion of 'a culture of integrity."

In other words, ethical behaviour emanates from generally accepted norms of personal and social ethics and finds reflection in ideals to which the state subscribes. This is the crux of principles of governance. The society sets standards reflective of the general moral conscience or principles of social ethics, incorporates them in laws for the state to implement them and dispense justice, and thus obtain legitimacy and allegiance of the body politic.

On an earlier occasion in this very city, I had drawn attention to the long standing Indian belief in righteousness and to Gandhi*ji's* 'Seven Social Sins' that are inscribed on a tablet near his Samadhi at Raj Ghat. Both inexorably propel us to a unified value system, applicable to private and public life.

The doctrinal position is thus clear. We have also been blessed with appropriate social institutions; the challenge now is to identify, in their functioning, the gap between profession and practice and focus on what Amartya Sen has termed "social realisation".

Public conduct and public policy, in actual practice, present for three dimensions for consideration:

First: Some aspects of private morality may have no impact on the ability of a public servant to execute his official functions; in other instances, private immorality may directly or indirectly impact his/her public functioning. All governments are managed by human beings and, as the American historian James Harvey Robinson noted, "No process has been discovered by which promotion to a position of public responsibility will do away with a man's interest in his own welfare, his partialities, race, and prejudices."

Second: The creation of the modern State structure has also displaced some of the source of moral impulses and initiative from the individual and the community to larger professional/corporate groups or State institutions. The individual functionary, to that extent, has been mechanised and depersonalised, loses personal empathy, and becomes a morally passive citizen.

Third: What is common to public morality and private ethics is a belief that the self and personal interest is not the sole point of reference in assessing public and private actions. Paul Appleby, who wrote a fine report on our public administration in the 1950s, defined a moral public decision in terms that remain relevant:

> "The action conforms to the processes and symbols thus far developed for the general protection of political freedom as the agent of more general freedom; ... leaves open the way for modification or reversal by public determination; ... is taken within a hierarchy of controls in which responsibility for action may be readily identified by the public; ... and embodies as contributions of leadership the concrete structuring of response to popularly felt needs, and not merely responses to the private and personal needs of leaders".

II

A study of State structures since ancient times would reveal that personal failings in the discharge of public functions, public scandal and the consequent clamour for correctives have incrementally led to the evolution of a framework of public morality. Kautilya categorically asserts that "a king who flouts the teachings of Dharmashastras and the *Arthashastra* ruins the kingdom by his own injustice". Good rulers observed this "to redress the wrongs, to extract recompense from the oppressor, to give justice, and listen to the words of his subjects with his own ears, without any intermediary." Thus elements of public morality were deduced from the individual example of public conduct.

In this context, it would be useful to examine the basic elements of public morality relevant to a multi-cultural democracy such as ours. Some of its ingredients can be identified:

In the first place, a healthy spirit of optimism about the ability of public service to serve public interest is an essential element of public morality. Public service without an optimistic outlook could degenerate into cynicism, manipulation or blatant pursuit of self-interest. It is only when one can see that possibility of public good in the ambiguities and uncertainties of public life and public policy that one can begin to work in that direction.

Secondly, the courage of conviction required to take decisions and sustain them despite opposition is essential for effective political and social action. Such courage needs to be summoned in simple issues such as refusing favours to friends and family or in momentous decisions of peace and war. Many instances of this can be found in our recent and earlier history.

Thirdly, public morality demands pursuit and dispensation of justice in an impartial, quick and even an impersonal manner. Injustice is a powerful motivator of human emotions, usually of rebellion and destruction. Every scripture in our multireligious society testifies to it.

In the fourth place, upholding the rule of law is an essential requirement of public morality in a modern democracy. John Locke's dictum - "wherever law ends tyranny begins" - has universal validity. Strict adherence to the law and basic honesty are integral to this element. The standard of probity must not be the 'Lowest Common Denominator' but the 'Highest Common Principle'.

Fifthly, a sense of empathy and compassion towards human suffering is needed for dealing with moral ambiguities in public policy and to prioritise resources and actions. A public service approach tempered with human decency, humility and willingness to compromise for the larger good help weather the rough ethical climate faced in public service.

III

Lest an impression of cosiness be created by the above, let me hasten to mention some substantive impediment. Customs and traditions are one aspect of it. Each one of us has a group identity and custom demands that special consideration be given to the members of the group, be it family, caste or tribe. As a result, personally upright individuals sometimes come across moral dilemma when confronted with complex public policy choices. For example, while helping family, clan or community members is a good private moral, it would tantamount to an unacceptable public evil and be termed nepotism. These instances can be multiplied and add a nefarious dimension to the conduct of public policy.

The same holds for an atmosphere of permissiveness and its amoral norms of measuring excellence.

In recent years, our public domain has witnessed a debate on the crisis of governance in the country. The palpable public disenchantment with it has directed the focus of the debate on the ethical dimension of the framework of governance. This too is reflected in the Report of the Second Administrative Reforms Commission which begins with a candid acknowledgment that governance is the weak link in our quest for prosperity and equity. It defines integrity as 'much more than financial honesty' and addresses the dual facets of institutional and individual corruption. It notes the 'growing permissiveness in the society to the phenomena of corruption' and calls for addressing 'the perverse system of incentives in public life which makes corruption a high return-low risk activity'.

A few of the other observations of the report tell the story candidly:

- Anti-corruption interventions so far made are seen to be ineffectual and there is wide spread public cynicism about them. This cynicism is spreading so fast that it bodes ill for our democratic system itself.
- Corruption has been aggravated by three factors: propensity to exercise power arbitrarily, enormous asymmetry of power in society, and policies that unintentionally put the citizen at the mercy of the state.
- Quality of politics is such that honesty is considered incompatible with survival. If public life attracts undesirable and corrupt elements seeking private gain, the abuse of authority and corruption become the norm.
- In a vast majority of cases of bribery, the citizen is a victim of extortion and is compelled to pay a bribe in order to get a service to which he/she is entitled.
- The escalating levels of corruption in various segments of our economy is resulting in large scale generation of black money, serious economic offences and fraud, and money laundering leading even to the funding of terrorist activities against the state, have created a grave situation.

Needless to say, each of these signals a departure from ethical and legal norms of the Republic. Moreover, the gains from the implementation of social security programmes, such as the Mahatma Gandhi National Rural Employment Guarantee Scheme and food provision through the Public Distribution System, are being diluted due to mal-administration and corruption.

The above, taken together, unavoidably lead to the conclusion that corruption in public life is today a threat to national security and we have to deal with it accordingly.

We have in place a loosely structured Code of Conduct for the three sets of actors in the public service domain—Civil Service, Legislature and the Judiciary. Regarding the first, the ARC has recommended that there be a set of 'Public Service Values' and a 'Code of Ethics' governing public service operations to be stipulated by law. In 2007, a Draft Public Services Bill was put in the public domain for comments and is yet to be introduced in Parliament.

In the case of the Legislature, the Rajya Sabha has adopted a code of conduct for Members enumerated by the Committee on Ethics. Members are also required to declare assets and liabilities and specified pecuniary interests. Somewhat similar procedures are also in place in the Lok Sabha. Regarding the Higher Judiciary, judicial ethics have been summarised in the 'Restatement of Values of Judicial Life adopted by the Chief Justices' Conference of India, 1999' and in "The Bangalore Principles of Judicial Conduct, 2002".

The legal and administrative steps taken so far to improve ethical norms in the executive, the legislature and the judiciary have been felt to be clearly inadequate. The need for a more purposeful, result oriented, approach is imperative.

A long time back the philosopher Aristotle had pointed out that moral virtue in humans does not emanate from nature and needs to be imbibed by habit. This habit has to be cultivated, individually and collectively. A survey of the Indian scene today suggests that this cultivation of habit is being neglected at every stage, at home, in school, and in the wider public domain. Instead, there is a pernicious preference for a moral vacuum. This has to change, must be changed. Only then would public morality be reflective of the righteousness that the sages, ancient and modern, talked about.

Nor is this merely a matter of cultural options or selective virtue; record shows that no nation has achieved greatness without attaining a high level of moral integrity in personal and social conduct.

Inauguration of the Diamond Jubilee Celebrations of 'Yarrows'
The National Academy of Audit and Accounts, Shimla
18 May 2010

I am delighted to be here today to inaugurate the Diamond Jubilee celebrations of the National Academy of Audit and Accounts. The surroundings are idyllic. 'Yarrows', said to have been so named by a very homesick Scotsman, is a national 'heritage' institution with a long and distinguished history.

The same is true of the Audit Department that has an illustrious history of over 150 years. As one of the oldest training facilities for the civil servants in the country, the academy has made a significant contribution to practices of good governance in the country. It has also emerged as an institution of excellence in public auditing and accounting in the global arena.

This audience is only too well aware that modern democratic states have evolved public audit as an important tool for ensuring accountability of the Executive to the Legislature, and through it to the electorate. Public audit was envisaged as an assurance to all stakeholders in a democracy that public resources, in their widest meaning possible, are utilised for public good, in compliance with the intent of the Legislature and the orders of the Executive.

The role of public audit in India was debated extensively by the Constituent Assembly. Shri T.T. Krishnamachari argued for changing the nomenclature from 'Auditor-General' to 'Comptroller and Auditor-General'(C&AG) citing functionality that covers "not merely audit but also control over the expenses of Government". Dr Ambedkar characterised the C&AG as "probably the most important officer in the Constitution of India".

These perceptions are reflected in Articles 148 to 151 of our Constitution. The status and functions of the Comptroller & Auditor General were amplified in the C&AG's Act of 1971.

The objective of public audit in our country has evolved from 'Regularity Audit' focused on probity, legality, propriety and compliance in public spending, to 'Performance Audit' that emphasises programme results and ultimate outcomes. This transformation also means that the C&AG now has to focus on risk analysis and containment, forecasting emerging trends and facilitating good governance.

Thus audit is no longer a stand-alone activity but is done in synergy with social audit groups, wider civil society and other stakeholders.

The ambit of audit has also expanded to include audit of revenues, audit of government commercial enterprises, audit of receipts and expenditure of bodies or authorities substantially financed from Union or State Revenues, technical guidance and supervision of audit of Panchayati Raj Institutions in most states, audit of accounts of stores and stock, and audit of grants or loans given for any specific purpose to any authority or body, not being a foreign State or international organisation.

Besides audit, another important function of the C&AG is compiling and submission of accounts.

Amidst a fast changing national and global economic landscape, government accounting has remained relatively static in the last fifty years.

The Government still follows cash basis of accounting and the financial reporting framework is based on book keeping rules rather than fundamental accounting principles. The current cash-based system does not record transactions where no cash has been paid or received even if liability may have been contracted or value received. It has not proved to be an accurate or effective instrumentality to focus on performance accountability.

Some years back the Government accepted the recommendation of the Twelfth Finance Commission to migrate to accrual based accounting. The first step in preparing a detailed road map for this and in formally formulating the Government Accounting Standards for the country was taken in 2002 with the formation of the Government Accounting Standards Advisory Board.

The suggested Accounting and Financial Reporting Standards on various themes are under the consideration of the Government and are yet to be notified. The migration process is expected to take at least another ten years. This accounting reform is of the utmost urgency and needs to be taken up immediately.

A systematic review of the working of public audit and of C&AG was undertaken by the National Commission to Review the Working of the Constitution and in its report submitted in 2002 to the Government made four recommendations on the subject:

1. The Commission argued for the need for a collegiate decision making system for finalising audit reports before submission to the legislature. Noting the example of Germany, France, Japan and Korea, it recommended the setting up of an Audit Board for better discharge of the vital function of public audit.
2. The Commission recommended that a healthy convention be developed to consult the Speaker of the Lok Sabha, before the Government decides on the appointment of the C&AG so that the views of the Public Accounts Committee are also taken into account.
3. It recommended that the considerations that apply at the union level in regard to the functioning of the office of C&AG should apply with equal force at the state level. The State Accountants General should be given greater authority by the C&AG, while maintaining its general superintendence, direction and control to bring about a broad uniformity of approach in the sphere of financial discipline.
4. To ensure professional soundness, efficiency and effectiveness, and noting the practice in Commonwealth countries of UK and Australia, the Commission recommended that the operations of the office of the C&AG itself, at the Union and State levels, should be subject to external audit by an independent body.

These recommendations deserve careful scrutiny and public debate in the context of the proposed changes to the C&AG (Duties, Powers and Conditions of Service) Act of 1971.

The last two decades have changed the ground rules for our economy in a fundamental manner. The total expenditure of the Central government has gone up ten times from around Rs. 95,000 crores in 1989-90 to around Rs. 10,00,000 crores in 2009-10. The most dramatic jump has been in transfer payments by the Central Government to the rest of the economy that has gone up over fifteen times from approximately Rs. 44,700 crores in 1989-90 to Rs. 6,4,000 crores in 2009-10.

The volume, mix, variety and legal structures employed for undertaking government expenditure have thus undergone a tremendous change.

Flagship social sector and infrastructure programmes of the government and provision for subsidies consume the bulk of resources. There has been a gradual evolution of the role of government from direct provision of economic goods and services and tight control of private enterprise, to broad regulation of economic sectors, promotion and facilitation of private enterprise and fair competition. Government funds are increasingly devolving through urban and rural local bodies, Special Purpose Vehicles, Non-Governmental Organisations and Public-Private Partnerships.

Effective use of public audit as an aid in enhancing governance and improving accountability demands that we seriously consider six key issues.

First: There has been an exponential growth in regulatory agencies in economic and social sectors tasked with ensuring coordinated development, fair competition and trade practices, minimum standards of operation and customer service and fair use of scarce public resources. Uniformity in audit treatment of regulatory bodies must be ensured, if necessary through statutory means, so that their accounts, performance, and decisions that directly or indirectly carry financial implications are brought under the purview of the C&AG.

Second: The existing provisions of the 1971 Act are restrictive regarding audit of public funds spent by NGOs, autonomous organisations, societies and trusts etc. In my view, any organisation that comes under the definition of 'Public Authority' in the Right to Information Act, 2005, as interpreted by our Courts and Information Commissions, should be subject to the audit of C&AG.

Third: Public audit can achieve its aims only if there is timely and unhindered access to records. One of the core principles deemed essential for proper public sector auditing by the 'Mexico Declaration on the

Independence of Supreme Audit Institutions' is 'unrestricted access to information'. Provisions of the RTI Act which has a time limitation for production of records and replies and has specific penalties for non-compliance are worthy of emulation in this regard.

Fourth: The efficacy of public audit is premised on effective follow-up mechanism on the reports of Supreme Audit Institutions submitted to the Legislature. An analysis by the C&AG found that out of the more than nine thousand audit paragraphs included in the audit reports for the years 1994 to 2008 that were presented to the Parliament, about 3000 audit paragraphs had not even received the first response from the Ministries, despite Government's agreement to a four month time frame for submission of Action Taken Notes to the PAC. The situation in State Legislative Assemblies is also similar. Regrettably, this weakens parliamentary financial control and ability to enforce accountability of the Executive to the Legislature.

Fifth: An equally pertinent issue is the lack of any statutory authority vested in the C&AG for summoning officials and seeking evidence on oath, undertaking follow-up to the Audit Reports, fixing responsibility on officials who may have caused loss to the exchequer or recommending disciplinary action as per conduct rules or criminal prosecution as applicable.

Sixth: The complex economic arrangements of our era demand that public debt management and provision of subsidies should be subject to public audit due to their significant impact on government budgets and burden of future generations. Finance Minister Shri Pranab Mukherjee in his Valedictory address at the Twenty-Fifth Conference of Accountants General last month sought the focus of public audit on containing expenditure on subsidies without adversely affecting the targeted beneficiaries of such subsidies.

The public auditors have played an important role in the development of our nation by their oversight of public accounts and expenditure and providing sound advice and assistance to the Legislature and the Executive in fulfilling their mandated functions. The National Academy of Audit and Accounts deserves the nation's appreciation for transforming young civil servants to professional auditors.

I once again congratulate the Academy's faculty and trainees and the entire Audit Department.

Second Annual Lecture at the Annual Lecture Series on 'Governance and Public Service'

Union Public Service Commission, New Delhi

3 May 2011

I am happy to participate in today's function. I wish to convey the country's, and my own, appreciation for the contribution of the Union Public Service Commission (UPSC) to nation-building by shaping the constitution and functioning of the higher civil service in the country.

It is a truism that an overwhelming majority of human beings live in politically organised societies that require for their normal functioning a set of persons entrusted with the implementation of laws and rules made by the polity for its welfare. The concept of civil services, as of judiciary and of defence forces, is inextricably linked to this requirement.

It is for this reason that every state in history has utilised the instrumentality of civil services, tailored to its requirements. These needs have changed with times, with the nature of the state, and with its end purposes. Some essential traits have nevertheless persisted down the ages. We can, therefore, read with benefit to this day Kautilya's short chapter on 'Service with a King' and its emphasis on the need to give advice at all times in accordance with dharma and *artha*.

The relevance of the civil servant to the ruler (individual or a collective) was perhaps best described by the medieval historian Ibn Khaldun: "You are", he wrote, "the ears through which they hear, the eyes through which they see, the tongues through which they speak, and the hands through which they touch."

This need to seek the best available talent, and condition it appropriately for the requirement of society and the state, was practised at all times in our own history. Modern India thus inherited an established tradition. Its imperative necessity was appreciated by the founding fathers of our republic. The end product was incorporated in Part XIV of the Constitution.

In the past six decades, the Union Public Service Commission has ably discharged its constitutional function in the recruitment of the higher civil services. The civil services, in turn, have responded in varying measure to their core mandate of dispensing social, economic and political justice. The framework of the political and bureaucratic executive has made a significant effort at ameliorating the quality of life of citizens and in doing public good.

In the same time span, however, the socio-economic and political context has evolved in good measure and substantive notions of justice and equality have filled the interstices of the constitutional principles and fundamental rights. This has brought about a virtual revolution in expectations.

It is therefore essential to comprehend the impulses at work. Together, they pose a set of six challenges:

First: Government interventions are now viewed by citizens through the prism and framework of rights. The days of the so-called mai-baap sarkar are over. Today, and particularly in matters relating to education, health, roads or good governance, the operative expression is right and entitlement. Increasing levels of literacy and economic success has contributed to this conceptual shift in some measure.

Second: Advances in technology, means of communication and interaction, and changes in civil society perceptions have multiplied manifolds the instrumentalities available to a common citizen to engage with the government, assert entitlements and rights, and challenge decisions of the government that impact adversely.

Third: Given the unsatisfactory record of dispensation of justice through the court process, the burden of dispensing it has shifted in considerable measure to the government, civil society and the public in general. Enhanced legal literacy, establishment of regulatory frameworks in various sectors, and reliance on administrative facilitation have enabled citizens to assert their rights without the need for interventions of courts. The role of civil servants and public service delivery has become critical in this effort.

Fourth: As an economy and as a society, we are in the process of transition from the use of controls and regulations to bring about desired public policies to harnessing of incentives and markets for the same. The market looms large in all spheres of personal and public life. It affects our choices of profession, ways of life, modes of living and entertainment, education, health care, and even, ideologies and belief systems.

Fifth: The broad framework of our social and political contract that sustains the legitimacy of the government and its interventions for public and social good is increasingly facing erosion. This has come about principally on account of the actual and perceived inequities of the growth process, marginalisation and impoverishment of segments of citizenry and also perhaps, a balkanisation of the mind. It has wider, perhaps disturbing, implications for our democracy and the rule of law.

Sixth: We have a young generation that is exposed to global standards of living and service, is impatient with the pace of change, and demands equal opportunity in sharing the fruits of development. This is more pronounced in urban areas, but equally true for rural India. Their despondency finds reflection in hostility towards elites in polity, business and industry and society; at times, it takes violent forms of protest targeted against the state, its structures and agencies. These manifestations retard growth, erode democracy and legitimise anarchy.

Emanating from the above, a set of questions come up for consideration:

- How should we deal with the huge asymmetries of power, and the socio-cultural propensity of tolerating its misuse through dilution of systemic and institutional safeguards?
- How can public policy bring the citizen to the centre stage of service delivery and governance, and not put him/her at the mercy of the State and its agencies, or of the market and its mechanisms? and
- What role can the civil service play in this regard?

I venture to think a good starting point is recognition that the civil services in our country represent the societal elite and that elite behaviour represents a significant challenge to the supremacy of Rule of Law.

We do not need to go far to substantiate this. The national and international media is full of reports of how the elite are able to subvert the Rule of Law with money or influence. Sections of society and polity even accept this as a way of life. As a result, Rule of Law norms are being sidelined or subverted through systemic discrimination and exclusion based on community, gender, class and other limiting and distorting considerations. Its impact on the quality of governance is all too evident.

The higher civil services in the country, therefore, must be role models of elite behaviour upholding the Rule of Law. This is not a homily; it is part of our constitutional scheme of things and a professional and moral obligation of a civil servant to the nation and to the citizens.

This necessitates an element of out-of-the-box thinking on quality and content issues pertaining to our higher civil services.

The UPSC, I understand, is already implementing some reforms in the recruitment pattern, especially in the syllabus and examinations. The issue of life-long cadres for All India Services, reluctance or inability to serve adequate period of careers outside the cadres whether at the Centre or other states, equitable access to posts covered under the Central Staffing Scheme, and possibility of lateral access into and out of the civil service are issues that could benefit from such out-of-the-box thinking.

A review of the performance of the civil service since independence would show that in terms of Sardar Patel's parametres, while the polity has delivered by giving constitutional safeguards to civil servants and implementing sound recruitment procedures, the political leadership has at times faltered on discipline and control and the civil servants themselves have often enough succumbed to the temptation of tailoring professionally sound advice to subjective considerations.

The need for introspection and correction is compelling; inaction is no longer an option, nor is reticence in the face of evident wrong. The need is also for a moral imperative that is comprehensive, not selective, and which emanates from and encapsulates constitutional morality.

We do need reiteration that civil servants are functionaries of the state and not of the government alone, that they are paid to render *honest* professional advice however unpalatable, and that they should be guided in their work by the principles and objectives, and the charter of rights and duties, enshrined in our Constitution.

Systemic improvement in governance and service delivery to citizens is an ongoing process and effort of the Union Public Service Commission in this regard deserves our appreciation. It is time to remember, and remind, that the objective in the final analysis is indeed 'Public Service'.

Book release: *Corruption and Human Rights in India* by Prof. C. Raj Kumar
India Habitat Centre, New Dehi
5 August 2011

The publication of this book is timely and touches a matter of public interest. It brings into focus the inseparable bond of two critical requirements for human will: equality and dignity. This is eloquently noted by Justice V.R. Krishna Iyer in his Foreword.

Prof. Raj Kumar outlines a comprehensive legal approach to fight corruption. He looks at the human rights implications of corruption and articulates a rights-based approach to fighting it. The case is well made that corruption is not merely a law enforcement issue that can be addressed through better laws or more stringent enforcement, but a phenomenon that violates the constitutional foundation of our democracy on the basis of which a rule-of-law society was meant to be established.

The book emphasises transparency in governance and ensuring accountability of the government as the key weapons to empowering citizens to address corruption. The comparative references in the book are exhaustive and give insight into the various models of combating corruption, especially in the Asian context. The 'Post Script' addresses the contemporary debate regarding the Lokpal, and the author has given his views on some of the contentious issues.

Corruption, whichever way it is defined, is essentially a governance issue. Every society in history has pronounced norms of governance to distinguish between a good and a bad ruler, a happy and an unhappy people. The only meaningful corrective to bad governance is good and responsive governance.

The Constitution of India prescribes justice, and equality of status and opportunity, to all our people along with the ideals of liberty and fraternity. It lays down an institutional framework for achieving these objectives. At the same time, Dr Ambedkar had administered a note of caution. His words remain relevant:

> "The working of the constitution does not depend wholly upon the nature of the Constitution. The constitution can provide only the organs of the state such as the Legislature, the Executive and the Judiciary. The factors on which the working of those organs of the state depends are the people and the political parties they will set up as their instruments to carry out their wishes and their politics. Who can say how the people of India and their parties will behave?"

The starting point of discussion, therefore, should be the efficacy with which the people of India and their political formations have operated the institutions. The successes, and limitations, have to be shared in equal measure. At the same time, any study of governance in practice cannot avoid the changes in citizen awareness emanating from experience and a deepening of their understanding of norms. This provides the backdrop to many of our current debates.

Three questions come to mind:

- Is the basic problem of countering corruption a lack of good legal framework, or an understanding of the human rights' implications of corruption?
- At a time when the phenomenon of corruption looms large on our public and personal arenas, what is the importance of politics and the political processes in addressing this malaise?
- What role do we assign to ethical conduct in public life and upholding of political virtue?

It is undeniable that public perceptions have evolved and that today our awareness of, and demand for, better governance is quantitatively and qualitatively greater. So is the awareness that deficit impinges on human rights guaranteed to citizens by national laws and international covenants subscribed to by us as a nation.

This heightened consciousness of rights is the result in good measure of the successful functioning of the institutional system and laws bestowed on us by the Constitution. Citizens have operated it through political parties as instruments to implement their agenda and work in accordance with their mandate.

Political parties are thus needed for exercise of political power and for conducting governance. Their credibility and efficacy are critical elements in bringing about stable polities that are essential for socio-economic progress. They are expected to set examples of democratic practice, influence the nature of political mobilisation, alliance formation and societal accommodation. They can facilitate conflict management. Political parties lie at the root of any debate on representativeness, societal conciliation, and governance that is accountable, stable and efficient.

Shortcomings, wherever identified, must be made good. At the same time, there is a peril to be avoided. Urgency in the search for solutions, or impatience with established political processes, or sheer frustration with the current state of affairs cannot, and should not, prompt us towards quasi-legal or extra-legal options. Any thinking towards solutions that delegitimise the constitutional process can do incalculable harm.

Likewise, it is incumbent on each of us, and especially those in public life, to respect the careful in-built balance between the Executive, Legislature and the Judiciary as contained in the Constitution. Eroding the balance, either through under-reach of one or over-reach of another, could lead to chaos.

The last question, on ethical conduct and public virtue, can only elicit one response. Negativity of mind and soul cannot but result in diminishing the public spirit needed to deliver public good.

I hope the publication of this book would ignite a public debate on the important subject of corruption and best means to counter it.

Yusuf Meherally Memorial Lecture
University Convocation Hall, Mumbai
23 September 2011

I am happy to be back in Mumbai and to address this distinguished gathering on the occasion of the Golden Jubilee of the Yusuf Meherally Centre.

Started in 1961 in the memory of noted freedom fighter Yusuf Meherally, and formally inaugurated in 1965 by then Vice President Dr Zakir Husain, the Centre evolved the focus of its efforts from promoting national integration and studying the problems of urbanisation, to rural development. The Centre's efforts to work out a replicable model of rural development had led to impressive micro-watershed development, intermeshed with organic farming, non-conventional energy, village industries and marketing of their products.

Yusuf Meherally played a leading role in peasants' organisations and trade unions. He was imprisoned many times and was elected the mayor of Bombay in 1942 when in Lahore jail. He coined the 'Quit India' slogan that Gandhi*ji* adopted in his final campaign for independence. A Socialist and founder of the Congress Socialist Party, he believed that his socialism was based, as he put it, "on aesthetic and ethical premises and not on economics". He was moved by human suffering and worked to alleviate it. His prison dairy of 1942, as also his work as Mayor of Bombay and as a member of the Bombay Legislative Assembly, bear testimony to his commitment to public causes. He was an early advocate of the Right of Recall on municipal councilors who had failed to serve their constituencies.

Today's function gives us an opportunity to ponder over the ideas and ideals of Yusuf Meherally, with a focus on those relating to urban governance.

The close interrelationship between urbanisation, economic progress and social evolution is insufficiently appreciated. We trace our historical heritage to the cities of the Indus Valley and the extensive urbanisation of that era. Yet, after Rome achieved the first distinction of a human settlement of one million people, it was not until the 19th century that London became the second city to reach this mark.

Since then, rapid urbanisation has literally changed the face of the planet. Within two centuries, the urban population increased from 2 per cent of the world population in 1800 to crossing the critical 50 per cent mark in 2009. The United Nations estimates that the urban areas of the world are expected to absorb the entire expected population growth of the next forty years and even draw in some population from rural areas. Most of this expected urban population growth is likely to occur in cities and towns of Asia and Africa. Until 1975, there were only three global megacities, with population of over 10 million–New York, Tokyo and Mexico City. Today, there are twenty-one megacities with three in India–Delhi at second place after Tokyo, Mumbai at fourth place and Kolkata at eighth place. As a matter of fact, Delhi and Mumbai are two of the world's four cities with a population of over 20 million.

There should be no doubt that the 21st century would indeed be an urban century, especially an 'Indian' urban century, with India expected to account for the largest urban population of over one billion in fifty years from now.

Cities would continue to propel economic growth, prompt economic and social change, and spark widespread innovation and entrepreneurship. Today it is accepted that achieving growth rates of 9-10 per cent in GDP is critically dependent on a vibrant urban sector. The Eleventh Five-Year Plan argued that as urban sector contributes over 60 per cent of the GDP; it is a positive factor in overall development.

The draft Approach Paper to the Twelfth Plan notes that "to achieve rapid growth, the economy will have to overcome constraints posed by ... the complex problem of managing the urban transition associated with rapid growth". It quotes the 2011 census which shows an increase in the urban population from 27.8 per cent in 2001 to 31.2 per cent in 2011, and which is likely to exceed 40 per cent by 2030. It concludes that this would necessitate "a sufficiently long term focus on urban planning in the Twelfth Plan".

The time is therefore ripe for a national debate on urbanisation, and particularly, on urban governance.

Modern urban municipal institutions have a history of over three centuries in India. It was in 1687 that the Madras Municipal Corporation was formed and thereafter Calcutta and Bombay Municipal Corporations were created. In the early part of the nineteenth century, almost all towns in India had experienced some form of municipal governance. The 1935 Government of India Act brought local government under the purview of the state governments and specific powers were given. This was repeated in the Seventh Schedule of our Constitution in Item 5 of the State List.

In 1992, a major step towards the decentralisation and empowerment of local governments was undertaken through the 74th Amendment. It recognised local governments as the third tier of governance and stipulated greater responsibility and authority for them, including in planning for economic and social development, and mobilisation and utilisation of resources.

Four major areas of importance in urban governance, in my view, require immediate attention:

First: while the urban local bodies have found political protection through the 74th Amendment, the other aspects of decentralisation have lagged behind. Local government is the most neglected tier of government with functional and financial decentralisation not flowing from the state governments to the cities. Furthermore, there is lack of decentralisation within the city councils from the city centre to the peripheral wards, and lack of involvement of community groups and civil society stakeholders, women and other marginalised groups in decision-making and implementation.

Second: We need to radically elevate the role and prestige of managers of large urban agglomerations in terms of structural location in governance and in terms of their place in the political and economic scheme of things in the country. Megacities such as London and New York have empowered mayors who set the agenda for the development of the city and promote the economic progress and social development prospects in the city. Contrary to this, our metropolitan city managers do not enjoy appropriate political prestige or economic clout.

It is therefore essential for the mayors of our cities to get back the role that their predecessors enjoyed in the pre-Independence period. The skill sets and remuneration for our municipal personnel need to be adjusted appropriately.

Third: Our urban spaces and governance mechanisms have become the theatres for political conflicts and economic struggles. Our urban spaces have also been used for promoting reforms as well as for contesting such reform measures. Some seek privatisation of municipal services including through Public-Private Partnerships with governments merely functioning as regulators or facilitators; others say that this would institutionalise social and economic disparities.

The scale of investments and choice of projects to direct them have been subject to political pulls and economic pressures. While some critics speak of "elite capture" of our urban spaces and indeed of all 'urban commons', others bemoan that 'exclusionary' urbanisation is benefitting certain social groups to the detriment of others, and directing resources to large metropolises depriving small and medium towns of funds needed for infrastructure and essential services.

Fourth: The governance structures of our metropolitan cities differ significantly from each other. We have a distinct model for the National Capital Region. Other metropolitan cities are state capitals with their own Municipal Corporations. They experience competing claims emerging from diverse social, political and linguistic groups to appropriate urban spaces and opportunities for social and economic advancement. How the nation manages and addresses these claims is critical to keeping our urban spaces inclusive and preventing the metropolitan cities from becoming exclusionary and exclusivist.

We do need a public debate to ensure that our urban spaces remain 'national' in their character, that there is transparency and inclusiveness in urban governance.

We need to ensure that our cities do not succumb to narrow or sectarian monopolies.

Urbanisation cannot be prevented; it is in our own interest that we manage it better and direct it to serve our national goals and public interest. Equality of access to urban spaces, to availing of emerging social and economic opportunities, and to participation as equal stakeholders is essential to prevent social strife and economic conflict. Let all empower the third tier of urban local government in meaningful ways and let our cities not only survive, but thrive.

Annual Sardar Patel Memorial Lecture: 'Physical Integration and Emotional Inconsonance'
New Delhi

It is a privilege to be called upon to deliver the 2012 Sardar Patel Memorial Lecture.

Sardar Vallabhbhai Patel was an iconic personality, a close associate of Gandhi*ji*, a leader in the freedom struggle, a person who along with Jawaharlal Nehru was at the helm of affairs in the early years of our existence as a free country. Hs contributions were manifold; above all, history and generations of Indians will remember him as the man who presided over the process that resulted in the integration of the Indian states following the end of British rule and the termination of the "vague and undefined" relationship that princely States (together constituting 40 per cent of the Indian land mass) had with the United Kingdom as the paramount power.

The process of integrating 554 large and miniscule states was complex. It involved intricate negotiations on political, administrative and financial matters as also those relating to the armed forces of these units. It was almost completed by the time the Constitution of India came into force on 26 January 1950. Nevertheless, a passage in V.P. Menon's classic and first-hand account highlights what was not accomplished at that point:

> 'We had demolished the artificial barriers between the States inter se and the rest of India and had indeed laid the foundations for an integrated administrative and financial structure. But the real integration had to take place in the minds of the people. This could not be accomplished overnight. It would take some time for the people of erstwhile States to outgrow their regional loyalties and to develop a wider outlook and a broader vision.'

Menon goes on to quote Sardar Patel's apprehension in the matter:

> 'Almost overnight we have introduced in these States the super-structure of modern system of government. The inspiration and stimulus has come from above rather than from below and unless the transplanted growth takes a healthy root in the soil, there will be a danger of collapse and chaos.'

Passage of time was to show that this integration of the minds, not only by the residents of the erstwhile princely states but by citizens on the national scale was to be a longer process, at times torturous, and covered all regions and all segments of population in our vast land.

Nor was this unanticipated; as early as 1902, Rabindranath Tagore had observed that 'unity cannot be brought about by enacting a law that all shall be one.'

The constitution-making process reflected the concern for national unity. One aspect of it, legal and structural, put into place a parliamentary democracy; the other pertained to sociological and emotional dimensions. Emerging from the inherited pattern of centralised governance, the concern was to prevent Balkanisation as well as to accommodate what Sunil Khilnani has called 'layered Indianness' that specifically recognised linguistic and cultural identities. This was reflected in the end product—a union of states, described by Ivor Jennings as 'a federation with strong centralising tendencies'.

The imperatives of democracy were spelt out with great insight, and foresight, by Babasaheb Ambedkar in the closing days of the work of the Constituent Assembly. Effective functioning of democracy, he said, required focus on three aspects: firstly, holding fast to constitutional methods and abandoning 'the method of civil disobedience, non-cooperation and satyagraha'; secondly, not allowing anyone, however mighty, to subvert the institutions; and thirdly, not resting content with political democracy only and recognising the twin principles of equality (through one man one vote and one vote one value) and fraternity (through common brotherhood of all Indians). 'The sooner we realise', he added, 'that we are as yet not a nation in the social and psychological sense of the word, the better for us.'

Some years later, and speaking on national integration, Jawaharlal Nehru stressed the same point: "I lay stress on the unity of India', he said, 'not merely the political unity which we have achieved but something far deeper, the emotional unity, the integration of our minds and hearts, the suppression of feelings of separatism.'

The working of the Constitution in terms of the arrangements between the Union and the States in the context of 'a changing social, economic and political environment' has been examined on a number of occasions, the most recent being the Punchi Commission. Its Report submitted in March 2010 built on earlier works particularly of the Sarkaria Commission (1988), took note of the failure of expectations generated by it, and concluded with the observation that 'cooperative federalism will be the key for sustaining India's unity, integrity and social and economic development in future.'

In one of the questionnaires circulated by the Punchi Commission to stake holders it was enquired if, given the pluralistic identity of India, political and social developments and increased socio-political mobilisation around sectarian identities would pose a threat to the unity and integrity of the country? Furthermore, what could be done to ensure that the national vision and wider collective purpose are always paramount and do not get distorted? The answers received are not yet in the public domain.

In this context, another set of questions come to mind. While the debate on the functioning of the federal system is very much a part of the national political discourse, can the same be said for the realisation of fraternity? How far, and how well, have we as a people travelled on the path of social and emotional integration?

Record shows that in September 1961 Prime Minister Nehru convened a National Integration conference to find ways and means to combat the evils of communalism, casteism, regionalism, linguism and narrow mindedness that were becoming hurdles to maintenance of national unity and integrity. The Conference decided to set up a National Integration Council to address these matters and make recommendations thereon. The first meeting of the Council was held in June 1962. To date, fifteen meetings have been held in fifty years, with glaring gaps of over ten years between some of these meetings.

Could the frequency be suggestive of priorities? Perhaps the answer is to be found in a propensity to evade troubling questions until they begin to dent the certitudes or the major premises that envelop public discourse.

In 2005 Rajni Kothari had written about "a need to think beyond the merely political and tap the psycho-spiritual dimensions of Indian reality;" he concluded that "the Indian model of development is characterised by the politicisation of social structure, through a wide dispersal and permeation of political forms, values and ideologies." Other competent observers have noted democracy in India advancing "through the competitive negotiations between groups, each competing for their interests, rather than the diffusion of democratic norms."

A natural consequence of this is 'the politics of identity', perhaps even a Balkanisation of the Indian mind.

It is in the backdrop of these ground realities that the question of national integration is to be viewed. How do we bring about 'the integration of minds and hearts?

Many years back a political scientist had sought to delineate the contours of the desirable on this count:

"In the semantics of functional politics the term national integration means, and ought to mean, *cohesion* and *not fusion, unity* and *not uniformity, reconciliation* and *not merger, accommodation not annihilation, synthesis* and *not dissolution, solidarity* and *not regimentation* of the several discrete segments of the people constituting the larger political community ... Obviously, then, Integration is not a process of conversion of diversities into a uniformity but a congruence of diversities leading to a unity in which both the varieties and similarities are maintained."

A conceptual framework of this degree of sophistication would obviously require a comprehensive endeavour by the State and the society to ensure its implementation on an ongoing basis. It has to become part of the social discourse and of the educational curricula aimed at making the citizens imbibe the virtues of integration and eschew the vices emanating from its absence. Such an effort has to be to move beyond the presumed

Indianness in cultural terms or its spirited display on special occasions on which national integration and national solidarity are most obvious – in the face of an external enemy (1961, 1965, 1971 and 1998), a celebratory occasion like success in an international sporting event, an achievement of note by an Indian citizen or person of Indian origin, or a social or religious festival; above all, and on a fairly continuous basis, success stories in the film industry.

It is therefore essential to have a re-look at the basics of our methodology and of the contours within which it has worked. Our ground reality is a plural society; our operating radius is a democratic polity and a secular state structure, both based on a Constitution aimed at seeking justice, liberty, equality and fraternity for all citizens within a single political and juridical entity whose federal structure provides for separate legislative and executive powers for states but stipulates uniformity in civil and criminal jurisprudence, a single judiciary, a common All India Civil Service, a common armed forces, a common market, and a constitutional provision on sharing of financial resources between the centre and the states. The assumption was that political and administrative integration of the state would lead to an integration of hearts and minds of those who may speak a different language or follow a different faith or come from a different region, but would subscribe to and believe in a common Indian identity in which all other identities would be subsumed and also flourish at the same time.

This, however, has turned out to be insufficient. Hard issues agitating the public mind in different regions have come to the fore and seek acceptable solutions. B.G. Verghese has rightly observed that "as India's multitudinous but hitherto dormant diversities come to life, identities are asserted and jostle for a place in the sun." He lists among these issues of majority and minority, centre and periphery, great" 'this management of diversity within multiple transitions is a delicate and complex process aggravated by inexorable population growth."

One obvious reason for this is the ripening and deepening of the democratic process in the country, the awareness generated by it, and the terms and shape of the dialogue propelled by it. Another is the failure of the

State to comprehend the dimensions of change and the resultant failure to respond appropriately, without undue procrastination, and adapt existing mechanisms to newer requirements. As a result, the immediate has taken precedence over the remote; the obvious over the less obvious. There has been a shift of focus, perhaps a narrowing of the vision, with the national receding behind the regional or local. This is also evident in the domain of foreign policy where complex questions of national interest are involved and should not be impinged upon by transitory considerations.

The size and diversity of the Indian landscape adds to the difficulty of finding solutions. A population of 1.25 billion dispersed over 4,635 communities 78 per cent of whom are not only linguistic and cultural but social categories. The human diversities are both hierarchical and spatial. 'The de jure WE, the sovereign people is in reality a fragmented 'we', divided by yawning gaps that remain to be bridged.' Around 30 per cent of our people live below the official poverty line and the health and education indicators, for the population as a whole, despite recent correctives, leave much to be desired. There are, in addition, problems arising out of Naxalism and insurgency in some areas where the writ of the state runs in name only, demands for a better deal for the states of the union, as also for tribes, dalits and most of the minorities within them. Each of these also relates to the requirements of fraternity and the achievement of national integration.

A sense of urgency is thus imperative. How should we proceed? What institutional and policy devices can be availed of?

A beginning can, and must, be made with the loadstar of our national destiny, the Constitution. Experience shows that its provisions have been used creatively to expand the area of rights, to redress grievances, to allow greater space for federal units in specific areas. The need of the hour is to reinvigorate this process, to explore and make better use of existing constitutional provisions; above all, to ensure better delivery. Prescriptions of despair, unwise or impracticable, do not help the process.

A case in point is the working of our federal system. The underlying major premise is the Rule of Law. Without it, the carefully calibrated framework of power-sharing, and the jurisdictional allocation spelt out in the Seventh

Schedule, become irrelevant. And yet, this does appear to be happening. A knowledgeable scholar analysed the resulting situation earlier this year:

> "That coalition politics makes effective governance a challenge is not surprising… The more important question is what state politics and political parties are doing to the Indian federation. For federalism is not only about giving more powers to the states; it is also about preserving the integrity of those areas that lie within the exclusive preserve of the centre. Undermining the centre's governance over its own jurisdiction does not do any service to the federal idea. Today the Indian federalism is gravely endangered by populist imperatives originating in the states which encroach so far into the Union's as to enervate Parliament and the Union Executive."

This is not to say that genuine disagreements of perception and functioning do not or would not arise; the question is the presence or absence of a will to seek fair and equitable solutions within the ambit of the law. The only way to do so is through dialogue and adequate flexibility within the framework of the Constitution. The obvious platform for such a dialogue, besides the Parliament, is the Inter-State Council, belatedly established in 1990 under Article 263 on the recommendation of the Sarkaria Commission. Its meetings have been infrequent, except in 1997, and the political will to explore its full potential has clearly not been forthcoming. At the same time, the Council must desist from efforts to expand its ambit into matters unambiguously in the Union List of the Seventh Schedule, or to convert itself into a super federal executive, since both would be destructive of the delicate balance envisaged in the Constitution, a balance integral to the preservation of the Union itself.

The same holds good for constitutional safeguards for tribal areas where the potential of Schedules V and VI of the Constitution could have been realised in fuller measure and could have retarded if not prevented resort to violence in tribal areas arising out of their marginalisation. Nor is the situation any better with regard to the actual implementation of various programmes for uplifting educationally and economically some of the most backward of our minorities.

More instances can be cited. These relate to ethnic or communal violence in different parts of the country, the efforts to differentiate between resident and 'outsiders' when both are citizens, to differentiate between Indian and Indian on specious and malicious considerations. Each is a manifestation of parochialism that has crept into our body politic. Each derogates from the requirement of fraternity and thereby affects national integration. The responsibility for failures is shared by all.

The conclusion is unavoidable that the process of emotional integration has faltered and is in dire need of reinvigoration. A corrective is imperative and would lie in reaffirmation of the democratic process bequeathed to us by the founding fathers, adherence to the letter and spirit of the Constitution, rejuvenation of the institutions beginning with the Parliament and state legislatures, and reaffirmation of the sanctity of dialogue. These principles need to be imbibed and implemented at all levels of the polity and particularly in educational policy, in the workshops of the mind that mould the thought process of the citizens of tomorrow.

Culture and Heritage

"Our preference has been for the salad bowl rather than the melting pot. The question of striking a balance between globalisation and identity, between authenticity and modernisation, and between the desire to be oneself and the temptation to be like others, would thus remian a teasing one

Launch of the International National Trusts Organisation during the Twelfth International Conference of National Trusts

Hotel Ashok, New Delhi

3 December 2007

This is an international gathering of a different kind and I feel privileged to be here with you today at the formal launch of the International National Trusts Organisation. It is a rare sight to see such a congregation of conservation specialists in Delhi, sharing their experiences, debating and developing collective strategies to promote international cooperation in heritage management and conservation.

The need for international cooperation in heritage management has been recognised much before today's period of globalisation. The 'Convention Concerning The Protection of the World Cultural and Natural Heritage' adopted in 1972 by the General Conference of the UNESCO had clearly spelt out that the cultural and natural heritage of countries needs to be preserved as "part of the world heritage of mankind as a whole" and that "it is incumbent on the international community as a whole to participate in the protection" of this heritage to complement, and not in lieu of, the efforts of the concerned State. The Convention had also noted that the cultural and natural heritage is increasingly threatened with destruction not only by the traditional causes of decay, but also by changing social and economic conditions".

The formal launch of the International National Trusts Organisation brings the critical task of international cooperation of heritage conservation from the ambit of State actors to a rapidly globalising civil society. It takes conservation back to the people, the ultimate guarantors as well as the beneficiaries of the preservation of their heritage. This is happening against the backdrop of unprecedented economic growth and development taking place in India and in other developing countries. The theme of the

Twelfth International Conference of International Trusts, 'Heritage and Development', is thus very timely and appropriate.

Rapid economic development, good in itself, is also dislocating. Conventional social and economic mores of life are disrupted, people are displaced and uprooted by unseen forces beyond their control, social and cultural axes of reference are replaced and people suffer varying degrees of alienation, disconnect with the roots and conflict of their external environment with their internal cultural context. We are told that valuable biological heritage is lost, as many species of flora and fauna have become extinct; many spoken dialects and languages have died out. Sustainability as a concept applied to development has many dimensions related to conservation of our heritage.

Some of the other issues that have been chosen for discussion in this conference deserve the attention of policy makers, national trusts and civil society and the people of our countries. I wish to highlight three of them:

1. Conservation of heritage in regions affected by conflict and natural disasters is an issue that is ripe for international cooperation. We have seen in our own country that the process of rehabilitation and development in the aftermath of conflict and natural disasters does not accord a high priority to heritage conservation. It is understandable when resources are limited and the uppermost concern is to help people cope with the disaster and rebuild their lives. However, international assistance and cooperation could help mitigate the great damage to the heritage caused by natural disasters and conflict.
2. Heritage tourism is increasingly becoming important for resource generation in regions and societies that have inherited rich cultural and natural heritage. But heritage tourism also creates its own set of problems. It has been said that heritage tourism is negatively impacting the cultural, geographic and natural landscape of host societies. Questions have also been raised about equitable distribution of the costs and benefits of such tourism and about the role of local communities and civil societies in promoting

heritage tourism as opposed to the role of government and the corporate sector.

3. One facet of cooperation that has not been explored to its fullest potential while conserving our heritage is that of regional cooperation. It is very difficult to superimpose national boundaries over the complex map of inherited cultural, natural and intangible heritage of peoples. We in India, have been at the confluence of cultural and civilisational winds blowing from all directions. Various strands of our heritage owe their origin to different regions and peoples of the world. Conservation of heritage would immensely benefit from regional cooperation.

Governments around the world cannot ignore the increasing public concern at the potential damage to the environment and heritage as a result of the development process. Development, to be sustainable, must be inclusive, not just in economic terms but also in cultural terms. Those who have not benefited from the rapid growth of the recent past must be enabled and empowered to participate in the developmental process. The incredible diversity of our heritage, including those of the weaker and marginalised sections of our society, must be preserved.

I once again applaud the various national trusts, especially INTACH, for their remarkable work in conservation of heritage. The work of INTACH is also a tribute to the vision and dedication of its founder and its first Chairman, late Shri Rajiv Gandhi. I hope that INTACH will continue as a prime vehicle for civic action to save heritage and for educating the public in heritage awareness.

I congratulate the members of the Transitional Steering Committee for their work in bringing into being the International National Trusts Organisation. I wish the Twelfth International Conference of National Trusts all success in its deliberations.

Book release: ***Feroze Gandhi*** **by Shashi Bhushan**

New Delhi
25 August 2008

Lifting the veil from the conditions of the past is the purpose of the historian. This, as the historian Ibn Khaldun said, "Forces stubborn stray wisdom to return to the fold and induce corrective action."

Today's book resurrects a name from the past. This should not merely be an exercise in nostalgia even though it is permissible in the case of a public figure of yesteryears who was a freedom fighter, editor of a newspaper that played a role in the freedom struggle, a crusader for public causes, and a parliamentarian of eminence.

The present generation of Indians know precariously little of these. For this reason alone, Shashi Bhushan*ji* has done a great public service by drawing attention to Feroze Gandhi's role in the early years of the Republic.

There are two aspects of Feroze Gandhi's work that are of abiding relevance. One is what Shashi Bhushan*ji* calls "the ideological struggle waged in the fourth Lok Sabha" on the role of the State in the economy. The other is the role of parliament in scrutinising executive action.

Feroze Gandhi passed away in 1960. Five decades later the ideological debate has not disappeared; instead, it has developed new dimensions. The controversy over the SEZs (Special Economic Zone) makes this evident. The problems it has highlighted cannot be brushed away; they need to be addressed.

Equally relevant is Feroze Gandhi's approach to the role of parliament.

In January 2006, the United Nation's Research Institute for Social Development published a study on the role of the Indian Parliament as an Instrument of Accountability. It concluded that opposition parties are reactive rather than proactive and that the opposition uses Parliament more to impugn the credibility of governments than to exercise accountability for the sake of good governance.

Matters were perhaps better in earlier times.

Feroze Gandhi was a backbencher on the treasury side in the Lok Sabha. His concern for public good, nevertheless, remained paramount. Several instances of this are cited in Shashi Bhushan*ji's* book. The one that attracted maximum public attention was the Mundra case involving LIC's decision to purchase shares in companies of dubious standing in the market.

Feroze Gandhi raised the matter in the Lok Sabha in stentorian words: "A mutiny in my mind has compelled me to raise this debate. When things of such magnitude occur, silence becomes a crime". The discussion resulted in a judicial inquiry. Chief Justice Chagla, who conducted it, insisted on public hearings. "The public", he said, "is entitled to know on what evidence the decision is based".

This excellent precedent was not followed in the case of the 1992 and 200I inquiries. The resulting damage to the public's perception of its elected representatives is evident today and has furthered the view that "the politics of corruption and the corruption of politics fuel each other". Transparency International's latest Corruption Index gives India a score of 3.5 on a scale of 10. The loss of national energy, and of national wealth, is evident.

We do need to put a stop to the loot emanating from corruption, enforce the rule of law with greater diligence, and erase the creeping impression that we are a populist democracy rather than a constitutional one. Only heightened public awareness and a reasoned debate in the civil society and parliament could initiate it; only a determined effort and a plan of action could pursue its implementation.

A corrective is imperative. The example set by Feroze Gandhi is worthy of emulation.

Release of *Tragic Hero of Kashmir – Sheikh Mohammad Abdullah* by Ajit Bhattacharjea
New Delhi
30 September 2008

This book is living history at its best. It is the record of happening of a generation that is all but gone. For this reason alone, it is invaluable.

It is also a profoundly disturbing book. It reinforces the view that we are still in the process of learning about the momentous events relating to J&K in the early years of our independence.

There are snippets of information that help a reader understand a shade better the role of the principal actors. There are insights which are invaluable. The book does need to be read with some diligence, preferably with other material now in the public domain.

Some of the events mentioned and documented in the book have a contemporary relevance. Nehru's emphatic observations on the impulses behind the Jammu agitation in 1952-53 are a case in point. Sheikh Abdullah gave vent to his sentiments in the speech of 31 July1952 and Nehru stated the Indian position in his long letter of June 1953.

Two factors mentioned in the book are critical to the understanding of the approaches of different actors in J&K. The first relates to the pre-August 1947 period in which the focus of the struggle of people of the Valley was not against the British but against the Maharaja's rule. The second is the impact on the Jammu region of the land reforms implemented by the National Conference government.

Even a serious book on a serious subject recounts some humourous episodes. I found two rather amusing. The first cites V.P. Menon's account of the instructions given by Maharaja Hari Singh to his ADC on 26 October 1947. The second we have on the authority of Foreign Secretary Gundavia;

it relates to a discussion in early 1964 between Nehru and his Director of Intelligence Bureau. The latter dilated on the strength of legal case against the Sheikh; what followed was a typical Nehruvian outburst: "If a damned thing cannot be proved in four years and in six years, there's obviously nothing to be proved".

Annual Virasat Lecture
Sayaji Garden Museum, Vadodara
7 March 2009

It is a pleasure for me to be here in Vadodara on my first visit to the state. The occasion, by happy coincidence, is one that is dear to me. The Heritage Trust is a unique platform in the country; it brings together heritage professionals from diverse backgrounds for the cause of conservation and to sensitize our society and polity to turn more heritage-friendly. I therefore deem it a privilege to deliver the Virasat Lecture this year.

Allow me to begin with a set of questions. What is heritage? Why is it relevant? Why have societies down the ages spent time and effort in making subsequent generations imbibe it, transmit it and build upon it?

The simplest meaning of Virasat is inheritance or legacy. Related to it in this context is the term Aathar meaning trace, vestige or an ancient monument; hence the terms Ilm al aathar for archaeology and dar al aathar for museum of antiquities. This is what led the medieval Arab poet to say:

Tilka aathar-o-na tadallun alaina
Fa unzuru baad-o-na ilal aathar
These are our works, these works our souls display;
Behold our works when we have passed away.

Some of you may have had occasion to read the last chapter of Edward Gibbon's great history. It begins with a quotation from the 15th century historian Poggius introspecting on the ruins of ancient Rome, nine hundred years after the fall of the Western Empire. One sentence summed up the scene: 'The public and the private edifices, that were founded for eternity, lie prostrate, naked, and broken like the limbs of a mighty giant; and the ruin is the more visible, from the stupendous relics that have survived the injuries of time and fortune'.

Gibbon's own assessment is in a philosophical strain and can be true of a similar situation elsewhere in the world:

'The art of man is able to construct monuments far more permanent than the narrow span of his own existence; yet these monuments, like himself, are perishable and frail; and in the boundless annals of time his life and his labours must equally be measured as a fleeting moment'.

This fleeting moment, nevertheless, is invaluable and leads us to the next set of questions. What role does an understanding of the past, its context and construct, thus have on our perceptions of the present and our aspirations for the future?

It can be said without fear of contradiction that our generation has done more than earlier ones to give shape to it.

This audience is familiar with the work of UNESCO, its World Heritage Committee, and with its basic principle that cultural heritage of each is the cultural heritage of all. This was given a sharper focus in the November 1994 Nara Document on Authenticity in Relation to the World Heritage Convention which states that 'the diversity of cultures and heritage in our world is an irreplaceable source of spiritual and intellectual richness for all humankind' and that 'the protection and enhancement of cultural and heritage diversity in our world should be actively promoted as an essential aspect of human development'.

The responsibility is essentially national even though international assistance has been sought and given in many cases. How have we in India gone about it?

Article 51(A) of the Constitution of India, dealing with fundamental duties requires every citizen to value and preserve the rich heritage of our composite culture. After over three decades since this Article was inscribed in the Constitution, it is time to assess its impact on the perception and practice of heritage conservation and management. I would like to mention some aspects of it.

In the first place, heritage conservation has largely remained a top-down and a government-driven process with minimal involvement of citizenry and civil society. There are notable exceptions, and INTACH is one such. There are less than ten thousand monuments protected by the Archaeological Survey of India (ASI) and State Archeology Departments. Apart from these monuments, very few public spaces have been subject to heritage conservation frameworks. In comparison, Latvia, with a population of around 2.5 million, has over eight thousand protected heritage sites.

While the broader aim of heritage conservation through community development and a "bottom-up" approach with the community as a stake holder is acknowledged, its actual realisation is still a work-in-progress.

Secondly and despite minimal involvement of common people in conservation, the legislature, the judiciary and the media have increasingly played an important role in heritage conservation and advocacy. In terms of legislation, Punjab and Maharashtra have pioneered state-level legislation for heritage conservation. Executive regulations for heritage conservation have been notified in many states and have provided a framework for conserving buildings of architectural, historical and aesthetic value. These have also included environmental and natural features such as coast lines and rock formations. The Judiciary has played an important role in preventing demolition of historical structures and in stopping industrial or other activities that could damage heritage monuments.

Thirdly, heritage sites in India not only house historical monuments but also continuous areas of habitat for the local population. Conservation efforts have had to be balanced against housing and other infrastructural needs of urban planning and development. Historical cultural heritage, that is static, co-exists with living cultural heritage, that is dynamic and ever changing in response to the needs of those owning, living and using the heritage sites. It was only in very few instances that heritage conservation emerged as a vehicle for both economic growth and cultural regeneration.

A fourth point pertains to increasing globalisation and homogenisation and its adverse impact on cultural distinctiveness. What was taken for granted earlier now has to be explored and people have looked within, and to their past, to better understand who they are and to identify the quintessential values of their culture and civilisation. This process is more complicated in multi-ethnic, multi-lingual and multi-religious states, when identifying syncretic threads from the past has become important in building a broad-based framework of national identity.

Finally, national and community narratives of tangible and intangible heritage have not only become politicized but have in fact been used as instruments of political mobilisation. This has posed one of the most serious challenges to heritage preservation in India and in the South Asian region. The destruction of the Bamiyan Buddhas in Afghanistan and of the Babri Mosque in Ayodhya best reflect the manner in which issues of identity, shaped by fundamentalist approaches, have threatened archaeological and heritage sites.

How we interpret our heritage is a matter of perception, depth of knowledge and breadth of vision. Artificial lines resulting in the owning and disowning of the past do not stand the test of scientific historiography; nor do they serve the cause of national cohesion and through it the national interest. Jawaharlal Nehru described Indian culture like some ancient palimpsest on which the imprint of succeeding generations have unrecognisably merged. He had the insight to assert that 'If we were going to build the house of India's future strong and secure and beautiful, we would have to dig deep for the foundations'.

I can think of no better example to illustrate this vision than the work undertaken by the Heritage Trust and INTACH in ensuring that Champaner-Pavagadh Archaeological Park is designated as a UNESCO World Heritage Centre. It reflects the composite culture of Gujarat and the multi-cultural ethos of our nation. This site is a shining example of archaeological, historic and living cultural heritage that includes pre-historic sites and strong Hindu, Jain and Islamic influences in its history, monuments and even in the myths and legends surrounding it. It has contemporary relevance for the state and for the country.

The matter does not and must not remain confined to state agencies. Unless the common citizen understands the richness of our heritage, and is empowered to play a more direct role in preserving it, there is every danger that the diversity and the heterogeneity implicit in the idea of India would be corroded to the detriment of all of us.

Book release: Series *Islam in South Asia* edited by Prof. Mushirul Hasan
New Delhi
4 November 2009

A 'book release' is a very mundane expression that does little justice to the intellectual, and physical, endeavour involved in the writing or compiling a book. 'Unveiling' is a nicer, more anticipatory, term. It signals a movement from the unknown to the known.

Having settled this definitional matter, at least to my satisfaction, let me say I am delighted to be associated with today's function.

Professor Mushirul Hasan needs no introduction to this, or any other, audience. His eminence as a historian is in no need of commentary. His ability to delve into the nuances of intellectual history and culture, to explore marginalised voices, adds a dimension to the understanding of a period of our history in which new challenges disrupted traditional patterns of life and induced agonising adjustments.

What we have before us today is not a single volume but a set of six. This in itself is somewhat unique. These, taken together, contain what Ibn Khaldun would have described as "unusual knowledge and familiar if hidden wisdom". Together they provide a wide cross section of views emanating from or relating to Muslims and Muslim communities in South Asia over a span of two centuries. It is the history of a dialogue between the realm of religious symbols and the world of everyday reality, and of the interaction between them. The compilation is thematic and each theme is narrated eloquently through a diversity of voices. The editor's introductions to each of the volume need to be read carefully because they spell out the approach. His purpose is to uncover important, often overlooked, facets of Muslim thought and practice in South Asia and to portray the diversity of views on a very wide range of societal interests.

Ours, regrettably, is an age in which the 'spectre of Islam' seems to haunt many minds in different parts of the world. An artificial construct of an existential threat has taken the place of serious study of religion and culture in time and space. The publication of these volumes on *Islam in South Asia* is therefore timely. Roughly 480 million Muslims of the world, out of a global total of around 1.57 billion, live in South Asia. For almost a thousand years they have interacted with other faiths and cultures. Their experience is distinctive, their contributions noteworthy. A deeper study of these would help dispel many of the myths and stereotypes that have been developed or imbibed thoughtlessly. A century earlier the poet Akbar Allahabadi's looked at it despondingly and sought divine correctives:

> *"Be-had woh khafa hain Akbar se aur uski dua ye hai ki un-hain*
> *Allah baseerat aisi de apni ghalti ko dekh sakain"*

Professor Mushirul Hasan's approach is more practical: I am confident his six volumes would help the quest for this *baseerat.*

Inauguration of an international seminar 'Indian Culture in a Globalised World' on the Sixtieth Anniversary of the founding of ICCR
New Delhi
11 November 2010

This conference coincides, purposely, with the birth anniversary of a great Indian whose name is associated with this auditorium. I refer of course to Abul Kalam Azad whom Jawaharlal Nehru described as "an extraordinarily interesting companion" at a time when they were incarcerated in adjoining cells in a British jail. Many years later, Nehru compared him to "the great men of Renaissance, or, in a later period, of the Encyclopaedists who preceded the French Revolution, men of intellect, men of action."

It has been rightly said that Maulana Azad's thought process transcended national boundaries and imbibed the best of different worlds–Indian, West Asian and Western. He was prone to question the fundamentals. In one of his early essays he urged his readers "to break the chains forged by centuries of custom and habit, belief and practice, and adopt a new line of thought and action ... to acquire a new body, a new mind, a new imagination, new senses ..." He was thus responding to the intellectual stirrings of the age and was perhaps an early proponent of culture unbound by territoriality.

II

Our subject today verges on the amorphous. It seeks elucidation and linkages of three concepts: globalisation, culture, and Indian culture. While the first is commonly viewed solely as an economic phenomenon, the other two have been subjected to considerable philosophical and sociological analysis. All three tempt the uninitiated to wander off in a speculative labyrinth. Hence the need, as Hegel would have put it, "to see things with the eye of reason."

Even in its economic sense, it is essential to be clear about the meaning of globalisation. The concept is viewed in two distinct ways: in a positive sense to *describe* a process of integration into the world economy, and in a normative sense to *prescribe* a strategy of development based on a rapid integration with the world economy.

The economic aspect, critical though it is, does not cover the entire ambit of the phenomenon that has political, social and cultural dimensions. Much light on these was shed by the *Report of the World Commission on the Social Dimensions of Globalisation* published by the International Labour Organisation in 2004. The report brings out the point that economic globalisation has developed in 'an ethical vacuum' and has created 'global imbalances that are morally unacceptable and practically unsustainable.' It urges the need for basing it on 'universally shared values and respect for human rights and individual dignity'.

Other dimensions of globalisation are equally relevant. To the sociologist, it is associated with modernity, to international relations theorist with global governance, and to the men and women of science with a range of technologies and mediums that have qualitatively transformed human communications and connectivity.

The transformation in the processes and forms of connectivity has led, as in past ages, to a complex series of interaction between peoples and cultures. It has been suggested, and rightly so, that a culture is no longer a discreet world and is instead transformed 'to accord with a world of ruptured boundaries' that seek reciprocal recognition. The level and intensity of these interactions and the convergence of activities associated with them have been uneven rather than uniform and have depended on the totality of forces at work in specific cases. What is clear is that cultural hybridity, not cultural purity, is an unavoidable outcome. This goes hand in hand with the erosion of the traditional concepts of the nation-state, national economies and national culture and tends to produce new forms of global mass culture dominated or heavily influenced by new ways of expression and imagery.

Some definitional clarity is essential to this discussion. How, in the first place, do we define culture? For our purpose today, a working definition is available in UNESCO's *Universal Declaration on Cultural Diversity* adopted in November 2001. It defines culture as 'the set of distinctive spiritual, material, intellectual and emotional features of a society or social group, and that encompasses, in addition to art and literature, life styles, ways of living together, value systems, traditions and belief.' Acknowledging that cultural diversity is as necessary for humankind as biodiversity is for nature, it notes that globalisation creates conditions for dialogue of cultures and civilisations. The relevance of cultural interaction is highlighted in the Declaration's assertion that while creativity draws on the roots of cultural tradition it flourishes in contact with other cultures.

In our common parlance, culture has connotations to the idea of a fixed locality. Globalisation, and the complex connectivity that goes with it, thus threatens this understanding of culture and introduces the notion of mobility and a loosening of the linkage to specific area or territory. Nor do the latter remain uninfluenced by the process of this loosening and global cultural flows do invade the local space. To that extent, cultural practices remain at the heart of globalisation and shape it. By the same token these cultural flows, made inevitable through the complex connectivity unleashed, generate concerns because they bring about frequent confrontation with 'the Other' and induce debates about identity.

The Iranian philosopher Abdolkarim Soroush has addressed the question of cultural identity and cultural allegiance in terms relevant to our discourse. Identity, he asserts, is to be viewed as dynamic and evolving; he adds that "what causes fear of other cultures is the lack of a strong cultural digestive system and also the misconception that each culture is an indivisible monolith, accepting one part of which equals accepting the whole."

The problem of digestion, it must be admitted, is infinitely complex in a vast land like ours. Our preference has been for the salad bowl rather than for the melting pot. The question of striking a balance between globalisation and identity, between authenticity and modernisation, and between the desire to be oneself and the temptation to be like others, would thus remain a teasing one.

III

Before we consider the place of Indian culture in such a new world, perhaps not yet a brave one, an element of clarity is essential about it. Jawaharlal Nehru's precision of expression in the matter is noteworthy. Indian culture, he wrote, is "the palimpsest on which the imprints of succeeding generations have unrecognisably merged." Mahatma Gandhi expressed it differently. "I want the cultures of all lands", he said, "to be blown about my house as freely as possible but I refuse to be blown off my feet by any." These ideas have been amplified by the historian K.N. Panikkar and I can do no better than to cite a few relevant passages from a lecture delivered by him at Bangalore in 2004:

> The political history of India is characterised by a continuous cyclical process, centrifugal on the one hand and centripetal on the other ... The cultural make up of the nation is enmeshed in this political process ... The dynamism of Indian culture is derived from this diversity which moulded the cultural practices of the people ... the coming together of people of diverse cultural moorings and traditions had several cultural consequences. These have been variously conceived as synthesis, assimilation, acculturation, and eclecticism.... The crucial question is whether Indian culture is conceived as a static phenomenon, tracing its identity to a single unchanging source, or a dynamic phenomenon, critically and creatively interrogating all that is new ... The Indian Renaissance and the national movement recognised the positive significance of cultural plurality for national identity and sought to further the syncretic tendencies already present in social and religious life; hence the nationalist notion of unity in diversity.

The participants in this seminar include a great many scholars of eminence who would dwell on different aspects of Indian culture and the interest displayed in it by the world beyond our borders. I would, therefore, like to confine my remarks to some aspects of public policy for which the ethos of Indian culture has some relevance. I refer to the notion of accommodation of diversity in modern societies.

The uniqueness of the Indian experience is principally responsible for this. Our plural society is an existential reality; we have consciously adopted a democratic polity and a secular state structure. Our diversity emanates from the first characteristic, and is expressed through the second and the third. Diversity is an Indian passion: we live it, tolerate it, accommodate it, and relish it. Contestation is thus inherent, but it manifests itself most of the time in an agreed framework. A historian of modern India, Ramachandra Guha, has observed that "at no other time or place have social conflicts been so richly diverse, so vigorously articulated, so eloquently manifested in art and literature, or addressed with such directness by the political system or the media."

Accommodation of diversity is not an Indian preserve. In a world so full of variety, it must necessarily occur elsewhere too. It has been observed that 'homogenous national states are a pipedream.' Globalisation and its inherent connectivity and mobility have added to it in ample measure. The critical question then is of the manner in which individual societies respond to it.

A cursory survey of the past five decades unravels patterns of response ranging from rejection to accommodation in varying degrees. The progression of comprehension has not been uniform; in fact, in recent years and in many societies, regression is the dominant trend. The retreat has been both at the level of theory and of policy. In 1999 the Canadian scholar Will Kymlika proclaimed that "multiculturalists have won the day" in making their case for difference-conscious notion of justice and concomitant laws and policies in the liberal state. Recent experience, however, indicates a 'tendency to take multiculturalism as a description of a diverse society rather than a prescription for state policy.'

This distinction between *description* and *prescription* is critical to the accommodation of diversity. Most states in the modern world would meet the first criterion; a far lesser number, however, qualify for the second. Furthermore, there are some who live up to the ideal in fair weather only and regress under stressful socio-economic conditions. Such regressions add to social tensions and aggravate matters. A good many contemporary instances of the latter are fresh in public memory.

It is suggested by some that the tidal wave of economic globalisation carries with it the imperative of cultural homogenisation. Empirical evidence does not sustain this argument. A competitive edge internationally necessitates quality and creativity; the latter is influenced by the cultural environment in which the local rather than international plays the dominant role. The appreciation and celebration of diversity thus becomes an economic strategy as well as a cultural and political one.

IV

It is here that Indian culture has a relevance to the globalising world of today. Being the confluence of ideas, values and traditions it cannot but be inherently syncretic. While maintaining the purity of individual traditions, dance forms, music, literature and art, it accepts the authenticity of others and often synthesises them into newer and richer forms. The same holds good for manifestations of diversity in the daily life of the people, be it in language, cuisine, clothing, behaviour patterns. The imperative of a common market, and of a common political system, has induced intermingling. All of this finds reflection in popular culture and above all in films. The instinctive Indian impulse is to evade the either/or question and seek an approach that accommodates both. Fringe trends apart, assimilation and homogenisation are viewed neither as feasible nor desirable.

The richness of values secreted in the interstices of Indian culture was known and appreciated long before the era of present day globalisation. It left its imprint on the culture and civilisation of East Asian, South-East Asian, Central Asian and West Asian lands. The Western world too discovered some aspects of it in the colonial period. The new world now taking shape amplifies and magnifies them. Many factors contribute to it: the speed of connectivity, the number of Indians abroad, the popularity of commercial Hindi films and yoga and of the literary products of Indian writers in English, the projection and acceptance of the work of painters and sculptors etc in addition to philosophy and classical music, classical dances and other art forms. An overarching backdrop to these is provided by the emergence of India as a major economic and political factor on the global scene.

These traits of culture go beyond national experience in the political sense and are reflective of the genius of a civilisation. So long as Indians continue to imbibe and practise them, there is every reason to anticipate an expanding impact of Indian culture in the world of tomorrow.

I commenced this talk with Maulana Azad. Allow me to conclude with a Persian couplet recited by him urging receptivity to an audience:

Tafawut ast ma'ani shanidan man-o-tu
Tu bastan-e-dar, o man fateh-bab mi shawam
What you and I hear are different. You hear the sound
Of closing doors but I of doors that open

This openness of mind to ideas and practices is the principal ingredient of Indian culture. It is to be nurtured and cherished and must never be allowed to be tampered with for any reasons.

Inaugural function of the 150th Birth Anniversary commemorations of Rabindranath Tagore

Dhaka
6 May 2011

Visiting a neighbour is always a matter of happiness. The pleasure is enhanced manifold when the occasion is such a rarity. In history, as in cricket, a score of 150 is worthy of special mention; it becomes doubly so when it relates to a personality who cannot be situated in conventional terms, who transcends categories and national boundaries, and simply remains *sui generis.*

Some in this audience would recall that half a century back, we celebrated the Tagore Centenary separately and that you did it here notwithstanding many odds.

For these reasons, and more, I am delighted to be here today to represent the Government of India on this historic occasion emanating from the decision of the Prime Ministers of Bangladesh and India in January 2010 to hold joint commemorations to mark the sesqui-centenary of the versatile and multifaceted genius who both our nations and our people refer to as *Kobiguru, Vishwa-kavi* and *Gurudev* and whose pen wrote our respective national anthems.

We are looking forward to welcoming tomorrow in New Delhi the Hon'ble A.K. Khandker to join us in our National Inaugural Function. These parallel celebrations highlight the enduring impact of Rabindranath Tagore on our cultural and intellectual ethos.

We cherish it as you do; together we shall endeavour to enrich it for future generations.

It is well know that Tagore spent the most creative decades of his youth in Bangladesh where he absorbed the beauty of nature. Enchanted by the river Padma and on his *Padma* boat, Tagore produced some of his finest works.

It was here that the serene environs of Shilaidaha, Kushtia, Patisar and Shahzadpur worked their magic on young Rabindranath, thereby becoming an integral part of his inspirational canvas. "I knew not then", he said in the sylvan paradise of Shilaidaha, "that it was so near, that it was mine, and that this perfect sweetness had blossomed in the depth of my own heart".

It was here that Tagore was drawn closer to the toiling masses and took the opportunity to work tirelessly for their upliftment.

It was here that he began his pioneering experiments in education, rural reconstruction and development, as also in affirmative action to set right the existing social inequities. Much of his philosophy, world-view and vision can be traced to these highly productive years.

Madam Prime Minister

Your historic state visit to India last year laid the road-map for our bilateral relations. We have made considerable progress regarding implementation of the far-reaching decisions taken during your visit and remain committed to addressing your developmental priorities, strengthening bilateral relations and enhancing economic engagement.

Rabindranath Tagore represents much that is precious in our common heritage and has influenced our intellectual and cultural ethos in an enduring and distinctive manner. His vision and outlook binds us as perhaps nothing else can. Today's joint celebration is a momentous occasion and the first of its kind in the history of our two nations.

It is also recognition that Tagore was a man ahead of his time; his ideas on culture, gender, poverty, education, freedom, and a resurgent Asia remain relevant today. Tagore worked for one supreme cause, the union of all sections of humanity in sympathy and understanding, in truth and love. He expressed himself in an invocation penned in April 1919. It bears recalling in the troubled world that we live in:

> "Give me the supreme courage of love, this is my prayer, the courage to speak, to do, to suffer at thy will, to leave all things or be left alone.
>
> Give me the supreme faith of love, this is my prayer, the faith of life in death, of the victory in defeat, of the power hidden in the frailness of beauty, of the dignity of pain that accepts hurt, but disdains to return it."

Conferment of Honorary Doctorate for International Relations

Mevlana University at Konya, Turkey
12 October 2011

> "A man, never having seen water, is thrown blindfolded into it, and feels it. When the bandage is removed, he knows what it is. Until then, he only knows it by its effect".

When one comes to the city of Mevlana, and to a university bearing his name, it is only appropriate to commence with his wisdom about the difference between *feeling* and *knowing*.

Needless to say, I am delighted to be here and feel elated by the honoured bestowed on me today. I come as a traveller who has known of the destination but has taken long to reach it. The Persian saying *dair aayed, durust aayed* does help console me.

Turkey and India have known each other for centuries. Both were important pillars of a seamless, borderless world of culture, art, spiritualism and philosophy that extended from Maghrib and Andulusia in the west to all corners of Asia in the east, enriched humanity for over a millennium, assimilated and synthesised many distinctive local, cultural and ethnic features and displayed much diversity within unity. Both contributed to it in ample measure; both take pride in this heritage.

There are similarities and parallelism in this heritage. This is most vividly evident in mysticism, the great spiritual current that runs through all religions. In Islam it is called Sufism and the period from the ninth to fifteenth century witnessed the emergence of a great many masters in Iraq, Iran , Khurasan, Turkey and India whose teachings are revered to this day and have a mass following. Amongst them were Jalaluddin Rumi in Turkey and Moinuddin Chishti in India. They were virtual contemporaries; Chishti died in 1236 and Rumi in 1273.

Nor were they alone. Yunus Emre in Anatolia who died in 1320, became a folk saint in his lifetime and is regarded as an outstanding example of Turkish humanism. Consider the following:

We regard no one's religion as contrary to ours
True love is born when all faiths are united as a whole

And:

The man who does not see the nations of the world as one
Is a rebel even if the pious claim he is holy

"True faith", he observed succinctly, "is in the head, not in the headgear".

Almost a century and a half later Kabir, brought up in a weaver's family in northern India, was a folk saint in a similar mould who sought to find commonalities in faiths. The theme was pervasive in his utterances. I draw attention of this audience to the following:

Allah the Invisible pervades in us all
You must realise it in your heart
He is the same both in Hindu and the Turk
Says Kabir, after due thought

And:

If Allah dwells in a mosque alone,
What about the rest of space?
The Hindus believe that He abides in the image of the deity
The truth is missed in either case

And another:

Muslim's mosque and Hindu's temple
Make them follow separate paths

The Lord dwells in the heart of man
Both Hindus and Muslims miss that

The tradition, of reverence to mystics, and benefiting from their teachings of ascetic living, egalitarianism, and brotherhood of all faiths, continues to be a living reality in India and has contributed to the spiritual fertility of our society. An excellent example in modern times is one of India's greatest poets, Mohammad Iqbal, who drank deeply from the fountain of Konya; many of his works and individual poems are vividly reflective of the impact of Mavlana's teachings.

It is this backdrop of a plural society and a tradition of accommodation and synthesis that has allowed modern India and its democratic polity to develop and put into practice a secular polity. This is a basic feature of our Constitution and cannot be amended.

Thus for different reasons, and traversing different paths, modern Turkey and modern India reached the same destination, considered essential for our wellbeing in the modern world.

If convergence characterised the spiritual realm, physical distance, infrequent contacts and complex considerations of statecraft conditioned political relations between our two countries in medieval times. In the last century, Indian public's support for Turkey was evident during the Balkan War and Turkey's struggle after World War I to regain independence, identity and dignity was keenly watched and admired. In 1935 the author Halide Edib spent some time in India, met Mahatma Gandhi and other leaders of our freedom struggle, gave extensive lectures about modern Turkey, and wrote that India was "nearer to my soul-climate than any other country not my own".

II

Countries, like individuals, live by professed values and defined interests. The purpose of public policy is to develop the capacity to protect and promote these values and interests, and to respond to challenges.

The stability and fixed patterns and processes that were a feature of the Cold War period are today a matter of history. Instead, we face changing alliances and interests, new modes and instruments of conflict, and universalisation of normative standards of fundamental and human rights. This churning, and shift in world and regional power balances, will continue.

The unprecedented political and social challenges in every region of the world have been further compounded by the precarious global economic situation, described by Professor Jeffery Sachs as "the great failure of globalisation". It has, to quote en eminent Indian economist, "eroded social stability".

It is in this context that I wish to speak to you about India's world view.

Our view of the world stems from our civilisational heritage and experience of history. We do believe that every human irrespective of identity, affiliation, faith, nationality, gender or region has an inherent right to a better life, the development and utilisation of his/her capabilities to the fullest, and to participate and contribute in productive ways to their communities and nations.

States have a duty to their citizens to enable them to freely choose their paths to development and self-fulfillment.

Based on these premises, India has also stood steadfast to the basic principle of full sovereignty and independence of peoples, and their states, in an inclusive, representative, and increasingly pluralist world community.

We abhor any attempt aimed at disruption of the national unity and the territorial integrity of States, and seek the observance of the letter and spirit of the Charter of the United Nations.

We want to see an inclusive world order, a world united by partnerships based on mutual respect and benefit, not divided into blocs or alliances of competing interests. We believe that the benefits of globalisation must be inclusive, across and within nations. We remain convinced that dialogue and cooperation are the best way to address the new global challenges. Institutions of global political and economic governance, including the United Nations and Bretton Woods institutions, should reflect contemporary realities and not perpetuate historical contexts and divides.

The primary objective of Indian policy is to improve the lives of our own people through sustained development. For this we need a prolonged period of peace, a peaceful periphery and an enabling international environment that would allow us access to essential resources, technology, and permit free trade.

We cannot but notice the pockets of turbulence in our common area. India and West Asia have enjoyed cultural, intellectual and commercial ties since ancient times. The turmoil that some countries in West Asia and North Africa have experienced in recent months is a matter of great concern to us.

The people of the region seek to shape their own future and their wishes must prevail. However, violent means must be abjured by all sides. As a member of the Security Council since the beginning of this year, India has been underlining the need to resolve conflicts through political negotiations and diplomatic means, rather than through the use of force.

A primary cause of tension, instability and violence in the region is the situation in the Occupied Palestinian Territory. India fully supports the Palestinian people's struggle for a sovereign, independent, viable and united state of Palestine with East Jerusalem as its capital, living within secure and recognisable borders side by side and at peace with Israel.

The conflict is political and cannot be resolved by force. At the same time, protracted negotiations over decades have not achieved the national goals of the Palestinian people and have fuelled disappointment and anger.

India was the first non-Arab country to recognise the Palestinian State in 1988 and will support its aspirations in the United Nations.

The upheaval in Libya is characterised by a fast changing situation and the Transitional National Council has now acquired effective control. We believe that the normalisation of the situation should be in the hands of the Libyan people themselves–guided by democratic norms, respecting popular aspirations and preserving the sovereignty and integrity of Libya.

India has been in touch with the Transitional National Council in Benghazi and Cairo and has reiterated its willingness to extend all possible assistance to the people of Libya in their political transition, rebuilding and reconstruction activities.

We are concerned at the unfolding situation in Syria which has resulted in many deaths of civilians and security personnel. We deplore all violence, irrespective of who the perpetrators are. The Syrian government has announced some far-reaching measures and it should be given the time and space to implement them. The actions of the international community should facilitate an inclusive political engagement of the Syrian government and the opposition, rather than complicate the situation through threats of sanctions.

India firmly believes that observance of the rule of law is as important in international affairs as it is within countries and that the political, societal and economic destiny must be the choice of people. The international community has a role in assisting the process of transition, but that does not extend to imposition of external prescriptions.

The complex neighbourhood in which India is located has seen rapid and often, turbulent, change in the last thirty years. India has followed the same policy of dialogue, engagement and mutually beneficial cooperation that it urges on all international issues. Our neighbourhood policy seeks to articulate and promote the advantages of building networks of inter-connectivity, trade, and investment so that prosperity can be shared and the entire region can benefit from India's rapid economic growth.

Afghanistan, geographically poised between south and central Asia, is a neighbour with historic people-to-people linkages. The fratricidal conflict there is a threat to regional and international peace and security. It is India's view that the peace process should be Afghan-led, transparent, inclusive, and based on the acceptance of the Afghan Constitution. Our civilisational links with Afghanistan and our close friendship are embodied in the landmark Strategic Partnership Agreement that we signed during President Karzai's visit to India last week.

The international community must take effective measures to guarantee the sovereignty, territorial integrity and unity of Afghanistan. The Afghan people have suffered enough and must be allowed to decide their destiny without external interference, coercion or intimidation. India will participate in the forthcoming conferences in Istanbul and Bonn to contribute to regional and international initiatives to support Afghanistan's efforts at nation building.

We subscribe to the emerging patterns of partnership in Asia based on Asian regionalism, inter-regional dialogue forums with other regions, global and multilateral organisations, and robust bilateral cooperation.

We believe that no partnership architecture should be exclusive or exclusionary. It should neither be a reflection of the emerging redistribution of global or regional power nor should it be a platform for projection of narrow economic and political interests of a nation or group of nations.

Furthermore, all disputes must be settled peacefully, without resort to violence, or the threat of violence. These have been the principles that have guided India's 'Look East' policy, and increasingly our 'Look West' policy, in Asia.

The same cooperative approach is evident in our policy towards African countries. We are convinced that the people of Africa are its most precious resource. India has taken the lead in empowering them through technology, education and skill development. We have offered lines of credit worth US $5 billion and US $700 million in grant assistance for human resource development, transfer of technology and building new institutions.

All this adds up to an ardent policy of international cooperation. India, like Turkey, is a strong proponent of multilateralism and has been actively involved in the work of the United Nations. We believe reform and restructuring of the UN is necessary to make it better equipped to respond effectively in an era of transformational change in global affairs.

The call for democratisation cannot be limited to nations and states, but must also extend to global governance. We should test the validity of the proposition, expounded many years back by an eminent political scientist that 'a theory of legitimate power is inescapably a theory of democracy in the interlocking processes and structures of the global system'.

Our efforts at the restructuring and reform of the United Nations are ongoing, and support for reform and expansion from member countries is gathering momentum.

Unless there is a cooperative framework among states and peoples, today's challenges cannot be faced. A case in point is international terrorism. It is an immediate threat to all nations and knows no national boundaries. India has called for the adoption of a Comprehensive Convention on International Terrorism to help eradicate this scourge.

The same holds for the safety of sea lanes. Maritime commerce along the sea lanes of communication has been subjected to piracy being carried out with impunity from areas that are outside State control and not subject to international accountability.

Pandemics, global warming and climate change, sustainable development, and issues of equity, both within and across nations, pose substantial challenges to the international order. Each requires a cooperative and global approach.

III

As we survey this backdrop to our engagement and partnership, we must remember what binds us. Both our countries are secular democracies wherein the will of our peoples is embodied in the supremacy of our Parliaments. Turkey and India believe in the need to support and sustain our plural traditions and multi-cultural societies. Our economies are growing at an impressive rate leading to generation of incomes and employment opportunities to millions of our citizens and improving their standards of living.

Both the countries have faced terrorism and have collaborated at international fora on combating terrorism. We also have a common stake in the emergence of a cooperative multi-polar world order which recognises the legitimate aspirations of all countries, big and small.

We do not share physical borders, but we do have a vast common extended neighbourhood–in Central Asia, West Asia and the Persian Gulf. I am convinced that enhanced engagement between India and Turkey is in the interests of our peoples and regions, global peace and cooperation, and tolerance and peaceful co-existence among nations. Our joint efforts can result in a more balanced, inclusive and sustainable development for the benefit of vast sections of humanity.

IV

Allow me to conclude. It is evident that the world of tomorrow would be too small for discord, too interdependent for isolation, too evolved for prejudice. Perhaps Yunus Emre had anticipated it. I am fascinated by the following couplets:

Come let us all be friends for once
Let us make life easy on us
Let us be lovers and loved ones
The earth shall be left to no one..

Platinum Jubilee session of Indian History Congress
Punjabi University, Patiala, Punjab
10 December 2011

A non-historian in a houseful of those who worship at the Temple of Mnemosyne is an oddity. My presence in your midst, and the generous invitation that I accepted without cogitating on possible consequences, can perhaps be ascribed to an occasional propensity to succumb to temptation!

Be that as it may, I shall endeavour to live up in some measure to the expectation reposed in me.

Even though history was not the discipline formally pursued by me, I confess to having dabbled in it from time to time. I recall in particular reading an essay entitled *History and Philosophy* in which it was argued that 'history deals with mind and the operation of mind; and the supreme necessity is that the historian should bring a living mind to the understanding of the operation of man's mind'.

Nor can I forget Ibn Khaldun's dicta that "the pasture of stupidity is unwholesome for mankind" and that the historian, in his quest for truth, should "lift the veil" from the condition of the previous generations to "wash his hands of any blind trust in tradition".

History and historian thus remain critically relevant to our daily life, to the perceptions that shape our approach to contemporary questions, to the lessons that we tend to draw from proximate or distant past.

History, it is said, does not solve problems but does help understand them better. Its direct lessons are few, its specific morals rare. Toynbee noted that historians "generally illustrate rather than correct the ideas of the communities within which they live and work". He therefore sought to widen "the intelligible fields of study" of history into "groupings of humanity called a society" and study societies and civilisations in terms of challenge and response, progress and decay.

With or without conscious attribution, the historian brings to bear on his or her work a set of stated or un-stated major and minor premises. These, as Hobsbawm put it, "build barricades in the way of the historian, whose major task is not to judge but to understand even what we can at least comprehend."

E.H. Carr, whose little book was obligatory reading for undergraduates of an earlier generation, expressed the point somewhat differently. "The historian and the facts of history", he wrote, "are necessary to one another. The historian without facts is rootless and futile; the facts without their historian are dead and meaningless."

Since history records human activity, its ambit is vast, almost synonymous with life itself. The historian per force is compelled to make a choice of the domain of scrutiny–political, military, economic, social and cultural, intellectual, scientific and technological. Each domain is a record of change and of happenings leading to change.

The challenge for the historian is to assess the nature of change and its impact on the actors on the stage of history. The tools of assessment and the intellectual skill of the assessor, perhaps even predilection, thus become critical. As Lord Acton put it, "the main thing to learn is not the art of accumulating material, but the sublimer art of investigating it, of discerning truth from falsehood and certainty from doubt. It is by the solidity of criticism more than the plenitude of erudition that the study of history strengthens, and straightens, and extends the mind."

A particularly difficult area of work is contemporary history. Here the domains of the political analyst and the historian converge. Unlike the former, however, the latter has the benefit of relative detachment, the time to analyse happenings in the context of the past and freedom from the pressure of suggesting policy options.

II

History has societal relevance and plays a role in the shaping of identity. Since humans are social creatures and sustain themselves in social groupings, every individual per force has multiple identities--individual, family, group, national and international. Each is also a conglomerate of sub-identities, be it language, faith, food habits, economic activity, social or political affiliation, cultural and artistic pursuits. Identity is therefore always plural and efforts to compress it into a singularity are at best simplistic and misleading. We do need to bear in mind Amartya Sen's caution that "history and background are not the only way of seeing ourselves and the groups to which we belong".

It is here that, in the work of the historian, the past merges into the present and even ventures to shape the future. Ours is an ancient land that has witnessed the vicissitudes of ages. We are also a modern republic whose contours and parameters were carefully defined in the Preamble of the Constitution. These encapsulate essential ingredients of modernity. Jawaharlal Nehru understood them to mean democracy, religious tolerance, economic development and cultural pluralism.

And yet, there are contradictions that hamper the realisation of objectives. One set of these relate to our political ideal, our social and economic life and the quest to realise one-person-one-vote-one-value; the other to the civic idea of inclusion that defines citizenship and accommodates diversities. Both remain contested, often through purposeful obfuscation. Derogations, in whatever form, undermine the ideals of justice, liberty, equality and fraternity.

Thus the study of contemporary history, beyond the traditional paradigm of broad-brush political history, assumes a qualitatively different significance. We live in a world of nation states but the idea of a homogenous nation state is a pipedream. The sheer diversity of identities, 4635 communities according to the Anthropological Survey of India, is a terse reminder about the care that needs to be taken to put together the profile of a national identity. It has of necessity to be liberal and accommodative. Our ideal of citizenship, as the political scientist Gurpreet Mahajan puts it, "is marked neither by a universalism generated by complete homogenisation nor by the particularism of self-identical and close communities."

For this reason, history teaching at the school stage acquires critical relevance. Pupils should be made to learn why there is diversity in society so that they are able to understand this diversity in a historically grounded way, and thereby address its complex problems in a socially useful manner. The understanding has also to be inculcated that a proper perception of the past requires a serious examination of the values of that time.

A history teacher once said that "the pleasure of history teaching comes from alienating the familiar and familiarising the alien." Both require going beyond the stereotype. I venture to hope that there are some in this learned audience who would subscribe to this approach.

III

I would like to draw attention to one other matter. India and Indians have never lived in isolation and at all times interacted with the outside world. The last phase of this interaction, of British domination, has for good reasons been the subject of intensive historical scrutiny. One consequence, perhaps unintended, of this has been the neglect of the history of immediate and proximate neighbours. The period of British supremacy, rooted in the complex economic mechanism of modern colonialism, disrupted centuries old patterns of economic and cultural relationships.

Modern India has, with considerable success, sought to revive these contacts in the political, commercial and cultural fields. The same however cannot be said of endeavours in the realm of intellectual activity, particularly history. One looks in vain for good Indian historical studies pertaining to the immediate or proximate neighbourhood to the north, east or west of India. A principal casualty of this is our inability to discern their thought processes and perceptions directly and rely instead on transmission through other sources.

Allow me to substantiate the point with a few examples that I know of. A random search of Indian studies on Afghan history indicates no more than ten academic publications and of these, half relate to post-Soviet invasion of 1979. And yet, the works of S. Gopal, Dilip Kumar Ghosh, D.P. Singhal and Bisheshwar Prasad show the depth of scholarship on the subject. Why were these not followed up by the next generation of scholars?

The same holds good, in greater measure, for Indo-Arab and Indo-Turkish relations. Both bear the imprint of interaction in the struggle against colonial or imperial domination. Yet academic studies are few and most do no justice to the subject.

The situation is probably the same for Central and South-East Asian countries and is reflective of a wider problem.

I note from the Constitution of the Indian History Congress that one of its objectives is to promote study of "history of countries other than India." The conclusion I am tempted to draw is that this is being done inadequately. A random perusal of the *Indian Historical Review* and of the research projects of the Indian Council for Historical Research makes it evident. This, apart from its academic relevance, impacts on our understanding of neighbouring societies most relevant to us.

Perhaps it is time to inject a corrective and induce scholars to explore these areas.

Birth Centenary celebrations of Sachidananda Hiranand Vatsyayan 'Agyeya'

Kolkata

22 February 2012

It gives me immense pleasure to take part in the birth centenary celebrations of Shri Sachidananda Hiranand Vatsyayan, better known as 'Agyeya'. It is a matter of satisfaction that the Prabha Khaitan Foundation, the Sahitya Akademi and the Raza Foundation have taken the initiative in organising the celebrations in Kolkata.

Agyeya belonged to an era where it was possible to be a master of many crafts. As a towering literary personality, he initiated new and experimental trends in almost all genres of literary writings including poetry, short stories, criticism, novels, travelogues, essays and drama. He also ventured into journalism and took up causes of the poor and the oppressed. He was a patriot and a revolutionary freedom fighter on whom Chandrashekhar Azad left a deep impression. He was a polyglot, well-versed in Hindi, English, Sanskrit and Persian. He also had a stint in the Indian Army and took part in social movements for the benefit of the downtrodden. His interest also extended into academia, especially the teaching of Hindi.

The range of his interests and the deep philosophical underpinnings of his literary output, which at a certain level resonates with Vedantic thought, have established him as a literary figure in the footsteps of Vishwa Kavi Rabindranath Tagore.

To an extent, his pen name is most appropriate to his personality. Agyeya, 'the unknowable', was most in evidence in his poetry. The Experimentalist School, or the Prayogvada, was led by Shri Vatsyayan. The poet's canvas was wide and concerns diverse. It ranged from the problems of language and how it reflects the altered identity, a focus on silence and the power of utterance to summon meanings, and use of poetry as truth telling.

I would like to highlight four issues from the thoughts and the writings of Agyeya that have contemporary literary, political and social significance.

The first of these relates to the intricate relationship between literature and politics. Agyeya realised that the link between the two goes back to Vedic times. Indeed, Vedic hymns were used to win battles and the *Mahabharata* and *Ramayana* laid down the rules of war and royal conduct. He believed that "poetry on politics was the best use of poetry". Yet, he was careful to draw the distinction and warn that "patriotic poetry should not lead to an overemphasis on a religious-spiritual ethic or even religious nationalism." On the other hand, being completely anti-political too was not a solution.

Shri Vatsyayan felt that a "poet does not cease to be a citizen or a political person. Even a denial of involvement in politics constitutes political action. He asserted that poetry changes society because the poet has been influenced and has changed." His emphasis was not on politics or poetry but on the changes in the poet-citizen.

Second: Vatsyayan*ji* struggled to make Hindi a vibrant, volatile, alive and growing language–not a "standard, well regulated and universally accessible form" of Hindi which he felt would only be good for official notifications and regulations. While such a standardised and dry language might be useful for spreading literacy, he felt that the logic of literacy cannot be the logic of a national language. He very forcefully argued that a language cannot be an artificial creation like Esperanto but should be a growing, and therefore changing and stable language that grows from the depths of the minds of ordinary men and women.

Third: Agyeya bemoaned the fact that as our social and political life became complex, it has become very difficult to focus popular ire. Power and exercise of power has become more diffused. Kindly allow me to quote him in this regard:

> In today's politics, there is often confusion about whom one is fighting ... Power–tyrannous power–now has no face ... The struggle today is against the faceless enemy; that is why we are continually providing it new faces and looking for successors as one face after another disappears off the stage

> … The struggle is against an entire establishment, a system of power, which includes the government and the social order–and therefore, also ourselves.

Fourth: Agyeya gives us the definition of a great writer. According to him, a great writer "communicates to us a dimension of reality which extends our experience to its utmost range" and which might remain unnoticed if he had not showed it to us and which we cannot forget or ignore once it has been shown to us. By this definition, there is no doubt that he remains one of the greatest writers in Hindi literature whose writing have opened up many dimensions of reality to his readership.

Birth anniversaries provide us an occasion to pause on our routine and flow of habit and introspect on various aspects of our lives and look for meaning. Birth centenary celebration of a towering literary figure like Agyeya is also an occasion for us to think about the realm of individual possibility, depth of mental capacity and the complexity of linguistic intricacy.

Hindi was not the mother tongue of Agyeya yet it did not prevent him from becoming an exceptional Hindi writer. His fluency in English and in other languages was more in tune with the leaders of the Indian renaissance that emerged in Bengal. In fact, Agyeya acknowledged that his mind was "disciplined through the medium of English". He pointed to Ram Mohan Roy as to how someone with a "traditionally trained intelligence" could face the West through English.

I hope that the deliberations during the course of the centenary celebrations will focus on some of these issues. The life and work of Shri Sachidananda Hiranand Vatsyayan is an inspiration to our youth and any effort to popularise it deserves our full appreciation and support. I wish the deliberations all success and thank the organisers for inviting me to this function.

Prayer meeting in memory of Late Dr Abid Hussain

Chinmaya Mission, New Delhi
2 July 2012

It is difficult to speak about someone who personified life itself and lent vibrancy to whatever he touched. He was at all times involved, responsive, innovative, thought provoking.

He cultivated refinement without extravagance and knowledge without gasconading. Above all, he was humane and compassionate. There are many in this audience who would speak with knowledge about Abid saheb's significant contributions to different aspects of public policy. He did not look upon discussion as a stumbling block in the way of action and, instead, considered it an indispensable preliminary to wise action. It is said that once, in a discussion on brain drain, he cautioned against the peril of having brain in the drain.

Abid saheb possessed and displayed a remarkable capacity to prioritise. When he presented credentials in Washington, President Ronald Reagan asked him to explain the intricacies of our problems with Pakistan. Refusing to take the bait, he replied that in the limited time available, he would instead talk about trade and technology!

He represented the best of Hyderabad's old cosmopolitan culture, with all its refinements and fine touches. He perhaps also subscribed to some version of perennial philosophy, regarding each religious tradition as sharing a single, universal truth.

Abid saheb was a devotee of expanding horizons, would not be confined and, if asked, would refrain from subscribing to what a poet of yesteryears sought to depict as limitations of life:

"Fikr-e-ma-aash, ishq-e-butaan, yaad-e-raftagaan
Do din ki zindagi main ab koi kya kya kiya kare."

Instead, and on the same theme, he would have recited another couplet:

"Justujoo hai zindagi, zauq-e-talab hai zindagi
Zindagi ka raaz lekin doori-e-manzil main hai."

Such a man was our departed friend. He died as he lived–effortlessly–with his quest for receding horizons very much intact, now being pursued in another world, through another medium.

We have gathered here to offer comfort, not condolence to his near and dear ones, to salute him, and to celebrate his qualities of head and heart.

"Kya khoob aadmi tha, khuda magfirat kare."

Closing ceremony of the Commemoration of the 150th Birth Anniversary of Rabindranath Tagore

Vigyan Bhawan, New Delhi

7 May 2012

This is a rare privilege. On the 6th of May last year I had visited Dhaka to participate in the inaugural function of the joint commemorations to mark the sesqui-centenary of the versatile and multifaceted genius whose pen wrote our respective national anthems.

Today, I have the good fortune to participate in the closing ceremony of the joint commemoration.

The preceding twelve months have been witness to the vibrant expression of Tagore's legacy in our two countries and have reminded our two people of the continuing relevance for our times of his ideas and ideals.

It is indeed of enduring significance that the governments and peoples of Bangladesh and India have chosen such an occasion to renew their bonds of friendship and reaffirm their commitment to our shared cultural heritage and intellectual ethos.

While browsing through the facsimile of the original manuscript of Tagore's *Gitanjali* that I received from the Ministry of Culture, my attention was drawn to the following verse:

"I surely know the hundred petals of a lotus will not remain closed forever and the secret recess of its honey will be bared."

I believe something similar could be said of the enduring friendship, fraternity and affection of the peoples of India and Bangladesh for each other.

Prime Minister Sheikh Hasina has undertaken three historic visits to India: to New Delhi in January 2010, to Tin Bigha Area in October 2011 and in January this year to Agartala. Prime Minister Manmohan Singh visited Bangladesh in September 2011 and was accompanied by the chief ministers of some of our states bordering Bangladesh.

Each of these visits reinforced the firm resolve of our leaderships to further strengthen people-to-people links, settle outstanding issues and enhance trade and economic relations between India and Bangladesh.

Rabindranath Tagore was a multifaceted genius whose creativity spanned every form of artistic expression. His concerns ranged from global and universalist ones to practical and mundane issues. He established institutions to reflect his vision and through his travels, writings and actions demonstrated that the international brotherhood of man was not merely a theoretical construct.

He believed that national and human identities inherent in us need not be contradictory and that promoting one's culture should not preclude acceptance and respect for the culture of others.

He heralded the cultural rapprochement between communities, societies and nations much before it became the liberal norm of conduct.

Tagore was a man ahead of his time. He was one of the most creative exponents of an Asian sense in the early twentieth century. He wrote in 1932, while on a visit to Iran, that "each country of Asia will solve its own historical problems according to its strength, nature and needs, but the lamp they will each carry on their path to progress will converge to illuminate the common ray of knowledge."

His ideas on culture, gender, poverty, education, freedom, and a resurgent Asia remain relevant today.

Tagore worked for one supreme cause, the union of all sections of humanity in sympathy and understanding, in truth and love. He expressed himself in an invocation penned in April 1919. It bears recalling in the troubled world that we live in:

> Give me the supreme courage of love, this is my prayer, the courage to speak, to do, to suffer at thy will, to leave all things or be left alone. Give me the supreme faith of love, this is my prayer, the faith of life in

> death, of the victory in defeat, of the power hidden in the frailness of beauty, of the dignity of pain that accepts hurt, but disdains to return it.

We are fully appreciative of the efforts of the Government of Bangladesh for its initiatives to honour and perpetuate the memory and legacy of Rabindranath Tagore.

Book release: *Valmiki Ramayan* (three volumes) in Hindi and Persian by Sumer Chand

Nehru Memorial Museum and Library, Teen Murti House, New Delhi

8 May 2012

It gives me great pleasure to participate in this function, organised by Rampur Raza Library, to release the three volumes of the Persian version of the *Valmiki Ramayan* penned by Sumer Chand in the year 1715 and translated into Hindi and edited by Prof. Shah Abdus Salam and Dr Waqarul Hasan Siddiqui.

The Raza Library is a treasure house of inestimable value for the literary and cultural history of our country. Its collection of manuscripts of the medieval period is truly unique. These include rare copies of the holy *Qur'an*, a fourteenth century text of Rashiduddin's *Jami-ut-Tawarikh,* a fifteenth century manuscript of Firdausi's *Shah-Nama* and another of *Sad Pand-e-Luqman* bearing the signatures of Emperors Jahangir and Shah Jahan, and innumerable sixteenth and seventeenth century manuscripts on history and literature.

The *Balmiki Ramayan* is in Persian Nasta'liq script and like other manuscripts of that period, is beautifully illustrated.

This audience knows that *Ramayan* is accepted as the *adi kavya* and Maharishi Valmiki as *adi kavi*. It is closest to representing Indian culture, vision, values and importance of moral values in public and private lives.

Every social and linguistic group in India has adopted and made *Ramayan* its own. It has travelled beyond the shores of India and influenced societies and civilisations afar in contexts that are distinct and different from the cultural and religious milieu of India.

The centrality of the personality of Ram, in the cultural consciousness of India and Indians, is amply demonstrated in the poet Mohammad Iqbal's poem entitled *Ram*. One couplet says it all:

"Hai Ram ke wujood pe Hindostan ko naaz
Ehl-e-nazar samajhte hain usko Imam-e-Hind"

The functional quest, to know and understand better the traditions and thought processes of large sections of population, was the rationale for a medieval ruler or ruling group to seek a translation of such texts in their working language.

A similar, but earlier, example is Emperor Akbar's instructions to Abul Fazl to supervise the translation in Persian of the *Mahabharat*. This was published in February this year under the auspices of the National Archives of India.

Both of these, and innumerable other texts, are reflective of a catholicity of approach to good governance in a multi-religious society. Tolerance and accommodation, rather than bigotry, was widely practised.

This is of great contemporary relevance. It constitutes a building block and a cardinal principle of our state policy whereby a plural society has given to itself a secular polity and a democratic state structure. Practical experience has shown that this Indian model is superior to multicultural odysseys undertaken in many other modern societies.

I congratulate Rampur Raza Library for publishing this manuscript and its Hindi translation. I congratulate the translators for their efforts and hope that the Rampur Raza Library will continue to uphold its glorious intellectual tradition and undertake more such endeavours in the future.

Education and Higher Education

"What we need most urgently, therefore, is revolution in education which can trigger off the cultural, economic and social revolution we need

—Dr Zakir Hussain

Dedication Ceremony of the Centenary Faculty Block

National Institute of Advanced Study, Bangalore
13 January 2008

It is a privilege to be amidst this distinguished gathering today, in an institution reflective of the vision of J.R.D. Tata. His critical role in synthesising India's scientific, medical and artistic genius is under-appreciated.

I believe the concept of an institute for advanced study, dedicated to theoretical research and intellectual inquiry, emanated in 1930 with the one at Princeton made famous, amongst others, by Albert Einstein. Its purpose, 'to encourage the original, often speculative, thinking that produces advances in knowledge' has been fulfilled in good measure.

In India we made the first effort in 1964 with the Indian Institute of Advanced Study, Shimla. Its mentor was none other than President Sarvepalli Radhakrishnan. The aim was to facilitate free and creative inquiry into the themes and problems of life and thought.

J.R.D. Tata's approach, in 1988, was somewhat more focused. He recognised that in the Indian context a multidisciplinary approach and bringing together of civil servants and managers from industry, leaders in public affairs, eminent personalities and academic scholars from the natural and social sciences was important for public policy formulation and implementation.

We live in an age where the only constant is change. The physical, mental and virtual landscape around us is being rapidly transformed, imposing constant demands on individuals and institutions to adapt and reinvent themselves. In its wake one tends to lose sight of the inherent unity in nature and the impulse for harmony. It is this underlying harmony that binds the strands of human enquiry across various disciplines.

This was understood, even practised, in an earlier age when inter-disciplinary studies facilitated cross-pollination of ideas. Overtime, however, what commenced as a functional division of work tended to crystallise into rigid boundaries.

The problem has been accentuated by the structure of our higher education system and of our research institutions. Increasingly universities have parted ways with research and development activities; even within the universities, academic pursuits are rigidly delineated within specific departments. As a result, the intellectual output of our universities leaves much to be desired.

Against such a bleak backdrop, the National Institute of Advanced Studies (NIAS) is an oasis. The books, reports, working papers published by it bear testimony to the scope of work being done and are perhaps unique for an Indian academic institution. The study under the same roof of archaeometallurgy with primatology, sociology and anthropology with nuclear and strategic issues, philosophy with astrophysics and aeronautics, rural development and gender issues, philosophy and number theory makes for new and fascinating outcomes.

Such a multi-disciplinary approach is critical to the advancement of knowledge. Nor are such efforts in the realm of pure theory; I appreciate in particular the initiative undertaken by the institute in fostering an informed and in-depth debate on contentious issues such as river water disputes and nuclear non-proliferation by bringing together experts with differing views on to a common platform.

John Adams once said: "I must study politics and war that my sons may have liberty to study mathematics and philosophy. My sons ought to study mathematics and philosophy, geography, natural history, naval architecture, navigation, commerce and agriculture in order to give their children their right to study painting, music, architecture, statuary, tapestry, and porcelain."

In the final analysis, the pursuit of knowledge is an exercise of walking towards receding horizons. Each generation makes its own judgment about the success of the endeavour. The important thing is to create conditions conducive to undertaking the walk. NIAS contributes to this effort; so will the Centenary Faculty Block.

The Valedictory and the First Convocation

St. Xavier's College, Kolkata
18 January 2008

Homecoming is a feeling that is difficult to articulate. A sense of happiness is evident. So is a flood of memories. I return to St. Xavier's to express my gratitude to the college that initiated me in disciplines which became a lifelong passion.

I come also to salute an institution whose dedication to its mission is exemplary and foremost amongst them is a passion for excellence.

More objectively speaking, it is always a privilege for any alumnus to return to his alma mater after half a century, to interact with a new generation of students, to share perceptions, to catch up with their vision of a new world, and their hopes and aspirations in it.

History records that the rise and fall of civilisations is closely related to knowledge creation and its utilisation for human advancement through techniques of production and distribution. Human history, said H.G. Wells, "becomes more and more a race between education and catastrophe".

Hence education is critical to the well-being of a society. It is a public good, a basic human right, a fundamental right, and an important instrumentality for social and economic empowerment.

How then do we approach the question of education, in relation to itself and in relation to society?

Some in this audience may know of Lord Acton, the nineteenth century historian of liberty. He was dismissive of utilitarian education and was critical of universities "where nothing is studied for its own sake, but only as it will be useful in making a practical man". Notwithstanding an element of truth in it, bland advocacy of such an approach today would be socially irresponsible.

A few years back a Task Force of the World Bank on 'Higher Education and Society' concluded that in the world of the 21st century, global wealth will be reckoned in terms of knowledge, skills, and resourcefulness of people.

In a word, the way we work and the way we live both necessitate a change in the way we educate ourselves. The advancing tide of globalisation means that the quality of knowledge generated within higher education institutions, and its availability to the wider economy, is becoming increasingly critical to national competitiveness.

Education, therefore, has to respond to the imperative of a qualitatively new situation.

The challenge is to be met at all levels: primary and secondary and higher education. It is also to be addressed in institutions of vocational training. Logical sequence and pragmatic necessity both suggest a bottom-up approach. Good higher education must of necessity be premised on quality, universal, school education.

II

Where do we stand today? Some hard facts confront us. About 2 crore children are born every year. Around 7 per cent of the children do not attend school between the age group 6 to 14. Of the ones that do go through the primary and secondary schooling, about 75 lakhs appear in Class X and 38 lakhs in Class XII examinations. At both levels the pass percentage is 50-55 per cent. Only 6 per cent enter the university system and only 4-5 per cent opts for vocational education.

While the global picture about new schools and enrolment is impressive, does it tell us enough about the inroads made in the weaker and the deprived segments of society? Available data indicates that the percentage of children who do not attend school between the age group 6 to 14 from minority, SC and ST communities is higher than that of the general population.

There are other questions about the content and quality of primary and secondary education. Who teaches in these schools? What is the teacher-pupil ratio? What is taught? How is it taught? Are the teachers adequately trained? Are we training them in sufficient numbers?

Tenth Plan data shows that 'secondary education suffers from lack of access, low participation, and from equity and quality issues'. The all India average of the number of secondary and higher secondary schools per 100 sq. kilometre area is only four, and much below this in several of the larger and most populous states.

Once upon a time, teachers commanded social status and elicited respect. Do we still subscribe to these values in adequate measure, and translate that respect into action?

These questions about school education are relevant because schools constitute the base of the educational pyramid and determine the quality of the input into college and university education.

The next stage in the education pyramid is the question of higher education. The National Knowledge Commission, in its report on the subject presented to the Prime Minister in January 2007, summed up the situation:

'There is a quiet crisis in higher education in India. It is not yet discernable simply because there are pockets of excellence, an enormous reservoir of talented young people and an intense competition in the admission process. And, in some important spheres, we continue to reap the benefits of what was sown in higher education 50 years ago by the founding fathers of the Republic. The reality is that we have miles to go. The proportion of our population, in the age group 18-24, that enters the world of higher education is around 7 per cent, which is only half the average for Asia. The opportunities for higher education, in terms of the number of places in the universities, are simply not enough in relation to our needs. What is more, the quality of higher education in most of our universities requires substantial improvement'.

The report was emphatic in recommending a focus on expansion, excellence and inclusion: 'higher education needs a systematic overhaul, so that we can educate much larger numbers without diluting educational standards'. It proposed that the enrolment level be raised to 15 per cent by opening about 1200 new universities, by increasing public spending and diversifying sources of financing, by a thorough overhaul of the curricula and governance structures, and by making universities the hub of research.

In his address to the National Development Council last month, the Prime Minister gave details of the Eleventh Plan targets in education. "But all these ambitious investments", he added, "will bear fruit only if the central and state governments work purposefully to see that the results are in line with expectations and that the quality of these institutions do remain top class".

In the final analysis therefore increased resources, efficient delivery mechanisms and quality control will be critical to the success of the new approach. Dereliction on any count would impact negatively on the overall performance.

Two questions unavoidably arise:

- How are we placed today to achieve these?
- What correctives are essential for this purpose?

The ground reality is grim. We have at present over 350 universities and around 17,700 colleges. The total number of teachers is around 4.7 lakhs. The gross enrolment ratio, defined as the number of students enrolled as a percentage of the population in the 18-20 age groups, is around 10 per cent. The comparative figure for the most developed countries is over 50 per cent; the world average is around 23 per cent. It is clear that access to higher education in India needs to be improved significantly.

Enrolment in terms of overall numbers is one aspect of the matter; another is the question of equity. There are rural-urban disparities, with gross enrolment in urban areas being four times higher than in rural areas. The enrolment between States shows significant differences and there is a persistent gender disparity with gross enrolment of males being 50 per cent higher than that of females. As regards the poor and the marginalised sections of our society, and some minority groups, their enrolment in higher education is significantly lower than the national average. There are also overlapping categories between the various disadvantaged groups.

Consequently, the input into our higher education system is neither broad-based nor inclusive.

An equally relevant question is that of quality. Our principal pillar of higher education is the undergraduate college network. Undergraduate education accounts for over 85 per cent of enrolled students, seeking first degrees in arts, commerce and science. Of the 17,700 undergraduate colleges in the country, a mere 200 colleges are autonomous and 97 have been identified by the UGC as "Colleges with Potential for Excellence". Most of the remaining do not comply with the minimum infrastructural and academic standards.

The problems of access and equity are thus compounded by the question of quality. This is critical to educational institutions and needs to be analysed in five dimensions:

- Teachers. It has two aspects. On one side, our system does not reward teachers at the same scale as other productive sectors of our economy. Those who are covered by the UGC scales of pay (after the 5th Pay Commission) are a tiny minority; less fortunate are the teachers in state universities and in private colleges. The better ones among the teaching faculty are poached upon by business and industry, and more frequently by foreign academic and research institutions. We have not been able to retain and mentor our bright students who choose to remain as researchers or as faculty. On the other hand, however, the system of teacher accountability has virtually become non-existent. A solution would lie in providing better working conditions, equitable remuneration, merit-based selection, combined with a genuine work-assessment system and incentives for performance.
- R&D. Over the years, research and academics have tended to part company, and increasingly, R&D is taking place within the domain of designated government institutes or in industry-supported institutions. This has impacted adversely on the universities, has deprived society as a whole from the fruits of optimal effort, and is in sharp contrast to the situation in developed countries. Universities must, therefore, once again become the hub of research and capture the inherent synergies between teaching and research. This would also have a demonstration impact on students.

- Governance structure. This has remained static and not adapted to the fast changing socio-economic and demographic situation in the country. Autonomy and accountability have been locked into a zero-sum framework. Accountability does not imply uncontrolled interference; it does however stipulate a requirement to explain actions and have successes and failures examined in a transparent fashion within the framework of known rules. On the other hand, allegations of external interference for political or commercial considerations make disturbing reading and do no good to our institutions of higher education.
- Regulatory framework. This has not produced the desired outcomes. According to the National Knowledge Commission, 'it constrains the supply of good institutions, excessively regulates existing institutions in the wrong places and is not conducive to innovation or creativity in higher education'. We now have good experience of regulatory frameworks in other walks of national life, like telecom, capital markets and insurance. There is, therefore, no reason why the same effort and determination cannot be shown in regard to higher education.
- Financing. This is a matter of urgency. As the World Bank report put it, 'higher education institutions require sufficient financial stability to permit orderly development'. It is heartening that the government has placed education at the centre of the Eleventh Plan with an increase in central gross budgetary support from 7.7 per cent to 19 per cent. While government support is crucial for undergraduate education, professional education in India has, de facto, undergone privatisation, with the majority of seats now being in private institutions. The real challenge, then, is to maintain the balance between non-government financing, universal access and high academic standards.

In responding to the imperatives of our age, we must also deal with the phenomenon of globalisation and its impact on higher education. Two results are evident: education has become business, and there is business in education. Markets and globalisation are shaping the content of higher education and exercising an influence on the nature of institutions that impart higher education. These compel us to think. Professor Deepak Nayyar has suggested a proactive approach to the problem:

"We should not allow markets and globalisation to shape higher education. Instead, we should shape our agenda for higher education, so that we can capture the opportunities and avoid the dangers unleashed by markets and globalisation".

We have set for ourselves a national objective of building a knowledge society, an inclusive society, a humane society. The national effort directed at the educational pyramid must therefore harmonise the objectives and develop synergies.

One last word before I conclude. This is a convocation with a difference–that of an autonomous college. The students graduating today follow an illustrious lineage. They have demonstrated academic excellence. This was the easier part of the endeavour. As Xaverians, they bear a lifelong responsibility for a wider concern pertaining to humanity. Let 'Nihil Ultra'–the motto of this institution, be their guiding principle.

Nineteenth Convocation of the Indira Gandhi National Open University (IGNOU)

University Campus, New Delhi

16 February 2008

There is a sense of uniqueness about the occasion. University convocations are location-specific. Today, thanks to the tele-conference facility, thirty-eight centres across the country are participating in this convocation and no less than a hundred and fifty thousand would be recipient of degrees. Also unique is this university, the world's largest, having students from thirty-five countries.

The scale and numbers are staggering. It has been said authoritatively that higher education in our country is facing a crisis. However, every crisis carries within it the seeds of opportunity, of new possibilities for change and reform.

We have embarked on building a knowledge society. The ground to be traversed is depicted in a set of statistics:

- One third of India's adult population is illiterate; only 12 per cent of eligible children at school complete the 10th standard.
- Only 10 per cent of the population in the relevant age group is enrolled in higher education. In developed countries, the corresponding figures are between 30-50 per cent of the relevant population.
- A mere 5 per cent of the relevant age group graduate with degrees in India.
- With fourteen National and State Open Universities and around 130 'Distance and Correspondence' education institutions of conventional universities, distance education accounts for 24 per cent of the total enrollment in higher education in the country; IGNOU alone caters to 13 per cent of students enrolled in higher education.

- Questions of equity stare us in the face in relation to the enrollment in higher education. These relate to the rural-urban, inter-regional and inter-caste differences. They also relate to women, minorities and other marginalised segments of society.

Three crucial elements of higher education, quality, access and cost, have been locked into a zero-sum framework and compound the crisis.

The conventional brick-and-mortar campuses of higher education have long gestation periods for completion and have been unable to keep pace with growing demand. Increasing the access to higher education has concomitant requirements of enhanced budgetary outlays; increasing the quality of education in conventional campuses has meant increased cost; and, very often, increasing the access has also meant deterioration in the quality of higher education.

The biggest challenge is to provide quality higher education to the greatest number at minimum possible cost to the intended beneficiaries. How is this to be achieved?

It is here that open and distance education delivered through information and communication technology has the potential of providing answers. Increasingly, distance education has emerged as a critical link in achieving our goal of ushering in a knowledge society.

Distance education in our country has inherent characteristics that are insufficiently appreciated. A few of these need to be highlighted.

In the first place, distance education is inclusive and encourages marginalised sections of society into the fold of higher education. For instance, for the country as a whole, gross enrollment ratio in urban areas is four times higher than in rural areas; the gross enrollment ratio is much lower for SCs, STs, OBCs and for Muslims as compared to the general population; the ratio is 11 per cent for females as compared to over 15 per cent for males; the poor also have a low gross enrollment ratio, that is one fifth of that of the non-poor.

Serving the disadvantaged sections of the society was the primary focus of distance education in India. IGNOU itself has over 217 special study centers focusing on such marginalised groups as SCs/STs, minorities, women, jail-inmates, remote and rural areas and low literacy districts. Around 35 per cent of the fresh students enrolled last year in the university were women and around 25 per cent of them were SC/ST students. In our country, women make 40 per cent of distance education students as compared to 28 per cent in the conventional mode.

These are concrete outcomes worthy of emulation. The eventual entry of such disadvantaged and non-traditional learners into the productive workforce of the nation has tremendous implications for sustaining our economic growth and making it inclusive.

In the second place, open and distance education is the best means for skill enhancement and retraining; these are essential features of a knowledge economy. A significant component of our GDP is from the services sector where continued skill development is essential. This can be done in a cost-effective manner through distance education.

Thirdly, distance education is an ideal instrument for galvanising community education and action and energising civil society groups. This is an important aspect of our democratic polity and remains a key instrument for conservation of local and indigenous knowledge systems. It also serves as a useful link between communities and the global knowledge economy.

In the fourth place, distance education, by virtue of its openness, flexibility and delivery across multiple platforms, facilitates higher education of those with special needs. Our conventional universities have not been suitably reconfigured to cater to those with special needs, leading to their exclusion from higher education.

With all the benefits of open and distance education, it is unfortunate that there is still a sense of stigma attached to those who pursue distance education. The degrees of students of open and distance education are not accorded the same weight and credibility in the job market and even by academia.

Why are they treated like stepchildren of our higher education system? The answer probably lies in the DNA of our higher education system. We need to look at the following issues:

- Capacity building activity in higher education is currently focused on campuses rather than students and learners. This places a premium on products of a superior campus rather than the skill set of students.

- Systemic rigidity prevents movement across systems, institutions or academic programmes. Skills acquisition through academic credits and portability of credits across institutions is probably the answer.
- The focus in distance education has been on certification rather than skill enhancement and development of knowledge and competencies. This has compromised the quality of distance education. The need to develop quality benchmarks and standards is even higher in distance education than in conventional institutions of higher learning.
- The distance education system in India has remained insulated from industry and civil society. This goes against the inherently open structure of distance education. Strengthening partnerships with industry, NGOs and civil society would impart appropriate skills and training to students of distance education.

Comprehensive education involves training of the mind and of the body. The latter has not received its due attention in higher education institutions in India, and remains non-existent in the case of distance education. In keeping with the community development orientation of distance education, IGNOU could perhaps pioneer the creation of communal sports facilities at its regional and sub-regional centres. This would be a significant initiative in promoting physical fitness, sports and games in a community framework, as part of distance education.

Eventually, distance education deals with issues other than higher education–it lies at the confluence of development, education and public policy. It is a prime instrument to ensure sustainable and inclusive development and address the core issues of achieving universal education, improving health and reducing poverty.

Today, India is recognised as a leader in the developing world in the deployment and use of tele-medicine and tele-education. In fact, India is assisting states in Africa and East Asia in the establishment satellite-based tele-medicine and tele-education services. In this context, we need to ask ourselves if the majority of our citizens in remote locations within the country have access to and are able to avail of tele-medicine and tele-education services. Can such e-services be integrated and provided as community services at regional and sub-regional centres of open and distance education institutions?

Realising this promise of distance education requires concerted action of the government, academia and civil society.

It has been over two decades since open and distance education was initiated and evolved into the current institutional structures and processes. There is an urgent need to revisit the regulatory structures governing open and distance education institutions in the country, review their effectiveness, and ponder over the necessity for alternatives.

I congratulate the distinguished personalities on whom the university has conferred the degrees of Doctor of Science and Doctor of Letters (honoris causa). I felicitate the students graduating today and wish them all success in life. I am confident that education would continue to be a part of their lives as they seek to upgrade their skills, acquire new knowledge and improve their life chances and well being.

Dr Zakir Hussain Memorial Lecture
Zakir Husain College, New Delhi
2 March 2009

One cannot come to this college without a realisation of its place in Delhi's intellectual history. The Madrasa Ghaziuddin of the Moghul era has indeed been witness to, and participant in, a good deal of what transpired in a period of great change; it nevertheless retained its focus on education relevant to the times.

A footnote to the story indicates that a minor matter of protocol came in the way of the college counting among its teachers none other than the poet Asadullah Khan Ghalib!

The occasion of my visit is exciting as well as humbling. To deliver a memorial lecture instituted in honour of a great son of India is a privilege to be cherished.

Zakir Hussian was an exemplary human being. I was an undergraduate at Aligarh when he was the Vice Chancellor. One evening some of us were returning from a hockey match when, in the narrow pathways of the campus, he drove past at a slow pace. The car stopped a few yards ahead, he disembarked, came towards us and said: *"Kya aap logon ko ghar par yeh nahin bataya gaya ki buzurgoan ko salaam kar te hain?"* While most were stunned into silence, one of the group did respond: *"Buzurgoan ko salaam kar ne ka kya faaida jab woh salaam ka jawaab nahin dete?"* Zakir saheb's response was typical of the man: *"Mere bhai, agar moojh se kabhi aisi ghalti hui ho to maaf karna"*.

A generation later, Zakir Hussain is remembered by most people as a distinguished and erudite President of the Republic, and an embodiment of the old world courtesy and charm. Few but very few today bother to recall his work as a thinker and an educationist. His thinking was not an ivory tower exercise. His ideas evolved in practice; his laboratory was the institution in Okhla that is today a vibrant university. I refer, of course, to Jamia Millia Islamia.

Inspired by the Gandhian ideal, Zakir Hussain's focus was on training of the mind, body and soul to bring forth a complete human being. An essay in 1938 shed light on his perception of Jamia's primary purpose: to focus on challenging the perceived dichotomy between the requirement of faith and those of developing an Indian cultural identity in the most comprehensive sense.

Nor was he alone in this quest. The question of education of the youth was addressed by many of our leaders during the freedom movement. The most significant initiative in this regard was the Wardha Scheme of Education proposed after the All India National Education Conference held in October 1937 under the presidentship of Gandhi*ji*, and the Nai Talim that emerged from there.

It is useful to recall the Resolutions passed at this Conference:

First, that free and compulsory education be provided on a nationwide scale.

Second, that the medium of instruction be the mother tongue.t

Third, that the process of education throughout this period centre around some form of manual and productive work and that all the abilities to be developed from the training to be given should, as far as possible, be integrally related to the central handicraft chosen with due regard to the environment of the child.

Fourth, that this system of education will be gradually able to cover the remuneration of the teachers.

The first two Resolutions of the Wardha Scheme were incorporated into the Constitution of the Republic. The Right to Education is yet to be operationalised six decades after Independence. Adequate facilities for instruction in the mother tongue at the primary stage of education do not exist in all parts of the country.

The last two Resolutions of the Wardha Scheme continue to remain an unimplemented component of the vision of our founding fathers. The Nai Talim is, for all purposes, dead. Even Gandhian institutions in the country do not follow the Nai Talim in letter and spirit. Far from being self-sufficient, education has either become state supported, with questionable quality, or commercialised and elitist, out of the reach of common citizens.

The need for vocational training and skill development to facilitate employment is axiomatic for a country of our size and population. The need is more acute due to peculiarities of our demography, economy and the labour market. Let me mention a few of these.

In the first place, over 60 per cent of the total population is in the working age group with the child dependency ratio of over 30 per cent and old age dependency ratio of over 5 per cent. This indicates a predominantly youth profile.

Secondly, a majority of the work force have poor skill sets and levels of educational attainment. It is estimated that only 5 per cent of our labour force in the 20-24 age group has received vocational training compared to levels of 60-80 per cent in industrialized countries. Around 65 per cent of the work force is either illiterate or has only obtained literacy up to the primary level. Among those unemployed, around 70 per cent constitute those who are educated but without requisite professional skills. This illustrates the difference between possessing educational qualifications as distinct from skill sets required for jobs.

Thirdly, the overall labour productivity in India is much lower, even in comparison to other developing countries. Labour productivity in India, for example, is estimated at a quarter of the figure for Mexico.

In the fourth place, high dropout rates characterise our primary and secondary education. It is estimated that 90 per cent of school students who enter Grade I drop out by the time they reach Grade 12, accounting for over 180 million students. Yet, we only have around 3 million vocational training slots available in the country for a total labour force of over 400 million and the annual entry of 7-8 million new workers. Very few of these vocational training opportunities are available to school drops outs.

Finally, India is unique amongst developing countries that 93 per cent of its work force is employed in the unorganised sector producing around 60 per cent of the GDP. The structure of the formal vocational training system in our country is geared for the educated and does not cater to those with limited educational attainment working in the unorganised sector.

The diagnosis, ladies and gentlemen, is clear. The question now is about the proposed treatment. Its urgency is evident.

Skill training and employability cannot be addressed as standalone themes. Efforts towards vocational training must be geared towards increasing employability in the organised sector and improving the quality of jobs in the unorganised sector. The Draft National Employment Policy issued last year calls for linking skill training with the educational system and offering vocational education as an option at high school level of Grade 9. It also calls for extending functional literacy programmes to the majority of work force who have poor educational attainments. More importantly, the Policy seeks to make skill training an important component of large scale public programmes such as NREGA (National Rural Employment Guarantee Act), Sarva Shiksha Abhiyan, National Rural Health Mission and ICDS (Integrated Child Development Services).

The National Knowledge Commission has suggested four alternate delivery models for vocational training and for capacity expansion.

First, institution of a public private partnership framework to benefit from private sector delivery in training and to benefit from increased linkages between vocational training institutes and industry.

Second, a decentralised model that is inexpensive and scaleable and would focus on low intensity and low cost programmes at the local level based on existing infrastructure.

Third, distance learning modules for continuing education and skill upgradation of workers.

Fourth, computerised vocational training courses to leverage ICT (Information and Communications Technology) platforms and dovetail with similar efforts in areas of literacy and agriculture.

We need to reorganise and reorient our fragmented vocational educational system that is currently spread over 17 different organisations and departments. We also need to ensure the framework of skill standards, assessment and certifications that allows for mobility of credits and qualifications. Our accreditation and certification norms must align with global standards to empower our work force seeking employment abroad.

There is awareness in Government of the need for improving the access to, and scope of, vocational training in the country. The Prime Minister has noted that supply shortages of skills can constrain growth and that this shortage is felt not only in high-tech skills but also in basic skills, such as plumbers, electricians and nurses. To meet this skill shortage, the government is committed to opening new institutions at various levels of the knowledge pyramid, with particular emphasis on a Vocational Education Mission.

Given his close knowledge of matters educational, Zakir Hussain was candid about the limitations of what had been achieved. Addressing the Bombay University in 1967, he characterised education as the most powerful instrument of national development: "What we need most urgently, therefore, is revolution in education which can trigger off the cultural, economic and social revolution we need"'. He attributed failure to "proper type of educational leadership" and suggested that in addition to the traditional functions of teaching, research and leadership training, universities should pay attention to community service and adult education.

Three decades later there is evidence of some evolution; a revolution, however, is still awaited.

Zakir Hussain personified the quest for change. A younger colleague of his wrote that Zakir saheb undoubtedly subscribed to Mohammad Iqbal's advice:

Qanaat na kar aalam-e-rang o boo par
Chaman aur bhi aashiyan aur bhi hain
Tu shaheen hai parwaz hai kaam tera
Tere saamne aasman aur bhi hain
Isi rooz-o-shab main ulajh kar na rehja
Ki tere zamaan aur makaan aur bhi hain

I am confident that some young minds in this audience would come forth to provide this leadership and realise the vision of Zakir Hussain.

Forty-First Convocation

Indian Institute of Technology (IIT), New Delhi
7 August 2010

It gives me great pleasure to participate in the Convocation of a premier academic and research institution of the country. I congratulate the graduating students and those who have received medals and awards for their academic achievements. I also take this opportunity to congratulate Dr Anil Kakodkar who has been conferred the Degree of Doctor of Science (*Honoris Causa*) for his outstanding contributions and achievements in the field of nuclear science and engineering. Let me also congratulate the awardees of the Distinguished Alumni Award.

Each of you, by dint of your competence, is fortunate to be in this 'ecosystem' and associated with an institutional brand name that is globally recognised and represents the best that our academia has to offer.

The nation also appreciates the unsung efforts of the many dedicated and committed faculty of the IIT Delhi that have helped mould and transform the professional and personal growth of this student body.

Convocations are a 'rite of passage' from the academia; for you, professionals, it also marks your formal entry into a select group, very much an elite group, which has formidable alumni with very impressive achievements and contributions to the nation, and at the global level.

Convocations should also be moments of introspection about the purpose of education, its role in society and in the life of the nation. This is that rare, fleeting, moment in life when the individual can afford to steer clear of peer pressure, pursue one's convictions, sail into the unknown and chart unconventional paths.

Yours is a critical discipline. It has been said that while scientists study the world as it is, engineers create the world that has never been. Throughout history, engineering has been a key driver of human development and, along with technology in the wider sense, impacts on and shapes culture.

Despite this, it is insufficiently appreciated that engineering education is a key enabler of India's growth and a vital element in shaping our national destiny. While the effort predates our independence, questions remain about the ability of the present framework of engineering education to respond to national requirements in adequate measure. The quality of teaching, and employability of graduates is one aspect of it; the dearth of qualified and motivated faculty is another.

It is for this reason that the National Knowledge Commission called for "a new paradigm in regulation, accreditation, governance and faculty development" across the engineering education spectrum.

The task is complicated by individual and peer-group attitudes and preferences, and by the prevalent value system of society. Allow me to draw attention to some data that makes disturbing reading:

- Less than 1 per cent of IIT undergraduates in the country pursue Masters or Ph D courses within the IIT system.
- Less than 15 per cent of those graduating from IITs move towards teaching or research, whether in India or abroad.
- The IIT system produces less than 1.5 per cent of the total engineering graduates in the country but accounts for over 70 per cent of those pursuing Doctoral programmes in engineering and technology.
- In terms of international grading of academic output based on publications, citations of faculty, and patents applied for and granted, we fare poorly in comparison to even some developing countries. Only IIT, Mumbai and IIT, Delhi find a place in the 2009 Times Higher Education ranking of fifty engineering and information technology institutions. However, no Indian university, not even an IIT, figures in the top 100 of the Shanghai Jiao Tong University Institute of Higher Education's Academic Ranking of World Universities, or in the top 100 of the 2009 Times Higher Education World University Rankings.

Another set of figures, from the US National Science Foundation, depict the paradox. Students from India and those of Indian origin and numbering 35,300 accounted for over one-third of all foreign engineering students in the United States in 2009. Out of these, around 26,000 students were enrolled in Masters Programmes constituting over 65 per cent of all foreign masters students, and 5690 were enrolled in Doctoral Programmes constituting around one fifth of all foreign doctoral students.

These figures shed light on the opportunity loss for our academic institutions, and eventually to the nation, to benefit from the research potential and effort of the best and brightest graduating from our engineering institutions, including the IITs.

A focus at the top end, essential for excellence, does not obviate the need for correctives at other levels. This audience is well aware of the contours and dimensions of problems that confront us in areas of education in general and in skills development in particular. We need in the first place to focus on accessible learning, affordable learning, and applicable learning. We need to close the gap between policy intent and actual delivery. The requirement to up-skill or re-skill 500 million people by 2020 in order to meet growth requirements underlines the need for undertaking this on a war footing. Curricular reforms, faculty development and promotion of a spirit of entrepreneurship and innovation are imperative and compelling.

Moving away from the immediate issues of the state of engineering education in the country, it is noteworthy that the last two decades have visibly demonstrated the social and economic reach of technology and have thrown greater light on the less understood interface between technology and society. It underlines the need for consonance and for methodologies to achieve it.

The evolutionary context of any technology determines the purposes to which they would be deployed. Where such technologies evolve as societal products, they carry the ability to serve larger social purposes. Increasingly, in this era of globalisation transforming technologies are emerging in corporate contexts and are being deployed to primarily serve narrow corporate interests and stakeholders. Thus, the shrinking base of stakeholders in the development and deployment of technologies is fast eroding their political and social legitimacy. It is increasingly felt that these technologies are widening societal inequalities and deepening political conflict. The situation has also been compounded by the lack of political initiative and social impetus by national leaderships and community elders.

Two experiences in our own country illustrate the point. The Green Revolution in the 1970s and the IT revolution in this decade have been epochal technological influences on our society. Sociologists have analysed how the Green Revolution used technological substitutes to modernise parts of agriculture without necessitating social change or political intervention that might have called for massive land reforms. A prominent economist assed the impact and concluded that "technological changes ... contributed to widening the disparities in income between different regions, between small and large farms, and between landowners on the one hand and landless labourers and tenants, on the other". Others have argued that the Green Revolution reinforced the urban domination of the rural, industrial domination of the agricultural sector and the domination of the developed countries over the developing.

The Information Technology revolution of this decade raises similar issues. Most of the IT development has been geographically located around certain metropolitan and urban areas, increasing their densification and their ability to create, attract and accumulate more capital. This has prevented the territorial dispersal of tertiary sector and service industries, and of wealth generation and consumption, across the country and restricts access to transformative technologies to an elite group.

Technology diffusion to the masses has also become difficult due to lack of access to telecom infrastructure, electrical infrastructure or even literary skills and financial resources which the poor and the marginalised do not possess. A legitimate question arises whether the utilisation and deployment of information technology has been an enabler in equalising opportunities to all of our citizens to better their situation in life.

It would therefore seem that an essential concomitant of technological advance is the effort by society, including its professional segment of engineers and technologists, to ensure that it sustains and promotes social cohesiveness through necessary correctives. Technological, scientific or digital divides in societies cannot further the larger human cause. Today's professionals cannot function in isolation of the social and political context nor can they remain in ivory towers or professional silos.

One more dimension can be added to the argument. We know that the past informs the present and helps shape the future. A historian of eminence noted some years back that the 20th century ended in global disorder whose nature was unclear. At the same time, it was unquestionably the greatest period of human history in terms of science, technology and innovation. This trend will persist.

The American scientist Bill Hibbard wrote two years back that progress of biology, neuroscience and computer science will make possible in the foreseeable future technologies of mind and life that will invalidate the working social assumptions of societies. He concluded that "the technology of intelligence will bring enormous changes to the world, which can be for good or evil" and that "the public needs to understand and exercise collective, democratic control over this technology".

The graduating students today represent the young citizenry that constitutes the overwhelming majority of our population. It is for you to question if the technologies that you have imbibed and would develop in future are being co-opted in the massive social and political projects that our nation has undertaken since independence–of ameliorating the condition of each of our citizens so that they have access to opportunity to lead better lives and utilise their potential.

I once again congratulate the medal and award winners, Dr Anil Kakodkar, winners of the Distinguished Alumni Awards and all the graduating students and wish you success in your professional and personal endeavours. I am confident that the graduating students would live up to the oath that you have undertaken to be honest in the discharge of your duties, to uphold the dignity of the individual and integrity of the profession, and to utilise your knowledge for the service of the country and of mankind.

Inauguration of the 'National Education Day'

Vigyan Bhawan, New Delhi
11 November 2010

I feel greatly privileged to participate in today's function to celebrate the National Education Day and commemorate the birth anniversary of Maulana Abul Kalam Azad. This great freedom fighter, Islamic scholar, secularist and institution-builder needs no introduction to this audience. It remains to his credit that the course of modern independent India and indeed, our Constitution, were guided by his firm belief that democracy cannot function while citizens remain illiterate.

Maulana Azad made no compromises on national unity and on educating the citizens of India. He was an ardent advocate of Mahatma's Basic Education and of vocational training and adult education. He laid the base for higher education and for technological and scientific research and education that was instrumental in industrialisation and the recent emergence of knowledge-based industries. He was also clear about the primary purpose of education. In an address to the first meeting of the Central Advisory Board of Education, he said: "The primary aim of any system is to create balanced minds which cannot be misled."

The National Education Day is a fitting occasion to enquire into the need for, and role of, education in our national life. The National Policy on Education 1986 mentions the following:

- Education is essentially for all; this is fundamental to our all round development, material and spiritual.
- Education has an acculturating role; it refines sensitivities and perceptions that contribute to national cohesion, a scientific temper and independence of mind and spirit – thus furthering

the goals of socialism, secularism and democracy enshrined in our Constitution;

- Education develops manpower for different levels of the economy; it is also the substrate on which research and development flourish, being the ultimate guarantee of national self-reliance; and finally
- Education is a unique investment in the present and the future.

About 2 crore children are born every year. The Sarva Shiksha Abhiyan launched in 2001-02 as the main vehicle for providing elementary education to all children in the 6-14 age group has ensured almost universal access to primary education. It addresses the educational needs of over 19 crore children. Focused interventions have ensured that the gender gap in enrolment at elementary level has been reduced significantly. Furthermore, the Gross Enrolment Ratio in respect of SCs and STs has rapidly increased narrowing the gap with the rest of the population.

Yet, problems remain. The impact of the Sarva Shiksha Abhiyan in areas listed in Schedule V and VI of the Constitution, among SCs and STs, Muslim concentration areas and slums has not been very significant. While the issue of access has been largely addressed, the huge dropout rate at the elementary level of over 43 per cent is a cause of concern. It is more disconcerting that there are huge social gaps in dropout rates, with dropout rates at elementary level for SCs at over 52 per cent and that for STs at over 63 per cent. In large states like Uttar Pradesh, Bihar and Rajasthan, over 50 per cent of SC children do not even go beyond the primary level of education.

There are other important questions about the content, quality and outcomes of elementary education. Who teaches in these schools? What is the teacher-pupil ratio? What is taught? How is it taught? Do the students attain skill levels commensurate with their age and grade? Are the teachers adequately trained? Are we training them in sufficient numbers?

A critical element of the Eleventh Plan strategy in education was to achieve a paradigm shift from access to quality. Surveys done by NCERT (National Council of Educational Research and Training) on student learning and achievement have shown that outcomes have not been commensurate with the investment, especially in the case of mathematics and science.

The Annual Status of Education Report 2009 brings out some relevant and interesting facts. While 96 per cent of children in the 6-14 age groups in rural India are enrolled in school, average absenteeism is in the range of 25 per cent, going up to 40 per cent absenteeism on day of visit in states such as Bihar and Uttar Pradesh. Over 30 per cent of children in Grade One could not recognise alphabets or knew numbers from 1 to 9. The percentage of children in Grade 5 in government schools who can read at Grade 2 level has remained at 50 per cent for the last four years. In other words, half of the children in government schools in rural areas are three grade levels behind in terms of outcome and achievement. Around two-thirds of children in government schools in Grade 5 have been unable to do division problems. The Report also reveals that many students are resorting to paid private tuition across the country, in both government and private schools, and even at Grade 1.

This dismal picture of elementary education's quality and outcomes contrasts sharply with the achievement of near universal access, and the landmark legislation of the Right of Children to Free and Compulsory Education Act 2009.

We also need to focus on specific issues highlighted by the Mid-Term Appraisal of the Eleventh Plan:

First, systemic issues such as teacher absenteeism, single teacher schools and multi grade teaching need to be resolved.

Second, we need to address equity concerns of the disadvantaged, vulnerable social groups and urban-deprived groups with regard to access and retention.

Third, all quality issues impacting on the learning outcomes of children must be addressed as a priority.

We must remember that ensuring access to education without a commensurate focus on quality and outcomes will result in the 'right to education' remaining merely a 'right to schooling'.

The Thirty-First Convocation of the National Institute of Design

National Institute of Design campus, Ahmedabad
14 December 2010

I am happy to be participating in the Thirty-First Annual Convocation of the National Institute of Design. I offer my congratulations to students who have won prizes today as also to all of the graduating students. It is an important occasion for them, their families and their teachers. As products of internationally acclaimed institution in design education and research, I am confident that they would go on to make a mark in the key areas and institutions with which they will be associated.

The term 'design' evokes questions, and possibly suggests some answers. It was the philosopher Aristotle who held that "human nature is inclined to imitate"; he propounded the theory that 'art imitates nature'. This is also true of the idea of design. Both are reflective of human perception in its interaction with the external world. It therefore has elements and imprint of both the universal and the particular and seeks to develop and improve both.

While in a globalising world a measure of homogenisation is unavoidable, the genius and uniqueness of the local retains its place and adds colour and content to the final product; hence the need to draw upon it to the fullest measure.

The roots of Indian design go back to the urban architecture and town planning of Harappa and Mohenjo-Daro, to the highly skilled and intricate metallic, ceramic and stone sculptures, to sophisticated classical art forms in music and dance, to intricate and evolved dress materials and sartorial preferences.

Yet, an innovation that has helped many people lead normal lives such as the Jaipur Foot is not readily recognised as a design marvel.

Design was an important, yet under-appreciated, element during the freedom struggle. Gandhi*ji's* Ashram in Ahmedabad is nearby. It was here that the Father of the Nation applied himself to evolving an Indian idiom to the freedom movement, characterised by self-reliant systems of design and indigenous means of production.

Scholars have analysed how Gandhi*ji's* focus on the *charkha*, the Khadi cloth and Indian chappals represented uniquely Indian artefacts and designs, of everyday use of all sections of Indian society across the length and breadth of the country. They strengthened the element of identification with the freedom struggle and have come to represent symbols and message of this aspect of India in the modern era.

Gandhi*ji's* efforts to find a new idiom were propelled by the colonial legacy spanning architecture, costumes, products, literature, technologies and designs that explicitly or implicitly elevated colonial practices and showed 'native' practices, belief systems and culture in poor light.

In the post-Independence period, Jawaharlal Nehru understood the significance of the design element in espousing his vision of a modern nation. Even as the planning process focused on the temples of modern India, Nehru invited Le Corbusier to design a new city.

Design today is seen mainly from the lens of value addition, enhancing competitiveness, and improving quality of products and services. The National Design Policy enunciated three years ago notes that the vision behind initiating it is "to have a 'design enabled Indian industry' which could impact both the national economy and the quality of life in a positive manner'. It speaks of 'global positioning and branding of Indian designs' and 'raising Indian design education to global standards of excellence".

The design paradigm a few decades ago, however, was starkly different.

This Institute owes its origin to *The India Report* of April 1958 prepared by the famous American designers Charles and Ray Eames at the invitation of our government. What is perhaps lost sight of in the clamour for industrial design is the fact that the report was for 'a programme of training in design that would serve as an aid to the small industries'.

It is useful to recall some of the important conclusions drawn by the Report:

One: The change India is undergoing is a change in kind, not a change of degree. The medium that is producing this change is communication, not some influence of the West on the East.

Second: India faces this change with advantages of tradition and philosophy familiar with the meaning of creative destruction; with not having to make the same mistakes that others made in the transition; and with well-defined immediate problems of food, shelter, distribution and population.

Third: In the face of the inevitable destruction of many cultural values and in the face of immediate need for the nation to feed and shelter itself, a drive for quality takes on real meaning. If the new Republic has to survive, a relentless search for quality must be maintained.

Fifty years later, like Charles and Ray Eames, we must question how many of the design products of this Institute can rival the humble and ubiquitous vessel of everyday use–the *lota*. Like them, we must ask: "What are the *lota*s of our time that need to be designed to fulfill an existing need, with a focus on quality, cost and environment?"

We must question whether the search for quality has remained an essential characteristic in our society. We should also introspect how well we have addressed our immediate problems of food, shelter, distribution and population even as we lament the destruction of our cultural values. How many of us can follow the ideals of the *Bhagavad Gita* with which 'The India Report' begins, of working without desiring the fruits of work?

As you leave the portal of this Institution, I wonder how many among you would be interested in design that would serve real world issues. For example, keeping in view that more Indians have access to mobile telephones than to good sanitation facilities, how many would focus on designing low-cost and adaptive sanitation systems to address this pressing need of millions of our citizens.

In a resource scarce economy in the pre-reform era, Indians took recourse to *jugaad* and used their creativity, imagination and innovation. In this era of globalisation, when our 'real villages' have to compete with 'the global village', the problem for many designers is to fuse functionality with our cultural legacy and heritage. Such designs and products that are identified with our culture, our geography and our Indianness would distinguish and fetch a premium in the global market place of ideas, services and products.

As Indian designers catering to Indian consumers and designers located within the country, you would notice that your senses are well attuned to our diverse linguistic, cultural, religious and geographical make-up. This is an invaluable asset in our villages and in the global village. Each of these elements and influences is a source of innovation and initiative. You must treasure them, amplify them, and fine tune them as you move to the real world outside.

It is a matter of pride that the Institute is celebrating its Golden Jubilee. The alumni of this institution have brought laurels to it and to the nation. I am confident that your journey of the next fifty years would be equally exciting, challenging and innovative. You will face changes and challenges in the country and at the global level, and will be required to steer through them successfully. The country expects the faculty to train the next generations of Indian designers in these tasks.

Foundation Day Lecture 2010
University of Calcutta, Kolkata
20 December 2010

Higher Education–Challenges and Imperatives for Change

This is a rare privilege. I do feel flattered to be invited to deliver the Foundation Day Lecture of a great and famous seat of learning, India's oldest modern university, more so because of an ancient association of a few youthful years with this city. I also subscribe fully to what the Urdu poet Ghalib said about Kolkata which he visited around the year1830:

Kalkatte ka jo zikr kiya tu ne hum nasheen
Ek teer mere sine main maara ki hai hai
Ah me, my friend! The mention of Calcutta's name
Has loosened off a shaft that pierces to my very soul

Voltaire was perhaps unduly cynical when he describes history as "nothing more than a tableau of crimes and misfortunes." This is certainly not true of the history of this great city which is, in a sense, also the history of modern India.

Most of us associate the year 1857 with the First War of Independence, with the heroic deeds of many, as also with the eventual failure of the effort to overthrow the foreign yoke and seek freedom from bondage. Few today would associate 1857 with another event of seminal significance. It was on January 24, 1857 that the Calcutta University Act was enacted. It was the culmination of a process initiated by Lord William Bentinck and energised by his successor Lord Auckland. The conceptual input and framework had come earlier from Sir Charles Wood. Its purpose, and ambit, was unambiguously linked to a colonial purpose, namely "to confine higher education to persons possessing leisure and natural influence" over the minds of their countrymen and who, by attaining a higher standard of modern education "would eventually produce a much greater and more beneficial change in the ideas and feelings of the community."

The expectations from this endeavour were anticipated to be modest. The first Vice Chancellor, Sir James William Colvile, was candid about results. "We must recollect," he said in the first Convocation Address, "that we are not merely planting an exotic (tree), we are planting a tree of slow growth." His successor went against the tide of opinion in the British Indian establishment in the aftermath of 1857 and said three years later: "Educate your people from Cape Comorin to the Himalayas and a second mutiny of 1857 will be impossible."

These worthy gentlemen evidently could not discern the thirst for new knowledge among segments of the public, nor could they anticipate the use that would eventually be made of it. The alumnae of this institution played a great role in the freedom struggle as also in the furtherance of knowledge in all fields. The record does speak for itself.

The proclaimed and principal purpose of the university was, and is, 'Advancement of Learning'. There was an element of idealism about it. In a celebrated work published in November 1858, Cardinal John Henry Newman spelt out the idea of a university in terms worthy of reiteration:

> A university is a place of concourse, wither students come from every quarter for every kind of knowledge ... It is a place where inquiry is pushed forward, and discoveries verified and perfected, and rashness rendered innocuous, and error exposed, by the collusion of mind with mind, and knowledge with knowledge.... It is a place which wins the admiration of the young by its celebrity, kindles the affections of the middle-aged by its beauty, and rivets the fidelity of the old by its associations. It is a seat of wisdom, a light of the world, a minister of the faith, an Alma Mater of the rising generation.

Over the past century and a half, the ideal has retained its relevance. What has changed in response to the evolving external environment is the content, some of the methodology, and some of the end product. These were propelled by the enormity of change–political, economic, technological and cultural. A historian of our times noted at the turn of the century that "we are entering a fearful time, a time that will call on all our resources, moral as well as intellectual and material." In this endeavour, the intellectual inputs from seats of learning and research would impact decisively on the moral and material resources needed to respond to the emerging challenges.

The need to revisit the framework for higher education in the country has been felt in recent years. This was summed up in the 2008 Report of the National Knowledge Commission:

> The emerging knowledge society and associated opportunities present a set of new imperatives and new challenges for our economy, polity and society. If we fail to capitalize on the opportunities now, our demographic dividend could well become a liability. The widening disparities in our country will translate into social unrest, if urgent steps are not taken to build an inclusive society. And our growth rate, which is faltering now, will stagnate soon, if a sustainable development paradigm is not created.

II

A look at the ground reality is relevant to this discourse. Today we have 504 universities, with varying statutory bases and mandates. Of these, forty are central universities, 243 are state universities, 130 are deemed universities, five institutions established under state legislation, 53 are state private universities, and 33 are institutions of national importance established by central legislation. We have a total teaching faculty of around 6 lakhs in higher education.

The structure and quality of these institutions, and their output, was the subject of critical scrutiny in the Yashpal Committee Report of 2009, tasked to suggest measures for the renovation and rejuvenation of higher education. One of its observations is telling:

> Over the years we have followed policies of fragmenting our educational enterprises into cubicles. We have overlooked that new knowledge and new insights have often originated at the boundaries of disciplines. We have tended to imprison disciplinary studies in opaque walls. This has restricted flights of imagination and limited our creativity. This character of our education has restrained and restricted our young right from the school age and continues that way into college and university stages. Most instrumentalities of our education harm the potential of human mind for constructing and creating new knowledge. We have emphasized delivery of information and rewarded capability of storing information. This does not help in creating a knowledge society. This is particularly vile at the university level because one of the requirements of a good university should be to engage in knowledge creation – not just for the learner but also for society as a whole.

The report goes on to say that our universities remain one of the most under-managed and badly governed organisations in society, with constricted autonomy, internal subversion within academia and multiple and opaque regulatory systems. Furthermore, university education is no longer viewed as a good in itself but as the stepping stone to a higher economic and social orbit.

The report dwells on the increasing demand for expansion of private college and university level institutions necessitating an understanding of its implications in terms of the system's enrolment capacity, programme focus, regional balance, ownership pattern, modes of delivery, degree of regulation, quality and credibility as well as social concerns of inclusiveness. It points out that State universities and affiliated colleges represent the bulk of enrolment in higher education and remain the most neglected in terms of resources and governmental attention.

Targeted government interventions to enhance access to elementary education through the Sarva Shiksha Abhiyan have been successful in quantitative terms, even though problems remain with regard to content, quality and outcomes. You are also aware that one of the focal themes of the Eleventh Five-Year Plan is the expansion and enhancement of access to higher education.

Our Gross Enrolment Ratio in higher education is half of the world's average, two-third's that of developing countries and around a fifth that of developed countries. Even though we have been able to achieve an economic growth rate of 9 per cent of GDP despite low enrolment in higher education, it would not be possible for us to sustain such economic growth, maintain our competitiveness and enhance our productivity without at least doubling our higher education enrolment. Unless we can increase access and educational outcomes at secondary and tertiary levels, our demographic dividend might turn into a demographic liability.

Contrary to conventional wisdom, gross enrolment in higher education is not directly linked to economic growth and prosperity or to elementary school enrolment. Thus, for example, some of the economically and educationally backward states with respect to literacy rate and school enrolment, such as Orissa, Assam, Jharkhand and Andhra Pradesh have higher enrolments in higher education as compared to relatively better off states such as Tamil Nadu and Karnataka. It would seem that enrolment is a function of a variety of social, cultural, institutional and economic processes and is significantly affected by the availability of educational infrastructure and facilities.

In addition to expansion, the other two central themes of the Eleventh Plan are inclusion and excellence. This is recognition of the fact that expansion does not necessarily ensure automatic access to the marginalised sections of the society and that quantitative expansion without maintaining quality would defeat the basic objective.

III

There are five questions pertaining to higher education that need to be addressed urgently:

First: We must ponder whether the existing means of instituting new universities is desirable and sustainable. Currently, Universities can be established only through Central or State legislation or through recognition as Deemed Universities on a selective basis. Legislation has been accorded to many private Universities by some State Governments, and both Central and State governments have accorded statutory status to some institutions.

Second: Higher education cannot improve in India unless state universities, which are the backbone and represent the bulk of enrolment, are able to obtain greater funds, create new infrastructure and enrich their existing academic programmes. Anecdotal evidence suggests that the budget of one central university is almost the same or more than the budget of all state universities in some states. Just like the central government has assumed the responsibility for elementary education through Sarva Shiksha Abhiyan, it should also vastly enhance its support to state universities as a shared national enterprise. The Midterm Appraisal of the Eleventh Five-Year Plan takes note of this option and has observed:

> Many state universities including the old and reputed universities of Kolkata, Mumbai, Chennai and Pune are starved of funds and this allocation could be used for improving the conditions of the existing State universities and colleges which faces severe paucity of resources to help them retain their excellence and competitive edge.... The Central funding of State institutions should be linked to the reforms and a MOU signed between MHRD, UGC, States, universities and institutions for implementation of time-bound reforms and outcomes.

Third: A significant focus of reform should be the college system, numbering around 26000 colleges, where most of the enrolment in higher education occurs. Sadly, under graduate education does not get the attention it deserves in universities amidst paucity of funds for qualitative development and quantitative expansion of colleges. The government is planning to establish colleges in 374 educationally backward districts in the country, representing over 60 per cent of all districts, with shared funding between the state and central governments.

Fourth: We need to liberate education from the strict and fragmented disciplinary confines of our formal higher education structures. This has become a significant impediment in the creation of new knowledge, especially in view of our stated objective of creating a knowledge society. We need to remind ourselves that the Indian Nobel Prize winners in the early part of the last century were a part of our higher education set-up. We had then allowed free interplay between science and engineering, languages and the humanities, performing and fine arts. It was at the fringes of such inter-disciplinary interaction that new knowledge was produced and existing knowledge flourished. I am aware of academic administrators who bemoan that those pursuing Mathematics could not simultaneously study Sanskrit grammar in India despite sound academic and research logic of doing so, due to systemic rigidities of our university system.

Fifth: Higher education in our country must be an arena of choice, not of elimination. Increasingly, one notices that entrance and admission criteria and procedures are designed to screen out and eliminate, due to the adverse ratio of demand and availability, especially in disciplines with job potential or where the college or university reputation is likely to be a determining factor in employment. We must create avenues for skills training and vocational education so that entering universities does not become a default choice for the sake of employment, particularly for those who might not have interest in the subject or desire for higher education.

IV

Allow me to conclude, ladies and gentlemen, by pointing out that the entire gamut of issues dealing with the rejuvenation and restructuring of higher education in India is in the public domain for an open policy debate. In the near future, we would witness civil society, policy community, academia, the government and the legislatures debating issues ranging from regulatory and governance structures, academic and administrative reforms, capacity building and teacher training, and entry of individual and institutional foreign education providers. This is a positive development and must be pursued to its logical conclusion.

It is my hope that this distinguished audience, and students, would be part of the ongoing debates on higher education. Each of you is an important stakeholder in the process and must contribute to it, not only as members of the academic community, but more importantly as citizens of this Republic. It is only with active engagement that we can hope to mould higher education as an instrumentality to achieve the Constitutional vision propounded by our founding fathers.

Release of the Annual Status of Education Report ASER 2010

Teen Murti Auditorium, New Delhi
14 January 2011

It gives me great pleasure to be present here today to release the Annual Status of Education Report for the year 2010.

For the past five years, Pratham has undertaken this annual exercise of assessing and evaluating the outcomes of education of our children across the length and breadth of the country. As a huge non-governmental citizen-focused effort involving over 25,000 volunteers and covering over 700,000 children in 15,000 villages each year, it demonstrates that the well- being of our children is not just the government's responsibility, and that citizens can and should do more to initiate, propel and direct public policy towards public good.

These annual reports remind us that that the first requirement for good public policy is inculcation of scientific temper among the Executive, the Legislature, civil society and citizenry. While the imperative for ensuring access to elementary education to citizens is well understood and is enshrined as a fundamental right, the "quality agenda" is still not accorded the same priority.

ASER's simple, reliable and scientific methods of sampling and assessment on a nation-wide scale are important for highlighting the "quality agenda" in education. This is more glaring in the context of our public policy because we neither have an inbuilt evaluation culture nor adequate trained human resources with both technical knowledge and field experience to check and monitor outcomes.

A few questions do come to mind:

- Why is quality central to all education?
- What is its role in the classroom or in any other learning environment?

- If we do not tolerate a large gap between 'expectation' and 'delivery' in domains of economy, society and polity, how should we approach a significant 'performance gap' in education?

I would like to draw the attention of this distinguished gathering to the first and most important event in education at the dawn of the new century. It was in April 2000 that the World Education Forum at Dakar adopted the Dakar Framework for Action. It recognised that education is a fundamental human right, is the key to sustainable development and peace and stability within and among countries, and thus an indispensable means for effective participation in the societies and economies of the twenty-first century, which are affected by rapid globalisation.

The international community committed itself at Dakar to achieving free and compulsory universal primary education of good quality by 2015, and eliminating gender disparities in education. It specifically decided to improve all aspects of the quality of education so that recognised and measurable learning outcomes are achieved by all, especially in literacy, numeracy and essential life skills.

Quality indeed lies at the heart of the goal of "Education for All". What happens in classrooms and other learning environments is vitally important to the future of our citizens, and indeed to the future of our Republic. Education of acceptable quality must address basic learning needs, enrich the lives of learners and their overall experience of living and well being.

Evidence from around the world demonstrates that "efforts to expand enrolment must be accompanied by attempts to enhance educational quality if children are to be attracted to school, stay there and achieve meaningful learning outcomes". Public policy can address this challenge with a sharp focus on two issues–quality improvement in teacher training and curricular materials development. It is also essential that what students are meant to learn ought to be clearly defined, well-taught and accurately assessed. Ideally, this should not be limited to knowledge alone but also cover skills, attitudes and values.

There is one other aspect of the matter. Education governance and management at the grass roots and institutional level should be participatory and engage with local communities and cultures. We have made a positive beginning with the Right of Children to Free and Compulsory Education Act 2009. It mandates the constitution of School Management Committees consisting of parents, elected representatives of the local authority, teachers and local educationists, and tasked, *inter alia*, with monitoring the working of the school and maintenance of prescribed norms and standards.

I do hope this statutory initiative would be utilised for enabling parents and the local community a greater say in the monitoring of educational outcomes. Civil Society organisations such as ASER and Pratham have an important role in building technical capacity of the members of the School Management Committees.

Inauguration of the New Campus

The Gujarat National Law University
Gandhinagar, Gujarat
7 January 2012

I am happy to be here today in your midst to inaugurate your new campus. In a short span of six years, the Gujarat National Law University is on the path to achieving its vision of becoming a world class law university through steady progress in education, research,training and extension activities.

I commend your initiative to establish centres of excellence in specialised areas such as private and public international law, foreign policy and security studies, environmental law and climate change. Equally impressive is your effort to assist professionals, the judiciary and the government in reducing the backlog of cases.

It is relevant to recall here an observation made in 1927 by Justice Felix Frankfurter of the United States Supreme Court: "In the last analysis, the law is what the lawyers are. And the law and the lawyers are what the law schools make them."

This statement remains valid to this day. It emphasises the centrality of legal education for the effective functioning of a democracy and for upholding the Rule of Law.

A similar view was espoused by the Working Group on Legal Education of the National Knowledge Commission. It opined that "the vision of legal education is to ensure justice oriented legal education to contribute to the realisation of values enshrined in the Constitution of India", adding that "legal education must also inculcate the need to observe the highest standards of professional ethics and a spirit of public service".

The Working Group felt the role of legal professionals has expanded beyond that of advocates in courts and includes legislators, judges, policy makers, public officials, civil society activists as well as legal counsel in the private sector.

Thus the role and public function of law schools has vastly changed since independence. Besides meeting the needs of the Bar, law schools are expected to cater to the growing requirement of non-practising law graduates in trade and commerce, and non-profit oriented work. This is reflected in the preferences of the graduating students.

While considering the changing role of lawyers, it is useful to refer to the "Basic Principles on the Role of Lawyers" adopted by the Eighth UN Congress on the Prevention of Crime and Treatment of Offenders at Havana in September 1990. Five of the twenty nine principles bear repetition here:

1. All persons are entitled to call upon the assistance of a lawyer of their choice to protect and establish their rights and to defend them.
2. Governments shall ensure effective and equal access to lawyers for all persons within their territory, without distinction of any kind.
3. Governments shall ensure sufficient funding and other resources for legal services to the poor and other disadvantaged persons. Professional associations of lawyers shall cooperate in this regard.
4. Governments and professional associations of lawyers shall promote programmes to inform the public about their rights and duties under the law and the important role of lawyers in protecting their fundamental freedoms. Special attention should be given to assisting the poor and other disadvantaged persons so as to enable them to assert their rights.
5. Lawyers, in protecting the rights of their clients and in promoting the cause of justice, shall seek to uphold human rights and fundamental freedoms recognised by national and international law and shall at all times act freely and diligently in accordance with the law and recognised standards and ethics of the legal profession.

A look at the legal and judicial landscape around us does bring to mind a few questions:

- Is our legal and judicial system able to deliver justice to every citizen, especially the poor and the disadvantaged? Is substantive access to justice diminishing as the cost of quality legal service escalates beyond the reach of the common citizen? Is legal knowledge increasingly being deployed for the rich?
- Do those pursuing legal education have public service orientation and social engagement? Are they being inculcated with such an orientation at our law schools?
- Can we speak of justice delivery when the process takes two or three decades to reach finality?

Let us take the last issue first.

Today there is a pendency of over 56,000 cases in the Supreme Court, of which around 36,000 are arrears constituting cases which are more than one year old. The pendency in the High Courts and Subordinate Courts as of 31 December 2010 was around 3.2 crore cases, of which around 85 lakh cases are over five years old.

Reasons for delays in justice delivery are well known. Excessive adjournments are a primary cause; other reasons are shortage of resources and capacity, long-winded arguments by counsels, inadequate judge strength, delay in filling-up vacancies, and disproportionate concentration of work among some members of the bar, Furthermore, Alternate Dispute Resolution has not succeeded to the extent it ought to have. The Supreme Court recently bemoaned the frequent adjournments for the flimsiest of reasons in the case *Shiv Cotex vs Tirgun Auto*. The Hon'ble Judges said: "It is sad, but true, that the litigants seek–and the courts grant–adjournments at the drop of the hat. Adjournments have grown like cancer corroding the entire body of the justice delivery system."

Yet there are reasons for some optimism. The government last year approved the setting up of the 'National Mission for Justice Delivery and Legal Reforms' to implement the two major goals of increasing access by reducing delays and arrears in the system and enhancing accountability at all levels through structural changes and setting performance standards. A mission mode approach is proposed to improve the infrastructure of Subordinate Courts under the National Mission.

The government has also made available enhanced central funding for infrastructure in subordinate courts and has also accepted the recommendations of the Thirteenth Finance Commission to provide a grant of Rs. 5000 crores to the states for improving the justice delivery system over the five-year period 2010-15. It has also begun implementing "e-Courts Project" for district and subordinate courts and upgrading IT infrastructure in Superior Courts at a cost of Rs 935 crores and with a target to computerise 12000 courts by March this year.

Our progress on achieving the Constitutional promise of securing to citizens justice, social, economic and political, especially to the poor and disadvantaged, leaves much to be desired. In many instances, it is the State that is the biggest and enduring litigator, forcing citizens and businesses to sustain substantive and notional losses as cases drag on in the labyrinthine justice delivery system. The certainty of long gestation for resolution coupled with heavy costs to sustain the legal process has given large corporate and business entities added incentives to threaten or institute legal proceedings on civil matters. It is usually the individual citizen and the poor and marginalised among them, who bear the brunt of inadequate or non-existent Alternate Dispute Resolution mechanisms and extended judicial processes.

Litigators, some of whom are compulsive in the Indian context, have not fully internalised the externalities of their actions, especially because of long delays in delivery of justice and because they escape the full liability of the harm they cause to those at the receiving end of their litigation, as also to the public good. The deterrent impact of an effective law of torts is rarely felt and has been to the detriment of the citizen.

Barring fundamental rights whose violation can be challenged through a writ petition, legal rights, especially civil legal rights bear the brunt of judicial delays. While the economically better off have more staying power and are able to hire and deploy superior legal resources and knowledge to defend their economic interests and property, the poor are pushed into further penury to defend their meagre possessions and holdings against legal challenges. In the Indian context, defending legal and statutory rights that are non-fundamental, is time consuming and expensive and works against the poor.

There is one other aspect of the matter. It has to do with the ethics of the profession. The Law Commission of India in its Report No. 230 of August 2009 has presciently noted that "the ethics of lawyers has also become questionable". The Report states that though there is a Bar Council that "has to look after ethics of lawyers", it has "rarely taken action against tainted lawyers".

The need for introspection is imperative and should lead to an ethical renewal in actual practice.

Besides teaching and research, the academia is an arena for inculcating a culture of professional responsibility, ethical behaviour and public and community service among legal professionals. It is the place to make young entrants to the profession realise the importance of social responsibility in the practice of law and emphasise the social functions of legal institutions. The behaviour of young students here remains the guiding light for their later careers as lawyers and judges. It is here that one should be made to realise that the legal profession should be a helping and caring one, and not a selfish or exploitative one.

I am confident that the Gujarat National Law University would lead in imbibing a culture of community and public service among its graduates and adopt a leadership role in emphasising professional excellence and ethical conduct.

Forty-Fourth Annual Convocation

Utkal University, Bhubaneswar, Orissa
2 March 2012

I am happy to be here in your midst today. The world over, convocations are an important date in a University's calendar. Neither technology nor the changing face of academia has dimmed its luster.

Convocations are occasions to acknowledge intellectual excellence and achievement and also to remind the students that the pursuit of knowledge does not end with the portals of the University or with the acquisition of a university decree.

I congratulate the graduating students and the distinguished personalities who have been awarded the Honoris Causa. Their achievements and contributions are a source of joy and pride to the University and the nation. In honouring them, we also honour their *alma mater* and the values that they have nurtured in them. I also congratulate those students who have been awarded medals and prizes for their academic excellence.

Since time immemorial, education has been an important instrument for social and economic transformation. The technological revolution and the process of globalisation have not only enhanced its salience but transformed it into a precondition for economic growth. It is the key to enhance our competitiveness in the global economy. Ensuring equity in access to quality education for all, in particular for the marginalised in our society, is central to the economic and social development of India.

It was in April 2000 that the World Education Forum at Dakar adopted the Dakar Framework for Action. It recognised that education is a fundamental human right and is the key to sustainable development and peace and stability within and among countries.

The international community committed itself at Dakar to achieving free and compulsory universal primary education of good quality by 2015, and eliminating gender disparities in education. It specifically decided to improve all aspects of the quality of education so that recognised and measurable learning outcomes are achieved by all, especially in literacy, numeracy and essential life skills.

Quality indeed lies at the heart of the goal of "Education for All". What happens in classrooms and other learning environments is vitally important to the future of our citizens. Education of acceptable quality must address basic learning needs, enrich the lives of learners and their overall experience of living and well being.

Today, I wish to discuss a key element of the edifice of our human resource development that has come to plague all branches–elementary, secondary and tertiary education. I refer to the issue of quality, or the lack of, in our educational system.

We have achieved considerable progress in universalising elementary education through the Sarva Shiksha Abhiyaan during the course of the past decade. In this period, we have reduced the number of out-of-school children and succeeded in retaining the majority of children in school. The passing of the Right to Education Act and its implementation has transformed a human right into a fundamental right for all children to demand 8 years of quality elementary education.

A critical element of the Eleventh Plan strategy in education was to achieve a paradigm shift from access to quality. This, regrettably, is yet to be achieved. The Approach Paper to the Twelfth Five-Year Plan spells this out in words that I wish to share with this audience:

> Despite improvement in access and retention, the learning outcomes for a majority of children continue to be an area of serious concern. Several studies suggest that nearly half the children in grade 5 are unable to read a grade 2 text. Concerted efforts are required to ensure that a minimum set of cognitive skills are acquired by all children during eight years of elementary education. Thus, quality issues and determinants thereof such as ensuring availability of trained teachers, good curriculum and innovative pedagogy

> that impact upon learning outcomes of the children must be addressed on priority basis. Quality as mandated under the RTE shall have to be realized in tangible terms, failing which it will be difficult to wean students away from private tuitions that are prohibited under the RTE.

The situation is not significantly different in the case of higher education in the country. A look at the ground reality is relevant to this discourse. Today we have over 500 universities, with varying statutory bases and mandates. Of these, forty-four are central universities, 285 are state universities, 130 are deemed universities, 106 are state private universities, around five institutions are established under state legislation, and thirty-three are institutions of National Importance established by central legislation. We have over 30,000 colleges and a total teaching faculty of over 6 lakhs in higher education.

The structure and quality of these institutions, and their output, was the subject of critical scrutiny in the Yashpal Committee Report of 2009, tasked to suggest measures for the renovation and rejuvenation of higher education. It noted that "we have followed policies of fragmenting our educational enterprises into cubicles" and that "most instrumentalities of our education harm the potential of human mind for constructing and creating new knowledge".

The Report said that our universities remain one of the most under-managed and badly governed organisations in society, with constricted autonomy, internal subversion within academia and multiple and opaque regulatory systems. Furthermore, university education is no longer viewed as a good in itself but as the stepping stone to a higher economic and social orbit.

The Yashpal Report dwelt on the increasing demand for expansion of private college and university level institutions necessitating an understanding of its implications in terms of the system's enrolment capacity, programme focus, regional balance, ownership pattern, modes of delivery, degree of regulation, quality and credibility as well as social concerns of inclusiveness. It points out that State universities and affiliated colleges represent the bulk of enrolment in higher education and remain the most neglected in terms of resources and governmental attention.

Thus higher education in our country suffers the pincer effect of low enrollment and poor quality. The Approach Paper to the 12th Five-Year Plan calls for "a strategic shift from mere expansion to improvement in quality higher education" for which "the focus should be not only on larger enrollment, but also on the quality of the expansion".

There are four questions pertaining to quality in education that need to be addressed urgently:

First, across all tiers of education, we must shift focus to learning outcomes from the current emphasis on input indicators such as infrastructure, teaching faculty and staff employed and resources made available. Even as we move to cover the gaps in access, we must realise that lack of quality would increase the associated costs for students, to the industry hoping to hire them and to the nation in the long run. Poor quality of education, especially in the public sector, would negate fundamental and human rights of our citizens and deny them equal opportunity to fully realise their potential and lead fulfilling and rewarding lives.

Second, there is an urgent need to move away from the lure of branding and elitist education. The average institution must improve for overall institutional improvement in the human resource development sector. The enormous resources deployed for education in the last decade in terms of human and material resources must be justified by vastly improved learning outcomes. Government schools must deliver educational outcomes that are commensurate if not superior to those in the private sector. The booming tuition and coaching industry that stands as a monumental reflection of the institutional and systemic failure of education must be reversed so that centrality is accorded to classroom learning.

Third, State universities, and the 30,000 strong college system, which are the backbone and represent the bulk of enrolment, must obtain greater funds, create new infrastructure and enrich their existing academic programmes. Anecdotal evidence suggests that the budget of one central university is almost the same or more than the budget of all state universities in some states. Just like the central government has assumed the responsibility for elementary education through Sarva Shiksha Abhiyan, it should also vastly enhance its support to state universities and under graduate college education as a shared national enterprise in qualitative development and quantitative expansion.

Fourth, education in our country must be an arena of choice, not of elimination. Increasingly, one notices that entrance and admission criteria and procedures are designed to screen out and eliminate, due to the adverse ratio of demand and availability, in the entire spectrum from nursery school admissions to admission in IITs and IIMs. We must create avenues for skills training and vocational education so that entering universities does not become a default choice for the sake of employment, particularly for those who might not have interest in the subject or desire for higher education.

The key to improving quality, and indeed the entire edifice of our education system is to bring the focus back on teachers. We in India believe the Guru to be Brahma, Vishnu and Maheshwara. We are inheritors of a civilisational legacy that accords the highest place and respect to teachers. It is a matter of concern that our society and polity today does not accord that primacy and reverence to teachers.

The current system of teacher recruitment, teaching methods, performance assessment, incentive and reward structure and manner of accountability raises many questions. Far too often the focus, regrettably, is on completing the syllabus rather than on cultivating critical thinking skills and competencies. This needs to be corrected.

We should also depoliticise education and cease to view teacher appointments as patronage or largesse. Politically empowering teachers, while professionally disempowering them, is a disservice to the cause of education.

The need of the hour is to painstakingly rebuild the professional identity of our teachers, nurture their skills and professional competence through continuing education. It must be ensured that their work reflects our Constitutional values. The society on its part needs to recognize their work and reward them appropriately.

Allow me to conclude by drawing attention to the place of a university in the world of today and tomorrow. The Glion Declaration of 1999, emanation from UNESCO's World Conference on Higher Education, stressed that knowledge is neither a free good nor a natural resource; instead, it comes only to the prepared mind, coaxed into existence by personal reflection and inquiry, individual discovery, sophisticated research and costly exploration. In this venture, universities play a unique and crucial role.

The Declaration went on to elucidate this vision of universities in the contemporary world:

> They are the chief agent of discovery, the major providers of basic research that underlies new technology and improved health care, they are the engines of economic growth, the custodians and transmitters of cultural heritage, the mentors of each new generation of entrants into every profession, the accreditors of competence and skill, the agents of personal understanding and social transformation. In them on a daily basis, the young and the old seek to bring wisdom, insight and skills to bear in the daunting complexities of human affairs.

I venture to suggest that these words, encapsulating the purpose of a modern university, should be inscribed on the portals of all institutions of higher education.

I once again convey my congratulations to those who have been conferred the Honoris Causa and all the graduating students of the university.

The National Literacy Award Function
Lucknow, Uttar Pradesh
8 September 2012

I am happy to be here today, in the historic city of Lucknow, to participate in this function to mark the International Literacy Day 2012, organised by the National Literacy Mission Authority. It is an important event in our calendar, an occasion for rejoicing for the work done, as also for introspection about the distance still to be traversed.

Needless to say, literacy is a human right, a tool of personal empowerment and a means of social and economic development. It is one of the most important parameters for gauging, in conjunction with other social parameters, the development of a society.

Allow me to mention a disturbing fact. We have the largest number of non-literates in the world. Our literacy rate of 74 per cent, achieved in the last decade, is much below the world average of 84 per cent and is in sharp contrast to what has been achieved by some Asian countries like China, Iran, Myanmar and Sri Lanka.

We console ourselves with the fact that our national literacy rate at the time of independence was a little over 12 per cent and that significant progress has been made since with the literacy rate going up to 52 in 1991, 65 in 2001 and 74 in 2011.

It is also evident that the vast treasures of knowledge dispensed by our sages and scholars down the ages emanated from a very narrow base in numerical terms.

The paradox is that within our own country, uneven progress in the promotion of literacy has been made and wide disparities are noticeable. Thus Kerala has almost 100 per cent literacy. Himachal Pradesh and Mizoram have made remarkable progress. On the other hand, some other states record well below the national average. When this is viewed in conjunction with other social indicators like infant mortality and life expectancy, the linkage between literacy and quality of life become evident.

This audience is well aware of the steps taken in the past decade to promote literacy in all age groups in our population. The Constitution (Eighty-sixth) Amendment of 2002 and the Right to Education Act of 2009 address the problem at the base of the age pyramid. For those in the higher age groups–fifteen to thirty-four and thirty-five to fifty-nine–together constituting about 67 per cent of the population, and particularly its weaker and disadvantaged segments–specific initiatives were required to address the prevalence of non-literates.

This was the purpose of the National Literacy Mission with its objective of imparting functional literacy to all persons in the age group fifteen to thirty-five, defined as acquiring the skill of reading, writing and arithmetic and the ability to apply them to one's daily life and thereby ameliorate their condition by participating in the process of development.

Experience showed the need for further refinement and sharper focusing. Three years ago, on this day, the Saakshar Bharat, the new variant of National Literacy Mission, was launched by the Government. The prime focus of the mission is to establish a fully literate society through improved quality and standard of Adult Education and Literacy.

The purpose of the mission is to impart functional literacy to 70 million adults in the age group of fifteen years and above focusing mainly on women, SCs, STs, Minorities and other disadvantaged groups of the society in rural areas. The Programme is being implemented in the Mission Mode with institutional framework at national, state, district, block and Gram Panchayat levels. The institution of Adult Education Centre at the Gram Panchayat level is the backbone of the Programme.

The rationale of this emphasis is evident. Schedule Castes, Schedule Tribes and Minorities together constitute 44 per cent of our population. The socio-economic development of women largely depends upon their literacy level. Literacy of women thus plays a critical role in their empowerment. The Saakshar Bharat programme, therefore, gives special emphasis on women literacy. It is to be noted that while the male literacy rate has increased from

75 to 82.14 per cent during the last decade, the female literacy rate in the same period has increased from 53.67 to 65.46 per cent. This has reduced the gender gap from 21 to 16 per cent.

I am happy to learn that the Saakshar Bharat programme is being implemented in 372 out of 410 eligible districts spread across 25 States and one Union Territory. Adult Education Centres have been set up in one lakh Gram Panchayats and around 570 lakh non literates have been identified through door to door survey. Literacy classes have started functioning in 16 lakh Centres covering around 174 lakh learners. Out of these, around 144 lakh learners have been certified as literates in the assessment tests conducted by the National Institute of Open Schooling.

While quantitative data makes impressive reading, some questions do need to be asked about the quality of literacy imparted. How do we ensure it? If stagnation and quality deficit in educational outputs remain a fact of life, how do we ensure that it will bring forth capacity building and eventual employability? Since this programme is in a mission mode, how do we ensure continuity once the mission is concluded?

To take this initiative further, we need to gear up the machinery at all levels i.e. National Literacy Mission Authority, State Literacy Mission Authorities, Lok Shiksha Samities in Districts, Blocks and Gram Panchayats. The implementation structure needs to be consolidated and strengthened with involvement of not only the Government Authorities but also eminent organisations in the Non-Government and Private Sector.

Furthermore, development of Adult Education in India depends upon the adaptability of the literacy mission to the emerging changes in all segments of the economy. Instead of functioning as a transient agent, the mission needs to take shape of a regular and permanent mechanism. Such mechanism is to be established and continued not only at the level of various administrative authorities, but also at the levels of the civil society organizations, social partners, private sector, community and adult learners' and educators' organisations.

The success of the programme would also largely depend upon how effectively it is implemented by the Local Self-Government bodies and Panchayati Raj Institutions.

Finally, we need to create more public awareness and public opinion in favour of our battle against illiteracy. It is the tyranny of circumstances rather than free choice that makes a person non-literate. It is the duty of society to change the conditions in which illiteracy prospers.

Let us not forget that literacy today, with a focus on quality, is essential for social, economic and cultural development of our people and towards the creation of a knowledge society.

I urge every citizen to take up this challenge and contribute to free India from the clutches of illiteracy.

Environment and Climate Change

❝Any action on climate change must enlarge, not constrict, the possibilities for development and empowerment of the world's poor. The human aspiration for leading a life of dignity must not be the outcome of the dice of geography

Conference on 'Vision 2025–A Sustainable Roadmap for India'

The Energy and Resources Institute (TERI), Oberoi Hotel, New Delhi

1 November 2007

It is my privilege to address this important gathering on the issue of sustainable development. It is heartening that such distinguished personalities from India and abroad have converged here to discuss policy initiatives necessary for establishing a pattern of sustainable development in India and submit a policy document based on the deliberations here to governments and other stakeholders.

The Johannesburg Declaration on Sustainable Development of 2002 constitutes the landmark document reaffirming the commitment of world leaders to sustainable development. The following elements of the declaration are significant enough to merit repetition:

1. It recognises "poverty eradication, changing consumption and production patterns and protecting and managing the natural resource base for economic and social development" as "overarching objectives of and essential requirements for" sustainable development.
2. It identifies "the deep fault line that divides human society between the rich and the poor and the ever-increasing gap between the developed and developing worlds" as "a major threat to global prosperity, security and stability".
3. The leaders of the world assumed "a collective responsibility to advance and strengthen the interdependent and mutually reinforcing pillars of sustainable development – conomic development, social development and environmental protection – at the local, national, regional and global levels".

4. The leaders of the world committed themselves to "building a humane, equitable and caring global society, cognisant of the need for human dignity for all."

These principles constitute the fundamental markers for a sustainable road map for our country's development and evolution in the next two decades.

The seven themes of this conference–issues of access, agricultural development, urbanisation, infrastructure growth, energy security, governance of water and natural resource management–have immense demonstrative value for showing a less resource-intensive growth path. But the most important theme to demonstrate our commitment to building a humane, equitable and caring global society, recognising the need for human dignity for all and for lessening the fault line between the rich and poor is the issue of ensuring universal and equitable access to basic services. I wish to dwell on this subject in some detail today.

The Approach Paper to the Eleventh Five-Year Plan is titled 'Towards faster and more inclusive growth' and spells out the nature of the 'divides' in our country: between the haves and the have-nots; between rural and urban areas; between the employed and the under/unemployed; between different states, districts and communities; and finally between genders. The global inequalities between the developed and the developing countries increasingly find reflection in disparities within developing countries. The statistics speak for themselves:

- Seventy-seven per cent of our population, totaling 836 million people, has an income of around Rs. 20.
- The richest 10 per cent of the population account for slightly less than 30% of the share of expenditure and the poorest 10 per cent of the population account for less than 5 per cent
- The recent Merrill Lynch World Wealth Report notes that as of 2006, there are 100,000 Indians who are High Net worth Individuals with financial assets of more than US$ 1 million, and that this segment in India witnessed the second largest growth rate globally, of 20.5 per cent.

- Public expenditure on education in India is around 3.3% of GDP and on health is around 1.2 per cent of GDP.
- 80 per cent of children in the age group of 6-35 months are anaemic.
- Around 38 per cent of all children under three years face stunted growth, indicating chronic long-term under-nutrition. Over half of all children in the age group of 12-23 months have not received all recommended vaccines.
- Over 50 per cent of households do not have access to piped drinking water or to a toilet facility.

In our country, national averages of economic growth and human development are rendered meaningless as they obscure such deep inequalities. What we need is a database of human development indicators in India for different income groups. We have different worlds in the same country–the human development parameters of the richest 20 per cent are way above that of the poorest 20 per cent of the population. At the most basic level, it is the inequalities in accessing basic health and education that perpetuate this vicious cycle. Inadequate public spending on health and education forces the poor to spend a disproportionate amount of their income on these two heads or forfeit education and along with it, chances for upward social and economic mobility.

I now come to the third pillar of sustainable development–environmental protection. Climate change has emerged as the headline of environmental protection efforts. India, with 17 per cent of the world population has only 4 per cent of global GHG emissions. In per capita terms, India's Greenhouse Gas emissions of 1 ton/annum are just about a quarter of the global average of 4 tons per annum, 4 per cent of the US, 12 per cent of EU and 15 per cent of Japan. In a significant development, we have succeeded in effectively de-linking energy sector growth from economic growth. While our GDP growth rate exceeds 9 per cent, our current primary energy consumption growth rate is merely 3.7 per cent per year. This contrasts with the pattern seen in developed countries and even a few major developing countries where higher GDP growth has followed the traditional pattern of increased use of energy.

India wants that the multilateral process dealing with climate change must ensure that burden sharing is fair and take into account the primary responsibility for the present levels of Greenhouse Gases and not perpetuate poverty among developing countries. Prime Minister Dr Manmohan Singh has, at the Heiligendamm meeting of the G-8, expressed India's determination that our per capita Greenhouse Gas emissions are not going to exceed those of developed countries even while pursuing policies of development and economic growth. This stand of India has been acknowledged by some countries in the G8 as part of their position on climate change issues. We have always emphasised the principle of common but differentiated responsibility and respective capability.

But what about the national process dealing with the climate change issue? Within the country, we have significant regional and urban/rural variations in economic development and extent of industrialisation. We need to adopt the same position at the national level that we seek at the multilateral level. We need to generate state-wise data on per capita emissions. Urban areas and heavily industrialised states that significantly contribute to Greenhouse Gas emissions must have different financial and other responsibilities on climate change as compared to rural areas and economically less developed states.

The global structure of dealing with climate change should eventually develop local and state-level strata. If the cause of climate change is the production and consumption patterns, any study of these patterns can't be limited to nation-states. We need to study sub-national patterns so that sustainable development does not remain an issue of nation-states alone. In the final analysis, sustainable development is an issue of peoples. This is where we need to concentrate our efforts if the road map that you would discuss is to remain relevant.

I wish the conference all success and hope that the policy document emanating from it would benefit governments and all stakeholders.

The India Energy Conference organised by TERI and PetroFed
The Taj Palace Hotel, New Delhi
3 October 2008

Let me begin with a candid confession. I am propelled by twin sentiments: happy to be here today to inaugurate the India Energy Conference, yet diffident because its subject matter is much too specialised for me to make a meaningful contribution.

Why then did I accept your invitation? The answer lies partly in the centrality of the subject and partly in your stated objective of doing something different from usual conferences and present insights and understanding of the complexities of the Indian energy market.

This gathering has brought together decision makers from the government and corporate sector from India and abroad. As one of the fastest growth economies of the world, the energy strategy of the country is critical for the achievement of our development objectives. The deliberations of this conference would thus be of relevance.

Modern civilisation has been founded and furthered on the development of different forms of energy. Every nation that has made a mark in recent history has successfully harnessed the matrix of energy sources through discovery and invention for its progress and prosperity. This would be true of India also as we endeavour in the coming decades to attain our development objectives.

The 'Energy for Development' debate is and must be multi-dimensional. Access to energy and security of supply is one aspect of it; availability of energy to all segments of society is another. A third consideration is energy conservation and environmental sustainability.

The Parikh Committee Report of the Planning Commission had estimated that we need to increase our primary energy supply by 3 to 4 times and electricity generation capacity and supply by five to six times of the 2003-04 levels to sustain a growth rate of 8 per cent through 2030.

Where do we stand today?

In terms of our primary energy consumption today, the International Energy Outlook 2008 reports that coal accounts for 53 per cent of primary energy consumption in the country, oil for 31 per cent, natural gas for 8 per cent, renewables including hydropower for 6.8 per cent and nuclear power for 1.2 per cent. By the year 2030, it estimates that this mix would change substantially only in regard to natural gas and nuclear energy whose share is expected to go up to 12 per cent and 5.4 per cent respectively.

Your conference will devote much time to all aspects of the development of the hydrocarbon sector. On my part, I would like to raise a few questions pertinent to the wider discussion on energy:

- What is our energy policy vision and what objectives do we wish to achieve?
- Is there, in the demand-supply equation, a policy preference for interventions that target the supply of energy?
- What are the policy constraints for augmenting energy efficiency and for demand side management?
- What should be the role of renewables in our energy matrix and what are the constraints in promoting them?

II

Three propositions sum up the vision behind the government's energy policy:

- To meet the demand for energy of all sectors at competitive prices.
- Cater to the basic energy requirements necessary for survival of all households, if necessary through targeted subsidies for the benefit of the poor and the vulnerable.
- Achieve these through safe, clean and convenient forms of energy at minimum cost in a technically efficient, economically viable and environmentally sustainable manner.

In an ideal environment, one would expect that policy initiatives to achieve these energy policy objectives would look equally at both the supply and the demand sides.

On the supply side, the government is looking at pursuing all energy options both conventional and non-conventional, expanding energy resource base and diversifying the sourcing of energy, both internally and globally.

Demand management, on the other hand, is more difficult. It should include improved energy efficiency and lower energy intensity of GDP growth, and recognise that relative fuel prices ought to lead to the correct choice of fuel, energy form and technology.

A focus on demand management should also lead to competitive energy markets where government subsidies to the vulnerable are clearly targeted, and resource allocation and pricing decisions are market determined and subject to effective regulation. As the Parikh Committee noted, crucial social objectives of the State should ideally be met through direct transfers.

It has recently been estimated by Morgan Stanley that half of the world's population enjoys fuel subsidies. In effect, this means that a quarter of the world's petrol is sold at less than the market price.

Fuel subsidies are politically sensitive and have adverse consequences for government finances and the efficiency of energy use. All stakeholders therefore need to enquire if fuel subsidies are the most efficient way to protect the poor and vulnerable households.

An IMF working paper on fuel subsidies in five emerging economies has noted that the richest 20 per cent of households received on average 42 per cent of total fuel subsidies, whereas the bottom 20 per cent of households received less than 10 per cent of subsidies.

Thus universal and undifferentiated subsidies for petrol, diesel and LPG imply a substantial leakage of benefits to higher income groups. It also translates into a significant opportunity cost since these resources could otherwise be used for greater inputs into social sectors.

The ideal however is not always possible. Fashioning targeted fuel subsidies, or effecting direct transfers to poor households in a non-fuel subsidy regime, call for an effective social protection system that could safeguard the real incomes of the poor. This is as yet lacking.

III

Energy security is intricately linked to energy conservation. Infrastructure projects in the energy sector require long gestation periods and heavy capital outlays. A megawatt saved is much more than a megawatt produced, keeping in view the transmission losses and the opportunity costs. Energy conservation technologies are known and can be implemented in all end-use sectors.

This has not been achieved until now. The energy intensity of our growth has been falling and is estimated to be about half of what it was in the early 70s. We currently consume 0.16 kg of oil equivalent per dollar of GDP in purchasing power parity terms. This is significantly lower than China which is 0.23 kg of oil equivalent, US at 0.22 and a world average of 0.21.

Furthermore, current energy assessments only take into account marketed energy use whereas over 80 per cent of rural households in India still rely heavily on non-marketed energy sources such as wood and cow-dung for heating and cooking.

Thus with faster development, improving energy infrastructure and rising incomes, many households in rural India would seek to access marketed energy sources and energy-using equipment, making it imperative to focus on further reducing the energy intensity of our growth.

What is being done to cater to the emerging demand pattern?

In June this year the Prime Minister released the National Action Plan on Climate Change, with a special focus on enhancing energy efficiency in industry. The Energy Conservation Act of 2001 provides a legal mandate for implementing energy efficiency measures and it is anticipated that they would result in a saving of 10,000 megawatts by the end of the Eleventh Five-Year Plan in 2012.

Government is also committed to putting in place a market-based mechanism for trading of certified energy savings and developing fiscal instruments to promote energy efficiency.

It remains to be seen if these steps would have a meaningful impact on the losses in the transmission and distribution of electric power that currently stand at 36 per cent of the primary energy consumption. It is to be noted that the global average on this count is around 28 per cent.

IV

Finally, we come to the role of the renewable segment in the energy mix of the country. This, at present, accounts for 6.8 per cent of primary energy consumption. Hydroelectric power is its principle component. According to the International Energy Outlook 2008, most of the growth in renewable energy consumption in developing countries over the next 25 years is expected to come from hydropower. In the case of India, this would require new approaches to regional cooperation.

This audience is aware that the government has ambitious programmes underway to utilise renewable energy. The New and Renewable Energy Policy 2005 promotes utilisation of renewable energy sources through indigenous design, development and manufacture. This includes use of wind energy and solar energy for power generation. The government has recently declared the National Policy on Bio-fuels that aims at raising the blending of bio-fuels with petrol and diesel to 20 per cent by the year 2017.

This notwithstanding, two problems with regard to renewable energy sources need to be highlighted.

In the first place, most of the renewable energy systems are proving to be land intensive. This is particularly true of bio-diesel blending and of solar thermal electric generation. Such vast tracts of land may be difficult to acquire in our country.

Secondly, many renewable energy projects are facing problems of grid capacity in transporting renewable energy from areas of production to areas of consumption. We may need innovative ways of either redesigning current electricity grid networks or commission renewable energy systems in stand-alone mode and independent of the national grid.

The direct correlation between energy use and human development is well established. Our goal must remain to improve access to reliable, affordable, economically viable, socially acceptable and environmentally sustainable energy sources. We have no choice but to increase per capita energy consumption to provide to our citizens a minimum acceptable level of well being and welfare.

I do hope the conference deliberations would, while focusing on hydrocarbons, place them within the ambit of broader energy issues affecting us, and come forth with suitable policy options.

Global Summit on Sustainable Development and Climate Change
The Observer Research Foundation, Taj Mahal Hotel, New Delhi
24 September 2009

I am happy to take part in today's conference. The Observer Research Foundation is a familiar platform for me. The timing of this conference, coming in the run up to the Fifteenth Conference of Parties in Copenhagen, ensures that its deliberations would inform the national and global debate on climate change.

Climate change remains one of the most complex problems facing humankind today. It is expected to impact on the distribution and quality of natural resources, and consequently the developmental path of nations and the quality of lives of peoples across the globe. To developing countries like India, climate change imposes new challenges that may probably require negotiating new international and national political and economic arrangements, fashioning new technological interventions, and negotiating financial and technological transfers for mitigation and adaption to climate change.

An incontrovertible premise in the debate is the right of every human being to a life dignity. This needs to be assessed in terms of some basic indicators. Allow me to mention five of these:

- In terms of basic energy consumption for two essential requirements of household electricity and transport, the per capita energy use in India was around 18 tons of oil-equivalent per person in the year 2005. The corresponding figure for Pakistan was 41, for China 52, for Mexico 345, for Brazil 205 and the United States 1881.
- India, despite having 17 per cent of the world population and a rapidly growing economy, has only 4 per cent of global Green

House Gas emissions as compared to US and China that account for over 16 per cent each of global Green House Gas emissions.

- In per capita terms, India's Green House Gas emission of 1.1 ton/annum is miniscule when compared to over 20 tons for the US and in excess of 10 tons for most OECD countries.
- India's primary energy consumption growth rate was merely 3.7per cent per year despite a GDP growth rate, until recently, of around 9 per cent. This contrasts with the pattern seen in developed countries and even a few major developing countries where higher GDP growth has followed the traditional pattern of increased use of energy.
- Over 40 per cent of our population is without access to electricity.

Sustainable development is premised on sustainable production and sustainable consumption patterns across all nations. A complex reality of our world is insufficient and inefficient production, as also profligate and inadequate consumption of varying degrees. The climate change negotiations have thus resulted in various countries adopting different negotiating positions. These have ranged between absolute emissions, per capita emissions, current emissions and historical emissions. Equity, nevertheless, remains the operative principle and every citizen of the globe has an equal entitlement to the planet's atmospheric space, a common resource of humanity.

At this early stage of development, India has the opportunity to exercise the right choices on climate change and sustainable development issues. The National Action Plan on climate change portrays this vision as creating "a prosperous, but not wasteful society, an economy that is self-sustaining in terms of its ability to unleash the creative energies of our people and is mindful of our responsibilities to both present and future generations". Our national objective, it states, is the establishment of "an effective, cooperative and equitable global approach based on the principle of common but differentiated responsibilities and respective capabilities, enshrined in the United Nations Framework Convention on Climate Change".

Seminars are occasions for exchange of ideas. I on my part would like to raise a few for your consideration:

First, the question of equity and burden sharing is central to climate change debate. Lack of a global agreement on such an equitable formula is likely to cause the climate change negotiations to spill over to other multilateral, regional and bilateral negotiating platforms. This would further accentuate existing divisions such as North-South, East-West, Developed-Developing countries, etc.

Second, pursuit of equity at the international level needs to be reflected at the national level. There is significant variation in Green House Gas emissions of various states within the country. In the year 2000, for example, a study has estimated that the per capita emission of Madhya Pradesh was over 16 times that of Assam. As part of the national debate on climate change, we should discuss whether urban areas and heavily industrialised states that significantly contribute to Green House Gas emissions should have different financial and other responsibilities on climate change as compared to rural areas and economically less developed states.

Third, the climate change debate so far has been primarily government-focused with some participation of the civil society. This needs to be broadened to include the legislature, people's groups and grass root movements so that adaptation and mitigation options are discussed by those who are directly affected by climate change. The debate must be as inclusive as possible to enhance its legitimacy and credibility.

Sustainable development is an issue of the peoples of the world. The issue of development should continue to remain the focus of the global discourse. Any action on climate change must enlarge, not constrict, the possibilities for development and empowerment of the world's poor. The human aspiration for leading a life of dignity must not be the outcome of the dice of geography.

Inauguration of the India Water Forum

The Energy and Research Institute, India Habitat Centre, Delhi

13 April, 2011

The Energy and Resources Institute has a formidable reputation and I am happy to participate in today's function organised in association with the Ministry of Water Resources of the Government of India.

It is very appropriate that the theme of this first international convention is the challenges and opportunities of dealing with the twin issues of water security and climate change.

Water is an essential building block of life. Existence would be unimaginable without it. An Urdu poet had summed up the human sentiment about it:

Yeh aab o baad o khak ka jahan bahut haseen hai
Agar koi bahisht hai to bus yehi zameen hai
Beautiful is this world of water, air and dust
If there is a paradise then this indeed it is.

In our world of today, water is a critical national asset with geo-political and geo-strategic import. Water resources often transcend national boundaries. Successful public policy therefore has to be premised on establishing cooperative partnerships between governments, business and industry, non-governmental and civil society organisations and, above all, the individual users.

Water management systems have traditionally reflected existing socio-economic structures and governance mechanisms. The key challenges to water management today stem from changing demographics, shifting geo-politics, wide-spread poverty and under-development, climate change phenomena and shifting weather patterns, and the elements of globalisation and its attendant consequences.

Those formulating public policy regarding this vital resource must therefore cater to essential requirement and ensure sustainability of eco systems so that there is availability of adequate water for everyone. Prevention of greed, of waste and of conspicuous consumption must remain high on their agenda.

II

At the outset, it would be useful to look at some figures regarding our water resources.

India has 2.4 per cent of the world's area, 16 per cent of the world's population but only 4 per cent of the total available fresh water. Our main water resources consist of annual precipitation of around four thousand cubic kilometres and a broad estimate of trans-boundary flows from upper riparian neighbours of around five hundred cubic kilometres. Out of the total precipitation, annual availability from surface and ground water is estimated at 1869 cubic kilometres.

However, only 60 per cent of this at 1123 cubic kilometres is estimated to be capable of being put to beneficial use, 690 cubic kilometres of which is surface water and 433 cubic kilometres being replenishable ground water.

The twin indicators of water scarcity are per capita availability and storage. Our population has increased from 361 million in 1951 to 1.21 billion in 2011. Accordingly, the per capita availability of water for the country as a whole has decreased from 5177 cubic metres per annum in 1951 to 1544 cubic metres per annum in 2011, a drastic reduction of 70 per cent in sixty years. This meets the definition of a water-stressed condition which is per capita availability of less than 1700 cubic metres.

The situation is even more serious when we look at individual river basins. Nine out of twenty river basins in the country, with a population of over 200 million, meet the definition of water scarcity of a per capita availability of less than 1000 cubic metres.

We fare no better regarding the other indicator of storage. According to the Eleventh Five-Year Plan document, per capita water storage in the country is 213 cubic metres, as against over 6000 in Russia, 4700 in Australia, 1100 in China and 1960 in the United States.

It is estimated that by the year 2050, as per existing water use practices, overall demand for water resources would be 1447 cubic kilometres, around 30 per cent higher than assessed utilisable water of 1123 cubic kilometres. It is evident that only the adoption of better governance practices and enhanced efficiency would reduce this demand.

The annual extraction of groundwater in India at 210 cubic kilometres is the highest in the world. It provides for over 60 per cent of net irrigated area and has accounted for over 85 per cent of the addition to irrigated area in the last three decades.

The growing dependence on ground water has been at the cost of unsustainable over-extraction in at least a third of total area and population of the country, which has lowered the water table and adversely impacted rural drinking water. For example, in a six year period, ground water depletion in Rajasthan, Punjab, Haryana and Delhi was 109 cubic kilometres, double the capacity of India's largest surface water reservoir.

Finally, we must note that irrigation accounts for 85 per cent of water requirement, whereas drinking water accounts for 7 per cent with industrial, energy and other uses being of a smaller scale.

This data makes disturbing reading. It suggests that analysis and policy regarding irrigation is central to sustainable water management.

III

The picture of water security across the country is indeed one of major concern. Water availability and water quality issues plague the majority of citizens in both rural and urban areas. Gross irrigated area is not rising commensurate with our huge investments, with a big gap between potential created for irrigation and potential that is actually utilised. The problem of floods has been exacerbated due to degradation of catchment areas and loss of flood plains to urban development and agriculture. Water conflict has taken new forms with more menacing consequences.

Climate change issues have further complicated the water calculus. It is likely to alter precipitation received in our territory, the hydrology of catchments in upper riparian neighbouring countries, and the distribution and quality of water resources in the country.

The threats and challenges are significant and immediate. We have recognised and responded to the threat of water insecurity emanating from climate change. The National Water Mission has been established under the National Action Plan for Climate Change for 'conservation of water, minimising wastage and ensuring its more equitable distribution both across and within States through integrated water resources development and management'. It has suggested specific action points and has sought policy modifications in view of climate change concerns. Five of these merit close attention:

First, it has sought comprehensive reform on regulation of water resources. Such public regulation must ensure that the right of citizens and residents to minimum essential water supplies for health and hygiene is ensured; available water is equitably distributed across regions and categories of users; monitoring is done to ensure compliance with allocation and water quality; that there is creation, review and modification of water rights for various categories of users; create water prices for different uses; and create a system of penalties for polluting surface and ground water resources.

Second, policy planning must consider water as a unified resource, with the quantified hydraulic cycle becoming the main tool for understanding the water situation. Management of rain water and evaporation should supplement current strategies of managing rivers and aquifers. Thus, water balances, water budgeting, water accounting and water audits should be based on the hydraulic cycle and the interaction between rain water, surface water, ground water and evaporation.

Third, there is a need to establish legally-empowered, stakeholder-managed Basin authorities with wide powers for approving development and management plans and tackling emergencies and tasked with reducing conflicts and imposing penalties for misuse of water resources.

Fourth, improving water use efficiency in irrigation is critical for water management. For each large irrigation system, benchmarking and performance evaluation studies for each water year with complete water budget and efficiency related data should be put in the public domain for transparency and accountability. Subsidies should encourage irrigation efficiencies through piped and drip irrigation, and constructing storages for irrigation water at the user's end. Participatory management of irrigation systems would increase equity and reliability and reduce losses due to over irrigation.

Fifth, we need to launch a coordinated and time bound programme to improve the analytical capabilities of our water resource personnel in the various public and private agencies at the national, state and local government levels.

I fear that in regard to water we are living in the past and too many of us take water for granted. Like climate change, the idea of water scarcity must seep into consciousness and through it to the institutions and mechanisms of global and national governance and business and industry. The need to address the complexities of water management in the context of climate change is imperative.

Water shortages affect the most unlikely of industries. For example, severe water shortages and high water temperatures in 2003 in France led to the shut down or scaling down of production at the 58 nuclear power stations responsible for supplying over 75 per cent of total electricity. If nations and peoples ration the use of water for industrial purposes or change the pricing for such use, there would be significant changes in the business environment.

Water stress and scarcity would have a significant impact on the prospects of Indian companies operating in various sectors including agriculture and agro-industry, irrigation, mining, pulp and paper, iron and steel, and power generation. Regulators, investors and citizens alike must demand corporate water disclosure, including plans and policies for water consumption, use and disposal and whether environmental concerns have been addressed.

Today's convention, I venture to hope, would contribute to the realisation that water scarcity affects individuals, businesses and the national economy, that water is central to poverty alleviation and citizen empowerment, and that better water governance is a shared enterprise between all stakeholders–citizens, governments, civil society and industry.

International Conference on 'Strengthening Green Federalism: Sharing International Practices'
India Habitat Centre, New Delhi
29 October 2012

I am happy to be here today to inaugurate the 'International Conference on *Strengthening Green Federalism: Sharing International Practices*' being organised by The Energy and Resources Research Institute in partnership with and supported by Ministry of Environment and Forests, the Inter-State Council Secretariat, Government of India; the World Bank and the Forum of Federations, Ottawa.

I understand the conference brings together scholars and practitioners from federal systems across the world to share experiences, and to understand better the design and implementation of environmental policy in federations around the world.

Environment and related issues like environmental federalism are pertinent in today's age when the paradigm of sustainable development and environmental soundness has come to occupy the centre-stage in humanity's quest for socio-economic progress and prosperity in a world marked by finite and depleting natural resources.

Despite immediate preoccupation with the global financial crisis and its implications for the development agenda, most governments acknowledge today that a judicious balance between development and environment would be the key to comprehensive human security in the long run.

In some countries, however, the debate around this balance is still built around contestation and conflict, because the inter-linkages between eco-systems and the economy, between eco-systems and quality of life, between human and national security, are still not properly understood or perhaps not better articulated.

It is relevant here to recall the invocation in an ancient Indian prayer which emphasises oneness with environment:

> "Do not harm the environment; do not harm the water and the flora; earth is my mother, I am her son; may the waters remain fresh, do not harm the waters ... Tranquility be to the atmosphere, to the earth, to the waters, to the crops and vegetation."

Our judiciary has, in many instances, interpreted the Right to Life embodied in Article 21 of our Constitution, to include the right to a clean environment.

Culturally, legally, morally and existentially, therefore, we need to move to a deeper understanding and recognition of the fact that human wellbeing and even economic growth are underpinned by a clean and healthy environment.

Environmental issues manifest themselves at various levels–global, national, state and local–and call for action at each of these levels in order to ensure the most efficient and equitable delivery of the required high and low spillover public goods. Allow me also to touch upon a few matters that readily come to mind:

Forests and Climate Change, being a global issue, requires multilateral solutions with adaptive responses at national levels appropriate to specific regional and local requirements. Forests and biodiversity, terrestrial and marine, are global and national public goods; actions relating to them have long term implications so well spelt out by the noted American conservationist Edward O. Wilson:

> The worst thing that will probably happen–in fact is already underway–is not energy depletion, economic collapse, conventional war, or the expansion of totalitarian governments. As terrible as these catastrophes would be for us, they can be repaired in a few generations. The one process now going on that will take millions of years to correct is loss of genetic and species biodiversity by the destruction of natural habitats. This is the folly our descendents are least likely to forgive us.

We therefore need urgent global action on protecting the biodiversity, as was noted by the recently concluded 11th Conference of Parties to the Convention on Biological Diversity at Hyderabad.

On the Indian subcontinent, many bio-diverse rich eco-systems like the Himalayan eco-system, the Western Ghats and the Coasts, have a number of overlapping institutions that give rise to contradictory incentives which are detrimental to their protection. It is of course necessary that biodiversity be protected for the larger public interest, but it is also essential perhaps to think about how sub-national and local units which stand to lose from the conservation of these habitats be compensated.

Inter-state rivers are source of conflicts and acrimony between countries and between states around the sharing and use of water. Many of these conflicts result from a poor fit between ecosystems they represent and the institutions designed to manage them. A course correction is required.

Serious reflection and action is also required on issues of governance and institutional design wherein environment and development are concerned. In our context, the Thirteenth Finance Commission in its recommendations urged the need to "manage ecology, environment and climate change consistent with sustainable development" and to incentivise Indian states towards improved environmental performance through intergovernmental transfer of financial resources in the form of grants. The same point has been made by the Punchhi Commission on Centre-State Relations has acknowledged the importance of strengthening federal relations to protect the environments and addressed them in some detail.

The Approach Paper to the Twelfth Five-Year Plan (2012-2017) states that all levels of government need to act together to combat the challenge of Climate Change. The state governments need to develop a State Action Plan for Climate Change that can be dovetailed to the National Action Plan, by identifying vulnerable areas and communities, and by developing a state specific action programme for the above mentioned areas that will facilitate mitigation and adaptation action against the challenge of climate change.

Such strengthening of environmental federalism requires us to understand the constitutional provisions within each country to deal with the fine balance between environment and development. Does empowering the

Centre on environmental matters relative to the sub-national units create a more efficient framework to deal with environmental and developments concerns or would a more distributed, multi-polar framework be a better way to address the diversity of environmental problems and ecosystem management? How does the answer to this question vary depending on issues and context?

Strengthening environmental federalism also requires an engagement with the institutions and their capacity to take the mandated task forward. It raises a few questions:

- Where do we see compliance failure, excesses, and inadequacies?
- How do we ensure ecological sustainability while also addressing issues of equity and inclusiveness, not only in the use of natural resources but development in general?
- How do countries incentivise improved environmental performance? Do countries have a national policy of compensation to sub-national units for opportunities lost (forest preservation) or availed (mining, logging)?
- How will public participation and greater transparency and accountability help improve the balance?

Any move to strengthen environmental federalism will require the enhancement of capacities at the sub-national levels. I am happy that the conference has devoted a session on this issue.

I wish the conference success in its work over the next two days.

Foreign Policy Challenges

"India is not in any country's orbit but is rotating on its own axis as part of the great galaxy of nations

—Nehru's remark cited by Y.D. Gundavia

Seminar on 'Politics and Security'

Organised by India International Centre and Centre for Policy Dialogue, Dhaka
IIC, New Delhi
10 September 2007

I deem it a privilege to be invited to inaugurate today's seminar on 'Politics and Security', it being the third theme of the Indo-Bangladesh Dialogue. The dialogue itself has been in progress now for over a decade; more importantly, it has retained its autonomous character and has brought together persons of diverse political persuasions and intellectual backgrounds. It is a credible manifestation of civil society interaction between two countries.

I subscribe to the view that conceptual clarity and definitional precision help the process of analysis. A few questions, therefore, need to be posed to elicit responses relevant to the thought process:

- What do we mean by the terms politics and security?
- How do we define them in terms of content and impact radius of inclusion and exclusion–whose politics and whose security are we talking about?
- In what manner, and to what extent, does the civil society impact on these perceptions?

Answers to these questions are of relevance to the theme of this dialogue; it is important that we get them right.

For long, much too long, the paradigm of security and politics has been state-centric. The State was at the centre of the discourse. All politics revolved around it and was judged in terms of the interests of the state as defined by the wielders of state power. Experience, however, demonstrated the limitations of this approach.

Today, sheer necessity has propelled thinking to bring into focus two new paradigms of politics and security–the first, at the sub-national and micro-level, is the concept of human security; the second, at the supra-national and macro level, is the quest for solutions to problems of human security that transcend national boundaries and thus necessitate regional cooperation and structures imperative for its realisation.

More than a decade earlier, the UNDP's Human Development Report for 1994 shed useful light on the concept of human security and predicted that the idea would revolutionise society in the 21st century. It identified freedom from fear and freedom from want as two interdependent principal components of human security; both concepts are people-centered. In 2003 the Commission on Human Security, co-chaired by Prof. Amartya Sen and Mrs Sadako Ogata was instrumental, through its report, in placing the issue on the international agenda.

Ours is a world in which the nation-state, as perceived in recent history, has been transformed into what Philip Bobbitt has called the market-state. The upside benefits of the latter are global growth and development that transcends national borders. This is the argument for globalisation and for open markets and economic policies. By the same lethal logic, however, the downside risks to human security also are not bound by national boundaries. Transnational terrorism, global epidemics such as bird flu, HIV/AIDS, environmental problems such as global warming and natural disasters such as tsunamis and earthquakes and even debilitating economic events such as recession, currency crises, global stock market meltdown or drastic oil price hikes strike one and all–they do not respect borders nor go by citizenship.

This is unique to our age; previous generations did not have to deal with the global impact of local issues or the local impact of global issues. In such a context, interaction between countries and societies needs to move away from the traditional confines and accommodate these wider concerns.

The Indo-Bangladesh Dialogue, I hope, has included this dimension to relations between India and Bangladesh, to help demonstrate its relevance to the public in both countries.

The imperative is clear and emanates from a specific question. Do our people enjoy the most basic elements of security–freedom from want and from fear? If the definition of security were to be expanded, it would include the full range of human rights, full access to education and health care, good governance, economic options and opportunities for leading their lives to their full potential and with dignity, with freedom from vulnerability, want and hunger.

How then do we develop a local and national political discourse that makes this possible? How can we make such a path politically rewarding, for it to be a viable political option and ensure that it brings about economic synergies for it to be a viable economic option?

At the macro, supra-national level, the answer may lie in regional co-operation. Some indications of this are available in SAARC documents. At the 13th SAARC Summit held at Dhaka in 2005, the Heads of State or Government reiterated, and I quote: "That the peoples of South Asia are the real source of strength and driving force for SAARC and resolved to make regional cooperation more responsive to their hopes and aspirations". At the 14th SAARC Summit held at New Delhi this year, the leaders of SAARC countries agreed to build a "Partnership for Prosperity and work towards shared economic cooperation, regional prosperity, a better life for the people of South Asia, and equitable distribution of benefits and opportunities of integration among the peoples and the nations".

Despite these and other official proclamations, and considerable civil society pressure and persuasion, the honest truth is that institutional structures and systemic constraints come in the way of their realisation. Our delivery mechanisms remain a major impediment.

At the inter-state level, I believe as many as forty instrumentalities exist for dialogue between India and Bangladesh on matters that are of common concern and depend for success on inter-state cooperation. The missing element in these is sufficient political will. How to infuse this into the dialogue?

We have to admit that the traditional paradigm of politics and security has reached an impasse. The imperative of survival calls for an alternate approach. Would participants in this seminar respond to the challenge–for the common good of the people of Bangladesh and India?

I wish the seminar success in its work.

The Foundation Day

The Institute for Defence Studies and Analyses, New Delhi
10 November 2007

I feel privileged to be here with you today to celebrate the Foundation Day of the Institute for Defence Studies and Analyses. I also celebrate as an insider. Over the years the IDSA has carved out for itself a place in the fraternity of the regional and international community dedicating itself to matters strategic. These engagements have in some measure helped shape perceptions, and add a much needed Indian dimension to them.

"I think, therefore I am", said the philosopher René Descartes. By this logic, thinking should be a normal and universal human trait. Experience however reveals a propensity to avoid structured thinking and leave it either to superiors in the social or organisational hierarchy or to a small group charged to do so. Both amount to an abdication of civic responsibility since, as Pericles said a long time back, ordinary citizens are fair judges of public matters and discussion therefore is not a stumbling block but "an indispensable preliminary to any wise action".

At the other end of the spectrum governments, busy with the concerns of the moment, sometimes do not have the time and the energy to devote themselves in sufficient measure to matters in the domain of the possible, the probable and even the improbable. It is here that speculative but structured thinking demonstrates its relevance and helps bridge the gap between the worlds of ideas and action.

The sociologist Anthony Giddens, who was in New Delhi recently, described the present day world as "puzzling, strange, elliptical" in which 'we are far from being fully in control of the forces we have unleashed'. This is further complicated, as Philip Bobbit put it in a seminal work published a few years back, by 'the shift in the basis of legitimacy from that of the nation-state to that of the market-state' which questions much of what went with the doctrine of sovereignty. To think about the world of today in terms of security and foreign policy, therefore, requires cognition of what is decidedly new. Some of these are evident and can be mentioned:

- Revolution in Information Technology and the emergence of user-friendly technologies at the retail level leading to immense empowerment at the individual level.
- Globalisation, with its market integration and instantaneous media of communication, has created extensive interdependencies down to the village level.
- The end of the Cold War and the emergence of a more complex international order that lends itself much less to prototyping. Affiliations, alliances and identities are no longer exclusive–overlapping multiplicity is no longer merely an option, it has become a necessity.
- The concept of 'power' and 'influence' has undergone tremendous changes. Today, strong nation-states are much less feared than weaker ones. Non-state actors have been technologically empowered to unleash enormous destruction among states and societies. Soft power projections are as important as hard power instrumentalities.
- The political, economic and cultural DNA of nations acts as the limit of the potential that exists for development and flowering of peoples. The actualisation of this potential depends as always on the political and social environment of the day and the leadership available to harness the energies of the people.
- Fundamental human rights have obtained the widest observance and recognition in human history. They impose implicit and explicit codes of behaviour for nation states irrespective of national constitutions and domestic legislation.
- With the predominantly young profile of our population–over 550 million Indians are below the age of 25 years - patience with state interventions and facilitation for socio-economic development is wearing thin. People want income growth, enhanced standards of

life and actualisation of their potential at the earliest. The margin for delay and non-performance in this area is minimal. This is the leitmotif of this generation.

This then is one set of factors that impact on the security and foreign policies of countries, including our own. Needless to say, the traditional imperatives also remain in place. How then do we harmonise the two, respond to security imperatives and energise the policy impulse? This, to my mind, is the challenge of the day that requires to be addressed by the strategic community.

Any exercise in structured thinking is premised on conceptual clarity. Our terms of reference today pertain both to security policy and to foreign policy. In the first place, the two are not synonymous since national security has domestic dimensions as relevant as external ones. The concept of security itself has acquired depth and a new meaning; it now encapsulates non-traditional security and is focused on comprehensive human security.

Foreign policy, on its part, is not conducted in a vacuum on the basis of a wish list; it must perforce result from the manner in which a country persuades the external world to respond to its national vision (inclusive of its security requirements) and the supportive structure it brings to bear in terms of national capabilities.

II

I venture to suggest that India of tomorrow would attempt to locate itself in terms of such a basket of imperatives and perspectives. In doing so, it would still go back to the basic objectives enunciated by Jawaharlal Nehru in his Address on 7 September 1946, six days after the Interim National Government was formed. Its essence bears reiteration:

- 'We propose, as far as possible, to keep away from the power politics of groups'
- 'We believe that peace and freedom are indivisible and the denial of freedom anywhere must endanger freedom elsewhere and lead to conflict and war'

- 'We are particularly interested in the emancipation of colonial and dependent countries and peoples, and in the recognition in theory and practice of equal opportunities for all races'
- 'We seek no dominion over others and we claim no privileged position over other peoples. But we do claim equal and honourable treatment for our people wherever they may go, and we cannot accept any discrimination against them';
- 'India is on the move and the old order passes. We go forward to success and to freedom and well-being of the hundreds of millions of India.'

An observer of the Indian scene may well ask the question: do these considerations remain operative? The answer would be in the affirmative, as is evident from authoritative pronouncements made from time to time by public personalities and government leaders and most recently in the conclave organised by the Hindustan Times.

The focus thus remains on success, on freedom and on the well-being of our people and on a cooperative, non-hegemonic, world order. By implication, challenges to these in a changing situation become challenges to our security.

If there is one challenge that I wish to highlight today as being of critical importance and yet under-appreciated for its likely impact, it is the predominantly state-centric discourse of our national security policies. The protection of a state from external aggression and internal threats is increasingly seen as one component of a more comprehensive approach to security–that of human security. There is a need to look at security of individuals and peoples in this more holistic sense–where protection of individuals from all forms of violence, from hunger and disease, from natural and man-made disasters, from socio-economic and political inequity is the goal.

Undertaking this quantum definitional leap is critical if the discourse on national security and on foreign policy challenges is to evolve and progress. We also need to remind ourselves constantly that the primary purpose of conducting foreign policy, and of the effort to 'promote international peace and security' and 'maintain just and honourable relations between nations', is to do so in the interest of the People of India.

The complexity of the Indian reality, particularly in its economic, sociological and human dimensions, is the umbilical cord linking domestic and foreign policy; it conditions all aspects of the security perspective. The sources of strength, and weaknesses, of this reality need to be borne in mind by scholars devoting themselves to national security studies.

We live in an era where the only certainty is uncertainty. How do we convey our vision of our security and foreign policy to the world and our people? How do we synthesise the ambiguities and uncertainties into coherent policies and build support in our diverse polity and society? The only answer would be to place individuals and peoples at the centre of the discourse and debate. All around us are societies where the priorities were reversed, with dire consequences.

A word of caution may not be out of place. It is a folly to view the world in terms of black and white. The future of world peace and of the international community remains in balance because ambitions of control continue to surface to achieve, in Headley Bull's terms, dominance, hegemony or primacy. An alternative model, based on common ideals and common values, is yet to emerge. There is, however, hope that eventually sanity will prevail. Almost two decades after India proposed it in 1988, there is now talk in the United States itself of a phased reduction and elimination of nuclear weapons. Would some researcher in IDSA be tempted to explore the options from an Indian perspective?

The only approach to our security and foreign policy challenges is one of incremental success. This is a painstaking task that requires patience and clarity of purpose. I have no doubt that IDSA would continue to play an important role in this task by generating new knowledge and ideas, by paying greater attention to societal impulses, and by shaping Indian responses to challenges that may confront us in the years to come.

I wish the Institute all success in its work.

International Conference on 'Emerging Security Concerns in West Asia'
The Observer Research Foundation, New Delhi
21 November 2007

It is a pleasure to be back on a familiar platform. Familiarity in this case, however, is a disadvantage since I may be in danger of repeating what I might have articulated on previous occasions!

Many years back the British philosopher Gilbert Ryle had drawn attention to the dangers of expressions that are 'couched in syntactical form improper to the facts recorded'. This observation is relevant to our subject today since the theme of the conference begs definition and delineation. Unanimity of perception, of course, would have been ideal; since that is lacking, the two operative terms–'emerging' and 'security concerns'–need to be spelt out.

Centrality has been the curse of West Asia. It is hardly necessary to remind this audience that external security concerns pertaining to the region have been around for over a century. Writing in 1917, Marriott, a British Scholar, defined the Eastern Question as 'the problem of filling up the vacuum created by the gradual disappearance of the Turkish Empire from Europe'. In May 1917, Britain and France used the Sykes-Picot Agreement to acquire 'the right of priority in enterprises and local loans' in designated Arab areas of the Ottoman Empire and to deny any facilities to a third Power in the Arabian Peninsula and the Red Sea. In a parallel move, the secret Balfour Declaration of November 1917 carried the commitment for the 'establishment in Palestine of a national home for the Jewish people'. A decade earlier on 31 August, 1907, the Anglo-Russian Entente was signed, dividing Iran into three zones only one of which was under Iranian control. 'The Iranians', in Professor Nikkie Keddie's words, "were neither consulted on the agreement nor informed of the terms". That exercise, of division and occupation, was repeated during World War II.

These experiences with external powers left indelible marks on national perceptions.

The short point that I wish to emphasise is that 'emerging security concerns' cannot be viewed in a vacuum and in a single dimension; they need to be seen both from the internal and the external perspectives and in terms of the historical experience of individual societies. Furthermore, security perceptions vary greatly within nations and between them. Security is no longer viewed in military and nation-state terms. National security and regime security are not necessarily synonymous. Today we live in the age of human security. Progress in comprehension would therefore be possible only through de-segregation; generalisations would be possible only if we succeed in identifying common threat perceptions.

II

Any discussion of contemporary West Asia must begin with three questions:

What is happening in the region?

Why is it happening?

What is the way out? The answer to the first question is obvious. It focuses on a set of well-known situations:

- A Middle East Peace Process that is lingering on promissory notes whose encashment has been deferred repeatedly;
- A quagmire in Iraq that has dented the prestige and power of the United States;
- A failure to abandon the doctrines of 'Pre-emptive Strikes' and of 'Regime Change' despite the experience of recent years and sharply declining public support for it in the United States;
- Israel's failure to destroy the Hezbollah in Lebanon and Hamas in Gaza;
- America's stand off with Iran, and the threat to regional and world peace emanating from it;
- Enhanced external pressure on Iran to terminate its nuclear programme;

- Demographic pressures and a developing gap between commitment and expectation in West Asian societies;
- Failure of the 'Middle East Initiative' and the 'Greater Middle East Initiative' and of the attempt to democratise West Asian societies. Also, the impact of this on indigenous reform movements; and
- The little mentioned problem of water.
- There is no simple answer to the second question. West Asia has been and continues to be a pivotal factor in global geopolitics. These have been aggravated in recent years by a set of new considerations:
- Crisis of the Old Order and end of bipolarity;
- The attempt to impose a New Order.
- Failure to develop a security paradigm in the region and particularly in the Persian Gulf; and
- Ideological dimensions and their implications–defeat of Arabism and Arab nationalism, failure of the Left and the re-emergence of religious radicalism.

These factors do not function autonomously; instead, they interact on a continuous basis. Comprehensive analysis of these is not possible in the short time available to me this morning. One aspect, however, is worth highlighting; I refer to the interaction between the periphery and the core. In specific terms, this would refer to the role of Israel and Iran, and occasionally of Turkey, and the impact of their relationship on the core problems of contemporary West Asia.

An answer to the third question is contingent on variables of considerable size and diversity. One could begin by stating the factual situation as known publicly.

While the greater part of the region and its population are Arab, the principal factors in the strategic calculus are non-Arabs. Two are on the periphery–Israel and Iran, and one beyond it–the United States. The interaction of these with the region, and with each other, is having a decisive impact.

A beginning may be made with self-perceptions. The region, President Bush said in his State of the Union message earlier this year, is the venue of 'the decisive ideological struggle of our times'. As Undersecretary of State Nicholas Burns put it, it is the epicentre of American foreign policy.

On the other side is the view of Dr Martin Kramer, an Israeli-American scholar of considerable repute who also serves as senior Middle East advisor to Republican presidential hopeful Rudy Giuliani. He said in a lecture the other day that 'we must get ourselves back over the horizon and as much out of the Arab line of sight as possible' and, as was done by the British, French, Ottoman throughout history. 'Rule lightly, unless provoked. Delegate power and don't tamper with local customs. Using these rules, great empires dominated the Middle East for centuries. Our problem, though, is that we don't see ourselves as a great empire, and we don't want to rule anyone directly. We just want to transform them thoroughly'.

The operative expression in both sets of perceptions is a desire to dominate. The discussion is only about modalities.

Israel, a mid-twentieth century factor in the region, has not been able to translate its military superiority into a total, definitive, victory. Its invincibility was dented in the war with Hezbollah. This is not reflected in political perceptions where right wing political parties and a small but effective settler lobby has defied moves towards a meaningful peace process. The lack of a serious U.S. interest in the peace process has helped sustain it. The American West Asian policy is hampered by the "Israel test" to which it is subjected in terms of domestic politics. Israel's policy objective is to: (a) exhaust the Palestinians, riddle the West Bank with settlements, make impossible the emergence of a viable Palestinian state and (b) dominate the region militarily, technologically and economically.

Iran, driven by memories of the Revolution and the long war with Iraq, seeks to project a threefold desire: (a) acknowledgement of its regional weight, particularly in West Asia and the Persian Gulf (b) development of a technological capability to assist it (c) bring to an end, on equitable terms, to the regime of sanctions to facilitate access to badly needed technology and foreign investment for economic development. The stand off on Iran's alleged nuclear weapons programme is thus a political instrumentality resorted to maximise advantage in a complex negotiating process.

III

The state-centric security concerns in West Asia thus relate principally to the moves on the chess board of the United States, Israel and Iran in relation both to each other and to other actors in the region.

The United States today is not the Sole Super Power of the spring of 2003. The policies of unilateralism, 'creative destruction' and pre-emption have faltered. The U.S. has been mauled by non-state actors in Iraq; its policies have given an impetus to terrorism; it has lost domestic support for its Iraq policy; its unpopularity levels are alarmingly high in Arab and Muslim countries and its intentions are suspected. The financial burden of the war and the drain on the dollar has added to public concerns. The dissent in the national security establishment of the United States has become public. Francis Fukuyama wrote last month that when he penned the End of History 'the one thing I did not anticipate was the degree to which American behaviour and misjudgements would make anti-Americanism one of the chief fault lines of global politics'.

The imperatives in the Iran policy of the United States have to be viewed in this context. Suggestions about military action have emanated from time to time; doubts about its efficacy and wider implications have also been raised. The absence of decisive evidence of Iranian culpability has been a restraining factor. Non-proliferation experts like Dr David Albright have recently expressed the view that (a) Iran has not yet demonstrated competency at enriching uranium, (b) the programme 'still has a way to go', and (c) creative thinking should focus at direct negotiations without pre-conditions, but with some confidence building measures by Iran, between Iran, the EU and the United States. Dr Henry Kissinger, who was in Delhi recently, was cautiously optimistic about such talks taking place in 2008.

Israeli perceptions of Iran are nuanced. Since 1979 the relationship has been conditioned by ideology on the one side and geo-political interests on the other. The channels of communications have never completely closed. Iran's support to the Palestinians and the Hezbollah has been a strategic irritant to Israel. An Iranian success in developing a nuclear weapon capability would deny Israel the regional monopoly it has in the matter. Israel has been extremely active in mobilising American opinion against Iran. On the other hand, *Haaretz* magazine cited on 25 October 2007 a remark by foreign minister Tzipi Livni that 'Iranian nuclear weapons do not pose an existential threat to Israel'.

Similarly nuanced are the Iranian positions on the U.S. and Israel. The Iranian proposal of May 2003 for negotiations on a package deal was rejected by the Bush Administration; it does, nevertheless, contain elements for serious consideration. Iran in 2002 had also signalled its willingness to accept a 'Malaysian profile' in return for an easing of Israeli and American efforts to isolate Iran.

IV

So much for the periphery and the extra-regional actors. But what about the core? Why is it that all discussion on regional security in West Asia is not primarily centred on the Arab core? Even as we live in an age of multiple identities, the peoples of the region have not yet resolved their overlapping identities and the implications of such non-resolution are visible at key historical and evolutionary junctions.

The end of European colonialism in West Asia had unleashed three sets of forces whose complex interplay sets the background for all subsequent developments in the polity and society of Arab states:

1. The first is Arab nationalism; the concept that all Arabs are one nation was very strong in the immediate aftermath of the end of European colonialism. Later, conflict on who should steer the destiny of the Arab nation has led to a conscious downplaying of Arab nationalism. Today, the concept remains a significant cultural matrix but its impact on the Arab polity has diminished.
2. The second is the creation of nation-states in the areas vacated by the erstwhile colonial powers. The systems of governance in these nation-states have varied between kingdoms, emirates, sultanates and republics. The ruling regimes of some states had access to

unforeseen riches from hydrocarbon resources. The colonial masters left behind border problems and other disputes. Ruling regimes found it convenient to obtain allegiance by emphasising the interests of their nation-state over that of the Arab nation.

3. The third is Islam. In the initial stages, religious revival was sought to be fused with anti-imperialism and modern grass-roots political activism. The energies of this activism were later directed against the ruling regimes. In some cases, Islamist movements came to power, in others they were thwarted from taking power. What is undeniable is that Islamism retains significant political space in West Asia–co-opted in some regimes and hounded in others.

Political evolution, propelled by these three factors, was aided by vast changes taking place in Arab societies. Rapid urbanisation set the scene for mass indoctrination; Arab nationalism filled the lacunae until its demise in the wake of the 1967 War. Islamism readily provided a substitute. Its inherent anti-communism was looked upon with favour by the concerned Western powers. The point was proved at the time of the Soviet invasion of Afghanistan. The slogan of Jihad in terms of armed resistance was promoted by the states of the region (with some exceptions) and actively endorsed by the western powers.

To these various factors must be added the security threats, including terrorism, emanating from non-state actors in West Asia–a direct product of the political impasse mentioned above. A simplistic analysis of these is rarely rewarding. Domestic, regional, external and ideological factors combine to produce chemical reactions of varying intensity. In traditional societies sustained by a mix of religious and tribal norms, neo-patriarchy and non-participatory governance cause resentments that are subdued partially and for varying periods of time by largesse. Rapid inflow of wealth, on the other hand, brings in its wake social disruptions and awakened expectations.

Social systems also produce their anti-bodies. The youth who spent time in Afghanistan returned home Islamised and radicalised. They sought correctives from local rulers and their external friends. They found solace in traditional, religious, idiom. The rest of the story, in Algeria, Tunisia,

Egypt, and eventually in Jordan and Saudi Arabia is too well known to bear repetition. Iraq added its share in ample measure.

Islamism is an ideology of protest, and of change. Apart from slogans, it has little by way of a programme of social reconstruction. Suppression without other correctives, however, gives it a lease of life.

V

It is time to wind up. Diagnosis and commentary on the first and the second questions inevitably propel us towards the third. The correctives are suggested by the diagnosis itself.

The question is of the will to undertake it. Simple logic, however, is not synonymous with state logic!

Third International Congress of the Asian Political and International Studies Association

Academic Research Centre, University of Delhi, Delhi
23 November 2007

I confess I did not understand until quite recently the import of the adage 'accept in haste, repent at leisure'. The point was driven home to me when, some weeks after having accepted the invitation, I started thinking about the implications of the commitment and was gripped with trepidation at the prospect of standing before an audience of distinguished political scientists to expose the inadequacy of my thought process on so weighty a subject.

Having unburdened my conscience, let me thank the organisers of the 3rd Congress of APISA (Asian Political and International Studies Association) for conferring on me the privilege of inaugurating your conference. I am happy to do so, confident in the knowledge that your deliberations would clarify and amplify concepts and further understanding on a subject of crucial relevance to social well being.

I notice that since its inception, your Association has structured its work on the specific theme of Asia in the New Millennium. This makes sense since yours is an ASIAN association and rightly retains the focus on Asia, more so because the misfortunes of Asian history for a few centuries not only subjected it to colonial and neo-colonial domination but also ensured intellectual subordination by making the world Euro-centric. Terms like the Near East, Middle East and Far East entered the political vocabulary and Orientalism became an intellectual industry.

The focus on Asia has helped APISA explore specific areas of the Asian experience. The 1st Congress dwelt on development, democracy and security. The 2nd Congress focused on aspects of governance. The theme of this 3rd Congress is Asian concepts of justice.

I am, I confess, enthused by the theme and intrigued by it. The concept of justice is integral to social well being; for this reason, it must be reiterated on every possible opportunity. It is also in the category of universal values, rather than location-specific. Talk of an Asian concept may, therefore, convey an impression that there is something specific by way of a value addition or value subtraction. This, presumably, is not intended.

The primacy of Asia in terms of religious or ethical traditions is a matter of recorded history. Virtually all the world religions–Hinduism, Judaism, Zoroastrianism, Confucianism, Buddhism, Christianity, Shinto, Jainism, Islam and Sikhism–emanated in Asian lands. Each has an ethical system and thus an approach to the concept of justice. Even if we take Toynbee's categorisation of twenty one societies for his comparative study of civilisations, we find a majority of them emerging from Asia.

Let us take a closer look into the subject matter. The human being is a social animal. Living in society necessitates social arrangements that determine the division of responsibilities and ascribe rights and duties. Such an allocation is made on a basis that is broadly acceptable; this is considered the principle of social justice. In ancient Greece, Plato set out to enquire into the nature of justice and injustice and found justice to be the bond that holds society together. Aristotle amplified it in a statement of universal validity: "justice is the bond of men in states, and the administration of justice, which is the determination of what is just, is the principle of order in political society". Devoting a whole section of Nicomachean Ethics to it, he defined just behaviour as "a mean between doing injustice and suffering it".

The critical question for Aristotle, and for every society in history, was the determination of what is considered just–its median and its extremities. Plato concluded that justice is a public and private virtue, "best for the soul" irrespective of the rewards that may accrue "both in life and after death".

The quest for the nature of justice, however, was much older. The Indic world considered justice as synonymous with righteousness. In *Mahabharata* the sage Vamadeva stresses the need to act righteously: "There is nothing superior to righteousness. Those kings that are observant of righteousness succeed ... That king who disregards righteousness and desires to act with brute force, soon falls away from righteousness and loses both Righteousness and Profit". In practical statecraft, Kautilya, in the second century AD, could prescribe dispensation of justice as the duty of the King, adding that this was to be undertaken on the basis of Dharma, Evidence, Custom, and Royal Edicts. In this framework, ethical value is attached to Dharma which is based on truth; its observance, said Kautilya, leads to eternal bliss and its transgression to chaos.

Instances of considering justice as a religio-ethical notion, elsewhere in Asia and in different epochs, can be multiplied. The Muslim approach, for instance, was no different. The Qur'anic injunction "judge with justice" led to the conclusion that injustice is transgression. It is the counterweight to arrogance. Justice, said a medieval jurist, is the maintenance of the mean or of the just middle. It introduces, in Aziz Al-Azmeh's words, the notion of normative equity "not of equality or equivalence but of optimal proportionality among the unequal and uneven components of a composite".

II

Inherited tradition is one thing, albeit relevant and important. In the context of the contemporary world, however, it confronts three questions:

- To what extent has it been transmitted to modern societies in Asia and translated into state practice in a secular paradigm?
- How far does it conform to the global norms that have emerged in our times?
- To what extent have the new global norms been imbibed in Asian societies?

On a theoretical plane, and given the differences over the ultimate nature of good and bad in politics, a rational and practical basis for what is just needed to be worked out. The position was stated by the philosopher John Rawls:

"The unity of society and the allegiance of its citizens to their common institutions rest not on their espousing one rational conception of the good, but on an agreement as to what is just for free and equal moral persons with different and opposing conceptions of the good".

Dwelling on the role of justice in social cooperation, Rawls argued that "justice is the first virtue of social institutions" that take "the liberties of equal citizenship as settled"; as a result, "the rights secured by justice are not subject to political bargaining or to the calculus of social interests".

The modern concept of justice received international recognition in the Universal Declaration of Human Rights of 1948. It proclaimed "a common standard of achievement for all peoples and all nations", asserted equality before the law and equal protection of the law. These were amplified in the International Covenant on Civil and Political Rights and other international documents.

Any analysis of contemporary Asia, devoid of its modern history, would be partial and inadequate. The year 1498 marked the coming of the Portuguese. An Asian awareness of that seminal event was slow in coming. The new comer, however, realised it comprehensively and formalised it by an addition to the titles of the King of Portugal: "Lords of the Conquest, Navigation and Commerce, of India, Ethiopia, Arabia and Persia". Other conquerors followed and had different patterns of influence. All had a profound impact on the inner structures of Asian societies and upset the equilibrium of pre-modern institutions. Assessing the longer term impact of European imperialism, the historian K.M. Panikkar concluded that "the first and perhaps the most abiding influence is in the sphere of law. In all Asian countries the legal systems have been fundamentally changed and reorganised". This process involved a re-look at the principles of governance and a re-arrangement of institutional arrangements to give shape to them.

The most visible evidence of this was in India. In a book published in 1951 Sir Earnest Barker reproduced on its first page the Preamble of the Constitution of India and explained his reasons for doing so. "I am proud", he wrote, "that the people of India begin their independent life by subscribing to the principles of a political tradition which we in the West call Western, but which is now more than Western".

The ambit of the Preamble is comprehensive and interlinked. It is reflective of the sovereign will of a people to acquire for themselves the virtues in totality of justice, liberty, equality and fraternity. The operative line, for our argument today, is the commitment to secure to all its citizens

Justice, social, economic and political. This expression has been the subject of commentary and judicial interpretations. One knowledgeable commentator expressed it succinctly:

"The expression 'social and economic justice' involves the concept of 'distributive justice' which connotes the removal of economic inequalities and rectifying the injustice resulting from dealings and transactions between unequals in society... the ideal of economic justice is to make equality of status meaningful and life worth living removing inequality of opportunity and of status – social, economic and political".

He argues that the doctrine of equality embodied in Arts. 14 to 18 of Part III (Fundamental Rights) is to be understood in the light of social justice assured by the relevant Articles of Part IV of the Constitution. On this basis, therefore, social justice is a fundamental right.

It can be said, with some justice, that six decades of Independent India have been a journey to actualise the concept of social justice visualised in the Constitution. In the process, content has been added and the concept amplified. The debate is premised on contemporary, secular, norms of inclusive justice and does not seek sustenance from traditional concepts rooted in religion or tradition. While much has been done, the task as yet remains unfinished.

III

So much for the 'Plural Conception of Justice' and 'Social Justice'. But what about the issue of Transnational Justice–the third theme of this Congress. Because of associations rooted in history and culture, reinforced by the shared experience of colonial domination, the thought of an Asian dimension to the nationalist awareness of emerging India was not a strange one. An expression of it was the Asian Relations Conference of March-April 1947. A sense of Asian-ness emerged in India and, possibly, in other Asian lands. In 1997, the golden jubilee of that historic gathering was celebrated by convening another conference. At the end of it the delegates felt that "unless there is political and social understanding, economic cooperation is difficult to achieve and, for the attainment of the objectives of freedom, equality and justice a new international system characterised by an absence of want, fear and all forms of intolerance and based on peace, justice, equality and respect for freedom of all is essential".

The association of expressions 'freedom', 'equality' and 'justice' with the quest for a new international system is indicative both of a lacunae and of a desire to fill it in terms of the international system. Does this suggest an acceptance of universal norms in these matters? If so, has the theoretical framework for it been put into place? How far have individual Asian societies moved on the road to implementation of these norms. There are many in this audience who are in a position to answer these questions in generic and specific terms.

There is one other aspect of the matter. In Asia, there is a justifiable frustration about selective application of the existing modes of transnational justice. The provisions for robust international intervention in conflict situations in Asia are unevenly applied. In today's age of globalisation, domestic conceptions of justice as applied in democracies of the West must find application in the larger international arena. There can be no apartheid in the application of justice.

The matter goes beyond the realm of political theory. For several centuries, the history of the world was also the history of the suppression and domination of Asian lands. The termination of that process, in the middle of the 20th century, was the first step in the correction of that historical distortion; much more, however, needs to be done to prepare Asian lands to take their rightful place in the comity of nations and contribute in full measure to the development of a world that eschews the doctrines of dominance and, instead, tries to live by principles of cooperation. Economics is one aspect of the matter: Asia's share of global trade climbed from 16 per cent in 1980 to 27 per cent in 2003 and economists predict that Asia would provide the growth engine to world trade. They also opine that this would necessitate greater importance being given to corporate governance.

However, can good governance be selective and confined to sectors of human activity? Also, can governance be good without conceptual clarity about what is good? Is it possible, over a longer term, to govern the business sector on norms of fair play and mutual advantage while denying it to all segments of society that contribute to economic activity?

Whichever we look at it, selective good and selective justice is a recipe for trouble. A conceptual framework for justice, therefore, has practical implications and can only be viable if it is inclusive–at the societal, national and international levels. Asian societies, drawing upon their extensive heritage, undoubtedly would come to this conclusion and conceptualise it appropriately.

Inauguration of the Dr D.D. Kosambi Festival of Ideas
Goa
4 February 2008

THE IMPERATIVE OF WORLD PEACE

It is a pleasure to be in the salubrious surroundings of Goa. The encyclopaedic personality of Damodar Dharmanand Kosambi endeared him to scholars beyond the fields of mathematics and numismatics. Amongst them was the historian A.L. Basham, author of *The Wonder that was India*, who became a lifelong friend. On Kosambi's death, Basham wrote a personal tribute and said his initial impression was that his friend had only three interests in life–ancient India, mathematics and preservation of peace; for all of them, he added, "he worked hard and with devotion, according to his deep convictions". This was also the view of President V.V. Giri who chaired the Kosambi Commemoration Committee and wrote a foreword to a commemoration volume of essays published in 1974.

Kosambi was an active fighter for peace and, in the hay days of the Cold War, spent time analysing the causes that prevented peace. He held the view that peace was a prerequisite for development and that true peace required 'true democracy' where all men are truly equal and no one claims any superiority. His focus was on peace in the global community. There is little evidence to suggest that peaceful resolution of conflicts within societies was amongst his priorities. His thought process was driven by his ideological orientation; that, in fairness, would deserve a separate discourse.

My quest today would be to explore the passion for peace, and its relevance to the world in our own times.

II

We are confronted with a contradiction of serious dimensions. A look at human history makes evident the role of violence. At the same time the passion for peace is a perennial in human history. The philosopher Lao Tzu summed up its pre-requisites in the 5th century BC:

> If there is to be peace in the world,
> There must be peace in the nations.
> If there is to be peace in the nations,
> There must be peace in the cities.
> If there is to be peace in the cities,
> There must be peace between neighbours.
> If there is to be peace between neighbours,
> There must be peace at home.
> If there is to be peace at home,
> There must be peace in the heart.

The impulse was the same elsewhere, in another age. The medieval Italian scholar Marsilius of Padua commenced Defensor Pacis with a quotation, on the meaning of peace, from the sixth century Roman statesman Flavius Cassiodorus:

'Tranquillity, wherein peoples prosper and the welfare of nations is preserved, must certainly be the desire of every state. For it is the noble mother of the good arts. Permitting the steady increase of the race of mortals, it extends their power and enhances their customs. And he who is perceived not to have sought for it is recognised to be ignorant of such important concerns'.

Marsilius concluded that 'we ought to wish for peace, to seek it if we do not already have it, to conserve it once it is attained, to repel with all our strength the strife which is opposed to it'.

The quest for peace, as a human trait, is not synonymous with peace amongst human groups. The latter is characterised by conflict and the resultant need, through force or compact, to enforce order. The need for a final authority was felt in all groupings; the sanction for it was at times human, at others attributed to an extra-human impulse. Sovereignty in this form existed before it was conceptualised.

While peace among members of a group–society or state–was sought to be achieved through a compact or a final authority, harmony between groups or states was perceived to be a qualitatively different exercise. Domination was one form of achieving it; hence the expressions Pax Romana, Pax Britanica etc. that crept into political vocabulary. This was not found to be perpetual or all embracing. Hence the need for conflict management or resolution through rules of behaviour that came to be known as international law of peace and war.

A methodology for conflict resolution is to be found in all societies. Kautilya refers to six methods of seeking conciliation. In modern times, the conceptual and the practical endeavour to seek peace between nations took shape in post Renaissance Europe. Publicists like Grotius pioneered it; theoretical depth was added by philosophers like Immanuel Kant in his tract on Perpetual Peace wherein he argued that peace must be established through conscious effort based on a mutuality of interest. The Kantian perception of this interest is worth recalling:

'The spirit of commerce, which is incompatible with war, sooner or later gains the upper hand. As the power of money is perhaps the most dependable of all powers included under the state, states see themselves forced, without any moral courage, to promote honourable peace and by mediation to prevent war wherever it threatens to break out'.

Kant was ahead of his times in considering commerce as a promoter of peace. The dominant impulse in the eighteenth and nineteenth centuries was promotion of commerce through domination and war. The other viewpoint, nevertheless, had its votaries. In 1909, Sir Norman Angell published The Great Illusion wherein he argued that modern commerce made war necessarily unprofitable, even for the technically victorious country; success in war, he added, was an illusion.

Serious thinking on the futility of war, however, had to await the experience and bloodletting of World Wars I and II. In August 1945 Prime Minister Atlee committed Britain to utilise atomic energy 'not for our own ends but as trustees for humanity in the interest of all people in order to promote peace and justice in the world'. President Truman did likewise. The Preamble of the UN Charter begins by expressing a determination 'to save succeeding generations from the scourge of war'. Removal of threats to peace thus became a primary purpose of the United Nations. Five decades later only partial success can be attributed to it and war, defined as organised violence between states, is still considered an instrument of policy to achieve objectives.

In a seminal study published in 1987, the historian Paul Kennedy surveyed the interaction between economics and strategy to study the manner in which great powers in modern history grappled with economic growth, technological innovations, the spiraling cost of weapons, and changes in the international scene and power equations. He concluded that:

"Whatever the likelihood of nuclear or conventional clashes between the major states, it is clear that important transformations in the balances are occurring, and will continue to occur, probably at a faster pace than before. What is more, they are occurring at the two separate but interacting levels of economic production and strategic power …

"The present large powers in the international system are thus compelled to grapple with the twin challenges that have confronted all their predecessors: first with the uneven pattern of economic growth, which causes some of them to become wealthier (and, usually, stronger), relative to others; and second, with the competitive and occasionally dangerous scene abroad, which forces them to choose between a more immediate military security and a longer-term economic security".

In such a context, the effort necessarily remains confined to the management of global insecurity. Boutros Ghali's Agenda for Peace was structured on that premise. Much work has been done in the past decade and a half to develop the framework for peace keeping, peace building, and conflict prevention. The approach, however, is riveted on prevention rather than cure.

In 1988 Prime Minister Rajiv Gandhi told the United Nations that "in consequence of doctrines of deterrence, international relations have been gravely militarized" and that "peace which rests on the search for a parity of power is a precarious peace". He proposed a time-bound Action Programme for a Nuclear-Free World and the initiation of negotiations to establish a Comprehensive Global Security System under the aegis of the United Nations.

After having ignored this and other suggestions for nuclear disarmament, an initiative has recently been taken by some establishment personalities in the United States. Concerned over nuclear weapons "falling into dangerous hands", they have "called for a global effort to reduce reliance on nuclear weapons, to prevent their spread into potentially dangerous hands, and ultimately to end them as a threat to the world". A world without nuclear weapons requires "the necessary political will to build an international consensus on priorities". This, they concede, cannot be done "without the vision of moving towards zero, we will not find the essential cooperation required to stop our downward spiral". These views were most recently articulated in an op-ed in *The Wall Street Journal* on 18 January this year.

III

The strategic paradigm, as hitherto understood, offers no escape from the possibility of states resorting to war. This necessitates a qualitatively different approach if perpetual peace is to be made a human objective.

A new framework for world peace must begin with conceptual clarity about the meaning of words in our vocabulary. Can peace be defined as absence of conflict? If so, it could be no more than a tactical happening of a transitory nature involving no value judgment or commitment to such a judgement. A study of the semantic history of the term itself is revealing. The impression of contention, hostility, conflict (armed or unarmed) is ever present; so is its acceptability in a certain sense. A cynical observation by Oscar Wilde is perhaps an apt reflection on human perceptions: "As long as war is regarded as wicked, it will always have its fascination. When it is looked upon as vulgar, it will cease to be popular".

Early in the twentieth century the philosopher William James had recognised the obstacles confronting a pacifist approach. "The war against war", he wrote in 1906, "is going to be no holiday or camping party. The military feelings are too deeply grounded to abdicate their place among our ideals until better substitutes are offered than the glory and shame that come to nations as well as to individuals from the ups and downs of politics and the vicissitudes of trade".

A century later Robert Fisk has referred to the same problem in his monumental work *The Great War for Civilisation*:

"Governments like it that way. They want their people to see war as a drama of opposites, good and evil, 'them' and 'us', victory or defeat. But war is primarily not about victory or defeat but about death and the infliction of death. It represents the total failure of the human spirit."

The truth is that, in the realm of world politics, the avoidance of war is perceived, as Hedley Bull put it, "as a goal subordinate to that of the preservation of the state system itself ... and as subordinate also to the preservation of the sovereignty or independence of individual states ... the subordinate status of peace in relation to these other goals is reflected in the phrase 'peace and security' which occurs in the United Nations Charter".

So how do we go about demonstrating the vulgarity of war and war-like activities, erasing the association of ideas that lend it credibility, and exposing its implications for humanity? Can a war be waged against war? The challenge is a formidable one.

In order to develop a rational approach, it is essential to consider the matter from four perspectives:

- The impracticality of war in the nuclear age;
- The inefficacy of power politics;
- The emergence of new imperatives for conflicts, and their implications;
- The unavoidability of inducting a sense of justice in the conduct of relations between individuals, groups and nations.

War in the nuclear age has become inconceivable. Its implications were spelt out, among others, by George Kennan in The Nuclear Delusion published in 1982. The impulse to acquire nuclear weapons, as a currency of power, is nevertheless pervasive and, as with all new technologies, becoming easier by the day. According to Dr Mohamad El Baradai of IAEA (International Atomic Energy Agency), "soon there could be 30 virtual nuclear weapon states on the horizon". The only rational option, therefore, is to move for universal, comprehensive, nuclear disarmament through international agreements of the type already concluded with regard to biological weapons

(1972) and chemical weapons (1997). In such a scheme of things, there can be no exceptions.

Power politics and the quest for dominance, hegemony or primacy would inevitably be a recipe for instability that, in the global system, cannot but induce states to resort to arms. Patterns of these may wary; the National Intelligence Council of the United States has assessed that "the likelihood of great power conflict escalating into total war in the next fifteen years is lower than at any time in the past century, unlike during previous centuries when local conflicts sparked world wars". Local or regional wars would nevertheless continue to erupt. Every such conflict would be disruptive of development and enhance human misery. A new mechanism for conflict prevention is thus essential.

A new, and hitherto unexplored area for future conflicts resides in the imperatives of the current and future competition for resources, of climate change and of wider environmental questions. Economic historian Angus Matterson has noted that humanity's average real income per head has risen 10-fold since 1820. The increases however have been widely divergent. Technology and resource availability have been critical to the effort. At the same time, an emerging contradiction is also becoming evident. Technology continues to improve but declining availability of resources is generating fear, and responses bordering on panic.

The UNEP's (United Nations Environment Programme) Global Environment Outlook published in October 2007 pointed out that 'we are living beyond our means' and need to consider environment, development and energy crises as one rather than separate issues. It stressed that while governments are expected to take the lead, other stake holders are just as important to ensure success in achieving in sustainable development: 'Our common future depends on our action today, not tomorrow or sometime in the future'.

The conclusion of the UNEP report shifts the focus from the state to the public: 'while governments are expected to take the lead, other stake holders are just as important to ensure success in achieving sustainable development. The need couldn't be more urgent and the time couldn't be more opportune, with our enhanced understanding of the challenges we face, to act now to safeguard our own survival and that of future generations'.

IV

The picture that emerges can be summed up in a set of eight prepositions:

- The new paradigm of human existence has to be premised on comprehensive security, covering both conventional and non-conventional security.
- Experience indicates that competitive security results in confrontation and conflict.
- The prospect, and intensity, of conflicts can be controlled and lessened through a globally applicable scheme of disarmament beginning with nuclear disarmament.
- The alternative is cooperative security premised on accommodation of competing requirements.
- Such accommodation would require a point of reference, a principle that can help reconcile differences and disagreements and impede their aggravation.
- Such a principle can only be based on the concept of justice which enables us to choose between different possible arrangements that determine the division of advantages on an equitable basis, and assign rights and duties. 'When justice is destroyed', said Manu, 'it destroys; when justice is protected, it protects'.
- A global society based on justice has no place for war since both greed and aggression would be curtailed by its operative principle.
- The actualisation of such an objective cannot be left solely to state action and must involve active participation of 'other stake holders' in the civil society

There would be many who would consider such an approach utopian and impractical and would contrast it with the realistic and practical. The answer would lie in working out the implications of such 'realism'–namely, a steady march by humankind towards self-destruction. In other words, peace must be demonstrated to be good in value terms as also in practical term since war can be demonstrated to be genuinely harmful.

In the final analysis, then, we see merit in Kosambi's vision that peace was a pre-requisite for development and that true peace required true democracy where all human beings are equal.

The struggle for world peace must therefore be a quest for equality, justice and democracy. The modalities of furthering it would inevitably be conditioned by public awareness and public action.

The Indian Ocean Naval Symposium Seminar 2008
Vigyan Bhavan, New Delhi
15 February 2008

Once upon a time the commander-in-chief of a rising land power, unfamiliar with seafaring and uneasy about it, asked one of his field commanders to describe the sea and seafarers to him. The officer dutifully reported:

"Verily I have seen a great creature [that is, the sea] ridden by a small one [that is, man]. When it is calm it renders the heart with anxiety, and if it is agitated it leads the mind into confusion. On it certainty shrinks and doubt increases. Those who are on it are like a worm on a twig; if it bends he is drowned, and if he is saved he is astounded".

In another region of the world, in the island of Bali, the traditional belief considered the sea to be full of demons; hence to be approached with care if not avoided.

In both cases, perhaps, the immenseness of the body of water and the mysteries in its depths acted as a deterrent.

These examples can be multiplied. History is witness to great land powers failing to comprehend the relevance of the sea as an instrument of statecraft. The historian Paul Kennedy attributes the rise of European powers, sixteenth century onwards, to 'technological change and military competitiveness'; he may have added, with equal justice, that seafaring was an equally relevant ingredient of promoting trade, competing with rivals, and eventually overcoming them.

The fact nevertheless remains that for a good percentage of humankind, the sea is not in the same category of familiarity as the land. This may be no more than an accident of natural history and the manner in which humans assumed a centrality on this planet. On the other hand, certain facts relating to this planet of ours may suggest correctives to such a slanted approach.

Earth is a planet of oceans. They constitute 71 per cent of its total area. In a very real sense, they sustain life on earth. Cheap transportation is possible through them. They are in increasing measure a source of food, energy and minerals.

The Indian Ocean is the third largest ocean in terms of area but unquestionably the first in terms of its impact on human civilisation. The reason for this is obvious; some of the oldest civilisations took shape and blossomed in lands around the Indian Ocean or the seas adjacent to it. They interacted with each other principally through trade. For this reason alone, a gathering of people from Indian Ocean lands would provide a useful collection of perspectives.

II

Today's conference, I believe, goes beyond an exercise in history and ethnology. Its timing and purpose are sharply focused on the world of today and tomorrow. A look at recent history provides the perspective.

The Portuguese discovery of the sea route to India was of such critical importance that the King of Portugal thought it fit to reflect it in his formal titles. Its wording is to be noted: 'Lord of Conquest, Navigation and Commerce, of Ethiopia, Arabia, India and Persia'. Their hegemony lasted for two centuries, to be replaced by the British who followed the pattern and the new jewel in the Crown justified the additional title of Empress of India.

The end of the British era saw the enhancement of the role of the United States. Alongside, the Cold War witnessed superpower rivalry extended itself in the Indian Ocean littoral. In each of these, the external impulse remained the dominant one. The littoral states themselves had little or no input into it.

Whatever be the past, the imperative today is of a qualitatively different situation in the Indian Ocean littoral. The external impulses have in good measure given way to internal dynamics of individual societies. This, however, is not easily comprehended and older patterns of thinking persist.

A few years back a scholar in Honolulu delved in futurology pertaining to the Indian Ocean:

'We do not yet understand the political geography of the twenty-first century. However, no region is likely to feature as prominently in that geography as the Indian Ocean due to its combination of oil, Islam and the likely rise–and probable mutual rivalry of both India and China. Indian Ocean regionalism, or regional integration, remains quite retarded when perceived through an economic lens. Sadly, however, it is the converse conclusion that seems warranted when the region is perceived through the prism of geopolitics and nuclear weapons'.

This prognosis, and many other similar ones, is premised partly on the location specifics of the Indian Ocean and partly on the known behaviour pattern of states. It is argued, with regard to the first, that unlike the Atlantic and the Pacific Oceans, the Indian Ocean can be accessed through several choke points and thus necessitates intense policing. With regard to the second, it is asserted that only one-fifth of the total trade flowing through the Ocean is conducted among the countries of the IOR (International Offshore Rule), that 80 per cent of it is extra-regional, and that local conflicts in the Indian Ocean littoral have the potential to acquire international dimensions in view of the need to safeguard the Sea Lines of Communication (SLOC). These are augmented by actual and potential threats, of varying intensity, from non-state actors. In addition, most of the contemporary international conflicts from Iran-Iraq war, to Operation Enduring Freedom and Operation Iraqi Freedom have taken place in the Indian Ocean Region.

There is merit in both sets of arguments. The quest for security of SLOCs is most vividly demonstrated in the case of Japan where, as shown by Euan Graham in an excellent study published in 2006, it has been the lifeline of the economy and seen as the core security concern. Given the nature of the trade passing through the Indian Ocean, the logic holds good for a great many other regional and extra-regional states.

In this globalised world of today, 95 per cent of world trade is conducted through the sea. Around 100,000 ships transit the expanse of the Indian Ocean annually. Roughly 40 per cent of this sea-borne trade is accounted for by the Straits of Malacca. The Persian Gulf and adjoining region accounts for 50 per cent of the world's containerised cargo and 33 per cent of bulk cargo. Every day 15.5 million barrels of oil, or 40 per cent of the entire global oil trade passes through the Straits of Hormuz and 11 million barrels of oil pass through the Malacca and Singapore Straits.

At the same time, the argument of securing maritime traffic or lessening the vulnerability of sea-lanes has also been used as a rationale to build up naval capabilities and thus give rise to questions about intentions.

The SLOC argument, valid in itself, is nevertheless reflective of partial reality. The ocean is admittedly a channel of communication; it is also a resource both for basic forms of existence and for sustaining advanced forms of civilisation. It supports life on earth, regulates temperatures, humidity, rainfall and seasons. It can and does generate catastrophic convulsions affecting the human race.

Any discussion of the ocean therefore, must be multi-dimensional and reflective of four aspects:

- The security paradigm
- Disaster management
- Oceanic resources
- Environmental questions.

Solutions, likewise, would need to be comprehensive and balanced rather than slanted in favour of one aspect, however weighty.

III

Throughout recorded history, maritime security has been the prime concern of states and of their nationals undertaking international trade. In an earlier era, piracy by entrepreneurs for themselves or on behalf of states was common. Then came a time when the balance of advantage was found to lie in the suppression of piracy. The same pattern was followed in regard to slave trade. Economic interests and prevailing moral norms played and continue to play a role in shaping perceptions as is evident by the present-day measures against narcotics. Some would no doubt recall that in another age a great European power used its military superiority to dump opium on an Asian people in order to correct trade imbalance.

In the past, initiatives for maritime security generally emanated from a strong power driven principally by express or tacit hegemonic perceptions. They received cooperation at times and aroused apprehensions at others.

In conceptual terms, the requirement of maritime security is of necessity linked to threat perception. In the period of the Cold War, security perceptions were based on identified threats and on the need to contain them. The approach, therefore, was cooperative amongst allies and competitive in relation to perceived enemies. In the period after 1990, the focus shifted and attention came to be riveted on questions of common concern. The expectation was that a more comprehensive cooperative approach, on a non-discriminatory basis, would gradually take shape. It would not dispense with the traditional paradigm of requiring naval power to defend territory or essential national interests but would, instead, add a dimension that would minimise if not eliminate the need to resort to the use of force.

In practical terms, maritime security is to be considered at three levels:

- Measures to create transparency–these include advance notice of exercises and of ship movements.
- Measures to build confidence–these could be undertaken through joint exercises, training, joint naval hydrographic operations, joint task forces for policing and agreement on avoidance of incidents at high sea.
- Measures to build security–regular gatherings of littoral states, user states and other stakeholders to discuss matters of concern and undertaking initiatives to establish regional maritime security mechanisms.

This gathering, I venture to hope, is indicative of a broad acceptance of the need to take these three sets of measures to further maritime security in the Indian Ocean Region. Overtime, these may lead to what a distinguished Indian had described many years back as an "Indian Ocean Panchayat, a self-governing council or collective Ombudsman empowered to take decisions on behalf of the community, settle disputes, and suggest ways to prevent disputes."

The voyage even to this point has not been eventless. The recent effort at pursuing security at choke points in the Indian Ocean was highly selective and predominantly extra-regional. It emanated from the Global War on Terror (GWOT) and the Iraq War, and is focused on the western Indian Ocean, the Persian Gulf, Gulf of Aden, Red Sea, Gulf of Oman and the Arabian Sea and extends out to Pakistan's border with India. It functions through a Coalition Task Force known as CTF 150 and includes ships principally from the navies of the United States, UK, Australia, Germany, Italy and France. Its three non-NATO members are Australia, New Zealand and Pakistan. The Task Force is mandated to prevent terrorist attacks on maritime targets, and disruption of shipment of arms and material to terrorists in Persian Gulf and thereby secure the ocean for use by 'legitimate mariners'. It is currently led by the Pakistani Navy.

An initiative aimed at the eastern choke point was taken in August 2005 when the governments of Indonesia, Malaysia and Singapore convened a meeting at Batam for creating a forum for the purpose of making a framework of cooperation to enhance the safety of navigation, environmental protection and security in the Straits of Malacca and Singapore while respecting the sovereignty and sovereign rights of littoral states. In September 2006 the three states convened a larger meeting under the International Maritime Organisation's Protection of Vital Shipping Lanes Initiative. It was attended by thirty-four countries included eleven Indian Ocean littoral states.

Also in September 2006, the Regional Cooperation Agreement on Combating Piracy and Armed Robbery Against Ships in Asia came into force involving ASEAN (Association of Southeast Asian Nations), Japan, China, South Korea, India, Bangladesh and Sri Lanka. Subsequent meetings have reinforced the need for cooperation between the littoral states, user states and users of the Straits of Malacca and Singapore. A cooperative mechanism has also been established.

The difference between the two approaches, in respect to the western and the eastern choke points respectively, is significant. The former primarily involves the extra-regional powers and gives the impression of being hegemonic; the latter primarily involves the littoral and user states and is focussed on cooperation. This gathering would, undoubtedly, make its own judgements.

IV

Security against anticipated threats is one aspect of the matter. In human terms, situations created by natural disasters and accidents are equally relevant. Tsunamis and cyclones take a heavy toll every year. 70 per cent of the world's natural disasters take place in the Indian Ocean region. Environmental disasters, oil spills etc hold the potential for large-scale damage. These happenings do not respect national boundaries. The response, accordingly, has to go beyond national efforts to be meaningful. A very good example of international cooperation is the effort mounted after the December 2004 tsunami. The Indian Navy undertook a commendable operation on that occasion. More recently, the Indian Navy provided help and succour to the victims of the earthquake in Indonesia.

The innate sense of curiosity of the human mind, and the progress of science, has opened the doors on the mysteries of the sea. These, when unravelled, indicate the immensity of resources that the oceans possess. These can be accessed rationally or irrationally. Our generation has not been slow to learn lessons from the past. Hence the comprehensive effort that resulted in the UN Convention on the Law of the Sea and the subsequent agreement to create the International Seabed Authority charged with the responsibility to organise and control all mineral-related activities in the international seabed beyond the limits of national jurisdiction.

The exercise of regulating the exploitation of the common heritage of mankind has some teething problems that, hopefully, would be overcome. While exploratory ventures have been made, the consensus at this stage is that technology for economic mining of the ocean depths is probably a decade away. This interval is a blessing; deep-sea ecosystems are the main reservoirs of global biodiversity and the scientific and legal framework for protecting them and minimising the potential environmental impact of such mining is yet to be put in place.

V

Given the diversity of ocean-related activities of humankind, the responsibility of undertaking them is shouldered by various segments of society. Each of these requires an atmosphere of peace and stability. The maintenance of peace is a politico-military exercise necessitating intelligent use of available resources to achieve desired ends. The challenge always is to ensure that contention and cooperation are in harmony. The totality of objectives sought to be achieved in the Indian Ocean region by the littoral, hinterland and user states can only be achieved through a methodology of cooperation.

It has been said, with justice, that the narrative of conflict, as advanced by belligerents, is always one of grievance. The causes, conditions and consequences of conflict almost invariably relate to economic, social and environmental factors. Each of these is better addressed by common endeavour.

The Indian Ocean Region is among the fastest growing regions of the world. The existing structure of cooperation in this broad region is primarily based around five groupings, namely ASEAN, GCC (Gulf Cooperation Council), SAARC, SADC (Southern African Development Community) and SCO (Shanghai Cooperation Organisation). These are not formally linked to each other; their overlapping and overarching framework is an implicit recognition of each other's sensitivities and concerns. It is also reflective of the tenuous equilibrium of the region. An earlier effort, to create an Indian Ocean Rim grouping, did not produce the desired results.

Within the region, and around it, are important political and economic powers that have a stake in peace, stability and progress. They could form the nucleus of an eventual Asian Economic Community.

India is and will remain a maritime nation. In keeping with its maritime heritage, its overseas presence would be based on its soft power and cooperation.

- With 7516 km long coastline, twenty-seven islands of the Lakshadweep chain and 572 islands of the Andaman and Nicobar chain, thirteen major and 185 minor ports and a merchant shipping fleet of over 750 ships, the security imperatives are compelling.

- Disaster management in a multilateral framework of cooperation for speedy and effective relief operations is an important element of our maritime approach.
- India is a UN-recognised pioneer investor in deep-sea mining and has been allotted a mining area of 150,000 sq. kms in the central Indian Ocean. In addition, the EEZ (Exclusive Economic Zone) of India is set to increase to 2.54 million sq. km. Furthermore, around 20 per cent of our overall petroleum demand is met by offshore production.
- Environmental issues are now global themes and India has a vital stake in the approaches towards management of global environmental issues.
- By disposition, and by inherent capacities, India is well placed to be part of bilateral and non-discriminatory and inclusive regional and multilateral arrangements for maritime security, in consonance with international law and respecting the sovereignty of littoral states.

The evolution of perceptions takes time. The key to the future, in the words of Prime Minister Manmohan Singh, is the development of new synergies. This needs to be a comprehensive endeavour. A convergence of interests in the maintenance of peace and in the creation of a co-prosperity area would greatly facilitate the effort. This gathering of the Chiefs of Navies of the Indian Ocean region attends to one aspect of the matter.

The Inauguration of the Seminar on 'India and the Gulf'
Association of Indian Diplomats, India International Centre, Delhi
23 February 2008

India and 'the Gulf'

I am delighted to be here today, amidst friends, and to talk about a subject that, by accident rather than design, became a lifelong pursuit.

Confusion about nomenclature is avoidable. The correct name of this body of water is the Persian Gulf (PG). This is recognised by the United Nations, the US Department of State, and by historical maps of the region. This confusion about name is reflected in practical usage; at times we are exclusive and make 'the Gulf' synonymous with the GCC, and at others we include all the littoral states in the term.

The Persian Gulf, and its littoral states, has been described as India's 'proximate neighbourhood'. Our task then is to locate India in relation to the PG states. This necessitates identifying the perception, in self, of the other: to determine (a) how we see these states and (b) how do PG states perceive India? Both are necessary to bring about a convergence of interests and the establishment of mutually beneficial relationships.

Iran occupies the whole of the northern coast of the Persian Gulf and has a coastline of 2440 km; Iraq, by contrast, has 58 km. The narrow entrance to the Persian Gulf in the Straits of Hormuz is controlled on the one side by Iran and on the other by Oman. This entire sub-region is:

- Within the security parametre of India and within the operational radius of the Indian Navy;
- Principal source of imported hydrocarbon energy supplies;
- Principal destination for manpower exports that provides

employment to 4.5 million Indian nationals whose remittances exceed to US$ 9 billion per annum;

- A major trading partner with whom the overall economic engagement is of the order of US$ 75-80 billion;
- An increasingly important destination for Indian projects, and IT services;
- An increasingly important source for investments into India;
- Having an India-friendly and Indian-friendly orientation and desirous of enhancing its political, economic and technological interaction with India.

The focus of Indian interest, now and in the foreseeable future, is on the imperative necessity of (a) regional peace and stability (b) friendly regimes (c) access to oil and gas resources of PG (d) freedom of navigation in PG and through the Straits of Hormuz, and (e) continued access to regional markets for Indian trade, technology, investments and workforce. Within this general framework, the challenge for India is to develop policy approaches relevant to each of the littoral states.

The Persian Gulf states perceive India as (a) an emerging major power in their neighbourhood (b) a major destination for their primary exports (c) a possible venue for investments (d) a major source of skilled manpower that is acceptable in security terms and (e) broadly acceptable in cultural terms.

Domestic stability and regional peace are prerequisites for the Persian Gulf States to continue playing their role as the principal suppliers of oil and gas. These states, however, are also undergoing social, economic and political transformation that is generating tensions that need to be managed carefully in terms of domestic and external pressures. The imperatives of the 'youth-bulge', in particular, necessitate immediate responses in terms of social and political reforms. There is a near-consensus that these reforms need to be evolutionary. The earlier expectation that political change can be expedited has now been abandoned in favour of stability.

Developments on the domestic scene in each of these states need to be watched and analysed carefully. The forthcoming Majlis elections in Iran may suggest changes in political equations there. Stability and cohesion of Iraq remains an open question. Saudi Arabia and the other GCC states have appeared to imbibe the germs of political change. Kuwait's example of the succession question being settled in parliament, rather than in the ruling family, may have wider implications. In Saudi Arabia, King Abdullah has put in place an Allegiance Commission charged with implementing succession procedures; its efficacy is yet to be tested. The challenge in the immediate future is for the ruling establishments to renew their legitimacy through a process of political liberalisation, cooption and accommodation. Each society would develop its own road to participatory governance, and should be allowed to do so without external imperatives.

Complexity characterises inter-state relations in the region. These relate to threat perceptions and national interests and need to be reconciled. The process would neither be short nor easy but must nevertheless be undertaken. The littoral states themselves are showing growing awareness of this.

Islamism is an ideology of protest, and of change. A perceptive observer has noted that "Wahabism constructed from above was a pillar of the status quo. Wahabism from below has become the mortal enemy of the same status quo". The pressures emanating from Islamist groups and tendencies are unlikely to subside and may gather momentum in the light of the successes recorded by these trends in Egypt, Lebanon and Palestine. At the same time the low levels of political activity in the GCC states, and the ingrained culture of tribal consensus that persists despite urbanisation, is likely to keep these trends within manageable bounds. In Iran, and notwithstanding the power struggle within the establishment, the primary orientation of policy will be reflective of national identity and interests.

The economies of all the Persian Gulf states would continue to prosper in the wake of high oil and gas prices. This would benefit all sections of these societies. Their integration in the global economy would increasingly reduce the local peculiarities. The structural changes now underway, pursuant to a policy of economic diversification away from hydrocarbons, cover areas of interest to Indian business. These include education, healthcare, construction services, insurance and banking, business and financial services, and tourism. An area of analysis should be the impact on India of possible changes in the skills-mix of manpower requirements of GCC countries.

Exercises in futurology have been undertaken, some in terms of pure economic growth and others in terms of variable politico-economic scenarios. No inter-state war appears likely in the region. Divergent security perceptions, however, would continue to prevail. Iran would remain apprehensive of external attempts at regime change or an attack against it. Iraq's threat perception would be focused on national unity and possible external interference.

Non-traditional threat to the security of the Persian Gulf states, or to their economies, can arise from (a) political mismanagement in domestic terms leading to instability and economic disruption (b) violence and terrorism directed at regimes and resulting in domestic instability (c) military action against a regional state by regional or extra-regional states resulting in retaliatory action that could disrupt shipping in the Persian Gulf and prevent / hamper the export of oil. All interested parties (including India), therefore, need to develop contingency scenarios to safeguard their interests.

Recent years have witnessed debates about an alternate security architecture for the Persian Gulf. NATO has been proposed as an option. Some regional states, and opinion makers, have gingerly suggested a role for larger Asian states like China and India. Iran's focus remains riveted on a cooperative security regime of the littoral states. The smaller littoral states, however, seek security in the involvement of Western powers. This debate needs to be monitored closely. The example of CTF 150 is suggestive of an inclination to keep India away from practical arrangements for security of sea lanes in this general area.

All these factors necessitate close and continuous study, and rigorous research, of the region. This, I am afraid, is not being done in adequate measure. The totality of India's interest demands that the 'Look East' policy be supplemented now by a 'Look West' policy.

The need of the hour is to put these studies on a firmer footing on the basis of cooperation between the academia and the business community.

Knowledge of operative languages, and familiarity with the region through frequent field-trips, has to be a pre-requisite for such an endeavour.

Today's seminar, I venture to hope will underline the imperative necessity of such an approach. It would be in our national interest.

Inauguration of the Eighteenth World Congress

International Physicians for the Prevention of Nuclear War
Mavlankar Hall, New Delhi
9 March 2008

I am happy to be here at the inauguration of the Eighteenth World Congress of International Physicians for the Prevention of Nuclear War. The pioneering work of the organisation and its efforts for peace, health and development need no mention here; it has been awarded the Noble Peace Prize. Conferences of this nature help in better understanding of the causes of armed conflict, especially from a public health perspective, and build grassroots awareness of the immense health and environment consequences of nuclear war. The involvement of students and youth as part of these conferences brings in the much-needed dimension of spreading awareness among the future decision makers.

This distinguished audience needs no reminding that the first resolution of the UN General Assembly of 24 January 1946 was adopted unanimously and sought the elimination of atomic weapons and all other major weapons adaptable to mass destruction from national armaments and the control of atomic energy to ensure its use only for peaceful purposes. The horrors of the use of nuclear weapons have convinced all responsible nations that elimination of nuclear weapons is necessary. The International Court of Justice had in its advisory opinion of 8 July 1996 concluded that "there exists an obligation to pursue in good faith and bring to a conclusion negotiations leading to nuclear disarmament in all its aspects under strict and effective international control". The nuclear disarmament discourse has been enriched by the contributions of the Non-Alignment Movement, various members States including India and even the community of Non-Governmental Organisations.

While there is agreement on the principle, the practical means and approaches necessary for realising this vision have been the subject of much debate and divergence of opinion. It was India that first proposed an end to nuclear testing in 1954. The principles for a Nuclear Non-Proliferation Treaty (NPT) were first proposed by India in 1965. India eventually refused to sign the NPT when it became clear that, instead of addressing the central objective of universal and comprehensive non-proliferation, the treaty only legitimized the continuing possession and multiplication of nuclear stockpiles by those few states possessing them.

I am reminded of what the Late Prime Minister Shri Rajiv Gandhi said in a speech before the United Nations. He argued: "We cannot accept the logic that a few nations have the right to pursue their security by threatening the survival of mankind ... nor is it acceptable that those who possess nuclear weapons are freed of all controls while those without nuclear weapons are policed against their production. History is full of such prejudices paraded as iron laws: That men are superior to women; that white races are superior to the coloured; that colonialism is a civilising mission; (and) that those who possess nuclear weapons are responsible powers and those who do not are not."

India aspires for a world that embodies this vision of Late Shri Rajiv Gandhi, of a non-violent world, free from the scourge of nuclear weapons. We have always held that progress towards nuclear disarmament will require mutual confidence in the international community to conclude universal, non-discriminatory and verifiable prohibitions on nuclear weapons leading to their complete elimination. We believe that the following elements constitute actionable and concrete steps towards achieving nuclear disarmament and have placed them for debate before the international community:

1. Reaffirmation of the unequivocal commitment of all nuclear-weapon states to the goal of complete elimination of nuclear weapons;
2. Negotiation of a convention on the complete prohibition of the use or threat of use of nuclear weapons.
3. Negotiation of a nuclear weapons convention prohibiting the development, production, stockpiling and use of nuclear

> weapons and on their destruction, leading to the global, non-discriminatory and verifiable elimination of nuclear weapons with a specified time frame.

An op-ed in *The Wall Street Journal* of 15 January 2008 by George Shultz, William Perry, Henry Kissinger and Sam Nunn has again focused on nuclear disarmament noting that the spread of nuclear weapons know-how and material has brought us to "a nuclear tipping point". They emphasised the need for a global dialogue that includes non-nuclear and nuclear nations to discuss, among other issues, "turning the goal of a world without nuclear weapons into a practical enterprise among nations, by applying the necessary political will to build an international consensus on priorities". Yet, it is worth noting that six decades after Hiroshima and Nagasaki, the focus of international efforts is still on "applying the necessary political will to build an international consensus on priorities". It is a measure of the distance we need to travel to realise the vision of universal nuclear disarmament. The theme of the Congress, 'Peace, Health and Development', is timely.

The 'First Foundation Day Lecture'
Rajiv Gandhi Centre for Contemporary Studies, University of Mumbai, Mumbai
31 March 2008

India and the World: A Vision for the Future

I am happy to be back in Mumbai University. It is a privilege to be invited to deliver the Foundation Day Lecture at the Rajiv Gandhi Centre for Contemporary Studies.

Rajiv Gandhi was a visionary who focused on the future of this great land of ours. He was also a realist who appreciated that a vision of the future must of necessity be anchored in the present and build upon it.

A professor of theoretical physics said some time back that the future 'will resemble a fairy tale'. This would undoubtedly be true of scientific advancement. Decades earlier the astronomer Nikolai Kardashev went further, to explore the world beyond the year 2100 in terms of its energy sources; his bench marks were the sun, the galaxy and the universe itself as the sources of energy. These perceptions, and similar other prognosis of the future, pose a question: how would social developments synchronise with this degree of change?

"The owl of Minerva", wrote the philosopher Hegel, "spreads its wings only with the falling of the dusk". He meant that philosophy understands only in hindsight. Would the speed of change and the compression of time impact on this process?

Anticipating the nature, direction and pace of change in societies involves a threefold exercise of visualising a better future based on projected scientific advancement, developing the requisite technological and societal instrumentalities, and doing so in the light of cumulative human experience.

I would like to proceed on this basis to develop a vision of the future, and India's place in it. An exercise in futurology pertaining to a society and its place in the association of societies needs, however, to go beyond production and distribution numbers and focus on changes in awareness and perceptions. For this reason, a longer time span is unavoidable.

Can we then look at India and its place in the world, in and beyond 2050?

II

India in 2050 would be the most populous country of the world. Its population of 1.5 billion would exceed that of China by about 50 million. Goldman Sachs in its report on the BRIC (Brazil, Russia, India and China) economies in December 2005 has estimated that by 2050, India would be the third largest economy after China and the US. Our GDP would be slightly over half of that of China and around three quarters of that of the US. Somewhat similar projections have come from the World Bank and some other assessment agencies.

Demography would have a wider impact. By the middle of the century and given the projected fertility rate, the population of Sub-Saharan Africa would be between a billion and a half and two billion. Sixty-two per cent of the world's people would be in Africa, South Asia and East Asia. Asia's share alone of the world's GNP would go up from the current one-third to about half.

It is only fair to add that despite these economic projections, the shape of the world in 2050 would depend on what happens in the intervening decades.

The challenges would be many. An Indian perspective, on the shape of India's future, would need to answer a set of six questions:

- What would be the contours and dynamics of the Indian society?
- What would the size and weight of the Indian economy?
- Would technological change–particularly in areas of food production, health and energy–keep pace with our needs?
- Would we improve upon our delivery mechanisms to fulfill the requirements of an inclusive society?

- What would be our capacity to deal with disasters in the shape of pandemics?
- Would the external environment remain benign? If not, what would be the nature and extent of external challenge? Would it hamper the achievement of our primary socio-economic goals? What would be the Indian impact on the external world?

Conflict, opines Sunil Khilnani, 'is written into the idea of India'. His prognosis of future lines of conflict include caste injustice, religious differences, economic inequality, environmental degradation and competition for resources, internal migration, political rights and recognition, rural/urban populations, present future generations, the regions versus the centre, and rival nationalisms and states.

Conflicts in societies can be resolved, moderated, aggravated. How would we address these questions in the coming decades? The shape of India in the second half of the 21st century would depend in great measure on our ability to respond to these challenges.

Amongst the first of these relates to caste. As Professor Srinivas put it, caste is both a structural principle of society and a dynamic force in interest articulation, collective mobilisation and social movement. It thus impacts on all aspects of social life. A paper in the 'Economic and Political Weekly' in October last year summed up the situation:

'India today is caught in a querulous debate over developing reservation policies for groups and communities suffering from economic exclusion associated with caste, gender and religious identity'.

It concluded that 'far from fading as India modernizes, the problem of discrimination remains a serious one—even at the very top of the human capital hierarchy'.

To what extent would it drain national energy in the later decades of the century?

Would we succeed in developing an inclusive framework broadly acceptable to those who feel deprived?

The religious plurality of India is a fact of life. Most accept it; some rejoice in it, some others bemoan it. Virtually every fifth Indian belongs to a religious minority and cherishes its identity. The constitutional framework is accommodative and has stood the test of pressures. The challenge lies in translating legal equality into the elimination of deprivation and discrimination that are finally being recognised.

Would the corrective process of empowerment, as an imperative of harmonious and inclusive development, be undertaken in years rather than decades?

A major obstacle to a unified national impulse is the 'balkanisation of the mind' that is increasingly evident despite political unity, and the unity of the market that has been achieved. We cannot claim the benefits of globalisation and the attendant mobility in services on the world stage sector and at the same time deny it within the country itself.

What would be its implications?

The matter has wider ramifications from our perspective. In 1993 Patrick Moynihan, in a book consciously entitled *Pandemonium* (which is the capital of hell in Milton's *Paradise Lost*), wrote about ethnicity in international affairs and ended with a plea: 'make the world safe for and from ethnicity'. Fifteen years later, in the current issue of the journal 'Foreign Affairs', the historian Jerry Muller has surveyed the enduring power of ethnic nationalism and concluded that "since ethnonationalism is a direct consequence of key elements of modernisation, it is likely to gain ground in societies undergoing such a process". It is, he adds, 'among the most vital –and disruptive – forces in many parts of the world'.

How then do we immunise India from this incipient virus in the coming decades?

These challenges cannot be wished away. They need to be comprehended. The corrective to each has to be a deliberate effort, rooted in the consciousness of the civil society itself, so that it can overcome social and political lethargy and develop alternatives. The vanguard in the effort has to be the youth; their optimism, hopefully, would be infectious.

III

Given the parametres of growth the challenge to the polity would be to make it truly inclusive. A prerequisite for this would be production, since there can be no distribution without it. Economic success and prosperity would also rest on three factors, namely the human development of our people, the success of our large market to attract investment and technology, and good governance.

Education is the most critical determinant of empowerment of people. It gives them skills and life chances and turns them into productive members of societies. Ensuring access to basic health and education as part of public services and irrespective of the ability of citizens to pay for such services is the prime responsibility of governments. Our record in this regard has so far not been bright. The Eleventh Plan promises greater movement towards fulfilling the constitutional obligation of providing free compulsory education of good quality to all children up to the age of fourteen years. This would determine the extent to which we can transform our human potential to development, growth and personal well being.

Much has been said in recent months about agriculture. It supports more than half a billion people, provides employment to 52 per cent of the workforce and remains the backbone of the economy; it is also in a state of stagnation. The National Commission on Farmers noted in its report in October 2006 that the time is opportune for "revitalising our agricultural progress by making agrarian prosperity and food security and sovereignty the bottom line for government policies and priorities in agriculture and rural development'"so as to "reverse the decline and restore confidence in our agricultural capability". A number of good new schemes have been initiated; the efficacy of the delivery system would be critical to their success. Success stories are indeed there; how do we make them the rule rather than the exception?

It is widely acknowledged that both for reduction of poverty and for sustainable growth the power of agriculture must be unleashed. This, as the World Development Report 2008 put it, 'requires a productivity revolution in smallholder farming'. Agriculture-related R&D would be critical to the effort. Thus new techniques need to be developed for arid and semi-arid land farming where rural distress is most acute.

Reforming agriculture is also about enhancing the quality of public services in rural India. Small and marginal farmers who earn meagre livelihoods from agriculture need to be supported by social security and non-farm employment to enable them to live decent lives. Development of land and water resources should be seen as the obligation of the state rather than a burdened peasantry. Agricultural marketing and extension systems also need immediate reform.

Agriculture must also be ready to deal with the dangers of climate change and global warming. Eventually this will have its own impact on rural poverty. Climate shocks such as droughts and floods drastically reduce long-term opportunities for human development. High poverty and low levels of human development limit our capacity to manage climate risks, especially for the vast majority of our population that is poor.

Agriculture cannot be left as residual activity for the elderly. The interest of the youth in agriculture requires attention. This would be possible, as the Swaminathan Report put it, 'if farming becomes economically rewarding and intellectually stimulating'.

Spatial inequalities have not been limited to economic development alone; they have extended to human development indices. The quality of sanitation, health, education and other public services vary widely across multiple dimensions – rural/urban, various states and districts, gender etc. These have impacted on migration flows as people move towards high growth areas with better employment and income earning opportunities. Such migrations are always accompanied by community-focused friction and attendant social and political problems.

Managing and smoothening migration flows would be an important component of ensuring social stability and economic growth in the future.

How quickly would we develop the requisite instrumentalities for it?

These factors would constitute the domestic backdrop in which India would interact with the outside world.

IV

The primary duty of the state in any society is to protect it from external aggression and internal disturbance. The typology of threats faced by us since independence can be summed up in the following:

1. Threats emanating from the nature of the international order: These include international arrangements that threatened our security, political or economic interest and thereby constrained our policy options.
2. Ideological threats: These include external or domestic attempts to posit an alternate view to the basic structure of the Indian state and its core values of secularism, pluralism and peaceful coexistence of multiple identities within the national framework. Examples of this are the two-nation theory, fundamentalisms of all hues, and various separatist and secessionist movements.
3. Territorial and resource disputes: These relate to territorial and water disputes with neighbours.
4. Internal threats: These range from religious and political dissatisfaction, ethnic, regional and caste-based grievances, separatist agendas, ideological movements motivated by economic deprivation or injustice, traffic in narcotics and drugs, and terrorism in all its forms and manifestations.

It would be unrealistic to assume that all of these would disappear by the year 2050. Two things, however, would change. The first would be an upward movement in our capacity to deal with them. India of the future, after the application of the correctives mentioned above, would be more prosperous, more inclusive, more accommodative and more confident of its ability to resolve complex social issues. Its charter of rights and duties would be more pervasive; its commitment to the achievement of justice more purposeful. This in itself would lessen the gap between civil society perceptions and those of the state on the one hand and, on the other, expand the state's menu of choices in its endeavour to resolve external disputes.

The second factor would be a change in the nature of the external world and the resultant changes in the terms of our interaction with it. Attention needs to be paid to it and its implications. The parameters of the nation-state are shrinking. New norms like human rights and globalisation, new threats like pandemics and environmental changes, and new technologies for global communications cast doubt on claims of sovereignty. A new form of state is emerging. Phillip Bobbitt has called it the market state and visualised three possible versions: The Meadow, The Park and The Garden:

"In a meadow all is profusion, randomness, variety. A park is for the most part publicly maintained, highly regulated with different sectors for different uses. A garden is smaller, more inwardly turned–it aims for the sublime, not the efficient or the just".

Every market state, he adds, will make historic choices among these or other possible models. He dilates on the implications:

"So long as the state's legitimacy is a matter of ensuring the welfare of its citizens, then the globalisation and interdependence of its economy, the vulnerability and transparency of its security and the accessibility and fragility of its cultural institutions will increasingly deny the state that legitimacy. As a result, individual states will change–they are already changing–to reacquire legitimacy by creating a new basis on which they may claim it. A change in the constitutional order of states will eventually recreate the nature of the society of states and its constitutional order".

The wider challenge, then, would be to synchronise multiple impulses–to accelerate change at home and accommodate ourselves to change abroad.

India of the future, in the best case scenario, cannot be and will not be isolationist. It would interact with the external world as an important member of the comity of nations. Its economic weight would be felt without overt demonstration. Changes in the nature of its economic capabilities would lead to a change in the nature of its economic engagement with the external world. It would seek peace, promote cooperative security, eschew hegemonic temptations, demonstrate its successful model of a plural society, and share its developmental experience with those in need of it.

India's external impact would be most profound in its demonstration of the working of the triad–its plural society, its democratic polity and its secular state structure. At a time when multiculturalism has come under strain in many parts of the world, our accommodative pluralism, capacity to give space to fellow citizens and ability to draw the circle wide enough to be inclusive would rate as enduring contributions to the human race.

Would this match our physicist's fairy tale?

A less optimistic picture cannot be ruled out. If tensions in our society do not subside, our output would suffer and impact adversely on our external impulse. Alternatively, a less benign external environment would unavoidably cause deviations from our chosen course and demand greater inputs and resource diversion. That, in turn would demand greater social cohesion.

Either way, the key to success abroad lies at home.

The Al-Farabi Kazakh National University
Almaty, Kazakhstan
9 April 2008

I am privileged to be invited to this prestigious University and deeply appreciate it. Even greater is the honour bestowed on me by the decision of the University.

Mohammad bin Mohammad bin Tarkhan Abu Nasr al-Farabi was a Central Asian polymath and one of the greatest scientists and philosophers of the Islamic world in his time. He was also a cosmologist, logician, musician, psychologist and sociologist. Amongst his woks read to this day is Al-Madina al-Fadila in which, inspired by Plato, he explained his concept of the Perfect City. It is truly befitting that this University with a distinguished history of over seventy years and contribution to the development of native science, technics, culture, and higher education should bear Al Farabi's name.

We live in interesting times. When I see the young students of this university I see the energy and dynamism of youth, their restlessness and impatience for better lives and happiness and their hope and optimism for the future. We too are a young nation. Over 550 million Indians, out of a total of a billion, are below the age of twenty-five years. The young are also the seed bearers of tomorrow's leaders. Both our countries have been fortunate in having wise leaders at critical points of our histories.

Leadership, like all resources, is scarce; its domain and platforms are contested. A leader, by definition, stands apart; but he does not stand alone. He must ensure continuous nourishment from the group he leads; in turn, he enriches the group by his leadership. The challenge for an open society is to ensure this.

In India, we have set for ourselves a national objective of building a knowledge society, an inclusive society, and a humane society. The most daunting task for our new leaders is the human development of our people. Their mandate is to explore and exploit all the possibilities for socio-economic advancement and personal fulfillment of our citizens. They also have to lead them to it. The young are resourceful, enthusiastic, willing to work hard; they have neither the patience to wait for extended periods to realise their aspirations nor does today's economic environment permit them the luxury of time that an earlier generation had.

I am tempted to quote Martin Luther King Jr. He said:

"Human progress is neither automatic nor inevitable. We are faced now with the fact that tomorrow is today. We are confronted with the fierce urgency of now. In this unfolding conundrum of life and history there is such a thing as being too late … We may cry out desperately for time to pause in her passage, but time is deaf to every plea and rushes on. Over the bleached bones and jumbled residues of numerous civilisations are written the pathetic words: Too late."

As I stand today before you, three issues appear self evident:

- The first is the physical proximity of Central Asia to India.
- The second is the historical continuity of an interactive relationship between us based on ties of civilisation, culture and trade.
- The third is an imperative of the emerging world system where globalisation is compressing distances and speeding up communication.

The old paradigms of economic relations are no longer valid. Similar is the case with the old paradigms of security. We live in a world where the imperative need for cooperative approaches in the security and economic arena asserts itself to overcome previously insurmountable obstacles. Today we do face problems in physical connectivity between our countries. We can rest assured that the compelling logic of this age will lead to solutions to overcome this.

Our approach to the world is naturally a function of our values, our history and geography, and of how we define our interests. India's main focus since independence has been to improve our people's lives through inclusive economic development within a pluralist, secular, equitable and democratic framework. In making this effort, India has also decisively demonstrated that democracy and development are compatible and necessary for ensuring sustainability. The primary task of our foreign policy has been to enable the transformation of India's society and economy, restoring traditional patterns of dealing with the world, and building strategic autonomy of choice.

Judging by the results, our foreign policy choices have served the nation well. For more than two decades, India has recorded average annual GDP growth of around 6 per cent. In the last four years, this has risen to around 9 per cent. Historically unprecedented transformations and improvements in the people's living standards have taken place in India in the last few decades. Yet, much remains to be done. If we are to abolish mass poverty in India, we need to grow at 8 to 10 per cent every year until 2020. We need considerable effort, correct public policy choices and a supportive and peaceful international environment.

Our foreign policy is also based on principles and a broad national consensus. The vision of our leaders like Mahatma Gandhi, Jawaharlal Nehru, Indira Gandhi and Rajiv Gandhi has led to the emergence of a secular polity. We share the values of fundamental human rights and freedoms with other democracies. Our values and civilisational heritage make us a barrier against fundamentalism and terrorism and a factor of peace and stability. We also seek maintenance of friendly relations with all countries, resolution of conflicts through peaceful means and equity in the conduct of international relations.

We firmly believe that global threats demand global responses and equitable sharing of responsibilities. India has actively pursued the strengthening of multilateral institutions, in particular the United Nations. We are committed to the comprehensive reform of the United Nations, including its Security Council.

Relations between India and Kazakhstan have always been warm, friendly and close. Both our countries are multi-ethnic, multi-linguistic, multi-cultural societies committed to countering fundamentalism, religious extremism and terrorism. Our views coincide or converge on all major regional and international questions.

I am confident that stronger and deeper relations between Kazakhstan and India will further contribute to increased prosperity and security not only for the peoples of our countries, but also for the region and the world.

International Conference 'Towards a World Free of Nuclear Weapons'
Hotel Maurya ITC, New Delhi
10 June 2008

To deliver a valedictory address is to begin with twin apprehensions: that whatever is to be said has been said, or that what is going to be said may be outrageously at variance with what has been said!

In either case, the speaker would be deprived of what Dr Samuel Johnson termed "frigid tranquility".

For being in this interesting position, I have to thank an old and dear friend!!

Any discussion necessitates clarity about concepts. In terms of the theory of statecraft, war has always been considered an instrument of policy. Pursuit of war necessitates weapons, defined as tools to gain advantage over an adversary. Improvement in the quality of weapons, and invention of new ones, is a logical outcome of the human trait to seek excellence, for success in subduing a political and military adversary by inflicting unacceptable damage.

The impulse to invent weapons of mass destruction, including nuclear weapons, was part of this process. Each new weapon system also propelled assessment of its implications in tactical and strategic terms. Both processes were accelerated in the second half of the twentieth century.

Every invention, apart from its novelty, has to prove its utility. Mass destruction in the Spanish civil war was vividly depicted by Picasso's 'Guernica'; less than a decade later, it was typified by London and Dresden. In the case of the nuclear weapon, the utility was brutally demonstrated at Hiroshima and Nagasaki. The scale of destruction there propelled consideration of the implications of the new weapon.

An early recognition came in the shape of the Baruch Plan of June 1946. It was rejected by the Soviet Union for reasons that were evident. In 1948,

General Omar Bradley told an American audience that "the only way to win an atomic war is to make certain it never starts".

None appreciated the implications better than the scientists. In July 1955 the signatories of the Russell-Einstein Manifesto spoke "not as members of this or that nation, continent, or creed, but as human beings, members of the species Man, whose continued existence is in doubt".

The venue of this conference is important; so is its timing. India has been an ardent advocate of prohibition on the production and use of nuclear weapons. Jawaharlal Nehru in 1954 spoke of the fear that "would grow and grip nations and peoples and each would try frantically to get this new weapon or some adequate protection from it." Prime Ministers of India proposed prohibition in 1978 and again in 1982. In 1988 Rajiv Gandhi sought "not a marginal adjustment in the machinery of nuclear confrontation, nor a partial or temporary scaling down of the arms race", but "a world which is rid of nuclear weapons". His Action Plan for a World Free of Nuclear Weapons was comprehensive in its scope, passionate in its appeal, and clinical in its reasoning and analysis.

The idea was considered utopian.

Despite this, and in the initial euphoria at the end of the Cold War, the global momentum for a less unpleasant world led to the conclusion of the universal and non-discriminatory Chemical Weapons Convention, with its intricate and intrusive verification mechanism. Significantly, however, the argument for outlawing it was not extended to nuclear weapons.

In regard to matters nuclear, the world has witnessed changes over the past decade and a half. This audience is knowledgeable about it. India herself has emerged as a nuclear weapons state.

On one side it is argued that the imperative of realism leaves no option but to accept the reality. On the other, those distressed over the fraying of world order and apprehensive of the "normative cost of silence" advocate a more assertive approach. "This is a time", writes Professor Richard Falk in his recent book *The Costs of War*, "when realism and idealism are increasingly fused in their call for a future world order based on law and justice, but this cannot be made to happen without the engagement of the peoples of the earth acting as detribalized citizens without borders."

Three questions arise:

- Is the logic of 'realism' unassailable?
- Does it hold good for the world of tomorrow?
- Has the argument for disarmament, and particularly for nuclear disarmament, ceased to be relevant for the survival of the human species?

The case for the possession of nuclear weapons needs to be assessed in strategic, legal, political, financial, developmental and environmental terms. This would unavoidably widen the ambit of discourse.

In the first place and according to the Federation of American Scientists, the global stockpile of nuclear warheads today remains at more than 20,000. Of these, more than 10,000 warheads are considered operational, of which a couple of thousand are on high alert, ready for use on short notice. The approach is premised on the doctrine of deterrence; the latter, however, remains inherently unstable, prone to human error or folly; the probability of the annihilation of the human race through the use of these weapons thus remains high, and must be considered unacceptable.

Secondly, nuclear armament ends up being, in its implications, anti-poor and anti-development. Stephen Schwartz, in his 1998 book *Atomic Audit* on the comprehensive cost of the US nuclear weapons programme, has estimated that the US spent around $6 trillion in total. The arms race led the former Soviet Union to the point of exhaustion and disintegration. The resource drain of other nuclear-weapon states would be equally high in proportionate terms. This level of spending by nuclear weapon states cannot but deny national resources for developmental or other purposes for public welfare.

Thirdly, the development, production, stockpiling and use of nuclear weapons results in immense, irreversible and unforeseen damage to the environment. As far back as 1987, the Report of the World Commission on Environment and Development, (known as the Brundtland Report), affirmed that "among the dangers facing the environment, the possibility of nuclear war is undoubtedly the gravest". It noted that the "whole notion of security as traditionally understood in terms of political and military threats to national sovereignty must be expanded to include the growing impacts of environmental stress"; it concluded that "there are no military solutions to 'environmental insecurity'."

Fourthly, there have been fundamental changes in the nature of conflict and of the structure of international relations. Conflict in the post-Cold War era has acquired new characteristics: it is not a classical inter-state conflict; it is fuelled by identity based factors and issues of economic and social justice; and there is a drastic increase in the role of non-state actors. Weapons of mass destruction that were fashioned for inter-state conflict and their associated strategic deterrence doctrines premised on state behaviour have little relevance for the new reality.

II

The case for possession and use of nuclear weapons stands dented and lends credence to the need to re-think its fundamentals. Any endeavour on this basis must necessarily be rooted in legality and morality and be capable of demonstrating the advantages emanating from it.

How is this elusive goal to be attained? In exploring options, we need to remember that the community of nations has put in place agreements to outlaw chemical and biological weapons.

The question of legality poses problems. On a reference from the UN General Assembly on 'threat or use of nuclear weapons', the International Court of Justice gave an Advisory Opinion in July 1996. It decided that in customary or conventional international law there is neither an authorisation nor a prohibition of the threat or use of nuclear weapons. While it opined that such a threat or use would be contrary to the rules of international law applicable to armed conflicts, it noted that the current state of international law does not permit the Court to conclude definitively whether such threat or use would be lawful or unlawful in an extreme circumstance of self-defence, in which the very survival of a state would be at stake.

The distinguished audience here is cognisant of the UN General Assembly resolutions passed each year by a large majority reaffirming that "any use of nuclear weapons would be a violation of the Charter of the United Nations and a crime against humanity" as declared in its resolution 1653 (XVI) of 24 November 1961.

This reveals the desire of a very large section of the international community to move forward along the road to complete nuclear disarmament.

On the other hand, we have the annual re-affirmation of the Chapter VII Security Council Resolution 1540 of 2004 stating that proliferation of nuclear weapons "constitutes a threat to international peace and security".

Put together, we get two sets of assertions:

1. Use of nuclear weapons is a crime against humanity;
2. Proliferation of nuclear weapons is a threat against international peace and security.

Between the two ends of this spectrum, falls the question of production, possession and threat to use of nuclear weapons. It is an irony of Realpolitik that these have so far not been perceived to constitute a threat to international peace and security.

The ICJ (International Court of Justice) addressed but did not resolve a critical question: Would a higher priority be accorded to the survival of the state if the survival of humanity itself were at stake?

A Dissenting Opinion summed up the legal dilemma: "The case as a whole presents an unparalled tension between State practice and legal principle". "When it comes to the supreme interests of State", it noted, 'the Court discards the legal progress of the Twentieth Century, puts aside the provisions of the United Nations Charter of which it is the principal judicial organ, and proclaims, in terms redolent of Realpolitik, its ambivalence about the most important provisions of modern international law".

This impasse was reflected most recently in the Report of the UN Disarmament Commission on 25 April 2008 at the end of its Three Year Cycle of Deliberations. Releasing the Report, the Chairman of the Commission said that even set against the relatively low expectations, the results were meagre.

"There was a stark contrast between the state of the world and the cooperation of the United Nations Member States in the Commission. Therefore, the credibility question is inescapable, and in time, each and every one of us should be able to answer it".

The only way to resolve the impasse is to do it on a different plane. The modern state system is premised on the model emanating from the Peace of Westphalia. The reality of the sovereign state today, however, is very different from its theory. In 1991 Javier Perez de Cuellar had called upon the international community to help develop a "new concept, one which marries law and morality".

Such an effort of bringing together law and morality would help initiate the process of resolving the dilemma highlighted by the ICJ in its Advisory Opinion. The process would then take us back to the Russell-Einstein Manifesto's focus on the human being: "Remember your humanity, and forget the rest. If you can do so, the way lies open to a new Paradise; if you cannot, there lies before you the risk of universal death."

To transform vision into reality, a plan and a timetable on the pattern of the Rajiv Gandhi Action Plan would be essential. We have seen that, hitherto, nuclear disarmament has become almost synonymous with nuclear non-proliferation. A change would be possible only through such an Action Plan.

For much too long, ladies and gentlemen, the question of disarmament has remained in the exclusive domain of states and their experts. Is it not time now to open a window or two to let in the fresh breeze of global public opinion? We are aware of the beneficial results produced by such an approach in other areas that transcend state sovereignty.

Given the immobility of the current disarmament process, a new methodology may be worth a try.

International Seminar on 'Changing Political Context in South Asia and Prospects of Security and Regional Cooperation'

IDSA and ICRIER, New Delhi

5 November 2008

I feel privileged to be here amidst such a distinguished audience. Over the years the IDSA has provided the impulse for such gatherings of scholars and analysts. The end products add to the compendium of knowledge.

The attention of this conference, I understand, would be on dimensions of change in South Asia and its possible implications.

The logic of geography is compelling. For India, the neighbourhood radiates in concentric circles, buttressed by history, cultural affinities and economic necessities.

Our political commitment to closer ties with our neighbours in South Asia is serious. India's security interests are better served if our neighbours evolve as viable states with moderate and stable political and social environments and vibrant economies.

We wish to see South Asia at peace with itself, leading to ever widening circles of security, peace and prosperity in the region.

The theme of this seminar is twofold: security and regional cooperation. Both need to be understood in themselves as also in their mutual relationship. Their logical manifestations could be (1) security exclusively in national terms (2) regional security cooperation (3) regional economic cooperation and (4) a mix of all these resulting in comprehensive security. In terms of linkages, it would be valid to ask if the perceived regional economic cooperation is to be the first step in our quest for regional security cooperation, or vice versa.

Perceptions, as this audience is well aware, have changed overtime. At one point security in the conventional sense offered a menu of choices in regard to security cooperation and suggested options ranging from alliances to collective security, security regimes and security communities. At a later stage, frameworks for communication and dialogue emerged. Each of these was experimented with; results varied from region to region.

Regional economic cooperation has tended to be influenced by a set of factors relating to intra-regional relations and convergence of political interests and cultural compatibility. The potential for economic cooperation is stymied when historic fears cloud security perceptions.

II

South Asia presents a varied picture towards the end of 2008. In some areas, forces of change are resonating noticeably. Bhutan has opted for a new system of governance through a constitutional monarchy. Change is the message of the election in Maldives last week. Nepal has witnessed historic transition from a monarchy to a democratic republic with a new leadership, and a new constitution in the offing. Pakistan has reverted to civilian rule with a new Parliament and a democratically elected President.

Less specific are the readings on Bangladesh and Sri Lanka. The former seeks a return to constitutional democracy and the latter an end to internecine strife.

The conflict in Afghanistan remains a source of considerable concern and calls for innovative solutions premised on national unity.

India, having registered rapid growth in recent years, is itself moving into a period of state and national elections.

The move towards popular and democratically elected governments in South Asia, however, has not eclipsed the existing challenges to governance in all the countries of the region. Poverty and economic disparities coupled with ethnic and social divisions have created political and social fault lines that have been exploited by non-state actors with their own agendas.

Human Development indices of most countries of South Asia are not flattering and it would a miracle if the targets of the Millennium Development Goals are achieved.

Yet, economic growth has continued as most of the South Asian countries have liberalised and moved towards market economies. Regional cooperation has made headway within the framework of SAARC which itself has expanded to include Afghanistan as well as nine observers.

New initiatives on the operationalisation of the SAARC Food Bank, establishment of the SAARC Development Fund, setting up of the South Asian University, the launching of negotiations to bring services into SAFTA and signing of the Convention of Mutual Assistance in Criminal Matters are significant for regional integration.

The question that one must ask is whether the changed and changing political context in many SAARC countries would confine itself to domestic politics or go beyond it to develop a changed context for security and economic cooperation with India? In other words, do the new political elites in our neighbourhood harbour a new paradigm of bilateral and regional cooperation?

We have to admit that the traditional pattern of bilateral state-to-state relations has already been transformed in varying degrees as a result of globalisation. Governments today do not control information or patterns of human interaction. Across the region, we see a web of connectivities between political actors, media centres, civil society organisations and commercial entities. Common people freely exchange views and ideas on their governments and their lives.

The prospects of security and economic cooperation are thus correlated to the ability of states to broad-base their relations beyond the traditional frameworks.

Let me venture to summarise some overarching themes that characterise the emergence of this new political context.

First, there is recognition of the importance of good relations with India and an advocacy for closer economic and political relations. There is also a desire for updating, where relevant, the existing instrumentalities of such cooperation to reflect the new ground level realities. The question for renegotiating existing treaties has been raised in this context.

Second, India on its part has tried–incrementally and non-reciprocally–to incentivise economic cooperation through confidence building measures.

As a result, some in our neighbourhood have begun to feel that a prosperous and economically vibrant India is an opportunity for them to reap both economic and political benefits.

Third, political elites are increasingly emphasising that the desired economic outcomes transcend investments, growth or development. The focus is on the human development of people, the quality of the lives of citizens and even Gross National Happiness!

Fourth, all countries in South Asia realise that globalisation would be meaningless without the improvement of intra-regional connectivities. Informal trade and third country trade is still predominant with formal intra-regional trade constituting under 5 per cent of South Asia's overall trade.

On the other hand, negative security perceptions continue to cloud cooperation in tackling trans-national and cross-boundary issues. These include security concerns such as terrorism, drug-trafficking and money laundering, as well as economic and developmental issues such as food, water, climate change and energy security.

Some initiatives need to be mentioned. India has taken the lead in building infrastructure for intra-regional trade in the full knowledge that the economic importance of intra-regional trade is considerable for the smaller regional economies. Taking the theme of connectivity forward, the SAARC transport ministers identified specific corridors for implementation linking Nepal, Bhutan, India and Bangladesh. A draft Motor Vehicles Agreement and a draft Railway Agreement are also being negotiated.

The expectation is that cross-border trucking and container movements, improved regional air and rail links and upgraded customs and trade facilitation would knit our neighbourhood in a network of mutually beneficial economic partnerships contributing to long term political and social stability.

Such partnerships are the need of the hour and can help address problems that cannot be solved nationally. Two instances of these lie in (i) rivers and flood control; and (ii) energy generation, energy trade and energy transit. Both are critical to the achievement of development goals of the countries of South Asia.

Experience elsewhere in the world shows that political constraints need not be permanent barriers to economic cooperation and that the latter could help create a climate of opinion to resolve conflicts.

III

We live in times of great change. The challenges we confront overflow national frontiers. The public in South Asia has, in diverse ways, signalled its impatience with the politics of the status quo. This is most evident in the younger generation. It is now for the governments to think innovatively and encapsulate this impulse in national policies.

History is witness to occasions when bold thinking has led to creativity. Why should South Asia be an exception and remain embedded in the unproductive routine and ritual of six decades?

Would it then be altogether unrealistic to hope that South Asian cooperation would seek to achieve the following?

- Free travel and trade across frontiers, a euro-style single currency, environmentally sustainable and regionally balanced development.
- Security coordination resulting in Joint action on crime and terror.
- Speak with a single voice and work closely together on trade issues and development policy.
- Develop a mechanism for dispute resolution.
- Coordinate approaches on major foreign and defence policy questions?

The meandering River of Time is mighty and can flow in many directions. The answers to the above questions lie in harnessing it for common good and regional betterment. The analyst should go beyond identifying the obstacles and pitfalls to suggesting solutions. I venture to hope that today's conclave would be part of such an effort.

Book release: *India's Nuclear Policy* by Shri Bharat Karnad

India International Centre, Delhi

12 November 2008

This is a substantive book, authoritative and densely written with 158 pages of text and 875 end notes. Its subject can only be described as deadly serious. Professor Karnad, who needs no introduction to the strategic community, has done it with the same thoroughness that characterised his earlier tome, published in 2002. It will certainly provoke debate.

There has been and continues to be a good deal of informed, and even more uninformed, discussion on nuclear weapons in the global context. In the vocabulary of economics, a monopoly of possession gave way to an oligopoly. It resulted in a set of rules emanating from the game theory.

The assumptions and rules were disturbed when the nuclear weapons debate developed a regional context. The new arrivals, however, developed their own game theory. This, despite the sceptics, has held ground for over a decade.

The theological certitude of an earlier era has now given way to doubt in some quarters.

A third dimension however was bound to emerge, and did. It relates to cross-category interaction. What would happen when a player in the regional category has to interact in nuclear terms with a global player of the first category?

II

Prof. Karnad's focus is on 'the working of India's nuclear strategy and posture'. He takes on board India's doctrine of 'credible minimum deterrence' (CMD) and seeks to examine it in a 'militarily sustainable stance' and, as he puts it, 'with the nitty gritty of realising a credible, effective, and survivable thermonuclear force'. He develops this argument to show that the direction of India's nuclear strategy and posture, to quote him again, 'are headed clearly away from the minimalist notions of nuclear deterrence'.

Analysing this theorem in depth, he concludes that 'it is the indecisiveness and lack of will of the Indian political leadership to take hard national security decisions that is the weak link in the deterrence chain'.

Prof. Karnad's conclusion, based on scenario-building and war games in the strategic community, is even more specific: "If India does not speedily close the gap in the size and quality of its strategic forces, which gap can in a crisis be psychologically debilitating, China with its 'stronger nuclear capability' will hold the whip hand".

I find the scenario disturbing in terms of its assumptions.

The first of these relates to the doctrine of nuclear deterrence. There is a credible body of opinion that considers the doctrine a recipe for instability. Possession generates the impulse to further develop, and modernise, existing stock piles. This necessarily has a reaction leading to escalation.

Secondly, the emergence of actual or potential regional nuclear weapon powers is a reality. Each case has an impulse and a calculus of its own. Containment carries in itself the germs of a breakout, resulting in proliferation. It may thus result in the opposite of what is intended.

Thirdly, the conclusions about decision-making by the political leaders in a democracy are far too sweeping to be relevant. Competence or lack of it has a wider rationale and is not to be associated with a particular type of leadership. Democracies can be competent or incompetent; so can dictatorships including military dictatorships. Enough examples from recent and not-so-recent history can be cited for both types of situations. No segment of society has a monopoly of wisdom. Successful societies have invariably been examples of cooperative harmony.

Fourthly, the propensity to identify potential military adversaries has wider implications and, to my mind, should be eschewed. The world we live in is far too complex and far too rapid in its transformation to encourage definitive formulations. What Heraclitus said on flux has to be kept in mind.

States have interests, not friends or enemies. These interests can be adjusted and reconciled.

Finally, the impact of globalisation on national security needs to be factored in. It affects state capacity and autonomy. We are currently witnessing the consequences of financial globalisation.

III

No discussion on national security can be unidimensional. The rationale for military security and weapons systems is one aspect of the matter. The real debate today is about human security and about non-military threats. Many of these are trans-national. The challenge is to develop both a psychological propensity and technological capability to respond to the latter. How would we develop a credible minimum deterrence to these? Would this not be a relevant priority for the strategist as the twenty-first century and its threats unfold?

Book release: *Challenges and Strategy: Rethinking India's Foreign Policy'* by Ambassador Rajiv Sikri

Federation House, New Delhi

13 April 2009

Ambassador Sikri has written a book that compels introspection. His basic premise is that the world has changed and continues to change. India's capabilities and capacities have also changed and are changing. This requires rethinking policy objectives and the methodology for attaining these objectives.

Sikri analyses India's position in the world in terms of an arc of prosperity to the east, an arc of energy to the west, and an arc of instability extending from West to Central and South Asia. Cutting across there are vital sea lanes and communication channels. His suggestion is that India should be a major player in the complex geo-strategic game that is unfolding. He proposes that India "must play its role as conscience keeper of the world," and do so by "looking beyond the West and its troublesome neighbours like Pakistan and China and find its niche in the world."

In general terms, Ambassador Sikri's thesis may be optimistic, even idealistic. For one, states are propelled by Machiavellian impulses and cannot be conscience keepers. Professed nobility of sentiments and piety in purpose generally camouflages more mundane objectives. On specifics, however, he does identify lacunae in the approach that seems to have prevailed in the recent past. One example of it is West Asia; another is Central Asia.

An impression seems to have gained ground that West Asia, particularly the Persian Gulf region, is good for certain purposes only. These are (a) energy supplies (b) employment for our nationals (c) a limited amount of off-shore business. The wider strategic aspects of relationship with a region in proximate neighbourhood appear to have been put aside.

A case in point is Gulf security. The present arrangement of competitive security, based on inclusion and exclusion, is inherently unstable and is increasingly being recognised as such. Sikri suggests an ARF-like approach and proposes a Gulf Regional Forum for dialogue on the question.

In December 2005 a GCC foreign minister suggested a three-pronged gulf security framework. The first would be GCC, Yemen, Iraq and Iran as regional pillars; the second would be a unanimous Security Council guarantee for the sovereignty and territorial integrity of all Gulf Countries; the third is to strengthen the international component and necessitate engagement with 'the emerging Asian powers, especially China and India.'

The proposal hints at an Indian role. This should be premised on our core concerns: (a) stability in the littoral states (b) freedom of navigation in the Persian Gulf and the Strait of Hormuz (c) security of sea lanes (d) availability of an interdiction capacity to safeguard Indian shipping. An essential prerequisite for such an engagement would be more vibrant political relations with all the states of the Persian Gulf littoral.

The book has a number of interesting insights on economic diplomacy and energy security. The chapter on 'US and Nuclear Issues' offers on pages 185-188 a perception somewhat at variance with the public picture.

In a changing world, foreign policy tactics have to remain flexible. The National Intelligence Council of the United States, in its scenario building for 2025, states that in the next ten years China and India are expected to achieve near parity with the US in two different areas: India in scientific and human capital and China in government receptivity to business innovations. We therefore have to be patient and diligent, work our way up, and not be overtly anxious to get there prematurely.

One last point. Most foreign policy analysts seem to overlook domestic factors and constraints. The pace of our progress would also depend on the speed at which we overcome domestic strives that retard our progress. These questions cannot be wished away; to do so successfully, we have to keep in mind and implement the basic principles of the Indian polity.

Book release: *For the Honour of India: A History of Indian Peace Keeping* by Lt. Gen. Satish Nambiar

USI, New Delhi

29 May 2009

I am happy to be back at the premises of the USI and to release this book that gives an authoritative account of the valiant contribution of our soldiers towards maintaining international peace and security. The book owes its origin to a suggestion of President Kalam; the effort of General Nambiar and his team of collaborators are impressive and commendable.

The term 'peacekeeping' does not figure in the Charter of the United Nations. The impulse for it comes from the first of the four Purposes of the UN, enunciated in Articles 1 of the Charter. Secretary General Dag Hammarskjold, who was said to have had 'almost a religious respect for the Charter', referred to peacekeeping as belonging to 'Chapter Six and a Half' of the Charter.

Over the years, peacekeeping has undergone massive expansion covering today 18 operations deployed in five continents encompassing over 140,000 personnel and budgeted cost exceeding US$ 7 billion. Its methodology has been subjected to periodic reviews, the most comprehensive of these being the Brahimi Panel Report of August 2000.

This book deals with three distinct aspects of Indian peacekeeping:

1. Peacekeeping through the institutional mechanism of the United Nations;
2. Peacekeeping undertaken through a multi-national/international commission such in the case of Indo-China;
3. Peacekeeping undertaken through bilateral formats such as the IPKF and Operation Cactus in the Maldives. These two were propelled by national security imperatives and are a category apart.

Experience of the last two decades indicates that India's policy preference in an increasingly complex global security scenario is for peacekeeping interventions through UN mechanisms.

Some characteristics of UN peacekeeping are noteworthy:

First, peacekeeping operations have multiplied since the end of the Cold War. While there have been only seventeen operations during the period 1948-1991, there have been around forty-five since 1991. The much anticipated New World Order commenced with a heavy dose of global disorder!

Second, peacekeeping operations have increasingly complex mandates and this is reflected in their nomenclatures–Truce Supervision, Military Observers, Verification, Transition Assistance, Confidence Restoration, Preventive Deployment, Stabilisation and Hybrid Operation, to name a few.

Third, UN peacekeeping operations have become the sole prerogative of the Security Council that defines their mandates and monitors their operation. Troop contributing countries that bear the human, and increasingly the material cost of peacekeeping, are consulted on a semi-formal basis but do not have a defined role in shaping mandates and in mission planning. The countries that do have a say in Council Resolutions often do not participate in their implementation. It is now not remembered that in the Cold War period there were two peacekeeping operations established by UN General Assembly mandates–the First UN Emergency Force and the UN Security Force in West New Guinea. These operations were characterised by negotiations with the participating countries where mission planning was done through an Advisory Committee of member states. Their operational and mission models deserve further study.

Fourth, peacekeeping is straying from traditional mandates. While consent of the parties, impartiality of peacekeepers and the minimum use of force remain cardinal principles, deviations have been devastating. Furthermore, peacekeeping is sought to be juxtaposed into nation-building. The irony of promoting democracy and nation-building through armed peacekeeping is indeed stark.

Fifth, there is an increasing trend to regionalise peacekeeping and even to give post-facto endorsement to unilateral action. This raises disconcerting questions since it is only the United Nations that has the universal legitimacy and credibility to undertake this role.

UN Peacekeeping is a product of structural necessity of the global order and the institutional innovation of the United Nations 'to save succeeding generations', as the Preamble of the Charter put it, 'from the scourge of war'. Its theology is still evolving. The underlying dilemma, of reconciling the principle of state sovereignty with the imperatives of a globalising world committing itself to universal norms that transcend national borders, remains unresolved. The emergence of a global civil society, and the enhanced commitment to principles of human rights and other emerging norms for group and state behaviour, is propelling us towards modified patterns of conduct nationally and globally. At the same time selectivity, rather than universality based on principled adherence, determines conduct. The imperative of global order today demands peacekeeping on a vast scale, but the spirit and application of innovation to the UN structures and the Charter principles is lacking.

Despite this, India's commitment to peacekeeping in general and the UN peacekeeping in particular needs no reiteration. We have contributed nearly 100,000 troops, participated in more than forty missions and 130 of our peacekeepers have made the supreme sacrifice and laid down their lives while serving in UN missions. Some of them are being honoured today at the UN Headquarters. We have acquired vast experience in peacekeeping and have the intellectual capital from our own experience in nation-building to tackle the complex scenario that today's peacekeeping faces. Our military, paramilitary and police forces have the requisite experience to match the challenge. The establishment of the Centre for United Nations Peacekeeping under the aegis of the United Service Institution of India has institutionalised this experience to make it available to other countries.

This book is timely. I am confident that besides enlightening the general public, it will facilitate a more focussed policy debate on the principles and mechanics of peacekeeping.

The Fourteenth Field Marshal K.M. Cariappa Memorial Lecture
DRDO Auditorium, New Delhi
7 October 2009

Insecurity and the State: Emerging Challenges

I deem it a great privilege to be invited to deliver the Fourteenth Cariappa Memorial Lecture. The first Indian chief of the armed forces of modern India was a legend in his own lifetime and will undoubtedly remain so in the annals of history. Cariappa's greatest contribution, said Field Marshal Manekshaw, "was that he taught the Indian Army to be apolitical". By doing so, as General Raghavan put it in an earlier Lecture, he "set the foundations of civil military relations in India".

My pleasure at being here today also has an element of the subjective. The Field Marshal was, several decades earlier, a very distinguished predecessor of mine as High Commissioner to Australia. I called on him prior to my departure and he offered a valuable piece of advice. "Do not waste your time in Canberra, young man", he said; 'go out and meet the real Australians'.

I heard more about his work in Australia from his, and my, neighbour on Mugga Way in Canberra the late Sir Harold White who was Australia's first National Librarian. Cariappa is remembered to this day for his impromptu action in cleaning personally the brass plate at a war memorial; he was the founder-president of the Commonwealth Club at Canberra. Records also shows that he maintained a high public profile on some issues and was openly critical of the White Australia policy that characterised the official approach in that period to immigration from 'new' commonwealth countries. An Australian historian has noted that "his critics notwithstanding, Cariappa had a significant impact on progressive opinion in Australia."

Field Marshal Cariappa was a soldier of World War II, part of an imperial army in a global contest that produced a victor and a vanquished but, in Henry Kissinger's words, "ended with a geopolitical vacuum". The responsibilities entrusted to him in 1948 by a newly independent India were, however, of a different nature. The challenges were immediate even if the security paradigm in that early period was considerably simpler.

So much for history and recollection! Let me return to the world of harsh reality. I intend today to probe the concept of insecurity. I would argue that unless we understand it clearly in all its dimensions, our endeavour to craft comprehensive national security for the world of tomorrow would remain elusive.

II

The historian Eric Hobsbawm concluded his 1994 work *Age of Extremes: the Short History of the Twentieth Century* with a prognosis:

"The future cannot be a continuation of the past, and there are signs, both externally, and, as it were, internally, that we have reached a point of historic crisis. The forces generated by the techno-scientific economy are now great enough to destroy the environment, that is to say, the material foundations of human life ... Our world risks both explosion and implosion. It must change ... If humanity is to have a recognisable future, it cannot be by prolonging the past or the present. If we try to build the third millennium on that basis, we shall fail. And the price of failure, that is to say, the alternative to a changed society, is darkness".

A number of questions arise. Is perception of this change reflected in current thinking on national security and strategies pertaining to it? Is national security synonymous with, or apart from, the security of citizens? Do we comprehend insecurity not merely in state-centric and military terms but also to cover insecurity pertaining to food, water, energy, other resources, pandemics, environment and, as Walter Lippman put it a long time back, "core values"? How would they impact on national strategy in the world of tomorrow? Would it restrict or expand our choices in seeking security?

The traditional approach to security is state-centric and for good reason. The *raison d'être* of statehood is provision of security for its citizens, and to a lesser extent its residents, in both its internal and external dimensions. The post Second World War global order is premised on states acting as net security generators and providers and thereby contributing to systemic stability. The experience of the last six decades, and especially since the end of the Cold War, shows that real life veers quite significantly away from text book assumptions. Many of the states have radiated insecurity towards their citizens and residents and thus destabilised their own societies and polities. This has led to state failures and implosions in the internal dimension and to regional and even global crises in the external dimension. One cannot escape the harsh conclusion that states have, quite often, been significant contributors to individual and systemic insecurity.

A good recent instance of it is the study on Global Trends 2025 published by the National Security Council of the United States in November 2008. It is based on wide ranging interaction with think tanks in America, Europe and China. Allow me to cite its conclusion on the likely shape of the international system:

'By 2025, the international system will be a global multipolar one with gaps in national power continuing to narrow between developed and developing countries. Concurrent with the shift in power among nation-states, the relative power of various non-state actors–including businesses, tribes, religious organisations, and criminal networks is increasing. The players are changing, but so too are the scope and breadth of transnational issues important for continued global prosperity … The next twenty years of transition to a new system are fraught with risks. Strategic rivalries are most likely to revolve around trade, investments, and technological innovation and acquisitions, but we cannot rule out a nineteenth century-like scenario of arms races, territorial expansion, and military rivalries … This is a story with no clear outcome … (These) trends suggest major discontinuities, shocks, and surprises.'

Assessments emanating from credible studies elsewhere are on somewhat parallel lines. They focus on multipolarity, interdependence, and changing nature of conflicts. Concepts like interpolarity and hybrid wars have acquired relevance. Other matters having security implications like governance, drugs, money laundering and immigration have been added to the framework. Each seeks a strategy to respond to a new situation; each compels a review of the security paradigm, and our response to it.

The Barcelona Report in 2004 focused on the capabilities needed by the European Union for dealing with situations of severe insecurity and for achieving 'freedom from fear'. It proposed a Human Security Doctrine for Europe in a set of seven principles. These were listed as the primacy of human rights, clear political authority, multilateralism, a bottom-up approach, regional focus, the use of legal instruments, and the appropriate use of force. The report was selective in its approach to human security.

A more holistic view was taken in 2001 by the UN Secretary General Kofi Annan. "We must," he said, "broaden our view of what is meant by peace and security. Peace means much more than the absence of war. Human security can no longer be understood in purely military terms. Rather, it must encompass economic development, social justice, environmental protection, democratization, disarmament, and respect for human rights and the rule of law."

In such a framework the inescapable conclusion would be that absence of any of these would signal an element of insecurity.

In an interesting book on new perspectives of security, Professor T.K. Oommen argues that security is the conjoint concern of three pillars–state, market and civil society; as a result, only "a society free from genocide, culturocide and ecocide may be conceptualised as a secure society." The sources of insecurity, he holds, tend to feed on one another and aggravate it. In more specific terms the India Social Development Report 2005 used six indices, namely demography, healthcare, basic amenities, education, unemployment and poverty, social deprivation–to assess the security perception of citizens in states of the Indian Union.

The substantive point that emerges is the felt need to assess security in a wider perspective. This is easier said than done. The human mind is not a tabula rasa; the response patterns of the past do condition its reactions. The challenge for the strategist is to overcome these and think beyond the obvious. Even in military terms, Donald Rumsfeld chose the expression "known unknowns and unknown unknowns" to highlight the predicament. While developing response patterns, it would be relevant to recall Sun Tzu's dictum that the acme of skill is to subdue the enemy without fighting; hence the need to "attack the enemy's strategy". For the world of tomorrow, however, the 'enemy' has to be defined in wider terms. In one of Arthur Clarke's stories there is a fascinating portrayal of a situation in which 'the ancient battle between man and insect' is decisively settled in favour of the latter. The same may hold for other contestations with nature. The human strategist would need to visualise the improbable, perhaps even the impossible. He should have the ability to combine innovative, perceptive and holistic insights and yet be realistic enough to be comprehensible. The challenge is real; it is also bewildering.

It is essential, in the first place, to comprehend insecurity. The dictionary meaning is fear or anxiety stemming from a concrete or alleged lack of protection. It could relate to individual or collective insecurity, could be self-centered, state-centric or society-centric. Its manifestations and sources could be multifarious. It could emanate from natural or human causes. For purposes of today's analysis, our focus would be on collective insecurity that affects particular segments of the population or even society as a whole. A typology of insecurities, present and anticipated, thus needs to be developed. This takes us to the very purpose of being in a society.

Hobbes depicted the pre-society stage as one in which life of a person was "nasty, brutish and short". Others dwelt on an essential implication of being in society. "The strongest man", said Rousseau, "is never strong enough to be always master, unless he transforms his power into right, and obedience into duty". Hence the need for an association which takes upon itself the obligation to, in Rousseau's words, "defend and protect with the whole force of the community the person and property of every associate." Furthermore, fear is not a correlate of underdevelopment and, to use Ashis Nandy's felicitous phrase, is to be found "in the interstices of anxiety" even in the most developed societies.

Consequently the community encapsulated in a territorial state seeks collective and, by implication, comprehensive security and, in today's world, does so without wishing to be homogenised and deprived of identities within its fold. The same would hold for the global community.

An observation made in the Report of the 6th ARF Security Policy Conference held in May 2009 is indicative of some new thinking. Noting that as a result of globalisation the international community has become more vulnerable to non-traditional security threats, it underlined the importance of 'a whole-of-society approach' to respond to these questions. It observed that 'both traditional and non-traditional security threats need to be balanced in terms of setting priorities and policy planning.'

What then should be the priorities for the world of tomorrow in terms of elements of insecurity and the imperative to address them?

III

It is evident that given the structure of the international system, traditional and more recent norms of state security would remain in place in the foreseeable future and make ever increasing demands on resources of individual states. The sustainability of the effort, however, would be a debatable question and there are some lessons to be derived from the last decade of the Cold War that demonstrated the inability of one of the contestants to cope with the burden. Equally relevant would be George Washington's caution about the impact on free societies of 'overgrown military establishments'. These apart the right to wage war, a traditionally accepted attribute of state sovereignty, stands circumscribed by the Charter of the United Nations in 1945. It enjoined Member States to refrain from 'the threat or use of force' in their dealings, except for Purposes of the UN and in self-defence as defined in Article 51. This, of course, has not prevented inter-state wars; it has, nevertheless, put into place the constraint of legitimacy of state action. Introspection by some of those involved in decision-making has now brought forth new categorisation: wars of necessity and wars of choice. Terminological refinement, however, has its own problems. Gradually but surely the concept of wrong, of illicit action, is beginning to seep into the discourse; it ventures into the 'unexplored normative potential' and would constitute a major advance in conceptual terms. Despite it, inter-state wars remain an option even though the easier availability of the weapons of mass destruction and the demonstrated futility of their use does seem to act as a deterrent on major conflagrations.

Going beyond the traditional security paradigm, the ambit of discussion does not remain confined to maintenance of state sovereignty and territorial integrity. Once we begin to address other threats, two characteristics rapidly emerge. We find, in the first place, that the initiating actors and eventual recipients are states as well as individuals and groups; secondly, because the latter do not always fall within the ambit of a single state, it necessitates departures from the traditional structure of command and compliance. The latter, in effect, would often depend upon demonstrated good rather than its a priori acceptance. Both, together, necessitate a paradigm shift.

Another aspect is the nature and diversity of challenges. Together they demonstrate the inefficacy of unilateral action and the imperative of a comprehensive and cooperative approach. The terms of this cooperation, and their equity, remain work in progress. Since paucity of time does not permit a detailed scrutiny, I shall endeavour to illustrate the point by referring to a few obvious but relevant aspects.

A case in point is terrorism. It has domestic and external dimensions that are not mutually exclusive. Some states indulge in it as an act of policy to conduct, what Kautilya called, 'secret war'. The Security Council has described terrorism as any act "intended to cause death or serious bodily harm to civilians or non-combatants with the purpose of intimidating a population or compelling a government or an international organization to do or abstain from doing any act". Globalisation and technology has made it trans-national in organisation and reach and devastating in its impact; hence the approach, mechanisms, and commitments developed through various Security Council resolutions as also the innumerable bilateral and regional arrangements that are unevenly implemented. These are essentially focused on preventive or punitive steps, on the dismantling of the infrastructure of terrorism, and do not deal sufficiently with the mental orientation that leads to terrorist acts. The latter emanate from a radicalisation of the mind induced by an ideological or faith-based impulse and propelled by a perceived grievance. Combating terrorism thus becomes a sociological and political effort as much as a security one.

Another threat of trans-national dimensions is pandemics. Their impact on societies is and would be devastating, apart from the havoc they bring about in terms of loss of human lives. A Princeton University Project in 2006 visualised the scenario in the wake of an apocalyptic pandemic. It is worthy of being cited in some detail:

'The global economy could grind to a halt, if not collapse entirely. Stock markets would fall, travel would cease, trade would be inhibited, and productivity would decline precipitously. In addition, the costs associated with directly tackling the crisis would be astronomical. Worse still would be the consequences of differential dying … we can plan on huge global disparities in the nationality and socio-economic status of victims. The repercussions of a catastrophe with such disparities would likely linger, fester, and cause rage for generations. Even in the industrialised world, trust might be obliterated as individual states hoard and nationalise vaccines that can be produced within their borders. In a post-pandemic world … dangerous patterns of inter-state behavior might emerge that resemble those prevalent before World War II.'

The report recommended that 'we must broaden our understanding of national security so that health and development experts are included at every stage of the threat assessment and decision-making processes and not just consulted after the outbreak of a crisis.'

Despite these suggestions, an acknowledged expert wrote in the Wall Street Journal on May 2 this year that the United States remains 'under-prepared for any pandemic or major outbreak, whether it comes from newly emerging infectious diseases, bio-terror attack or laboratory accident.' Visualising the consequences can at best a matter of conjecture; a worst-case apocalyptic vision of the future was portrayed last year in the film Doomsday in which a whole country, quarantined for decades to contain a deadly virus, reverted to lethally primitive form of existence.

As for our own capabilities, a sober assessment would show that these are modest and the recent experience in regard to H1N1 was instructive. Given the global health trends there is a good case for creating, nationally or multilaterally, one primary facility and one backup facility for the production of vaccines and therapeutics expressly for emerging and re-emerging infections.

Similar arguments hold for environment and climate change. These too are not coterminous with political units. At the national level and despite the good work done by a number of dedicated environmentalists, public awareness is still in its infancy and there is merit in Vandana Shiva's observation that "the environmental movement can only survive if it becomes a movement for justice." Official efforts, on the other hand, have often sought to strike an uneasy balance between competing pressures.

Awareness at the international level of the need for conservation and management of resources for sustainable development was initiated in the UN General Assembly as early as 1988, was highlighted by the Rio Summit of 1992 and thereafter allowed to linger while governments negotiated from narrow national perspectives. An acknowledgement that changing climate poses a threat to stability and human security has been slow to emerge. In his Nobel Lecture in December 2007 Dr R.K. Pachauri drew attention to some instances in recorded history of the link between climate and security. He laid stress on "the equity implications of the changes that are occurring and are likely to occur in the future." He defined peace as "security and the secure access to resources that are essential for living. A disruption in such access could prove disruptive of peace". He listed these essentials as (1) access to water, (2) access to sufficient food, and impact on (3) public health, (4) biodiversity, and (5) security of settlements particularly in Asian and African mega-deltas and small islands.

Despite frequent articulation of principles, especially at Kyoto and Bali, the harsh reality is that individual nations and particularly those in the developed world are dragging their feet on implementing their commitments.

Two conclusions emanate from these examples of dimensions of insecurity, transcending national frontiers and beyond solutions in the traditional security paradigm. They suggest that solutions have to be sought in a multilateral framework of equals; they also have to be equitable. The process would be tortuous and slow and would depend on the speed with which the gravity of the emerging threats sinks into public perceptions and governmental action.

IV

Let me return to the question of the ambit of insecurity posed in the earlier part of this lecture. It clearly goes beyond challenges to state sovereignty and its territorial integrity. It is also evident that comprehensive security needs to focus on citizens and their right for a dignified existence. This does not limit the role of the State; instead, it changes it. The responsibility of the citizen and of the civil society is to keep the state glued to its purpose. This, in our case, is inscribed in the Preamble of the Constitution. From this emanates the imperative, at the conceptual level, to redefine the social purpose: to ensure that each citizen is assured freedom from fear and from want so that he/she is able to partake of all other activities open to a citizen. Such an endeavour at the national and global levels would help bring forth a new world, more in consonance with a sustainable existence in tune with human rights and the environment. Its rationale would be practical necessity and the imperative of survival, rather than utopian idealism. It would require adding new dimensions to the concept of threat assessment.

The need for a new approach to comprehensive security is underlined by a survey of both the traditional and non-traditional threats faced by us in the past three decades. The data is in the public domain. It presents a complex picture; it is also indicative of a certain imbalance in our allocation of resources and in the efficacy of their utilisation. This suggests a need for correctives directed at capacity-building in societal structures and, in the security framework, a rationalisation based on qualitative upgrading and quantitative resizing.

No venture into futurology can altogether rule out less optimistic scenarios. There is always the possibility that evolution in thought and practice may not happen along the lines visualised in the foregoing. The result would be an optimisation of insecurity. Insanity, goes a Lebanese proverb, has seventy gates. Reaching any of these would be entry into the capital of hell, aptly called Pandemonium by the poet John Milton.

Avoiding such an outcome would require collective community effort based on sober reasoning grounded in a set of agreed values and objectives. This is achievable since, as a 14th century historian said, "the pasture of stupidity is unwholesome to mankind".

'Emerging China: Prospects for Partnership in Asia', Conference

Indian Council of World Affairs and Association of Asian Scholars
Sapru House, New Delhi
21 November 2009

I am happy to be here at this seminar organised by the Indian Council of World Affairs and the Association of Asia Scholars. Sapru House itself has a place in the evolution of our foreign policy thinking. Established in 1943, the Council is tasked to promote the study of national and international affairs. More than a generation of scholars, analysts and diplomatists has passed through its portals.

It was here that Jawaharlal Nehru, with his vision of Asia forged in the fires of the struggle for freedom that raged across the entire continent of Asia, organised the Asian Relations Conference in 1947 as a non-governmental gathering.

Human societies live in time and space. A historian has noted that in the year 1500 each one of the great centres of world civilisation was at a roughly similar stage of development, some more advanced in one area but less so in others. Subsequent events were to show that initiative, technological innovation, intellectual liberty and a flourishing economic base provided the critical mix that allowed the West to dominate the world for almost five centuries.

The Asian Relations Conference was held at the end of one era and at the threshold of another. One theme of the conference was the contours of the awakening of Asia; another was cooperation and partnership among the countries and peoples of Asia. The objective was spelt out by Nehru: "We propose to stand on our own feet and to co-operate with all others who are prepared to co-operate with us."

Six decades later, the continent stands at the threshold of another Asian era. In this period the Nehruvian vision of Asia, indeed the geographical unity of the continent so to speak, has ceased to matter for geo-politics or economics. Asia developed, but the development was perceived and reflected in individual countries, sub-regional and trans-regional groupings. Japan emerged from the ruins of the Second World War as an important economic powerhouse, South East Asia has witnessed rapid economic growth and there has been a dramatic change in the economic, military and political profile of China. India has developed at a much faster pace in the last decade bringing millions out of poverty and showing that substantive social and economic progress is possible through democratic governance.

In this period, even as India and China enunciated the Five Principles of Peaceful Co-existence as the corner stone of inter-state relations, the bilateral relations between them did not always conform to those very principles. Yet, as Prime Minister Rajiv Gandhi presciently put it in 1988: "What must not be forgotten in a listing of differences is a listing of commonality in our world outlook. There has been significant parallelism in the views expressed by India and China on a wide range of issues relating to world security, the international political order, the new international economic order, global concerns in regard to environment and space".

A glance at the Asian map shows that over a wide arc extending from West Asia, through Central Asia, to South and South East Asia to East Asia, Indian and Chinese interests intersect. Active partnership between New Delhi and Beijing and mutual sensitivity to each other's concerns is thus vitally necessary if stability, security and prosperity in the shared spaces in their near and distant neighbourhood are to be effectively ensured.

The leaderships of India and China during the past two decades have cooperated in creating mutual political and economic stakes for mutual benefit. Economic cooperation between us has become a principal driver of our strategic and cooperative partnership for peace and prosperity. Yet, cooperation does not preclude competition. We realise that countries compete in global markets and such competition is constructive and beneficial rather than adversarial.

The post-Cold War world also demands that we readjust our theoretical models of state behaviour. Traditional concepts of polarity, alliance building, balance of power and spheres of influence have to contend with the impact of globalisation where opportunities for, and threats to, human welfare and national progress have a global character. How India and China deal with various trans-national challenges such as terrorism, illegal migration, smuggling of drugs and arms and pandemics would affect large parts of Asia. The joint vision of the leaderships in India and China is to ensure a global order in which our simultaneous development will have a positive impact for our peoples and economies, as also for the rest of the world.

II

Allow me to dilate a little on conceptual frameworks. Partnership in Asia has primarily taken four forms. The first is one of Asian regionalism. Asia has been primarily reduced to the total of its constituent sub-regions like GCC, SAARC, SCO, ASEAN, BIMSTEC and the MGC (Mekong-Ganga Cooperation) framework. The second means of partnership has been through inter-regional dialogue forums like Asia-Europe Meeting (ASEM) and APEC (Asia-Pacific Economic Cooperation). The third framework is one of global and multilateral organisations. These include the UN and its specialised bodies, the IMF and World Bank, WTO and WIPO (World Intellectual Property Organisation), Asian Development Bank etc. There also exist thematic organisations such as the G-20, Organisation of Islamic Conference and the League of Arab States. The fourth framework is that of bilateral relations between countries of Asia.

The last decade has seen two contradictory trends at work. Even as market-driven globalisation is a reality, the global political and economic institutional framework has weakened and is evident in the diminished role and influence of bodies such as the United Nations, IMF, World Bank and WTO. Nations have resorted to regional political and economic institutions to resolve problems and cooperate for mutual gain. This phenomenon is most visible in the economic arena. With progress being stalled in the Doha round of trade negotiations, countries of Asia have concluded regional and bilateral free trade and economic partnership agreements creating the so-called "noodle bowl" of Asian regionalism, spurred on by the inability of global multilateral bodies to address the

Asian economic crisis in 1997 and leading to the emergence of the ASEAN+3 framework.

The evolution of community building and partnership in Asia thereafter led to the launching of the East Asia Summit (EAS) process. The first Declaration issued in Kuala Lumpur called for the EAS to be an open, inclusive, transparent and outward looking forum. The ultimate vision is one of Asian economic integration by converging the Free Trade Agreements among Asian countries into an Asian Regional Trade Agreement. This could, later, lead to the creation of a broader Asian Economic Community.

III

Partnership and cooperation among Asian countries is a necessity to take advantage of the opportunities emerging as a result of the region's increasing economic integration, as also to face the common threats of terrorism, proliferation of weapons of mass destruction, energy shortage, security of sea lanes, pandemics, natural disasters and others. China is an important element of this architecture of cooperation, as are India, Japan, Korea, ASEAN, Australia, New Zealand and all other Asian sub-regions.

The future weight and success of Asia is the sum of the success of each of these national and regional components and the tenacity of their inter-linkages. Long-term security and stability in Asia is dependent on the ability of Asian countries to build mutual stakes in one another. Every framework that can further this process should be encouraged and welcomed. A few caveats however would be in order:

1. No partnership architecture or process should be exclusive or exclusionary. It should seek to bring into the fold as many Asian nations as possible and articulate an inclusive, open and transparent process of community building.
2. Community building in Asia should not be a reflection of the emerging redistribution of global or regional power nor should it be a platform for projection of narrow economic and political interests of a nation or group of nations.

3. Soft regionalism based on informal dialogue and consultation mechanisms, consensus building and open structures is a better alternative to hard regionalism based on rigid and definitive institutional structures, inflexible mechanisms and formal dialogue.
4. A multitude of formal cooperation structures could lead to a pick-and-choose policy for 'forum shopping'. The "noodle bowl" of free trade agreements and comprehensive partnership agreements is overflowing and the impact of these numerous bilateral and multilateral agreements on trade efficiency is an open question. Eventually, there would be no alternative to effective and functioning global multilateral institutions such as the United Nations, IMF, the World Bank and the WTO to ensure that there is a fair, transparent, open and rules-based global political and economic order.

Before I conclude, and in a gathering of strategic thinkers and analysts, it is relevant to recall the words of a master of statecraft of the nineteenth century. Nations, he observed, travel on the stream of time which they neither create nor direct but upon which they can "steer with more or less skill and experience." I am confident that this conference would make a contribution to this compendium of skill and also come forth with some practical suggestions about how trans-Asian connectivity can be achieved in an early time frame.

Golden Jubilee Celebration of the National Defence College

Tees January Marg, New Delhi
27 April 2010

I am happy to be here today to join you in commemorating the Golden Jubilee of the National Defence College (NDC). Through five decades of sustained work the college has earned reputation and respect amongst its peers in the world.

The primary purpose of the establishment of the NDC was to instruct senior service and civilian officers in the 'wider aspects of higher direction and strategy of warfare.' It represented a systemic attempt to synergise the various dimensions of a principal objective of social order, that is, to seek security and develop the capacity to face challenges to it.

The meaning and content of these concepts has evolved with time and human progress. Security today is viewed as human security. It goes beyond state security in the traditional sense and encompasses environmental protection, resource security, sustainable development, basic amenities, good governance, social justice, and human rights. War too now has a meaning that transcends the one given to it in textbooks of strategy or international law. Concepts like *interpolarity, hybrid wars* and *networked adversaries* have acquired relevance and are re-shaping strategies and tactics.

The collective impact of these perceptions dilutes the traditional paradigm and induces a comprehensive review of concepts and practices. Such an approach excludes compartmentalised thinking.

The challenge for the strategist therefore is to think beyond the obvious, visualise the improbable perhaps even the impossible. A tsunami, a pandemic, a global financial meltdown, a volcanic eruption of the type witnessed in Iceland earlier this month are indicative of the type of challenges that national planners may have to confront in addition to the traditional ones. Each of these would necessitate inter-agency planning and implementation.

Here lies the relevance of institutions like the NDC where a pooling of knowledge and experience is intended to shed new light on questions of comprehensive security and to bring forth policy options.

Equally important are the "higher direction" aspects of the Course and the question of management and leadership. These are critical to success in any organization. Captain Liddell Hart, a strategic thinker of an earlier era, penned a passage that to me has continuing relevance. Allow me to share it with you; it may, or may not, resonate:

> A study of history, past and in the making, seems to suggest that most of mankind's troubles are man-made, arise from the compound effect of decisions taken without knowledge, ambitions uncontrolled by wisdom, and judgments that lack understanding.... Men who are helped to authority by their knowledge continually make decisions on questions beyond their knowledge. Ambition to maintain their authority forbids them from admitting the limits of their knowledge, and calling upon the knowledge that is available in other men.

Developments in the last two decades have changed the world and the way we interact with it nationally and globally. The end of the Cold War, the induction of new technologies, the implications of globalisation, the debate about the place of state sovereignty in world politics have, together, undermined in varying degrees the foundations of the pre-1990 world.

Alongside, the receding horizons of science have given a new profile to genomics and neuroscience, offering a new definition of human nature and leading, in the view of some competent observers, to the possibility of "promethean powers to repair and even redesign that nature."

It is here that two questions of immense importance confront us: What is the nature of the threat today? How prepared are we, nationally and globally, to cope with the implications of the changes that events and our own actions have unleashed?

An answer to the first question is inextricably linked to our perception of insecurity. Beyond traditionally politico-military threats, any impediment to national development to achieve an inclusive and equitable society would be considered a threat. The dimensions of human security were spelt out by the UNDP many years back. More recently, the *India Social Development Report 2005* used six indices to make an India-specific assessment. Correctives to some of these lie in the domestic sphere while some others are of a regional or global nature and can only be addressed through wider cooperation.

A sober assessment would show that the national will and national capacity is being impacted adversely by the sub-national and the supra-national. The State, as Professor Barry Buzan has observed, "is less important in the new security agenda than the old one. It still remains central, but no longer dominates either as the exclusive referent object or as the principle embodiment of threat."

How is this to be achieved? What are the pitfalls?

The challenge, in the first place, is to craft methodologies by which the State can still act effectively within constraints, be they of national law or of multinational covenants. This is possible because increasingly trans-national threats to common good are evoking collective responses. Heightened awareness has helped. The trends are clear even if the pace is uneven.

Secondly, while providers of security are primarily State actors, the threats to security of states is increasingly moving beyond the sovereign space to include non-state, sub-state or trans-state actors. The technological changes and quicker communication and transportation have become force multipliers to such non-state actors. The instrumentalities available to State actors to deal with such threats have to be adapted or modified accordingly since traditional deterrence models may not be effective when confronted with cellular organisations and their decision making structures.

Thirdly, it is important to acknowledge conceptually and in empirical terms that security of states and security of societies is not necessarily synonymous since there can be state actors that disregard accepted norms of good governance and thereby induce insecurity. This gives rise to doctrines on intervention. Recourse to it complicates matters and causes untold hardship to affected societies. A societal or political version of nano-medicine that seeks out a diseased tissue and pathogens and spares healthy tissue from collateral damage is yet to emerge.

Finally, and given the experience of the first decade of this century, the 'multi-polar' world that is tending to emerge encapsulates within its fluidity opportunities as well as risks and therefore calls for careful navigation.

"Few countries of the world", according to the Annual Report for 2009-2010 of the Ministry of Defence, "face the range of security concerns that India faces today." Addressing these concerns, internally and externally, remains a matter of the highest priority. Institutions like the National Defence College contribute to the national effort. The NDC deserves appreciation for its structured study of dimensions of national security in our increasingly complex global environment. The officers who have graduated from here have contributed to it in good measure. The college can be justly proud of its Alumni.

I am confident that the next fifty years of the National Defence College would be equally productive.

Prague Security Studies Institute
Ministry of Foreign Affairs, Prague, Czech Republic
7 June 2010

Some Aspects of Global Governance in the 21st Century

I claim to be resident of a city of considerable antiquity. It is one of eight cities built successively on the same stretch of land on the banks of a river. I, therefore, cannot but be fascinated by another city of ancient vintage. Legend has it that the founding deity of Prague visualised 'a large town whose glory shall reach the stars'. The beauty and architectural splendour I see here testify to this prophesy.

Geography and history have bestowed on Prague a centrality that is evident. It has for centuries witnessed ideological and political contestations in central Europe and is today an active participant in the making of a new Europe.

For all these reasons it gives me great pleasure to be here today at the Prague Security Studies Institute. The Institute's formidable reputation for contributing to policy debates makes it an appropriate venue to think aloud and explore policy options for the world of tomorrow. I thank the Institute for inviting me to address this distinguished gathering today.

Ours is an era of great change–political, economic and technological. Humankind has benefited from it, though in unequal measure. Some live in affluence and prosperity unmatched in history; others are less fortunate. The levels of disparity between peoples, nations and societies are starker than ever before.

The impact of change is pervasive. Concepts, values and systems are in flux. The sanctity of the Westphalian Order of State sovereignty has been dented by international covenants and practices. Globalisation has accelerated it by the imperatives of what the historian Philip Bobbitt has called the 'Market State'; technology has added to it. Clarity nevertheless evades us; the sociologist Anthony Giddens has described the present day world as "puzzling, strange, elliptical" in which 'we are far from being fully in control of the forces we have unleashed'.

It is evident that we need a new global consensus, a new paradigm for assessing performance.

Many in this audience would recall that in 1992 Vaclav Havel had called for a redefinition of modernity. "Man's attitude to the world", he said, "must be radically changed". He then went on to elaborate the concept:

> It is my profound conviction that we have to release from the sphere of private whim such forces as natural, unique and unrepeatable experience of the world, an elementary sense of justice, the ability to see things as others do, a sense of transcendental responsibility, archetypal wisdom, good taste, courage, compassion and faith in the importance of particular measures that do not aspire to be a universal key to salvation. Such forces must be rehabilitated.

I concede it may not be altogether easy to implement such a vision in its totality. Nevertheless, today we have the objective conditions for economic and political emancipation of a majority of humanity since technology and political evolution have exponentially multiplied the strands of connection, movement and circulation between states of peoples, ideas, goods and services.

We are also in a better position than ever before to suggest for observance, norms of social behaviour appropriate for the requirements of the age, remembering Aristotle's dictum that moral virtue does not emanate from nature and has to be imbibed by habit.

Converting this potential for change into reality represents the most significant governance challenge, nationally and internationally.

Governance has been a subject of debate since the advent of civilisation. Greek philosophers dwelt on it. In the 4th century BC, the Indian strategic thinker and administrator Kautilya maintained that the objective of governance was "the happiness and welfare" of the subjects of a state: "in the happiness of his subjects lies his happiness; in their welfare his welfare". An 11th century AD medieval scholar wrote that the God-ordained duty of the king was "to close the doors of corruption, confusion and discord" so that people may live in constant security.

Global Governance is today understood as a minimum acceptable framework of norms, principles and rules needed to tackle global problems and achieve global objectives, and that are upheld by a broad institutional framework, including multilateral, regional and international organisations, national governments, the private sector and civil society. These objectives include eradication of poverty, mitigation of conflict, achieving minimum standards of health and education, environmental sustainability, upholding human rights and addressing the problem of hunger. Good governance is about leadership, sensitivity to the concerns of others, and upholding of basic norms of equity, justice and fairness. It is essentially about humanity defined in universalistic terms.

The dimensions of the problem, and the complexity of the task, unavoidably bring forth disjuncture and challenges. Allow me to mention a few of these.

We know, in the first place, that while the primacy of nation-states has not ended, their absolute control over their territory and their citizens has been partly ceded to trans-national, multilateral, global and regional institutions and mechanisms. This upward power shift is still a work-in-progress as exemplified by the experience of the European Union.

Secondly, governance at the global and national levels confronts the old dilemma of a choice between normative standards and realpolitik. The unacceptability of a chauvinistic concept of the nation-state must go hand in hand with a similar undesirability of an unequal global order. The latter is most evident in the institutional inadequacy of the global political and financial institutions. A sustainable argument for global governance cannot overlook David Held's observation that 'a theory of legitimate power is inescapably a theory of democracy in the interlocking processes and structures of the global system. It is a theory of the democratic state within the global order and the theory of the impact of the global order on the democratic state'.

A third reality to be registered is the state of flux characterising the contemporary world order. The past two decades have witnessed bipolarity conceding ground to unipolarity and then to multipolarity. Affiliations and identities are no longer exclusive, and overlapping multiplicity has become a necessity rather than an option. Alongside, globalisation and homogenisation have had an adverse impact on cultural distinctiveness of peoples and nations. The articulation of who a people are, and what the quintessential values of their culture and civilisation are, is a more difficult process today. This is more so in multi-ethnic, multi-lingual and multi-religious states, or groupings of states, when identifying snycretic threads from the past has become important in building a broad-based framework of national identity.

A fourth point to be noted is that unknown to the casual observer and undocumented in its minutiae, the disparate elements of global governance are welding treaty-based global and multilateral organisations and national governments with the evolving global discourse on rights, democracy, legitimacy, and international cooperation. National governments, peoples, corporate entities and civil societies, who may or may not have similar value systems, are cooperating in transnational networks for achieving common objectives. Some are old, strong and cross-cutting alliances, while others are recent loose groupings focused on limited themes. The future evolution of this process has important consequences for all of us.

Even when there is a convergence of views and recipes, the experience of individual societies remains critical to correctives. It is in this context that I wish to speak of my country. India is one-sixth of the world in terms of population, is a vibrant democracy and is a microcosm of the diversities that characterise our world. It has been rightly called 'the largest multicultural society in the world.'

I wish to highlight three aspects of our experience for your consideration.

First, and the most important, is the accommodation of diversity and acceptance of multiple identities. We have been fortunate in implementing it due to our civilisational heritage and innate capacity for synthesis. In the words of a distinguished academic, "the Indian Constitution was well ahead of its time not only in recognising diversities but also in providing for representation of the collectivities in the formal democratic structures." The special provisions for guarantees or affirmative action in eight broad categories–caste, class, tribe, backwardness, religion, region, sex and language–is evidence of this approach for securing justice and ensuring cultural autonomy in a composite culture within a framework of a quasi-federal structure. Accommodation of diversity has thus been consciously incorporated as a distinctive feature of the Indian state. It implies that a standardised image of an Indian cannot be constructed.

Second, rapid economic and human development has raised new issues of identity and integration. Living in isolation is not an option in the era of globalisation; there are, however, many ways of living together. Integration is necessary and desirable; assimilation is neither desirable nor practical. Throughout our history, we have seen identities being built on a series of inclusions and exclusions reflective of ground realities. The challenge for us in the future, as in the past, would be to maintain a balance in favour of inclusions.

Third, it has been said that societal "conflict is written into the idea of India" and that some of the dimensions of such conflict include caste injustice, religious differences, economic inequality, environmental degradation and competition for resources, internal migration, political rights and recognition, issues arising out of a federal structure and competing claims of rural-urban populations, present and future generations, and rival perceptions of nationalisms. The constant effort of our polity, through its democratic churning, has been to address societal conflict through accommodation and good governance and realise the vision of an India that is more prosperous, more inclusive, more accommodative and more confident of its ability to resolve complex social issues.

The Indian approach to multiculturalism is to 'aspire towards a form of citizenship that is marked neither by a universalism generated by complete homogenisation, nor by particularism of self-identical and closed communities'.

At a basic level, global governance is deeply impacted by the quality of governance of nations. I would like to conclude by noting that both of our countries have been fortunate to be blessed with vibrant democratic polities and dynamic economies. Our peoples and leaders are committed to peace, freedom and justice for all. Our mutual cooperation and our role in the various regional and global groupings would substantially contribute to better profiles of global governance in this century.

No discussion of global governance in the contemporary context would be complete without attention being paid to what has been called the 'Hydra-Headed Crisis' confronting the world. The reference, of course, is to the overlapping, even interlinked, economic and financial, security, and environmental threats that have emerged so sharply in the past year or so. They are interlinked and impact the capacity of players on the global stage. They also reflect on national and global governance, demonstrate the limitations of national governance and the inadequacy of existing global mechanisms.

The experience reiterates the imperative need for restructuring institutions of global governance to make them more representative, more effective and more dedicated to the common, rather than sectional, good.

Meeting of Members of Parliament held in honour of the President of the United States of America, The Honourable Barack H. Obama

Parliament House, New Delhi

8 November 2010

This is one of those infrequent occasions when the Rajya Sabha and the Lok Sabha Members come together for a meeting to honour, and hear, a visiting dignitary of great eminence. Our guest today is from one of the world's oldest democracies and we, in the largest, rejoice in welcoming him.

Relationships between countries, Mr President, are reflective of a complex web of considerations. Some of these are ephemeral, others more durable. The latter pertain to principles and values that transcend material considerations. Elements of what has been called the American Creed with its focus on liberty, constitutionalism, the law, democracy, individualism and political and cultural egalitarianism inspired and influenced our own Constitution.

We admire the tenacity of the American spirit and its capacity for introspection and course correction. You have demonstrated both during your presidency. The troubled world we live in necessitates it. We appreciate your initiative to "seek the peace and security of a world without nuclear weapons" and to take concrete steps towards it. We ourselves have been for long an advocate of non-discriminatory and universal nuclear disarmament.

In over six decades of Independence, India has endeavoured to impart substance to the principles of liberty, equality and fraternity and to promote political as well as social and economic justice. We have accommodated diversity. Above all, we have sought to eschew conflict and promote peace.

The United States and India, Mr President, have much to do together. Our areas of agreement are considerable, and expanding. We venture to hope that our two countries would work purposefully for an open world based on the principles of equity and dedicated to peace, freedom and prosperity for all people. We both repose faith in John Rawls' dictum that 'rights secured by justice are not subject to political bargaining or to a calculus of social interests.'

We are geographically removed from each other but face similar threats and challenges and have to be sensitive to each other's concerns and critical interests. As vibrant democracies we cherish the right to disagree within a framework of our endeavour for the common good.

We are confident that your visit would bring our two people closer, help create a world order free from the evils of extremism, intolerance, injustice and terrorism, and devoted to the pursuit of new vistas of humanism and technological innovation in the service of humankind.

Inauguration of the Indian Council for World Affairs Conference titled 'India and GCC Countries, Iraq and Iran: Emerging Security Perspectives'

New Delhi
20 November 2010

I thank the Indian Council of World Affairs for inviting me today to inaugurate this seminar on a subject of considerable relevance. The presence of a good number of scholars from many lands testifies to it.

I note that the organisers have riveted attention on the terra firma rather than on a body of water about whose nomenclature dictionaries are sought to be re-written. This is perhaps a good example of the art of evading choices and managing contradictions!

Our focus today is on eight countries that constitute a sub-set of the West Asian region. Their location and contiguities are relevant. Six of them (Bahrain, Kuwait, Oman, Qatar, Saudi Arabia and the United Arab Emirates) are members of a regional grouping–the Gulf Cooperation Council while the other two–Iran and Iraq–are physically in the sub-region and share commonalities with all others as also with some countries beyond the region.

Given the geography, security perceptions are unavoidably interlinked and turbulence within or around the area usually has a wider impact.

Some in this audience would recall the title of Ibn Khaldun's great work on history. It is *Kitab al-Ibar* (*Book of Lessons*). It would be no exaggeration to say that in relation to our subject of discussion, lessons of history are of relevance. One of these, pertaining to the concept of dominance and exclusivity, is particularly note worthy. It can be dated to the arrival in the region of the Portuguese in 1498. They were followed by the Dutch who in turn were replaced by the British. The British dominance lasted till 1970. In the past four decades, various bilateral and multilateral, regional and extra-regional, combinations for security have been explored. Like the earlier versions, selectivity and exclusion rather than inclusion have been their dominant trait.

These perceptions have focused on military security aimed at ensuring the safety of the trade routes by sea; they remain a principal impulse for the littoral states as also for their trading partners the world over. An unstated major premise is maintenance of political stability and, by implication, regime security. In a wider context, however, this view of security is limited and inadequate. A more holistic approach was articulated by the UN Secretary General Kofi Annan in 2001. "We must," he said, "broaden our view of what is meant by peace and security. Peace means much more than the absence of war. Human security can no longer be understood in purely military terms. Rather, it must encompass economic development, social justice, environmental protection, democratisation, disarmament, and respect for human rights and the rule of law."

In such a comprehensive framework, deficit on any of these counts would signal an element of insecurity. A holistic approach of this nature, essential for a fuller understanding of security and insecurity, is perhaps beyond the scope of this conference focused as it seems to be on a more traditional paradigm.

It is evident that given the geo-political imperatives of these eight littoral states of the Persian Gulf, security perspectives and threat perceptions do not converge. Nevertheless, and in relation to this international waterway, some common elements can be discerned. In the first place, the concerned states want to prosper and avail of the benefits of development. Secondly, the Gulf lands are essential for the economic health of the world since they are a principal source of hydrocarbon energy as well as a major market for industrial goods, technology and services, For these reasons, to use Curzon's phrase used in another context in 1903, "the peace of these waters must be maintained". Interestingly enough Gulf security, in the words of a Saudi scholar, "was an external issue long before it was one among the Gulf States themselves".

The essential ingredients of such a requirement would be (a) prevalence of conditions of peace and stability in the individual littoral states (b) freedom of access to, and outlet from, Persian Gulf through the Strait of Hormuz (c) freedom of commercial shipping in international waters in the waterway (d) freedom to all states of the Gulf littoral to exploit their hydrocarbon and other natural resources and export them (e) avoidance of conflict that may impinge on the production of oil and gas and on the freedom of trade and shipping and (f) assurance that regional or extra-regional conditions do not impinge on any of these considerations.

In December last year a senior dignitary in the region described the objectives of Gulf diplomacy as "mutual understanding, coexistence, good relations with our neighbours and the establishment of strong relations based on the principles of reciprocal advantage and the realisation of the good of all." These principles by themselves are unexceptionable and widely subscribed to. The devil is in the un-stated major premise, and in threat perceptions that do not converge sufficiently.

The challenge, then, lies in seeking this convergence in areas of security, politics and economics and in developing procedures that would help bring it about. Experience shows that convergence is achieved only through a painstaking process of developing a (minimum) common threat perception, in maintaining it over time and in developing the mechanism for minimising risks to common security and maximising the benefits of cooperation. Such a process requires agreement on dialogue procedures.

Record shows that the resources of the region were initially controlled by extra-regional private commercial entities that had played a pioneering role in the discovery and development of these resources. They were strongly supported by their governments. The process of establishing national control over these resources was at times torturous and painful. Eventually, however, the mindset of an earlier era gave way to the common sense approach of inter-dependence of the producer and the consumer. Access to resources thus became more relevant than physical control.

I mention this because some residual perceptions of the earlier period do at times cloud the market vision even now and need to be dispelled.

II

In this backdrop, I propose to explore answers to three questions: How does the prevailing situation affect India and Indian interests? What should India do to sustain and secure its interests? What could, and should, be the Indian contribution to the promotion of peace and security in the sub-region?

The strategic relevance of the sub-region to India has to be located geographically, historically and in economic terms. The distance from Mumbai to Basra is 1526 nautical miles while Bander Abbas and Dubai are in a radius of 1000 nautical miles. Contact through trade and movement of people has roots deep in history, testified to by archaeological finds and written record. Fascination with India is reflected in Kitab Ajaib al-Hind by Buzurg ibn Shahriyar of Ramhormuz, a 10th century AD collection of sailor's tales. Many proverbs pertaining to India are to be found in the colloquial language of the lower Gulf. Familiarity with India and Indians at individual and family levels, Mumbai-Hindustani, Mumbai-Biryani and Bollywood films contribute to it in good measure particularly in the GCC countries.

Given this proximity, it is hardly surprising that in the period after 1975 there has been a significant spurt in economic linkages between the region and India. Changed and changing requirements and capabilities have contributed to it and will continue to do so in the foreseeable future. It is significant that given the affinities of the past and the experience of recent decades, the public and political establishments in the littoral states are India-friendly and Indian friendly.

The quantitative parametres of this relationship can be specified:

- We import over 63 per cent of our crude oil requirement from these eight countries of the Persian Gulf. Its worth in money terms, in 2009-10, stood at over $49 billion. Given the rate of growth of the Indian economy, these figures can only go up in the future.
- These eight countries account for over 22 per cent of our total trade as of 2009-10 amounting to around $105 billion. They account for a quarter of our imports totalling $72 billion and 18

per cent of exports totalling around $33 billion. Six of these eight countries, barring Oman and Bahrain, figure among the top 25 countries in terms of total trade.

- UAE is our top trading partner with a total trade of $43.5 billion, ahead of China at $42.4 billion and the US at 36.5 billion. It is our largest export destination accounting for 13 per cent of our exports amounting to $24 billion and the second largest source of our imports after China, totalling $19.5 billion.
- Saudi Arabia is our fourth largest trading partner with a trade of $21 billion, and Iran our ninth largest trading partner at $13.4 billion.
- An Indian non-immigrant workforce of around 6 million works in these countries, principally in the GCC states. Of these, 1.6 million are in Saudi Arabia and 1.2 million in the UAE. The composition of this workforce has changed over the years and many more professionals and specialised technical skills are to be found amongst them today. The remittances of this workforce, through banking channels, stands at around $30 billion per annum. They help support six million families and contribute in some measure to economic activity in some of the states of the Indian Union.
- The two-way investment profile, modest at present, is expected to grow with the growth of the Indian economy. The GCC countries have become an important destination for Indian projects and IT services.

The sub-region is also within the security parameter of India and within the operational radius of the Indian Navy. The latter's participation in the anti-piracy operations in the Arabian Sea is a case in point. If needed, it can escort shipping and interdict forces hostile to it.

The focus of Indian interest therefore is, and would remain, on the desirability of having (a) friendly governments (b) regional peace and stability (c) access to oil and gas resources of the region (d) freedom of navigation in the Persian Gulf and through the Straits of Hormuz (e) continued market access for Indian trade, technology, investments and workforce and (f) security and welfare of the Indian workforce, particularly in times of distress emanating from disturbed local or regional conditions.

A state of preparedness for responding to other contingencies should also be catered for, in consonance with the developing dimensions of maritime security.

It would therefore be fair to opine that India is reasonably comfortable with the status quo. However, the apprehension of an unstable status quo also looms over the horizon. Misgivings about intentions motivate it; divergence of perceptions and policy about extra-regional politico-military presence adds to it; so does what had been called 'an undeclared arms race.' One may add to this disruptive challenges emanating from non-state actors and new technologies. The requirement clearly is to seek understandings and arrangements that would cater to the threat perceptions and essential interests of all regional and extra-regional stake holders and thus stabilise the regional situation on a longer term basis.

III

Despite the successes of the GCC, attempts to foster a comprehensive Gulf regional cooperation have a history of over three decades and are replete with failed strategies of local or global hegemony. There is therefore an imperative need for developing a security order that is seen as equitable by all the states concerned.

There are ideas and precedents elsewhere that can be drawn upon beneficially. Asian regionalism and community-building has remained, albeit unevenly, an important framework for cooperation and framework within the continent. We thus have strong regional organisations focused on constituent sub-regions such as ASEAN, GCC, SAARC, SCO, BIMSTEC and the MGC. The Asian Development Bank, in the context of East Asia, has characterised the challenges of regional cooperation as including "providing regional public goods, managing spillovers among economies, exercising Asia's influence in global economic forums, liberalising trade and investment, and helping to improve national policies in which the region has a vital stake".

It is evident, that these challenges exist in the Gulf region too, and that a Gulf regionalism that is outward looking, flexible and dynamic, consistent with regional diversity would contribute to regional and global welfare, peace and security. This would also enable these nations to take advantage of the opportunities emerging from enhanced economic integration, as also to face the common threats of terrorism, proliferation of weapons of mass destruction, securing energy exports, security of sea lanes, tackling pandemics, natural disasters and others.

What could or should be the guiding principles of a Gulf regionalism that is in the interest of all regional and extra-regional stakeholders? A few of its essential ingredients can be mentioned:

It should not, in the first place, be exclusive or exclusionary. It should instead articulate an inclusive, open and transparent process of community building.

Secondly, it should not be a reflection of the emerging redistribution of global or regional power nor should it be a platform for projection of narrow economic and political interests of a nation, an alliance or a group of nations.

Thirdly, soft regionalism based on informal dialogue and consultation mechanisms, consensus building and open structures would help in establishing cooperative and beneficial norms of state behaviour ,and

Finally, it must not be seen as means to limit state sovereignty but as instrumentalities to address complex regional problems through cooperation and partnership.

Like in East Asia, Gulf regional cooperation and community building should include important stake-holders like India, China and Japan as also all other principal beneficiaries of energy supplies and open sea lanes. A Persian Gulf littoral that is integrated through a web of regional cooperative structures will offer more opportunities for socio-economic advancement of its peoples and lay the foundation for eroding political rivalries and harsh nationalist impulses and for bringing about regional stability and peace.

For us in India, a 'Look-West' policy towards this part of West Asia, aimed at engaging in this dynamic, would thus be as relevant for safeguarding and promoting India's interests as its Look-East policy that has been in place for some years.

I am confident that this conference would shed useful light on these perceptions and contribute to the effort. I wish it all success.

Book release: *Tinderbox: The Past and Future of Pakistan* by M.J. Akbar
Hyatt Regency, New Delhi
11 January 2011

This book is vintage MJ—incisive analysis, brilliant passages, wide sweep, bold judgements. One could agree or disagree, but read one must.

I was intrigued by the title and had to look up the dictionary meaning of the term Tinderbox. It is defined as a small container holding flint, fire steel and tinder, used together to help kindle a fire. I assume the author intends to depict a flammable or an explosive mix.

Also intriguing is the subtitle: *The Past and the Future of Pakistan*. Both themes are valid and worthy of discourse. Ventures in futurology, however, would be more productive if they analyse the present more thoroughly in all its ingredients. This would necessitate closer scrutiny of the ethnic, regional and sociological aspects to comprehend the volatility that characterises the scene. No less relevant are the direct and indirect consequences of the involvement of the state, and segments of society, in quest of regional strategic objectives.

The book dilates on a concept. As with other ideas, their interpretation and actualisation is time and space specific. Some in Pakistan seeking empowerment and legitimisation read into it a political agenda and a military strategy. A great many scholars and practitioners of Islam the world over would interpret and practice it differently. Nor should it be forgotten that in the eighties of the last century, the term was lauded and lionised in many of the chancelleries of the world!

One aspect of the past needs a corrective. It is purveyed that the Muslims of British India opted for a separate homeland in 1947. Who and how many exercised the option? It is forgotten that universal adult suffrage did not exist prior to 1950. Voting rights were based on property, taxes, service in the military forces and literacy and were enjoyed by about 11 per cent of the population. Commenting on the election of 1946, the historian Ayesha Jalal has observed that in the Punjab, only a third of the total votes was cast.

In retrospect, it is evident that partition was the result of a political adjustment at the elite level, rather than of a mass desire to separate. It did enormous harm. Choudhry Khaliquzzaman, wiser after the event, observed that the 'Two-Nation' theory "never paid any dividends to us and proved positively injurious to the Muslims of India and on a longer term basis for Muslims everywhere".

Maulana Azad's assessment, and prognosis, cited by Mr Akbar in the concluding pages of the book, does remain the last word.

And yet, one cannot confine oneself to a diet of mishaps of the past, or even an unhealthy one of the present. "The pasture of stupidity", said Ibn Khaldun," is unwholesome to mankind." Wisdom and practical common sense would necessitate course correctives in Pakistan and the people there would find their way of doing it. We, as immediate neighbours, have a vested interest in the stability and well being of Pakistan and its people.

Annual Lecture 2011
Association of Indian Diplomats, India International Centre (IIC), New Delhi
11 March 2011

The Challenges to Indian Diplomacy in the 21st Century

This is one of those occasions when pleasure and apprehension come together: happiness at being with members of one's own tribe, and misgivings about the responsibility assigned. Ambassador Satish Chandra and his colleagues on the Executive of the AID had something to do with it but, as the saying goes, from the hands of a friend a stone is an apple!

I am required to speak on the challenges to our diplomacy in the twenty first century. The difficulty I confront is with the audience! How do I lecture to a group most of whose members know as much about the subject as I do; some, in fact, know much more.

There is yet another problem that I have at times encountered in the recent past. It is summed up in an Iraqi proverb: 'When you speak, do not fear; when you fear, do not speak'. In what manner then do I speak and yet observe the etiquette and the ritual emanating from what a philosopher, in another context, called 'My Station and its Duties'?

Within these constraints, I shall endeavour to be as coherent as possible. I would focus on the next four decades till about the middle of the century since no projections can realistically be made beyond it now nor can we predict the impact on society and politics of scientific or technological innovations that may surface later in the century.

II

Diplomacy is the conduct of relations among political entities aimed at reconciliation and accommodation of viewpoints and interests. It is both a function and a determinant of international order. The task of the diplomat, to use a blunt fifteenth century expression, is to seek the preservation and aggrandisement of his own State.

Many in this audience would recall Bismarck's remark that players on the world stage travel on the stream of Time which they can neither create nor direct but upon which they can steer with more or less skill and experience. They would also remember the words of another realist, Henry Kissenger, who recommended "patient accumulation of partial successes" as a desirable methodology.

Both dicta have relevance. Our own experience of over six decades as a player in the international arena would sustain it in good measure.

It is our stated objective to seek a global order that assures our interests, safeguards the autonomy of our decision-making, and is conducive to the achievement of rapid, sustained and inclusive development of the country. This necessitates policy that combines 'firm commitments to our core national values with dynamic adaptation to changes in the international environment'.

What then are our interests as a people and as a State? Primacy has to be accorded to social cohesion and territorial integrity. The post-independence decades have witnessed political, emotional and market integration in great measure. The much apprehended Balkanisation did not come about. Challenges nevertheless remain and in places have become acuter. A certain 'Balkanisation of the mind' has surfaced. It emanates from regionalism and pursuit of identity politics in the wake of the deepening of the democratic processes; it also arises out of non-inclusive development. Our inability to address these in sufficient measure allows space for sub-national, sectional and non-state actors with agendas that pose threats to social cohesion and national security. These in turn detract from our ability to perform in a fuller measure on the global stage.

The world today recognises our emerging role. Our assets are considerable; so are the expectations. Demography and the demographic mix give us an advantage over most others. By the year 2050 we would have a population of 1.8 billion, a labour force of one billion, and the second largest economy of the world. Our defence capabilities would grow proportionately. These together would position us for being a significant player in the multi-polar international system that is now taking shape.

The typology of threats faced by us since independence shape perceptions and may be viewed in three broad categories: (a) internal and ideological threats emanating from attempts to challenge the Constitution, its functioning, or its core values; (b) threats principally from neighbours and relating to territorial or water disputes; and (c) threats emerging from the global order and arrangements that threaten or could threaten our security, political or economic interests and thereby constrain our policy options.

It is evident that of these, the second and the third fall squarely in the domain of foreign policy and therefore of diplomacy. They would, nevertheless, be impacted upon by the dynamics of our societal forces, the strength of our economy, and our technological capability to meet increasing requirements in areas of food production, public health and energy in step with the imperative of inclusive development and human security. A quality deficit in performance, low levels of accountability in governance, and what has been called the 'malpractice of democracy', are handicaps that can and must be overcome. Diplomacy cannot overlook these domestic impulses.

Let us now look at the foreign policy challenges that are likely to confront us in the foreseeable future.

In the first place and in terms of geography, our immediate neighbourhood would be critical for regional stability and cooperation and the accretion of comprehensive national power by India. Asymmetry is a fact of life in South Asia and the history of conflict and animosity is deep and scarring. Our emergence as a global player is dependent in some measure on our ability to resolve or manage contentions to ensure a peaceful and secure neighbourhood, with meaningful economic, cultural and political ties. Would we be able and willing to give a stake in our development and growth to our neighbours, thereby helping them consolidate their state structures and ward-off centrifugal and destabilising forces of terrorism, aggressive nationalism, secessionism and poor governance?

The need for unconventional policy options in implementing such an agenda need hardly be over-emphasised, especially while dealing with amorphous state and elite structures, pursuing ambiguous and opaque security objectives.

The second challenge would be the emergence of Asia, as probably the most important locus of global power. This has been called the Asian Century and the first decade has given ample evidence of the changing nature of global economic and financial flows and emerging geo-political dimensions. Indian diplomacy will have to deal with the architecture, mechanics and the implementation of Asian economic and security cooperation that is likely to bring together regional organisations such as ASEAN, Asian powers such as China, Japan, South Korea, Australia and Russia and outside powers such as the European Union and the US.

Our "Look East Policy" must transform into a "Move East Policy" of our economic, political and cultural engagement resulting in intense exchanges of goods, services, peoples and ideas. As we move to complete the noodle bowl of FTAs (Free Trade Area) and CEPAs (Comprehensive Economic Partnership Agreement)with the region, the next challenging phase would be to realise the vision of an Asian Economic Community with seamless connectivities. Community building and partnership in Asia through a transparent, inclusive and open process would best lead to an Asian awakening that benefits all constituents of the continent and all stakeholders.

The third challenge would be to create an enabling international environment for unhindered economic development and growth, including through mutually beneficial arrangements concerning raw materials and markets for goods and services. The hunt for resources–mineral, energy, agricultural and human–would only intensify in the years to come and would necessitate resource diplomacy focused on maintenance of stable international resource markets, their efficient regulation and safety of related transport and shipping lanes. It should reasonably insulate functioning resource markets from intervention of state actors. Indian economic diplomacy would also be called upon to manage political risks involved in international trade, business and investments for Indian business; facilitate the movement of Indian human resources across business and sovereign jurisdictions; and attract foreign investments, technology and expertise to the country.

The fourth challenge is to foster a rule based international order underpinned by strong and functioning multilateral institutions. Security, economic development, stability and public welfare would increasingly be indivisible in a globalising world. An effective multilateralism premised on intense engagement and dialogue between a plurality of actors is the best institutional guarantee in an increasingly multi-polar world beset with global problems–whether on terrorism, natural disasters, global warming and environmental issues, pandemics or financial and economic crises.

The institutional architecture of global governance, however, is still an anomaly reflecting post-World War II and Cold War perceptions. Indian diplomacy is actively involved in initiating the process of making the international order reflective of contemporary realities through reforms in the United Nations system and the Bretton Woods institutions. It would be called upon to manage this process in tune with our interests and take the process to fruition, carefully balancing power and principle.

The fifth challenge is to evolve a consensual approach, along with all major and minor powers, of dealing with the regimes regulating global commons. We would need to articulate our role in fashioning, maintaining and implementing these regimes in accordance with our national interests. The global commons of the sea, air, space, Polar Regions and the cyber world are global public goods and our willingness and capability to contribute to their security, growth and stability, as per common but differentiated responsibilities, would only grow in future.

A sixth challenge is the requirement to respond in real time to unanticipated happenings, political, economic or environmental and to have at hand the intellectual and organisational resources to do so adequately.

Our diplomacy would have to maintain our strategic autonomy of action and policy while dealing with the accretion of national power and the calls by other state and non-state actors for "responsibility" in exercising it. It would, by its actions, pronouncements and conduct, have to carefully meander through the twin banks of State sovereignty and global order, of recognised multilateralism and selective coalition building, of universal equity and hard national interest.

III

This audience knows only too well that the practice of diplomacy is characterised by continuity and change: continuity of some aspects of its methodology amidst an ever changing content. On methodology, Richelieu's dictum about the need 'to negotiate continuously, directly as well as in more devious ways and in all places' would hold good for all times.

Representation is central to the process of diplomacy. The world of the 21st Century would increasingly be polycentric and multi-layered, necessitating diplomatic representation at various levels and with the state, multilateral and non-state actors of relevance. As this process gathers momentum, our Foreign Office and diplomats would need to deal with two distinct stakeholders:

- Internally, with a multitude of other state and sub-state agencies with external interests, wishing to exercise diplomatic and quasi-diplomatic functions;
- Externally, with new non-state actors engaged in diplomacy-like functions.

The first problem of representation is the need for the external competencies of different government departments to be well integrated with our bilateral and multilateral diplomatic structures and mechanisms. This is particularly true of Ministries of Defence, Finance, Home, Commerce and Industry, Petroleum, Coal, Mines, Agriculture, Water Resources, Human Resource Development, Atomic Energy and Space. The same would hold for the state governments that are looking for enhanced international exposure and official presence outside India, with unique branding for purposes of attracting tourists, capital, technology and expertise.

States that are in border areas have a natural cultural and economic interest in our foreign policy orientation towards our neighbours. Furthermore, changes in the international situation are impelling state governments to seek some form of diplomatic representation. Policy areas that fall within their jurisdiction such as environment, agriculture, public health, transportation, law and order, and culture are increasingly coming under the ambit of multilaterally negotiated conventions and regimes. Thus, for example, state governments would be called upon to devise and implement the bulk of the adaptation and mitigation strategies under Climate Change related Environmental Agreements. Likewise, FTA and CEPA agreements entered into with other nations or regional organisations, or commitments made under WTO agreements, impose obligations and constraints in areas of jurisdiction of state governments.

Thus, Indian diplomacy would have to creatively deal with the pressures for such sub-State Diplomacy and devise means to address the concerns and facilitate achievement of the objectives of our state governments. While the Ministry's institutional response has been to open Branch Offices in a few State Capitals, a more robust institutional and systemic response rooted in mandatory dialogue and consultation mechanisms with sub-national territorial units might need to be crafted for the purpose.

The second problem of representation, in its external dimension, is more problematic. Classical diplomacy has been the exclusive preserve and domain of nation-states. As we survey the practice of diplomacy worldwide, we observe that the departure from the classical definition is very definitive. A range of new non-state actors have emerged on the global scene to engage in diplomatic or quasi-diplomatic activities to further their objectives. These include NGOs focused on environment, human rights and labour issues, international sports bodies, professional federations, business and multinational corporations and academic institutions.

Our diplomacy would have to find means of representation with, and access to, these new actors and engage with them to defend and promote our national interests. Traversing these uncharted waters would be tricky and would have to be carefully calibrated in view of the strong linkages of many of them with Indian civil society and NGOs, Indian business and industry, our Pravasi Bharatiya Community, and our polity and economy.

IV

In a delectable quote, the late Mr Y.D. Gundevia cited Jawaharlal Nehru's remark that that India's foreign policy 'was so simple that even an Ekkawala in Lucknow could claim to understand it'. Mr Gundevia added, more substantively, that India was not in any country's orbit but was rotating on its own axis as part of the great galaxy of nations.

Interestingly enough, a report on Global Trends 2025 published in 2008 by the National Intelligence Council of the United States had this to say about India:

India's growing international confidence, derived primarily from its economic growth and its successful democratic record, now drives New Delhi towards partnerships with many countries. However, these partnerships are aimed at maximising India's autonomy, not at aligning India with any country or international coalition.

As in the past, it will be the job of Indian diplomacy to explain our axis to the world and to our citizens. Our Ambassadors, true to their calling would remain, in the words of Nizam-ul-Mulk, 'generally censorious and always on the look out to see what faults and what virtues there are' in the nations to which they are assigned.

The First National Conference on International Relations
India Habitat Centre, New Delhi
22 October 2011

I am happy to participate in this conference, claimed to be the first of its kind, of scholars and practitioners of international relations from all over the country. This initiative of the Ministry of External Affairs deserves our appreciation.

I confess I am somewhat puzzled at the characterisation of today's initiative as being part of 'public diplomacy'. Words have meanings and concepts have connotations. Neither of the two is immutable; yet, new meanings and connotations do require explanations and justifications. Diplomacy, to be productive, cannot be conducted publicly; the public, on the other hand, has every right to be informed about its outcomes.

The dictionary meaning of diplomacy is 'management of international relations'. Textbooks on the subject refine it to mean 'the peaceful conduct of relations amongst political entities'. The interest of the general public in it, as in other aspects of public policy, is evident. We thus have three categories of persons who profess to relate to diplomacy: those who are charged to conduct it, those whose pursuit in life is to analyse it from an academic or expert perspective, and those who interest themselves in a general sense in its processes and results.

It is evident that bringing together practising professionals, academics, and interested members of the public, for a healthy exchange of views and ideas is a normal part of the business of government in all aspects of national activity. There is no reason for it to be different in regard to external relations or be given a different nomenclature.

India lives in a community of nations and is an active participant in it. We have a population of 1.2 billion, an economy of nearly two trillion dollars, a capacity in some measure to project power in immediate or proximate neighbourhood, as well as the wherewithal to become a knowledge society. Together they sustain the claim to have both hard power and soft power and the ability to enhance both in good measure and thereby enhance national power.

A prerequisite for these is a sound knowledge of the world, of the equilibrium of power, of the dynamics of current or anticipated changes, and of the manner they impact on India and Indian interests. Each is a function of incisive scholarship in which conceptual frameworks and microanalysis would lend credence to the national effort.

How well are we prepared to shoulder this responsibility? How do we fare in comparison to our peers among players on the global stage?

The need for the study of international relations is self-evident; its absence, in fact, evokes questions. The harsh reality, however, is that the study of international affairs in our country is episodic, emotive and inadequate.

Three aspects of the matter need to be considered. The first relates to the need to conceptualise our own experience as a player on the global stage; the second to the requirement of in-depth study of countries and regions of relevance to us and the acquisition of analytical and linguistic tools, required for such studies; the third to the manner in which this experience and knowledge is to be related to our present and future policy options.

Record would show that our performance on each of these counts is less than adequate; given our intellectual resources, the output should have been better in terms of quality and content.

The need for correctives is thus evident. It is here that a platform like today's, where concerned scholars and researchers from all parts of the country could exchange ideas and experiences with practitioners, would be of great relevance. Its rationale is self evident; its success would lie in concrete correctives, not platitudes.

Academics analyse the conduct of international relations and diplomacy. Diplomats, on their part, put together the building blocks of diplomacy and use them for achieving national objectives in international relations. The former can choose areas of interest of their research; the latter, usually, have tasks thrust on them by the tidal waves of daily developments from all the corners of the globe.

Yet, it is vital that they interact and exchange notes. The academic has one resource that the professional does not–the time to study and analyse a problem in all its dimensions. The academic also has the option of dissent, of thinking unconventionally, suggesting courses of action that may be perceived to be risky and need not bear the weight of either history, or future expectation, that would distort decision-making.

Our understanding of countries and people that we deal with cannot be based solely on academic output of foreign institutions. We need to evolve a uniquely Indian understanding, based on the historical context of our relations with other nations and peoples, as also contemporary realities and concerns. We need our own culture of strategic thought.

A first step towards this end should be acquisition of linguistic skills. This is one area where there is an acute national shortage of skilled professionals, well versed in the languages and idiom of other countries and peoples. I would urge this distinguished gathering to deliberate on this aspect and work out the means through which we can create a national resource-base of language professionals which can be tapped not only by government, but also by academia, media, industry and business.

Another requirement is the sociological analysis of societies, particularly of countries most relevant to us and to ascertain their core concerns, interests, obsessions and inhibitions, and response frequencies.

There is another aspect that deserves closer scrutiny. Serious academic analysis in the field of international relations is not possible without access to archival records. Unfortunately, despite significant strides in transparency, especially through the Right to Information Act, archival documentation is so scanty that our researchers are forced to rely on declassified documents of foreign governments. We do need to bring our rules on this in line with the practice of other advanced and open societies.

It is my sincere hope that this is not a one-off conference and that there would be regular and institutional interactions between the two broad groups represented in this audience. This would lead to better academic research and more productive policy making.

I wish you all success in your deliberations over the next two days.

National Seminar on 'India and Central Asia: Perspectives on Bilateral and Regional Cooperation'

Centre for Research in Rural and Industrial Developement, Chandigarh
17 October 2012

I came to the Centre for Research in Rural and Industrial Development almost five years back to deliver the Haksar Memorial Lecture. I am therefore happy to be on familiar territory once again, to share my thoughts on a subject of considerable importance.

A gathering of scholars to discuss Central Asia is relevant for more than one reason. The region is in our proximate neighbourhood and is therefore of geopolitical salience. The surprising thing is that we do not know enough about it.

Historically speaking, the geographical term 'Central Asia' came into the vocabulary of European scholars and governments only in the middle of the nineteenth century. In the year 1900 the famous Russian historian Victor Barthold could find little about the recorded history of the area before the Arab conquest of seventh to eighth centuries. A seminar organised by the Embassy of India, Tashkent in March 2000 sought to collate available information, mainly archaeological, on the relations between India and Central Asia in the pre-Islamic period. On the other hand, we do have sufficient evidence of conquerors and conquests, of movement of people, and of trade in the medieval and pre-modern periods. The National Archives of India have recently published an interesting travelogue of Munshi Mohan Lal who accompanied the British envoy Alexander Burns to Turkisṭan in 1831 on what was called 'a knowledge-gathering' exercise. Burn's own account, of course, remains a classic.

In more recent times, both Czarist Russia and the Soviet Union kept it a virtually 'closed' region. This changed with the demise of the Soviet state and the emergence of the five republics, the so-called 'stans', as independent entities, eager to retrieve their cultural identities, benefit from their economic resources, and play a role on the world stage. By the same token the geo-political space, and its accompanying benefits, vacated by the erstwhile Soviet Union, was sought to be taken by others.

CRRID is therefore to be complemented for undertaking this initiative of seeking perspectives on the potential for cooperation between Central and South Asia for peace, security and development.

My impression is that different aspects of modern Central Asia are being studied in different research institutions in the country and the need of the hour is to enhance coordination and cooperation amongst them to avoid overlapping, ensure better utilisation of available resources and, eventually, more meaningful inputs for our foreign policy objectives. Greater attention also needs to be devoted to language skills and the study of social impulses in individual societies. Diligent field work is essential for both and must be undertaken.

II

This audience knows well that foreign policy formulation rarely begins with a clean slate. Its building blocks, instead, consist of ground realities. Aspirations and objectives help give it shape; the baggage of the past is sought to be avoided but is rarely achieved comprehensively. Success thus lies, as Henry Kissinger put it, in "patient accumulation of partial successes."

It is thus evident that the new ground realities in the post-Soviet period called for a redefining of India's strategic interests in the region. Our primary interest was stability in the region. The task of diplomacy was to build new relationships and protect and enhance economic and commercial interests. We were successful in the first and are still struggling with the second.

Culturally, and apart from historical linkages and affinities, the access given to India during Soviet times through the establishment of a consulate general in Tashkent, allowed us to promote educational and commercial exchanges with Uzbekistan.

Over the past two decades and despite being land locked, Central Asia emerged as one of the fastest growing regions in the world, and has displayed considerable development potential. It is resource rich in terms of oil, gas, gold, cotton, rare-earths, has relatively advanced infrastructure and human capital, and enjoys the benefit of a strategic location between Asia and Europe. Many of the Central Asian Republics have embarked on market-oriented economic reforms to boost private sector competitiveness and economic performance. As a result, leading and aspiring powers are active in the region in quest of natural resources, energy pipelines and transit routes leading to wide ranging geopolitical considerations pertaining to security, prevention of drug and arms smuggling, and countering terrorism and fundamentalism.

India's own approach to the region has evolved over these twenty years and has recently been spelt out in its *'Connect Central Asia'* Policy. This is focused on identification and furtherance of mutually beneficial interests, development of access routes and options, sharing of developmental experience in nation building, offering economic and technical assistance, and furtherance of cultural and educational cooperation.

Pursuant to it, we have entered into Strategic Partnership agreements with three of the five Central Asian Republics–Kazakhstan, Uzbekistan and Tajikistan and have increased co-operation and dialogue between specialised security agencies and the defence forces.

Furtherance of trade and economic co-operation with the region, beginning with Afghanistan, hinges on connectivity which in turn, is intrinsically dependent on access-route options and its policy and practical implications. The easiest route, through Pakistan and Afghanistan, appears totally dependent on a good mix of human wisdom and divine intervention; both seem elusive in the foreseeable future! A second point of access, through Iran and Afghanistan, is a real possibility and appears now to take shape through the proposed development of the Chabahar port and the completion of the Zaranj-Delaram highway. A variant of this for Central Asian states, dependent on the upgrading of railway network in Iran, could be the Iran-Turkmenistan route. Both would require fine tuning of policy and longer term financial commitments. Other options, through China or Russia, would be grossly uneconomical.

Other elements of the twelve-point *'Connect Central Asia'* Policy are in various stages of initiative and implementation and have evoked positive responses from the Central Asian States. The emphasis on our political approach being non-prescriptive, while holding on to our own value system, is timely.

No discussion on Central Asia and its immediate neighbourhood would be complete without taking on board the challenges arising out of the situation in Afghanistan. The lesson of history is that hegemonic prescriptions do not sustain themselves and result in greater chaos. The entire region would therefore benefits if realistic alternatives are thought of and Afghanistan drawn into a cooperative regional economic and security framework so that nation-building there could proceed based on economic development, social harmony, rule of law and participatory democracy in consonance with the wishes of the Afghan people. Such an approach should be underwritten by the United Nations and all interested powers.

Though India is not part of any regional grouping so far, our role in regional fora like the Shanghai Cooperation Organisation and Conference on Interaction and Confidence Building Measures in Asia would serve to strengthen India's renewed links with the region. India's engagement in Central Asia is also part of our belief in a multi-polar world.

The world of tomorrow cannot and must not be visualised on the patterns of a past that resulted in misery and bloodshed. India wishes to eschew archaic concepts of Great Game and Grand Chessboard and, instead, be a partner for peace, stability and economic development in the region. India also hopes that the people of Central Asia do not give quarter to fundamentalism and religious extremism in their respective societies since these trends are disruptive and hamper progress.

Indian Muslims

"To deny discrimination and pretend all is well is to fly in the face of facts. But agitation against discrimination can arouse the very emotions that foster discrimination. The solution of the Muslim problem lies in a resolution of this dilemma by devising a form and context of agitation which heals old wounds and inflicts no new ones. This resolution can be achieved by regarding discrimination as what it is; a problem of Indian democracy to be resolved within the framework of national integration. This is best done by associating men of goodwill of all communities in the task of making a success of Indian secularism

—A.G. Noorani
2003

Annual Convocation of Jamia Millia Islamia
New Delhi
30 October 2007

"Ba naam-e-khudavand jaan aafareen
Hakeem-e-sokhan dar zubaan aafareen"

A diplomatist by profession, an academic by courtesy, and the holder of a public office perhaps by the fall of the dice is called upon by you not only to participate in the most solemn of occasions in the academic calendar of a university but also to share the inadequacy of his thought process with this audience. Prudence would have counselled restraint; my own association with the Jamia, however, induced me to take the bold step of venturing into the unknown.

A few weeks back, and while trying to restore some order in the books in my study I came across a little booklet on the *Founders of Jamia Millia Islamia*, penned by an old teacher of mine, Syed Mohammad Tonki. It contains a perceptive remark:

> *"Jamia ki aik haisiyat tahreek ki hai aur doosari aik idaare ki. Tahreek main woosat-e-amal o fikr aur aik tarah ki hamagiri hoti hai; iddara mahdoor daaire main rah kar khaas haalat ke mud-e-nazar kaam karta hai aur apni baqa ke liye samet-ta aur fikr o amal ko samait-ta hai"*

The first identity created the second; having done so, it expected the second to carry the banner of its progenitor. This is one aspect of the matter. My purpose today, however, is to probe some of the unstated premises of the first in the hope that these might shed light on what continues to be a teasing question for Muslim thinkers in India and elsewhere—that of reconciling tradition and modernity in all its ramifications in social and political life of the community.

II

In its most obvious sense, the foundation of Jamia was a protest against the political conformity of Aligarh in the context of the period immediately after World War I. Maulana Mahmood Hasan Sahib described it as *hukoomat-e-waqtiyah ki parastish*. This protest was not a flash in the pan, did not happen by accident, and was not confined to a narrow section of opinion. Instead, it emanated from a basic premise that perceived the established political order [illegible] unjust.

[illegible]d the protest go beyond it? If so, how far did it go and with what conte[illegible]n essay by Dr Zakir Hussain in 1938 shed light on his perception of Jamia's [illegible]ary purpose:

> *"Jamia k[illegible]h se bara maqsad yeh hai ki Hindustani Musalman*
> *ki aaindah [illegible]gi ka aisa naqsha tayyar kare jis ka markaz*
> *mazhab-e-Islam [illegible]r oos main Hindostan ki quami tahzeeb*
> *ka woh rang bhare jo [illegible] insani tahzeeb ke rang main khap jai".*

The focus of this was on challen[illegible] the perceived dichotomy between the requirement of faith and those o[illegible]eloping an Indian cultural identity in the most comprehensive sense. Za[illegible]ahib conceded that this objective was somewhat opaque in the minds of [illegible]amia fraternity. Some others at Jamia spoke in the same vein. Abid Hus[illegible] urged the need to create an alumnus who is "*insan-e-kamil, sachcha M[illegible]nan aur pacca Hindustani*". Perhaps there was, in the background, a [illegible]nance of Syed Ahmad Khan's concept of *amal-i-saleh* [illegible]ing the argument further, Mohammad [illegible] sources of the Indian sense of unity. Written in 1962, his perception remains relevant four and a half decades later:

"We can become united only if we create within ourselves individually and in consonance with our dispositions and our taste an overriding passion for a unity which can bear the moral burden of the wrongs we have committed and the mistakes we have made. The acceptance of this approach to unity will be a spiritual effort and can succeed only if it receives sustenance and power from the traditions of religiousness which are a part of our history. The State by declaring itself secular has thrown out a challenge to each and every citizen to show that he can enrich civic life by drawing inspiration from the institutional religion which he professes".

The citizen responded to it in varying measure. The core question of Indianness, however, does stand settled.

The objective of creating an identity comprehensive enough to encapsulate both Indianness and Muslimness in the plural, democratic and secular ethos of contemporary India also required creative thinking addressed to changing situations of a modernising India. The task of converting this into a plan of action became, and remains, the principal challenge to contemporary Muslim thinking. Underlying any such endeavour is the tension between the twin concepts of tradition and modernity. To what extent have these been addressed?

In this context, an observation of Professor Akbar Ahmad is to be noted. "The postmodernist age in the 1990s" he wrote in 1992, "hammers at the doors of the Muslim ijtihad; Muslims ignore the din at their peril. Before they creak open the door, however, they must know the power and nature of the age and for that they must understand those who represent it".

Does this suggest the inevitability of a single, unavoidable, pattern of response? If so, it overlooks the diversity of the Muslim situation and the resultant complexity of the response patterns. The Muslim world has expanded beyond its traditional boundaries; the inherited paradigm of Muslims living principally in Muslim-majority societies, and thinking in terms of those societies, has now acquired different dimensions. Muslim communities in India, China and Russia have sought to develop locally relevant response patterns; the same is true of Muslim communities in the United States and in the member states of the European Union. None of these have been devoid of pain. There is therefore relevance in Tariq Ramadan's observation that while globalisation causes the old traditional points of reference to disappear, it at the same time awakens passionate affirmations of identity. As a result, he notes, Muslim communities in the West are 'living through a veritable silent revolution'.

Awareness of identity and the desire to develop it is one aspect of the matter; the capacity to actualise is another; a third is the desire to strike a balance between identity and what Professor Ramadan has called for an authentic dialogue with fellow citizens aimed at mutual enrichment. It is here that empirical evidence is of crucial importance. How much of an effort was made (and is being made) to give a comprehensive response to the challenge? What areas of community life were addressed? What obstacles were encountered? What was the success achieved?

Some answers to these questions are now available, thanks to the Sachar Committee Report on the social, educational and economic condition of the Muslim community in India. The Committee set out to collect 'authentic information' particularly on equity-related questions and succeeded in quantifying the extent of deprivation. It reported that 'the topic of education was raised most frequently in the representations (made to it), followed by reservation, employment and security related issues'. It identified with some precision the areas of State failure, suggested urgent corrective action, and recommended that this 'should sharply focus on inclusive development and the 'mainstreaming' of the community while respecting diversity'.

The default by the State in terms of deprivation, exclusion and discrimination is to be corrected by the State; this needs to be done at the earliest. Political sagacity and public opinion play an important role in it. Besides it, however, there is another default; here I refer to the inadequacy of the autonomous effort by the community itself in relation to its social perceptions. How has this been approached? Is there a veritable silent revolution underway in the thinking of the Indian Muslim?

Firqa-bandi hai kahein aur kahein zaatain hain
Kya zamaane main panaph-ne ki yahi baatain hain?

It is evident that significant sections of the community remain trapped in a vicious circle and in a culturally defensive posture. Tradition is made sacrosanct while the rationale of tradition is all but forgotten. *Jadeediyat* or modernity has become a tainted expression. Such a mindset constrains critical thinking necessary both for the affirmation of faith and for the wellbeing of the community. The instrumentality of adaptation to change–*Ijtihad*–is frowned upon if not ignored altogether. Forgotten is its purpose, defined by the late Sheikh Abul Hasan Ali Nadwi as "the ability to cope with the ever-changing pattern of life's requirement". Similarly, al Ghazali's delineation of the ambit of Maslaha–protection of religion, life, intellect, lineage and property–provides ample theoretical space for focused thinking on social change.

III

Has this focused thinking, resulting in corrective action, taken place? One could scrutinise a few of the most obvious examples. Syed Ahmad Khan was acutely aware of the problems in an era of painful change. He confronted the view that ijtihad is no longer necessary:

> We must remember that circumstances keep changing and we are faced daily with new problems and needs. If therefore we do not have living mujtahids, how shall we ask those who are dead, about questions which were not material facts of life in their time. We must have a mujtahid of our age and time.

Despite this, he was diffident in regard to follow up action and his concept of amal-i-saleh remained devoid of the requisite degree of practical comprehensiveness. Similarly Dr Mohammad Iqbal stressed the need to reconcile the elements of permanence and change in Muslim societies and the resultant necessity of *ijtihad* in every generation. "Modern Islam", he said, is not bound by the "voluntary surrender of intellectual independence":

> *"Taqleed se naakara na kar apni khudi ko*
> *Kar ooski hefazat ki yeh gauhar hai yagana"*

In practical terms, however, Iqbal leaned on the side of caution; his philosophical legacy, in the words of Fazlur Rahman, has not been followed 'largely because he has been both misunderstood and misused by his politics-mongering followers'.

The one exception to such an approach was Maulana Azad who advocated a move away from a narrowly juristic view in favour of a mental renascence to achieve the highest moral and spiritual values of Islam. In opting for this approach he, as Mohammad Mujeeb put it, 'stood absolutely alone' and could not gather a following.

As a result, and despite the quantification of the extent of social backwardness, community effort to ameliorate it has remained confused and inadequate.

Let us look at the situation in its totality. Muslims in India today number about 150 million and constitute a significant segment–13.4 per cent–of Indians. 51.9 per cent of this population is below the age of twenty and 60.6 per cent below the age twenty- five. Muslims have the highest child sex ratio of any social group in the country—986 girls per 1000 boys. They are more urbanised than the general population. On the other hand, the literacy rate among Muslims is 59.1 per cent, against a national average of 65.1; it is even lower in the case of female literacy. 40.7 per cent of the Muslims are in the OBC category (15.7 per cent of the total OBC population of the country) and a small segment in SCs. The incidence of poverty among urban Muslims is even higher than among the urban SCs/STs is well above other OBCs, and is almost double of the national average. These figures speak for themselves in terms of the imperative for correcting social imbalances resulting from social immobility.

In the face of multiple challenges, is prioritisation possible or even desirable? Should education precede social reforms, or follow it? Should both wait for a lessening of threats to physical security and the obvious manifestations of exclusion? How is the collective will to be generated for simultaneous, across-the-board, movement?

IV

What is the way out? It would seem, given recent history and prevailing perceptions, that the following are unavoidable:

Develop a clear understanding of the modern world and the social and intellectual forces emanating from it. Sufficient evidence of this is available, in the Indian context, in the course of a citizen's daily life;

Seek conceptual clarity about tradition and modernity. Tradition is a double-edged sword; it is used both to deny change and to justify it; alternative uses of tradition are thus a major battle ground. Some years back Abdul Hamid Abu Sulayman, a Saudi Scholar had drawn attention to the 'psychological impediments' that have impeded the Muslim mind in the analysis of 'its intellectual legacy or what it holds as sacred'. The argument on tradition and modernity requires to be turned around; a formulation by another scholar therefore merits attention: 'Rather than viewing modernity as a source of light, dispelling the darkness of tradition, we should instead imagine tradition as a beam of light, refracted by the prism of modernity';

Comprehend the concepts of Ijtihad and Maslaha in the light of contemporary Islamic thought in different parts of the world, and a willingness to use them to address contemporary problems in Indian Muslim society. Mohammad Arkoun, for instance, has urged the need to rethink the historical situation so that 'critical thought, anchored in modernity but criticising modernity itself and contributing to its enrichment through recourse to the Islamic example' could open a new era in social movements. The manner in which Asian Muslim societies like Indonesia, Malaysia, Iran and Turkey have addressed the questions of knowledge and gender deficit needs to be studied, perhaps emulated;

Undertake a structured effort, on the basis of the above, to confront the evils of ignorance and stagnation through a sustainable programme of education and social reform. Such an effort would need to focus on autonomous correction of social customs hampering progress, particularly the ones with a tenuous base in religion; the priority areas of attention would need to be on primary and middle levels of education, on the education of girls, on vocational training, and on a wide-ranging awareness programme relating to rights of citizens and the facilities available to them by law but often denied in practice.

Reinvigorate the traditional practice of charity through focused philanthropy, and impart a new dynamism to the management of Awqaf to derive maximum benefit for the community. There are, according to the Sachar Committee, a total of 4.9 lakh registered Wakfs in the country having a current market value of about Rs1.2 lakh crores (1,200 billion). Some of these properties are in adverse possession and the State must help retrieve them; the majority of them are misused by individuals and institutions; if put to 'efficient and marketable use they can generate at least a minimum return of 10 per cent which is about Rs 12,000 crores per annum'.

Collect and publicise success stories, of individual and community initiatives, that do exist in different parts of the country.

None of the above would be a substitute for, or dilution of, well documented and justified demands for affirmative action by the State within the framework of Articles14, 15(4) and 16(4) of the Constitution and the various programmes announced by the government pursuant to the Sachar Report. Instead, they could become a critical foundation on the basis of which maximum benefits can be derived from these schemes.

We need to remember that in any form of therapy, patient cooperation is essential.

We have to remind ourselves that in the India of today, time is of critical importance.

We could recite with benefit a couplet of relevance:

"Aghyar mehr mah se bhi aage nikal gaye
Uljhe huwai hain subh ki pehli kiran main hum"

What may be the modality of change? Who can be its flag bearers? The bourgeoisie wrote Karl Marx "has historically played a most revolutionary part in changing societal relations". The Muslim middle class, however, is weak and hesitant as an agent of social change. The literacy and development gap in regard to Muslim women adds to this handicap; so do perceptions of physical and economic insecurity.

The agents of change would thus have to be new grass-root community leaders principally emanating from the youth who constitute the biggest segment in terms of numbers and who are better placed to understand its demands and aspirations. Their effort would need to focus both on legitimate demands on the State and on the mobilisation of internal resources of the community for the empowerment of the marginalised. Above all, it would need to imbibe the advice given by Maulana Azad in October 1947:

> *"Tabdiliyon ke saath chalo, yeh na kaho ki hum is taghghur ke liye tayyar na thei".*

I conclude where I commenced: the role of Jamia Millia Islamia. Its achievements in recent years have been noteworthy. It has shown itself receptive to new ideas and creative practices. The institution is now a part of the academic landscape of the country. Having reached thus far, could some in the Jamia community now also think of a larger mission that is, in a sense, part of its original mission, so eloquently enunciated by Zakir sahib? Success in such an endeavour would benefit Indian Muslims and enrich India itself.

Lastly, I felicitate the young women and men who have been formally honoured today and who are leaving the precincts of the academia to enter a harsher world. They need to retain at all times their enthusiasm and optimism. They must remember that the horizon of knowledge is ever receding; the quest for it, therefore, does not end with a university degree. On the contrary, it is the first step in a grand participatory venture of building a new India.

Inauguration of the World Summit of Aligarh Muslim University Alumni
Aligarh Muslim University (AMU), Aligarh
18 October 2008

This is homecoming and therefore in no need of ceremony. Today however is a special occasion and I am grateful to the university for having invited me to it.

"Aap ke saam-ne khare ho kar ek sawal bhi zehan main uth-ta hai:
kya kahoon aur kyun kar kahoon?

Is bazm main woh kahte hain hame, mouqe ke muwafiq baat karo
Aur hum ne yeh dil main thaani hai, ya dil ki kahain ya kooch na kahai"..

Yesterday Aligarians the world over celebrated Sir Syed Day and finished the evening by devouring little or not so little quantities of biryani and shahi tukra. It was the occasion to honour the memory of the Founder of this great institution. The tenacity of the practice is indeed admirable:

Jahan jaa-ain wahan teera fasana cheirh daite hain
Koi mehfil ho tera rang-e-mehfil yaad aata hai.

Many of the success stories of recent decades are here with us today. For this reason, and on the morrow of Sir Syed Day, it is time to recall the message of Syed Ahmad Khan, do some introspection, some cost accountancy.

This institution came into existence in 1875 in response to a specific need, and on the basis of a vision. Its mission was to bring the fruits of modern education to the Muslim of India. This included inculcating a spirit of rational thinking and scientific enquiry. Allama Iqbal summed up the requirement in a couplet:

"Is daur main taleem hai amraz-e-millat ki dawa
Hai khoon-e-fasid ke liye taleem misl-e-naishtar"

The mission succeeded to a point, but failed to go beyond it. The results of that failure are evident and in no need of elaboration.

Two questions do arise: Why did it happen? How can it be corrected?

Let us candidly admit that our failure was conceptual as well as practical. We failed to appreciate that educational advancement cannot be sectional, nor can it be attained in a vacuum divorced from social change and without changes in levels of consciousness about evolving requirements of the world around us, nationally and internationally.

Let me be specific:

- We succumbed to selectivity, and did not appreciate the true worth and imperative necessity of education for all, beginning with primary education. As a result illiteracy levels remain above the national level and, until quite recently, only sections of the well-to-do were exposed to modern and higher education.
- There was an inordinate delay in appreciating the need for female literacy and its relevance for educating new generations.
- While *shikwa* about our condition was valid, there was no need to carry it to the point of incapacity for autonomous action. We failed to take note of, emulate and adapt, the initiatives taken by other communities in creative ventures in the field of education independent of government agencies.
- While adhering to the traditional virtue of charity, we did not (exceptions apart) appreciate the need for organised philanthropy for public purposes.

All this happened while the pace of change in modern India gathered a new momentum. To participate in this exciting venture, relevant education became a pre-requisite.

Much is happening nationally in the field of education. The requirement of a knowledge society, however, is yet to be met. Our Gross Enrolment

Ratio in higher education remains at 11 per cent and compares poorly with China's 22 per cent and 54.6 per cent of the developed world. The government proposes to raise it to 15 per cent by 2012 and 21 per cent by 2017.

The challenge now before us is to ensure that all segments of the public benefit from it in equitable measure. This can only be achieved in a proactive mode, on the basis of an agenda relevant to the world of tomorrow.

We also need to understand that failure to participate would lead to marginalisation, and that mediocrity means irrelevance.

II

Every challenge is also an opportunity. What can and should be done by the Aligarh fraternity at this juncture? Could it become a catalyst? If so, what practical steps beckon us?

The corrective has to commence at the foundations of the societal structure. I would suggest that we lay the foundations of a new approach through the following eight steps:

- Ensure that in our own respective localities every child actually goes to primary school.
- Ensure that all children, boys and girls, complete eight years of schooling.
- Ensure that after class eight, children either proceed to class ten or go to a vocational training centre.
- Identify and assist those qualified to enter universities or professional institutions. Inculcate in them a spirit of competition. Affirmation of identity is a legitimate pursuit; seeking special dispensations will not get us very far.
- Draw the maximum benefit from the scholarship schemes announced by the government in recent months.
- Mobilise opinion for channelling income from Awkaf for setting up new educational and professional institutions. This has been done in some places and the practice needs to be universalised.

- Endeavour to go beyond charity to organised and focused philanthropy so that adequate resources are mobilised for medium and large scale interventions in the educational sector.
- Seek equity, not concessions, form the State and draw practical lessons from success stories of others, including our own elsewhere.

This wider setting is relevant to the Alumni's understandable concern for the institution so dear to us.

For many of us, however, this is not the university in which we spent our youth.

We live in fast changing times. The AMU of yesteryears had lesser numbers, greater space, fewer pressures. On each count today, the situation has worsened. This has impacted adversely on the output in diverse ways and has become a matter of concern. Innovative thinking, rather than nostalgia, is the call of the hour.

Funding by the government takes care of salaries, pensions and normal expenses of the university. This is substantial but leaves insufficient amounts for developmental purposes–for re-equipping of laboratories, opening of new courses, up-gradation of facilities, construction of new hostels etc. Alumni support in some other universities in the country has ameliorated these in good measure and there is no reason why AMU Alumni cannot do likewise.

Infrastructure is one aspect of a new agenda. More important is the quality of the intake and the crafting and content of courses. AMU needs to respond to the challenges of the twenty-first century, of a knowledge society and of a globalising world. Some of what is taught, and the way it is taught, has become irrelevant. Reorientation of courses of study and of the methodology of teaching has become a necessity.

At the same time, the hallmark of a good university remains the quality of research undertaken by its scholars. To further the frontiers of knowledge, it must retain a balance between theoretical and applied research.

A report produced by the university recently, aimed at raising the potential in teaching and research, has identified problems pertaining to accountability, teaching performance and research output. These need to be rectified expeditiously.

III

Within the ambit of a university, the specific requirements of higher education, professional education and distant education have to be met. None can be neglected. In the final analysis, a university has to be responsive as well as responsible; responsive to societal demands and responsible to its role of guiding reflection and policy-making in a society. An imbalance between the two would be detrimental to the institution and a loss to the society.

I wish this conclave success in its deliberations. It should go beyond *nashistand, guftand, barkhastand* and come forth with practical suggestions on what the Alumni can do to help the AMU reorient itself. Only then would it be said with conviction:

Kuch ho raha hai ishq o hawas main bhi imtiaz
Aaya hai ab mizaj tera imtehan per.

The Khuda Bakhsh Memorial Lecture
Khuda Bakhsh Oriental Public Library, Patna
12 December 2009

IDENTITY, CITIZENSHIP AND EMPOWERMENT

I am privileged to be invited here to deliver the Khuda Bakhsh Lecture on the occasion of the death centenary of Khan Bahadur Khuda Bakhsh. My thrill at the honour bestowed is subdued by the realisation of my own inadequacy.

Maulavi Mohammad Bakhsh and his son Khuda Bakhsh are known to us by their simplicity, dedication to a cause and single mindedness of purpose. This institution is amongst a handful of its kind in the world. It is a unique collection of Persian and Arabic manuscripts, described by a visitor as "an enclosed garden of precious things." These testify to the richness of the civilisation of Islam to which India and Indians contributed in no small measure. One characteristic of it is the diversity of the cultural dialogue conducted over centuries between peoples of diverse stocks and traditions and the interaction between Islamic values and the historical experience of Muslim communities.

The late Professor Mohammad Mujeeb concluded his monumental work *The Indian Muslims*, published in 1967, with what he termed "a note of warning". "Generalisations about the Indian Muslims", he wrote, "can only be partial statements of truth and would, therefore, be misleading." Commenting on the inadequacy of prevailing historical perception, he added that "the Indian Muslims are judged by the non-Muslims and, vice versa, the non-Muslims by the Muslims, as if the historical record of one party could be separated from the record of the other, and each party answerable only for itself."

Equally relevant is Richard Eaton's observation about the "diverse variety Indian Islamic traditions" that reflect "both the dynamism of Islam and the fluidity of Indo-Islamic identities."

Both judgements signal uniqueness. They were arrived at after encyclopaedic surveys of a thousand years of political, intellectual and cultural history in which the past journeyed into the present. Every stage of this journey was marked by debate and dissent, reflective of what were perceived to be prevailing challenges. It is therefore of critical relevance to India of today that counts 160 million Muslims amongst its citizens who constitute 13.4 per cent of the population of the country.

There is also an external dimension to this identity. India is not a part of the 'Muslim World' but is not away from it; not a Muslim majority state in statistical terms yet home to the third largest community of Muslims in the world; not a society focused on Muslim welfare only but one in which the Muslims, as an integral part of a larger whole, constitutionally claim the attention that every other section does. The Indian Muslim community also has a history of engagement with the larger Muslim world and has contributed in intellectual, cultural and material terms to its enrichment.

My endeavour today is to explore two aspects of the interaction that has characterised the Indian experience:

- Have the Muslims allowed their parameters to be frozen in time and taken too much for granted?
- Have they been sufficiently critical? Is there a need of newer impulses to respond to new situations?

Both relate to the debate within the community as also to interaction with the wider national and international community. Both have a contemporary relevance. Both are emotive and could be evaded if the instinct of caution were to prevail:

Udhar mashkook hai meri sadaqat
Idhar bhi badgumani kam nahi hai

The effort, nevertheless, must be made.

II

The discussion needs to be posited in the contemporary Indian reality. Ours is a pluralistic society, a secular polity, and a State structure that is democratic and based on Rule of Law. Plurality is an existential reality; responding to its imperative, the Founding Fathers of the Republic crafted the Constitution endowed with the values enunciated in its Preamble: a Sovereign, Socialist, Secular, and Democratic Republic dedicated to the achievement of Justice, Equality, Liberty and Fraternity. Each of these enunciates a comprehensive agenda; some objectives have been achieved; others remain work in progress. These political virtues are in essence interlinked and inter-dependent and cannot be considered as replacements or substitutes. Some are of older vintage, other are of recent origin.

The Indian reality pertaining to its Muslim population has another dimension. This was portrayed in the Sachar Committee Report of 2006 that examined the ground situation pertaining to identity, security and equity, highlighted facts emanating from official data, and made recommendations for corrective and affirmative action.

What conclusions do we draw from our experience of six decades in terms, firstly, of the conceptual framework and, secondly, of the actual experience?

Let us begin with plurality. It is a social reality that has manifested itself in different ways in different periods of our long history. It was cherished and relished:

Gul haai ranga rang se hai zeenat-e-chaman
Ai Zauq is jahan ko hai zaib ekhtelaaf se

Pluralism indicates the presence of differences and marks a departure from policies aimed at annihilating the other; it however remains silent about the public status of these communities. Cultural pluralism of the past thus existed within acknowledged structures of authority and did not seek to place it in a framework of equality. The contemporary constitutional framework of equality and secularism, however, provides it a different enabling atmosphere. "In today's India," writes Asim Ray, "tolerant pluralism is totally meaningless and impotent unless it is thoroughly rooted out of its traditional mores, and is relocated on the basis of equalitarian and egalitarian principles". Such relocation, he adds, can only be achieved if all religious groups dedicate themselves to an overarching spiritual ideal of living together. This brings forth "three interconnected ideas: repudiating the idea of the State as belonging to the dominant group; replacing assimilationist and exclusionary nation-building policies with policies of recognition and accommodation; and acknowledging historic injustice and offering amends for it." This imposes obligations on the State to promote equal treatment. It must, as Gurpreet Mahajan puts it, acknowledge and accommodate diverse cultural communities as equal partners: "Only when the diversity that comprises the totality is reflected in the universal can communities have a sense of identity and equality."

The same holds for secularism. The concept itself, mentioned though not defined in the text, is accepted as part of the basic structure of the Constitution. It pertains to three sets of relations in a society: between religion and the individual (freedom of religion); between the State and the individual (citizenship); and between the State and religion (separation of State and religion). The basic debate in India on the meaning and content of secularism has ranged on two principal approaches, namely (a) neutrality of the State vis-à-vis religions to ensure a basic symmetry of treatment between citizens of different religious communities and (b) prohibition of religious activities in the functioning of the State. The former implies respect for and implementation of rights given to religious minorities. The record of six decades shows that flawed practice has at times tended to dilute these principles. The devil, as always, lies in the detail of implementation and the 'major premise' in the functioning of the State machinery. There is also a need to probe Asghar Ali Engineer's observation that "increasing democratisation should have meant more secularisation, but increased democratisation is resulting in greater communalisation." The inevitable conclusion is that patterns of political mobilisation in the country have not always adhered to our constitutional ideals and have exacerbated societal fault lines.

In regard to State structure, the Constitution prescribed the form of political democracy. This has produced good results and empowered the citizenry. The working of the democratic process, however, has lent weight to Ambedkar's foreboding about the contradiction between political equality and social and economic inequality and about the need to have one man one vote and one vote one value. The inequality trap thus created, as the Report of the Expert Group on Diversity Index put it last year, 'prevent the marginalised and work in favour of the dominant group in society.' As a result, it adds, 'unequal economic opportunities lead to unequal outcomes which in turn lead to unequal access to political power. This creates a vicious circle since unequal power structure determines the nature and functioning of the institutions and their policies. All these result in persistence of initial conditions.' The debate is also beginning to focus on the relationship between caste and class and between caste and minority; it has been argued that 'the politics of inclusion has to go beyond caste inequalities as deprivation and discrimination are widespread and not confined to a single community or group'. The situation is aggravated, in actual governance, by the fraying of the Rule of Law norms.

On all three counts, therefore, practice has fallen short of the promise. What has been its impact–physical and psychological–on the largest minority? What has been the direction of debate within? How, and to what extent, has it interacted with the larger citizen body and sought solutions?

III

Insecurity, frustration and uncertainty characterised the Indian Muslim mind in the immediate aftermath of Partition. Evidence of the official attitude in earlier years, cited by Ramachandra Guha, leaves little room for doubt. Balraj Puri summed up the position succinctly in an essay written in 1993: "Their expectations were low and fears high … Gradually, the mood of withdrawal and resignation gave way to consciousness of rights, assertion of identity and protests against perceived injustices …" The grievances (with some important local variants) centred on five core concerns: security, employment and reservations, Urdu, Aligarh Muslim University and Muslim Personal Law. The community's internal discourse on these as also in the wider Indian circle is, therefore, of relevance. It was articulated through the *ulema*, political leaders, intellectuals and the general public. In many cases, these categories over-lapped; their responses varied. The record of six decades suggests an unduly defensive approach, sporadic and emotional rather than systematic and rational. The internal discourse repeated an old lament:

> *"Ab who altaf nahin, hum pe enayat nahin*
> *Baat ye kya hai ke pahle si madaraat nahin"?*

Suggestions for possible corrections were few, unfocused and far in between. On the other side, the wider community and the political class preferred to be in a state of denial. As a result an inter-community dialogue to seek correctives did not emerge; this enhanced distances.

Security concerns and the inability of the State apparatus, from time to time, to ensure physical security still tend to condition reactions across the board. It has affected visibility in public spaces and induced ghettoisation with all its attendant consequences. The same holds good for livelihood concerns. The government's follow up actions on the Sachar Committee Report has made some impact but many of the grievances persist, as is evident from the thrust of testimonies given in the meeting organised recently in New Delhi by a civil society group. Some of the recommendations for corrective action emanating from the meeting need to be given a closer look.

The patterns of differentiation in the employment of Muslims in the public and private sectors as well as deprivation from other forms of State largesse, identified by the Sachar Report and other studies, combined with low performance levels in education, has caused economic hardship and given a fresh impetus to the demand for reservations, notwithstanding its evident limitations. Some of the state governments have seen merit in it and responded in varying degrees. The Ranganath Mishra Commission, whose report is yet to be made public, is said to have recommended specific steps based on assessment of backwardness irrespective of religion. More is likely to be heard about this in the coming months and years.

In regard to Urdu, there is sufficient evidence to show that it suffered from deliberate official neglect in some of the states. Jawaharlal

Nehru complained about it to the Chief Ministers as early as 1954. Half a century later and belying the requirement of Article 350A, large segments of a generation have grown up without knowing their mother tongue. Equally glaring is the failure of Urdu-knowing people to nurture the language, particularly among the youth. The general public, apart from occasional couplets and more frequent melodies in Mumbai movies, considers Urdu synonymous with Muslims with its teaching confined to madrasas or universities but rarely undertaken in normal schools. An international conference on Urdu language in 2003 recommended that 'in order to protect Urdu in its land of birth, while it flourishes abroad, a national movement for the revival of Urdu commanding strong political will is the need of the hour'. There is little evidence of this taking shape. What was said many years back still holds good: "*Sad salah jalse huai, magar is se zubaan ki yaad to qaim rahti hai, taraqqi nahin hoti*". Thus the onus for salvaging Urdu rests primarily with those who claim it as mother tongue and those who value its inherent strength and beauty and its substantial contribution to Indian literature and culture.

The demand for the acknowledgement of the distinctive, minority, character of the Aligarh Muslim University (to rectify a Supreme Court ruling of 1965) has been a persistent one but seems to have lost its centrality in community perceptions with the emergence of good quality minority-run institutions of higher and professional education in several states and the resultant erosion of AMU's all-India identity and character. It remains to be seen if the attempt now underway to reincarnate the AMU in different parts of the country and link it to the mother institution by an umbilical cord of uncertain quality and character would necessarily serve better either the purpose of minority education in specific minority-concentration areas or do away with the demand to restore the minority character of the university.

The concern over protection of Muslim Personal Law from parliamentary legislation is of later vintage and surfaced only in 1972 in the wake of a suggestion that an effort be made to move towards a uniform civil code. The debate has thrown up polarised positions and generated more heat than light. More relevant is the argument that the provision of Article 44 does not demand a 'mechanical application of a single family law to the entire nation by one stroke of legislation' since it goes against its rationale and ignores ground realities. This is supported by the Supreme Court's observation that 'a uniform law, though it is highly desirable, enactment thereof in one go may be counter-productive to the unity and integrity of the nation' and that 'the mischief or defect most acute may be remedied by process of law in stages'. This notwithstanding, the need for segregating harmful social custom from religious law per se does stare the community in the face and seeks a response; so does the precedent set by a number of Muslim countries to codify the law relating to marriage, divorce and succession. "Voluntary surrender of intellectual independence", to use Allama Iqbal's phrase, does not signify a vibrant community; nor is self-imposed isolation an answer.

IV

Do these readings become an imperative for course correction? Do they provide sufficient social and political momentum for change? Our national objective is inclusive growth. The State has to ensure this in its policy formulation and, more importantly, in its implementation. Public support thus becomes an essential ingredient. It is here that the citizen body in its entirety has to shoulder its responsibility and try to dilute if not undo the binary construction of the social universe. By the same token, Muslim citizens need to acknowledge the insufficiency of their interface with the rest of the citizen body and the limitations of their initiatives on self-help in social and educational matters needed to bring about a qualitative change in approach. Egalitarian pluralism, in other words, propels counterpart obligations for both the Self and the other.

Many in this audience would know that the corrective was prescribed a long time back:

"Khuda ne aaj tak uss qaum ki haalat nahin badli
Na ho jisko khayaal aap apni haalat ke badalne ka"

There is, specifically, a requirement to address three challenges:

- Sustained, candid, and uninterrupted interaction with fellow citizens without a syndrome of superiority or inferiority.
- Involvement of all segments of the community, particularly women who constitute half the population and are to be empowered in social responsibilities as equal partners with Muslim men, and
- Self-empowerment in areas where competence already exists, making the best use of government assistance that is available, and creating capability to benefit from the opportunities being offered by an expanding economy.

A careful observer has summed up the requirement in blunt terms: *"Fiza aap ke haq main bhale badal rahi ho magar jab tak aap aage barh kar us se faaida nahin uthaenge, kuch nahin hone wala".*

The failure of communication with the wider community has tended to freeze the boundaries of diversities that characterise Indian society. People have tended to live together separately. As a result, stereotypes have been developed and nurtured. Many years ago Edward Said had portrayed western perceptions of Islam and Muslims: "For the right, Islam represents barbarism; for the left, medieval theocracy; for the centre, a kind of distasteful exoticism". In our country, mercifully, perceptions were less stark thanks to the cultural interaction of a thousand years. However, the politics of history text books has left its imprint on the mind of a good section of the public. Media images add to this. The past, however rosy or gory, will neither sustain the present nor help create a better future. There is therefore an urgent need to correct the image, go beyond identity issues and project a more holistic view of Muslims as normal human beings and fellow citizens with the same rights and responsibilities as other citizens. The requirement is of an authentic dialogue among equals about the universality of values. Its objective should be Gandhi*ji's* "union of hearts". Islam's emphasis on observance of ethical principles in interaction with all human beings should help Muslims to propel a positive image.

In regard to the status of women, the dead weight of tradition, poverty and communal politics has resulted in three deficits: (a) literacy (b) economic power resulting from work and income, and (c) autonomy of decision making. This has produced a pattern of structured disempowerment. It is most visible amongst the poor. It is therefore imperative to seek correctives through social awakening; in this effort religious texts are not an impediment, social custom is. The endeavour should be inclusive; the traditionalists, who have a wider social reach, have to be included and reminded of Islam's teachings on the status of women as also of the imperative of our times. What is needed is a virtual revolution in our approach to this question. The examples of education of women in Muslim societies like Indonesia, Malaysia, Iran and Turkey, and its eventual impact on the status of women in society, can be emulated with benefit. Given the ground situation, a beginning can be made by a time-bound programme of opening primary and secondary schools for girls in Muslim concentration localities. This, and the scholarship schemes being implemented by the government, should show some results over a five year period.

The third challenge is of empowerment and self-empowerment. The State can assist as it must, and is committed to do so; by the same logic, however, this only initiates the process and cannot be the end of it. The syndrome of victim-hood does not help and there are lessons to be learnt from the experience of other minorities. An expanding economy like ours needs active participation in emerging opportunities and in equipping the youth with skills to improve employability. In India of today, time is of critical importance; so is the need to remember that mediocrity means marginalisation. There are a great many success stories in small and medium businesses, educational institutions and in professions. These need to be studied, publicised and internalised. The process, admittedly, is unevenly spread and a much greater community and governmental effort is needed in the northern and eastern states. It can, nevertheless, be said that a new Muslim identity is emerging in different regions, language areas, professional groups, and social classes. It exudes confidence in varying degrees, refuses to shoulder the burden of the past, and is assertive about the rights due to it as citizen. They thus become partners in the promotion of inclusive development.

V

Let us look again at the characteristic of uniqueness. This has three dimensions: of India being a plural, secular and democratic State, of its Muslim minority being the third largest community of Muslims in the world, and of this minority's distinctive experience in terms of cultural contributions and dialogue. Indian Muslims constitute 10 per cent of the total Muslim population of the world. Other countries where Muslims live as significant minorities (Ethiopia, China, Russia and Tanzania) do not have the democratic framework or the record of cultural interaction; on the other hand, the Muslim numbers in individual Western countries are a miniscule percentage of their populations. The Indian experience and the Indian Muslim experience, therefore, could be of relevance to others also, particularly in the context of globalisation that has induced much greater mobility of people. More and more countries in the world, therefore, will be called upon to accommodate diversity within a framework of equality; many of them are encountering conceptual and practical difficulties. India thus offers an alternate working model of pluralism in thought and action.

Allow me to conclude by submitting that despite our credible record of accommodation of diversity, it would be a folly to consider it a finished product. A living society evolves continuously in terms of its perceptions and practices, including those pertaining to equality, plurality, secularism, human rights and minority rights. The deepening of the democratic process in the country, and heightened consciousness of egalitarian diversity, would unavoidably propel all segments of the population to exercise the moral muscle, explore the normative potential and question some of the traditional symbols, customs and prejudices. The social and economic rejuvenation of Indian Muslims is important for its internal dimension, as also for revitalising India's traditional engagement with, and contribution to, the Muslim world beyond our borders.

While the Indian Constitution was well ahead of its time in recognising diversities and in providing for representation of and affirmative action for identified collectivities in our formal democratic structures, there would come a time when we would need to revert to focus on redressing the deprivations of individual citizens, irrespective of their group affiliations.

Eternal vigilance, it is said, is the price of liberty. There is, therefore, a need to be vigilant, keep the process on a progressive track, and prevent regressions. The key seems to lie in a sincere, unconditional and uninterrupted dialogue and requisite corrective action within the framework of the Constitution. All segments of society, majority and minority, have a national duty to do so:

Mere ahl-e-watan yeh aadmiyat ka taqaaza hai
Muhabbat ka, sharaafat ka, hameeyat ka taqaaza hai

Inauguration of the Conference 'An International Dialogue Between Islam and Oriental Religions'
Jamia Millia Islamia, New Delhi
20 February 2010

Islam and Oriental Religions

Religious discourse is a ponderous subject. I claim no competence in it. Inter-faith dialogue is seemingly simpler but is in reality equally obtuse. Here, too, I claim no expertise. Both frighten away the novice and make the initiated cautious. Despite this, I succumbed to the request to present myself in your midst today. "Temptation", said George Bernard Shaw "should not be resisted":

"Rang-e-sharaab se meri neeyat badal ga-ie
Waaiz ki baat reh ga-ie, saaqi ki chal ga-ie"

The organisers of this conclave are to be congratulated for taking up a subject that is in dire need of an open discussion in our country. My personal inclination would be to dispute the title. It imposes a geographic definition on a theme that transcends geography. It categorises faiths or belief systems in terms of their region of origin. It severely limits a reading of the history of inter-faith dialogues.

This 'Oriental' distinction is significant in view of the results of the survey of the world's Muslim population done by the Pew Research Centre. It revealed that two-thirds of the world's 1.57 billion Muslims live in Asia. Islam, indeed, is as much an Oriental religion.

Be that as it may, and taking the subject on face value, I presume the intention is to examine the interaction of Islam with religions that originally emanated from the Indic and Sinic societies. These would principally be Hinduism, Buddhism, Sikhism and Jainism in India, Zoroastrianism in Iran and Confucianism and Taoism in China. One reason for this could be that while there has been an on-going dialogue between Islam, Christianity and Judaism in recent times, the same is not the case with other faiths mentioned above. Another reason, equally valid, is the religious diversity of the Indian society and the consequent need for a dialogue with the religious 'other'.

It is to be noted that all these faiths emerged in the Eurasian landmass and the vast majority of their adherents are to be found in geographically contiguous regions. Together they constitute over two-thirds of the world's population. The normal business of living brought them together from time to time in the past and does so today. Such social intercourse may include religious dialogue but is not necessarily synonymous with it. The frequency and intensity of this interaction varied with time and place. Despite the abridgement of distances due to modernisation, urbanisation and globalisation, the disappearance of traditional channels and modes of communication have impacted adversely on this interaction.

Inter-faith dialogue has emerged as a prominent civil society initiative between nations and groups in the post-Cold War world, amidst the 'Clash of Civilisations' debate and the raging ethnic and religious conflicts in various parts of the globe. The 'The Alliance of Civilisations' initiative under United Nations auspices connects people and organisations devoted to promoting dialogue among political, religious, media and civil society leaders, particularly between Muslim and Western societies. Other such dialogue frameworks include the Cordoba Initiative on improving Muslim-West relations, the Madrid Dialogue Conference that was a Saudi-Spanish effort, the Assisi interfaith work of the late Pope John Paul II and the Common Word initiative of Muslim scholars.

Despite the significant progress achieved, the record shows that inter-faith dialogue has remained confined to the select few and has not percolated to the public at large.

Religion, in a generic sense, covers both the articles of faith or creed and a set of rituals emanating from them. The two are connected but not synonymous. Furthermore, all systems of faith also promulgate certain universal values and principles of human conduct that are similar to each other. On a metaphysical plain thinking about Creator, the Purpose of Creation, and the relationship between the Creator and the Created often tends to run along parallel lines and reaches proximate conclusions. Once that level is reached, commonalities prevail:

"Hum muwahhid hain hamara kaish hai tark-e-rusoom
Millatain jab mit ga-een ajzaa-e-eeman ho ga-een"

Dialogues and discussions between adherents of different faiths have always taken place and are not a modern day novelty. Occasionally, they have been State-induced; more often, they emanated from individual or group initiatives.

This backdrop helps us address a set of questions. To what extent did this contact help the process of mutual understanding, particularly an understanding of each other's religions and systems of belief? What were the points of convergence and divergence? To what extent were these influenced by politics and state craft? What conclusions can be drawn from it? Above all, what needs to be done today?

II

The first, and unquestionably the most important in the Indian context, is the contact between Islam and Hinduism. This was not a single point happening in space and time and response patterns were not uniform. In southern India, Islam as a faith came through traders and had little difficulty in being accommodated. The story was different elsewhere in the subcontinent where Islam was often identified with rulers; here too, however, response patterns varied and their homogenisation did no service either to history or to proper understanding.

It is a truism that all social orders are impacted upon by belief systems as well as by politics. In order therefore to comprehend the interaction between the two, it is essential to distinguish between (a) a religious action that is politically relevant or conditioned and (b) a political action that is religiously relevant or conditioned. A good many examples in both categories can be found in history as well as in current practices.

An early example of Muslim perception of Hinduism is to be found in the Central Asian scholar Abu Rehan Alberuni's account written in the early years of the eleventh century. He candidly admitted the dissimilarities between the adherents of the two faiths, highlighted "the deeply rooted hatred" resulting from the invasion of Mahmud of Ghazna, and then went on to dwell on the essence of Hinduism:

"The Hindus believe with regard to God that he is one, eternal, without beginning and end, acting by free will, almighty, all-wise, living, giving life, ruling, preserving: one who in his sovereignty is unique, beyond all likeness and unlikeness, and that he does not resemble anything nor does anything resemble him."

In a similar vein Amir Khusrau in the fourteenth century said the Hindus are among those good people who believe in God— who is omnipotent and omniscient and is "pure Truth and inimitable Reality."

Another example of this approach was Dara Shikoh's *Majma-ul Bahrain* wherein he concluded, with regard to Indian monotheism, that "he did not find any difference, except verbal, in the way they sought and comprehended Truth." (*Juz ikhtilaaf-e-lafzi dar daryaaft o shenaakht-e-Haq, tafaawati na deed*).

In the twentieth century, Muhammad Iqbal went even further in a popular poem, *Hindustani Bachon ka Qaumi Geet*:

"Wahdat ki lai suni thi dunya ne jis makaan se
Mir-e-Arab ko aai thandi hawa jahaan se
Mera watan wahi hai, mera watan wahi hai"

These should have signalled a mutual appreciation of two systems of belief. The Mughal emperor Akbar and his prime minister Abul-Fazl came close to such an appreciation. However, compulsions of Statecraft directed the majority of rulers in an opposite direction. As a result, identities were principally sustained through the cultivation of prejudices rather than through spiritual and social values. Politics contributed to it in great measure.

Rulers were motivated by political and economic considerations; principles of their faith rarely guided their actions. The result of this approach was twofold: on one plane, the coming together of people in daily life impacted on habits and customs and induced acceptance of each other; on another, they lived together separately.

The chasm was sought to be bridged by the Sufis who, as one scholar put it, took religion from the classes to the masses; another described it as "a walking incarnation of inter religious dialogue". This achieved degree of success, had its imprint on the Bhakti movement, left some mark on perceptions but did not alter the wider picture. Over time, the negative perceptions congealed.

It is evident, therefore, that despite adequate knowledge and good intentions, misperceptions were allowed to prevail. Their impact on Indian society is in no need of commentary.

The need of the hour is to seek a more effective approach to further mutual understanding.

III

A beginning has to be made with the first principles of social order. This is a set of values that regulate social intercourse and dispense justice. These values, in a religiously homogenous society, are generally taken from religion or conditioned by religious precepts; in a non-homogenous one, however, the only available and acceptable course is to seek values common to all faiths, is subscribed to by the votaries of all faiths, and is not overtly offensive to any segment. Every society in its political manifestation accepts these common values; it also subscribes to a set of secular values. The historian Edward Gibbon dwelt on this in the context of ancient Rome in its republican period; his words remain relevant:

"The various modes of worship were all considered by the people as equally true; by the philosopher, as equally false; and by the magistrate, as equally useful. And thus tolerance produced not only mutual indulgence, but even religious concord."

Our requirement today is no different. We need to go beyond tolerance; the imperative for religious concord in a framework of equality is evident and compelling. This would be achieved only through a sustained, candid and uninterrupted dialogue without a syndrome of superiority or inferiority and with the objective of locating common values conducive to the maintenance of ethical standards essential for social harmony and furtherance of common objectives. The process of locating these values would bring forth other commonalities. Experience over time of shared public space and common national resources in everyday interaction, and mechanisms that blur boundaries through management of differences, would assist the process.

The quest for common values would not be a substitute for religions. All it would do is to locate a minimum of basic values on which consensus exists or can be developed; these would include faith in the unity of humankind and equality among human beings, contemplation, penance, ascetic living, justice, charity, truthfulness, help to poor and needy, contentment, self respect, tolerance and promotion of social peace and stability.

These values unite, they do not divide; they foster love, not hatred. Because they are embodied in all faiths, they transcend formal boundaries. Together, they would involve a commitment to a culture of peace, respect for life and non-violence, justice and social solidarity, truthfulness and human equality.

Commitment is one aspect of the matter, practice is another. The latter has to go beyond the circle of the select few and percolate to the masses. In the final analysis, we will be judged not by what we say, but by what we do. To do this meaningfully, institutional arrangements would be helpful; these would be means to an end, not the end itself.

IV

Today's conference is the beginning of a process debating how to foster dialogue between various faiths in East and South-Asian societal contexts. It is an affirmation that the process starts through cooperation among religious, cultural, political, educational, and media establishments with a view to consolidate ethical values and encourage progressive social practices.

Prof. Sarvepalli Radhakrishnan in his epic study of Indian philosophy has concluded: "The twin strands which in one shape or another run through all the efforts of the Indian thinkers are loyalty to tradition and devotion to truth ... The different views are not looked upon as unrelated adventures of the human mind into the realm of the unknown or a collection of philosophical curiosities. They are regarded as the expression of a single mind, which has built up the great temple, though it is divided into numerous walls and vestibules, passages and pillars."

Inter-faith dialogue should proceed on this Indian heritage that we have inherited. This heritage has no specific religious, linguistic or cultural label and no attempt should be made to keep it exclusive or make it exclusionary. The inclusiveness of our constitutional ideals derives its inspiration from this heritage and any process that further strengthens it is good for the nation and needs to be encouraged.

The message from this conference should be loud and clear:

Aa ghairiyat ke parde ek baar phir utha dain
Bichroan ko phir milaa dain, naqsh-e-duie mitaa dain

The International Seminar on 'Islamic Art and Culture'
Maulana Azad National Urdu University, Hyderabad.
30 December 2011

THE ART AND CULTURE OF ISLAM IN INDIA

I stand here with mixed emotions: happy to be amongst you, honoured by the invitation to speak on so weighty a subject, daunted by the enormity of the task, sobered by my own inadequacy. I therefore seek sustenance in two couplets that have remained a sound preamble down the ages:

"Ba naam-e-Khudawand jaan aafarein
Hakim-e-sukhan dar zubaan aafarein

Khudawand bakhshanda-e-dastgeer
Karim–e-khata bakhsh pozish pazeer

In the name of the Lord, soul-creating
Wise One, speech-creating in the tongue!

Lord forgiving, apt to help
Generous, fault-forgiving, excuse accepting"

The subject is vast, almost nebulous. The best that can be attempted is to touch upon some overarching themes. Islam has been a part of the Indian landscape for well over a millennium and has impacted on, and been impacted upon, in very many layers. A very good reason for it is the unique nature of Indian culture.

The doyen of historians of an earlier era, Dr Tara Chand of revered memory, delineated it with some precision:

> Indian culture is synthetic in character. It comprehends ideas of different orders. It embraces in its orbit beliefs, customs, rites, institutions, arts, religions and philosophies belonging to strata of society in varying stages of development. It eternally seeks to find a unity for the heterogeneous elements which make up its totality. At worst its attempts end in mechanical juxtaposition, at best they succeed in evolving an organic system.

Historical record makes evident the absence of mechanical juxtaposition. Islam as a faith, as a body of ideas and practices, came to India through human interaction in different ways in different parts of the subcontinent. This took place over time, and 'in a manner that was beyond social and political control'. The unifying factor for the adherents of the new faith was a common allegiance to Islam.

Beyond it, variations in doctrine and observances, and diversity in regional terms, remained; nor were the differences in rural–urban practices erased. Each left its imprint on art and culture.

II

A discourse on culture necessarily confronts definitional impediments. How do we define culture? One study compiled 164 definitions! For our purpose today we could accept the anthropologist Edward Taylor's definition and consider culture to be "that complex whole which includes knowledge, belief, art, law, morals, custom, and any other capabilities and habits acquired by man as a member of society". Emanating from this, the art and culture of Islam in India could be taken to mean such contributions inspired, made, or cause to be made, by persons or groups living here and professing to belong to Islamic faith.

It is known that within a few centuries from its inception Islam became a world religion with its adherents living in different countries imbibing, and shaping, the local environment.

The historian Ira Lapidus has neatly characterised this interaction as "a dialogue between the realm of religious symbols and the world of everyday reality … of interaction between Islamic values and historical experiences of Muslim peoples that has shaped the formation of a number of different but interrelated Muslim societies".

The nature of this interaction also depended on the type of contacts and the cultural level of the societies concerned. In regard to the first, there is sufficient evidence to show that Indians, particularly those all along the west coast, were familiar with various communities in western Asia in the period before the advent of Islam.

There were extensive trading ties with and through thc lands of Arabia, Persia, the Red Sea, the Persian Gulf, and beyond. Transient traders as well as settled communities were a frequent occurrence. The rise of a centralised state in the wake of the early Islamic expansion gave a considerable impetus to existing interaction.

India, therefore, was a known land, sought after for its prosperity and trading skills and respected for its attainments in different branches of knowledge. Baghdad became the seeker, and dispenser, of Indian numerals and sciences.

The *Panchatantra* was translated and became *Kalila wa Dimna*. Long before the advent of Muslim conquerors, the works of Al-Jahiz, Ibn Khurdadbeh, Al-Kindi, Yaqubi and Al-Masudi testify to it in ample measure. Alberuni, who studied India and Indians more thoroughly than most, produced a virtual encyclopedia on religion, rituals, manners and customs, philosophy, mathematics and astronomy. He commenced his great work by highlighting differences, but was careful enough 'to relate, not criticise'.

For our purpose today and given the time constraints, I shall opt for some selectivity in the choice of impact areas, and restrict my observations to the most noticeable ones: to architecture and painting in the realm of art proper and to history, literature, religious and philosophical speculation and Sufism in the wider area of culture.

This discourse took shape through rulers and the ruling class, scholars and intellectuals, and all those who interacted with and influenced the masses in general.

III

Historians have shed much light on the essential features of the Muslim rule and the ruling classes. In the first place, the State was not theocratic, notwithstanding the fact that throughout the medieval period the rulers in Delhi and in many other kingdoms were Muslim; they however 'paid scant attention to Islamic concepts of the State'. Kingship was absolute rather than conditional; governance was conducted through State-made regulations *(zawabit)* and not on the principles of *sharia*. The nobility (with a few exceptions) was a hierarchy of salaried officials. Over time, the imprint of Indian social organisation was clearly visible. Social interaction at different levels, and within those levels, diluted rigid norms and induced adaptability. Creativity followed.

One unavoidable consequence of the capture of authority anywhere is to reflect it physically. The mosque and the tomb in the religious domain and the palace, pavilions, town gates, gardens and landscape architecture in the secular domain thus became reflective of the new, changing, reality. So towards the close of the twelfth century—India saw the arrival of a totally distinct tradition of architecture. Its major characteristics, in the words of Professor Irfan Habib were:

> ... the use of arch, vault and dome, and the application of lime cement; it could achieve in consequence a lightness and grace that the earlier trabeate construction could not easily match. Its love of light and space and 'simple severity' seems to stand in sharp contrast to 'plastic exuberance' of the earlier Indian tradition.

This tradition of distinctive style evolved over a period of four centuries and produced regional variants. Competent observers have noted that in the Moghul period "the combination of scale, detail and good taste was sometimes breadth-taking and has seldom been surpassed." The mosques and tombs of that era, as also the landscape architecture in the shape of ornamental gardens, are too well known to be mentioned individually; their grandeur immortalises the architectural and building skills of the planners, engineers and craftsmen.

Provincial styles in architecture also blossomed. Ahmedabad and Mandu were distinctive. The Qutubshahi forts, mosques and monuments in the vicinity of the city of Hyderabad, and the Charminar, are too well known to this audience to be dilated upon. Scholars like Percy Brown have dwelt in detail on the stylistic evolution in this period.

Painting was another area of excellence. The Ajanta frescos are reflective of the high technical and artistic quality attained in the pre-Muslim period. Humayun, during his exile in Persia, developed a taste for Persian paintings and was able to bring back masters like Abdus Samad.

The Moghul style, in the words of Annemarie Schimmel, "developed from the interaction of the refined Persian style and the strong, lively, vision of the Hindu artists"; its evolution is well reflected in the miniatures of the *Tutinama* and the *Hamzanama*. It reached its peak in the reigns of Jahangir and Shahjahan. They, like Akbar, regarded painting as a means of bringing historical and romantic texts vividly to life. Jahangir in particular used paintings as a guide to physiognomy, to enable him recognise and assess nobles and as a scientific instrument to study flora and fauna. He mentions in his Memoirs the names of Abul Hasan and Ustad Mansur; their respective titles, *Nadir-uz-zaman* and *Nadir-ul-Asr,* speak for themselves. He also dwells on his own expertise on the subject in words that need to be quoted without abridgement:

> As regards myself, my liking for painting and my practice in judging it have arrived at such a point that when any work is brought before me, either of deceased artists or of those of present day, without the name being told me, I say on the spur of the moment that it is the work of such and such a man. And if there be a picture containing many portraits, and each face by the work of a different master, I can discover which face is the work of each of them. If any other person has put in the eye or the eyebrow of a face, I can perceive whose work the original face is, and who has painted the eyes and the eyebrows.

Yet another area of excellence was calligraphy. Suspicion of figurative art as idolatrous led to it; thus abstract depictions become a major form of artistic expression in Islamic cultures, especially in religious contexts. Fine handwriting was also regarded as an essential accomplishment for a noble man and "aesthetics was made an aspect of sovereignty." The emperors were not merely admirers of calligraphy, they were also practitioners. The Moghul artists like their Ottoman counterparts; developed new variations and formed pictures and figures out of words.

An impetus to the writing of history is particularly noticeable. In the period prior to the twelfth century there was, in the words of Narayanan Bandyopadhyaya, "a lack of recorded history", an exception to it being Kalhana's history of Kashmir.

In the subsequent five centuries historical writings flourished. The names are too many to be mentioned here. An early example is Ali bin Hamid Kufi's *Chachnama*.

Much more followed, in the pre-Moghul and Moghul periods. The wealth of material compiled by Jjuzjani, Barani, Abul Fazl, Badauni, Qazwini, Khafi Khan and others have made possible comprehensive study of that period.

Equally significant are the autobiographies of rulers; the most prominent of these were the *Babur Nama* and *Tuzk-i-Jahangiri*. Gul Badan Begum's *Humanyun Nama* could be counted in the proximate category.

Belief, consciousness and practice became a particularly rich area of interaction. On one side high value was placed on orthodoxy 'because it maintained the identity of a community against other communities and prevented an assimilation that could lead to the community disintegrating and being absorbed by others.' On the other, and living in a non-homogenous social milieu, the pious often communicated values through personal practice.

In this sense the values of faith, though not its theological content, reached a wider circle of the public. The popularity of different *Sufi* personalities is evidence enough of their reach. Thus there is merit in Professor Mujeeb's observation that "Sufism took Islam to the masses and in doing so it took over the enormous and delicate responsibility of dealing at a personal level with a baffling variety of problem."

Scholars have analysed the socio-cultural role of the *Sufi dargahs* in the cultural integration of the religious communities. The *Sufi* trends sought commonalities in spiritual thinking.

One example of it is *Dabistan-i-Mazahib*, a mid-seventeenth century work believed to have been written in Srikakulam (present day Andhra Pradesh) and described by an eminent scholar as "the greatest book ever written in India on comparative religion." Dara Shukoh went further in his *Majmu'-al Bahrain*, gave a Vedantic view of Universe and Truth and concluded "that the differences between Islam and Hinduism were merely verbal."

Alongside, the influence of Islam can be discerned in the vocabulary of preachers and saints of other faiths and *Bhakti* traditions.

The pattern of convergence or parallelism has been traced with precision by many scholars; their judgment is that some Islamic precepts and many Muslim practices seeped into the interstices of the Indian society and gave expression to a broader and deeper unity of minds expressive of the Indian spiritual tradition.

This tradition was aptly summed up by Allama Iqbal in his poem *Hindustani Bachon Ka Qaumi Geet.*

IV

To conclude, I can do no better than to go back to Dr Tara Chand's classic work *Influence of Islam on Indian Culture* written in 1922 and cite a telling passage:

> It is hardly possible to exaggerate the extent of Muslim influence over Indian life in all departments. But nowhere else is it shown so vividly and so picturesquely, as in customs, in intimate details of domestic life, in music, in the fashion of dress, in the ways of cooking, in the ceremonial of marriage, in the celebration of festivals and fairs, and in the courtly institutions and etiquette of Marathi, Rajput and Sikh princes. In the days of Babar, the Hindu and Muslim lived and thought so much alike that he was forced to notice their peculiar "Hindustani way"; his

> successors so gloriously adorned and so marvelously enriched his legacy that India might well be proud today of the heritage which they in turn left behind."(pp 141-142)

One last word about this venue; perhaps accidental, but altogether appropriate, a seat of learning, associated with the name of a personality who embodied in his person and his work the ethos and apogee of Indo-Islamic culture.

Book release: *Muslims in Indian Cities* edited by Laurent Gayer and Christophe Jaffrelot
New Delhi
10 September 2012

The subject of India's Muslim minority, and its socio-economic condition, has been the subject of considerable study in recent years. The debate has thus progressed from informed and less informed speculation to diligent collection and analysis of actual conditions based on ground data.

Indian Muslims are, in more ways than one, sui generic. They are 13.4 per cent of India's population; at the same time, they are the second or third largest Muslim community in our world of nation-states. They have lived in India's religiously plural society for over a thousand years, at times as rulers, at others as subjects and now as citizens. They are not homogenous in racial or linguistic terms and bear the impact of local cultural surroundings, in manners and customs, in varying degrees.

The Partition of India in 1947, a result of political calculus, compromises and adjustments of elites but not of population at large, adversely affected the Muslims in India, particularly in the northern and eastern states of the Indian Union. For several decades thereafter the socio-economic impact of that event on the Muslim minority remained largely un-tudied or understudied. Ad hoc government initiatives taken occasionally were poorly implemented.

In March 2005, the Government of India had set up a High Level Committee under Justice Rajinder Sachar to collect authentic information about the social, economic and educational status of the Muslim community so that it could be used for formulation of specific policies and programmes to address its socio-economic backwardness.

The Sachar Report has become a landmark and is being used by the Government for affirmative action in different areas. The extent to which it has succeeded is the subject of a lively debate. Amongst the many studies undertaken, I could mention the volume edited in 2010 by Rakesh Basant and Abusaleh Shariff and the Report published last year by Harsh Mander's Centre for Equity Studies. Both shed much light on the conceptual and practical limitations of the extant policies.

The volume before us today adds some useful empirical data to the debate. It is yet another example of the thoroughness and diligence of the CNRS, Paris and of its guiding light, Professor Jaffrelot, who needs no introduction to an Indian audience. It is a sociological study of the condition of Muslim communities specifically in a dozen urban centres. It explores patterns of segregation as well as of resilience. The concluding essay by the editors offers a nuanced view of social and territorial marginalisation through typologies and argues that Muslims are losing ground.

This conclusion may be contested on two grounds. In the first place, any generalisation for so large a number spread over a vast area, is hazardous. Secondly, and as the editors point out, the Muslims of India are not a homogenous entity. Different strata of the community have performed differently. The elite of a feudal past have lost ground but some amongst them have adapted themselves well in new callings. New elites have sprung up amongst those who in the past were socially under-privileged and are now doing well in terms of educational levels and economic wellbeing.

Above all, the realisation is dawning that as equal partners in a democratic polity governed by the ideals of social, economic and political justice, they can make the weight of numbers be felt in political decision-making and seek a fair access to it.

Locating Urdu in Present Day India

"We encourage he smallest tribal language in its own area, but many of us resent even the mention of Urdu, and yet Urdu is very much a child of India and is a vital and graceful aspect of our many-sided culture. I am deeply grieved at this narrowness of outlook which so frequently comes in our way

—Jawaharlal Nehru
1 August 1953

Inauguration of International Ghalib Seminar
Aiwan-e-Ghalib, Ghalib Institute, New Delhi
14 December 2007

اقبالؔ: ایشیائی بیداری کا شاعر

پروفیسر نذیر احمد صاحب!

مہمان گرامی، خواتین وحضرات!

ہم کہاں کے دانہ تھے۔ میری سمجھ میں یہ نہیں آیا کہ میرے دوست پروفیسر صدیق الرحمٰن قدوائی صاحب نے مجھے اس باوقار سیمنار کے افتتاح کے لئے کیوں چنا۔علامہ اقبالؔ کے کلام سے تو سب واقف ہیں مگر جو فلسفہ حیات ان میں پوشیدہ ہے اس کا اور اس کی نوعیت کا سمجھنا اتنا آسان نہیں ہے۔

بہر حال اس موضوع پر جو کچھ کہنا تھا وہ شمس الرحمٰن صاحب و دیگر کہہ چکے ہیں۔

علامہ اقبالؔ کی شاعری میں ایک چیز واضح ہے۔ ان کی نظر میں دنیائے اسلام اور عالم مشرق کی پسماندگی کا اصل سبب ایک ذہنی رجحان ہے جو نئے خیالات اور نئے تاثرات کو سماج سے الگ تر رکھتا ہے۔ انہوں نے اس کا ذکر ایک چھوٹی نظم میں کیا جس کا عنوان تھا "نفسیاتِ غلامی"۔

سخت باریک ہیں امراض امم کے اسباب
کھول کر کہیے تو کرتا ہے بیاں کوتاہی!

اسی انداز میں وہ دوبارہ دیکھئے کہتے ہیں...

ے نظر آتے نہیں بے پردہ حقائق ان کو
آنکھ جن کی ہوئی محکومی وتقلید سے کور

انہوں نے اپنے دَور کے مشرقی ممالک اور حکومتوں کا مطالعہ کیا اور ان کو ناکافی پایا۔

ے میری نوا سے گریبانِ لالہ چاک ہوا
نسیم صبح چمن کی تلاش میں ہے ابھی
نہ مصطفےٰ نہ رضاشاہ میں نمود اس کی
کہ روح شرق بدن کی تلاش میں ہے ابھی!

علامہ اقبالؔ اردو کے ان اولین شعراء میں سے تھے جنہوں نے شاعری کا استعمال سماج کے مسائل پر روشنی ڈالنے کے لئے کیا اور ان مسائل کا حل تلاش کرنے کے لئے ہر فرد کے نظریے میں تبدیلی لانے کے علمبردار ہوئے۔

ے دل بیدار پیدا کر کہ دل خوابیدہ ہے جب تک
نہ تیری ضرب کاری ہے نہ میری ضرب کاری ہے

اسی بات کا ذکر انہوں نے چند اشعار میں کیا جب وہ افغانستان میں تھے۔

ے تری دعا سے قضا تو بدل نہیں سکتی
مگر ہے اس سے یہ ممکن کہ تو بدل جائے!
تری خودی میں اگر انقلاب ہو پیدا
عجب نہیں ہے کہ یہ چار سُو بدل جائے!
تری دعا ہے کہ ہو تیری آرزو پوری
مری دعا ہے تری آرزو بدل جائے!

یہ تو واضح ہے کہ علامہ اقبالؔ کا پیغام خصوصاً امت مسلمہ کے لئے تھا جو عالم مشرق کا ایک بہت بڑا جزو ہے۔سوال یہ ہے کہ کیا یہ پیغام دوسروں کے لئے بھی تھا؟

ایک مثال ساقی نامہ میں ہے جہاں ''گراں خواب چینی'' کا ذکر ہے۔

ایک دوسری مثال ''خضر راہ'' میں ملتی ہے جہاں سرمایہ اور محنت کے ذکر میں حضرت خضر کا پیغام ان الفاظوں میں مزدوروں تک پہنچایا گیا...

اٹھ کہ اب بزم جہاں کا اور ہی انداز ہے
مشرق و مغرب میں تیرے دور کا آغاز ہے

میرے ذہن میں، خواتین وحضرات، یہ چند سوال ہیں جن کا جواب میں نہیں دے سکتا، ماہرین اقبالیات دے سکتے ہیں۔

مجھے پورا یقین ہے کہ یہ سیمنار ازحد درجہ کامیاب ہوگا۔

میں غالب انسٹی ٹیوٹ کو مبارکباد دیتا ہوں کہ انہوں نے اس میں شرکت کے لئے اتنی بڑی تعداد میں معروف اور معزز علماء کو جمع کیا ہے۔

Inauguration of the Hali Mela
Hali Park, Panipat, Haryana
22 November 2008

I am happy to be here today to participate in honouring a great son of Panipat. Altaf Hussain Hali was an eminent scholar who added new dimensions to Urdu literature. He was a pioneer of social and educational advancement amongst Muslims of India.

Hali lived in troubled times. He witnessed the loss of freedom, the subjugation of India to the British rule, and the totality of its implications for society.

Allama Hali's principal contribution to Urdu literature lies in his natural, matter-of-fact style, in his pioneering work on literary criticism and in his very effective use of the quatrain (Rubai) as a form of poetry to convey a moral message. In an early edition of the Rubayat, the publisher said in his introduction that these were more relevant to the times than those of Omar Khayyam. The purpose, he added, was "*Bachoon ki taalim, nau jawanoan ki tafreeh, budhoan ki naseehat, deendaroan kin hidayat aur dunyadaroon ki ibrat.*"

Let me cite a few examples:

I. On the close connection between good and bad:

"Jo loag nekiyon mai mash-hoor bouhat
Hoan nekiyon par apni na maghroor bouhat
Neki hi khood ek badi hai, ger na ho kholoos
Neki se badi nahi hai bouhat door".

II. On the difference between knowledge and ignorance:

"Hain jehel main sab aalim-o-jaahilhumsar
Aata nahin farq uske soo unko nazar

Aalim ko hai ilm upni naadani ka
Jaahil ko nahin jehl ki kuch apni khabar"

III. On changing fortunes:

"Bus bus ke hazaaroan ghar ujar jaate hain
Gar gar ke alum laakhoan ukhar jaate hain
Aaj uski hai naubat to kal uski baari
Ban ban ke yoonhi khel bigar jaate hain".

IV. On the difference between talking and action:

"Jo karte hain kuch, zubaan se kehte hain woh kam
Hote nahin saath jama, dum aur qadam
Barh ta gaya jis qadar keh husn-e-guftaar
Bus utne hi ghat-te gaye kardaar main hum".

V. He who has no faith in life can do no great work:

"Dunya ko hamaisha naqsh-e-faani samjho
Roodaad-e-jahan ko ek kahaani samjho
Par jab karo aaghaz koi kaam bara
Har saans ko umr-e-jaawedani smajho".

Maulana Hali's attitude to social problems is reflected in an early example of a feminist poem, *Chup ki daad,* where he describes with great sensitivity the plight of women and notes the emergence of new trend of opening doors of education to them.

Hali was associated with Syed Ahmad Khan and the Aligarh Movement. His views on education are best reflected in his 1907 address to the annual session of the All India Muslim Educational Conference. He identified the relevance of modern education to employment and urged the Muslims to make their own efforts to redress the situation.

He advised Muslim youth not to confine their quest to government jobs but to seek expression of their talent and genius in crafts and in technical education. He quoted with approval of a European scholar who said that "nations that depend for livelihood on government jobs lose their creativity and are doomed while those who opt for industry and trade prosper".

This piece of advice is as relevant today as it was a hundred years back.

I think I can end with a couplet of Hali that is reflective of his relevance to me and many others:

"Bohat lagta hai dil suhbat main uski
Who apni zaat main ek anjuman hai".

Book release: *Muraqqa-e-Chughtai*
Jubilee Hall, Hyderabad
1 August 2009

It gives me great pleasure that this beautiful collection of poetry and paintings is being released today in the city where it was created. In 1928, the patronage and encouragement of arts by Mir Usman Ali Khan provided impetus to the young Abdur Rehman Chughtai to make possible the nearly impossible task of imparting a concrete form to *The Uncreated Garden* of the thought of Ghalib with his pen and brush.

At the time of the publication of his collection, Chughtai wrote: "The objective behind publishing this collection is to give a concrete shape to the spirit of that Asian culture of which Ghalib was himself the greatest protagonist. I hope that the publication of this collection of paintings will help in infusing a new life into those impressions which are gradually growing very dim." These words sound truer after eighty years.

Andhra Pradesh Urdu Academy and Mr Abdur Raheem Ansari deserve accolades for realising the importance of the objective of the great and skilled artist of India and reviving this everlasting masterpiece which had almost lost its sheen under the dust of so many passing years. For this, we owe a gratitude to them

Whether it is a play by Shakespeare, a novel by Dickens or the *Shahnamah* of Firdausi, generally when the word and the writing are rendered into a painting, they seem to have been captured on the silver screen or the canvas of a painter because, as opposed to a painting, the word leaves it to our mind to fill in all shades of colours, which has limited scope. Especially, to render a couplet into a painting is like capturing the imagination. Chughtai has given ample evidence of his excellence by absorbing in his colours the entire range and depth of Ghalib's metaphor.

Some of the couplets selected from the *Diwan-e-Ghalib* by Chughtai basically have the elements of painting in them:

"Sab kahan, kuchh lala o gul mein numayaan ho gain
Khaak mein kya suraten hongi ke pinhaan ho gayin"

But the real mastery of Chughtai consists in capturing on the canvas those couplets which are inspired by merely a thought or an idea:

"Wo firaq aur wo wisaal kahaan
Wo shab o roz o maah o saal kahaan"

The only stage that has remained unattained is the last one which Chughtai did not strive to attain and rightly so:

"Use kaun dekh sakta ke yagaana hai wo yakta
Jo dui ki boo bhi hoti to kahin do chaar hota"

Many years ago, the late Professor Rasheed Ahmed Siddiqui wrote: "Ghalib imparted a new consciousness and a new horizon to Urdu ghazal. Fired by Ghalib's imagination, ghazal became the power and destiny of Urdu. Ghalib discovered the image and the destiny of ghazal and introduced ghazal to such a world as had the entire wherewithal to facilitate realisation of all the poetic possibilities and potentials of Urdu."

These ideas have been reproduced for the layman in a poem entitled *Azmat-e-Ghalib* by a little known poet. Two of its stanzas read like this:

"Konsa naghma tere she'r ke taaroN meiN nahiN
Falsafi bhi tere ash'aar meiN kho jaata hai
Aik soofi tere naghmoN ka sahaara le kar
Jalwa e Zaat ke afkaar mein kho jaata hai
Teri shokhi, teri rindi, teri masti le kar
Aa gaya aik naya 'aariz e Urdu pe nikhaar
Wo fasaahat, wo balaaghat, wo zaraafat teri
Ban gai daaman e she'ri pe darakhshanda bahaar"

Inauguration of the World Urdu Editors' Conference

Jubilee Hall, Public Gardens, Hyderabad
30 December 2011

Today's distinguished gathering is a proclamation to the world: *Saare jahan main dhoom hamari zubaan ki hai,* and it gives me great pleasure to be amidst you on this occasion.

This conference testifies to Urdu being a living language, an international language, a language whose speakers are to be found from far east to far west and everywhere in between, a language so captivating and enchanting that *ahl-e-Urdu* propose to carry it in the life hereafter:

> *"Isi main ho gi Khuda se bhi guftagoo Maikash*
> *Ke roz-e-hashr bhi hogi meri zuban Urdu"*

Much has been written about Urdu literature, prose and poetry, about the unique capacity of the language to accommodate, adapt, synthesise, and evolve. Those having a superficial acquaintance with it know Urdu for its romantic poetry; others, more familiar with the history of our freedom struggle recall with pride the 17 May 1857 issue of Maulvi Mohammad Baqar's newspaper *Dehi Urdu Akhbar* that came to be known as '*Inqilab* edition'. A generation later Pandit Ram Prasad Bismil wrote the famous poem whose opening lines became the battle cry of freedom fighters:

> *"Sarfaroshi ki tamanna ab hamare dil main hai*
> *Dekhna hai zour kitna baazu-e-qatil main hai"*

This spirit, of questioning authority, was imbibed by Urdu journalism for about a century and brought forth the well known couplet:

Khaincho na kamanon ko na talwar nikalo
Jub toup muqabil ho to akhbar nikalo

August 1947 witnessed the end to British rule. By a twist of fate, that event had an unwelcome consequence for Urdu journalism. As Gurbachan Chandan has put it, *"is taqseem se sawa sao saal purani Urdu sahafat ka sheeraza bikhar gaya aur yeh do hisson mai but gaye"*. This is not the occasion to go into details of that momentous happening:

"Beet gaie jo dil pe na pooch"

The focus of today's conclave is on the present and the future of Urdu journalism in a world that has been transformed by technology and its impact on public perceptions and behaviour.

II

This is a conference of editors who know only too well the challenges confronting print journalism today. To my understanding, they fall into two categories: those of a general nature pertaining to the calling of journalism and those specific to Urdu Journalism. A distinction also need to be made between the business of publishing newspapers and the discipline and art journalism.

The media is the Fourth Estate in a democracy and plays a major role in informing the public. It thereby shapes perceptions and helps define a people's political and non-political agenda. It is the watchdog of public interest. In an earlier age, this was the preserve of the print media; today, it has to be shared with other media platforms and devices emanating from the technological revolution of the past two decades and its impact on the generation, processing, dissemination and consumption of news.

Two other considerations are relevant. Firstly: The traditional media was essentially editor-driven and, owner interests notwithstanding, bore the imprint of individual editors. Secondly:It tended to subscribe to a code of journalistic ethics. Neither was impregnable yet both sustained their character in normal times.

Today, and as a result of the new media devices being available and the commercial considerations involved, the demarcation between journalism, public relations, advertising and entertainment has been eroded. Each of these impacts on the role of the editor and the code of ethics observed hitherto.

The first challenge, then, is to develop methodologies of retaining the essence of these attributes in the new surroundings of the newspapers. The second is to sustain the reputation for dependability for authentic news and sober analysis that is not tainted by sensationalism so often displayed by the electronic media. A third, of eternal relevance to the profession, is Walter Lippmann's caution that more than pressures and intimidation "is the sad fact media persons can be captured and captivated by the company they keep, their constant exposure to power."

The problems confronting the Urdu print media include the above and in addition have many of a unique nature having disturbing dimensions. Some of these relate to readership and its areas of interest.

It is a truism that every publication targets a set of people preferably in different age groups interested in acquainting themselves with authentic news and comments. This, in the case in the case of Urdu publications, is to be on those knowing the language. The difficulty here is that despite the overall increase in population, the percentage of Urdu speakers to the total population has registered a noticeable decline. Thus the younger age group does get excluded in some parts of the country. One implication of it is the effort by the newspapers to focus on the older age groups. The development stories, of particular interest to the youth, thus tend to be down played; by the same logic, older and familiar grievances remain disproportionately in focus. Responsible publications can perhaps do more to mould taste and cajole the readership in the direction of contemporary issues.

Other problems of Urdu media relate to resources—advertisements, news gathering methodology and adaptation of new technology. Each of these is related to size and demands of readership. A good newspaper, however, should cater both to public demand and to the needs to shape this demand. Only then would it be in a position of opinion-maker. News coverage needs to move away from the purely sectional interest to what would satisfy a wider audience.

At the same time, there is some silver lining:

> *"Shaam-e-gham laikin khabar daiti hai subh-e-eid ki*
> *Zulmat-e-shab main nazar aae kiran ummeed ki"*

Technological modernisation has set in. Some of the larger media groups have invested in Urdu editions. This is indicative of growth in readership.

III

Before I conclude, I would like to pay tribute to Hyderabad's past and continuing services to Urdu. Some years back a friend had given me a copy of Professor Agha Haider Hasan Mirza's dictionary *of Daccani Expressions*; it is revealing of the capacity of the language to adapt and evolve local variants. I personally find it delightful reading.

In our own times there are essayists like Mujtaba Hussain sahib whose pen portraits of persons and places leave an indelible mark on the minds of readers. Also to be mentioned is Allama Aijaz Farrukh's work *Hyderabad Shehr-e-Nigaran* that sheds much light on the people who contributed to a culture that that was distinctly Hyderabadi and which, regrettably, is less evident today.

The Nizam Urdu Lecture
University of Delhi, Delhi
6 January 2012

Challenges for a Homeless Language: Urdu in Present-day India

"Yeh mai khana hai, bazm-e-jum nahin hai
Yahaan koi kise se kam nahin hai"

It is said that the chancellor of a university should be seen infrequently and heard rarely, if ever! For this reason, and some others, I do feel privileged to be invited to deliver the Twenty-Second Nizam Lecture of the University of Delhi.

Some in this audience may know that I spent close to four decades in the profession of diplomacy, trying to explain to foreign governments and audiences the Indian impulses and responses emanating from our heterogeneity and unique socio-cultural complexity. One aspect of this was the multiplicity of languages. My message was decisively understood whenever I asked them to examine an Indian rupee currency note to count the languages in which its monitory value was written!

Historians and political scientists have written about the intense debates on the language question in the Constituent Assembly. The outcome was reflected in Part XVII of the Constitution and in its Eighth Schedule. This did not settle the matter. Some years later we witnessed the emergence of the impulse for linguistic homogeneity seeking expression in territorial identity. It was sought to be satisfied through the States Reorganisation Commission whose report was tabled in Parliament in 1955.

It is to be noted that most of the twenty-two languages now listed in the Eighth Schedule find territorial expression in a 'home state'. A notable exception to this is Urdu which despite its spread across many states finds itself to be in a condition of homelessness, with all its attendant consequences. Sindhi is in a similar position except for the fact that the total number of Sindhi speakers is 2.57 million.

Today, I wish to draw attention to some aspects of the homelessness of Urdu.

II

Besides being an officially recognised language, Urdu also has an official language status for some specified purposes (whose details vary and condition the impact substantively) in Andhra Pradesh, Bihar, Delhi, Jammu and Kashmir, Jharkhand and Uttar Pradesh.

According to the Census of India 2001, there were a total of 51.5 million Urdu speakers in the country, amounting to 5.01 per cent of population and constituting the sixth largest language group. Five states (Uttar Pradesh, Bihar, Maharashtra, Andhra Pradesh and Karnataka) account for 41.5 million of the Urdu speakers. If you add Jharkhand, West Bengal, Madhya Pradesh, Tamil Nadu and Delhi to it, the figure reaches 48.55 million. Data also reveals that the percentage of Urdu speakers was 5.25 and 5.18 in the census of 1981 and 1991 respectively.

This decline, in a framework of overall increase of population and more specific demographic data, raises a question. Why is the number of Urdu speakers declining when the areas and groups generally associated with the language have registered normal increases in population?

Does this suggest a pattern of language abandonment? Why does this happen? An explanation in a wider context was given by Professor Abram de Swan in a paper published in the European Review in October 2004:

> "People who abandon their native tongue do so because they move elsewhere or take up something else and in this new existence they have higher expectations of a different language. Or they neglect it because another language is preferred at school, by public authorities, or in courts of law, and their own language is treated with disdain. Or they have to stop using it because they are ruled by another nation that imposes its

> language on them, and, having lost heart, they no longer take care to preserve their own language."

He went on to add that since "every language is a product of the collective creativity of people expressed over hundreds or thousands of years, its disappearance is an irreversible loss of culture."

Where then do we look for an explanation for the decline of Urdu speakers? Since language is principally a matter of affiliation and usage, giving it up is unlikely to be voluntary or an act of 'enlightenment' and must necessarily emanate from some form of compulsion or necessity. Hence the key to our primary question has to be sought amidst the factors cited by Professor de Swan and, of the three possible situations visualised by him, the answer seems to be in the second—namely, language at school level and in use by public authorities.

Allow me here to cite two sets of facts emerging from official data or pronouncements:

In a question answered in the Rajya Sabha on 12 August 2011, the Ministry of Human Resource Development stated that Urdu is not being taught in Kendriya Vidyalayas in various states since in none of them twenty or more students opted for the language, adding that for the same reason, no posts of Urdu teachers were sanctioned.

The simple conclusion to be drawn is that students who know Urdu do not make it to Kendriya Vidyalayas in the minimum numbers prescribed. The data has other implications since these schools are primarily for transferable central government employees.

In a study completed shortly before his death last year, the late Dr Omar Khalidi of the Massachusetts Institute of Technology(MIT) had examined the state of Urdu literacy in India as gauged through school education and raised five questions:

- How many students in primary schools have Urdu as the language of instruction?
- How many learn Urdu as one of the subjects under the three (or four) language formula?

- Have the various levels of government–central, state, and local–facilitated or obstructed learning of Urdu in various states?
- To what can we attribute the uneven levels of Urdu literacy in various states?
- What are the other institutions, besides schools run by the state, involved in promoting Urdu literacy?

Khalidi's conclusions on the first two questions, based on available official data, reveal that Urdu literacy in terms of Urdu medium enrolment in primary-secondary schools is highest in Maharashtra and Bihar, less so in Karnataka and Andhra, and least in Uttar Pradesh and Delhi. In terms of percentages of total enrolment for the year 2007-2008, it was 6.53 in Maharashtra, 5.2 in Bihar, 5.9 in Karnataka, 2.8 in Andhra, 1.0 in Delhi and 0.40 Uttar Pradesh.

The answer to the third and fourth questions requires delving into recent history. Here I can do no better than to recall Jawaharlal Nehru's own assessment. In a confidential letter to chief ministers on 16July 1953 he spoke of "a pettiness in mind, narrowness in outlook and an immaturity" that characterised "a deliberate attempt to push out Urdu which is spoken and written by a large number of people". This was repeated two weeks later, and in a wider framework, in the letter of August 1:

> We encourage the smallest tribal language in its own area, but many of us resent even the mention of Urdu, and yet Urdu is very much a child of India and is a vital and graceful aspect of our many-sided culture. I am deeply grieved at this narrowness of outlook which so frequently comes in our way …

Nehru repeated his views in the matter in the Hyderabad session of the All India Congress Committee in October of the same year. A Union Home Ministry circular of July 1958 mentioned the need to provide Urdu language teaching at the primary stage to children having it as mother tongue, and some other related facilities. It did not refer to Article 350A of the Constitution nor did it invoke Article 347.

The American scholar Paul Brass, in his 1974 book *Language, Religion and Politics in North India,* shed much light on the policy and procedural methodology by which some states succeeded "in diverting large number of Urdu speakers" from the path of education in their mother tongue.

Narrow political perceptions and mistaken identification of language with a community thus led to a unilingual approach and prevailed over the linguistic diversity of a plural society and the ethos of the Constitution.

In 1972, the Government of India Resolution that had set up the Gujral Committee to ascertain ways for the promotion and development of Urdu stated that 'Urdu is not the concern of any one state government or of any community; the responsibility for its development has also to be shared by the Central government'. Its recommendations received in 1975, as also of the Ali Sardar Jaafri Committee in 1990, to the extent they have been implemented, have not altered the picture meaningfully. Nor has the National Council for Promotion of Urdu Language, established in 1990, registered a significant success in its primary objective. The *pashemani* remained formal rather than corrective.

"Meri zuban pe shikwae ahl-e-sitam nahin
Mujh ko jaga diya yahi ehsaan kum nahi"n

III

Lamentation about the past is relevant only to draw lessons from it. Our concern today should be with the present, and the future. Where does Urdu stand now on the basis of the data cited above? What is its place in our social and cultural life, our political and economic life? How can its attributed affiliation to a specific community, with all its un-stated suggestions, be overcome to recapture its rightful place in the kaleidoscope of languages and cultural patterns of India? How can it be rejuvenated, its future be made livelier?

On one plane, the official acknowledgement of Urdu is extended with unfailing regularly. Anniversaries are observed, patronage given to 'mushairas'. Its limitations are obvious: *"Is se zubaan ki yaad to qaim rahi hai, taraqqi nahin hoti"*.

This dichotomous approach was commented upon many years back by Sahir Ludhianavi:

"Ghalib jise kahte hain Urdu ka hi shair tha
Urdu pe sitam kar ke Ghalib pe karam kyon ho"

A commentator observed in a newspaper last year that "Urdu has been kept alive by the Hindi cinema, FM radio, madrasas and occasional recitation of couplets in Parliament".

He drew attention to Professor Gopi Chand Narang's remark that "Urdu is like a patient on oxygen at the fag end of his life. This is the last generation of Urdu".

'Bollywood' films have unquestionably played a major role in keeping alive the usage of Urdu. The historian Ramachandra Guha has referred to its rationale in a perceptive chapter in *India after Gandhi*. From a different angle, Ira Bhaskar and Richard Allen have shed much light on the *Islamicate Cultures of Bombay Cinema* to highlight the points of intersection between history, culture, language, community and contemporary tensions and to demonstrate, as they put it, its "cultural and political value … in the plural and multicultural imagination of India".

The role of madaaris is noteworthy. They have sustained Urdu in difficult times in the context of their curricula of studies and have helped take it to a segment of the younger generation. By the same token, however, the effort has been community specific and confined to those of its members who preferred a madrasa, generally for economic reasons, to normal, state-run, schools. At the same time, confining Urdu to the madaaris also impacts on what is historically an essentially secular, occasionally libertarian, temper of the language:

"Dharkanen sadyon ki jis main, kaif be-bakana hai"

Languages are learnt and sustained for a variety of reasons. They are, in the first place, imbibed at home as a mother tongue and supplemented through primary (and secondary) schooling in it. This necessitates availability of schools, text books and teachers provided either by the state or local authority or through community efforts. Secondly, languages are learnt through economic compulsions and in quest of economic opportunities. It implies participation in wider and prevalent community patterns of education and employability and the requisite effort by society to make available educational institutions and teachers. In the third place, a language may be learnt as a preferred elective for social or religious prestige or academic excellence.

The challenge for a declining language is thus at two levels. The child's inherited awareness of the mother tongue is part of his or her personal, social and cultural identity and has to be shaped and consolidated by structured instruction to enable him or her to proceed from illiteracy to basic literacy. Thereafter, the instrumental motivation and contours of language revival must necessarily be shaped by economic factors. In most multilingual societies (including India), the latter is a function of dominant language for administration, business and inter-regional and international communications. The picture here is evident, and fully accepted.

The situation is different with regard to the mother tongue. It is a fundamental right of citizens, under Article 29, to conserve their distinct language and script. The objective of Article 350A–'for every state and every local authority within the state to provide adequate facilities for instruction in the mother tongue at the primary stage of education to children belonging to linguistic minority groups'–however remains unachieved for a great number of Urdu speaking children. In some cases their linguistic identity is overlooked or ignore; in others primary school arrangements remain non-functional by the absence Urdu language teachers and textbooks. The persistence of these defaults raises doubts about the sincerity of the effort.

The conclusion is inescapable that this is a case of multiple failures: on the part of the state in its constitutional obligations, of the Urdu speaking communities in their cultural duty to be assertive in seeking to learn and sustain the language, and of individual families for not making the additional effort required for doing so.

IV

What, then is to be done? An observation by a Senegalese poet is of some relevance to this discussion and I would like to bring it to the attention of this audience:

> "In the end we will conserve only what we love. We love only we understand and we will understand only what we are taught".

The imperative need is to find ways of teaching Urdu to those who declare it to be their mother tongue. The task has to begin with the primary school and should continue at least in part of the secondary school. The problem would be resolved if in the Three Language Formula evolved and accepted under the National Language Policy—Urdu is assigned the same status as its sister Indian languages. This, regrettably, is not forthcoming in government schools in some states and in others through tardiness in recruitment of teachers and publication of text books etc. The deficiencies in the implementation of safeguards for linguistic minorities in different states are recorded with some precision in the forty-fifth Report of the Commissioner for Linguistic Minorities for the period ending June 2007. It asserts that 'the constitutional safeguards provided for the linguistic minorities can only become real when there is necessary supportive legislation'.

Until more assertive state action is taken the only alternative, therefore, is organised effort at the family and Urdu-speaking community level. The experience of declining-language communities elsewhere in the world would be relevant in this context. A good example is the practice of the Jewish community in the United Sates of undertaking weekend instruction in Hebrew. Other examples of successful language revival are Catalan in Spain and French in Canada.

Alongside, the need to keep alive the effort to make the State to honour constitutional obligations in regard to those who claim Urdu as their mother tongue has to be galvanised. Public opinion and electoral pressures do produce results, as has happened in several states of the Indian Union. We have at all times to remember that justice is the first of the four principles enshrined in the Preamble of our Constitution and, as the philosopher John Rawls put it, " the rights secured by justice are not subject to political bargaining or to the calculus of social interests".

There are, nevertheless, some silver linings on the horizon. Urdu newspapers and magazines have survived the decline and have shown signs of a revival. Corporate media has shown interest the Urdu press. Books in Urdu continue to be published and are inexpensively priced. Several Urdu television channels (apart from Doordarshan-Urdu) have come into existence and seem to survive commercially. The music industry continues to prosper on Urdu ghazals, songs and qawwalis.

One other factor of relevance needs a mention. Urdu is now an international language and is being studied and promoted beyond the Indian subcontinent. The internet is assisting the effort in good measure. It would indeed be a tragedy of profound dimensions if the language would regress and disappear in the land of its birth.

The question, in the final analysis, also pertains to our perception of Indian pluralism and of the ambit of Indian culture. Is it to be inclusive or exclusive? Has it to be characterised by catholicity of approach or otherwise? Do we retain what has enriched it in the past and continues to do so today, or discard for considerations emanating from illiberal outlook?

"Kisi bhi shama se be-zaar ho kyon koi parvana
Yeh kya is daur ka diwana-pun hai hum nahin samjhe"

Note: Refer to the Annexure on pg. 786 for original Urdu speech

Media

> An uncontrolled pen serves but to destroy
>
> —Gandhi

The IPI India Award for Excellence in Journalism 2007

Teen Murti Bhawan Auditorium, New Delhi

19 December 2007

I consider it a privilege to be invited to this function and address this distinguished gathering on the occasion of the presentation of IPI-India Award for Excellence in Journalism 2007, being conferred this year on the *Outlook* magazine, 'for its investigative journalism and its pursuit of the truth.'

I extend my warmest felicitations to the Editor-In-Chief and his team. I am confident that this Award would motivate them to seek even higher levels of excellence.

The role that the press plays in sustaining and nourishing the democratic roots of our polity is sometimes lost sight of in the daily din of political and social life. Yet, a free press is neither a privilege nor a luxury for any democracy; it is a basic necessity for democratic survival.

The Indian press can look back to a distinguished record. While some of the earliest newspapers in the country in the eighteenth and nineteenth centuries, such as the *Bengal Gazette* and the *Calcutta Journal*, advanced the cause of free speech and attempted to use journalism for protecting public interest, others used journalism for societal reform and emancipation.

From about the beginning of the nineteenth century, politically conscious Indians focused attention on the freedom of the press. Increasingly, Indian newspapers became identified with the freedom struggle. In 1886 the Viceroy, Lord Dufferin, took note of the role of the nationalist press:

"Day after day, hundreds of sharp-witted babus pour forth their indignation against their English oppressors in very pungent and effective diatribe. In this way there can be no doubt there is generated in the minds of those who read these papers a sincere conviction that we are all of us the enemies of mankind in general and of India in particular.'

As a result, stringent laws were put on the statute book. Surendranath Banerjea, one of the founding fathers of the national movement, became the first Indian to go to jail in performance of his duty as a journalist.

Gandhi*ji* brought forth a new era in Indian journalism. He was probably the first editor in the history of Indian journalism to have started a newspaper for the express purpose of breaking the law governing the publication of newspapers. His political and social messages were conveyed through the press. He was also one of the first editors prosecuted for sedition. Nor was he alone; many other leaders of the freedom movement suffered the same fate but remained undeterred.

The diversity of the Indian press in the pre-Independence period was as heterogeneous as the Indian polity. This, along with boldness, has become the core DNA of our press. Both are cherished assets in an open society.

The socio-economic changes of the last two decades have highlighted a facet of the Fourth Estate that was hitherto less adequately appreciated. Amongst the pillars of democracy, only the media has an identifiable business and commercial persona. Today's media organisations are large business entities with thousands of employees and huge financial and other assets. While their primary professional duty is to their readership for keeping them informed and appraised with news, views and ideas, the commercial logic brings in a new set of stakeholders; I refer to the shareholders of these companies.

These developments have brought into play a new set of considerations that guide the professional decisions of the press. The days of the great editors who had a decisive say in newspaper policy on public issues are perhaps a matter of the past; instead, we have a basket of considerations in which the demands of professional journalism are carefully balanced with the interests of owners and stakeholders of media companies and their cross media interests.

The interplay of these conflicting demands is evident and subject of public debate. The phenomenal growth in the media industry, and intense competition in it, induces editors and journalists to look as much at the top line and bottom line growth as at headlines and editorial content. A recently published study on the state of India's democracy carries an observation by an eminent journalist that "even editors who support the liberalisation of the Indian economy have become increasingly concerned over the growing control that advertisers wield over news content". He expresses the apprehension that the media's "growing distance from its historic role as the provider of public information threatens to transform communities of citizens into islands of consumers."

The problem may well aggravate since the print media is estimated to grow rapidly due to increasing literacy, booming economy and the opening up of this sector to foreign investment.

Today one hears about newspapers where the news pages are outnumbered by advertisement content, where the distinction between editorials and advertorials is very thin, where the pressures for accelerated reporting overtake the need for accurate reporting and where there appears to be a congruence of sting journalism, reality shows and propaganda. There are complaints of erosion of news values and of a focus on personalities rather than issues and processes. The emergence of the Internet and 24x7 television reporting has put additional pressure on the print media. These developments lead to a few questions:

1. Who sets the terms of the public debate?
2. Is there enough media space for the marginalised, the dispossessed and the vulnerable? Have sections of the media developed stereotypes?
3. Has the media upheld the social and political compact that our people have given to themselves through our Constitution?

There are no easy answers to these questions. The room for introspection remains.

Despite the above, there is good news that is heartening. The 2006 World Press Freedom Review of the International Press Institute dealing with India begins by referring to India as "still one of the very few examples of a deeply rooted democratic system in Asia". It recognises the complex and sometimes conflicting socio-political developments in a multi-cultural and multi-religious society and notes that "media in such a society needs to reflect all aspects of society and cover a spectrum of opinion [as] only a free and diversified media can represent society and at the same time become an example of self-tolerance".

I applaud the India Chapter of the International Press Institute for instituting this award. The IPI has a distinguished record of globally defending the freedom of the press. An award of this nature would spur media organisations to work for professional excellence and the higher good of public interest.

Inauguration of the Varghese Memorial Lecture
Constitution Club, New Delhi
28 January 2010

Indian Media in the New Century

Till yesterday, I was under the impression that I was simply to *inaugurate* the Varghese Memorial Lecture series, my somewhat illogical mind therefore propelled me to the belief that the inauguration would constitute a formality devoid of any strenuous mental and physical exercise of articulating one's own perceptions!

The folly of my ways, mercifully, was detected in time!! All is well that ends well and I therefore have no hesitation in saying that it gives me great pleasure to inaugurate the memorial lecture series instituted by the Mangalam Group in the memory of its founder Late Shri M.C. Varghese.

The life of Shri M.C. Varghese, his rise from a newspaper boy to the head of the Mangalam Group, remains an inspiration to every journalist, entrepreneur and social activist. Shri Varghese used journalism as an instrument in his crusade against social evils, especially the dowry system. His efforts to promote art, literature and education have left a lasting impression.

The topic for this year's memorial lecture is timely. The Indian media today is indeed a new phenomenon. The statistics themselves are staggering. It is estimated that we have:

- over 400 million TV viewers
- over 400 million mobile phone users
- over 300 million newspaper readers
- over 150 million listening to the radio and
- around 50 million using the internet.

Media content has thus rapidly permeated our lives through various formats that are constantly being upgraded through new technologies.

However, the most important change in this century is neither these mindboggling numbers nor the dazzling new technologies. The purpose of journalism and the objectives of media enterprises have undergone a fundamental change. The evolution of the process bears recalling.

The pre-Independence period witnessed the use of newspapers for reform and emancipation and for advocacy in social and public discourse. The media also became a principal instrument in the fight against colonial rule and in consolidating our national consciousness. Political journalism was the staple and provided the sense of purpose.

In the post-Independence era, the media was caught between asserting the fundamental right of freedom of speech guaranteed by the Constitution and the pursuit of the commercial motive.

By the 1990s, our tradition of a free press had been firmly established. However, the winds of economic liberalisation brought with them the elements of the market economy that have changed the DNA of our media organisations. Four of its principal features need to be noted:

First: There has been a rampant growth of broadcasting media, principally television, along with new delivery modes such as Satellite TV, Cable TV, Mobile TV, IPTV, etc. The print media too has grown and India is today estimated to be the world's second largest print market. The phenomenon of convergence between news media, entertainment and telecom has meant that the demarcation between journalism, public relations, advertising and entertainment is rapidly eroding.

Second: It is now clear that amongst the pillars of democracy, it is only the Fourth Estate that has an identifiable business and commercial persona. Today's media organisations are large business entities with thousands of employees and huge financial and other assets. Thus their primary professional duty to their readership has been diluted by the commercial logic of catering to the interests of the shareholders of the holding companies.

Third: Commercial success of media organisations has become a function of advertising revenues rather than subscription and circulation figures. The advertisers have thus replaced the recipients of media products. By the same logic, circulation figures, meant to attract advertising, became more important than content.

Fourth: The pursuit of profit has altered the profile of the media entrepreneur. Today, a media enterprise is seen as a necessary subsidiary for a growing business enterprise, a political party and even individuals seeking to leverage public influence for private gain. On the other hand deception, opaque flow of political information, or slanted economic data prevents political and economic actors from exercising rational and well considered choices. They impede the democratic process and could lead to public disenchantment.

In this context, the recent practices of leveraging political and economic content in our media for overt and covert revenue generation have the malevolent potential to tarnish our polity and even destabilise the economy. This has led the Editors Guild and the Press Council to investigate the phenomenon of electoral malpractices of paid news and coverage packages.

The public purpose of journalism that guided us in an earlier era thus stands changed. How many of us remember that Gandhi*ji* was probably the first editor in the history of Indian journalism to have started a newspaper for the express purpose of breaking the law governing the publication of newspapers; or that he was also one of the first editors to be prosecuted for sedition.

In a changed and changing world, it would be useful to remember that vibrant journalism in a democracy is watchdog journalism. It monitors the exercise of power in the State and stands for the rights and freedoms of citizens. It informs and empowers citizens rather than entertains and titillates them. Vibrant journalism is based on professional ethics and should be the rule rather than the exception it has come to be.

Before I conclude, allow me to draw attention to three questions on which introspection is necessary:

Is there a public debate on issues of concern to the common citizen?

Is sufficient media space given for the concerns of the marginalised, the dispossessed and the vulnerable?

To what extent has our media contributed to upholding the social and political objectives of the Constitution?

The Bhashayi Patrakarita Mahotsav 2011 (Prabhash Prasang)
Indore, Madhya Pradesh
15 July 2011

It gives me immense pleasure to be visiting Indore and inaugurating the Bhashayi Patrakarita Mahotsav organised by the Indore Press Club to commemorate the 75th Birth Anniversary of distinguished journalist Late Shri Prabhash Joshi.

Joshi*ji's* career and life serve as a shining example worthy of emulation by all journalists. He was not only a distinguished editor but represented the voice of the people. He used simple language and local idiom to communicate the issues of the masses. He was a strong votary of ethics and transparency in media.

His approach was summed up in a pithy observation: "*Sabki khabar le, sabki khabar de.*"

We have been witness in recent years rapid, and unprecedented, changes in our society, economy and polity. These have also transformed the Indian Mass Media System. The growth in its scale, reach and influence, however, has not been matched by corresponding sensitivity towards non-commercial and non-market dimensions.

This aspect is of relevance because the media is the Fourth Estate in a democracy. It plays a major role in informing the public and thereby shape perceptions and through it in the national agenda. Its centrality is enhanced manifold by increased literacy levels and by the technological revolution of the last two decades and its impact on the generation, processing, dissemination and consumption of news.

Two other consequences of the change need to be noted:

- Media platforms and devices for consumption today vary between traditional, non-conventional and the experimental. They span traditional print, audio-visual and digital modes. Convergence between news media, entertainment and telecom has meant that the demarcation between journalism, public relations, advertising and entertainment has been eroded.

- Increases in per capita income, discretionary spending capability, attractiveness of India as a market and as a destination of foreign investment, have all reinforced the centrality of the Indian mass media system.

As a result, media outlets assume importance not only for marketing and advertisement but also for the 'soft power' aspects of businesses, organisations and even nations. Media entrepreneurship today is a necessary condition for any growing business enterprise, a political party and even individuals seeking to leverage public influence for private gain.

Furthermore, the trend towards globalisation has empowered individual citizens through increased movement of goods, capital, services and ideas. Economic liberalisation and spread of digital technologies have aided it. New media has brought forth new means of individual empowerment, allowing the expression of individual ideas, opinions and identities.

II

I would like to explore today the implications of these changes brought in by new media.

The necessity for media to function effectively as the watchdog of public interest was recognised in the freedom struggle. The Founding Fathers of the Republic realised the need to balance the freedom of expression of the press with a sense of responsibility while such freedom is exercised. Adherence to accepted norms of journalistic ethics and maintenance of high standards of professional conduct was deemed to be a natural corollary.

Gandhi*ji*, a journalist himself, cautioned that "an uncontrolled pen serves but to destroy". Jawaharlal Nehru warned that: "If there is no responsibility and no obligation attached to it, freedom gradually withers away. This is true of a nation's freedom and it applies as much to the Press as to any other group, organisation or individual."

It is no exaggeration to say that media represents the sector of the economy, that is the envy of others because of the extremely buoyant growth rates witnessed over the last two decades, in an environment characterised by minimal or no regulation. The sole statutory, quasi-judicial body set up for media regulation in the country is the Press Council of India. While it aims to preserve the freedom of the press and maintain and improve the standards of press in India, it has no way of imposing punishments or enforcing its directions for professional or ethical violations.

In the absence of any other government regulator, the focus has shifted to self-regulation by the media organisations, individually or collectively. Collective self-regulation has failed because it is neither universal nor enforceable. Individual self-regulation has also failed due to personal predilection and the prevailing of personal interest over public interest.

It is relevant to note that, to an extent, the most effective *de facto* media regulator happens to be the advertisers and sponsors who determine the bulk of the revenue stream of our media industry. Their aims and desired outcomes, however, might not align with public policy goals of the government or markers of public interests and may, instead, stand in opposition to them.

III

The common citizen, who is a consumer of media products, is thus faced with a piquant situation. While economic deregulation has been the dominant trend of the recent past, it is premised on a dynamic market place with a system of independent regulation, especially competition regulation, to prevent cartelisation, abusive behaviour by dominant firms and corporate transactions that derail the competitive processes in the market.

When the government, the polity, the market and the industry are unable to provide for full-spectrum systemic regulation that protects consumer welfare and public interest, who will step in to address the gap? As we debate the issue of media regulation, the following aspects need closer scrutiny:

First: The objective of regulation in democratic societies such as USA, France and others is to enhance diversity, competition and localism among media outlets and to promote public interest with a focus on upholding constitutional values, protecting minors and limiting advertising. Intrusive content regulation is minimised because those who are aggrieved can resort to legal means in the knowledge that the justice delivery system will address their grievances in a reasonable time period.

Unfortunately, the same cannot be said about our justice delivery system. The time taken to settle court cases deters individual citizens, and even corporate entities, from seeking legal options and forcing the search for alternate tools of administrative justice and facilitation for grievance redressal.

Second: We have not had an informed debate in the country on the issue of multiple-ownership and cross-ownership nor a cogent national media policy that covers print, radio, television, cable, DTH (Direct-to-Home) platforms, video and film industry, internet and mobile telephony.

In most developed countries, rules on cross-ownership and multiple-ownership are intended to prevent emergence of monopolies and cartels and promote competition. Many states in India have a few media groups dominating both the print and electronic media. At the national level, we have seen the emergence of a handful of media conglomerates spanning the entire media spectrum. Its impact on moulding public opinion, generating political debate and safeguarding consumer and public interest is a moot question.

Third: India is among the few democracies without active media watch groups engaged in objective analyses of the media, discerning prejudices and latent biases, and subjecting the media to a dose of their own medicine. For an industry that has over fifty thousand newspapers and hundreds of television channels, systematic media criticism is non-existent.

What this means is that in the absence of government and industry regulation, even civil society has been unable to provide an effective *de facto* media regulatory mechanism.

Fourth: No discussion of media regulation can ignore the recent controversy over 'paid news'. The last speech of the late Prabhash Joshi*ji* dwelt on this at some length.

We need to introspect whether the strategy of relying on advertisement rather than subscription as the main revenue source for media outlets has created a difficult set of ethical problems for the media industry as a whole. Once content ceased to be the revenue driver for a media outlet, the effort to leverage it as a direct revenue source began. The inability of the industry and the Press Council to go public with its report on paid news is also another pointer to the problems of self regulation and the 'culture of silence' in the entire industry when it comes to self criticism.

Fifth: The structural biases of the development process have favoured urban areas over rural ones, metropolitan areas over other urban areas, English-speaking over those speaking other Indian languages, the middle and upper classes over the others who constitute the vast majority of our citizens, and the service sectors over other areas such as agriculture.

These biases have prompted the media industry to resort to 'sunshine journalism' where the focus is on the glass that is quarter-full rather than that which is three-quarters empty! When media portrayal is of a life that is always good, optimistic, going with the tide of those with discretionary spending power and their causes and pet themes, the role of the media as a defender and upholder of public interest relegates to the background and its commercial persona takes over, replete with its allegiances to the market and the shareholders.

Sixth: No discussion of media regulation can ignore the slow erosion of the institution of the editor in Indian media organisations. When media space is treated as real estate or as airline seats for purpose of revenue maximisation strategies, and when media products are sold as jeans or soaps for marketing purposes, editors end up giving way to marketing departments.

IV

One might ask, if the situation is so stark, what can be the way forward?

A good starting point would be for all stakeholders of the media industry to realise that the ethical underpinning of professional journalism in the country has weakened and that the corrosion of public life in our country has impacted journalism.

It is for the journalistic community to take the initiative and seek to address the various concerns regarding the profession. At the same time, all categories of regulation or binding guide lines must be strengthened with a view to securing and defending public good – by the government, the media organisations and the industry, civil society, advertisers and sponsors, and the audience and readership of the media.

Today's function by the Indore Press Club is an occasion to debate how the values of transparency and professional ethics that were the guiding compass of Shri Prabhash Joshi, can continue to inspire today's journalists.

We should not forget that vibrant journalism in a democracy is watchdog journalism that monitors the exercise of power in the State, stands for the rights and freedoms of citizens, and informs and empowers citizens rather than entertains and titillates them. Vibrant journalism always springs from the bedrock of professional ethics. Our media, and democracy, are fortunate that we have shining examples of journalists who not only embody the ethical dimension, but sadly, also laid down their life for the same.

Allow me to recall in conclusion a remark of the eminent American journalist of yesteryears, Walter Lippmann. "The real danger to the press", he said, "springs not so much from the pressures and intimidation to which it may be subject but from the sad fact that media persons can be captured and captivated by the company they keep, their constant exposure to the subtleties of power."

Inauguration of the National Press Day Celebration

India International Centre, New Delhi
16 November 2011

It gives me great pleasure to inaugurate the National Press Day. In over forty-five years of its existence, the council has fulfilled to a significant extent its mandate, as a quasi-judicial body, of preserving the freedom of the press and of maintaining and improving the standards of press in India, and adjudicating complaints.

Ours is an age of great change–social, economic, political and above all technological. Each has impacted on our individual and collective thought processes. Major premises are being revisited and the certitudes of an earlier era called into question. The answers are often disconcerting, in many cases tentative.

The theme of today's celebration is 'Media as an instrument of public accountability'. A useful starting point of discussion would be to enquire into the basic premise of being a democracy.

An essential feature of democracy is constraint on unlimited exercise of power. Democratic practice seeks to bring about accountability of actions of institutions and individuals in an objective, verifiable and transparent manner. While common understanding of constraints on power is limited to exercise of 'public power' by state actors, it is important to remember that it also extends to 'private power', of non-public authorities, especially when such entities acquire or exercise power traditionally associated with state structures.

It is a truism that humans are social creatures who formulate rules of interaction aimed at furtherance of harmony and common good and avoidance of anarchy. Rules and rule-based regulations are thus essential and unavoidable, more so in a democracy that eschews arbitrary exercise of power.

Another truism is that some form of media has been integral to human civilisation since time immemorial. Its principal purpose, to *inform*, remains unchanged. Technological innovations like the invention of paper and the printing press, radio transmission, TV broadcasting, and the World Wide Web have spawned new media platforms and devices for consumption.

Today, the convergence between news media, entertainment and telecom has meant that the demarcation between journalism, public relations, advertising and entertainment has been eroded.

The new trends in technological development and media conglomeration characterised by an emphasis on commercial values and outcomes, pose challenges to traditional public service values in news broadcasting.

How do they impact the lofty ideal of journalism–of communicating reliable, accurate facts in a meaningful context?

This aspect is of relevance because the media is the Fourth Estate in a democracy. It plays a major role in informing the public and thereby shape perceptions and through it the national agenda. Its centrality is enhanced manifold by increased literacy levels and by the technological revolution of the last two decades and its impact on the generation, processing, dissemination and consumption of news.

Media outlets today assume importance not only for marketing and advertisement but also for the 'soft power' aspects of businesses, organisations and even nations. It is a harsh reality that media entrepreneurship is now a necessary condition for a business enterprise, a political party and even individuals seeking to leverage public influence for private gain.

It would be instructive to study how other democratic systems have dealt with the media revolution and the convergence of communication technologies. Three stable democracies, namely the United Kingdom, the United States and Australia can be studied for best practices.

In December 2000, the United Kingdom published a White Paper entitled *A New Future for Communications* in Britain. It suggested conceptual restructuring to bring together the five sectors of telecommunications—television, radio, broadcasting standards and radio spectrum allocations under a single-umbrella communications regulator. In addition, it proposed covering access, choice, content and competition.

The White Paper proposed a new three-tiered regulation of broadcasting so as to provide a level playing field between the broadcasters, depending on the extent of their public service role. It stressed that all broadcasters be subject to minimum standards, impartiality in news, provision of protection of minors and access of people with disabilities.

Emanating from this, *The Communications Act 2003* established the Office of Communications (OFCOM) as the regulator for all communications industries to further the interests of citizens and consumers. It was tasked with ensuring optimal use of electro-magnetic spectrum, availability of electronic communication services, a wide range of TV and radio services of high quality, maintaining plurality in broadcasting, applying adequate protection for audiences against offensive or harmful material, and against unfairness or infringement of privacy.

The British experience of transition from a multi regulator to a single umbrella regulator, accountable to Parliament, and covering telecommunications, broadcast media and wireless spectrum, indicates that turf battles between economic sectors, government departments and individual companies have to be carefully managed in the midst of building a national consensus and enacting legislation.

The experience of the United States and its Federal Communication Commission in regulating communications by Radio, Television, Wire, Satellite and Cable for over seventy-five years is also instructive. It promotes competition, innovation and investment in communications, encourages the best use of spectrum and revises media regulations so that new technologies can flourish alongside diversity and localism. American law imposes limitations on multiple ownerships and cross-ownership of media establishments across radio, television and print media to prevent emergence of monopolies and to ensure adequacy of independent media voices in the market that could serve public interests, localisation of news and bring about diversity.

In the case of Australia, it is The Australian Communications and Media Authority (ACMA) which is responsible for the regulation of broadcasting, the internet, radio communications and telecommunications sectors. In its role as a broadcast regulator, the ACMA plans the channels that radio and television services use, issues and renews licenses, regulates the content of radio and television services, including digital services, and administers the ownership and control rules for broadcasting services.

The regulator enforces statutory control rules based on license area and audience reach, limitations on multiple and cross-ownership, limits on foreign control of the mass media, regulations on transfer of media operations and media groups, and determines acceptability or otherwise of media diversity. It seeks to bring about programme diversity, help foster a national cultural identity, bring about fair reporting of news and ensure respect for community standards.

While media outlets in Australia have the main responsibility for ensuring that the broadcast content reflects community standards, most aspects of such content are governed by codes of practice developed by industry groups. The regulator registers these codes once it is satisfied that the codes contain tcommunity safeguards and are a product of public consultation. National content and children's programmes on commercial television are regulated by compulsory programme standards determined by the regulator after consulting the industry and the general public.

You would notice that the experience and practice of other democracies indicates that media licensing and regulation is seen as a normal and essential activity to help its functioning as the watchdog of public interest. One is reminded of Gandhi*ji's* dictum that "an uncontrolled pen serves but to destroy".

In our country today, media represents a sector of economy that is the envy of others because of the extremely buoyant growth rates witnessed over the last two decades, in an environment characterised by minimal or no regulation. In the absence of any other government regulator, the focus has shifted to self-regulation by the media organisations, individually or collectively.

Collective self-regulation however has yet to succeed in substantive measure because it is neither universal nor enforceable. Individual self-regulation has also failed due to personal predilection and the prevailing of personal interest over public interest.

In an address at the Indore Press Club earlier this year, I had mentioned that while economic deregulation has been the dominant trend of the recent past, it is premised on a dynamic market place with a system of independent regulation, especially competition regulation, to prevent cartelisation, abusive behaviour by dominant firms and corporate transactions that derail the competitive processes in the market.

Two questions arise here. In the first place: Who will step in to address the gap when the government, the polity, the market and the industry are unable to provide for full-spectrum systemic regulation that protects consumer welfare and citizen interest?

Secondly: Can the constitutional safeguards on freedom of speech be used to evade regulation of the commercial persona of media corporates and groups? Where does public interest end and private interest begin?

The experience of other countries shows us the way. The ongoing national debate on the subject should involve all stakeholders leading perhaps to the publication of a White Paper. This should lead to further consultations and evolution of a broad national consensus so that appropriate frameworks can be put in place combining voluntary initiative, executive regulation and legislative action, as appropriate.

Such an effort can cover issues of multiple-ownership and cross-ownership, content and diversity, and a cogent national communications policy that covers print, radio, television, cable, DTH platforms, video and film industry, internet and mobile telephony, and electro-magnetic spectrum.

Our democracy is poorer without active media watch groups engaged in objective analyses of the media, discerning prejudices and latent biases, and subjecting the media to a dose of their own medicine. For an industry that has over 50,000 newspapers and hundreds of television channels, systematic media criticism is non-existent in India. This should be remedied and I hope your deliberations would address this important aspect.

A related matter pertains to the recent controversy over 'paid news'. It has been debated extensively in the Press Council and other fora, including Parliament. It is a matter of some satisfaction that the 'culture of silence' on the subject is being replaced with an attempt to grapple with this malaise at multiple levels.

Finally, I venture to hope that your debate would also focus on the erosion of the institution of the editor in our media organisations. When media space is treated as real estate or as airline seats for purpose of revenue maximisation, and when media products are sold as jeans or soaps for marketing purposes, editors end up giving way to marketing departments.

I would like to conclude by saying that all stakeholders–the government, the media organisations and the industry, civil society, advertisers and sponsors, and the audience and readership of the media–must address the various concerns regarding the profession and work towards securing and defending the public good.

Presentation of the Ramnath Goenka Excellence in Journalism Awards 2010-11

Taj Palace Hotel, New Delhi
16 January 2012

I am happy to be participating in this function to pay tribute to Ramnath*ji's* memory.

Today, as we identify and recognise the excellence and contribution of distinguished journalists, we should pause and remind ourselves that the profession, and indeed Indian democracy, has been immensely enriched by this great publisher who built *The Indian Express* as an institutional example of good journalism, with intense passion and vision.

"Mr Newspaper", as B.G. Verghese characterised him, come to embody the fight for the fundamental right of freedom of speech and of the press. As a Gandhian and a freedom fighter, a politician and an industrialist, a citizen and an activist, he remains an exceptional personality of his time. He was India's Pulitzer. The Awards instituted in his name to celebrate excellence in journalism, are a fitting tribute to his courage and commitment.

The world as we know is experientially shrinking and it has changed the paradigm of production, transmission, and consumption of media products. Three aspects of it, pertaining to journalism, are note worthy:

First: It has become evident that technology is neither value-neutral nor inherently equity-driven. It takes on the form and structure of the society where it operates. It is only an instrumentality and not a panacea. The hard work of defining and implementing a value system and a vision for an organisation, a society or polity cannot be substituted by technology.

Second: Convergence between news media, entertainment and telecom has eroded the demarcation between journalism, public relations, advertising and entertainment. So is the case between business, commerce, philanthropy, politics and profession. It is not clear where public interest ends and private interest begins, where profit ends and the not-for-profit begins, where government ends and the non-government begins, where one's fist ends and the other's nose begins. This has significantly enhanced the complexity of our working and personal lives and created new ethical dilemmas that lie at the core of many issues of public debate today.

Third: The public purpose of journalism that guided us in an earlier era has changed. Gandhi*ji* was probably the first editor in the history of Indian journalism to have started a newspaper for the express purpose of breaking the law governing the publication of newspapers. He was also one of the first editors to be prosecuted for sedition. It was this public purpose of journalism that had propelled Ramnath*ji* into the newspaper business.

In a changed and changing world, it would be useful to remember that vibrant journalism in a democracy is watchdog journalism. It monitors the exercise of power and influence in society and stands for the rights and freedoms of citizens. It informs and empowers citizens rather than entertains and titillates them.

Vibrant journalism is based on professional ethics and should be the rule in a democracy, rather than the exception it has come to be. Our media, and democracy, are fortunate that we have shining examples of journalists who not only embody the ethical dimension, but sadly, also laid down their life for the same.

The media is the Fourth Estate in a democracy. It plays a major role in informing the public and thereby shape perceptions and through it the national agenda. Adherence to accepted norms of journalistic ethics and maintenance of high standards of professional conduct is deemed to be a natural corollary.

Experience shows that the best guarantee for safeguarding the public interest is to have strong and independent-minded editors. Today, they are an endangered species. The slow erosion of the institution of the editor in Indian media organisations is a reality. When media space and media products are treated solely in terms of revenue maximisation strategies, editors end up giving way to marketing departments.

Media norms are an issue of public debate. I have two points to make in this regard:

In the first place: The objective of norms in other democratic societies is to enhance diversity, competition and localism among media outlets and to promote public interest with a focus on upholding constitutional values, protecting minors and limiting advertising. Intrusive content regulation is minimised because those who are aggrieved can resort to legal means in the knowledge that the justice delivery system will address their grievances in a reasonable time period.

Unfortunately, the same cannot be said about our justice delivery system. The time taken to settle court cases deters individual citizens, and even corporate entities, from seeking legal options. This makes imperative the search for alternate tools for redressal of grievances.

Secondly: We have as yet not had an informed debate in the country on the issue of multiple-ownership and cross-ownership nor a cogent national media policy that covers all platforms. This is at variance with the practice of other developed democracies. The impact of the emergence of a handful of media conglomerates spanning the entire media spectrum in moulding public opinion, generating political debate and safeguarding consumer and public interest is a moot question.

The matter assumes urgency in the wake of moves towards consolidation in the media sector. While the entry of large corporates into the media sector is to be expected, especially to address the growing capital requirements, ensuring transparency and instituting effective and independent oversight in consultation with the industry could address such concerns.

I would like to refer to one other aspect of the profession. The structural biases of the development process have favoured urban areas over rural ones, metropolitan areas over other urban areas, English-speaking over those speaking other Indian languages, the middle and upper classes over the others who constitute the vast majority of our citizens, and the service sectors over other areas such as agriculture.

These biases have prompted the media to resort to 'sunshine journalism' where the focus is on the glass that is quarter-full rather than that which is three-quarters empty! When this occurs, the role of the media as a defender and upholder of public interest does get dented and relegated to the background.

I would also take the opportunity today to seek better development and harnessing of the human capital of journalists. Just as IT and other industries train their personnel after recruitment, the press must take the lead in training and professionally updating journalists. Failure on this front by the editors and managers of the media would prompt imposition of professional standards by outsiders, as was recently done by the Supreme Court of India.

Issues of ethics and professionalism of the media appear to invade all aspects of our lives–political, economic and social. Even a distinguished gathering such as this meant to honour the blessed memory of Ramnath*ji* and honour excellence in journalism is not immune from allegations centred on ethical issues. It is for you, the journalist community, to take the initiative and seek to address the various concerns regarding the profession.

I congratulate all the awardees and wish them many more years in the service of their chosen profession and the nation.

Minorities, Disadvantaged Groups, Gender Issues

"Today, even our urban and metropolitan spaces constrain persons with disabilities. National standards on minority rights need to move in step with international norms. The tribal population suffers from geographical and social exclusion. More women are gaining access to education but equality in education is still lacking. Such a development is critical in the process towards improving equality between men and women

Annual Day Celebrations
Lady Shriram College, New Delhi
10 March 2008

Gender Challenge for Modern India

I accepted Dr Gopinath's invitation with some trepidation and kept hoping that the programme would require me to do no more than release a pigeon of peace, cut a ribbon, launch the college magazine and generally do the things that vice presidents of countries the world over are so well drilled to do.

I discovered a bit late that I would have to sing for my afternoon cup of tea! Entrapment, however distasteful, does facilitate the thought process!! I decided to lean in favour of the contentious, to think aloud, and to explore the dimensions of the gender challenge to modern India. LSR, with its stated mission of 'empowering women to assume leadership', is an appropriate forum for such an endeavour.

Ours is a land in the throes of change. The functional mantra is growth; the guiding principle is inclusive growth. The underpinning for both is the constitutional stipulation of equality and prohibition of discrimination on grounds of religion, race, caste, sex or place of birth. It is, according to Article 51A, a fundamental duty 'to renounce practices derogatory to the dignity of women'.

In terms of principles, therefore, citizens of India should be a satisfied lot. In actuality, they are not. Their dissatisfaction is of various kinds and has many dimensions. Gender inequality is one of them. It affects half the population and is found in all parts of the country and at all levels of society.

The journal *Manushi*, in its first editorial in January 1979, raised a question: Is it possible to talk of women as an undifferentiated mass? Its answer was in the affirmative: Despite factors dividing women from each other, 'if we look at the nature and basis of women's oppression, we discover that our sex determines our common predicament in a very fundamental way'. The editorial asserted that the initiative for an alternative has to come from "toiling women" who alone are "capable of providing the leadership and the militancy that is required to bring about radical changes in this unjust system". It raised a battle cry: "Let us re-examine the whole question, all the questions. Let us take nothing for granted. Let us not only redefine ourselves, our role, our image–but also the kind of society we want to live in".

Three decades later, we need to assess the results achieved and the efficacy of the approach.

Law-making in any society is reflective of social perceptions and of social aspirations. This band-width defines the contours of the social discourse. Law, as Harold Laski put it, "is always made in terms of what life has meant for those who make the law".

India as a society has been around for a long time and has a collective as well as a recorded memory. The former is on different planes and is nuanced; the latter is linear and reflective of the dominant perception that still remains in public consciousness and influences thinking and action at the societal level. It is this, which lies at the root of the gender problem.

In such a context, policy interventions of the State are aimed at correcting the persecution, discrimination and exclusion to which women are subjected. The instrumentality is affirmative action at levels where the reach of state authority is significant. We however know from experience in diverse fields that state regulation is a blunt instrument and correctives through it have limited impact on consciousness.

It was Jawaharlal Nehru who said "you can tell the condition of a nation by looking at the status of its women". Let us then look at some facts:

- Women are around 48 per cent of the total population. The maternal mortality rate in India at 407 per hundred thousand live births compares poorly with figures of 92 in Sri Lanka, 56 in China and 130 in Vietnam. The Tenth Plan goal of reducing the maternal mortality rate to 200 per thousand live births by 2007 has remained unfulfilled.

- The child sex ratio that has declined from 945 in the 1991 Census to 927 in the 2001 Census. The combined gross enrollment ratio for primary, secondary and tertiary education for females at 60 per cent is lower than that for males that stands at 68 per cent. The adult literacy rate for females at 47.8 per cent is significantly lower as compared to males at 73.4 per cent.
- Out of a total workforce of 397 million, 124 million are women. Of these, 106 million are in the rural areas and only 18 million in urban areas. While the workforce participation rate of urban women has gone up marginally, the participation of rural women has remained almost constant for over a decade.
- There are significant wage differences between men and women across all categories. Wage differentials between males and females in both rural and urban areas have gone up by around one third between 2000 and 2005.
- Gender related crimes have increased over the years.
- While lip service is paid to it, adequate representation of women at decision-making, and implementation, levels of the polity remains the subject of intense debate.

These details can be amplified. They lead to the unavoidable conclusion that poverty in our country is increasingly getting a feminine profile. We are thus confronted with a problem that is social as well as economic. To evade the problem is to aggravate it. It needs to be addressed in both its dimensions simultaneously.

A recent ILO study has observed that women continue to be 'an untapped potential' in South Asia. It states that economic empowerment of women depends upon their access to labour markets which, in turn, requires 'equal access to education and equal opportunity in gaining the skills necessary to compete in the labour market. More women are gaining access to education but equality in education is still' lacking. Such a development is 'critical in the process towards improving equality between men and women'.

Education, and equality in education, is thus a critical element in the agenda of correctives that should be sought.

The more difficult aspect pertains to social perceptions woven in the interstices of the mind and sanctified by tradition. Government legislation, experience shows, is an inadequate deterrent. The lead in changing these perceptions and practices has to be taken by individuals and groups in different strata of society. Social reformers like Mahatma Jyotibha Phule and sociologists like M.N. Srinivas have dwelt on the root causes of the problem. The need of the hour is to go beyond ritual slogan-mongering. The *Manushi* editorial had talked of the 'whole question'. Today in the dominant discourse we find it reduced to some questions, more of interest to the educated and the middle classes than to the 'toiling masses'. As so often in the past, change has been co-opted. Will this suffice?

Gender justice, remains unachieved. The task of attaining it remains formidable; it remains urgent. Success would open the hitherto untapped reservoirs of energy. It would transform Indian society.

Over the years, the LSR alumna has occupied important leadership positions in academia, government, management and other professional fields. Perhaps the time has come to add an activist gender-justice dimension to the scoreboard of success.

Presentation of National Awards for the Empowerment of Persons with Disabilities

Vigyan Bhawan, New Delhi
3 December 2008

I feel privileged to participate in the ceremony today to present the National Awards. It has been a humbling experience and a lesson on what human spirit can do. It is also significant that this function is part of the annual observance of the International Day of Persons with Disabilities, which aims at promoting and understanding disability issues and mobilising support for the dignity, rights and well being of persons with disabilities.

The awards presented today have a forty year history of recognising the contributions of those who have made a difference in the empowerment of the persons with disabilities. This is especially significant because these outstanding contributions at the grassroots level by individuals and institutions stand in contrast with the vast gap that the State is yet to traverse in meeting its own goals of mainstreaming disability in the development and social justice agenda of the nation.

It is estimated that there are approximately 650 million persons with disability worldwide, constituting roughly 10 per cent of the global population. Around 80 per cent of these persons live in developing countries. It is also well understood that there is a strong correlation, and perhaps even bi-directional causation, between disability and poverty. The World Bank estimates that 20 per cent of the world's poorest people, who live on less than one dollar a day, are persons with disabilities.

Contrast this global picture with available national statistics. The 2001 census and 2002 NSSO (National Sample Survey Organisation) figures for persons with disabilities are a very low 2.13 and 1.8 per cent of the population respectively. Compare this with figures of 20 per cent for Australia and New

Zealand, and in our neighbourhood, 7 per cent for Sri Lanka, 6.3 per cent for China and 5.6 per cent for Bangladesh.

As we can see, the first major battle is to accurately and credibly define disability. In our country, the discrepancy between the official figure and the reality can be traced to the fact that the definition of disability used in the Census is at significant variance from our legal and policy framework as also from the UN Convention on the Rights of Persons with Disabilities. Civil Society Groups have pointed out that the question on disabilities is amongst the last in the census questionnaire and many times the question is never asked, citing cultural fears.

The legal framework regarding persons with disabilities begins with the Constitutional mandate of equality, freedom, justice and dignity for all individuals. Article 41 of the Constitution mandates the State to make effective provisions for securing the right to work, education and to public assistance in case of disablement, subject to the limits of the economic capacity and development of the State. We have also enacted the Persons with Disabilities Act of 1995 and brought in a comprehensive National Policy for Persons with Disabilities in 2006.

The translation of our policy objectives into tangible socio-economic outcomes that better the lives of persons with disabilities and empower them leaves much to be desired. The transition from a welfare-based approach to a rights-based approach since the Ninth Plan was forward looking and empowering. But the slow pace of implementation of the various enabling legislation and lack of accountability for non-implementation, has meant that the enjoyment of rights has been subject to the efficiency of the implementation. Even after thirteen years, we have been unable to ensure that each Ministry reserve not less than 3 per cent of their annual outlay for the benefit of disabled persons as per the Persons with Disability Act, 1995 nor have we been able to set up accurate statistical information gathering and monitoring mechanisms at various levels.

It is recognised the world over that creation of a barrier free environment for persons with disabilities must start with public buildings and facilities and must be written into vehicular design codes for public transport, municipal and civil regulations, constructions codes and building bye-laws. We have lost valuable time during the past decade when our economy grew at an impressive pace and thousands of buildings have been built, roads laid and mass transport systems established. If only we had ensured implementation in this period, facilities required for the disabled would have been available in a significant number. Today, even our urban and metropolitan spaces continue to constrain persons with disabilities. I may add there are excellent exceptions also. As a beginning, we should resolve to ensure that every government facility that caters to persons with disabilities should enjoy a barrier free environment.

The need of the hour is marrying fundamental and human rights with social justice and development goals. Disability, like gender is not a stand-alone thematic issue. It needs to be part of all programmes, policies and legislation with the objective to achieve equality in all political, economic and social spheres. It cannot remain confined to the government alone. It must bring in all stakeholders including civil society, international organisations and even the private sector and media within a cooperative framework for empowering persons with disabilities.

The National Policy for Persons with Disabilities recognises that such persons are valuable human resource for the country. It is long overdue for the nation to deliver on the promises made for providing equal opportunities to persons with disabilities, protecting their rights and ensuring their full participation in society. We need not reinvent the wheel. All we need to do is to realise the objectives of our legal and policy framework and include persons with disabilities in all aspects of our development and social justice programming.

Inauguration of the Annual Conference of State Minorities Commissions
New Delhi
20 January 2009

This platform has an air of familiarity about it! Notwithstanding the role reversal from being a host to the chief guest, I am happy to be here with you today, once again to cogitate on questions that impact on the socio-economic development of the country.

Let me begin by stating the obvious: We are a free people, living in a free country. Ours is a plural society and a secular polity that has a democratic state structure. Our rights and freedoms are guaranteed by the Constitution.

Each of these blessings has to be counted, realised, cherished and protected. Good citizens therefore seek to strengthen this edifice just as some others develop devices to weaken it. The tussle is unending; it necessitates careful and continuous scrutiny.

Ours is a land whose diversity includes religious minorities. Every sixth Indian is in this category. In absolute terms, it amounts to almost 200 million people. In law, they are beneficiary of all rights; in fact, deprivation exists and has been acknowledged. This has impacted on the overall progress of the country.

The National Commission for Minorities (NCM) and the state commissions were created in response to a felt need to safeguard minority interests and to infuse confidence in them. Experience has shown that the procedures to redress grievances remain somewhat ineffective, principally on account of a lack of will, and tardy responses, from the concerned state agencies.

I hope this meeting would come up with practical solutions to this problem. The government, on its part, could consider equipping the NCM with the instrumentality of investigation of the type given to the NHRC (National Human Rights Commission) and the Commission on Scheduled

Castes. Likewise, the option of legislation similar to 'The Scheduled Castes and the Scheduled Tribes (Prevention of Atrocities) Act, 1989' could be explored for the minorities.

There are three broad and inter-related dimensions to consider while discussing the question of minorities–Identity, Security and Equity.

Issues of identity are always complex, especially in a plural society. They nevertheless exist. The Sachar Committee Report shed light on aspects of it pertaining to our Muslim citizens. Some of this holds good for Christians too. Both result from a reluctance to imbibe a plural ethos. Neither is conducive to the idea of India enunciated in the Constitution. Both need to be contested. A liberal democracy has to be a tolerant one, accommodative of diversity in word and deed. Any other course would result in abridgement of rights.

Security concerns continue to be a matter of concern in the light of recent and not-so-recent happenings in different parts of the country. A disturbing aspect of it is the failure of the state to provide security. Confirmation of this comes from judicial pronouncements. A corrective can come, as it has in many instances, from public opinion and civil society activism. More needs to be done on this count.

On equity issues, the Sachar Committee Report on the socio-economic and educational status of Muslims depicted the nature and extent of deprivation or exclusion in education, employment, housing, health, municipal infrastructure, bank credits and other services provided by the government or public and private sector entities. Reports on other minorities highlight their individual problems.

The policies and programmes initiated in the wake of the Sachar Report are indicative of the corrective action under way. The key to success lies in close monitoring of the implementation at ground level.

Last year the Report of the Expert Group on Diversity Index recommended, on a wider canvass, the setting up a Diversity Commission and Diversity Implementation Boards as institutional mechanisms for affirmative action and policy targeting. Another Expert Group Report in 2008 suggested the creation of an Equal Opportunity Commission to give shape to the equality jurisprudence of the Constitution and to ensure inclusive growth. Support for both needs to be galvanised so that it culminates in enabling legislation.

The aim should be to minimise if not avoid 'inequality traps' that hamper the marginalised and work in favour of the status quo.

We have travelled a considerable distance in enforcing the human rights of individual citizens. A similar endeavour in regard to minority rights needs to be made since both form part of the charter of rights. Furthermore, and in today's world, national standards on minority rights need to move in step with international norms.

Rights of minorities have acquired renewed salience in the last two decades. The 'Declaration on the Rights of Persons Belonging to National or Ethnic, Religious and Linguistic Minorities' adopted by the UN General Assembly in December 1992 noted that minorities "contribute to the political and social stability of States in which they live" and that promotion of minority rights would contribute to the strengthening of friendship and cooperation among peoples and states.

Each one of you has a mandate that goes beyond committees, reports and political debates. The expectation from citizens belonging to minority communities, indeed from all citizens, is clear–to focus on socio-economic and political outcomes that embody the letter and spirit of our Constitution. This has to be done in a manner that brings about quantified outcomes in a framework of transparency and accountability.

I am confident that you would address this task in all seriousness.

Inauguration of International Seminar on 'Adivasi/ST Communities in India: Development and Change'

Institute for Human Development, New Delhi

27 August 2009

It gives me great pleasure to inaugurate this international seminar organised by the Institute for Human Development. The choice of the theme is appropriate. It covers a range of issues of local, national and global importance relating to the well-being of Adivasi communities in India.

A look at recent history provides a perspective. The political, social and cultural heterogeneity of India was amply reflected in the deliberations of the Constituent Assembly. The Objectives Resolution was tabled by Jawaharlal Nehru in December 1946. It sought to secure social, economic and political justice, equality of status, of opportunity, and before the law to all the people and promised adequate safeguards for minorities, backward and tribal areas, and depressed and other backward classes. The contours of the debate were quantified by Jaipal Singh of Chotanagpur who, speaking on behalf of, as he put it, "millions of unknown hordes ... unrecognised warriors of freedom, the original people of India who have variously been known as backward tribes, primitive tribes, criminal tribes and everything else", supported the Resolution.

Jaipal Singh also gave vent to long standing grievances and articulated the problem candidly:

"If there is any group of Indian people that has been shabbily treated it is my people. They have been disgracefully treated, neglected for the last 6,000 years....This Resolution is not going to teach the Adivasi democracy. You cannot teach democracy to the tribal people; you have to learn democratic ways from them. They are the most democratic people on earth. What my people require is not adequate safeguards ... We do not ask for any special protection. We want to be treated like every other Indian.... The whole history of my people is one of continuous exploitation and dispossession by the non-aboriginals of India punctuated by rebellions and disorder, and yet I take Pandit Jawaharlal Nehru at his word. I take you all at your word that now we are going to start a new chapter, a new chapter of Independent India where there is equality of opportunity, where no one would be neglected."

Six decades later, ladies and gentlemen, a few questions need to be answered:

- Has the experience of six decades been different from that of the earlier millennia and have Adivasis been treated with greater attention and justice?
- Have Adivasis been afforded the equality of opportunity?

The reality is unpalatable and the data speaks for itself. Compared to other sections of our society, the tribal population has the lowest Human Development Index. The literacy rate of the STs at 47.1 in the 2001 Census is far below the national literacy rate of 64.84. Tribal children suffer from high dropout rates and low female literacy. They also have high infant mortality rates and malnutrition as compared to other population groups. They suffer from geographical and social exclusion, high poverty rates and lack of access to appropriate administrative and judicial mechanisms. Low level of infrastructural endowments and growing gap in infrastructure creation in tribal areas, as compared to the rest of India, has further diminished prospects for progress.

For the 85 million Scheduled Tribes in India, the struggle to retain their identities and seek empowerment through our Constitutional framework has not yielded commensurate outcomes. I therefore wish to highlight a few points for the consideration of this audience:

First: Over 80 per cent of the Scheduled Tribes population works in the primary sector, with 45 per cent of them being cultivators and 37 per cent being agricultural labourers. Land thus represents the most important source of livelihood, emotional attachment and social stability in tribal communities. It is critical for cultivation horticulture, forestry and animal husbandry. The Draft National Tribal Policy testifies to it and notes that 'alienation of tribal land is the single most important cause of pauperisation of tribals, rendering their vulnerable economic situation more precarious.'

The Forest Rights Act of 2006 represents an important step in attempting to reverse the marginalisation of our tribal people. It gives legislative teeth to the Constitutional provisions for protection and development of Scheduled Tribes, provides them a level playing field and casts tribal rights in a new matrix based on community control and customary access. It acknowledges the immense hardship caused to the Scheduled Tribes due to insecurity of tenurial and access rights and forced relocation due to State development interventions. Quick implementation of the provisions of this Act by various State governments would go a long way in realising the vision of our Founding Fathers and ensuring that economic development and social progress is inclusive.

Second: The Constitution of India provides specific social, economic and political guarantees to the Scheduled Tribes. In the social dimension, these are covered under Articles 14, 15(4), 16(4), 16(4 A), 338 (A) and 339 (1). The economic provisions are covered under Article 46, 275(1) and 335. The political provisions are very elaborate and are spelt out in Article 244 and 5th and 6th Schedules of the Constitution, as also in Articles 330, 332, and 243 (D).

The extent to which the Constitutional provisions have been implemented and the normative guarantees translated into policy are a matter of ongoing debate. Civil society groups and activists have pointed out the manner in which the application of the Indian Forest Act 1927 and The Land Acquisition Act 1894 has caused marginalisation and hardship to the Adivasis. They also note that Fifth Schedule provisions to prevent application of such laws to Scheduled Areas had not been invoked.

Third: In comparison to other disadvantaged communities and groups, the Adivasis have been less effective in constituting themselves as a Pan-Indian interest group and in articulating their grievances through the formal political system. This could partly be attributed to lack of national homogeneity in the context and mechanisms that have led to the exclusion and oppression of the Adivasis. Geographical dispersion of the Adivasis and lack of iconic leadership with a national appeal also prevents effective political mobilisation. To a lesser extent, our education system and our media are also to blame for the lower profile accorded to the predicament of Indian tribes.

Fourth: The development paradigm of independent India has led to, in the words of the Draft National Tribal Policy, tribal communities witnessing "their habitats and homelands fragmented, their cultures disrupted, their communities shattered, the monetary compensation which tribal communities are not equipped to handle slipping out of their hands, turning them from owners of the resources and well-knit contented communities to individual wage earners in the urban conglomerates with uncertain futures and threatened existence'.

Across the nation gigantic industrial, power, irrigation and mining projects representing the current development paradigm have caused Adivasi protests against land acquisition and displacement. Aligning our development needs with Adivasi rights and enhancing their Human Development Index is the need of the hour. This is also essential to prevent violent manifestations of discontent and unrest in our tribal areas emanating from exclusion and alienation.

Fifth: It has been lost sight of that many Adivasis straddle multiple dimensions of deprivation and vulnerability. Besides being Scheduled Tribes, many of the Adivasis are also religious and linguistic minorities. It is very important that the protections afforded by the Constitution to the religious and linguistic minorities be fully made available to tribal communities that qualify.

I hope this seminar would act as a powerful tool for public advocacy on the extent of deprivation of Adivasis in the country and means to address them. I am confident that your deliberations would be immensely helpful for formulating policies conducive to Adivasi development.

Fifty-Nineth Annual Convocation
Shreemati Nathibai Damodar Thackersey Women's University, Mumbai
30 March 2010

Gender in National Discourse–The Road Ahead

I am happy to participate in today's ceremony. Convocations are to academic life what festivals are to social life: they signify rites of passage, the passing of seasons, a celebration of achievement, a benediction for facing the harsh world beyond the portals of the university.

Convocations are also occasions to draw lessons from the experience of life remembering, as Tennyson said:

"Yet all experience is an art wherethro'
Gleams that untravell'd world whose margin fades
Forever and forever when I move"

This university is a testament to the vision and effort of Dr Dhondo Keshav Karve over a century ago to ameliorate the depressing socio-economic condition of widows and women in India. His dictum that education was an essential element in empowering the women of India and making them self-reliant and self-confident remains valid to this day. Maharshi Karve's foresight was complemented by the contribution and support of Sir Vithaldas Thackersey.

The motto of the university–'*Sanskrita Stree Parashakti*–An enlightened woman is a source of infinite strength'–has universal validity. As the first women's university in India and South Asia, and being endowed with a uniquely national jurisdiction, SNDT has come to represent excellence in higher education for women.

II

I propose to share some thoughts today on an issue of contemporary relevance; I refer to the question of Gender in our National Discourse. What are its contemporary contours? Where do we go from here?

The discourse of course is of older vintage and social scientists have traced its evolution, limitations and nuances. For our purpose today, and if we take the era of Independence as the point of reference, there is no doubt that the principle of gender equality constitutes a basic feature of the Republic and is enshrined in the Constitution. The Preamble and the sections on Fundamental Rights, Fundamental Duties and Directive Principles are unambiguously explicit. The Constitution not only grants equality to women and prohibits discrimination, but also recognises their marginalisation and empowers the State to adopt measures of positive discrimination in their favour.

These constitutional provisions have been reinforced by the Supreme Court which has held that the equality clause in the Constitution does not speak of mere formal equality before law but embodies the concept of real and substantive equality which is an essential ingredient of social and economic justice.

Legal equality is one, perhaps the easier, aspect of the matter; societal reality is quite another. In a land as old and a society as diverse as ours, the dead weight of tradition conditions perception and practice, tells its own story, and reveals a chasm between the two. Equally disturbing is the proclivity to underplay the latter and the impulses leading to it.

It is necessary to delve into the underlying, unstated, sources of the problem. It has been argued that the identification of women with their physical bodies is the root cause of their oppression in a patriarchal culture and society like ours: “Most often women are denied the rights to emotional, mental, psychological and physical spaces. The fact that the female body is constantly under pressure to conform and mould into prescribed social and cultural roles brings into question the spaces that need to be protected as well as rights to be claimed so that women’s bodily integrity is respected”.

A few years back Professor Amartya Sen identified seven types of gender inequality in two broad categories, natality and post-natality, and stressed the need to recognise that "gender inequality is not one affliction but many, with varying reach on the lives of women and men, and of girls and boys"; hence the need, as he put it, "to take a plural view of gender inequality, which can have many different faces (and) can vary from region to another, and also from one period to the next."

This gap is quantifiable. The census data on declining sex ratio is well known. Discrimination and disparity begins even before a woman citizen is born. The saga of missing baby girls in wide swathes of rural and urban India has resulted from the marriage of ancient prejudice with modern technology and rising incomes.

A quarter of pregnant women do not receive pre-natal care and less than half of births are attended by skilled health staff. There is a high incidence of maternal under-nourishment and of under-nourishment of girls over boys. Female primary school enrolment rates are lower compared to boys and this is reflected, eventually, in the female literacy rate in the 15-24 age groups. Similarly, the female economic activity is lower and so is female participation in professional and technical work.

In terms of representation in structures of power, and while things have changed qualitatively at the grass root level, the participation of women in political decision-making at middle and higher levels is abysmally low. Less than 11 per cent of the seats in Lok Sabha are held by women. The situation is worse in the case of state assemblies where less than 8 per cent of the lawmakers are women.

A recent National Survey of Household Income and Expenditure conducted by the National Council of Applied Economic Research brings forth glaring disparities in the economic sphere. It shows that (a) women comprise a mere one third of Graduates and Post Graduates in the country (b) of the women graduates, 35 per cent are housewives, (c) 88 per cent of salaried jobs are held by men, (d) across most occupation types, non-graduate women earned less than half of that earned by men, and (e) for graduates with salaried jobs, men earned a third more than women.

It took us over four decades after Independence to allow women citizens to pass on their nationality to their children without reference to their spouse and over five decades to receive explicit statutory protection from domestic violence. To this day, a woman citizen's ability to unambiguously transmit her caste, tribal or domicile status to her offspring along with attendant benefits is ambiguous, and subject to a case-by-case determination.

The conclusion is inescapable that while all citizens are equal, women citizens are clearly less equal than men. The basic design of patriarchy still holds sway, sustained in good measure by the institution of early marriage and by real-life aberrations in property rights.

Is it then surprising that India ranked 114 out of 155 countries in the Gender Development Index of the World Bank?

III

To understand this inequality, we must realise that gender is not interchangeable with women. It refers to both women and men and the relation between them. Gender roles are not fixed, are learned as part of socialisation, are influenced by culture and traditions, and can be changed through education, socio-political and legislative interventions.

Gender equality has been defined to mean that 'the rights, responsibilities and the opportunities of individuals will not depend on whether they are born male or female and that the perceptions, interests, needs and priorities of women and men will be given equal weight in planning and decision making'.

The foregoing poses a question. How is gender equality to be promoted and ensured as a basic feature of our Constitution and as a necessary outcome of internationally accepted standards of human rights and women's rights to which India subscribes in full measure?

The National Policy for Empowerment of Women 2001 outlines three policy approaches:

1. Judicial/legal empowerment–by making the legal system more responsive and gender sensitive for women's needs.

2. Economic empowerment–by mainstreaming gender perspectives in the development process, enhancing women's capacities and access to economic opportunities.
3. Social empowerment–through focused efforts on education, health and nutrition.

In terms of operational strategies, the National Policy has called for gender development indices, gender disaggregated data, gender budgeting, Women's Component Plan in the five years so that not less than 30 per cent of benefits/funds flow to women, and gender sensitisation.

The policy, committing itself to building and strengthening partnerships with civil society and women's organisations, is silent on the methodology for the eradication of traditional prejudices and practices that impact adversely on women.

Meaningful action on these critical issues, clearly, lies in the realm of civil society. Experience has shown that women empower themselves by gaining power and control over their own lives. Governments and societies can facilitate these processes by raising awareness, expanding choices available to women, increasing women's access and control over resources and through targeted interventions to eliminate gender discrimination and inequality.

It would also be a serious fallacy to look at women empowerment as a zero-sum game leading to a loss for men. Women cannot be empowered without the active participation of men.

The time has come to move beyond tokenism. Legitimising gender equity in the minds of people is a complex process and women's empowerment per se is only part of the solution. The *India Social Development Report 2006* noted that "social development fractured along gender lines has to become a concern for society as a whole", adding that "it is absolutely imperative that the process of women's empowerment is located in broader structural, social and political structures" by assigning a greater role to men in engineering social changes in institutional rules.

The challenge then is the need to create a new consciousness and wider constituencies beyond the obvious.

A beginning has to be made at home. Domestic arrangements are central to the organisation of gender relations. Some years back, an official document acknowledged that the family in India "has not been a cradle for nurturing democratic values ... the need for a democratic family structure is a major challenge for families and not just for women."

We need to acknowledge candidly the tensions that emanate from the universalisation of citizenship and adult franchise in a democratic polity and a diverse socio-economic and cultural milieu. As a result, the citizen does have multiple identities and unavoidably reflects them in power structures in which he/she is a participant.

The responsibility for resolving the resulting dilemma thus rests principally on the individual and the group rather than on the state. The latter can at best put in place formal structures and undertake a measure of inducement through the educational system that must be geared fully and comprehensively for the purpose.

IV

Ours is a society in the throes of change. The value system itself is in a melting pot. No foolproof recipe is known to exist. It is in the nature of things that mistakes will be made as we proceed to actualise gender parity. Freedom, said Rabindranath Tagore, "cannot be called freedom unless one has the right to misuse it". The only anchor for the citizen is the Constitution and what Ambedkar called "constitutional morality". Both require unswerving commitment in word and deed.

The State's responsibility on gender issues is not in doubt and it is committed to bringing about gender equality. Equally important is the role of other stakeholders, individually and collectively. Many of you in this audience, when you confront life beyond the sheltered environment of the university, may witness or confront gender discrimination. At that juncture, you would be called upon to act on the basis of your convictions. That would be the occasion for public policy activism to counter these social evils, for the good of a better, more inclusive, society.

Social reform is a relay race in which the baton has to be carried forward incessantly. The national discourse on the gender question has traveled a good distance and gathered momentum. It should remain focused on promotion of meaningful equity and on enhancing choices.

Allow me to conclude by congratulating the graduating students, the award winners and the rank holders. I wish them every success in their professional endeavours and in their personal life. I urge them to have the confidence that a better future can be created by their personal effort, however modest it may be.

Eighth *India Today* Chief Ministers Conclave

Hotel Hyatt Regency, New Delhi
19 November 2010

I am happy to participate in the Eighth *India Today* Chief Ministers Conclave on the 'State of States Report.' I commend the *India Today* Group for initiating and sustaining a debate on the social and economic development of states through quantitative reference points so vital for policy making on a range of development themes.

I take this opportunity to congratulate the states who have been awarded today for specific aspects of governance and of human and socio-economic development.

It is universally acknowledged that one dimension of the Indian genius pertains to excellence in mathematics. This also manifests itself in our fondness for statistics. Quantitative data, however, often does not dwell on quality and tells the story partially. There is need therefore to exercise caution and ensure that such data does in fact reflect the *actual benefits* of developmental schemes reaching the citizen body in all its segments and age groups.

This year's report is on 'Development in Times of Naxalism'. The theme poses the problem and suggests a linkage between the two. The prime minister has noted that "in many areas, the phenomenon of Naxalism is directly related to underdevelopment" and that "exploitation, artificially depressed wages, iniquitous socio political circumstances, inadequate employment opportunities, lack of access to resources, under developed agriculture, geographical isolation, lack of land reforms–all contribute significantly to the growth of the Naxalite movement".

Much of the same thing has been said for years by distinguished police officers who have had firsthand experience of working in Naxal infested areas.

The Naxalite movement emerged four decades earlier. Its geographic spread covering over 160 districts of the country makes it a prime developmental and national security concern. The challenge of reconciling the imperatives of development, equity and national security continue to confront the state apparatus and the civil society.

No analysis of the ground reality can escape the centrality of the problem to the 70 million tribal population of Central India, spread over ten states of the Union. These citizens score the lowest in the Human Development Index when compared to other population groups. They suffer from geographical and social exclusion, high poverty rates and lack of access to appropriate administrative and judicial mechanisms. Low level of infrastructural endowments and growing gap in infrastructure creation in tribal areas, as compared to the rest of India, has further diminished prospects for progress.

I wish to highlight a few aspects of this question today. These relate to forest rights, the lack of effective implementation of constitutional and statutory provisions for tribal populations, the difficulties faced in their political mobilisation, the need for a new development paradigm in tribal areas and the multiple vulnerabilities of the tribal people.

Firstly: Over 80 per cent of the Scheduled Tribes population works in the primary sector, with 45 per cent of them being cultivators and 37 per cent being agricultural labourers. Land thus represents the most important source of livelihood, emotional attachment and social stability in tribal communities. The alienation of tribal land is the single most important cause of pauperisation of tribals, rendering their vulnerable economic situation more precarious. This is sought to be reversed by the Forest Rights Act of 2006.

In her Address to Parliament in June 2009, the President of India emphasised the need to ensure distribution, by end of December 2009, of title deeds to all eligible claimants under the Act. Sadly, while some States and some districts within states have achieved excellent progress in the distribution of titles, other states and districts are lagging far behind.

Secondly: The Constitution of India provides specific social, economic and political guarantees to the Scheduled Tribes. In the social dimension, these are covered under Articles 14, 15(4), 16(4), 16(4 A), 338 (A) and 339 (1). The economic provisions are covered under Article 46, 275(1) and 335.

The political provisions are very elaborate and are spelt out in Article 244 and 5th and 6th Schedules of the Constitution, as also in Articles 330, 332, and 243 (D). Specific responsibilities have also been assigned to Governors and to the Central Government.

The actual implementation of these Constitutional provisions is a matter of some concern. The same holds for the manner of implementing of the Indian Forest Act 1927 and the Land Acquisition Act 1894.

Thirdly: In comparison to other disadvantaged communities and groups, the Adivasis have been less effective in constituting themselves as a Pan-Indian interest group and in articulating their grievances through the formal political system.

Many Adivasis also straddle multiple dimensions of deprivation and vulnerability. Besides being Scheduled Tribes, many of the Adivasis are also religious and linguistic minorities. It is therefore essential that the protections afforded by the Constitution to the religious and linguistic minorities be fully made available to tribal communities that qualify.

The violent manifestations of discontent and unrest in our tribal areas, emanating from exclusion and alienation, calls for serious introspection. Our development paradigm has led, in the words of the Draft National Tribal Policy, to tribal communities witnessing 'their habitats and homelands fragmented, their cultures disrupted, their communities shattered, the monetary compensation which tribal communities are not equipped to handle slipping out of their hands, turning them from owners of the resources and well-knit contented communities to individual wage earners in the urban conglomerates with uncertain futures and threatened existence'.

Across the nation gigantic industrial, power, irrigation and mining projects representing the current development paradigm have caused Adivasi protests against land acquisition and displacement. An equitable solution to this has to be found. Inclusive growth necessitates aligning our development needs with Adivasi rights and enhancing their Human Development Index.

I am confident that the deliberations of this Conclave would lead to a better understanding of the issues involved and, hopefully, better implementation of the constitutional and legislative provisions for safeguarding the rights of our tribal population and ensuring its socio-economic development.

Nineteenth Convocation of North-Eastern Hill University

Shillong

30 September 2011

This is my first visit to the state and I am enchanted by the idyllic surroundings of Shillong.

I also feel privileged to attend today's convocation at an institution tasked with advancing knowledge and improving social and economic conditions and welfare of the people of the North-Eastern region. It has succeeded in significant measure not only in evolving specialised courses and research programs but also tuning the curriculum to the conditions and needs of the north-eastern region. The leadership, faculty and staff deserve our appreciation for their effort in moulding it into a 'University with Potential for Excellence'.

I take this opportunity to congratulate the graduating students who will be moving out to their chosen careers and courses of higher learning.

It is the task of the State, and the duty of society, to ensure that the principle of equity is an essential concomitant of its pursuit of welfare for citizens without regard to religion, race, caste, sex or place of birth. Much has been achieved, much remains to be done. One significant ingredient of the latter, relating to almost half of our population, is gender equality. I therefore propose to discuss some aspects of it today.

The principle of gender equality, and of affirmative action to ensure it, is writ large in the Constitution and has been reinforced by Supreme Court rulings. Societal reality however is not in consonance with it. Socially constructed roles of men and women define a person's role in society, economy and household. As a result and in order to camouflage reality, we resort to tokenism and often parade exception as the rule.

Gender works its debilitating impact over lifetimes and generations, and impedes a person's access to human capital formation, full range of citizenship functions, economic opportunities, social emancipation and political participation.

Five dimensions of inequality and discrimination resulting from gender need to be considered. These relate to demographics, nourishment and health, literacy, participation in economic activity and political representation.

The first is reflected in cold data: According to the provisional figures of Census 2011, there are 586.46 million females as compare to 623.72 million males, giving a sex ratio of 940 females to 1000 males. Compared with the sex ratios of the ten most populous countries in the world, we stand ninth, with only China at 926 behind us. In our own region, Myanmar, Sri Lanka and Nepal have more females in their population, while Pakistan and Bangladesh with a sex ratio of 943 and 978 have in comparison done better.

It is a matter of concern that the sex ratio in the age group 0-6 years continues to decline since 1961 and stands at 914 in Census 2011. Among our own States, the only silver lining is provided by Mizoram and Meghalaya having child sex ratio in this age group at 971 and 970 respectively.

Secondly, we have one of the highest incidences of under-nutrition among women in the world. In over 35 per cent cases relating to adult women in the country in the 15-49 years age group, virtually every third woman suffers from chronic energy deficiency. This level is higher than all countries in sub-Saharan Africa except Eritrea. Likewise, in over 55 per cent cases relating to adult Indian women, every second woman suffers from iron deficiency anaemia. Here too most countries of sub-Saharan Africa do better. The attendant impact on quality of life, access to opportunities for social and economic advancement, and ability to realise and harness their human potential is evident.

In the third place, our health indicators are weaker as compared to our level of development. The Draft Approach to the Twelfth Five-Year Plan acknowledges that while there has been progress, the targets of the Eleventh Plan are yet to be met with Infant Mortality Rate remaining at fifty per 1000 live births in 2009, Maternal Mortality Ratio at 212 per 100,000 live births and only 73 per cent of deliveries in institutions.

In regard to education, the Annual Status of Education Report 2010 shows that in all of rural India, 5.9 per cent of girls in the age group 11-14 years were out of school. According to Census 2011, though there has been more rapid improvement in female literacy, there still exists a gender gap of 16.7 percentage points.

Fourthly, the level of female economic activity is lower and so is female participation in professional and technical work. The Five-Year Strategic Plan of the Ministry of Women and Child Development for 2011-2016 notes that work force participation rate of women in urban areas is a mere 14 per cent as compared to 54 per cent for men. Even in rural areas, it is 31 per cent for women whereas it is 55 per cent for men. Women's share of organised sector and public sector is less than 20 per cent. They have an even lesser share of central government employment, of less than 8 per cent.

In regard to the fifth, and while things have changed qualitatively at the grass root level, the participation of women in political decision-making at middle and higher levels is abysmally low. Less than 11 per cent of the seats in our Parliament are held by women. The situation is worse in the case of state assemblies. Women hold less than 10 per cent of ministerial positions at the Centre with a single cabinet minister, and there have been only five women judges of the Supreme Court since independence, constituting around 3 per cent of appointments.

Thus the picture of discrimination and deprivation that emerges is disturbingly stark. It took us over four decades after Independence to allow women citizens to pass on their nationality to their children without reference to their spouse and over five decades to receive explicit statutory protection from domestic violence. To this day, a woman citizen's ability to unambiguously transmit her caste, tribal or domicile status to her offspring along with attendant benefits is ambiguous, and subject to a case-by-case determination based on the personal laws applicable to her community and specific laws applicable to her region.

The conclusion is inescapable that while all citizens are equal, women citizens are clearly less equal than men and, as Justice Krishna Iyer once put it, "the laws themselves are lawless where women versus men are involved".

It is necessary to examine underlying sources of the problem. Gender inequality, in Amartya Sen's words, is "a far reaching social impairment". It emanates from the basic design of patriarchy that is pervasive and has still to be challenged adequately. Gender equality should lead to the rights, responsibilities and the opportunities of individuals being independent on their being male or female and the perceptions, interests, needs and priorities of both women and men being given equal weight in planning and decision making.

What have we done to bring this about? A beginning had been made with The National Policy for Empowerment of Women 2001 outlining three policy approaches:

1. Judicial/legal empowerment–by making the legal system more responsive and gender sensitive for women's needs.
2. Economic empowerment–by mainstreaming gender perspectives in the development process, enhancing women's capacities and access to economic opportunities.
3. Social empowerment–through focused efforts on education, health and nutrition.

In terms of operational strategies, the National Policy has called for gender development indices, gender disaggregated data, gender budgeting, Women's Component Plan in the five years so that not less than 30 per cent of benefits/funds flow to women.

Almost a decade later, the launch of the National Mission for Empowerment of Women in March 2010 is an important development that will enable coordinated assessment of current government interventions and align future programmes so as to translate the recommendations and approaches of the National Policy into reality.

At the same time and given the deep rooted nature of the problem we have to recognise that government interventions, though essential, are insufficient. Better results will be produced by women citizens empowering themselves and being encouraged to do by enlightened segments of public opinion.

An important focus area for policy and action is asset ownership. Even as the country has witnessed good economic growth in the past decade, the benefits of such growth and macroeconomic initiatives to women are mediated through their position in homes and workplaces, and access to, and ownership of, productive assets.

In developmental terms, therefore, asset redistribution is perceived to be more effective than income redistribution in empowering and addressing gender differentials in property rights, division of labour, mobility, ability to resist violence, and access to healthcare, education, and transformative technologies.

A recent project by IIM Bangalore based on a large-scale household survey in Karnataka state on women's access to and ownership of assets has revealed that apart from some jewellery, women hold little or no assets. There exist huge gender inequalities for key productive assets such as land or residence, ownership of business or vehicles, and even communication tools such as mobile phones. Women owners were less than half or at times less than a third of the number of male owners of assets, and their assets were of lower value, poorer quality and were less productive. Even in a metro such as Bangalore, less than a quarter of women had cell phones compared to around half of the men surveyed, whereas only 12 per cent of women owned vehicles as compared to over 50 per cent of men.

Even more startling was the fact that for asset acquisition, natal inheritance overwhelmingly benefits men and discriminates against women, with over 50 per cent of the men reporting asset acquisition through their natal homes as compared to around 15 per cent of the women. The vast majority of assets owned by women, of over 70 per cent, were either self-acquired, or obtained through marital or spousal inheritance.

The World Development Report 2012 released by the World Bank ten days ago argues that gender equality is a critical determinant of development outcomes and makes for smart economics. Besides calling for action in addressing human capital issues, closing earning and productivity gaps between women and men, and giving women greater voice within households and societies, the report for the first time seeks limiting the perpetuation of gender inequality across generations. This is an important aspect so that inequity, marginalisation, discrimination and stereotyping are not transmitted across generational cycles.

As the graduating students leave the portals of this university, they would do well to remember Dr B.R. Ambedkar's observation that "the degree of progress which women have achieved" is a true measure of progress of a community.

The Seventh Meeting of Women Speakers of Parliament on Gender Sensitive Parliaments

Central Hall of Parliament House, New Delhi

3 October 2012

I am privileged to be here today for the inaugural session of the seventh meeting of Women Speakers of Parliament, organised by the IPU, on the theme 'Gender Sensitive Parliaments'. Its stated purpose is to highlight the role of women speakers as catalysts for generating gender sensitivity in legislatures.

Women constitute nearly half the number of humans in any society and are equal share holders. In the words of a Human Development Report, they "must be regarded as agents and beneficiaries of change. Investing in women's capabilities and empowering them to exercise their choices is not only valuable in itself but is also the surest way to contribute to economic growth and overall development".

It is therefore paradoxical that despite great changes in past decades in large parts of the world on matters relating to gender equality, the core issues affecting women such as social equality, equal access to education and employment, equal pay for equal work, and equitable share in decision-making, still remain largely unresolved.

This calls for serious reflection. In the first place, we need some conceptual clarity. Gender equality is specific and quantifiable; gender equity less so; gender sensitivity, on the other hand, is an amorphous concept capable of varying and at times evasive interpretations.

Furthermore, analysis would need to assess whether patriarchy and its present-day remnants are a phenomenon of nature or a social construct. If the latter (as would appear obvious in the world we live in) then the required correctives should be injected in the interstices of individual societies to help re-shape social and political perceptions.

Experience has shown that women's issues do not relate merely to problems that can be resolved through ad-hoc measures. They pertain to the core of social organisation, to economic and political structures and relationships. More importantly, they relate to attitudes, prejudices and stereotypes that translate into certain unacceptable social value judgments.

Correctives therefore are imperative at the base of the social pyramid. Gender sensitivity, in other words, is more a bottom-up process rather than a top-down one.

There is no denying that as women come to control the levers of society and the State–business, media, legislature, administration and judiciary–their status in society, and its impact on gender relations, will register changes. We need to strengthen this process by creating a level playing field where women enjoy equality of opportunity and freedom of expression to realise their full potential. Legislative bodies can, and must, contribute to it in full measure. This is necessary but not sufficient. More remains to be done.

Global data tells its own story. In 1990, the United Nation's Economic and Social Council endorsed a target of 30 per cent women in decision-making positions in the world by 1995. By that year, however, only 10 per cent of the world's parliamentarians were women. The situation is no better today. According to a recent IPU survey, the world average of Women Members of both the Houses combined constitutes only 20 per cent of the total.

National experiences are relevant. In India, we have found that bottom-up approach has yielded better results. The gender profile in the Parliament of India is woefully lopsided with women constituting only around 11 per cent of the total membership. Legislation reserving 33 per cent of seats for women was passed in one House and has since been pending in the other.

On the other hand, a constitutional amendment in 1993 mandated reservation of one-third seats for women at the local level bodies, namely, the Panchayats and Municipalities. This has been a historic beginning for the effective participation of women in the decision-making process at the grassroots level. Today, women number 1.2 million among the nearly 2.8 million representatives elected to local bodies. Before reservations, the percentage of women in this area was merely 4.5 per cent; now it has gone up to 40 per cent. This is perhaps the largest ever representation of women in elected bodies anywhere in the world.

I venture to hope that the deliberations of this meeting would focus on a set of specific questions:

Which policies and practices will strengthen gender equality in different societies?

What should be done by Parliaments to encourage and foster gender equality and become role models for it?

Since Presiding Officers of parliaments do not initiate or control governmental agendas and legislation, what specific role can be visualised for speakers in the furtherance of gender equity and sensitivity?

The responses we get would be a step forward in the right direction to ensure gender equity and equality in our societies, thereby achieving participative and representative democracy in greater measure.

Parliament and Matters Legislative

“The quality of governance in a democracy will critically hinge on the quality of business transacted in the Parliament

Speech by Hon'ble Chairman, Rajya Sabha
(after felicitations were offered to him on being elected)
Parliament House, New Delhi
13 August 2007

An individual in a multitude of a billion becomes a celebrity when summoned by your sovereign decision to become the thirteenth incumbent of this august office of the Republic. The virtue of the democratic process is obvious. Equally evident is the burden of the twin responsibilities entrusted. The enormity of the task induces humility.

I am overwhelmed by the warmth of your welcome and the confidence you repose in me for the stewardship of this office. I can hardly find words to express my gratitude. I do pledge my utmost effort to discharge my duties with fairness and impartiality and to make every effort to protect and defend the rights and privileges of this Council.

Ours is a parliamentary democracy whose form and objectives are inscribed in the Constitution. Its institutions have stood the test of time. We, nevertheless, need to reiterate and reinvigorate our commitment to them and to their operational modalities. In such a system, the majority to my right and the minority to my left, both play an equal part. Here, I can do no better than to recall the words in this House of the first Vice-President of India, Dr Sarvepalli Radhakrishnan of revered memory and I quote: "A democracy is distinguished by the protection it gives to minorities. A democracy is likely to degenerate into tyranny if it does not allow the opposition groups to criticise fairly, freely and frankly the policies of the government. But, at the same time, minorities also have their responsibilities. Well, they have every right to criticise, their right to criticise should not degenerate into willful hampering and obstruction of the work of Parliament. All groups, therefore, have their right and have their responsibilities."

Over the years, this House has developed rules of procedure and conventions for the conduct of business. These have been amplified by the rulings of the chair. They constitute an invaluable compendium. The assigned duty of the chair is to ensure that all play by these rules. The referee in a game of hockey or football does carry coloured cards in his shirt pocket. A good game, however, is one in which the need to use these cards does not arise. It is my fervent hope that with your cooperation, the latter mode would characterise our common endeavour.

Hon. Members, even though I am a new comer to this august body, as a citizen I am not unaware of its deliberations. Much has been done, continues to be done and would be done here to promote the national agenda. In an era of rising expectations, however, our work has to respond to changing perceptions and requirements of the people and particularly of the weaker sections of our society. They, after all, constitute the overwhelming majority of our population.

The challenge lies in the need to ensure equitable distribution of the fruits of development. The challenge also is to seek justice through substantive equity and meaningful fraternity. The will to do so is one aspect of it. Institutional efficacy and a delivery mechanism is another. Both are integral to the process of change. Delays aggravate matters. We need to recall Macaulay's caution: "Excesses of people are directed against those whom they suspect of interfering with the public good." Each of these imposes an additional responsibility on the representatives of the people. A few days back, my very distinguished predecessor rightly observed, "The quality of governance in a democracy will critically hinge on the quality of business transacted in the Parliament."

I make bold to suggest that an awareness of this would be a first step in meeting public expectations.

I conclude with an Urdu couplet that has often been a fair guide to me personally:

"Justuju hai zindagi, jue-talab hai zindagi
Zindagi ka raz lekin doori-e-manzil main hai"

Sixtieth Anniversary of India's Independence

Central Hall, Parliament House, New Delhi
15 August 2007

Anniversaries are occasions for rejoicing, and for introspection. We rejoice over our achievements and successes; we introspect about our limitations and failures.

The reasons for rejoicing are evident. Sixty years after 1947, India's progress is evident. Doubts about our capability have given way to certitude. Our achievements in every sector of national activity are noteworthy. We are a nation of consequence in the comity of nations, respected and sought after.

Equally evident are grounds for introspection. The point of reference has to be the Preamble to our Constitution and the three objectives inscribed in it: Justice, Liberty and Equality. The content of each is spelt out. Justice has to be dispensed in social, economic and political terms; liberty has to be of thought, expression, belief, faith and worship; equality means equality of status and opportunity.

Record shows that we have achieved each of these in considerable measure; scrutiny reveals that much more needs to be done. Noticeable sections of our population remain deprived of an equitable share in the fruits of development, their aspirations of a better life unfulfilled. The hope, nevertheless, remains. They may agree with the contents of an Urdu couplet:

"Ab bhi khizan ka raj hai lekin kahin kahin
Goshe chaman chaman main ghazal-khwan huai to hain"

We need to ponder over other matters too. There was an apprehension in the early years of independence of physical balkanisation; it proved to be unfounded. A more distressing trend, increasingly evident, is the balkanisation of the mind. It needs to be addressed. The challenge is to promote Indianness in all its diversity.

Our success in establishing and sustaining procedural democracy is acknowledged. Gandhi*ji* reminded us of some pitfalls. Democracy, he said, "is a great institution and therefore it is liable to be greatly abused. The remedy therefore is not avoidance of democracy but reduction of possibility of abuse to a minimum". Substantive democracy would also need a much greater measure of justice in terms of participation and representation.

The same holds for governance. Civil society vigilance provides a badly needed corrective. The growth in public awareness is to be welcomed; its content, however, needs to bc substantive rather than sensational.

Our objective of a plural society, a democratic polity and a secular state structure has to be reaffirmed and reinvigorated. Each of these is a source of strength; together they demonstrate the uniqueness of our system.

The generation that fought for Independence is all but gone. Those who consolidated the gains of freedom through difficult decades contributed their share in full measure. India of the future, however, principally belongs to the youth. They would shape it through their vision, aspiration and hard work. They must not succumb to the temptations of cynicism in regard to civic institutions.

Today, on the sixtieth anniversary of our Independence, we pay homage to the countless men and women who made sacrifices in the quest for freedom. Today, we rededicate ourselves to their ideals and pledge ourselves to the building of modern India.

Inauguration of the Fourteenth All India Whips' Conference

Mumbai

4 February 2008

This distinguished gathering brings together persons who are an essential instrument for the functioning of parliamentary democracy. I therefore deem it a privilege to be asked to inaugurate it.

A 'whip' is defined as "an official appointed to maintain discipline among, secure attendance of, and give necessary information to, members of his party". Each of these is essential for the proper functioning of a legislature. This is recognised by convention and is sanctified by an Act of Parliament.

It is said that whips 'make a House' and 'keep a House'. They have multiple functions:

- Facilitate the functioning of the legislature and optimise its output.
- Be the channel for communicating party policy, on a day to day basis, to the rank and file of the party in the legislature and function as barometer for gauging their opinion;
- Act as counsellors to their members and advisors to party leadership;
- Function as the channel for dispensing favours and for enforcing discipline.

Knowledge of human nature and amiability are considered essential requirements for whips. They must know when to cajole, when to persuade, and when to threaten. One recent study has highlighted their role 'as arm-twister, bully and Machiavelli all rolled into one'.

Any commentary on the functioning of our parliamentary system is therefore, by implication, a comment on the efficacy or otherwise of the institution of whips. A generalised assessment, however, does not provide us all the answers, particularly with regard to their primary function touching upon their role in the functioning of legislatures.

Why do democracies have elected legislatures? What purpose do they serve? The answer to the first question lies in the term 'representative and participatory governance'. The second was answered by Dr Sarvepalli Radhakrishnan, the first Chairman of the Rajya Sabha. "Parliament", he observed, "is not only a legislative but also a deliberative body". The first is driven by the government of the day; the latter by public opinion and opposition pressure. This point was authoritatively stated by Sir Ivor Jennings:

"The true function of the House is to question and debate the policy of the Government. In doing so, it can bring home to the government the unpopularity of a particular line of policy. Democratic government rests upon public opinion".

Thus deliberation is essential for three reasons:

- Effective oversight on the work of the government;
- Explaining policy to opposition parties and the public;
- Informing the government of opposition and public concerns.

The extent to which these functions are discharged is less a matter of opinion and more of facts.

The basic principles of parliamentary government are well known. The government shall, as long as it can maintain a majority, be able to secure such legal powers as it considers necessary for administration and that the minority, however small, shall be able to criticise that administration. The spirit of the system requires that stout opposition be combined with cooperation so that both the majority and the minority are able to discharge their respective functions.

The yardstick of public expectations is the only way to measure the effectiveness of the functioning of our legislatures. How successful have our parliamentary institutions been in making the system work? The story is told in this data made publicly available:

- The number of sittings in the Rajya Sabha has come down from an annual average of 90.5 in the first decade 1952-61 to 71.3 in the decade 1992-2001, a decline of 20 per cent. The comparative figures for the Lok Sabha are 124.2 and 81.0 or a decline of 34 per cent.
- The picture in regard to the state assemblies is even more revealing, with the average now being in the range of twenty to fifty sittings every year.
- The annual average of the number of bills passed by Parliament has come down from sixty-eight in the decade 1952-1961 to 49.9 in the decade 1992-2001. Assurances given on the floor of the House are being fulfilled with lesser regularity.
- About 5.28 per cent of working time was lost due to disruptions in the Eleventh Lok Sabha. This rose to 10.66 per cent in the Twelfth Lok Sabha and to 18.95 per cent in the Thirteenth. In the current Lok Sabha, 21 per cent of the time has been lost due to adjournments. The loss of time in the Rajya Sabha has been particularly high in recent years.
- Some of the lost time is made up by late sittings. Nevertheless, the impact of disruptions remains on the public mind. Party whips are mute spectators to such disruptions and thereby fail to discharge their primary duty of facilitating the functioning of the legislature.
- Political groups do not observe sufficient care in the selection of their representatives in legislatures. Nearly 23 per cent of MPs elected in 2004 had criminal cases registered against them; over half of these are cases of a nature that could lead to imprisonment of five or more years. The situation is worse in the case of MLAs. This too has a negative impact on public opinion.

You would recall that in 1997, on the occasion of the Golden Jubilee of our Independence, the two Houses of Parliament adopted unanimously an 'An Agenda for India' resolution. One section of it related to the need to preserve and enhance the prestige of Parliament. Three specific commitments were made in the resolution:

- Maintaining the inviolability of the Question Hour
- Refraining from transgressing into the official areas of the House, or from shouting slogans
- Desisting, invariably, from interruption or interference with the Address of the President of the Republic.

Ten years later, record shows that each of these solemn commitments has been observed in the breach. It is a damning indictment before the bar of public opinion and is viewed as such by the civil society and the media. It has done damage to the institution of elected legislatures and to the functioning of Indian democracy. One observer has chosen to describe our system as merely an 'electoral democracy'.

Some questions unavoidably arise and beg for answers:

- Is not disruption of proceedings during the Question Hour a breach of privilege of individual members who await answers to admitted starred questions, and supplementary questions?
- Are members of legislatures immune to public opinion?
- Do members indulging in disruption understand the implications of being paid, full-time, public servants in the technical meaning of the term?
- Why can our legislators not function as legislators do in other democratic systems?

We need to remind ourselves that there is a difference in being a public figure and a legislator. Every public figure is not a legislator; the latter consciously accepts the obligations of his/her office and cannot accord a secondary place to his/her duties in the legislature. Regrettably, and often enough, the lure of the legislature is no longer for the laudable purpose of representation and is, instead, seen by some merely as a stepping stone to more attractive positions.

The deliberative functions of the legislature are decidedly in decline. All sides of the House bear responsibility for it. The Treasury benches shy away from substantive discussion of issues of public concern; the opposition prefers to resort to the so-called Zero Hour only to mention these issues in hyperbolic terms. Deliberation is thus reduced to a zero sum game. Policies are offered to the public as products; the electorate is denied a peep into the process.

The whole process reflects adversely on parliament as an institution of accountability in a democracy. This has serious implications for democracy itself.

What then can be done, by way of a corrective, to restore to parliament and other legislatures the centrality they should have and were intended to have? Such a corrective has to be at two levels simultaneously: to restore the sanctity of the Question Hour and to re-establish the legislature as the primary forum for debate on public policy. Perhaps the following could be considered by this conference and of the political parties represented here:

- Each member of a legislature, at the time of taking the oath of office, should subscribe to the three points relating to the functioning of Parliament mentioned in the 1997 Resolutions.
- The deliberative role of the Parliament must be restored by increasing the number of its sittings per annum to about 130 days. The comparative figures for the British and Canadian Parliaments are in excess of 140. The US Congress is in session, on an average, for over 150 days in a year.
- If time is lost due to disruptions it should be compensated for, the same day, by sitting beyond normal hours.
- The chair should take up with the whips, on a daily basis, incidents of violation of behavioural norms by members. The rule about naming members should be invoked whenever necessary.
- The practice of resisting debate, or mention, of contentious issues should be eschewed and both government and opposition should specifically commit themselves to deliberate on issues for which a request is made by at least one-third or one-fourth of the members of the legislature.
- Exceptions apart, interventions in debates are short on substance and long on rhetoric. One reason for this is the absence of a

> substantive research base at the disposal of many members. Such a base needs to be provided on the pattern of the Congressional Research Service in the United States.

The writing on the wall is clear. The instrumentalities at the disposal of our legislatures have either been blunted or become dysfunctional. The single most important issue of concern today is the decreasing credibility of our legislatures as effective institutions capable of delivering public good and contributing to effective formulation of laws and public policy. What is needed is a review of the functioning of legislatures in their day to day work in order to optimise their productivity.

There are successful precedents to such an initiative. It will be recalled that in 1993 the Parliament created the Departmental Standing Committees to 'make parliamentary activity more effective, make the Executive more accountable and to avail of expert and public opinion where ever necessary'. This has introduced depth in the consideration of legislative proposals; there is, of course, room for improvement, and for greater interaction with the public.

This is your fourteenth conference. The functioning of parliamentary democracy depends in great measure on the manner in which you shoulder your responsibilities as whips. Your recommendations would be of great value.

The greater challenge, however, would be to implement them. We would do well to recall Dr Ambedkar's advice. "The working of the Constitution", he said, "does not depend wholly upon the nature of the Constitution. The Constitution can provide only the organs of state such as the Legislature, the Executive and the Judiciary. The factors on which the working of those organs of the State depends are the people and the political parties they will set up as their instruments to carry out their wishes and their politics. Who can say how the people of India and their parties will behave?"

Address to the Senate of Kazakhstan

Astana, Kazakhstan

7 April 2008

It is a privilege for me to address this august gathering. I bring warm greetings of the people of India, of the Members of our Parliament and of the Government.

History in India and Kazakhstan goes back to ancient times and has common strains and points of convergence. Our regions were agricultural societies in the old world and evolved into urban civilisations. We had cultural relations and trade contacts. The Saka tribes and the Kushana Empire symbolise this. So does the Silk Route which played a seminal role in transporting not only commodities for trade, but more importantly knowledge and ideas. Illustrative examples of these are the flow of Buddhism from India to Central Asian lands and eventually to China, and the flow of the ideas of Sufism from Central Asia to India.

Our recent past too has commonalities. We are multi ethnic, multi religious societies with secular State structures. India is a vibrant democracy and Kazakhstan has opted for a democratic mode of governance. We are growing economies committed to inclusive development and better living standards for all sections of our society. We have understood the importance of managing diversity and are harnessing it for the wellbeing of our people.

India's diversity is staggering. We have twenty-four languages that are recognised by the Constitution of India with 844 different dialects that are practiced in various parts of the country. An Indian currency note reflects this diversity–you can find seventeen languages on it. Followers of all the major religions of the world are found amongst the citizens of India.

At a time when multiculturalism has come under strain in many parts of the world, our accommodative pluralism, our capacity to give space to fellow citizens and our ability to draw the circle wide enough to be inclusive has greatly contributed to stability and development.

Constitutions are reflective both of the genius of a people and of the requirements of a society, the challenges faced by it, its responses, hopes and aspirations. Each constitution, therefore, is unique. Commonalities of form do however exist. A country may be democratic or non-democratic; its structure may be unitary or federal; its legislature may be unicameral or bicameral; its form of governance may be presidential or parliamentary. What matters, in the final analysis, is the effectiveness of the response to the requirements of the situation.

In this context and since no one has a monopoly of truth or wisdom, exchanges of information and of experience have been found to be beneficial. This is done on common fora like the Inter-Parliamentary Union or through bilateral exchanges.

I had occasion recently to read the address of His Excellency Nursultan Nazarbayev, President of the Republic of Kazakhstan, on 6 February 2008 and was struck by his observation that "the status and power of Kazakhstan's People's Assembly have increased" and that this institution "needs strengthening through all means available" since it is essential both for strengthening the nation and for sustainable economic development.

These words are reflective of wisdom and maturity of approach.

Some of you may be aware that India gained its Independence in 1947 and has, in the past six decades, developed and deepened democratic institutions based on universal adult franchise at three levels in our polity. We have a bicameral federal parliament, state assemblies in each of our thirty states, and 240,000 village level assemblies. At this grass-root level, we have 3.6 million elected representatives; 37 per cent of the latter are women. Today, India is not only the world's largest democracy but is also one of the most innovative in accommodating diverse, often conflicting, demands.

Since I have the honour of addressing the Senate of Kazakhstan, it would be appropriate to share with you our experience of the second chamber at the national level.

The Rajya Sabha or the Council of States is one of the two chambers of the Parliament of India. It has a membership of 245 (including 12 who are nominated). Its 233 elected members are chosen by the members of the state assemblies according to the system of proportional representation by means of single transferable vote. The term of a member is six years and one-third of the members retire every second year.

The two chambers of our Parliament have been conferred equal powers except on some issues. The Lok Sabha or the House of the People has the sole jurisdiction on money matters, voting on demand for grants and on 'making or unmaking governments'.

The makers of our Constitution envisaged the role of the Rajya Sabha along three axes:

- As a legislative chamber of elders discussing, revising or delaying legislation as per need.
- As an institution where interests of the states of the Indian Union could be projected and safeguarded.
- As a deliberative chamber where greater and diverse experience is brought to bear on questions of significance.

The essence of democracy is participatory governance. Experience the world over has shown that this ensures responsiveness and transparency. The mechanism for it lies in the functioning of legislatures and the institutional structures created for the purpose. In the Parliament of India this is achieved through Questions, Motions of different categories on matters of public importance, Resolutions and regular discussions. Through each of these, the government is obliged to respond to general or specific queries. In recent years, the requirement of transparency is also attained through the Right of Information Act passed by the Parliament in 2005.

The domain of parliament is the totality of state policy. In today's globalised and inter-dependent world, this covers every aspect of external relations. Interactions between parliaments and parliamentarians offer opportunities to appreciate the mutual concerns and perceptions on crucial issues and challenges that confront people in different countries of the world. This assists the promotion of inter-state relations. Parliaments thus have an important role to play in strengthening bilateral relations between our countries.

It is heartening to learn that there is a Special India Friendship group in the Mazhilis of the Kazakhstan Parliament. I am happy to see that a group of parliamentarians from Kazakhstan visited India last year. Such exchanges must further increase and lead to deepening of the friendship and understanding between our countries and peoples.

In the world of today and tomorrow, relations between countries would necessarily focus on mutually beneficial cooperation. This would be true of countries big and small, rich or poor, developed or developing. Such cooperation would require matching of requirements and capabilities. This general proposition holds good for cooperation between Kazakhstan and India.

One significant area of cooperation could transform our relationship. President Nazarbayev in his address to the nation in February this year talked about the need to expand high quality education services. He called for the implementation of 'the programme for the further development of professional and technical education' and noted that such a programme should provide for 'the attraction of foreign scientists and teachers to the areas of education most useful to the national economy'.

It is here that India can make a useful contribution to Kazakhstan. The quality of our professionals be they engineers, doctors or information technology experts, is very high and they have contributed in significant measure to the growth of our services sector during the last decade. Both governments could therefore explore the potential for cooperation in the higher education sector by sending Indian professionals to Kazakhstan and training Kazakh students and professionals in various disciplines in India. The private sector and civil society in both countries should also be actively involved in such cooperation.

As regards economic interaction, it is heartening to see that bilateral trade with India has increased from about US$ 60 million in 2002 to about US$ 196 million in 2007 showing considerable growth. However with the economies of both India and Kazakhstan also registering impressive growth in recent years, there are wide ranging opportunities for both countries to expand the areas of economic cooperation. Greater economic engagement between India and the countries of the region is not only mutually beneficial for the countries but also for the whole region and the world.

I have extended an invitation to Chairman Tokayev during our discussions. I do look forward to receiving him in India.

I am confident that cooperation between both our countries would continue to make good progress for the betterment of people of both our countries.

Inauguration of the Seminar 'Evaluating Committees and Committee System: Changing Contours of Governance and Policy'

The National Social Watch Coalition, New Delhi
18 November 2009

It gives me great pleasure to attend today's seminar organised by the National Social Watch Coalition. The subject matter of the seminar is very topical. Committees, of one form or another, have become central to modern governance. Their utility is underestimated and far removed from the common saying of committees being 'a group of the unwilling, chosen from the unfit, to do the unnecessary.'

Since our Independence, India has emerged as an excellent illustration of a successful parliamentary democracy at work. We have synthesised our cultural and religious diversity and pluralism with a democratic polity. This was possible because of the three elements of the Indian template of parliamentary democracy:

1. Responsible government, stemming from ministerial responsibility, the requirement that the cabinet enjoys the confidence of the House of People, and the President as the trustee of executive power.
2. Representative government, where representativeness includes balancing local, regional and national imperatives; adherence to party positions while undertaking espousal of individual views and judgments; and finally balancing of interests along the lines of gender, economic class and the weaker and marginalised sections of society.
3. Responsive government, where responsiveness is at various tiers of governance–national, states and Panchayati raj institutions. It also means transparency, accountability, public consultation and citizen engagement with the political process.

The Indian Parliament has performed its essential legislative, deliberative and accountability functions with a fair degree of success. Parliamentary committees have become 'mini legislatures' helping Parliament in scrutinising executive and legislative action. They are a link between Parliament and people on one hand and administration and Parliament on the other. Parliamentary committees have a history of around four centuries. They have been the subject of popular praise and even of royal anger. The declaration of 1629 by Charles I against the Commons included a charge of 'extension of their privileges by the Standing Committees'.

Allow me to quote an Australian Parliamentary Study on the utility of the Standing Committee system:

"First: Acting as Parliament's watch dog; assisting in forming a judgment independent of the minister's point of view;

Second: Being a sounding board for the Parliament's reaction to contemplated legislation, regulations, etc;

Third: Acting as a safeguard against hasty, ill considered, legislation due to prior consultation of all interests concerned;

Fourth: Being a place for unprejudiced discussion of problems in an atmosphere where party barriers are substantially eliminated;

Fifth: Being a place where interest groups may be heard by groups of members, and views thereby transmitted to parliamentarians; and

Lastly, acting as a means of enhancing, the standing of Members of Parliament in relation to the government of the day, by their informed contribution to the subject area of the committee."

In view of the subject matter of today's seminar it would be pertinent to look at the functioning of the Department Related Parliamentary Standing Committee system during the last fifteen years. One of my predecessors, Shri K.R. Narayanan, had described the committee system as "a new phase in the evolution of our Parliamentary system" and with an intention "not to weaken or criticise the administration but to strengthen it by investing it with more meaningful Parliamentary support." I believe that the following observations merit your attention:

First: The number of constituents that an Indian Member of Parliament represents is among the largest in the world. The grassroots expectations from a Member of Parliament; range from routine administrative facilitation at district, state and national levels, to ushering in development projects and employment prospects for the constituents.

The Parliamentary reality is very different. An individual Member of Parliament finds that his parliamentary performance is determined in great measure by his political party. It is the party which decides his participation in and time allocation for debates, the broad contours of his view on major policy and legislative issues, and eventually his vote on legislative bills. Many a time, the party's decisions are backed with the issuance of a whip.

Second: The dawn of twenty-four hour media coverage has had a significant impact on the performance of Members of Parliament. Plenary sessions of the House are covered live by the media and have witnessed frequent disruptions and adjournments when members desire to project their enthusiasm on critical issues to their constituents and to their parties.

Third: While ministers have access to their ministries to provide information, undertake research and to seek counsel even during plenary sessions of the House, Members of Parliament do not have such established mechanisms to come to their support. They are expected to independently employ staff both for research and constituency management.

The department related standing committees have addressed most of these problems. Every Member of Parliament is a member of one of the committees. Since the deliberations of the committees are neither televised nor made public, an individual member is in a position to freely air views and opinions on policy issues and legislative bills even if they are not in consonance with those of his Party. Officials of ministries and departments, independent experts and civil society representatives also proffer their advice in a free and frank manner to the committees. This has immensely assisted the work of the standing committees.

One can conclude that to a large extent, the standing committee system has improved parliamentary debate through reports that have enhanced the information available in the public domain, has held officials to account, and influenced the government on major policy and legislative issues.

I offer three suggestions that could help further improve the standing committee system:

First: The lack of ministerial participation in department related standing committees significantly curtails the efficacy and outcomes of the committee process. While heavy demands made on the time of ministers is understandable, their contribution to the work of the standing committees would be very important because political inputs can only be provided at the ministerial level. Perhaps there is a case for looking at the British model and our own parliamentary select committees and joint select committees where ministers dealing with the subject matter are included as members.

Second: We need to build a political consensus so that the room for political and policy expression in Parliament for an individual member is expanded. This could take many forms. For example, the issuance of a whip could be limited to only those bills that could threaten the survival of a government, such as Money Bills or No-Confidence Motions. In other legislative and deliberative business of Parliament, this would enable members to exercise their judgment and articulate their opinion.

Three: Every effort must be made to intensify public engagement and indeed, enchantment, with Parliament and politics. A recent poll in Britain undertaken by the Hansard Society has revealed that around two-thirds of the British population does not feel that they have a good understanding of how Parliament works and only half of the population recognises that Parliament and government are not the same entity. It is also significant that 54 per cent of those polled felt that the media had the most impact on the everyday lives of people whereas only 26 per cent cited the Westminster Parliament as having such an impact.

These are not isolated phenomena. A poll in India might reveal similar results. Parliamentary outreach to the common citizen must receive the highest priority of both the Parliament and the government. Engagement with the standing committee process would be a promising initial effort. The role of civil society and of organisations such as the National Social Watch Coalition is very important in mobilising citizen engagement with the polity and Parliament.

Presentation of Outstanding Parliamentarian Awards

Parliament House, New Delhi

18 August 2010

This is an occasion for celebration of excellence This Award was initiated, belatedly in my view, in 1995 and I congratulate the Indian Parliamentary Group for sustaining it.

I take this opportunity to extend my felicitations to Shri Priya Ranjan Dasmunshi, Shri Mohan Singh and Dr Murli Manohar Joshi for being the distinguished recipients of the Outstanding Parliamentarian Award for the years 2007, 2008 and 2009.

By the recognition bestowed on them today, they have joined the ranks of the select few who have been so honoured. In each case, the honour was preceded by sustained and seminal contribution to the functioning of our parliamentary democracy.

This audience is well aware that discussion and persuasion are amongst the pre-requisites of democracy. To be elected, a candidate has to persuade the voter; after being elected, and in the legislative chamber, the representative needs to persuade others to his/her viewpoint. In both cases, persuasion emanates either from cold reasoning and hard logic or is based on rhetoric that reinforces probable knowledge with an appeal to the sentiments and emotions of the audience. Often, it has elements of both.

The skilled parliamentarian uses both. He or she is at times a cold logician; at others "a bird on the unopinioned wing", perhaps inspired by some higher power within. There are also occasions when the rhetorician is simply "inebriated" by the exuberance of his/her verbosity. The objective in each case is to prevail in discussion.

The Parliament of India has witnessed these skills in good measure and benefited from them. Long time parliament-watchers have also opined that the skilled parliamentarian is tending to become a rarity. This should be a cause for concern.

It is said that we are by nature argumentative. If so, parliamentary deliberation should thrive in our midst. A contrary trend, however, often tends to surface. In it, oratorical skills are replaced by lung power and discussion is sought to be drowned in noise and disruption. It creates momentary excitement, but is no substitute for persuasion. It detracts from the dignity of Parliament and invites public scorn.

The democratic process in a free society like ours makes available to the citizen various means for expression of views on issues of public interest and concern. It also assigns specific roles to the elected representative for whom the choice of form and forum becomes critical. Legislation, deliberation and seeking accountability are the three principal areas of activity that must be explored on a continuous basis within the legislative chamber. The three award winners today and many others before them earned name and fame by skilful indulgence in each of these. They set standards worthy of emulation.

I do hope that the Outstanding Parliamentary Award would induce others in this gathering to strive to improve the parliamentary discourse and thereby lend weight and substance to the most important edifice of our democracy.

Centenary Celebrations

Bihar Legislative Council, Patna
12 April 2012

To come to one of the most ancient seats of governance in the country is to share in a fleeting moment some of its illustrious history.

It gives me great pleasure to participate in the centenary celebrations of the Bihar Legislative Council. I convey my heartiest congratulations to the present and former members of the Council and to the Government and people of Bihar.

The Bihar Legislative Council has a noteworthy past. It is intricately connected to the movement for the formation of the State of Bihar during the early days of our freedom struggle. It was on 25 August 1911 that a recommendation was made by the Government of India for formation of the Council under the Indian Councils Act 1861 and Government of India Act 1909 (as amended in 1912). The first sitting of the Council was convened on 20 January 1913 at Bankipore.

Bihar's legislature turned bicameral under the Government of India Act 1919 and under the Government of India Act 1935. After Independence, the Bihar Legislative Council was summoned on 16 February1950 and has continued its glorious democratic tradition ever since.

It is a matter of record that over the years, the Council distinguished itself by taking initiatives for public welfare. It was the Council's initiative that resulted in women getting voting rights, in the provision of educational facilities to children of Patna, and the opening of Tibbi and Ayurvedic dispensaries.

The Council's pioneering experiment in holding the 'Child Assembly' sessions allowed children from different parts of the state to present their problems and demanded urgent solutions.

The observance of a centenary is an appropriate occasion for introspection on its objectives and vision and the path it has traversed; it also provides an opportunity for prognosis on its role in the foreseeable future.

I propose to use this opportunity to ponder over the importance of bicameralism and the significance of the Second Chamber in Parliamentary democracies, especially where State structures are decentralised or regionalised.

Bicameralism has a long history and is in vogue in many lands. John Adams, one of the Founding Fathers of the American constitution, wrote in 1776 that "since the legislative power was sovereign, it required the balance of constituent interests within its institutional structure. Elsewhere, the need to have representation of unrepresented or under-represented segments of opinion as also to provide opportunity for second thoughts on proposed legislation has provided the rationale for it."

In our country, and during the drafting of the Constitution, somewhat divergent perceptions were voiced. The Constitutional adviser for the Union constitution committee specifically noted that Second Chambers were important for representation of special interests of classes, as a check on hasty and ill conceived legislation of the Lower House and to provide equal representation to different constituent units. Gopalaswami Aiyangar supported the creation of the Upper House for similar reasons and concluded that "the balance of consideration is in favour of having such a Chamber and taking care to see that it does not prove a clog either to legislation or administration".

The matter, however, was viewed differently when it came to the issue of State Legislatures. The Government of India Act 1935 had provided for a unicameral state legislature for all Provinces except for the six Provinces of Madras, Bombay, Bengal, United Provinces, Bihar and Assam. The Provincial Constitution Committee in its meetings in June, 1947 decided that as a general rule all State Legislatures should be unicameral, and that Second Chambers may be constituted in States where special circumstances existed.

Speaking in the Constituent Assembly in January, 1949 Professor K.T. Shah supported the need for a Second Chamber in the Central Legislature but was tentative about their relevance in Units, concluding that "the place of the Second Chamber may be left entirely to the units themselves".

The Chairman of the Drafting Committee, Dr B.R. Ambedkar spoke in a similar vein and said:

> I cannot say that I am very strongly prepossessed in favour of a Second Chamber. To me, it is like the Curate's egg – good only in parts. All that we are doing by this constitution is to introduce the Second Chamber purely as an experimental measure. We have not, by the Draft Constitution, given the Chamber a permanent place, we have not made it a permanent part of our Constitution. It is a purely experimental measure ... and there is sufficient provision … for getting rid of the Second Chamber.

The number of legislative councils in the country today remain in number the same as at the time of our Independence–six. Today, the legislatures of Andhra Pradesh, Bihar, Jammu and Kashmir, Karnataka, Maharashtra and Uttar Pradesh are bicameral. The people of these states have found the Second Chamber useful and have retained it. But a few questions do arise:

- Does the Second Chamber in the States represent different interests than those represented in the First Chamber?
- Does the Second Chamber introduce a different kind of expertise that is useful for informed deliberation and law making as compared to the First Chamber?
- Has the Second Chamber succeeded in making legislation harder to pass with enhanced consideration of the merits of such legislation that would be the case in its absence?

An honest answer to these questions suggests that the glass is half-full.

To comprehend the context, we need to dwell more closely on the twin concepts of political representation and democratic space. Both are critical to reinforcing the legitimacy of our democratic institutions and in ensuring responsiveness of government to the needs of citizens.

Two questions come to mind: How representative are our elected representatives? What can be done to enhance their representative-ness and thereby add to their capacity to reflect the concerns of the citizen body?

In all the elections conducted under the Constitution, formalistic representation has been a success. The near-continuous whirring of the electoral cycle has meant that at the Central, State and Local government levels, regular and periodic elections ensure that citizens are represented in political and governance institutions.

However, the first-past-the-post system of electoral representation has produced its own set of problems. Electoral record for the Lok Sabha elections shows that in the past five general elections the number of winning candidates who secured 50 per cent or more of the valid votes polled has varied between 121 and 221; it was 121 in 2009.

Earlier, the Venkatachaliah Commission had surveyed the record of three general elections to conclude that over two-thirds of the members of the Lok Sabha and almost 90 per cent of the members of some of the State Legislative Assemblies were elected on a minority vote.

A cursory analysis of the huge discrepancy between percentages of votes polled and seats won in elections points to what a perceptive observer of our electoral scene has rightly called the "paradox" of a deepening representative democracy coexisting with a thinning of the very idea of representation. This paradox, he adds, "plays out differently in different domains of the democratic arena and most commonly takes the form of an encounter between a dynamic political process and an inflexible institutional response".

While legitimacy of representation is one matter, the issue of accountability of representatives is equally pressing. The ability of citizens to hold their representative to account for failing to act in accordance with their wishes or for lack of adequate responsiveness to them is critical for a functioning democracy.

It is essential that we consider our polity and electoral system in the context of our experience of the last six decades, the mandate of our constitutional framework and the future outcomes that we desire from them for the benefit of our citizens.

It needs reiteration that our citizens today seek enhanced representativeness, prompt societal accommodation and conciliation, implementation of constitutional and international safeguards to vulnerable groups, provision of accountable, stable and efficient governance, enhanced legislative oversight and the development of effective and internally-democratic political parties.

Allow me to add that structures and functions are not frozen in time and need to respond to changing requirements of the public and its urge for democratic space and expression.

It is here that the role of the Second Chamber in states comes into focus. I would argue that Legislative Councils widen political participation in our society, give opportunities for political representation to professionals and eminent citizens from outside the realm of political parties, and bring the voice of the third tier of government–the Local government–to decision making and law making processes. They act as a break on hasty legislation.

Legislative Councils are an important optional institution incorporated by our Founding Fathers to cater to special circumstances of states. Their utility is in enhancing inclusive and participatory governance and strengthening the pillars of democracy.

The Bihar Legislative Council is standing testimony that the 'experimental measure' referred to by Dr Ambedkar has succeeded in enlarging the circle and widening the participatory ambit of our democracy.

Yet, a word of caution is in order. Any legislative institution is only as effective as the Executive desires it to be. One disturbing trend of the past few years is the declining number of sittings per year of Legislative Assemblies and Councils in the country, sometimes declining to single digits! This is not conducive to facilitating effective and efficient functioning of our democracy. We must do everything to increase the number of sittings of our legislative bodies.

Sixtieth Anniversary of the Parliament of India

Parliament House, New Delhi

13 May 2012

It is a privilege to participate in this historic function to mark the Sixtieth Anniversary of the Parliament of India.

We celebrate the occasion with happiness, humility and hope: joy at the distance travelled; humility in remembrance of the sacrifices made by our people; hope and expectation for a radiant future for the nation and its citizens.

The functioning of our Parliament, based on universal suffrage, is a testament to our brand of democratic politics. It was unimaginable, in scale and reach, at the inception of the Republic.

Perfection eludes human creations. Nevertheless, our Parliament has been successful in good measure in representing and harmonising the diversity of our social and political interests, and in moving forward on the basis of commonality and inclusion, rather than superiority and exclusion.

While much has been achieved, more needs to be done to attain the lofty objectives so succinctly delineated in the Preamble of the Constitution.

New imperatives propel us. We do need to respond meaningfully to awakened expectation of a new generation in a changing world.

Sixty years is a good time to assess the working of Parliament in two critical areas of its functioning: ensuring accountability and oversight of the executive, and deliberation and law making.

Both tend to exhibit declining efficacy. The institutional mechanisms and procedural norms for ensuring accountability are being progressively underused. There is a perceptible drop in the working days of Parliament. Deliberation is less frequent; legislation is at times hasty.

An impression is afoot in some quarters that diligent parliamentary work is less rewarding in political terms. Despite it, excellent work is being done in some in parliamentary committees. Public awareness of this, through appropriate means, is essential in this age of instant information.

Our citizens know, must know, that Parliament is central to economic reform and development as these hinge on bringing about new laws, amending old ones and harmonising differences. As we see nation after nation suffering from fiscal problems, we are reminded of the key responsibility of Parliaments around the world in prudent fiscal management and ensuring financial accountability.

Earlier today, both Houses of Parliament have resolved to reinvigorate their working. These supplement the resolves and resolutions of yesteryears. Despite it, sceptics amongst the citizen body, seeking faster outcomes in practical terms, may well be induced to recall an Urdu couplet:

"Tere va'de par jiye hum, to yeh jaan, jhoot jana
Kih khushi se mar na jate agar etibar hota"
Had I lived on your pledge, I would surely have lost life
Out of sheer joy and ecstasy, if I had believed in it.

We must therefore restore our legislatures to their earlier norms of functioning. It is all the more necessary to restore such salience to the Parliament as we negotiate a difficult economic and social evolution in an era of globalisation, international economic churning and an unstable external strategic environment.

Our collective resolve on this historic occasion must be, to use the words of Jawaharlal Nehru, to restore "the majesty of Parliament".

Fourth Dr B.R. Ambedkar Memorial Lecture on 'Some Questions on Elections, Representation and Democracy'
New Delhi
17 December 2012

Some Questions on Elections, Representation and Democracy

I deem it an honour to be invited to deliver the Fourth Dr B.R Ambedkar Memorial lecture.

Babasaheb Ambedkar was a towering personality in the early years of our Republic. He was a distinguished political leader, eminent constitutionalist, jurist, thinker and a radical social reformer. He was also a rationalist and an iconoclast. As Chairman of Drafting Committee of our Constitution, he is often called 'Father of the Indian Constitution'.

His exemplary work for the upliftment of marginalised and deprived sections of our society has given him a very prominent place in the pantheon of the architects of Modern India.

Our Founding Fathers had the vision to comprehend that given India's ethos, diversity and requirements a representative parliamentary democracy was the most suited form of political system. Today, we have emerged as the world's largest democracy characterised by regular, free and fair elections based on universal adult suffrage to determine the will of the people as to who should be entrusted with the duty of governance.

The entire exercise of an Indian General Election is mind boggling: in 2009 the electorate numbered more than 714 million; it was catered to by 10 lakh polling booths in which about 50 lakh personnel were deployed. 360 parties put forth candidates. The average voter turnout was 59.7 per cent.

As elections are the bedrock of any functioning democracy, a citizen is entitled to assess their efficacy in quantitative and qualitative terms and, for this purpose, examine the mechanism for their conduct and the adequacy of the end product.

The electoral methodology adopted and practised by us is the single member plurality system, otherwise known as the First-Past-the Post (FPTP) system. The traditional arguments in its favour are that (a) it tends to provide a clear-cut contest between two or more major parties (b) its working is easy for voters to understand (c) it allows individuals who are not members of a political party to run as independents (d) it tends to produce stable governments and (e) it is likely to produce a strong opposition party.

Despite the above, the system is not universal and critics have commented on its limitations. These relate to the (i) disconnect between the vote share and the number of seats won (ii) propensity to over-reward major parties and under-reward smaller parties (iii) likelihood of smaller parties with strong regional base getting a 'seat bonus' and winning more seats than their corresponding share of the popular vote.

Experience of six decades propels us to question the certitudes of the First Past the Post system, consider its limitations, and acknowledge that there are a number of areas in the process that need to be looked at for corrective and improvement.

The changed context has to be borne in mind. There has been since 1989 what Yogendra Yadav has called "a fundamental transformation in the terrain of politics which in turn is anchored in the process of social change." As a result, the participatory base of electoral democracy has expanded. There has also been a "fractionalisation of the political space."

A number of government committees since 1990, have cogitated on the question of reforms relating to different aspects of the electoral process. These have dealt principally with criminalisation in politics, funding of elections, election campaign procedures and reform of election expenditure laws. Their objective was to improve the efficacy of the system and attend to the lacunae that came to notice. Some of these, like the Law Commission Report of 1999 and the National Commission to Review the Working of the Constitution (2001) also touched upon the question of qualitative improvement in the degree of representative-ness of the elected candidates.

Useful suggestions have also emanated from civil society groups; think-tanks and NGOs have likewise contributed to the discussions.

The most recent effort in this direction is in the shape of the Background Paper on Electoral Reforms initiated in December 2010 by the Ministry of Law and Justice and co-sponsored by the Election Commission of India. It confines itself to "explore options for electoral reforms within the framework of the current system and will not address these larger structural issues." Pursuant to it, a Core Committee has held regional consultation in seven state capitals; in some of these views on systematic reforms have also been expressed.

II

My purpose today is to dwell on one aspect of this debate and probe the concept of the *representative-ness of the elected representative*. The question has a theoretical dimension as well as an empirical one. Dr Ambedkar's vision of "one person, one vote, one value" is yet to be realised and may have to await a more egalitarian social milieu. In terms of existing reality, an elected candidate in our system is one who has secured a plurality, not a majority, of votes cast in his/her electoral constituency. Here some questions arise:

- Did the candidate obtain a majority of total votes or a majority of the votes cast? If the latter, would it constitute a *majority* in terms of the democratic principle of 50+1? If not, and in case the electoral decision reflects the will of a minority of the total electorate, how and to what extent would the candidate be considered *representative*?
- If this pattern is repeated in a good many other constituencies, could a situation arise in which an elected assembly has a majority, or good percentage of the majority party or combination, of members elected on a minority vote in their own constituencies?

- Would such a body be considered representative of the electorate as a whole? Would such a situation derogate from the principle of majority rule?

A look at the empirical data provides some justification for raising these questions. In the first general election in 1952, the percentage of successful candidates who secured less than 50 per cent of the votes cast was 67.28. This figure went down to 58.09 per cent in 1957. In the 13th, 14th, and 15th general elections in 1999, 2004, and 2009 respectively, it was 60.03, 75.87 and 82.68 respectively.

The conclusion is inescapable that a majority of elected members of the Lok Sabha in recent years, and even earlier, won on a minority of votes cast in their constituencies. This is compounded by the absence, in our system, of compulsory voting. Thus if a candidate is elected on 30 per cent of the votes cast and if the percentage of polling is the constituency is 60, then the positive mandate secured by the candidate is 30 per cent of 60 per cent, that is, just 18 per cent of the total electorate.

Such an outcome has a distorting impact on the composition of the elected legislature. This is vividly demonstrated by the vote-share seat-won data relating to all the fifteen Lok Sabhas.

The situation is no better, perhaps worse, in State assembly elections with percentage of returned candidates on minority of votes cast going above 70 per cent in several cases.

What are the ramifications of such an outcome? Observers have noted that it induces candidates to focus on securing votes of a segment of the electorate and thereby accentuate or reinforce social divisions based on caste, creed, faith or language. For this purpose, and despite formal legal or regulatory constrains, candidates or their supporters do succeed in invoking narrower loyalties to further electoral appeal. The excluded or marginalised social groups 'then indulge in strategic voting.' Divisive tendencies and social conflict is necessarily the end product.

The foregoing would suggest a need to revisit the electoral procedures to ensure a greater measure of representative-ness in the elected representatives of the people. This is essential to achieve in greater measure the purpose of democratic form of governance.

III

Suggestions have been made with regard to possible correctives to the present system. Principal among these are (a) Mixed Compensatory Proportional Representation on the German model and (b) Second Ballot System to achieve a 50 per cent +1 result. Their merits need to be carefully assessed in terms of our conditions.

- The 'German model' or the List System requires that the overall representation of parties in legislature be based on the proportion of valid votes (at least 10 per cent of the total) obtained by them. Fifty per cent of the legislators will be elected from territorial constituencies based on FPTP system. This will ensure a link between the legislator and the constituents. The balance of 50 per cent will be allocated to parties to make up for their shortfall based on proportion of votes. The party list for the latter will be selected democratically by its members. To operate this system, each voter will be required to cast two votes, one for each category. An essential prerequisite of this system is legal regulation of the internal functioning of political parties. It also requires a more literate electorate.

A diluted version of this model, suitable for 'Indian reality', was considered by the 1999 Law Commission Report on Electoral Reforms. It suggested that recognised political parties obtaining at least 5 per cent of the total votes be considered to be eligible for allocation from 25 per cent of the seats earmarked for party lists.

- The Second Ballot system involves a run-off between the first two contenders in an election if neither of them obtains less than 50 per cent of the votes cast. It retains most of the advantages of

> the present system but would ensure that parties and candidates seek a wider mandate from the electorate, broaden their vote catchments, and thereby minimise appeal to parochial sentiments which is becoming a source of concern in terms of social cohesion.

The basic premise, and requirement, in a democratic election is to ascertain through the ballot, the wish of the majority of voters in the constituency concerned. It cannot therefore be argued that the First-Past-the-Post system now in vogue, whatever may have been the compulsions for adopting it, is theoretically valid or practically the most desirable. As a mature democracy, and one in which correctives in the electoral procedures continues to be work in progress, there is a need to debate the representative-ness of the representative regardless of political convenience or administrative constraints.

This fundamental corrective in the electoral system can and must be added to other electoral reforms proposed by the Election Commission of India and others and are under consideration of the of the government, as indicated in the reply given by the government in the parliament recently. There is also a strong case for accelerating the process.

IV

'Conditions Precedent for the Successful Working of Democracy' was the title of a lecture given by Dr Ambedkar in December 1952. He defined democracy as "a form and method of government whereby revolutionary changes in the economic and social life of the people are brought about without bloodshed." He listed seven conditions as essential for the successful functioning of democracy and said there should be (a) no glaring inequalities in society (b) a strong opposition (c) no tyranny of the majority over the minority (d) equality in law and administration (e) observance of constitutional morality (f) functioning of moral order in society (g) public conscience.

Ambedkar concluded the lecture by mentioning some cases of failure of democracy and said "we ought to be very cautious and very considerate regarding our own future".

Six decades later, we have to concede that the glass of democracy remains half full. We have practised electoral democracy mechanically without making it fully representative. Our electoral procedures and practices have accentuated rather than diminish social cleavages. We have yet to succeed in eradicating electoral malpractices. We have allowed money power in all its manifestations to distort electoral outcomes. Our political process depicts ideological decadence and a declining observance of constitutional morality. Our society exhibits a disturbing disregard for moral order and public conscience and, in the words of an eminent academic, "the lines between legality and illegality, order and disorder, state and criminality, have come to be increasingly porous."

Are we on a slippery slope? There is, clearly an imperative need for rejuvenating our commitment to the values, objectives and the judicious balance of the Constitution.

Public Health

❝India bears a huge burden of the global case load of chronic diseases. These diseases are preventable and cause a huge loss to the national economies, communities and families

Eighteenth Convocation

The Tamil Nadu Dr M.G.R Medical University, Chennai
20 September 2008

I am happy to be in the historic city of Chennai. It is a privilege for me to be invited to address the Eighteenth Convocation of this university.

Convocations are special occasions. They mark the graduation of knowledge seekers from the sanctuary of the academia to the realities and vicissitudes of life outside it.

Convocations also provide opportunity to honour the best and brightest in our academic, social and public life. Today, eight eminent personalities have been honoured with the conferment on them of Doctor of Science (*honoris causa*) in recognition of their immense contribution and excellence. I warmly congratulate them and hope that their example would inspire many more students to emulate them.

We live in vibrant, fast changing times. The India of today is significantly different from what it was on the morrow of freedom. Wider horizons beckon us. Opportunities are greater, so are challenges. Both confront the young graduates as they move into their working lives and careers in a society where monetary compensation and material comforts are increasingly viewed as the sole determinants of success.

At the same time, every calling in life has its own imperatives. In your case, the contours of dharma were first indicated in the ancient Oath prescribed in the fourth century BC by the Father of Medicine, Hippocrates of Cos. This has been reiterated in all cultures. In our country, it is undertaken through the Oath stipulated by the Indian Medical Council (Professional Conduct, Etiquette and Ethics) Regulations, 2002. Its operative clauses are service to humanity, practice of profession with conscience and dignity, and the primacy of the patient's health.

Chapter V of these Regulations calls on physicians as 'good citizens and possessed of special training 'to engage on public health issues as part of their duties to the public and to the profession.

I would urge you, individually and collectively, to ponder on the import of these pledges and what they would mean in your professional life day by day.

In the presence today of a new generation of men and women dedicating themselves to the noble calling of medicine, I would like to dwell on some aspects of our public health policies.

The Economic Survey 2007-08 indicates that 'India's position on health parametres compared even to some of its neighbours continues to be unsatisfactory'. It notes that "inadequacies in the existing health infrastructure have led to gaps in coverage and outreach services" and that "wide inter-state, male-female and rural-urban disparities in outcomes and impacts continue to persist".

Our high maternal mortality rate of 450 per hundred thousand live births compares poorly with figures of 58 for Sri Lanka and 45 for China.

Likewise, on the other key health parametre of infant mortality rate, our figure of 56 deaths per thousand live births is significantly worse in comparison to the figure of 12 for Sri Lanka, 23 for China and 54 for Bangladesh. The situation is the same for the under five mortality rate and life expectancy at birth.

These are not mere statistics. These are issues of life and death and go to the very core of the right to life and survival.

These are also matters of moral and political obligation. The State, according to Article 47 of the Constitution, 'shall regard the raising of the level of nutrition and the standard of living of its people and the improvement of public health as among its primary duties'. These remain substantially unfulfilled six decades after Independence.

Why has this happened? How can it be remedied?

The first obstacle is conceptual. Health and health policies are not usually looked at from the prism of social justice. Yet, as the Commission on Social Determinants of Health set up by the WHO notes, "social justice is a matter of life and death (as) it affects the way people live, their consequent chance of illness and their risk of pre-mature death". Promoting health equity and eradicating avoidable inequalities in health are vitally dependent on the public policy focus on the social determinants of health. The Commission calls for improving daily living conditions across the population spectrum and a strong public sector role accompanied by a strengthened government and governance dedicated to equity.

As you are aware, our healthcare policies have primarily been predicated on State action, with State responsibility for healthcare and free medical care for all, including for those who are able to pay for those services. Yet, pressures on budgets and public expenditures combined with inadequacies in the governmental machinery for healthcare delivery have led to sub-optimal outcomes.

The advent of economic liberalisation and globalisation has led to the emergence of a strong private sector, including in medical education and healthcare. Surprisingly, however, we have not been able to evolve a coherent and consensual policy on the role of the private sector; nor have we succeeded in articulating the public duties of private professionals in key sectors such as healthcare.

What are the choices before our citizens in terms of healthcare?

The government spends around 1 per cent of GDP on health whereas private expenditure on health is four times the government expenditure. Government expenditure on health as a percentage of total government expenditure is around 3.5 per cent. Our citizens spend over 75 per cent of the aggregate expenditure on health as out-of-pocket expenditure incurred towards private practitioners of various kinds.

The burden of curative treatment is thus primarily borne by citizens who have to mainly rely on private health services. The choice is thus stark – limited and weak public health service network or expensive and elaborate private health services. If the poor have the misfortune of facing a life threatening health condition, should they either incur heavy debt for requisite health services or suffer morbidity and mortality?

A recently published survey of BPL households, undertaken jointly by Transparency International India and Centre for Media Studies, indicates the levels of corruption in regard to access by the poor of hospital facilities.

It need not be this way. Health need not be transformed into a tradable quantity as a result of a switch to market orientation and advocacy to review the role of public sector. From the viewpoint of the citizen, accessibility and cost would and should remain the determinants.

Inequities arise when vital public services such as education and health are not recognised as basic and fundamental human rights but are left to the harsh vagaries of the market place.

Such inequities further deepen when the government and the regulators of the health sector and the medical profession cannot adequately articulate and assign useful and practical roles to the private sector as also public duties for private professionals.

Private medical practice in the country remains a dominant presence in the health sector. It is troubling that some of its important features do not promote health equity. Let me mention a few:

1. Private medical practice has primarily remained urban with a proliferation of hospitals and clinics in towns and cities. This process has been substantially aided by the emergence of doctor entrepreneurs in the country.
2. Private tertiary healthcare is increasingly getting corporatised through company structures and even listing on the stock markets. One reads today of large investments in private healthcare and establishment of hospital chains across the country with private equity and venture capital funding.
3. This commoditisation of health services has meant that the interest of shareholders and other stakeholders have at times assumed precedence over the interest of patients. In many of these corporate hospitals, the focus is as much on valuation, operating profit margin and return on capital as on medical and health metrics.
4. Even as India has emerged as a destination for 'medical tourism' due to the high quality of private medical services, the public service role of the private hospitals has not been commensurate. Though many such private hospitals have been provided government land at concessional rates and favourable customs and tax treatment,

there are questions regarding their commitment to provide free or concessional treatment to poor patients.

5. The legal structure of a private health facility today ranges from a charitable trust, a registered society, a private limited company or a public limited company. In each of these cases, they are regulated by different bodies for distinct administrative and financial aspects. Industry or professional self-regulation bodies do not exist for accreditation, setting up standards and for institutional licensing. In the absence of any other regulatory and accreditation structures for such private health services, patients have the sole recourse to consumer courts and other such fora.

The government's role as public health service provider is adapting to the changing scenario. It would appear that such a role is being complemented with an ancillary role of a health facilitator, primarily through government support for enhancing health insurance coverage. Some of these schemes that so far have been tried in limited geographical and occupational contexts and with limited coverage have been successful. Some of the examples include the Rashtriya Swasthya Bima Yojana for BPL card holders, the Health Insurance Scheme for weavers and the Rajiv Gandhi Shilpi Swasthya Bima Yojana for artisans. Some of the state governments have also initiated their own health insurance schemes, such as the Rajiv Aarogyasri Community Health Insurance Scheme in Andhra Pradesh and the Yeshasvini Cooperative Farmers Health Insurance Scheme in Karnataka.

Health insurance provides a way of risk pooling and cost sharing among various segments of the population. The expansion of the health insurance sector is currently focused on urban areas and the middle and upper classes. Necessary secondary and tertiary infrastructure in rural areas is inadequate for effective health coverage to sections that cannot afford health insurance premiums.

Health insurance, in the final analysis, is not a panacea because, on its own, it would be unable to address the enormous inequity in healthcare provision. Government would continue to be looked upon as the prime provider for secondary and tertiary healthcare by the poorer segments of our population. Such prime responsibility of governance cannot be outsourced.

It has taken us six decades for the right to primary education to be debated and considered as a fundamental right of the young citizens of this nation. Let us hope that it would not take another six decades for healthcare access to be considered a fundamental right of our citizens.

I particularly appeal to the graduating students today to ponder over their role to make this happen. More than at any other time in our history, you would be called upon to perform the inherent public duties of your profession even as you pursue your careers in the private sector. In doing so, you also need to see how the promotion of a healthy lifestyle could be furthered since prevention is always a better option than cure.

I wish you professional success, happiness and decades of service to humanity.

Fourth Convocation

Chhatrapati Sahuji Maharaj Medical University, Lucknow
6 January 2009

It gives me great pleasure to be the chief guest at the Fourth Convocation of the Chhatrapati Sahuji Maharaj Medical University. It carries the weight of history and the legacy of impressive achievements of its distinguished alumni. As the first residential medical university in the country, it had performed a pioneering role since its inception almost a century ago.

I take this opportunity to felicitate the students graduating today, and those who have won medals for their academic excellence in specific disciplines of medicine.

The distinguished awardees of the Honorary Degree in Sciences fully deserve the recognition bestowed upon them for their outstanding contributions to medicine, medical education and public service.

Convocation is a "rite of passage" from the academia; for the professionals it also marks their formal entry into a select group having its own ethics, norms and codes of conduct.

In the case of men and women of medicine, the contours of dharma were first indicated in the ancient Oath prescribed in the fourth century BC by the Father of Medicine-Hippocrates of Cos. This has been reiterated in all cultures. In our country, it is undertaken through the Oath stipulated by the Indian Medical Council (Professional Conduct, Etiquette and Ethics) Regulations, 2002. Its operative clauses are service to humanity, practice of profession with conscience and dignity, and the primacy of the patient's health.

Chapter V of these Regulations calls on physicians "as good citizens and possessed of special training" to engage on public health issues as part of their duties to the public and to the profession.

I would urge you, individually and collectively, to ponder on the import of these pledges and what they would mean to you in your professional life.

II

We live in changing times. Rapid economic growth of the past decade has not only lifted many of our people from poverty but also brought about highly uneven access to the fruits of development along multiple dimensions of region, class, community and gender.

Let me illustrate the latter point with reference to public health, and on the authority of the WHO. The World Health Report 2008 highlights three conclusions:

- that the responses of the health sector to the changing world have been 'inadequate and naïve';
- that "left to their own devices, health systems do not gravitate naturally towards the goals of health for all through primary healthcare";
- that "health systems are developing in directions that contribute little to equity and social justice and fail to get the best health outcomes for their money".

The report specifically outlines five common short comings of healthcare delivery:

1. Inverse care, where people with the most means and with lesser healthcare needs are largest consumers of healthcare leaving those with the least means and greater need for healthcare with minimal access.
2. Impoverishing care, where lack of social protection and large out of pocket expenses push the sick into grinding poverty.
3. Fragmented care, where excessive and a narrow focus on specialised curative care discourages a holistic approach to healthcare.
4. Unsafe care, due to poor safety and hygiene standards and other avoidable adversities that more often impact the poor.

5. Misdirected care, where the potential of primary prevention and health promotion to prevent up to 70 per cent of disease burden is neglected with a clustering of resource allocation around high cost curative services.

Within our own country, and indeed in the state of Uttar Pradesh, available data clearly points to the significant gap between the aspiration of citizens for good quality public healthcare and the reality.

The data for Uttar Pradesh from the National Family Health Survey of 2005-06 brings out the following:

- Around half of the women in the age group between fifteen to fifty and 85 per cent of children under three years in the state suffer from anaemia;
- Around half of the children are stunted and underweight;
- Less than a quarter of children have been completely immunised;
- Infant mortality in Uttar Pradesh is seventy-three per thousand live births as compared to the all-India figure of fifty-seven;
- Less than 10 per cent households in the state have access to piped drinking water in comparison to the all-India figure of 42 per cent; only 43 per cent of households in UP have electricity as compared to 68 per cent nation-wide; 33 per cent in the state have access to toilet facility as compared to 45 per cent India-wide.

The life expectancy at birth is fifty-six years in UP as against seventy-four years in Kerala. It would thus seem that the state you are born into determines how long you would live. The meaning of this for the 180 million population of Uttar Pradesh is profoundly disturbing.

These figures have national relevance since Uttar Pradesh is home to one-sixth of our population.

It is to be recalled that the state of health of citizens is a component of the globally and nationally accepted parametres of human development. On this count, and as the State Planning Department has noted, "UP continues to languish at a low level of human development".

III

These facts pose a question: what can state policy, and the medical profession, do to address it?

The matter needs to be considered in terms of perceptions, policy, infrastructure, budgetary allocations and administrative procedures, role of the public and private sectors and mechanisms for medical insurance. Each of these calls for a serious public debate. Allow me to highlights some aspects:

In the first place: Uttar Pradesh has the highest loss in the country due to premature death and disability from non-fatal illness. There is an imperative need to address this through explicit commitments in policy and programmes. The focus has to be on reduction in infant mortality.

Secondly: Substantial investment in physical infrastructure is imperative. The population covered by a sub-centre in UP is 7080 and the average distance is 3.4 kilometres while the national average is 5109 and 1.3 kilometres respectively. As a result, only 9 per cent of the state's population makes use of government facilities for treatment of ordinary ailments with the rest depending on private healthcare. Over 11 per cent of the population is not able to access medical care due to locational reasons, and even when they do access, there is no guarantee of sustained care.

Only 11 per cent of population of Uttar Pradesh receives antenatal care compared to 85 per cent in Kerala and only 11.3 per cent are institutional deliveries for UP compared to 96.6 per cent for Kerala.

This state of affairs has disastrous consequences for the poor. According to the state's Planning Department, "health expenditure is the second biggest cause of rural indebtedness" and "over 40 per cent of hospitalised persons borrow heavily or sell assets to cover expenses and 25 per cent Indians fall below the poverty line because of hospital expenses while in Uttar Pradesh this figure is around 34 per cent".

Thirdly: Greater attention must be paid by policy makers to management and service delivery reforms. There is a high vacancy list in our PHC (Primary Health Care)s and hospitals. The Planning Department of UP has noted "the reluctance of doctors to serve in rural areas has become a major impediment in the government's ability to provide health services to the rural population". A World Bank study estimated that absenteeism among doctors at PHCs is around 45 per cent.

The WHO has called for "replacing disproportionate reliance on command and control on one hand, and laissez-faire disengagement of the state on the other, by the inclusive, participatory, negotiation based leadership". Modalities for these changes need to be developed expeditiously.

Fourthly: Alongside augmentation of physical infrastructure there is a compelling need for enhancing the human resources in the health sector. There is an acute shortage of doctors and paramedics. UP has eleven medical colleges, and faces a deficit of twenty-four medical colleges based on the norm of one medical college per 50 lakh population. There are less than 5900 sanctioned posts of nurses for the whole state and over 800 of these remain vacant. It is estimated that in the next six years, UP would need around 1lakh nurses.

Fifthly: Preventive healthcare must regain the primary focus, with concomitant resource allocation. Cost effective interventions have been suggested by the National Commission on Macroeconomics and Health in regard to infant mortality, nutrition, tuberculosis, smoking and tobacco use and unsafe sex. According to the Commission, reduction in childhood mortality may raise the life expectancy at birth of an Indian by over three years, and our GDP by over 4 per cent.

Sixthly: We must effectively integrate provision of private sector health services with those provided by the public sector. The government and the regulators of the health sector and the medical profession have not adequately articulated and assigned useful and practical roles to the private sector as also public duties for private medical professionals. Industry or professional self-regulation bodies do not exist only for accreditation, setting up standards and for institutional licensing of private health facilities in the country. This regulatory lacuna must be immediately addressed both at the centre and state levels.

And finally, we must take note of the growing importance of health insurance for various segments of the population. Central and state governments are enhancing their support for health insurance coverage in limited geographical and occupational contexts, with some success. Some of the examples include the Rashtriya Swasthya Bima Yojana for BPL card holders, the Rajiv Aarogyasri Community Health Insurance Scheme in Andhra Pradesh and the Yeshasvini Cooperative Farmers Health Insurance Scheme in Karnataka.

Health insurance provides a way of risk pooling and cost sharing among various segments of the population. While this is not a panacea, Uttar Pradesh could look at the successful experience of other governments and seek to emulate where possible.

V

I wish to appeal to the students graduating today to ponder over their professional role and the societal expectation of them. You would be called upon to perform the inherent public duties of your profession even as you pursue your careers in the private sector. How many of you would venture to work in rural areas and for how long? How many would pursue your profession within the state?

Your decisions on some of the policy and ethical issues would have far ranging implications for Uttar Pradesh, and for the country. Remember that each one of you matters in the much delayed and arduous task of providing basic healthcare to our citizens.

I wish you professional success, happiness and decades of service to humanity.

The J.R.D. Tata Awards for Population and Reproductive Health Programmes to the Best Adjudged States

Population Foundation of India, New Delhi
9 January 2009

It is my privilege to be the chief guest at the presentation ceremony of the Fourth J.R.D. Tata Awards for the best performing states on Population and Reproductive Health Programmes.

The Population Foundation and its work stand as a tribute to the vision, initiative and tireless work of J.R.D. Tata to address the population problem of the country and its impact on the prospects of our development and progress.

This distinguished audience today bears testimony to the success of the Foundation in fashioning an alternative paradigm to address of population question, by doing it through the civil society. It is the affirmation of an equitable, decentralised, rights-based and participative approach to human development, one aspect of which is population stabilisation. Its concomitants are access to affordable health care, education, sanitation, safe drinking water, and empowerment of women.

I take this opportunity to congratulate the Chief Minister of Sikkim and the Health Minister of Chhattisgarh for receiving the Fourth J.R.D. Tata Award for Population and Reproductive Health Programmes for the year 2008.

Their performance proves that political will, and a determination to bring about change, is as important as resources.

The website of the Foundation displays the population clock. Just before I left for this venue, it read 1,279,906,779. It also indicates that there are twenty-nine births in India every minute. This amounts to 41,760 births a day. Of these 2380 die every day amounting to a mortality rate of fifty-seven per thousand live births.

Such high infant mortality feeds into high wanted fertility, demolishing all efforts at reducing the total fertility rate.

Confronted with these figures, one is propelled to re-visit the National Population Policy 2000 and its layered targets.

The immediate objective of NPP was to address the unmet needs for contraception, health care infrastructure, and health personnel, and provide integrated service delivery for basic reproductive and child health care.

The medium-term objective was to bring the TFR (Total Fertility Rate) to replacement levels by 2010, through vigorous implementation of inter-sectoral operational strategies. The long-term objective was to achieve a stable population by 2045, at a level consistent with the requirements of sustainable economic growth, social development, and environmental protection.

In pursuance of these objectives, a set of seven National Socio-Demographic Goals, to be achieved by 2010, were set out:

- Address the unmet needs for basic reproductive and child health services, supplies and infrastructure.
- Make school education up to age fourteen free and compulsory, and reduce dropouts at primary and secondary school levels to below 20 per cent for both boys and girls.
- Reduce infant mortality rate to below thirty per 1000 live births.
- Reduce maternal mortality ratio to below 100 per 100,000 live births.
- Achieve universal immunisation of children against all vaccine preventable diseases.
- Achieve 80 per cent institutional deliveries and 100 per cent deliveries by trained persons.
- Achieve 100 per cent registration of births, deaths, marriage and pregnancy.

Available data indicates that almost none of the objectives of the National Population Policy 2000 and the targets for the year 2010 are likely to be achieved.

The total fertility rate is unlikely to reach replacement level before 2015, while some of the laggard and big states would reach that level only after 2021. The infant mortality rate is unlikely to reach the target of 30 per 1000 live births even by 2025. The accompanying legislation for making the right to education the fundamental right is still a work in progress, and more than 50 per cent of our children are yet to be fully immunised. The statistics on maternal healthcare are also not encouraging with over 50 per cent of births not being either institutional deliveries or deliveries by trained persons.

This is not to deny our significant achievements. Since Independence, we have drastically improved overall literacy and female literacy and enhanced life expectancy for our citizens. Our efforts, nevertheless, have fallen short of the targets we set for ourselves.

How is this gap to be covered? As a lay person, I wish to offer two themes for consideration.

First: The demographic map of India is extremely diverse and heterogeneous. There are significant differences between states in the achievement of basic demographic indices, resulting in disparities population size and growth trends. There are wide inter-state, male-female and rural-urban disparities in outcomes and impacts.

Over ten states and union territories have achieved replacement levels of fertility. The growth rates continue to be high in Bihar, Uttar Pradesh, Madhya Pradesh and Rajasthan. Here we see a striking confluence of high fertility rates with low literacy and low health indicators and lower levels of socio-economic development. These states accounts for 40 per cent of our population and expected to contribute half of our future population growth. We thus need to focus on these states with renewed vigour, with full coordination between central and state governments, and active involvement of civil society institutions.

Secondly: More emphasis should be paid to 'demographic decentralisation' through devolution of responsibilities and resources to the Panchayati Raj Institutions (PRIs) in formulating and implementing area specific policies and programmes relevant for population stabilisation. They need to be involved in micro-planning and monitoring at local level to improve implementation of the programme and ensure effective community participation.

So far service deliveries under family welfare programmes have been administered entirely through official agencies. These have achieved sub-optimal results and necessitate a search for alternative modes of service delivery.

The answer lies in the 73rd and 74th constitutional amendments that created a meaningful role for local self-governance. The time has come for activating the third tier of government to address the population problem through speedy devolution of financial and human resources and powers.

We live in an era where a nation is judged by the human development level of its people–standards of health care, nutrition and level of education; by the human rights and fundamental freedoms enjoyed by its citizens; by the access to development and progress for all the vulnerable and disadvantaged sections of its society.

It is here that we must prove to ourselves that we have succeeded as a nation; and thereafter, prove in the comity of nations that we are a great and a responsible nation.

We need to note that without timely and effective public policy interventions, the demographic asset could turn into an enormous liability. Demographic stabilisation must therefore become a policy imperative and converted into a national movement.

I once again congratulate Chhattisgarh and Sikkim for their performance and urge other states to emulate them.

National Rural Health Mission Award Presentation Function

Vigyan Bhawan, New Delhi
12 April 2010

It gives me great pleasure to participate in today's function marking the completion of five years of the National Rural Health Mission (NRHM), the most ambitious rural health initiative to have been launched since Independence.

I congratulate the award winning states for their success in implementation of the mission and in the progress achieved in making quality health services accessible and affordable to the poorest households in the rural parts of the country.

It has to be said at the outset that the NRHM was necessitated by the extremely poor primary healthcare infrastructure. Regional disparities aggravated it and hampered the implementation of health-related programmes such as sanitation, drinking water, hygiene and nutrition.

This mission had a unique thrust. It establishes a functional, community owned, and decentralised health delivery system with inter-sectoral convergence so that parallel action on a wide range of socio-economic determinants like gender, social equality, water sanitation, education etc. is undertaken.

It thus marks the shift from a programme or scheme mode to a health system mode.

A high-profile International Advisory Panel of experts undertook a mid-term evaluation of the mission. Its conclusion is noteworthy:

> "What the NRHM has been able to accomplish in a relatively short period of time is to create much higher level of demand for public health services from the ground up. This in turn, we believe will force the systems and processes to function better in order to meet this surging demand".

The panel noted that the significant areas of achievement include putting in place an Accredited Social Health Activist for every thousand of the population, creating greater awareness about infant and maternal healthcare, raising institutional deliveries and number of outpatients and providing untied funds at all levels of facilities along with flexibility for outreach of services.

The commitment of Government of India to the mission is premised on the belief that reforming and revitalising the public health system is not a hundred metre race but a marathon where citizens and the government need patience, perseverance, dedication and focus on the ultimate goal. Through the NRHM, therefore, the central government is facilitating the leadership of state governments in setting public health priorities and emphasising human resource and governance reforms.

In the remaining period of the mission, there are five key challenges to be addressed:

First: As noted by the International Advisory Panel, healthcare delivery in rural India is almost entirely curative; the sole exception to this is prenatal checkups for pregnant women. Curative healthcare had been the focus of planned efforts for a long time due to the burden of communicable diseases and the necessity to build up health infrastructure in the rural areas.

At the same time and as a nation, we cannot afford to accord a lower priority to preventive and promotive healthcare. In the long run, the immense benefits of preventive care for improving national productivity and efficiency of our business and industry should not be under-estimated.

Second: Human resource management is a critical aspect of the immense scaling up represented by the NRHM. The Hon'ble Minister of Health and Family Welfare has already announced some innovative measures focused on expanding the pool of available rural health professionals and has unveiled incentives for encouraging other health professionals to work in rural and difficult areas.

With concurrent focus on nursing education and skills up gradation for Accredited Social Health Activists and Aanganwadi workers, the human resource problem can be addressed to a large extent.

Third: The success of any large scale integrated programme would depend on appropriate setting of output and outcome targets. The International Advisory Panel has recommended that the central and state governments should enter into MOUs for benchmarking of outcomes and has also suggested that the mission would be more effective if it paid for outputs rather than fund the inputs.

The performance audit of NRHM conducted by the Comptroller and Auditor General has also recommended prescription of disaggregated state-wise targets in view of the overall national targets set by the ministry. It has suggested that progress may be measured state-wise on the basis of disaggregated targets and data and that national targets should reflect the inter-state and intra-state variations that existed before the Mission was implemented.

Fourth: Convergence is a powerful theme in the area of human development and inclusive growth. Compartmentalisation and specific scheme/programme based approaches would not yield optimum results for the resources expended. The NRHM seeks an inter-sectoral convergence approach to synergise women and child development, hygiene and sanitation, nutrition, water, public works and Panchayati Raj institutions. This is a huge effort and requires the convergence of government and civil society efforts.

Fifth: Approaches to public health must look at the different stages of health transition at state and district levels so that appropriate strategies could be adopted. The district is, and remains, the basic unit for all interventions under the mission.

Health transition has three components: (a) demographic transition involving lowering the mortality and fertility rates; (b) epidemiological transition of a shift from communicable to non-communicable and lifestyle diseases; and (c) social transition where people develop capabilities to better manage their health and nutrition and are equipped to take full advantage of the various components of the public health system.

The wide variation in the three components of health transition across various districts in India indicates the complexity that needs to be addressed to achieve the goals of NRHM.

Today's function is a landmark where we celebrate the success achieved so far and prepare diligently for the challenges ahead. We have raised hopes; we have propelled demand: through both of these the citizens seek accessible, affordable, accountable, effective and reliable healthcare in rural areas. We should not expect forgiveness if we fall short of these aroused expectations.

The National Florence Nightingale Award Ceremony 2010

Vigyan Bhawan, New Delhi
12 May 2010

It gives me great pleasure to be present in today's function and give away the National Florence Nightingale Awards to outstanding nursing personnel on the occasion of the birth anniversary of Florence Nightingale and the International Nurses Day. I also take this opportunity to heartily congratulate all the awardees and their families on this occasion and place on record the deep appreciation of the nation for their hard work and professional commitment to their patients and to public healthcare.

As a developing country with a population of over 1 billion, we face enormous socio-economic challenges; the challenges are even more complex in the realm of human development. We have to achieve the targets of the Millennium Development Goals and complete the unfinished agendas regarding communicable diseases, maternal and child healthcare and strengthening our primary healthcare network in both urban and rural areas. Rapid economic development has also meant dealing with issues of health profile transition such as those related to premature burden of non-communicable diseases which have emerged as a major public health concern accounting for around half of all deaths in the age groups of 30-60.

Nursing is critical to putting in place an efficient, affordable and comprehensive healthcare system and ensuring healthcare delivery in an equitable manner. The theme for this year's International Nurses Day– 'Delivering Quality, Serving Communities: Nurses Leading Chronic Care'– is appropriate as there is a massive increase in death and disability resulting from chronic disease. Unlike popular perception that chronic diseases are a developed country problem, 80 per cent of deaths worldwide due to chronic diseases occur in low and middle income countries. The WHO has concluded that it is the poor and the disadvantaged who have to disproportionately bear the increasing burden of chronic diseases due to widening health gaps between and within countries.

India bears a huge burden of the global case load of chronic diseases. For example, out of the 246 million people globally suffering from diabetes, India has the largest number of 41 million people with diabetes. The situation in the case of cardiovascular diseases, cancer and chronic respiratory diseases is broadly similar. These diseases are preventable and cause a huge loss to the national economies, communities and families.

Nursing personnel must understand the magnitude of this health challenge and take coordinated action to promote healthy lifestyles, prevent disease and provide health care to those in need. The International Council of Nurses has this year called upon each of the world's 13 million nurses to act as 'role models, educators and change agents among their families, friends, work places and local communities to promote healthier lifestyles ... to help stem the tide of chronic disease'. I urge each one of you to heed this call.

The immense shortage in nursing personnel is a significant impediment in achieving our public healthcare objectives. India has only eight nurses per ten thousand population in comparison to Sri Lanka which has fourteen, Indonesia which has thirteen, Thailand at thirty-seven and Maldives at thirty-three. We have a nurse to population ratio of 1:1100 as compared to developed country averages of 1:150. It is also estimated that of the 10.35 lakh registered nurses, active nurses pursuing the profession in the country are only around four lakhs.

It is also anomalous that there are more doctors than nurses in the country and for every three doctors there are two nurses. In comparison, in most developed countries, there are three nurses per doctor.

There are also significant regional disparities in the location of nursing educational institutions and availability of nursing personnel in the country. Over 60 per cent of the nursing educational institutions are in southern and western India whereas the greatest shortfall of nursing personnel is in the high focus states in northern and eastern India. We have a huge gap of around 10 lakh nurses who need to be trained in a time-bound manner to meet the shortfall and to achieve the Bhore Committee recommendation of a nurse to population ratio of 1:500.

On a different note, it must be acknowledged that nursing is not perceived as an attractive professional option in many areas in our country. One is compelled to introspect about the possible cultural and social reasons behind it.

The government remains committed to enhance resources for health care and bring about reforms and convergence in service delivery. The efforts of the Hon'ble minister of Health and Family Welfare have resulted in a vastly enhanced allocation during the Eleventh Plan period with a focus on increasing the overall availability of nursing personnel and an emphasis on skills up gradation for nurses.

While we readily perceive the role of quality nursing care in the provision of high-end private healthcare to our citizens and foreigners, it is often forgotten that it is the General Nursing and Midwives along with the Auxiliary Midwives and Lady Health Visitors who have been instrumental in taking preventive, promotive and rehabilitative primary healthcare services to the doorsteps of our citizens. It is they who are the face of our public health services in the vast reaches of rural India and provide vital maternal and child care health services to the community.

Presentation of the International Gandhi Award–2009

Gandhi Memorial Leprosy Foundation, Wardha

1 July 2010

For me this is a privilege and pilgrimage. I feel privileged to participate in today's programme at Wardha. This city has been witness to momentous and historic events during the freedom struggle and has thereafter become a place of pilgrimage for those upholding Gandhian values of service, sacrifice and compassion.

This is my first visit to the city and I am privileged to be here to give away the International Gandhi Awards.

The recipients of the awards this year, Dr Vijay Kumar Pannikar and the Vidarbha Maharogi Seva Mandal represented by its president Dr Motilal Rathi, deserve our appreciation for their untiring efforts over many decades for the cause of leprosy elimination and for their service to leprosy affected persons.

Their efforts have made a significant difference in the lives of many leprosy affected persons and have facilitated their rehabilitation and resettlement in society. On behalf of the International Gandhi Award Committee, and on my own behalf, I extend my congratulations to the awardees and urge them to continue their good work.

As a disease, leprosy has affected humans for over 2000 years with references in ancient Indian literature dating back to about 600 BC. But with little information about the disease and about modes of treatment until the 1950s, it remained a mystery for humans.

Medical ignorance did not, however, prevent social stigma. Leprosy had been construed as a divine curse and a result of immoral behaviour, with a 'leper' representing someone who is physically and morally unclean, deserving of blame for contracting the disease, and hence, for ostracism.

Mahatma Gandhi had a special concern for leprosy patients, even at a time when there was no specific cure for leprosy. He understood that there are two aspects of the disease–first, the medical dimension and secondly, the social dimension. He worked to end the social stigma associated with the disease and to bring about the reintegration of leprosy patients in the mainstream of society.

The introduction of Multi-drug Therapy in the early 1980s has changed the scenario for the disease, curing over 13 million leprosy cases and bringing down the prevalence rate in the nation from around 150 per population of ten thousand in 1983 to less than one per population of ten thousand today. By the end of 2005, India had achieved the goal of eliminating leprosy as a public health problem at the national level.

Still, it is important to remember that we have not eradicated the disease. The states of Bihar and Chhattisgarh and the Union Territory of Dadra and Nagar Haveli have a prevalence rate of over 1 per population of ten thousand and are yet to achieve elimination. They constitute over 10 per cent of the country's population and contribute around one-fifth of the recorded case load in the country.

If analysed at the district level, 80 per cent of the districts have eliminated leprosy, with 15 per cent of districts witnessing moderate prevalence of between one to two per ten thousand of the population and around 4 per cent of our districts having a severe prevalence of between two to five per ten thousand of the population. It is important that the national effort to eliminate the disease continues and is more geographically focused on these areas.

We still face daunting challenges in the post-elimination era of leprosy. India still accounts for over half of the new cases of leprosy recorded worldwide. It is estimated that there are around one million leprosy patients with disabilities in the country. We need to further reduce the leprosy burden, prevent disabilities and deformities and empower those who have been disabled by the disease and reduce social discrimination through advocacy and targeted information campaigns.

For Bapu*ji*, his life was his message. His personal example in tending to leprosy affected persons and his efforts to integrate them into normal community life had highlighted the importance of eliminating the social stigma attached to the disease and in generating awareness throughout the country regarding leprosy.

While the government and civil society have taken up this task, I believe there is great merit in going back to the Gandhian focus on the individual citizen. Each one of us in our own sphere must show greater awareness about leprosy and proactively take steps to end the social discrimination and bring about the social integration of the leprosy affected persons.

Sixteenth Convocation

The National Institute of Mental Health and Neuro Sciences (NIMHANS), Bangalore
20 January 2012

It gives me great pleasure to participate in today's convocation at this premier multidisciplinary institute for patient care and academic pursuit in the frontier area of Mental Health and Neuro Sciences.

With a distinguished history of over a century and a legacy of excellence, the graduating students of NIMHANS have every reason to be proud of their alma mater and look forward to their professional and personal futures with confidence and optimism.

With a spectrum of activity that stretches "from the bench to the bedside", it has emerged as an institution of global repute in the field of Neuroscience and Behavioural science. I extend my best wishes to all graduating students and wish them all success in their professional and personal endeavours.

This audience is aware that we have in place a comprehensive framework of laws and policies pertaining to mental health. Some of you will recall the infamous Eradi fire tragedy that evoked the conscience of the nation to the plight of those affected with mental illness in our society. Subsequently, the catalysing impact of the Supreme Court intervention resulted in greater resource allocation and enhanced policy intervention to mental health. The National Programme was restructured in 2003 and funding increased from around Rs 28 crores during the Ninth Plan period to over Rs 400 crores in the Eleventh Plan.

Despite this, our expenditure on health as a proportion of the GDP remains at 1.27 per cent and is very low as compared to international standards. Over three fourths of the total expenditure on health constitutes private sector expenditure, of which over 90 per cent is borne out-of-pocket by private households. Less than 5 per cent of such out-of-pocket expenditure is spent on anti-psychotic or anti-depressant medication.

A review of the human resources focused on mental health is also revealing. We have:

- twenty psychiatrists per ten million population as compared to the global average of 120;
- six neurosurgeons per ten million population in comparison to the global average of 20;
- five psychiatric nurses per ten million population to the global figure of 200;
- five neurologists per ten million population to the global figure of 30;
- three psychologists per ten million population to the global figure of 60;
- three social workers per ten million population to the global average of 40.
- Even in terms of mental health infrastructure, we have twenty-five psychiatric beds per million people as compared to the global average of 169.

A few questions do come to mind. Allow me to share them with you:

- Have we succeeded in our attempt to integrate mental health care provision as part of the primary health care delivery system? Are our general physicians and paramedical staff manning the primary health centres and sub-centres sensitised to problems of mental health?
- While inadequacy of specialists to staff mental health services is recognised, have we made efforts to update undergraduate medical curricula so that our doctors are skilled and trained in diagnosing and handling persons suffering from common psychiatric conditions seen in general settings?
- Have we given attention to enlarging the pool of non-medical professionals such as psychologists, social workers, occupational therapists and para-medical staff such as psychiatric nurses, all of whom are key elements of mental health service provision?

- Have we succeeded in evolving a community mental health service approach where people can be effectively treated and integrated into society? Do our mental health professionals prefer the safety of specialist institutions to moving out into the community?
- Have we involved non-health sectors such as education, labour, social welfare, urban development and law in improving the mental health of our communities? Do we include mental health indices as part of general health information and reporting systems to help set priorities, identify emerging trends and direct interventions appropriately?

That there exists a huge gap between the demand for mental health service provision and supply is not in doubt. Over two-thirds of those who suffer from mental illnesses do not receive the treatment that they ought to. Improving the infrastructure and human resources for supplying mental health services is one aspect of the problem.

The more serious issue relates to the stigma of mental illness in the country. While we have made enormous strides in de-stigmatising patients of HIV/AIDS through public education and awareness campaigns, we have not been able to replicate the same regarding mental disorders. We must reduce the stigma and discrimination through public awareness.

We must also focus our efforts specifically on vulnerable population groups such as women, children, those facing social or familial isolation, drug or alcohol addicts, natural or man-made disaster victims and those working or living in conflict zones. These population groups need proactive appraisal of their mental health condition and timely intervention if necessary.

Rule of Law, Human Rights, Terrorism

> "If we fail, we shall have a festering sore, which will eventually poison the whole body politic and probably destroy it
>
> —Jawaharlal Nehru, October 1947

Convocation

Indian Law Institute, New Delhi

5 November 2007

To one not formally lettered in the discipline of law, it is indeed a rare privilege to be invited to deliver the Convocation address of the Indian Law Institute. Some familiarity with political science, supplemented by decades in the profession of diplomacy did, however, familiarise me with aspects of law and helped me in some measure to fulfill Blackstone's requirement that public duty cannot be discharged 'without some degree of knowledge in the laws'.

This is a joyful occasion and I am happy to be a participant in it. A new group of young people is stepping out to join a profession whose relevance remains undiminished. A law school does not undertake to teach success. Its aim, said Judge Oliver Wendell Holmes of the U.S. Supreme Court, is "not to make men smart, but to make them wise in their calling" and to make them learn "how to make facts live".

Law, remarked the jurist Carl Friedrich, is "frozen history". Record shows that the formulations of law have borne the imprint of human experience; this experience demonstrates a simple thesis: that humankind is a social creature whose existence in society is predicated on norms of behavior. Thus Sir Paul Vinogradoff defined law as "a set of rules imposed and enforced by a society with regard to the attribution and exercise of power over persons and things". These rules are strengthened through recognition and thereby carry the element of consent based on a society's sense of equity and justice. Whenever the latter is perceived to be lacking an appeal is made, as Vinogradoff put it, "from Caesar to a better informed Caesar" thought to be capable of delivering justice.

Having decided upon the unavoidability of rules, every society in history addressed the question of the rule-giver and the law-enforcer. Here, the answer provided by Aristotle still holds good: "When men are alike and equal, it is neither expedient nor just that one man should be the lord of all, whether there are laws, or whether there are no laws, but he himself is in the place of law". From this arose, in terms of desirability and legitimacy, the idea of participatory governance or democracy. A condition of this legitimacy is the exclusion of arbitrary governance and the commitment of the State, firstly to its own laws and, secondly, to their uniform application.

The term 'Rule of Law' is now a part of our daily vocabulary. Critical study, nevertheless, requires scrutiny of the self evident and the obvious. The classic enunciation is to be found in Albert Dicey, who needs no introduction to this audience. To him, the essential ingredients of Rule of Law were (a) the absolute supremacy of regular law (b) equality before the law (c) access to justice and development of law by the judges on a case by case basis.

In terms of the institutions of the State, the classical approach to Rule of Law implies their functioning in terms of the limits prescribed by the constitution of the State so that the possibility of the enactment in Montesquieu's words of "tyrannical law", or their execution in a tyrannical manner, is excluded and is further safeguarded by the judicial power discharging its functions independently of the legislature and the executive.

Over time and in different societies, these principles have been challenged, amplified and modified. Upendra Baxi has sought to read the Rule of Law as "going beyond a mere division of functions in modes of governance; to him, it is the rule of good law and is as such reflective of the struggle of a people" "to make power accountable, governance just, and state ethical". Professor Baxi opines that "the Indian constitutional conception of the Rule of Law links its four core notions: rights, development, governance and justice". An interesting early example of this approach is to be found in the Declaration of Delhi of January 1959 by the International Congress of Jurists. It recognised the Rule of Law as:

> a dynamic concept for the expansion and fulfillment of which jurists are primarily responsible and which should be employed not only to safeguard and advance civil and political rights of individuals in a free society, but

> also to establish social, economic, educational and cultural conditions under which his legitimate aspirations and dignity may be realised.

This approach has been upheld in judicial pronouncements. Rule of Law, said the Supreme Court in Dalmia Cement (Bharat) Ltd v Union of India (1996) 'is a potent instrument of social justice to bring about equality in result'.

II

The concept in theory is thus clear enough. What about the practice?

On 15 August this year we celebrated the sixtieth anniversary of our Independence. The moment was simultaneously historic, celebratory and introspective. We celebrated the strength and depth of our democratic system based on the Constitution and introspected about the obstacles confronting democratic governance. One informed commentator noted that "the Rule of Law is still not sufficiently protected in the Indian society" and challenges to it 'continue to undermine Indian democracy and pose grave threats to governance'.

This perception of inadequacy is important enough to be examined in greater detail.

Two years back, a senior law officer of the government addressed this question candidly and sought to answer specific questions:

- Have the constitutional organs of the State – the Legislatures, the Executive and the Judiciary – discharged the obligations placed on them by the Constitution?
- Have they functioned within the limits set forth by the Constitution?
- What is the perception of the public with regard to their functioning?
- To what extent is the perceived erosion in their working the result of intra-institutional and inter-institutional problem?

His conclusions were stated bluntly:

1. The Rule of Law in India is under serious threat;
2. There is widespread popular disillusionment;

3. There are cancerous developments eating into the fabric of each institution and each is destroying itself from within;
4. If these trends are not arrested, they are bound to be destructive of the Indian State in the long run.

In a similar vein but commenting on the wider picture, civil society groups in the country and abroad have observed that 'the Rule of Law in India is in a downward spiral' and that the primary responsibility for it lies with the 'delayed justice dispensation system'.

It would appear that both in terms of the procedural technicalities, and substantive content, there is a sense of unease with regard to the working of the Rule of Law.

Why has this happened? The answer is to be sought in the functioning, or mal-functioning, of the institutions of the State that have led to 'cancerous development'. An institution-wise assessment would therefore be in order.

The United Nations Research Institute for Social Development published in January 2006 a study on 'The Indian Parliament as an Instrument of Accountability'. It concluded that Parliament is increasingly becoming ineffective in providing surveillance of the executive branch of the government. One part of this is attributed to the behaviour pattern of the MPs and the wastage of time that could otherwise be devoted to legislative duties and scrutiny of executive action; another reason is the increasing complexity of modern governance and the resultant need for greater professionalism in legislative work. The requisite correctives are not forthcoming. As a result, 'a hobbled legislative has ceded ground not to the executive or external forces, but to the judiciary'.

In regard to the executive, the balance between its political and professional components has been disturbed; this is evident in the functioning of the civil service and particularly of the police. Thus 'the myth of authority', on which the power of the state depends, has been dented and has resulted in what Mr Fali Nariman has called "executive under-reach"

The traditional public esteem for the judiciary has been reinforced by its activism in contrast to the failure of the executive to apply correctives on matters of concern. This is particularly true of its good work in expanding the ambit of rights. On the other hand, lack of access to justice, the high cost of it, delays in the delivery of justice, lack of a mechanism for accountability and allegations of corruption have, together, given rise to doubts and added to the pervasive pessimism about the efficacy of institutions. One law officer has also expressed concern over the 'increasing disregard of the salutary doctrine of precedents'.

Another area of concern is the excessive zeal reflected at times in pronouncements of members of the judiciary. Some observers have asserted that "the Supreme Court has given up any formal pretence to the doctrine of the separation of powers". This is perceived to upset, as the Hon'ble Speaker of the Lok Sabha has observed, "the fine constitutional balance and the democratic functioning of the state as a whole". The caution administered by Chief Justice Stone of the U.S. Supreme Court, therefore, has relevance: "While unconstitutional exercise of power by the executive and legislative members of the Government is subject to judicial restraint, the only checks on our own exercise of power is our sense of self-restraint".

It is evident that the careful balance visualised in the Constitution has been disturbed. The first step in redressing it would be to reiterate its major premises:

- The People of India are the sovereign and gave themselves the Constitution.
- The objectives sought by the People through this Constitution are inscribed in its Preamble. Thus Justice, Liberty, Equality and Fraternity are not gifts of the State; instead the State is the means, and its institutions the modality, through which these objectives are to be achieved.
- The State has the Rule of Law as its dharma and mode of governance. Its spirit pervades the Constitution in its totality.
- The State is not merely an agent of political order but is vested with enormous responsibilities for socio-economic development and is expected to undertake it. Both in terms of Fundamental Rights and Directive Principles, the Constitution visualises an interventionist state.

III

Public concern over the inefficacy of institutions is evident enough. If this is to be translated into correctives, the argument and its premises would have to be widened. In a narrow, technical sense, the realm of law stands apart from the realm of morality. If however Rule of Law is understood to be a rule of good law, then the moral quality of goodness would need to be injected in its interstices. These problems were anticipated by the framers, as is evident from Ambedkar's words of caution to the Constituent Assembly:

"The working of the constitution does not depend wholly upon the nature of the constitution. The constitution can provide only the organs of the State, such as the Legislature, the Executive and the Judiciary. The factors on which the workings of those organs of the State depend are the people and the political parties they will set up as their instruments to carry out their wishes and their politics. Who can say how the people of India and their parties will behave".

Ambedkar's foresight in anticipating the source of problems is evident from yet another remark:

"On the 26 January 1950, we are going to enter into a life of contradictions. In politics we will have equality and in social and economic life we will have inequality. In politics we will be recognising the principle of one man one vote and one vote one value. In our social and economic life, we shall by reason of our social and economic structure, continue to deny the principle of one man one value. How long shall we continue to deny equality in our social and economic life? If we continue to deny it for long, we shall do so only by putting our political democracy in peril. We must remove this contradiction at the earliest possible moment else those who suffer from inequality will blow up the structure of democracy which this Constituent Assembly has so laboriously built up'.

Would it be an exaggeration to say these words are an eloquent, and sufficient, commentary on the multiple crises that confront the Republic within the Parliament and in far flung corners of the country?

The unravelling of social consensus, anticipated by Ambedkar, has come about principally on account of the inequities of the growth process and also, in a sense, due to a balkanisation of the mind. This has wider implications since democracy and the Rule of Law are inextricably connected to each other; a decline in one would inevitably impact the other adversely. For this reason John Adam's premonition, leaning on the side of excess, is nevertheless a warning that should be heeded: "Democracy", he said, "never lasts long. It soon wastes, exhausts and murders itself. There never was a democracy that did not commit suicide."

No serious observer of the Indian scene can deny the signs of waste and exhaustion. The challenge then is to address the problem both in its totality and in its individual segments and endeavour to seek a consensus afresh. This would need to take into account the imperatives of entitlement and empowerment, translating each of these into state policies, and develop the resolve to implement them. It would also require a commitment from the media and the civil society to uphold the Rule of Law.

A mind trained in law is an invaluable asset. Our Law schools have an important function in promoting advocacy and legal knowledge and shaping the common man's understanding of the Rule of Law. Legal education has an important role to play in the establishment of a law-abiding society. However the increased interest in the legal profession, evident from enhanced enrolment in law courses, has not translated into a greater respect for law.

The Indian Law Institute has fulfilled an important role in promoting legal research and in cultivating the science of law. In the years to come, many of the young people graduating today would serve the country in upholding the Rule of Law, not only as a legal professional or as an academic, but also in diverse fields of public life and national activity. As they go through life, they would do well to remember the advice given by an Englishman who was not a lawyer but had much to do with law: "Because law is a part of life it must enter into relations with those parts of life by which it is largely determined".

Fourth Convocation
Vardhaman Mahaveer Open University, Kota
15 May 2008

Accommodation of Diversity: The Indian Practice and the Global Debate

I am happy to be in Kota, in a place of history, in an institution of higher learning where the enthusiasm of the youth interacts with the experience of the elderly.

It is indeed a joyous occasion for the university, particularly as it is honouring its Founder—Vice Chancellor, Prof. V.R. Mehta, with an honoris causa. This is a fitting recognition of his immense contribution as an eminent educationist and a noted political theorist.

A university is a playground of ideas, a place where the human mind is allowed to roam freely to examine critically the achievements of the past, the endeavours of the present and the prospects of the future. It is a platform for free thinking. For this reason, it is critical to the mental good health of a people.

Every free and healthy society must, therefore, allow this free play to its universities. By the same logic, places of higher learning have an obligation to discharge this responsibility in full measure.

II

An ancient philosopher is credited with the remark that "you cannot step in the same river twice". We can say the same about the world of today. The pace of change is unbelievable.

We cannot re-live the past, not even yesterday.

We can anticipate the future, but must do it in the knowledge that we have often been wrong, both with regard to human affairs and in relation to technological change. The human mind, given to reflection on changes in human condition, is thus unavoidably late on the scene. This reflection, nevertheless, is invaluable.

We in India live in an ancient land, in a society enriched by time and experience, amidst fellow citizens who are united in their commitment to India and Indian-ness. But as Sunil Khilnani has noted: "There was one very important feature of the project of defining Indianness.... The State did not try to impose a uniform definition of a national culture, it did not molest local loyalties - although it did frequently try to persuade such loyalties to adopt wider horizons. It respected the element of choice - for religions, regions, languages and above all for individuals - in deciding the issue of how to be an Indian. And it recognised that its citizens might choose to maintain simultaneous allegiances to a variety of things: nation, region, religion, language - such loyalties were not seen as necessarily competitive or exclusive identities."

Accommodation of diversity is thus a civilisational heritage of our societal evolution and survival over centuries and enshrined by the conscious choice of the Indian people as a distinctive aspect of the Indian state. A standardised image of an Indian cannot be constructed; if presented, it is partial, incomplete, misleading.

Our long history and rich experience has blessed us with the intellectual depth and practical tools of moulding our diversity into an integrated whole that is richer than its parts.

The mantra for our professed creed is a plural society, a democratic polity, a secular state structure. Our endeavour, in practical terms, is to draw an inclusive circle so that none is excluded.

The plurality of our society is a fact of life. Democracy and secularism are the results of conscious decisions taken by the People of India and enshrined in the Constitution. The objective was to create a structure of equality and justice for all and allow the plurality to flourish within it.

Three questions are often posed to us. How far have we succeeded? What remains to be done? How can others benefit from our experience?

- In six decades of independent existence, we have consolidated our physical integrity, sustained and deepened democratic structures, widened the circle of inclusiveness, and taken meaningful steps towards social justice. Our economic, scientific and technological development is note worthy. The strength and unity of our market is admired and envied.

- On the other hand caste, region, language and religion continue to dilute our national cohesion; an Indian continues to be singled out in some part of India or the other for differentiated, often derogatory, treatment on one or more of these grounds.
- Some have difficulty in accepting that justice and meaningful equality necessitates affirmative action.
- Some are reluctant to concede that a single citizenship entitles us to move, reside and work freely within the boundaries of India and without extra-legal hindrances.
- Some often forget, despite our glorious heritage in spirituality, that faith is a matter of individual choice dictated by conscience and not subject to overt or covert state or social regulation.
- Some are failing to invest the institutions of democracy with functional efficacy and seem oblivious to public disenchantment with this trend.

In sum, each of the core values of pluralism, democracy and secularism are perceived to be under siege and need to be rejuvenated.

III

There is a basic difficulty about our understanding of pluralism. It is a societal reality, not a creation of the State. One question however does arise: have we invested enough in strengthening and deepening the concept of pluralism so that it is embedded in our consciousness? Experience shows that:

- Pluralism involves energetic engagement with diversity;
- Pluralism is not just tolerance but the active seeking of understanding across lines of difference;

- Pluralism is not relativism but the encounter of commitments, of holding our deepest differences not in isolation but in relationship to one another;
- Pluralism is based on dialogue, of speaking and listening in a process that reveals both common understanding and real differences.

The proper pursuit of pluralism therefore necessitates a continuous inter-community, inter-faith and cross-cultural dialogue aimed at understanding and accommodating diversity. It has deep roots in our cultural history but is not being pushed with sufficient vigour by our society and polity today.

Such a dialogue is essential to promote an atmosphere of integration in which persons of different ethnic or religious groups come together in an equal association of a common political community to promote common values.

Integration is freely undertaken; it is very different from assimilation that involves absorption and loss of identity and is sought to be achieved through covert or overt coercion.

We are familiar with the implications of this distinction. Throughout our history, we have noted that identities have been built on a series of inclusions and exclusions reflective of ground realities. The challenge has been to maintain a balance in favour of inclusions.

The effort has been successful because identities do not remain in watertight compartments and because our everyday life has necessitated a networking of identities. In the light of this experience, the effort to narrow the circle is foolhardy. It is nevertheless there and must therefore be taken note of, and countered.

The significance of sustaining and strengthening the plural fabric cannot be overstated for the simple reason that it constitutes the end product of centuries of societal evolution, the bedrock of the State structure and, in the final analysis, of national security.

No society in the world is homogenous. No society is static. We are familiar with the implications of urbanisation. The question of accommodating identity and pluralism has been faced by others also, more specifically in the context of globalisation which brings forth a paradox: that while traditional points of reference disappear, a passionate affirmation of narrow or sectional identities is awakened often leading to virtual self-exclusion.

It would be useful to see how other societies have dealt with the question of accommodating or managing diversity. For our purpose today, the prime examples are in the Western world, principally reflected in the experience of the United States, some member States of the European Union, and Canada. The principal difference is that diversity in India is in situ, whereas in the West, diversity and the need to accommodate it stems primarily from immigration. It is a different issue that when it comes to accommodating indigenous diversity as in the case of Aboriginal issues, most Western countries have had a poor record. Amends continue to be made on this count, and the apology of the Australian prime minister is one such example.

In some of these, the starting point was the concept of mono-culture, in others the 'melting pot' or 'multiculturalism'.

The first presupposes a homogenous nation-state. An eminent scholar has called it 'a pipedream' since culturally homogenous populations are a rarity in a modern state. Any attempt to attain it is effectively hampered by globalisation and the mobility of people.

The other end of this exclusivist paradigm is represented by the 'melting pot' approach premised on cultural assimilation of new arrivals over a period of time. This was ardently advocated in the United States in an earlier period when the immigrants were principally from Europe and African-Americans and American Indians were excluded from the ambit of civic rights.

The concept of multiculturalism took shape in the second half of the twentieth century in the United States and Canada (and to a lesser extent in Australia). It allowed immigrants to express their ethnic, cultural, religious and linguistic identities and obliged all public institutions, through legislation, to accommodate such identities and contribute to the final product.

The situation in the European Union varies considerably. It has developed supra-national regional governance structures that accommodate the diversity of state structures, languages, religions, ethnicities and legal systems. Yet, for all the brilliance of its normative legal and rights structures, the situation has deteriorated in vast areas of the Union in recent years on account of the terrorism debate.

Many sections of opinion in Western societies have succumbed to the temptation of associating terrorist acts with people of a religious affiliation or immigrant background, forgetting their own, and global, experience in recent decades at different places and points of time. Record shows that adherents of all faiths, without exception, have at some time or other been guilty in the matter and that faith-specific analysis of acts of terrorism is inadequate, misleading and harmful to social cohesion and political stability.

These reactions also bring out the limitations of the immigrant multicultural model created through state intervention. The ability of the multicultural model to sustain itself in times of pressure has come into question.

IV

The Indian approach needs to be assessed in the context of the global experience. Unlike the countries of the West, the Indian social structure and its demographic mix is not of recent origin. This was aptly expressed half a century ago by Humayun Kabir and I can do no better than to recall his words:

"From times immemorial, India has been the meeting place of the conflicting races and civilisations. From times immemorial, she has tried to achieve a unity for the heterogeneous elements, which makes up the totality of her life. Hers is perhaps the oldest civilisation with an uninterrupted history. Most of her contemporaries have ceased to exist. She has not only survived but also maintained and developed a continuous culture ... Whence this vitality that overcomes destruction and death? The story of India's culture unravels the secret of that vitality and that wisdom. It is a story of unity and synthesis, of reconciliation and development, of a perfect fusion of old traditions and new value".

This synthesising ethos is a living reality and is variously described as 'unity in diversity', 'pluralism and tolerance', 'living together separately', 'salad bowl', 'thali' etc. In the absence of a constitutional definition of secularism, this has also led us to understand secularism as *sarva dharma samabhava* (equal respect to all religions). Our Judiciary has clarified it to mean - a) non-discrimination on grounds of religion; b) the State shall have no religion of its own; and c) all persons shall be equally entitled to the freedom of conscience and the right freely to profess, practice and propagate religion. The Constitution lends it a supportive framework of justice and equality. Public opinion sustains it in varying measure; so does popular culture and everyday economic activity all over the country.

Despite this, serious aberrations have surfaced from time to time. There have been occasions when individuals failed, when agents of the State were negligent or complicit, when the State itself faltered. Jawaharlal Nehru had anticipated such failures and cautioned against it in October 1947: "If we fail, we shall have a festering sore, which will eventually poison the whole body politic and probably destroy it".

The failures are often systemic and necessitate revisiting the concept to lend it greater vigour. This can be ensured by developing, and implementing, a commitment to egalitarian and equalitarian pluralism. The *sarva dharma samabhava* should intersect, in words and in spirit, with the constitutional principles of non-discrimination, the right freely to profess, practice and propagate religion and of the State having no religion of its own. A few practical measures would assist the process:

Consider community disharmony a threat to national security and deal with it in the same manner as other such threats;

- Be uncompromising in the implementation of laws and regulations.
- Educate all sections of the public, and particularly the youth and students, about the uniqueness of our structure and the benefits flowing out of it; and
- Develop a civil society awareness to pursue relentlessly cases of state failure or of individuals and groups who may be culprits.

Some of you may have come across in your readings Edmund Burke's remark that 'the only thing necessary for the triumph of evil is for good men to do nothing'. As citizens, therefore, each one of you has a duty to participate in strengthening this important aspect of our structure of governance.

I conclude by felicitating all those who have earned their degrees today. I wish them all success in the days ahead.

Krishan Kant Memorial Lecture
Constitution Club, New Delhi
28 July 2008

I deem it a privilege to be invited to deliver the Fifth Krishan Kant Memorial Lecture.

There are many ways of recalling the memory of the late Krishan Kant*ji*; each of these is equally valid. To most, it would be sufficient to remember him as a former vice president of India, a former chairman of the Rajya Sabha, a governor of eminence, an active and innovative parliamentarian and a public figure of note.

This would not do justice to the totality of work.

Krishan Kant*ji's* concern for civil liberties and fundamental freedoms was evident in his work as the founding General Secretary of the People's Union for Civil Liberties and Democratic Rights. He exemplified the pledge of the Servants of the People Society: to be a "national missionary for the service of the motherland".

Shri Krishan Kant was an ardent believer in the importance of good governance. He had the unique experience of seeing the federal structure of the Republic at work at both the centre and the state levels. He said on one occasion that "while bad politics may impair good governance, good politics is an essential requirement or the context in which good governance becomes possible".

It follows that a good structure is essential but not sufficient guarantee for good governance; also that the citizen cannot be oblivious to the nature and content of politics, particularly when it threatens to deviate from norms of goodness.

The health of the polity thus needs to be assessed on both counts. We are fortunate in being blessed with a structure of governance suited to accommodate the diversity of our nation and the multiple identities of our people.

The architect of the Constitution, Dr B.R. Ambedkar, accurately described the nature of our political structure. "Though India was to be a federation", he said, "the federation was not the result of an agreement by the states to join in a federation. Not being a result of an agreement, no state has the right to secede from it. Though the country and the people may be divided into different states for convenience of administration, the country is one integral whole, its people a single people living under a single imperium derived from a single source".

Thus the creation of the Indian 'federation' has been a top down, rather than a bottom up, process. The states are the end product, not the initial impulse, of the federating process. For this reason, the Constitution-makers chose to define India as a Union of States; the word federation itself finds no mention in the Constitution.

This approach did not develop in a vacuum and bore the imprint of the last phase of British rule. The intent of the Government of India Act 1935, which formed the basis of our Constitution, was 'to hold India to the Empire' rather than to expedite the handover of power. Its structure of a Federation based on the union of provinces was intended to create powerful provincial leaders who, as the historian Bipan Chandra has noted, would "safeguard their administrative prerogatives and would, therefore, gradually become autonomous centres of power" and thus weaken the central leadership.

It was for this reason, and with a view to overcome this deficiency, that the Constituent Assembly crafted a Constitution that avoided, as Ambedkar put it, "the tight mould of federation" and was instead "both unitary as well as federal according to the requirements of time and circumstances".

This requirement of circumstances played itself out in the following decades. The first period, till about 1988, was aptly described as "blood pressure at the centre, and anaemia at the periphery". Thereafter, a reverse process emerged and by mid-to-late 1990s concern had turned to symptoms of fragmentation.

II

Half a century on, some questions about federal functioning do arise:

- To what extent has the structure sustained itself?
- Has politics helped or hampered it?
- What correctives, if any, are now deemed essential?

The short answer is that the structure has evolved with democracy and federal practice reinforcing each other to an extent that the Constitution-makers may not have anticipated. This has resulted in new challenges that must be faced. Fortunately, the Constitution itself is in a position to provide most of the correctives. The great imponderable is the willingness of the system to seek them.

Any observer of the Indian scene would concede that the constitutional framework become the main vehicle for giving expression to regional, linguistic and other sub-national identities of our people. The reorganisation of states, creation of linguistic states, recognition through statehood of regional, ethnic or environmental uniqueness and creation of a third tier of local government are instances of the deepening of the regional and local structures of governance. These are no mean achievements.

In a similar manner the expression of multiple identities has been sought, with varying degrees of success, through the actualisation of rights guaranteed in the Constitution.

Each of these has been generally (though not exclusively) attained through broadly democratic processes. It has been furthered by the regionalisation of the political party system. There were 53 political parties in the first general election and 14 of these were national parties; in the 2004 election, 230 parties participated and only 6 of these were in the national category. A direct result of this has been the dawn of coalition politics.

This regionalisation has also induced a balkanisation of the mind that has impacted adversely on questions that transcend local and regional horizons.

Side by side, however, is the economic integration of the country with the unity of the market providing a national cohesive of substantial dimensions.

The dynamics of politically-induced change, and economic imperatives, produced contradictory results. On the one hand, universal franchise brought forth local elites of caste and class whose interest groups sought to capture the instruments of power; on the other hand the 73rd and 74th Amendments has allowed women, scheduled castes and scheduled tribes to begin to shake up the local power structures.

As a result, the structure visualised for the smooth functioning of the Centre-State relationship has often been stressed. One reason for this is the inherently asymmetric nature of the relationship particularly in the case of fiscal arrangements and transfers between the Centre and the states. A significant quantum of financial devolution from the Centre to the states comes through mechanisms that were not envisaged in the Constitution.

A further complication is the fact that taxation powers of the Central government cover subjects that have significantly boosted Central tax revenues whereas state tax revenues have been relatively inelastic. Nor is fiscal devolution to the third tier any better and the states behave in a similar fashion with regard to Panchayati Raj institutions.

Other points of stress relate to what are known as the 'emergency provisions' of the Constitution. The most famous of these is Article 356 that, in the view of many observers, has been "used, abused, misused and overused". On the other hand, instances in which the Union has actually discharged its 'duty' towards states in terms of Article 355 are hard to come by. Other questions relate to competences, to the methodology for the deployment of central forces, role of governors etc. The jurist Fali Nariman is critical of the trend in the judiciary to lean on the side of "a strong centre" and has advocated "new judicial thinking on the subject of Indian federalism" focused on more equal rights (financial and political) for the states.

III

The Indian federal practice is not merely a theoretical issue. It has emerged as one of the most important vehicle for managing our enormous diversity, enabling expression of the genius of our people and running the nuts and bolts of a modern nation state. We have innovated and adapted the federal model to our unique needs. However, pressing challenges remain and three of these need to be mentioned here:

Firstly: The most important challenge is instituting means of conflict resolution among the various vertical and horizontal levels of the state. The Constitution provides under Article 263 for the setting up of an Inter-State Council. Its mandate though is primarily deliberative, advisory and recommendatory and the experience of its functioning in arbitration and conflict resolution has not been encouraging. The judiciary has tended to refrain from intervening in inter-state and centre-state disputes, leaving it to the polity to politically mediate and resolve such disputes. This has become a very difficult, if not an impossible task, especially when different political formations are at the helm of the administrative units that are party to the dispute.

Secondly: Indian federalism is increasingly competitive at the economic and fiscal level. Allegations of political considerations influencing the quantum of financial transfers from the Centre to the State governments have been made. Some have even questioned the constitutional division of the powers of taxation. International Grants-in-Aid and competitive seeking of investments by State governments have queered the pitch. The challenge of placing fiscal transfers in a transparent and rule based framework is pressing. The nature of central intervention in reducing the debt of State Governments and correcting developmental imbalances should also be addressed. It is hoped that the 13th Finance Commission, constituted in November 2007, would suggest solutions to these grievances.

Thirdly: The devolution of functions, finances and functionaries to Panchayati Raj institutions has been, in the words of minister Mani Shankar Ayer, "uneven, fitful and subject to reversal". Fifteen years have passed since the 73rd and 74th Constitutional Amendments and the time has come for both the Central and State governments to deliver on their pledges of decentralisation and grassroots empowerment.

IV

A prerequisite for the satisfactory delivery of these and other correctives is what Shri Krishan Kant called "good politics". The problem had been anticipated by Dr Ambedkar. I can do no better than to recall his words:

> The working of the constitution does not depend wholly upon the nature of the Constitution. The constitution can provide only the organs of the state such as the Legislature, the Executive and the Judiciary. The factors on which the working of those organs of the state depends are the people and the political parties they will set up as their instruments to carry out their wishes and their politics. Who can say how the people of India and their parties will behave?

Where do we stand today? There is a pervasive sense of pessimism about the efficacy of institutions. A performance audit would show that the instrumentalities at the disposal of our legislatures have either been blunted or become dysfunctional. The single most important issue of concern is the decreasing credibility of our legislatures as effective institutions capable of delivering public good and contributing to effective formulation of laws and public policy.

In regard to the executive, the balance between its political and professional components has been disturbed; this is evident in the functioning of the civil service and particularly of the police. Thus 'the myth of authority', on which the power of the State depends, has been dented and has resulted in what has been called 'executive under reach'.

Even the judiciary has not been immune to allegations of corruption and concern has been expressed about the absence of a mechanism of accountability other than the process of impeachment.

A less scrutinised aspect of the functioning has been the role of political parties in the promotion or otherwise of democratic and federal functioning. Did Ambedkar have a premonition on this count too?

More disturbing questions have also been raised. Is representative government the same as responsive government? Do practices of governance satisfy the requirements of Rule of Law?

Three years back, a senior law officer of the government addressed this question candidly and concluded that the "Rule of Law in India is under serious threat, that there is widespread popular disillusionment, that there are cancerous developments eating into the fabric of each of the state institution and each is destroying itself from within, and that if these trends are not arrested, they are bound to be destructive of the Indian State in the long run".

In a similar vein but commenting on the wider picture, civil society groups in the country and abroad have observed that "the Rule of Law in India is in a downward spiral' and that the primary responsibility for it lies with the 'delayed justice dispensation system".

Surveying the functioning of our democracy, political scientist Pratab Bhanu Mehta notes that "the lines between legality and illegality, order and disorder, state and criminality have come to be increasingly porous".

Mehta sums up with a line from the poet Yeats: "The best lack all conviction, while the worst are full of passionate intensity".

Dismal though the picture may be, it cannot be allowed to dampen the will. In the final analysis, therefore, there is no option but to go back to Gandhi*ji's* dictum that "politics without principle is a sin".

Only this can be the basis of good politics; only good citizens can bring it about; only this will retain and sustain the spirit of the Constitution and lead to the fulfilment of its objectives.

Let me end where I began–on Krishan Kant*ji*. A line from an Urdu couplet provides an appropriate epitaph: *"Kya khoob aadmi tha khuda maghfirat kare"*

The Conference of Governors
Rashtrapati Bhavan, New Delhi
17 September 2008

The past two days have been highly educative and I would therefore like to join others in thanking Rashtrapati*ji* for taking this initiative.

The Constitution endows the governor of a state with a specific set of responsibilities. The executive power of the state is vested in the governor whose responsibility, in terms of the Oath of office, is to preserve, protect and defend the Constitution and devote himself or herself to the service and well-being of the people of the state.

The governor is also an integral part of the legislature of the state, has the right to address it or send messages to it. Needless to say, these powers and functions are to be discharged as per the provisions of the Constitution and within the framework of a democratic polity.

Today I wish to draw attention to three aspects of the governor's work. These relate to:

- The non-functioning of legislatures
- The role of governors as chancellors of sttate universities
- The governor's responsibility when the well-being of a section of the people of the State is seriously jeopardised.

My observations are based on knowledge that is in the public domain.

With regard to the first, the blunt truth is that state legislatures have virtually ceased to function in the sense in which legislature is expected to function in a democracy, that is, to be both a legislative and a deliberative body. The deliberative aspect of its work is to question and debate the policy of the government. This is seriously jeopardised by the duration of sessions—rarely exceeding two weeks and at times as little as three days.

A conference of the presiding officers of state legislatures in 1995 had recommended that state assemblies should meet for at least 60 days in the case of small states and 100 days in the case of larger states. The recommendation was reiterated in 1998. These have been completely ignored and, instead, a random sampling indicates the following:

- In the larger states for the years 2006 and 2007, the highest score was 59 days (Karnataka in 2007 closely followed by 56 in West Bengal in 2006) and the lowest was 23 (Gujarat in 2006 and 2007).
- In the smaller states for same years, the highest score was twenty-eight days (Puducherry in both years) and the lowest was thirteen (Haryana) in 2007.

It is time to focus on the perils of disuse. There is sufficient discussion in the media and in civil society about wasted public expenditure due to partial functioning of legislatures. In such a dismal situation, should the governor be a mere spectator and allow the Constitution he/she is charged to preserve and defend be violated in spirit if not in form? Instead, can the governor use the prestige of the office innovatively to initiate and develop a non-partisan debate about the longer term damage it can do to democratic politics, and to seek a broad consensus on a more productive approach to the functioning of legislatures?

My second point relates to the role of governors as chancellors of universities. Several governors have alluded to it and Shri Arjun Singh*ji* has indicated the action under way. I am given to understand that in quite a few cases in different states, differences over nominees for these posts have resulted in inordinate delays. These have an adverse impact on the institutions concerned. Furthermore, state governments are prone to issue diktats to vice chancellors on the day to day functioning of universities and thereby impinge on their autonomy. My suggestion is that the pattern and practice followed in the case of the Central Universities that have the President of India as the visitor be adopted in the case of State universities.

This would strengthen the governor's role in making these appointments and also shield the universities from the vicissitudes of the political debate.

My final point concerns social peace. The governor is required to devote effort for the well-being of all sections of the public. These include the weaker sections and the minorities. Recent and not-so-recent happenings bring out instances where the official machinery has defaulted in the discharge of its duties. Many of these have been identified by the Supreme Court. This has generated unease and insecurity among the minority segments of the citizen-body. Communalism of various hues is threatening the already fragile social fabric. Any selectivity in tackling it would be detrimental to the constitutional principles of equality and secularism.

The Constitution assigns responsibilities to governors. Secreted in the interstices of the constitutional text are its spirit and the purpose for which institution was created. These need to be explored in the context of the changing requirements of our times.

Golden Jubilee International Conference
Indian Society of International Law, New Delhi
2 February 2009

I am happy to participate in the Golden Jubilee Celebrations of the Indian Society of International Law. The society's work has been significant in terms of its scope and impact. It has fostered the study of international law in the country. Its publications, with a focus on the concerns of the developing countries of Asia and Africa, have been instrumental in the evolution of some aspects of international law.

International law took shape with the dawning of the realisation that anarchy cannot be the operative principle in the community of states. This necessitated the enunciation of rules. Some of these were induced by the desire for co-existence and to minimise or regulate conflicts; others took shape to facilitate cooperation. A third set of rules, of a normative nature, emanated from the ideals developed through interaction. Over time there has been progress, as Professor Richard Falk put it many years back, from consent to consensus.

The last three decades have witnessed the metamorphosis of international law from a tool for the regulation of formal diplomacy between states and coordination of international intercourse to an elaborate canvas covering complex areas of transnational concerns such as trade, economy and development, nuclear energy, outer space, human rights and environment. While this is an indication of the vitality of international law, it has also led to a certain fragmentation, of conflicting and incompatible principles, rule systems and institutional practices.

In this context, note has to be taken of some recent trends in the developments of international law and the manner in which it is sought to be legislated through the mechanism of the UN Security Council invoking

Chapter VII of the Charter. The responsibility for the maintenance of international peace and security has been interpreted to include the creation of new States, active role in nation-building and reconstruction efforts in conflict zones, establishing ad hoc international criminal tribunals, of humanitarian intervention and to bind non-State Parties to any international treaty.

Such an approach is reminiscent of an earlier era and compels one to reiterate the dictum that "a theory of legitimate power is inescapably a theory of democracy in the interlocking processes of the global system." The endeavour to broad base and democratise the international decision-making must therefore remain high on the agenda of all those who advocate a law-abiding international community.

In this 60th year of the Republic, it is relevant to recall that Article 51 of our Constitution exhorts the State to foster respect for international law and treaty obligations. Despite considerable progress, a fuller realisation of Fundamental Rights and of the Directive Principles incorporated in the Constitution is hampered by the enormity and diversity of the challenges in a country of over a billion people. It is therefore relevant to ask how and where the norms and principles of international law can be invoked to address these questions.

For a variety of reasons, India has not signed or ratified some treaties that are accepted by most members of the international community. Correctives could nevertheless be sought, and have been sought, in what is accepted as customary international law on the basis of the operating principles of 'justice, equity and good conscience'. There are a number of instances in which the Indian judiciary has relied upon international conventions and covenants in interpreting constitutional provisions and stating the law where legislation did not exist and where more can be done.

One example of the latter is the Visakha case in 1997 on sexual harassment when the court relied upon the Beijing Principles of Independence of Judiciary and Convention on elimination of Discrimination against Women. Another is the NHRC's order (17January 2003) on the Right to Food, relying on the Universal Declaration of Human Rights and the International Covenant on Economic, Social and Cultural Rights.

Even in the case of international humanitarian and human rights laws, and despite the fact that India has not subscribed to (1) the two Protocols additional to the Geneva Conventions of 1977 (2) the Rome Statute of the ICC (International Criminal Court) and (3) the 1951 Refugee Convention, a beginning was made by the NHRC after the Gujarat violence of 2002. It held the State responsible for significant human rights violations in its jurisdiction, whether committed by State or non-State actors. It demanded that victims of human rights violations have access to prompt and effective legal systems and to individual or collective reparations proportionate to the gravity of violations, including restitution, compensation, rehabilitation, satisfaction and guarantees of non-repetition.

The same holds good for the Refugee Convention. If accession is not considered feasible, an option may be either to have legislation providing for a framework for refugee status determination and protection or take executive action under the Foreigners Act of 1946 to create a class of foreigners called refugees under Sections 3(1) and (2) of the Act.

These matters are the subject of considerable debate; an instance of this is the unofficial National Consultations on the International Criminal Court.

The problems created by the dramatic expansion of the scope and instrumentalities of international law should not blind us to the significant success achieved in ameliorating the welfare of mankind. International Human Rights and Humanitarian Law have expanded their scope and application to become one of the most comprehensively regulated branches of international law. A great number of their rules have been recognised as part of customary international law.

The last two decades have witnessed the emergence of the five principal themes:

First: There is an almost universal acceptance that human rights, the Rule of Law and democracy at the National and International levels are interlinked and belong to the core values and principles of the Comity of Nations.

Second: It is now recognised that large scale violations of human rights and international humanitarian law could be construed as threats to international peace resulting in Security Council intervention. While this has meant that the Security Council has assumed the role of a guardian of International Humanitarian Law and Human Rights, problems continue to be posed due to the selectivity and subjectivity seemingly guided by realpolitik and interests of the Permanent Members of the Council.

Third: Alongside the increasing salience of human rights and international humanitarian law, there is a disturbing trend of various types of exclusion being practiced such as particularism, fundamentalism and nationalism that are against the universal humanitarian principles and human rights. This pattern of behaviour by some states of the international community is not in consonance with the principles of good governance and Rule of Law, and the purposes and thc principles of the Charter of the United Nations.

Fourth: There has been a drastic increase in the numbers and complexity of the role of non-state actors in areas that were traditionally considered to be the preserve of state action. This ranges from armed conflict, regulation of the economy and society including law and order functions, environmental protection, international trade and air transport and even protection of human rights and refugee rights.

The role of non-State actors challenges the traditional framework of international law when they resort to arms, violence and terrorism to achieve their objectives, either within their own state or in other states. Response patterns to these situations have tended to exhibit disconcerting levels of subjectivity.

Fifth: The Cold War period was a time of relative stability for the international system; it was preceded and succeeded by severe conflict, immense economic, social and political turmoil. The focus of the international community has now shifted to the wider question of comprehensive human security. International law has followed this trend. As a result questions of climate change, measures to address natural and man-made disasters and to counter global pandemics are increasingly the subject matter of international law.

The emergence of new nation states and non-state actors in the post cold war world, the empowerment of sub-state actors including individuals and groups and the creation of supranational actors and mechanisms have tested the traditional concept of state sovereignty. The tension continues between those who extol the virtues of the international legal discourse of the last two decades and those who criticise it citing that its underlying jurisprudential approaches conceal or ignore the deployment of power. The 'democratic deficits' and 'lack of level playing fields' that characterise international fora today have led to the criticism that they perpetuate organisational forms of hegemonic international law.

This leads us to a dilemma. If there is a significant gap in the espousal and implementation of international law, if enforcing mechanisms of international law are either non-existent or subjective in their approaches, and if the middle ground between idealism and realism is shrinking, could one justifiably question the future of international law in the contemporary world? Should we, in the words of Headley Bull, conclude that "it is better to recognise that we are in darkness than to pretend that we can see the light"?

The answer probably would be that in our globalised world, the process and impact of globalisation needs to go beyond economics and trade policies and result in universal adherence to the core and fundamental values of humankind. This admittedly would be an erratic and uneven process; it would test our patience and commitment. Governments, civil society and peoples all over the world have to be prepared to do what is right.

The objective of international law, in the final analysis, is orderly discourse among states for the good of humanity. This is best furthered in conditions of peace which, as an American statesman put it, "is a coin which has two sides–one is the avoidance of the use of force and the other is the creation of conditions of justice". In the long run, he added, "you cannot expect one without the other".

Let me conclude by pointing out that anniversaries are occasions for introspection, for measuring the distance traveled and for realising that the road ahead does have receding horizons. It can only be traversed on the basis of moral clarity.

Seventeenth Annual Convocation of the University of Kashmir
University Campus, Srinagar
20 June 2009

"B' naam-e-khuda-vand jaan aafarin
Hakim-e-sukhan dar zubaan aafarin"

It is difficult to come to Kashmir and not be reminded of an admiring visitor's description penned many centuries back:

"Kashmir is a garden of eternal spring. Its pleasant meads and enchanting cascades are beyond all description. There are running streams and fountains beyond all count. Wherever the eye reaches, there are verdure and running water."

Time does not dent the beauty of nature. Time does allow humans to enhance the benefits they derive from it. Time, regrettably, does not stand still. We never step into the same river twice; nor can we use a time machine to re-live a gone by era. This university campus, and its endeavour in different branches of knowledge, suggests a desire to move with time. It would undoubtedly please the spirit of saints and rishis who inhabited this land in yesteryears and imparted so much of wisdom and spiritual solace to the people.

I am happy to participate in today's ceremony. Convocations are to academic life what festivals are to social life; they signify rites of passage, the passing of seasons, a celebration of achievement and benediction for facing the harsh world beyond the somewhat sheltered academic environment. The motto of the university–From Darkness to Light–exemplifies the transition that graduating students undergo.

Convocations are also occasions to draw lessons from the experience of life. I too may be permitted to do so. Let me begin by recalling a couplet addressed to students of my own alma mater a long time back by a poet very well known to you:

"Auron ka hai payam aur, mera payaam aur hai
Ishq ke dard mand ka tarz-e-kalaam aur hai"

My message today pertains to the world of tomorrow. We live in an era of rapid change. A quarter of a century back an eminent historian wrote on the need to prepare for the twenty- first century; he offered the prognosis that instead of a "new world order" we confront "a troubled and fractured planet whose problems deserve the serious attention of politicians and public alike." The man and woman in the street, he added, know that their world is changing; they demand political responses in addition to technological ones.

I venture to suggest that these matters are of critical relevance to a society like ours. India is engrossed in challenges of development and political empowerment. It is one-sixth of the world in terms of population and is a microcosm of the diversities that characterise our world. It has been rightly called 'the largest multicultural society in the world.' The accommodation of diversity has been an Indian trait down the ages, made possible by an innate capacity for synthesis.

How do we use this asset in the future?

In what manner can we harness it for accommodating the competing demands of identity, autonomy and integration in a world that is perennially shrinking and inter-dependent?

How would this translate into institutions and practices?

How would it impact on the daily lives of citizens? What may be the pitfalls that need to be avoided?

What, in concrete terms, should be expectations of youth from society?

A healthy society faces these, and related questions, and responds to them meaningfully.

II

The process of social cohesion proceeds from small groups to larger ones; each step enlarges the common agenda and reveals points of convergence and divergence; each divergence necessitates a choice: rejection or adjustment in the wider framework. In this manner rights and duties, as also adjustment and accommodation become integral to social life. The process also reveals a desire to distinguish between what is shared and what is held close to the chest. The latter generates the impulse for self-management or autonomy, to the exclusion of those who participate in managing the realm of what is shared. It thus becomes an essential characteristic of identity and reflects on patterns of governance. When transferred to the sphere of public life, it takes the shape of several autonomies– horizontal, vertical, political, fiscal and cultural - that may be sought. In this sense, autonomy ceases to be an exceptional principle in a democracy and, instead, becomes one of its essential ingredients functioning, in the words of one scholar, as "autonomies in perpetual dialogue among themselves, linked by respective responsibilities to retain …" .It needs to be admitted straight away that the question of identity, integration and social cohesion is complex and necessitates conscious and continuous efforts at calibration of challenges and responses. It requires identification and justification of areas of autonomy and integration.

Two other terms, deprivation and alienation, are contextually relevant in relation to groups. The former signifies persons who find themselves disadvantaged or lacking for reasons beyond their control; the latter denotes estrangement, social isolation and powerlessness. Both impact on social cohesion.

A clear distinction is to be made between assimilation and integration. The former implies the blending or fusing of minority groups or cultures into the dominant society or culture. It is usually reflective of the desire of the dominant group on grounds of cultural nationalism and is resented and resisted by minority ones. Integration, on the other hand, implies the movement of minority groups and the underprivileged sections of a society, without erasing their identity, into the mainstream of the society to give them full access to the opportunities, rights and services available to the members of the mainstream. It is always a two-way street and thus goes hand in hand with social solidarity.

III

The debate on identity, autonomy and integration was part of the Indian discourse in the Freedom Movement and in the formative period of the Constitution. In the words of a distinguished academic, "the Indian

Constitution was well ahead of its time not only in recognising diversities but also in providing for representation of the collectivities in the formal democratic structures." The special provisions for guarantees or affirmative action in six broad categories–caste, class, backwardness, religion, region, sex and language–is evidence of this approach for securing justice and ensuring cultural autonomy in a composite culture within a framework of a quasi-federal structure driven by an overriding imperative of maintaining territorial integrity.

Closer scrutiny shows that the multiple identities so recognised are amplified in our Constitution for legal and operative purposes and total as many as thirteen–identities grounded in religion; identities grounded in language; caste identities; tribal identities; community identities, such as in the case of the Anglo-Indian community; class identities, such as in the case of the socially and educationally backward classes; racial identities, notably prohibiting discrimination on grounds of race and permitting notification of specific races or groups within races to be deemed to be Scheduled Castes; gender identities; identities grounded in region, place of birth or residence, especially in the context of prohibition of discrimination and provisions contained in Part XXI of the Constitution; identities based on age, such as those provisions relating to children and the aged; minority identities, whether based on religion, language, script or culture; identities grounded in descent, especially in the context of non-discrimination on grounds of descent; and identities based on occupation, such as agricultural or industrial workers, defence personnel or civil servants etc.

Accommodation of diversity has thus been consciously incorporated as a distinctive feature of the Indian state. It implies that a standardised image of an Indian cannot be constructed; if presented, it is partial, incomplete, misleading. Despite this accommodative framework, there have been acts of omission and commission impacting on identity and integration issues.

Perceptions have evolved nationally and globally and highlight areas that remain to be addressed. Democratic politics and economic liberalisation has also strengthened regionalist trends. Linguistic reorganisation has ceased to be the culmination of the process of expression of identities. Linguistically homogenous states have been subdivided over grievances of development.

New demands for statehood continue to be made on grounds of ethnicity, culture or regional grievances. The imperative of better governance adds a sense of urgency to these.

These impulses of identity assertion and recognition confront two contradictory trends at the micro and macro levels. On the one hand, forms of identity assertion at national and state levels combined with existing patterns of political mobilisation have been perceived as thwarting the impulses towards internal integration and consolidation. A modern market economy does not coexist with autarky. On the contrary, societal transformation resulting from economic growth and urbanisation has erased or downplayed certain identities while emphasising new ones. Each of these impacts the political agenda at local, regional and national levels.

At the other end of the spectrum, we are living in a global village where new integrating impulses have gone beyond national boundaries weaving nations into a common fabric of economic and financial architecture, shared membership of multi-lateral institutions and common value systems governing individual and state behaviour. Countervailing forces have also emerged. Thus, globalisation has produced a counter trend of resurgence of nationalism and of an emphasis on national and cultural identities. Domestically, one notices certain unhealthy trends towards a homogenising nationalism that flattens diversities, and has little respect for local cultures, value systems and ways of life.

IV

What do these developments mean to common citizens? What indeed is our vision of the interplay between identity and integration in the twenty-first century?

First: It is clear that living in isolation is not an option. It is nevertheless essential to realise that there are many ways of living together. Integration is necessary and desirable; assimilation is neither desirable nor practical. Throughout our history, we have seen identities being built on a series of inclusions and exclusions reflective of ground realities. The challenge in the future, as in the past, would be to maintain a balance in favour of inclusions.

Second: Political management of identities and ethnicities has tended to vary between accommodation, polarisation and manipulation. The only workable arrangement for a country of our diversity is accommodation in a constitutional and democratic framework. This necessitates negotiations with the State, and by the State. The politics of polarisation and manipulation practices should have no place in our country.

Third: In an evolving polity and a developing economy, institutional dynamism plays an important role in making the conceptual transition from plurality to multiculturalism. The latter 'is concerned with issues of equality: it asks, whether the different communities living together peacefully, co-exist as equals in the public arena.' Such an approach would result in 'a form of citizenship that is marked neither by a universalism nor generated by a complete homogenisation, nor by the particularism of self-denial and closed communities.' Such a vision of society would be contingent on the citizen body imbibing a new set of values.

Fourth: The youth in the age group of 15-35 years constitutes nearly 40 per cent of the total population of India. It is the same in the case of Jammu and Kashmir. This group represents the most vibrant and dynamic demographic segment and constitutes potentially a most valuable human resource. Youth empowerment would mean effective participation in decision making processes, with requisite knowledge, skills and capabilities. It is premised on attainment of higher educational levels and expertise by our young citizens, in line with their abilities and aptitudes, and access to employment opportunities.

How is it possible?

Two years ago I had, as the Chairman of the Working Group constituted by the prime minister on Confidence Building Measures, submitted a set of recommendations which also focussed on the Kashmiri youth. The issue was also addressed in the Report of the Working Group on Economic Development of J&K. The prime minister had expressed complete agreement with the view that implementation of the Working Group recommendations was the key to retaining the confidence of the people.

There is no option but to reconstruct the economy of the state ravaged by two decades of militancy. The potential of youth must be utilised to get out of the 'backwardness trap' of low economic activity, low employment and low income generation. Better education and health for the youth lead to inclusive growth where the poor continue to grow and benefit from it.

The graduating students today represent a minuscule and fortunate elite among youth having obtained tertiary education. We need to focus on creating adequate facilities for technical and vocational education, for skill up-gradation and improving employability of youth. New opportunities in services sector, including in the IT industry, must be made available to the youth of Jammu and Kashmir.

The youth of Jammu and Kashmir, like in the rest of the country, want to fulfil their potential, lead lives with dignity and honour and contribute to their communities and the nation. The government is committed to enable this and thus herald a new future for the people of Jammu and Kashmir.

How realistic is such an approach? The answer seems to lie in our experience with other innovative norms that challenged orthodoxy. The processes of devolution of power to Panchayats and Nagar Palikas, the acceptance of the need for transparency in governance, the insistence on fundamental rights and observance of human rights norms, are instances of new perceptions impacting on state practice. Each proclaims a new beginning; none can yet claim perfection; all need to be pursued vigorously. The challenge, as Richard Falk would put it, is for "morally sensitive and forward-looking political forces" to "seek unexplored normative potential." No segment of public is better qualified to do it than the youth. For them immobility, retreat, or disinterest is not an option.

I felicitate the students graduating today and wish them success in life. They would, I venture to hope, hold aloft the banner of the University and adhere to its motto. As citizens they should remember Edmund Burke's dictum that "the only thing necessary for the triumph of evil is for good men to do nothing." To do so meaningfully, they need to heed Allama Iqbal's advice:

"Jab tak na zindagi ke haqaiq pe ho nazar
Tera zajaj ho na sake ga hareef-e-sang."

The focus, above all, has to be on self development:

aamir-e-khudi kar, asar aahe rasa daikh.

Valedictory Function of the International Conference of Jurists on International Terrorism and Rule of Law

Vigyan Bhawan, New Delhi

22 November 2009

I am happy to participate in the Valedictory Function today of the International Conference of Jurists. Your deliberations have been wide ranging and the conference has highlighted the centrality of Rule of Law for issues that impact critically on our daily lives – violence, public safety, maintenance of law and order, economic development, poverty eradication, empowerment of women and marginalised sections of society, regulation of business and industry, and environmental sustainability. A principal concern has been the scourge of terrorism that is disruptive of all civilised life.

Rule of Law as a concept has two dimensions: formal and substantive. The first pertains to a system or a procedure and is referred to as the Rule by Law rather than by persons; the second relates to its substantive content. The latter seeks to ensure compliance with the law in a transparent, efficient and accountable manner. Its success depends on the value system of a society and of those in charge of governance.

This distinguished audience is well aware of recent trends in the study of the Rule of Law. Political scientists have argued that an organic development and entrenchment of Rule of Law in a developing country context requires three essential conditions: (i) certainty, meaning equality before law and absence of arbitrary abuse of authority; (ii) perpetuity, the ability to bind future regimes and officials of the state to today's rules and institutions and (iii) certitude that resort to violence is legitimate and controlled.

There is a teasing aspect of the matter also. Societies and polities differ on the purpose of Rule of Law; is it an instrument of the state structure for achieving the objectives of the state, or is it the bedrock of the state structure ensuring respect by the government for the sovereign authority of the people and the fundamental rights of its citizens?

In India we remain committed to democratic governance, transparency, inclusive development and the implementation of Rule of Law. Our practice, however, has been marred by lapses resulting in a failure to deliver it in sufficient measure. The supremacy of Rule of Law has been challenged by corruption and the malicious influence of money power; both are made possible by departure from norms of good governance.

Corruption is an ailment that is pervasive, cancerous and multi-dimensional. In moral terms it corrodes the social and political fabric of society and increases injustice; in its legal implications, it results in disregard for the Rule of Law; in its developmental aspect, it tends to distort the decision-making processes and is wasteful of resources. It shakes the legitimacy of the state, erodes sovereignty of the state and its capacity to exercise sovereign functions including ensuring law and order for the citizens. It has emerged as a significant threat to national security.

The second challenge to the supremacy of Rule of Law is elite behaviour. National and international media are full of reports on how the elite are able to subvert the Rule of Law with money or influence. A large swathe of society and polity even accept this situation as a way of life. While the normative elements of legal and political systems seek to establish the Rule of Law, the reality of systemic discrimination and exclusion based on community, gender, class and other limiting and distorting considerations is compelling.

Our globalised world is characterised by enhanced levels of resort to violence by State and non-State actors. Legal systems in many countries have resorted to doctrines of necessity to incorporate 'exceptional' and 'extraordinary' legislation to deal with this surge of violence. This has impacted the primacy of Rule of Law with all its attendant implications. The challenge for governments and legal fraternities across the globe is to deal effectively with violence within the framework of 'normal' laws and respect for human rights and fundamental freedoms.

The Human Rights Day Celebration

Mavalankar Auditorium, New Delhi

10 December 2009

It gives me great pleasure to address this distinguished audience today on the occasion of the Human Rights Day. This day commemorates the proclamation in 1948 by the United Nations General Assembly of the Universal Declaration of Human Rights as a common standard of achievement for all peoples and nations.

Though human rights entered the lexicon of national and international law in the twentieth century, the concept that these are rights inherent to human dignity and not the gift of any political sovereign existed much earlier. The Declaration of the Rights of Man adopted by the National Assembly of France in 1789 declared that 'the ignorance, neglect or contempt of the rights of man is the sole cause of public calamities and the corruption of governments.' Over time, human rights came to be considered universal, indivisible, interdependent and integral to state structure and global order. Thus every State came to be known by the rights it maintained.

Modern human rights law emerged at the end of World War II in response to violations and atrocities witnessed in that conflict. The Charter of the United Nations, the Genocide Convention and the Universal Declaration were its first manifestation. These were amplified in two International Covenants adopted in 1966. Over the next three decades, a comprehensive structure of individual, group, gender and child rights was put in place, along with a modicum of operational guarantees.

The Constitution of India, crafted with considerable diligence around the time the Universal Declaration was proclaimed, reflects the ideals of our freedom struggle as also many of the latter's principles. It has provisions and guarantees for safeguarding the entire gamut of civil and political rights.

The Preamble to the Constitution is a reflection of the Constitutional tight-rope walked by our Founding Fathers. It characterises 'dignity of individual' and 'unity and integrity of the nation' as core values and hints at the need to strike a balance between them in all actions and efforts of the state. It guarantees Fundamental Rights and enunciates the Directive Principles of State Policy. The record of six decades shows that judicial and legislative innovation on the issue of human rights has been a work-in-progress. There have been significant Constitutional amendments on the subject of Fundamental Rights. The Supreme Court's interpretation of Fundamental Rights has been critical in this regard, especially on two counts. The first relates to what Justice Krishna Iyer termed "Judiatrics", by which the apex court has incorporated some of the Directive Principles of State Policy into Part III of the Constitution. It held that Provisions of Part III and IV are supplementary and complementary to each other. The second has been the reading of enabling provisions of international covenants and treaties into the constitutional guarantees of Fundamental Rights and thereby enlarging the meaning and scope of human rights.

Our courts have commendably discharged their responsibilities in accordance with the 'Bangalore Principles' on 'The Domestic Application of International Human Rights Norms'. They have reiterated that international human rights instruments provide important guidance in cases concerning fundamental human rights and freedoms and that it would be proper judicial process for national courts to have regard to international conventions and norms where domestic law is uncertain or incomplete.

The most important legislative intervention on human rights has been the enactment of The Protection of Human Rights Act 1993 that enabled the constitution of a National Human Rights Commission. It has also provided for the constitution of State Human Rights Commissions and Human Rights Courts. The NHRC has been given a broad mandate to inquire into complaints of human rights violations or negligence in the prevention of such violations by a public servant, visit jails or detention centres, review statutory or constitutional safeguards for protection of human rights and recommend measures for their effective implementation, study international instruments on human rights, promote research on human rights and spread human rights literacy.

At the time of establishing the NHRC, it was the expectation of civil society and human rights activists that the Commission would represent a quantum leap in the institutional mechanism for protection of human rights in the country. An assessment sixteen years later would indicate that the Commission has done pioneering work, especially regarding its focus on the rights of women and children, custodial deaths and human rights literacy. Its landmark observation on the Gujarat communal disturbances underscored the 'primary and inescapable responsibility of the State to protect the right to life, liberty, equality and dignity of all those who constitute it … and ensure that such rights are not violated either through overt acts or through abetment or negligence'. The Commission adopted emerging human rights jurisprudence when it held the State responsible 'not only for the acts of its own agents, but also for the acts of non-State players acting within its jurisdiction'.

The same assessment would also show that the work of the NHRC has been in the nature of incremental and uneven growth. The glass, it would seem, is half-full and suggests the need for more work to ensure compliance with prescribed norms and procedures by the State agencies.

One way of assessing the efficacy and impact of the NHRC is in terms of 'The Paris Principles' relating to the Status of National Institutions on Human Rights, adopted by the UN General Assembly in 1993. It is to be recalled that the National Human Rights Institutions of South Asian countries did resolve at a conference in April this year to appeal to their governments for support to become fully compliant with Paris Principles, including on administrative and financial autonomy.

Two other factors are of relevance. Today we live in a world that has changed drastically since the proclamation of the Universal Declaration of Human Rights and the adoption of our Constitution. The emergence of new nation states and non-state actors in the post cold war world, the empowerment of sub-state actors including individuals and groups and the creation of supranational actors and mechanisms have tested the traditional concept of state sovereignty. This makes evident the resulting tension between those who extol the virtues of the international legal discourse including human rights discourse of the last few decades and those who criticise it citing that its underlying jurisprudential approaches and mechanisms for enforcement and application conceal or ignore the deployment of power.

It is now recognised that large scale violations of human rights and international humanitarian law are not mere domestic or internal concerns of states, but could be construed as threats to international peace resulting in some form of Security Council intervention. While this has meant that the Security Council has assumed the role of a guardian of Human Rights and International Humanitarian Law, problems continue to be posed due to the selectivity and subjectivity seemingly guided by realpolitik and interests of the Permanent Members of the Council.

As a founding member of the United Nations, a leading democracy that houses one-sixth of humanity and is working for their empowerment and development, India stands fully supportive of the increasing salience of human rights at the national and international planes. It opposes exclusions sought on grounds of 'particularism'. It is our hope that responsible state behaviour in our region and in the world at large would widen the support for principles of good governance and Rule of Law, and the purposes and the principles of the Charter of the United Nations.

I would like to add one last word about ideals. The realisation of one set of ideas does not, should not, distract us from walking towards the receding horizon. The transition from bestowed rights to inherent rights, from some rights to some people to all rights to all people, has signified quantum leaps. These also bring out the critical difference between the acknowledgement of a right and the realisation of a right; hence the need for constant review of the instrumentality made available to citizens, individually or in groups.

Furthermore, there is no reason to believe that the cosmopolitan and globalised world of the twenty-first century would remain static in terms of its perceptions on morality and rights and would eschew the imperative of exercising the moral muscle to put in place a plural, humanitarian and egalitarian morality to underpin comprehensive global human security.

Twelfth Convocation of the University of Hyderabad

Shilpakala Vedika, Hyderabad
22 June 2010

It is not customary to begin with a disclosure. Yet, I owe it to this audience to admit that the persuasive powers of the chancellor and the formidable reputation of this seat of learning were sufficient to induce me to come here today and feel happy about it.

Add to these Hyderabad's own cosmopolitan essence. The founder of the city in the sixteenth century decreed that it should be "a replica of paradise itself". Few down the ages disagreed with the outcome. Diamonds from nearby mines gave it fame and centrality and textiles commercial significance. It spawned a charmingly rich language and a composite culture. A Qutb Shahi poet summed up its place in the world: *"Dakan hai angina, angoothi hai jag."*

None would have then realised that the closing years of the twentieth century would make the city a Koh-i-noor in terms of modern science and technology. It speaks volumes for Hyderabad's genius for accommodation and change while holding on to the thread of excellence. The University of Hyderabad, occupying the first position in a recent ranking of Indian universities, is itself a good example.

II

Convocations are occasions to honour intellectual achievement. The pursuit of knowledge, however, is not subject to formal barriers and inquiry in any of its branches does not end with the acquisition of a university decree. The mind trained to think logically and critically does not cease to function. This often brings it face to face with reality at variance with tradition and to which it feels compelled to respond. It is here that the two worlds, within the academia and beyond it, come together.

There is a perception that in a gone by era; a university was an idyllic and isolated enclosure where knowledge was pursued for its own sake unrelated to mundane utilitarian requirements of the lesser world beyond its portals. The reality, however, was somewhat less prosaic and not devoid of a carefully crafted umbilical cord to society and its spokes-persons. It was also subject to change. Today it is candidly accepted that teaching and research in a university, and the advances in knowledge it produces, should in considerable measure be related to the changing needs and demands of society. The centrality of social purpose thus stands underlined. The really teasing question pertains to its ambit.

Some weeks back, I came across an introspective essay by Professor Stephen Chan, who teaches International Relations at the School of Oriental and African Studies, University of London. Seeking a new internationalism and exploring different cultural traditions, he dwells on the prevailing contest between what he calls "assertions of certainty" and described them as "about the best form of coercion to apply in any international moral impasse". He urges the need to speak publicly and with imagination about complex things, and challenge orthodoxy with correctives. "The idea", he adds, "is to think, and not be either led or simply moved by images of distress". "The concerned citizen", he concludes, "should be motivated by five principles: transparency, lack of arbitrariness, accountability, compassion and redress."

There is nothing altogether novel about any of Chan's five principles; yet, taken together, they do offer a road map for action. This youthful audience, blessed with a critical faculty and brimming with excellence in their chosen disciplines, knows only too well that responsibilities of citizenship cannot be forsaken nor can they be delegated or postponed since eternal vigilance is the only way to safeguard liberty and rights and, as Edmond Burke put it, "the only thing necessary for the triumph of evil is for good men to do nothing".

Some of you would, as I would, like to explore this further. What are the legal and the moral imperatives for the citizen? What is the most feasible manner in which his/her responsibilities can be undertaken? Both are inextricably linked to, and influenced by our perception of the human character and of the world we live in. It unavoidably influences the shaping of the future.

Let us consider the latter. The term human has a certain connotation. A random perusal of the dictionary suggests a number of associated terms: humane, humaneness, humanism, humanitarian, humanitarianism, humanity, humanise, humankind, and humanly. Each of these depicts an aspect being human and thereby becomes prescriptive in some measure if the claim to be human is to be sustained. It becomes clearer when put alongside its antonym which suggests its negation or opposite. Furthermore, and to use the words of the UN's Universal Declaration of Human Rights of December 1948, the ambit of humanity and therefore of human rights extends to 'all peoples and all nations.'

Those of you familiar with political philosophy would recall the argument by which Aristotle had distinguished between "a good man" and "a good citizen" and concluded that the virtue of the two "cannot be always the same" except in the case of a perfect state. He then defined a good citizen as one who should know "how to govern like a free man and how to obey like a free man". He or she should, as a later philosopher put it, appreciate both the necessity and the moral imperative of being free.

These attributes of citizenship were refined down the ages. A famous example is the Funeral Oration of Pericles, recorded for posterity by the historian Thucydides. Two of the attributes cited by him have universal validity: firstly, that citizens "are fair judges of public matters", and secondly that "instead of looking on discussion as a stumbling block in the way of action, we should think it is an indispensable preliminary to any wise action at all."

A citizen is endowed with rights, is a participant in public life not on sufferance but by right, does so as an equal and not as a subject. The raja-praja concept that has such an established place in our daily vocabulary is a relic of an earlier era and has no basis in today's legal structure. Its persistence, nevertheless, sheds much light on the psychological baggage that we sub-consciously carry.

It is essential to remember that the modern democratic State has specified the citizen's charter of rights; it also dwells on the duties of citizenship. We do not have to look for instances because we ourselves are the model. The Constitution of India is one of the best examples of a constitution that blends the rights and duties of citizenship harmoniously. In terms of sheer numbers and scale, the extent of human freedom and liberation that was granted was unprecedented in human history. It has stood the test of time and has been widely acclaimed.

III

The charter of rights of citizens is spelt out in the Constitution of India in the chapter relating to fundamental rights. These pertain to six broad categories: the right to equality, right to freedom, right against exploitation, right to freedom of religion, cultural and educational rights, and right to seek constitutional remedies. Some other rights are interspersed in other sections of the document, e.g. protection against arbitrary taxation, freedom of trade, commerce and intercourse, and group rights of certain classes. The text is underscored by an overarching framework of constitutional morality.

Many years after the Constitution was finalised and proclaimed, a section on Fundamental Duties was added, based on the perception that successful functioning of a democratic polity necessitates active participation by citizens in the processes of governance through assumption and discharge of responsibilities by the citizen body. This approach has been accepted by the courts of law.

You would note that Article 51A of our Constitution contains a set of eleven duties of citizens described as *fundamental*. Three of these need to be highlighted in the context of our discussion today. These pertain to the promotion of harmony and spirit of common brotherhood, development of a scientific temper, humanism and spirit of inquiry and reform, and striving for excellence in all levels of individual and collective activity. These have to be read with the requirements of justice and fraternity so clearly enunciated in the Preamble of the Constitution.

I dwell on this because you, the highly educated among our citizens, bear a special responsibility in this regard. As you leave the sanctuary of the university and step into the world beyond it, it is appropriate to remind you of this compendium of rights and duties and of the need to reiterate your commitment to them. This would assist you in assessing the direction in which we as a citizen-body are travelling, as also to explore correctives where needed.

It has been observed by an eminent public figure that we are today "desperately groping for a political culture based on integrity". One obvious reason for this is the dilution of system of values at the individual and collective levels. Views to the contrary are also around. Some, espousing pragmatism, propel us towards the dogma that politics is the art of the possible. The first is reflective of anguish, the second of smugness.

Here again, as in the case of the conceptual framework of humanity, the ambit and implications of terms like integrity and *possible* have to be clearly understood. Integrity stands for moral excellence and honesty; its absence would suggest immorality and dishonesty. In the same way, a term like 'possible' leaves open a range of possibilities including the acceptance of the immoral and the dishonest.

It should therefore be possible to argue that our quest for humanity and integrity does, lead us to an approach in which we proactively seek and induce values that are human, humane, moral and honest, values and practices that contribute fully to the public good in terms defined and prescribed by the Constitution,; thus is made the transition from what is ordinarily possible to what may be perceived as *impossible*.

Many decades back Gandhi*ji* had identified *Seven Social Sins*. They are inscribed on a tablet near his Samadhi at Rajghat. This identification is essential but not sufficient. The need of the hour is to redress the wrong, to apply the corrective, to change.

IV

Lest it be suggested that the foregoing is in the realm of the philosophical and the ideal, let me hasten to stress that a deficit of integrity and constitutional morality is wasteful of resources and harmful to the public good in material terms. This is substantiated by the reports of the Comptroller and Auditor

General, the Public Accounts Committee of the Parliament and the India chapter of the Transparency International. Thanks to the RTI, a good deal of information is otherwise also available in the public domain. Together they reveal a disturbing pattern of departures from norms of integrity.

Further afield, the same holds good in varying measure for our commitment to norms of human rights, humanity and justice inscribed in the Constitution and supplemented or amplified in customary international law and international covenants subscribed to by the Republic of India.

The need for correctives is thus evident. Public awareness is one aspect of the matter, focused public action is another.

It is clear that being a citizen and being a good citizen are far from being the same thing; the former is a legal fact while the latter demands participation in and contribution to the common good. Furthermore, and depending on the nature and extent of participation in civic burden and activities, it is possible to categorise citizens into three types: (a) those that are personally responsible, (b) those who participate in social activities within the established structures and values, and (c) those who go beyond the first two categories and critically assess situations to improve upon them and actively seek realisation of goals and values enshrined in the Preamble of the Constitution. The first is essential and obligatory; the second is desirable and necessary; the third would set us upon the path of full realisation of our potential as a society.

There is, of course, a fourth–an unmentionable category of those who flout rules, evade responsibilities, and disgrace by their behaviour the civic community to which they belong. A mature society would ostracise them, a less mature one would endure the burden while seeking a corrective.

The commitment of a society and polity to educating, grooming and nurturing its citizens, eventually manifests itself in the latter's approach to civic participation, standards of personal responsibility and adherence to constitutional morality. Thus a substantive contribution to the shaping of citizens can be made and educational institutions, including those of higher learning, can play a major role in this national effort.

One other aspect of the matter bears scrutiny. Technology and globalisation have ensured that isolation is no longer an option and that we have to live in the world and with the world. This necessitates an acceptance of global standards, rules, and norms of behaviour but without sacrificing our identity and values.

Pluralism and accommodation of diversity is a characteristic of our societal reality. The Indian approach to multiculturalism, in the words of an eminent academic, is to "aspire towards a form of citizenship that is marked neither by a universalism generated by complete homogenisation, nor by particularism of self-identical and closed communities".

This model is of wider relevance in an era that seeks to define the contours of a twenty-first century citizen who would have a national as well as a transnational identity.

The foregoing considerations help us to recapitulate the three of the eleven aspects of Article 51A and assess their relevance. A diverse and stratified society like ours requires social harmony for its cohesion, and needs a scientific spirit and excellence to seek and attain all round development. To promote and attain these is among the principal duties of citizens and this is to be undertaken proactively rather than passively, with a spirit of seeking justice and achieving fraternity.

This then is the task for the citizen body, and particularly for those like yourselves who are stepping into world beyond the portals of this seat of learning.

Every individual has an ideal, and an idiom for expressing it. This would be true of each of you. I have, speaking personally, often found a few couplets of the poet Mohammad Iqbal of considerable relevance and would like to share them with you:

"Sitaroan ke aage jahan aur bhi hain
Abhi ishq ke imtihaan aur bhi hain

Qanaat na kar aalam-e-rang-o-boo par
Chaman aur bhi, aashiyaan aur bhi hain

Tu shaheen hai parwaz hai
Tere saamne aasman aur bhi hain".

"There are worlds beyond the stars
Tests of passion yet to come

Content be not with the colour and scent around you
There are other gardens, other nests too

Thou art a falcon, flight is thy destiny
There are other skies that await you".

I congratulate the select few rewarded for excellence and all those who have received their university degrees today. I wish them happiness in personal life and success in professional pursuits. I urge them to remember at all times that they are citizens of this country and, by virtue of that, claimants of rights and obligated to discharge duties.

National Seminar on Electoral Reforms

C. Achyutha Menon Study Centre and Library, Kanakakkunnu Palace, Thiruvananthapuram

8 July 2010

This seminar focuses on a theme vital to the functioning of our democracy and I am, therefore, happy to be here to inaugurate it. The C. Achyutha Menon Study Centre and Library plays an important role in the intellectual and academic life of Thiruvananthapuram and has served as an important platform for social science research.

The subject matter of the seminar intersects the domains of theory and practice and has implications for both. This distinguished audience is aware of these. There is, nevertheless, a need to revisit the concepts, premises, definitions and domains since systematic restatements do help in clarifying the form of facts under scrutiny.

Political scientists in the audience know of the debate initiated way back in 1967 by the publication of Hanna Pitkin's thesis on the idea of representation, and of her definition of political representation as a public institutionalised arrangement where representation emerges not from any single action by any one participant, but from the overall structure and functioning of the system. For this reason political representation is different from private representation; the former is intrinsically and inevitably transformative and creates for a dispersed and diffused constituency an interest or a principle that did not pre-exist the act of representation. Political representation could take different forms; it could be formalistic, symbolic, descriptive or substantive. Any of these puts in place a set of markers, of authorisation and accountability, to assess the efficacy and success of the exercise of representative democracy thus undertaken.

II

It is relevant to recall that the Aims and Objectives Resolution moved by Jawaharlal Nehru in the Constituent Assembly on 13 December 1946 stressed that "all power and authority of this Sovereign Independent India, its constituent parts and organs of government, are derived from the people". Pursuant to this We the people of India' resolved in the Preamble of the Constitution to constitute India as a Republic dedicated the attainment of Justice, Liberty, Equality and Fraternity. The text spelt out the essential detail: a representative, parliamentary, democracy based on adult franchise; the sub-text anchored it in Rule of Law. Judicial pronouncements have amplified and highlighted four elements pertaining to these essentials:

1. A democratic setup is a part of the basic structure of the Constitution. It proceeds on the capacity of the people to elect their representatives and faith in the representatives to represent the people.
2. Democracy proceeds on the basic assumptions of popular sovereignty where the country is governed by the representatives of the people and that there exists equality among citizens in arriving at decisions affecting them.
3. There can be no democracy without periodical elections to ascertain popular will. These should be free and fair, in reality and form.
4. Democracy is not just a mechanism of forming and running a government but represents a matrix of relations between citizens which allows for every citizen to live his/her life to the fullest, in dignity, and able to develop, exert and enjoy his/her capabilities.

Our subject today is electoral reforms. Its various dimensions have been debated in governmental and non-governmental fora. Many suggestions have been made. Some have been incorporated in the framework of rules; others remain on the table. The debate, to my mind, is selective rather than comprehensive.

Our Founding Fathers adopted specific electoral systems for specific institutions of the State. While elections to the Lower Houses of the Central and State legislatures were on the basis of adult suffrage and first-past-the-post in delimited constituencies, elections to the Upper Houses was on the basis of proportional representation through a single transferable vote. A similar electoral system of proportional representation through a single transferable vote with different electorates has also been prescribed for the elections of the president and the vice president.

Since every decision has a context, a re-look at the occasion and the legislative intent is educative. The issue of representativeness came up for discussion in the Constituent Assembly in the Report on Minority Rights that was submitted on 8 August 1947. In the debate that followed, one Member moved an amendment suggesting Qualified Joint Electorates and stipulating that a Scheduled Caste candidate before being declared elected "shall have secured not less than 35 per cent of the votes polled by the Scheduled Castes in the elections for the reserved seat". He argued that it was important to demonstrate the Scheduled Caste representativeness of a victor in a seat reserved for Scheduled Castes. Another Member argued that "there should be confidence in the minds of the minorities that their views are properly represented in the legislature by persons in whom they have confidence and in whose election they have a reasonably fair voice". Yet another proposal was for abolition of reserved constituencies and introduction of a system of proportional representation with multi member constituencies by means of cumulative vote for election to the Lower Houses of legislatures.

In response, Dr Ambedkar gave three reasons for preferring the first-past-the-post system over the proportional representation system:

- Absence of a high level of literacy essential for proportional representation.
- Apprehension of a fragmented legislature that would impede stable government and maintenance of law and order.
- Disruption of the agreement already arrived at between the various minority communities and the majority community.

It would be recalled that the Two-Member Constituencies (Abolition) Act of January, 1961, abolished the Two-Member and Three-Member

Constituencies to which elections took place in the 1952 and 1957 General Elections.

How well has the first-past-the-post system worked? Electoral record for the Lok Sabha elections shows that in the past five General Elections the number of winning candidates who secured 50 per cent or more of the *valid votes polled* has varied between 121 and 221; it was 121 in 2009. Earlier, the Venkatachaliah Commission had surveyed the record of three general elections to conclude that over two-thirds of the members of the Lok Sabha and almost 90 per cent of the members of some State Legislative Assemblies were elected on a minority vote.

A perceptive observer of our electoral scene has rightly focused on what he calls the "paradox" of a deepening representative democracy coexisting with a thinning of the very idea of representation. "This paradox", he adds, "plays out differently in different domains of the democratic arena and most commonly takes the form of an encounter between a dynamic political process and an inflexible institutional response."

III

Given this record and six decades after these formational structures were put in place, a few questions unavoidably come to mind:

- What is the representative-ness of the elected representative? Our system works on the principle of *plurality* rather than of *majority.*
- Why has the electoral system of first-past-the-post to the Lower Houses of legislature produced fragmented legislatures and systemic instability since the third decade of the Republic, of a nature that was associated with the proportional representation system?
- Has the dis-proportionality between the share of votes obtained and the share of legislative seats won, eroded credibility and representativeness of our legislators?
- Is there merit in the suggestion that the government and the election commission conduct a careful and full examination of the introduction of a two-round system, with the second

round conducted between the two leading candidates in each constituency on the day after the first round? Is the time opportune now to conduct such an examination in consultation with all political parties?

- Does the current electoral system encourage a politics defined by 'who you are' and 'where you live' rather than 'what you believe in' and 'what you want to achieve'?
- What can be done to address the grievance of under-representation and unequal access to political power emanating from the Muslims? The data is compelling and disturbing.
- How are we to overcome the implications, in terms of the principle of one person, one vote, one value, of the 84th Amendment that froze the number of seats in the Lok Sabha and the State Legislative Assemblies till the year 2026?

Electoral systems are important because they translate the votes of people into legislative seats and hence into exercise of political power. Their credibility and representativeness are critical elements in bringing about stable polities that are essential for socio-economic progress.

Electoral systems also have an undue influence on the evolution of party systems, their role and their cohesion. They can encourage inner-party democracy or can suppress dissent. Electoral systems can also influence the nature of political mobilisation, alliance formation and societal accommodation. They can spark societal conflict or facilitate conflict management.

It is thus important for us to consider our electoral system in the context of our experience of the last six decades, the mandate of our constitutional framework and the future outcomes that we desire from our polity.

Any debate on the question of electoral system reform must look at enhancing representativeness, promoting societal accommodation and conciliation, incorporating constitutional and international safeguards to vulnerable groups, providing accountable, stable and efficient governance, enhancing legislative oversight and encouraging the evolution and development of effective and internally-democratic political parties.

I have attempted today to focus on some dimensions of electoral reforms which, I believe, have not been sufficiently addressed. I believe we should also guard against mechanistic analyses and suggestions for electoral reform. One analyst has opined that reforms "cannot be introduced by legislative fiat, but require the hard labour of politics and self-transformation". Are our polity, political parties, their leaderships and our elected representatives ready and prepared for this hard labour of politics and self-transformation?

The Durga Das Basu Centenary Celebrations
New Delhi
2 February 2011

To venture into the realm of law, for someone untutored in the discipline, can fairly be described as foolhardy. Greater, much greater, is the quantum of folly when such a venture is in the field of constitutional law, a calling located at the intersection of law, jurisprudence and political philosophy, and dealing with the interpretation and implementation of the Constitution itself and thereby touching upon the most fundamental relationships in society.

And yet, this is precisely the sin now being committed by this speaker before this august and learned audience. *Mia maxima culpa* is easier said than undone and the only mitigating factor to cite in defence is to submit that the incitement to commit the wrong came from none other than a very high ranking law officer of the Republic!

Since sins committed cannot be undone, the remaining option is to seek forgiveness through penance and repentance.

Well endowed with human frailties, I can only promise an honest try.

Durga Das Basu needs no introduction to students of law and to all those who seek to further their understanding of the robust text of our Constitution. His treatises on the subject, firmly entrenched in voluminous case law, have become standard source of reference. A celebratory exercise is thus very much in order.

Human history shows that legal codes are either bestowed or made. Once in place, an understanding of the text, and the context, requires comprehension of both. This takes the form of commentaries. We do not know if such commentaries existed on the ancient texts of Hammurabi, or Solon. We do know that *Manusmrti* attracted nine complete commentaries. We also know that medieval canonists in Europe or the faqihs in Muslim societies did dilate a good deal on the intent and purpose of their respective codes.

In modern times the classic work, of course, is Judge William Blackstone's *Commentaries on the Laws of England* published in 1776. More relevant for our endeavour today is Joseph Story's *Commentaries on the Constitution of the United States*, published in 1833. The purpose of the latter, in Judge Story's own words, was to bring before the reader "the true view of (the Constitution's) powers as seen by its founders and confirmed and illustrated by the actual practice of government".

This practice, in no small measure, included the interpretation of the constitution by the courts. It is true of both the United States and of India; both helped induce a spirit of constitutionalism amongst the citizens. Some landmark judgments of our own Supreme Court testify to it.

II

It has been said by an eminent authority on the working of our Constitution that the framers 'spun a seamless web' of three strands focused on (a) protecting and enhancing national unity and integrity, (b) establishing the institutions and spirit of democracy and (c) fostering a social revolution to better the lot of the masses. The framers believed that the three strands are mutually dependent and inextricably intertwined. The efficacy of the functioning of each strand, and a harmonious relationship of each with the other two, was considered by the founding fathers an essential requirement.

Given the constraint of time, and at the risk of selectivity, I would like to confine my remarks today to some aspects of the second strand and think aloud about some features of democracy at work in our society.

The concept of democracy has been dilated upon down the ages. It is premised on the dignity and freedom of the individual. To Aristotle, democracy meant the rule of "the poor and the majority"; "the preferred form", he opined," was one that upheld the supremacy of the law". Rousseau, on the other hand, considered "democracy so perfect a form as to be fit only for 'a nation of gods'." In modern times it is considered, as political scientist

David Held put it, "a universal formula for legitimation for a broad range of radically different societies and their respective modes of governance and political participation"

Whatever the form, an essential ingredient of modern democracy is its participatory character through a set of institutions agreed upon by the citizens and incorporated in laws, practices and conventions. The efficacy of these institutions thus becomes the litmus test for assessing the success of democratic practice.

This assessment is to be done in two segments and relates to the 'hardware' and 'software' of democratic principle and practice. Most observers agree that in the past six decades we have internalised in some measure the 'hardware of democracy'—by this, I mean the mechanisms, mechanics, institutions and procedures of our parliamentary democracy. Citizens are cognisant of periodic elections to elect their representatives to the parliament, state legislatures and local government. They remain acutely aware of the Executive and the benefits and pitfalls of dealings with it. They are knowledgeable in some measure of the judicial process.

This audience knows that parliamentary democracy necessitates government that is *Representative*, *Responsible*, and *Responsive*. The first implies balanced representation of all segments of the body politic; the second necessitates ministerial responsibility to the elected legislature; the third makes incumbent responsiveness at various tiers of governance – national, state and local – as well as transparency, accountability, public consultation and citizen engagement with the political process.

While representativeness and responsiveness are important, allow me to dwell here on the responsibility of the Executive as its impact on the citizenry is direct and immediate.

One needs to begin at the beginning. I subscribe to the view that the Constituent Assembly of India debates should be essential reading for all those wishing to comprehend the intent and purpose of the Founding Fathers who, despite political and ideological differences on some issues, managed to reconcile them and arrive at workable formulations.

While introducing the Draft Constitution in the Constituent Assembly in November 1948, Dr B.R. Ambedkar outlined two significant criteria that guided the Drafting Committee to suggest a Parliamentary democracy. He said:

- "A democratic executive must satisfy two conditions. It must be a stable executive and it must be a responsible executive."
- "In the Parliamentary system, the assessment of responsibility of the Executive is both daily and periodic. The daily assessment is done by members of parliament, through questions, Resolutions, No-confidence motions, Adjournment motions and Debates on Addresses. Periodic assessment is done by the Electorate at the time of the election which may take place every five years or earlier. The daily assessment of responsibility is far more effective than the periodic assessment and far more necessary in a country like India. The Draft Constitution in recommending the Parliamentary system of Executive has preferred more responsibility to more stability."

Thus, and apart from law-making, assessing the responsibility of the Executive on a daily and periodic basis constitutes the single most important element of being a Parliamentary democracy.

Our record on periodic assessment is good and universally acknowledged. Citizens can, however, legitimately enquire if those entrusted with the daily assessment of the Executive have discharged their duties? Also, and on an increasingly complex set of issues, have they legislated after due deliberation and given themselves sufficient time to do so meaningfully? Statistical data reveals a steady decline in the annual number of sittings of Parliament and of state legislatures.

As a result, and in the view of many competent observers, the idealised view of legislature as a deliberative body is a far cry from reality. Instead, the legislature has in the public mind become 'a site for adversarial combat rather than of deliberative clarity'. Consequently, 'disruptive adjournments have become the main tool of parliamentary opposition rather than reasoned argument'.

The other element that deserves scrutiny is the 'software of democracy'. How many citizens are aware of the spirit and the core values that inform the Constitution and the morality that guides it? How well versed are the functionaries in the political system aware of the software of our democracy?

The problem was recognised and addressed by Dr Ambedkar. He conceded that "the new institution of democracy was only 'top dressing on Indian soil that was essentially undemocratic', adding that our people have "yet to learn constitutional morality". It is not a natural sentiment but has to be cultivated. He therefore felt that the diffusion of constitutional morality throughout the body politic was indispensable for the peaceful working of a democratic Constitution, since any powerful and obstinate minority may render its working impracticable, without being strong enough to conquer ascendancy for themselves.

Ambedkar identified a few essential ingredients of constitutional morality:

1. "A paramount reverence for the forms of the Constitution, enforcing obedience to authority acting under and within these forms yet combined with the habit of open speech, of action subject only to definite legal control, and unrestrained censure of those very authorities as to all their public acts combined too with a perfect confidence in the bosom of every citizen amidst the bitterness of party contest that the forms of the Constitution will not be less sacred in the eyes of his opponents than in his own."
2. "Holding fast to constitutional methods of achieving our social and economic objectives" and "abandoning the bloody methods of revolution" and "the method of civil disobedience, non-cooperation and satyagraha". Where constitutional methods are open, there can be no justification for such unconstitutional methods which are "nothing but the Grammar of Anarchy".
3. Ensuring "Bhakti or hero-worship" in politics, which is a "sure road to degradation and to eventual dictatorship".
4. Ensuring that political democracy is followed by social democracy, a way of life which recognises liberty, equality and fraternity as the principles of life forming "a union of trinity" where to divorce one from the other is to defeat the very purpose of democracy.

He also added a word of caution. It is perfectly possible, he said, to pervert the Constitution without changing its form by merely changing the form of the administration and to make it inconsistent and opposed to the spirit of the Constitution.

III

The experience of the last six decades, ladies and gentlemen, demonstrates our success in widening and deepening the mechanisms of democracy, both horizontally and vertically. We have transformed our dual polity into a three-tiered one by giving constitutional status to local government. In the process we have introduced many innovations including decentralised planning, reservations for women, and establishment of state election commissions and finance commissions. Democracy today touches the remotest hamlet and the poorest citizen in its working.

At the same time, we must recognise that the key to the problems and crises of governance relate to the 'software of our democracy' – either a lack of awareness of the values and morality of the constitution among citizenry and the polity or its deliberate disavowal.

What is the corrective? How, and where, should it be initiated?

The corrective to bad governance is good and responsive governance rooted in our constitutional values. It has to be across the board and cover all the institutions of the state and all segments of the body politic. It necessitates an ethical corrective, a rejuvenation of the value system, a closing of the gap between public and private morality.

In the political realm, and notwithstanding Edmond Burke's classic exhortation to the electors of Bristol, the starting point in today's world should be the political parties. They are the instruments of our people to implement their agenda and work in accordance with their mandate. They provide the life blood of the Legislature and the Executive, and constitute the best media of political and social change. They embody within them the possibilities of realising our constitutional vision, or of sidestepping it.

Political parties are needed for more than merely exercise of political power. Their credibility and representativeness are critical elements in bringing about stable polities that are essential for socio-economic progress. They set examples of democratic practice, influence the nature of political mobilisation, alliance formation and societal accommodation. By their actions, they can either spark societal conflict or facilitate conflict management. Political parties lie at the root of any debate on representativeness, societal conciliation, and governance that is accountable, stable and efficient.

The legal fraternity too has an important role in spreading the message of constitutional morality and strengthening the 'software' of our democracy. It can perhaps do so with greater efficacy by addressing what Upendra Baxi has called "its own pathologies".

Before I conclude, allow me to go back to Judge Joseph's Story and cite an immortal passage that concluded his great work:

> "The structure has been erected by architects of consummate skill and fidelity; its foundations are solid; its compartments are beautiful, as well as useful; its arrangements are full of wisdom and order; its defences are impregnable from without. It has been reared for immortality, if the work of man may justly aspire to such a title. It may, nevertheless, perish in an hour by the folly, or corruption, or negligence of its only keepers, THE PEOPLE. Republics are created by the virtue, public spirit, and intelligence of the citizens. They fall when the wise are banished from the public councils, because they dare to be honest, and the profligate are rewarded, because they flatter people, in order to betray them".

In a similar vein, Dr Ambedkar too opined that if things go wrong under the Constitution, "the reason will not be that we had a bad constitution' but because 'Man was vile"!

I, for one, would unashamedly assert that both hold good in equal measure for the edifice given to us by the Founding Fathers of our own Republic.

Annual Convention
Benaras Hindu University, Varanasi
12 March 2011

Nationalism and Internationalism in the World of Tomorrow

Varanasi overwhelms, and with good reason. The city of Lord Shiva, referred to in the Rigveda as Kashi or 'the luminous one', is a place of great antiquity as also of immense reverence. The poet, Asadullah Khan Ghalib who spent a month in the city around the year 1820, wrote a poem in Persian of one hundred and eight couplets in praise of it. A few of these are indicative of the perception:

"Ta'aal Allah Banaras chashm-e-bad door
Bahisht-e-khurram o firdaus maa'moor"
"May God keep the evil eye away
From this heavenly meadow of joy"

"Ba Gangish aks partau fugan shud
Banaras khood nazeer-e-khaishtan shud"
"When its beauty is reflected in the water of Ganges
Banaras becomes witness to its own beauty"

There can be, have been, other descriptions of the city and its inhabitants. The Chinese traveler Xuanzang testified to the religious, educational and cultural centrality of the city. Tavernier praises its buildings but did not approve of its narrow streets. The British orientalist Horace Wilson, quoted by Nirad Chaudhury, cited a Sanskrit couplet (true in equal measure of all centres of pilgrimage!) about the presence of religious vagabonds:

> For those who are ignorant of the revealed scriptures and sacred traditions, and who have abandoned purity and proper conduct, and for those who have nowhere else to go, for them Benares is the refuge.

Even the timelessness of an ancient city does witness changes. The establishment of Banaras Hindu University in 1916 was one such event of seminal significance. The name and fame of the institution is in no need of commentary. Founded by Pandit Madan Mohan Malviya, for generations of Indians, the university has come to represent the national spirit. It played a crucial role in the independence movement and has produced many great freedom fighters and builders of modern India.

For more than one reason, therefore, I am delighted to be amidst this gathering of scholars and seekers of knowledge.

Convocations are occasions for introspection and contemplation. A university brings together the best mind of a generation. It is a place where enquiry is pushed forward and discoveries made. It induces informed speculation. It is therefore an appropriate forum for thinking about the future and the role in it of us as a people at a time when the country has taken meaningful steps towards a higher and inclusive economic and development orbit and is geared to empowering millions of our citizens to lead lives of dignity.

This quest necessarily takes us to consider the domestic as well as the external environment that would shape the future.

II

William Golding, who won the Nobel Prize for literature in 1983, described the twentieth century as the "most violent century in human history". It witnessed massacres and wars and ended in global disorder. In the last decade of the century the historian Eric Hobsbawm concluded that "our world risks both explosion and implosion. It must change".

The new century, whose first decade has just ended, confronts this challenge. It is readily conceded that science, technology and innovation would be increasingly vital to the health and wealth of nations. A report, entitled 'The Scientific Century', published last year by the Royal Society, London had this to say on the subject:

> No-one can predict the twenty-first century counterparts of quantum theory, the double helix and the internet. But there is little doubt that advances in science and technology will continue to transform the way we live, create new industries and jobs, and enable us to tackle seemingly intractable social and environmental problems ...
>
> Ten years into this new scientific century, the world is slowly recovering from a severe financial crisis. Food security, climate change and health inequalities are rising up international policy agendas. And countries such as China, India and Brazil are reshaping the economic and political landscape.

The unstated premise of this thesis is that it would modify, mould or change the way we think not only about scientific challenges but also about social and political ones. We do know that globalisation and the interconnectedness of the contemporary world have induced in some measure conceptual 'globality' or consciousness of the world as one place. What we have not explored in sufficient measure is the impact of this new consciousness on some of our most cherished notions that have dominated thinking and shaped action for over two centuries.

One of these is the concept of nationalism.

Nationalism as a motivating force emerged in Europe in early nineteenth century. As an ideology it sought 'the organs of a sovereign state through which to express itself'. It exalted national interest, heightened rivalries and shaped history. It provided 'the glue that made possible the modern state and modern industry'. It assumed aggressive dimensions and its overflow into imperial channels resulted in much misery to the colonised people and caused justifiable responses. It will be recalled that the world community formally expressed itself against colonialism through the UN General Assembly Resolution 1415 of December 1960. The actual process of decolonisation took a little longer.

Indian nationalism can best be described as political articulation of anti-colonial consciousness. After Independence, the new Indian State espoused a set of values focused on the attainment of justice, equality, fraternity, democracy, religious tolerance, inclusive economic development and cultural pluralism. Levels of actual achievement vary; our commitment to them, nevertheless, is unwavering and has stood the test of six decades.

In no period was Indian nationalism xenophobic. It was and is accommodative and synthesising. Its major premise is an existential reality, namely the plural nature of our society. A democratic polity and a secular state structure give shape to it and sustain and nurture it. The end product has rightly been described as *sui generis.*

There was no dearth of sceptics. The older, colonial, mindset about the absence and prospect of an Indian nation and nationhood was supplemented by the emergence of new apprehensions about of capacity to self-govern, of balkanisation, of failure of the democratic experiment, of overcoming the agony of the multitudes, were articulated. Others had greater confidence; in August 1950, the British political scientist Earnest Barker put the Preamble of our Constitution on the first page of his book *Principles of Social and Political Theory* because, he said, "it stated in a brief and pithy form the argument of the book." With one-sixth of the world's population and the closest reflection of the diversity of humanity, we have been rightly called 'the largest multicultural society in the world.'

The debate on identity and nationalism was part of the discourse of our Freedom Movement and was conducted with some vigour in the Constituent Assembly. It bore the impact of global developments of that era. As a consequence, while the focus of the Constitution was on the individual citizen it was also, in the words of a distinguished academic, "well ahead of its time not only in recognising diversities but also in providing for representation of the collectivities in the formal democratic structures."

Closer scrutiny shows that the multiple identities so recognised are amplified in our Constitution for legal and operative purposes and total as many as thirteen identities grounded in religion; identities grounded in language; caste identities; tribal identities; community identities, such as in the case of the Anglo-Indian community; class identities, such as in the case of the socially and educationally backward classes; racial identities, notably prohibiting discrimination on grounds of race and permitting notification of specific races or groups within races to be deemed to be Scheduled Castes; gender identities; identities grounded in region, place of birth or residence, especially in the context of prohibition of discrimination and provisions contained in Part XXI of the Constitution; identities based on age, such as those provisions relating to children and the aged; minority identities, whether based on religion, language, script or culture; identities grounded in descent, especially in the context of non-discrimination on grounds of descent; and identities based on occupation, such as agricultural or industrial workers, defence personnel or civil servants etc.

Accommodation of diversity was thus consciously incorporated as a distinctive feature of the Indian State. The special provisions for guarantees or affirmative action for specific collectivities is evidence of an approach for securing justice and sustaining multiple identities in a composite culture within a framework of a quasi-federal structure, driven by an overriding imperative of maintaining territorial integrity.

Consequently a standardised image of an Indian cannot be constructed; if presented, it is partial, incomplete, misleading. India nationalism and the dynamic of the Indian State demand a recognition and appreciation of the existence of a plurality of identities, leaving it to the individual citizen to accentuate or downplay any of these at a particular point of time. The latter perception does result, and has resulted, in expressions of ethnic or mini-nationalisms and the emanating tensions. The challenge of resolving them remains work in progress. Homogenisation or assimilation, however, is not the answer; it is neither feasible nor desirable.

One other feature of Indian Nationalism in its formative period was noteworthy. It had a vision of the external world, not merely in terms of anti-colonialism but also about India's approach to foreign policy. Jawaharlal Nehru expressed it on 7 September 1946 in his first statement as head of the interim government; he amplified it in a speech in the Constituent Assembly on 4 December 1947. "The conduct of foreign affairs", he said, lay in "finding out what is most advantageous to the country". Article 51 of the Constitution set out for the Republic of India its vision of foreign policy and inter-state relations. It helped define our political identity and cultural individuality.

III

The experience of the modern Indian State has been somewhat analogous to that of other States in the international community. Sovereignty has been exercised to defend the state against external and internal challenges, provide economic security and seek what is most advantageous for the country and its citizens.

This quest for seeking what was in the interest of the country was not always an altogether autonomous endeavour. The second half of the twentieth century was a period of global transition in which states, confronted with trans-national challenges, yielded some sovereign prerogatives to larger, common, purposes. By the year 1992, Secretary General Boutros Ghali was able to conclude that the time of absolute and exclusive sovereignty had passed. He urged the member states of the United Nations "to find a balance between the need for good internal governance and the requirement of an ever more interdependent world".

It must be admitted candidly here that the principle is easier to concede in theory than in practice. The reason lies in the gap between the theory and practice of governance and in the imperative of what has been conveniently taken under the rubric of 'national interest'. As a result, we have subscribed to most international norms on the one hand but at times desisted from reading these into state policy and practice, on the other. The 'disconnect' becomes visible in times of stress on some of the core issues of governance.

Valid questions also arise about the determination and articulation of 'national interest'. The difficulty of distinguishing between the sectional and transitory good, and the larger and longer term good, comes to the fore. So does our explicit commitments to norms of the global community and the need to reconcile them with the imperatives of nationalism and state sovereignty.

It is evident that global issues by definition respect no borders, by their complex nature overlap disciplines and, by sharing a common ecosystem, are all in some way interrelated. Globalisation is a set of processes principally driven by new technologies, new economic relationships and the national and international policies of a wide range of actors, including governments, international organisations, business and civil society.

Despite this, we do not naturally think in global, inter-disciplinary, multi-factored ways. Two benchmarks, however, tend to influence thinking and performance on this and related questions; the first relates to the benefits that accrue from global thinking, the second to the obligations arising out of it.

In recent years we have set for ourselves a set of national objectives and others, observing the direction of our progress, have delineated the levels of development likely to be achieved by the year 2040 or 2050. Alongside and on a shorter time span, we have subscribed to a set of objectives incorporated in the UN's Millennium Development Goals for the year 2015. Both propel us, in different ways, to think globally. A scholar has rightly noted that 'the structural conditions that gave rise to modern nationalism have changed'.

Four sets of broader considerations arising out of globalisation pose challenges to state actors and to the state-system in the international order:

First: Political globalisation is reflected in the reorientation of the international political order. Political legitimacy and credibility have been linked to observance of norms pertaining to governance, accountability, civil society and citizenry that have been enunciated. This is most vividly observed in the post-cold war agenda of the United Nations and particularly of the Security Council. The implementation of new norms of human rights and of humanitarian intervention is illustrative and instructive; so is the referral of cases to the International Criminal Court.

Second: Economic globalisation manifesting itself through increased economic openness, growing economic interdependence, and deepening economic integration in the world economy. These confer both benefits and obligations.

Third: Cultural globalisation in recent times has been characterised by de-territorialised global production, distribution and consumption of cultural forms and information. This has resulted in cultural products such as films, music and sports of nations garnering significant revenue from, and exerting cultural influence among, external territories or agents. The circumstances that have enabled the emergence of today's league sports and the film industry and their peculiar global business models illustrate this point.

Fourth: A de-nationalisation of the state appears to be in progress. We increasingly encounter the role of supra-national and sub-national entities.

On the one hand, there are global problems that transcend national borders in their origin and impact. Pandemics, climatic and environmental disasters and economic or financial crises fall in this category and seek global solutions through international consultation, cooperation, and enforcement. On the other hand, a great many questions are better addressed by side-stepping the state at local levels through civil society groups functioning as real and virtual global communities.

Each one of the above restrain the exercise of unbridled sovereignty internally and externally and thereby brings about behavioural modifications on the part of the nation-state.

Despite these, countervailing forces have also emerged. Globalisation has produced a counter trend of resurgence of nationalism and of an emphasis on national and cultural identities. State actors have to contend with certain unhealthy trends emanating from this counter trend, towards a homogenising nationalism that flattens diversities, and has little respect for local cultures, value systems and ways of life.

IV

As we enter the second decade of the twenty-first century and the sixth decade of our Republic, a few questions come to mind:

- How do our citizens view their role in the Indian State, in sub-national, provincial and local units, and in supra-national regional and international organisations?
- Can accommodation of group rights, diversities, identities and status in a democratic state setup continue in a period of political or economic shock or crisis? Will common people, and their leaders, forsake an approach of multiculturalism for the assumed comfort of nationalism at the first sight of contraction of economic opportunity or political space?
- How will the States-system deal with trans-national political, economic and cultural communities, especially when these are based on ethnicity, language, economic interest or political congruence?

Answers to these questions would have a bearing on the continuing debate about nationalism and internationalism. The Indian model, in fact, may be of increasing relevance to the outside world in some parts of which questions are being raised about the efficacy and desirability of a multicultural approach.

In a lecture a few years back in New Delhi on 'The Nation-State in the Global Age', the sociologist Anthony Giddens had concluded that 'creating cosmopolitan nations – with an overall identity but happy in their diversity–is the main way in which an effective international agenda can be forged and furthered'.

I congratulate the students graduating today and wish them success and happiness in the world beyond the portals of this great university.

Satyendra Narayan Sinha Memorial Lecture

Patna

12 July 2011

I am happy to be back in Patna and to participate, today, in this function being held in the memory of Late Shri Satyendra Narayan Sinha. "Chhote Saheb", as he was popularly called, was an important political leader of Bihar, a distinguished Parliamentarian, and someone who had the interests of his state and people uppermost in his mind.

During his long public life of over six decades, Sinha*ji* made significant contributions in streamlining the education system of Bihar, motivated the youth and students to take an active role in politics, and ensured their representation in political affairs.

As many in this audience would know, Sinha saheb was also a strong votary of the rights of states in our constitutional scheme of things. As a chief minister, and as an eminent and long-standing Parliamentarian, he was in a good position to appreciate the delicate balance maintained by our Constitution between the centre and the states.

This balance is dynamic and evolving. I therefore propose this afternoon to touch upon a few challenges to our federal polity in a period of great change, nationally and internationally.

Out constitution was carefully crafted. It is a Union of States having features of both a Federation and a Union with a systemic flexibility that has allowed it to becoming a three-tiered polity with a single citizenship, and with the capacity to be either unitary or federal according to the requirements of time and circumstances.

The point was succinctly and authoritatively explained by the Chairman of the Drafting Committee of the Constituent Assembly, Dr B. R. Ambedkar. "The Drafting Committee", he observed, "wanted it to be clear that though India was to be a federation, the federation was not the result of an agreement by the states to join in a federation", adding that "the federation is a Union because it is indestructible. Though the country and the people may be divided into different states for convenience of administration, the country is one integral whole, its people a single people living under a single imperium derived from a single source."

While the Constitution does not use the term federal or federation, the Supreme Court has spoken of the Indian Union as quasi-federal and deemed it to be a part of the basic structure. Eminent international authorities have characterised it as 'a centralised federation' and as sui generis.

Six decades of experience as a Republic is perhaps long enough to assess the functioning of our federal structure that has been the principal instrumentality for accommodating the enormous cultural, linguistic, religious and ethnic diversity of India within the framework of a democratic polity.

It is possible to analyse the functioning of our democracy in three of its dimensions:

In the first place: There is a need to assess its efficacy as an instrumentality of managing diversity, coping with political and social challenges, enhancing the scope of political participation of citizens, deepening their engagement with the state and accommodating various identities of our citizens;

Secondly: We should enquire if political federalism has served our democracy well by controlling extra constitutional forces and enabling articulation of the aspirations of our citizens through a political process; and

Thirdly: We need to examined the operation of fiscal federalism through the various tiers of our democracy and indicate required correctives.

I think it would be fair to assert that our democratic setup has served us well in orienting our heterogeneous society towards its developmental goals and including in this endeavour all segments of our citizenry. Our success is in sustaining a secular, pluralist democracy focused on the vision of our founding fathers. Our commitment to diversity and to upholding the varied identities of our citizens is unparalleled.

We have also shown that this commitment is not a fair-weather strategy to be discarded at the first sign of political or economic stress, but a fundamental value. Our federalism has enabled this achievement despite immense national and global transitions.

At the level of 'political federalism' it can be said with confidence that India has been a pioneer in moving from a dual federalism to a multi-level functional cooperative federalism through the 73rd and 74th Constitutional Amendments.

We thus have a multi-layered federal polity starting from the Gram Sabha, the Gram Panchayat, Block and District Panchayats, Urban Local Bodies, the States and the Union. This transformation has brought a qualitative and quantitative difference to the nature of our political representation. From a small number of less than 5000 political representatives from the Union Parliament and the state legislatures, we today have the largest political representative base in the world of over two and a half lakh local governments, comprising over three million elected representatives.

The experience of a series of coalition governments at the central level and in many states during the last two decades has changed the working dynamic of our polity. Today, having strong state governments pursuing their developmental goals with dedication and success need not depend on the dynamics of political force at the Centre. The emergence of strong regional and sectional political parties who participate in governance at the local, state and central levels has further strengthened the federal impulse.

The constitutional scheme of distribution of powers continues to be the subject of argument, mostly rational, among political parties and constituent units of our federal set-up. Similarly, greater political and fiscal freedom to units lower down the political pyramid continues to be politically debated and negotiated.

Some of these issues are critical. The significant regional disparities in economic development focus attention on the important aspect of 'fiscal federalism'. It has been a difficult task of balancing the objectives of equity, efficiency and autonomy in federal transfers and to keep the process on-track as envisaged in our Constitution. Finance Commissions have played a constructive role in harmonising the revenue structures of the centre and the states and in resolving disputes with respect to distribution of revenues between them. Grievances regarding fiscal devolution mechanisms do exist, and continue to be aired and addressed through our polity. This dynamic of the political economy has strengthened the process and foundation of fiscal federalism in our country.

The question of eliminating fiscal barriers to inter-State movement of goods and in the utilisation of natural resources has raised political tension and adverse political mobilisation. They pose a significant challenge for the management of our federal polity, especially as we move from a 'cooperative' to a 'competitive' federalism with constituent units competing for investments, job creation opportunities, and grants from national and multilateral bodies to improve the standard of living of their peoples. A horizontal disparity in economic development among states coexists with intense competition, which at times also takes on political overtones.

Rapid economic growth, increased demand for commodity resources obtained from mining and buoyant commodity markets, and widespread poverty and under-development in mineral resource-rich states have provided the backdrop for a debate on 'resource federalism' in the country. The polity has had to face questions about the functioning of our federal set-up in the context of resource development, the balance between political participation, protection of human, legal and fundamental rights, economic and developmental priorities and local environmental and social responsibilities.

We are yet to find definitive answers to the question of independent regulators for offshore and onshore resource management, improving compensation and sharing of resource revenues and improving the institutional capacity to utilise the revenues generated for public interest.

It has also to be admitted that the potential of the mechanisms suggested in the Constitution remains under-utilised. A case in point is the Inter-State Council under Article 263. It was established by a Presidential Order in 1990 but remains somewhat dormant. The March 2010 Report of the Commission on Centre-State Relations piously proclaims that 'cooperative federalism' is the key in which 'Statesmanship should lead Politics'.

Is this happening? Yet another area where cooperation rather than contention should prevail pertains to inter-state water disputes and underlines the imperative need for better water governance on the part of all concerned.

I would like to raise one other issue for the consideration of this distinguished audience. While there has been criticism regarding the manner and extent of devolution of finances from the centre to the states, the issue of further devolution to local government has not been adequately debated. India has one of the lowest shares of local government expenditure compared to total public sector expenditure at around 5 per cent, as compared to the OECD average of around 30 per cent, over 50 per cent in China and 15 per cent in Brazil.

Likewise, the share of local government expenditure to GDP is less than 2 per cent in India compared to around 14 per cent in OECD countries, over 10 per cent in China and over 6 per cent in Brazil.

Thus while political federalism has worked very well at the third tier of local government, through regular elections, granting of constitutional status, reservation for women and marginalised communities and the granting of responsibility for planning for economic development and social justice, these have been rendered without corresponding movement towards fiscal federalism. The institution of the State Finance Commissions has not been harnessed enough to achieve fiscal devolution to the local government and thus achieve a more inclusive and effective decentralised governance in the country.

I venture to suggest that the time has come for all the constituent units of our federal setup to ponder on how to realise the full potential of our federal democracy for meeting the aspirations of our people.

Allow me to conclude on a conceptual note. Writing in 1956 the Canadian scholar W.S. Livingston drew attention to the social forces that mould federal political institutions. "The essential nature of federalism", he wrote, "is to be sought for, not in the shading of legal and constitutional terminology, but in the forces–economic, social, political and cultural–that have made the outward form of federalism necessary ... Federal government is a device by which the federal qualities of the society are articulated and protected".

Needless to say, this is all the more compelling in our changing world where the twin imperatives of globalisation and identity have to be continuously reconciled to achieve our stated socio-economic and political objectives.

Birth Centenary Celebrations of Late Shri R. Venkataraman

India International Centre, New Delhi
30 July 2011

It is a privilege to attend a function commemorating the birth centenary of a great son of India. The late president Ramaswami Venkataraman had an extraordinary career in public life as an eminent lawyer, trade union leader, parliamentarian and statesman. The journey from Rajamadam village to Rashtrapati Bhavan is an example of dedication, perseverance and concern for public interest.

Ramaswami Venkataraman contributed to the strengthening of the institutions of our republic. He was a practitioner of virtue in the classical sense, a stickler for propriety and decency, for doing what was right in accordance with his conscience and convictions. He believed that incumbency of public office necessitated decision making, and that doing right was more important than catering to personal preferences or quest for popularity.

It is a truism that the Indian reality is reflected in contrasting images. We have witnessed in our own times significant strides in economic growth, technological innovation and social change. We also see societal and regional inequalities, wide spread poverty and disease, and unrealised aspirations for a better life. Change has generated hope; the challenge to our political process is to transform this hope into reality.

Venkataraman*ji* believed in the Gandhian dictum that "self government is not a substitute for good government". He noted in the opening lines of his presidential memoirs that he viewed his role as one where the ideals of Lord Krishna, taught upon the battlefield, were tested. He believed that while the observance of one's dharma, and right conduct, was necessary for the efficient functioning of our democracy, it was nevertheless insufficient since the test of good governance lay in delivery of justice.

The key to the twin imperatives of observance of *dharma* and delivery of justice thus lies in adherence to propriety in public and personal behaviour and practice. Shri Venkataraman's life and conduct is a fitting example of such propriety. He remains a shining example worthy of emulation.

The question of propriety in politics, of political morality, is a perennial one. Kautilya dwelt on the perils of flouting the *Dharmashastras* and the *Arthashastra*. Others accorded differing priorities; Confucius stressed the primacy of virtue; Machiavelli espoused the 'virtue' of the ruler in terms of success and sustainability; Ambedkar spoke of "the paramount reverence for the forms of the constitution."

It is necessary to dilate on this matter since it goes beyond ideals and touches the very core of public behaviour.

While political virtue is important, it can neither be pursued in isolation nor can it be the sole guide for political action. Political virtue, combined with idealism and activism, can also degenerate into political anarchy, even tyranny. A classic case is Robespierre's famous oration on political morality wherein he argued that in revolutionary times the mainspring of popular government is both virtue and terror.

In any structured society and polity therefore, and especially in a republic such as ours, it is paramount that political virtue be wedded to the grammar of constitutional morality.

What are the ingredients of constitutional morality? We can do no better than to go back to the description relied upon by Dr Ambedkar. It involved, as he put it:

> "a paramount reverence for the forms of the Constitution, enforcing obedience to authority acting under and within these forms yet combined with the habits of open speech, of action subject only to defined legal control, and unrestrained censure of those very authorities as to all their public acts combined too with a perfect confidence in the bosom of every citizen, amidst the bitterness of party contest, that the forms of the Constitution will not be less sacred in the eyes of his opponents than in his own."

In other words, freedom with self restraint, recognition of plurality, consensus on constitutional processes, and absence of a claim to singularity in representation, are absolutely necessary. Constitutional morality, in the words of an eminent political scientist, requires that allegiance to the constitution is non-transactional, is not premised on specific outcomes.

It was conceded even by the constitution framers that such an outcome was not to be a natural process and required the development of healthy conventions.

How successful have we been in developing such conventions and adhering to them? How vibrant is our democratic process in the periods between elections? Has our democracy tended to become progressively non-deliberative? Is there a suggestion of disenchantment with the state and its institutions?

It is essential that there be public debate on these issues.

Today we witness, across the length and breadth of the country, political activism at grass-roots level. In some instances, such activism has sought to utilise Gandhian approaches, both in tactical and strategic terms. These socio-political movements co-exist alongside mainstream politics represented by the political parties and related electoral dynamics at the national, state and local government levels. Their causes vary from environment, farmers' issues, land acquisition problems, disputes regarding natural resources and mining activities, and public policy goals such as improving public service delivery and combating corruption.

Instead of focusing on solving socio-political problems through established constitutional processes, the search for solutions is increasingly moving towards quasi-legal, perhaps, extra-legal arenas. This has longer term implications. Delegitimising the political processes is unlikely to solve our problems. Likewise, seeking to erode the careful in-built balance between the Executive, Legislature and the Judiciary as contained in the Constitution, either through under-reach of one or over-reach of another, could lead to chaos.

We were fortunate that many of the Founding Fathers of the Republic were not only freedom fighters, but were deeply committed to putting in place institutions, systems and processes. They had idealism, were endowed with political virtue, and were deeply committed to the constitutional morality of the republic. Shri Venkataraman was from that political stock and hence imbued his public life with such an approach. There is merit in rejuvenating that spirit, and the commitment that went with it.

Inauguration of the Sesquicentenary Celebrations of the Calcutta High Court

Netaji Indoor Stadium, Kolkata

21 April 2012

Poets, writers and visitors have for long dwelt on the virtues of Kolkata. Today's gathering pertains to a lesser known, though equally relevant, aspect of the city's functioning–the dispensation of justice–and I am happy, indeed privileged, to be here today to inaugurate the sesquicentenary celebrations of the Calcutta High Court.

It was in 1862 that the high court was established in Calcutta as the first high court in post-1857 British India. The British presence in the city, of course, predated that momentous happening; it also had its own skewed patterns of behaviour. These aberrations were done away with by the establishment of the high court. It was a seminal event.

Since then, the high court has performed its functions with dignity and independence. It has contributed great jurists, eminent judges and talented members of the Bar who have established a name for themselves within the country and abroad.

Over decades this court also laid the foundation for the development of Indian jurisprudence in the field of constitutional, criminal, civil and commercial law. Its judges were not only influenced by evolving concept of freedom and liberty in Victorian England but applied such principles impartially in their judgments.

It is to the influence of this court and the principles enunciated by it that one can ascribe the attraction of the legal profession among socially and politically progressive Indians of the colonial era. A great many of them contributed to the Freedom Struggle. It will be recalled that our First President, Dr Rajendra Prasad started his career as a practicing advocate in this court.

II

Today, I would like to discuss a fundamental concept that has been one of the core principles enunciated by this court, and later on, by the Constitution of this country.

I refer to the concept of human dignity.

Human dignity expresses a particular understanding of the inner nature and worth of the human person and his or her proper relations with society. Human dignity is closely linked with the concept of justice. A human being's sense of intrinsic worth, wrapped in the concept of dignity and forms the basis of a moral demand for just and equitable treatment, which then could be fortified with legal provisions for such treatment.

In our own Constitution, the Preamble speaks of the resolve of the people of India to promote among all citizens "fraternity, assuring the dignity of the individual and unity and integrity of the nation".

Dr B.R. Ambedkar remarked in the Constituent Assembly that fraternity means a "sense of common brotherhood of all Indians–of Indians being one people". Our Founding Fathers had envisaged fraternity to preserve and promote individual dignity. Every citizen was expected to develop mutual respect towards the other and in the process endow each citizen with enhanced dignity and opportunity for improving the quality of life. The provisions of fundamental rights were guaranteed in the Constitution and Directive Principles were enshrined therein to orient the policies of the State so that every citizen could seek opportunities for growth and betterment.

Indeed, Prime Minister Jawaharlal Nehru often talked about individual worth and dignity. He clarified that while "democracy and socialism are means to an end, not the end itself", they went beyond the pale of political activity to include "a basic factor of dignity of the individual and giving him opportunities of growth and preventing the reverse of this in political and economic institutions".

Our courts have developed jurisprudence regarding dignity. In *Kesavananda Bharti Vs. State of Kerala,* the Supreme Court held that the entire structure of our Constitution was built on the basic foundation of the dignity and freedom of the individual which was "easily discernible not only from the Preamble but the whole scheme of the Constitution". In the celebrated *Francis Coralie Mullin Vs. Administrator, Union Territory of Delhi and Ors,* the Supreme Court through Justice P. N. Bhagwati observed:

> We think that the right to life includes the right to live with human dignity and all that goes along with it, namely, the bare necessaries of ... Of course, the magnitude and content of the components of this right ... must, in any view of the matter, include the right to the basic necessities of life and also the right to carry on such functions and activities as constituting the bare minimum expression of the human-self.

In *Prem Shankar Shukla Vs. Delhi Administration,* Justice Krishna Iyer observed that the "guarantee of human dignity" forms part of our constitutional culture. In *Naz Foundation Vs. Government of NCT of Delhi*, the Delhi High Court observed: "At its least, it is clear that the constitutional protection of dignity requires us to acknowledge the value and worth of all individuals as members of our society ... Human dignity rests on recognition of the physical and spiritual integrity of the human being, his or her humanity, and his value as a person, irrespective of the utility he can provide to others."

We are not alone in emphasizing the importance of human dignity. The Canadian Supreme Court in Law v. Canada (Ministry of Employment and Immigration), [1999 1 S.C.R. 497] attempts to define the concept of dignity in these words:

> Human dignity means that an individual or group feels self-respect and self-worth. It is concerned with physical and psychological integrity and empowerment. Human dignity is harmed by unfair treatment premised upon personal traits or circumstances which do not relate to individual needs, capacities, or merits ... Human dignity is harmed when individuals and groups are marginalized, ignored, or devalued, and is enhanced when laws recognise the full place of all individuals and groups within Canadian society.

These precepts are is in consonance with universally accepted norms. The Preamble of the Charter of the United Nations mentions the determination of the peoples of the United Nations to 'to reaffirm faith in fundamental human rights, in the dignity and worth of the human person, in the equal rights of men and women and of nations large and small'.

The Universal Declaration of Human Rights notes in its Preamble that 'recognition of the inherent dignity and of the equal and inalienable rights of all members of the human family is the foundation of freedom, justice and peace in the world'. Article 1 of the Universal Declaration proclaims that 'all human beings are born free and equal in dignity and rights'. These have been further reinforced in the International Covenant on Civil and Political Rights, the International Covenant on Economic, Social and Cultural Rights and the various international Human Rights treaties.

Thus, the blueprint for our nation building exercise as enunciated in the Constitution is premised on bringing about social and economic changes while upholding the dignity of the individual in all its dimensions and empowering the citizens to better their condition in life. Our Judiciary has made the dignity of the individual, secured by fundamental rights and guided by directive principles, a part of the basic structure of the Constitution.

This approach is shared by others who care for social justice. The eminent South African Judge, Albie Sachs, has noted that "respect for human dignity is the unifying constitutional principle for a society that is not only particularly diverse, but extremely unequal."

III

If one goes beyond the constitutional guarantees and looks around at the legal and judicial landscape, a few questions do arise:

First: Is our legal and judicial system able to deliver justice to every citizen, especially the poor and the disadvantaged? Is substantive access to justice diminishing as the cost of quality legal service escalates beyond the reach of the common citizen? Is legal knowledge increasingly being deployed for the rich?

Second: Can we speak of justice delivery when the process takes years to reach finality?

Today there is a pendency of over 56,000 cases in the Supreme Court, of which around 36,000 are arrears constituting cases which are more than one year old. The pendency in the high courts and subordinate courts as on 31 December 2010 was around 3.2 crore cases, of which around 85 lakh cases are over five years old.

The reasons for delays in justice delivery are well known. Excessive adjournments are a primary cause; other reasons are shortage of resources and capacity, long-winded arguments by counsels, inadequate judge strength, delay in filling-up vacancies, and disproportionate concentration of work among some members of the bar.

The Supreme Court recently bemoaned the frequent adjournments for the flimsiest of reasons in the case *Shiv Cotex vs Tirgun Auto*. The Hon'ble Judges said: "It is sad, but true, that the litigants seek – and the courts grant – adjournments at the drop of the hat. Adjournments have grown like cancer corroding the entire body of the justice delivery system."

It is evident that our progress on achieving the Constitutional promise of assuring the dignity of the individual and securing to citizens justice, social, economic and political, especially to the poor and disadvantaged, leaves much to be desired.

In many instances, it is the State that is the biggest and enduring litigator, forcing citizens and businesses to sustain substantive and notional losses as cases drag on in the labyrinthine justice delivery system. The certainty of long gestation for resolution coupled with heavy costs to sustain the legal process has given large corporate and business entities added incentives to threaten or institute legal proceedings on civil matters.

Thus it is usually the individual citizen and the poor and marginalised among them, who bear the brunt of inadequate or non-existent Alternate Dispute Resolution mechanisms and extended judicial processes.

Litigators, some of whom are compulsive in our context, have not fully internalised the externalities of their actions, especially because of long delays in delivery of justice and because they escape the full liability of the harm they cause to those at the receiving end of their litigation, as also to the public good. The deterrent impact of an effective law of torts is rarely felt and has been to the detriment of the citizen.

Barring fundamental rights whose violation can be challenged through a writ petition, legal rights, especially civil legal rights bear the brunt of judicial delays. While the economically better off have more staying power and are able to hire and deploy superior legal resources and knowledge to defend their economic interests and property, the poor are pushed into further penury to defend their meagre possessions and holdings against legal challenges.

In the Indian context, therefore, defending legal and statutory rights that are non-fundamental, is time consuming and expensive and works against the poor.

What then can be done to redeem the promise of our founding fathers and deliver on the Constitutional guarantees and guiding principles?

I believe the legal profession must reclaim the hallowed ground that it occupied during our freedom struggle and in the early years of the fledgling republic. The need for introspection is imperative; it should lead to an ethical renewal in actual practice in terms of the canons of judicial ethics so eloquently enunciated by the former chief justice R.C. Lahoti in February 2005 in the First M.C. Setalvad Memorial Lecture.

Judicial processes and procedures must be streamlined, infrastructure should be strengthened, and the entire chain of subordinate judiciary must be subjected to an overhaul and renewal. Let us all say NO to excessive adjournments; say NO to long-winded oral arguments by counsels; say NO to delays in filling up vacancies of judges; and discourage, even penalise, compulsive litigation tendencies, whether of the State or of citizens.

Let us all remember the citizens, especially the poor and disadvantaged among them, now and always as we go about our daily work.

I once again convey my congratulations on the occasion of the sesqui-centenary of the Calcutta High Court, to the Judges and the Bar, and to the people of the state. I am confident that we all can look forward to many more decades of sterling service of the high court.

The Annual Bhimsen Sachar Memorial Lecture on 'Virtue in Public Life'
The India Islamic Culture Centre, New Delhi.
7 December 2012

I deem it a privilege to be invited to deliver the Bhimsen Sachar Memorial Lecture today.

Bhimsen Sachar was a freedom fighter, a political activist, an administrator and above all a person who advocated and practiced the core values of our freedom movement. As Chief Minister of Punjab on more than one occasion in the early years of our Republic, he shouldered the onerous responsibilities of putting in place administrative structures in the aftermath of a major disruption. He served with distinction as the governor in two of our states.

As a political personality occupying high public office, Bhimsen Sachar would have dealt with questions of governance. These are of a perennial nature and have been posed in all periods and to all systems; each faced challenges, including those of probity; each sought to developed appropriate responses.

Societies throughout history have functioned mostly on the basis of an un-stated consensus that provides the glue pertaining to social values, a set of do's and don'ts relating to the respective roles of the citizens and those entrusted by them with responsibilities of governance. The compact is in the nature of a trust. Record shows that points of tension arise whenever apprehensions develop about this relationship.

Many in this audience would agree that our society today, despite its firm moorings in religion and tradition, is increasingly prone to be amoral in the behaviour of its individuals and group components. Often, the connection between means and ends is being lost or side-tracked and the view is rampant that the end justifies the means, however devoid the latter may be of moral content.

The implications of this for individual and collective conduct are far reaching. Good and not-good, good and bad, moral and immoral, virtue and vice, are inclinations that determine individual and group action and experience has shown that disregarding them inevitably leads to moral anarchy and eventually to social decay. For this reason, societies in all periods of history have sought to put in place, and observe, norms though which virtue is promoted and vice eschewed.

Can the norms be accepted or discarded selectively? If so, who makes this determination, for what purpose, justification and duration? A good instance is the question of lack of probity in public life, a matter very much in our every day discourse though at times generating more heat than light.

The desire and need for a virtuous society is not just a metaphysical goal which lies in the ethereal realm of religion or philosophy but has tangible benefits for common good of humanity. Virtue in public life provides a necessary, if not sufficient, framework for sustained and harmonious political, economic and social progress in society.

Allow me to amplify. Virtue in public life goes beyond the normal clamour for probity in government and public administration and covers the entire spectrum of a citizen's public activity. Similarly, virtue is not restricted to absence of corruption in financial or monetary terms, but includes values such as service, sacrifice, faith, trust, courage, justice and ethical conduct. As the philosopher Aristotle put it, virtue is a disposition for excellence in the human soul. This virtue can be acquired.

In an article in *Young India* on 22 October 1925, Gandhi*ji* listed Seven Social Sins which he considered to be spiritually most perilous for humanity. These together constitute a good point of reference for any discussion on virtue in public life. Allow me, therefore, to reiterate them:

> "Politics without principles
> Wealth without work
> Pleasure without conscience
> Knowledge without character
> Commerce without morality

Science without humanity
Worship without sacrifice"

It is evident that each of the human activities listed here result in a socially relevant moral degradation if the concomitant virtue cited with it is absent. Hence the imperative need for imbibing and implementing them in social, and personal, behaviour patterns.

There can be other approaches to the problem. "Virtue in public life", an American academic wrote a few years back, "is less likely to be found in a clearer understanding of virtue and more likely to be found in a clearer understanding of public life", adding that "virtue in public life is to be found not just in the individual propensity to be ethical but more in the development of organisational rules and procedures, in virtuous leadership, and in the development rules and procedures, in various leadership, and in the development of virtuous public cultures."

Every society has in place a set of laws and regulations to deal with violations of rules requiring proper conduct by those who indulge in public affairs. The adequacy of these remains a matter of unending debate.

Beyond these, however, and in terms of principles and commitments, there are two aspects of the requirement of probity in public domain. In the first place, I would like to draw the attention of this audience to Article 51A of our Constitution that prescribes among the duties of citizens the requirement "to strive towards excellence in all spheres of individual and collective activity so that the nation constantly rises to higher levels of endeavour and achievement."

This requirement, of a quest for excellence, cannot evade the seven principles prescribed by Gandhi*ji* and necessitates a commitment for their implementation leading to probity in everyday life of a citizen.

In the second place, and in our world of today, societies and states no longer have the luxury of isolation. Instead, we have a community of states and a globalisation of values. National sovereignty is increasingly circumscribed by national commitments to global conventions. These, together, give teeth to the principles and behaviour pledges inscribed in the Charter of the United Nations.

For the purpose of today's talk the most relevant of these international commitments, having a direct impact on an essential aspect of probity, is the UN Convention against Corruption, adopted in October 2003 and somewhat belatedly ratified by India on 11 May 2011. This is a comprehensive document, has a direct relevance to the question of probity in public life and its rationale and objectives therefore need to be considered carefully.

The Preamble of the Convention states that corruption poses threats to the stability and security of societies undermines institutions, values of democracy, ethical values and justice, jeopardises sustainable development and the Rule of Law, has international ramifications, and leads to organised crime and money laundering involving vast assets thereby threatening political stability and development of states concerned. It stresses that the prevention and eradication of corruption is a responsibility of all states, puts in place a framework for observance, and urges in this endeavour international cooperation as well as support of individuals and groups.

The Preamble urges states to 'foster a culture of rejection of corruption'.

II

Given this requirement in terms of national and international norms and commitments, where do we in India stand in terms of perception and action in regard to this ailment?

The matter is very much in the public domain. It has been said with much justice that "evidence of corruption has moved from anecdotal to documentary", that it is Indian democracy's "inconvenient fact", that it violates human rights, constitutional rights and Rule of Law, and that "it undermines the very social fabric and the political and bureaucratic structure of the Indian society".

Our ranking in the global Corruption Perception Index is, to say the least, distressing.

The disease is not of recent origin but, in an earlier period, carried a social stigma less evident today. In 1949 the poet Josh Malihabadi had written a long poem entitled *Rishwat*. One couplet summed up the public opprobrium attributed to the ailment:

"Bhool kar bhi jo koi leta hai rishwat,chor hai
Aaj qaomi paagaloon main raat din yeh shour hai"

The perception of wide-spread corruption has widened and deepened in the public mind. Furthermore, there is a nagging apprehension that the administrative and judicial mechanism in place is inadequate as a deterrent. In January 2007 the 'Ethics in Governance' report of the Second Administrative Reform Commission concluded that 'anti corruption interventions so far made are seen to be ineffectual and there is widespread public cynicism about them.' This cynicism, it added, 'is spreading so fast that it bodes ill for our democratic system itself.'

It is evident that more effective corrective action is needed to restore public confidence. This has to be qualitatively different and must address three aspects of the matter simultaneously. These relate to (a) propensity, (b) opportunity, and (c) scope. It is essential to examine the role of each of these in the genesis and perpetuation of corruption:

- The *propensity* to resort to illegal or immoral means to achieve desired ends is increasingly pervasive in the wake of a sentiment that both traditional morality and constitutional morality have somehow become un-necessary and not in need of observance beyond the ritual of lip service. A culture of hedonism and of what Nehru called "vulgar display of wealth" does of necessity lead to a culture of inequality, very different from the requirements of justice, equality and fraternity to which we swear allegiance as citizens. The only viable corrective to this would lie in a concerted effort, in the family, the school, the work place, and the civic domain to rejuvenate and re-imbibe the required social values and, at the same time, put in place deterrents to ensure compliance.

Propensity could and does also emerge from situational compulsion caused by real or created scarcity, by intentional delays in the delivery of public service and the resultant moral dilemma faced by the seeker of a public service. The petty corruption thus generated has a differential impact on the less privileged whose capacity to resist is minimal. The ARC report cited above found that 'in a vast majority of cases of bribery, the citizen is a victim of extortion' and that 'experience has taught most citizens that there is a vicious cycle of corruption and they often end up losing much more by resisting corruption.'

- The same holds for *opportunity*. Successive reports of government commissions over five decades have suggested reform of procedures that would facilitate public service delivery, introduce transparency and thereby reduce opportunity to go astray. The Right to Information Act has helped rectify this in some measure; much still remains to be done. Rigorous training to inculcate the concept of service is essential so that it is rendered as a duty, not a favour.

The scope of what is considered corruption has to expand to cover the act as well as actors, both the taker and giver of bribes. This is of particular relevance in cases that go beyond petty corruption. A paper presented at a World Bank workshop some years back observed that "the problem of corruption lies at the intersection of the public and private sectors.

It is a two way street. Private interests, domestic and external, wield their influence through illegal means to take advantage of opportunities for corruption and rent seeking, and public institutions succumb to take these and other sources of corruption in the absence of credible restraints."

A survey by the Swiss consultancy firm KPMG in March 2011 showed that 'in many cases corruption is induced by the private sector', adding that 'a large number of respondents believe that corruption is a two-way street and people who pay bribes are as much to blame for the current environment as those accepting such payments. The regulation in India tends to focus on the bribe taker rather than the bribe payer and hence corporates do not shy away from adopting corrupt practices."

III

There are other dimensions to the problem. Given our social scene and traditions, nepotism in some form or the other is, tacitly or explicitly, considered a virtue. It is said to be 'a custom with infinitely more practitioners than defenders'. How is it to be defined in the Indian context of Kunba parvari? When and where does it violate canons of probity and becomes a corrupt practise? Has any government or public body sought to develop a framework to check it?

Much of the debate on dealing with the perils of corruption has dealt with the legal framework and law enforcement and the effort to make it produce better results. This is essential but not sufficient. An aspect of the fight against corruption, insufficiently addressed, is its impact on human rights and the extent to which it derogates the Rule of Law that ensures administration of justice by normal law courts, avoidance of arbitrary decision-making, and abuse of discretionary power.

It has been argued in this context that 'the human rights approach to corruption control mechanism makes the people of India central players in the corruption resistance movement' and that 'the law enforcement work of the government to ensure corruption free governance ought to be perceived as a part of the right of the people of India to seek a corruption-free government. Concomitantly, it then becomes the duty of the government to ensure that all its affairs are conducted in a manner that promotes transparency, accountability, and integrity in public administration.'

One clear benefit of such an approach would be to link up different ingredients of good governance and thereby synergise the quest for better governance and substantive rather than formal political legitimacy.

In the final analysis, therefore, a fourfold approach to treat this deadly social ailment and promote probity would lie in the combination of (a) ethical training in norms incorporated in legally enforceable Code of Ethics, (b) comprehensive protection of human rights, (c) a legal framework and regulatory practices that enforce clash of interest rules, and (d) laws and procedures that forbid nepotism in all its manifestations.

These steps would assist the attainment of 'excellence' in terms of the Duties prescribed in the Constitution. The endeavour is to be individual and collective. Here, as elsewhere, a Gandhian dictum is of relevance:

> "You must be the change you wish to see in the world."

Science and Technology

"As the Indian economy continues on the path of rapid, inclusive and sustainable growth, it will be necessary to ensure that India's capabilities in science and technology grow in strength ... Our science output has reached 3% of the global output in 2010. While this is heartening, the current rate of improvement is slow and falls short of global standards in many areas

—Twelfth Five-Year Plan (2012-2017)

Golden Jubilee Memorial Lecture
Indian Institute of Science, Bangalore
14 December 2008

It is a privilege to be invited to address this gathering, assembled to mark the centenary of the Indian Institute of Science (IIS).

I am also daunted by the prospect of sharing my thoughts with an audience of such eminence.

The postage stamps that have just been released are a nation's tribute to an institution of rare eminence. The Indian Institute of Science stands tall amidst institutions of excellence and has earned the right to celebrate its centenary.

By the same token, the IIS has imposed on itself the duty of sustaining its work in a new century before whose challenges; the ones of the last century recede into relative insignificance.

We in India have set for ourselves the goal of becoming a knowledge society. Beyond the slogan, however, is the realisation that the long march towards the destination entails a great deal of work aimed at ensuring access to knowledge of more and more people so that they become its beneficiaries meaningfully and in turn contribute appropriately.

This enhanced level of access to knowledge also implies a heightened awareness of the criticality of fundamentals, of basic research. It is here that the IIS must remain the torch bearer and I have no doubt that it would continue to be so.

I

The work of the scientist in relation to the priorities that individual societies set for them is of immense relevance. Let me illustrate this with reference to

India. In the first decade of independence, the government set forth their science policy with three objectives:

- To secure for the public the benefits accruing from the acquisition and application of scientific knowledge
- To promote the cultivation of science and scientific research—pure, applied and educational
- To ensure an adequate supply of research scientists and scientific personnel for the country's diverse requirements.

As is well known, much has been done in the past six decades to create an infrastructure of science and technology and endow it with the potential for advancement. Many notable landmarks have been reached. At the same time, significant gaps remain and are hampering achievement of targets. An HRD Taskforce in 2005 found that 'the quality and quantum of scientific research had been declining over the years' due to inadequate facilities, funds, declining enrolment and an acute shortage of qualified teachers in basic sciences, engineering, technology and medicine.

Allow me take a closer look at some of these.

The first relates to the paucity of scientists. This may sound paradoxical but is nevertheless reflective of ground reality. The prime minister referred to it in his address to the 2005 session of the Indian Science Congress and this has been amplified in the Report of the Steering Committee on Science and Technology and in the Eleventh Five-Year Plan.

The Plan accepts that basic research in science, engineering and medicine is a critical input for development. It has also stressed the need for making available equipment and facilities in colleges and universities, as also the need to create attractive career options for talented young scientists.

The old debate about 'basic research', 'directed basic research' and applied research and product development surfaced in the Steering Committee Report. The recommended solution attempts a balance: "while basic research should be encouraged, self-directed basic research should also receive substantially increased support".

The challenge now lies in converting these policy commitments into time-bound programmes.

Secondly, attracting young minds to the domain of science is often a matter of igniting interest. This is best done through inspiring teaching and creation of role models. There seems to be a disconnect here at two levels: between senior teachers and undergraduates, and between teaching and researchers. The net result is that the young science student is deprived of contact with sources of inspiration that may fire his/her imagination.

A few years back Jayant Narlikar had pointed out that a panel constituted for the decadal meeting of the Astronomical Society of India had only one of its thirty-seven members drawn from a university. The message, he said, was that "universities had best confined themselves to teaching while research institutes will look after research!" The Knowledge Commission has now drawn attention to the absence of interconnectivity between educational institutes and R&D laboratories and has suggested ways of bridging the gap.

My third point relates to the methodology of teaching science. I understand that nearly 50 per cent of school students fail in mathematics and science. What is needed is a culture of experiment-based learning. This would also involve re-training of teachers. How long would such an exercise take?

A related problem is the high level of vacancies in universities. A sample survey of forty-seven universities conducted by the UGC, for the academic year 2007-2008, shows an overall vacancy level of 51 per cent. The situation is particularly depressing in state universities where almost 90 per cent of students are enrolled. Some academic administrators attribute this, in part, to the poor quality of candidates; if so, it adds to the problem of quality that plagues many institutions of higher education.

My last point pertains to innovations and patents in the light of the generally voiced complaint that our national performance on this count is inadequate. Is this due to the absence of adequate linkages between research institutions and industry? Does our industry itself spend enough on R&D? Our modest performance is certainly not due to a lack of inventive genius. A report published in the *India-US Business Journal* in October last year cited a Harvard Law School study indicating that one in every ten inventions patented in the United States had an owner or co-owner with an Indian name.

Given our requirements, therefore, capacity building in science is the need of the hour. Only then would we be able to sustain technological advancement that is imperative for national development. Let me recall what Sir Mokshagundam Visveswaraya, an engineering genius of earlier years, had said: "To build a better nation, build better individuals", adding that "action, not sentiment, will be the determining factor". This certainly holds good for the scientific community that, to use Thomas Kuhn's phrase, "is an immensely efficient instrument for solving the problems or puzzles that its paradigm defines".

II

Our aspiration to be a hub of knowledge has other implications. In a conceptual sense, it necessitates promotion of knowledge about knowledge, its nature and character, its social and ethical content and their implications.

The latter problem has been posed by many down the ages; let me cite a fairly recent formulation by a scholar from the University of Leuven in Belgium:

> "Science is a mix of creativity and of goal-oriented effort, on the basis of our natural urge to know. On the way to its goal, science obeys certain laws, the rules of logic and rational reasoning being the most important ones. By having an impact on reality, scientists automatically and inevitably acquire a responsibility. Our work will have consequences, which we are not to ignore. Reflecting on our activities is the main target of ethics. Therefore, ethical reflection is related to science and to scientific progress."

This view may be contested but is not altogether isolated. An eminent British scientist, Professor Lord May of Oxford, said in his valedictory address as President of the Royal Society in 2005 that 'the scientific community should be energetically engaging the societal process to dispel 'the darkness of fundamentalist unreason'.

The matter has various dimensions. Two of these are relevant to our argument: the first pertains to rationality and logic; the second to the identity of scientists as moral creatures living in societies. Neither can be evaded and their connotations need to be probed.

The ancients considered humans as rational creatures. The process by which they reached this conclusion was somewhat complex. Aristotle divided the soul into three types: vegetable soul common to plants and animals and concerned only with nourishment and growth, animal soul shared by man and lower animals and concerned with locomotion, and the rational soul or intellect confined to humans.

At the same time, as Erasmus found, folly is perennial; hence the need to cultivate rationality since, as the historian Ibn Khaldun put it, the pasture of stupidity is unwholesome for mankind. Thus the process by which unreason is replaced by reason has to be both deliberate and continuous.

The process is one aspect of the matter, content is another. Should the scientific method and temper be confined to the domain of science in the narrower sense, or should they be imbibed as part of consciousness? Jawaharlal Nehru wanted all Indians to cultivate a scientific temper through the application of reasoning and the avoidance of preconceived notions and Amartya Sen has shown that the dialogic tradition of India plays a part "in supporting democracy, secularism and the pursuit of mathematics and science, and the use that can be made of dialectics in seeking social justice, against the barriers of class, caste, community and gender".

This audience is well aware of the role that heterodoxy has played in the emergence of new ideas and discoveries. The teasing question for the men and women of science is the application of this heterodoxy to the social realm. What should be questioned? To what extent should it be questioned? How is a balance to be struck between conformity and nonconformity?

One approach lies in State-centricity. The State is the keystone of the social arch and the final repository of the will of a society. In practical terms, however, the will of the State is the will of the government of the day and its claim to be obeyed, apart from narrow legality, lies in the content of that will and in the processes by which it is determined and communicated to the citizen-body.

The sceptic, on the other hand, draws attention to possible pitfalls. It was aptly stated by Bertrand Russell. Writing in the middle decades of the twentieth century about the growth of dogmatism and the power of governments over men's belief, he expressed concern over "the discovery that man can be scientifically manipulated, and that governments can turn masses this way or that as they choose, is one of the causes of our misfortunes".

Since historical record sustains both positions, an enquiring mind is lead to philosophical and practical questions about implications. This endeavour goes back to Arjuna's doubts in the debate in *Mahabharata*. In our own times, the scientist qua scientist is driven by the logic and impulse of work underway. Its implications may or may not be immediately discernable. The dilemma was stated by Robert Oppenhiemer in 1954:

"When you see something that is technically sweet, you go ahead and do it and you argue about what to do about it only after you have had your technical success."

The resulting choices tax the conscience. Should scientists work in a moral or ethical vacuum? Should they, instead, be what has been called citizen-scientists? Answers to these questions can only be sought in open debate and without a priori conclusions. Society facilitates scientific research and therefore has a right to know, perhaps also a right to judge; the latter right, however, has to be exercised with utmost care to ensure that such judgements do not stifle scientific research. At the other end of the spectrum, no free society can deny the right to dissent. The social responsibility of scientists has to be posited within such a framework.

Let me end with a quote from B.J. Marden written as early as in 1921: "May I venture, as a citizen, to make an appeal to men of science and to urge that the time has come when they should no longer stand aside from the social and political questions that vex the world? ... Science has made civilisation possible for mankind. It must now provide civilisation with that authority the lack of which is causing such waste of human energy today. Men of science alone have the power; they alone are above suspicion."

Before I end, I would like to wish all success to the Indian Institute of Science in its next hundred years.

Graduation Function

BARC Training School, Mumbai

26 August 2009

I am glad to be here today at the graduation function of the BARC Training School. Yours is a unique training facility that straddles the world of research and academia. It is a successful model where the teaching staff constitutes working scientists and technologists and class room teaching is as much about theory as it is about real life experiences. It is due to the collective and cumulative effort of this School that we have emerged as one of the few countries to have mastered the fuel cycle and have successful nuclear power and strategic programmes.

The scientists and engineers trained in this school have been, over a period of five decades, critical in underpinning excellent research and development work of the Department of Atomic Energy, producing the feedstock for our nuclear power programme, the isotope production and application programme and various other projects that constitute the technological infrastructure of the nation's nuclear effort.

It is relevant to recall that this praiseworthy facility is a product of the vision of our Founding Fathers and of their emphasis on the importance of fostering scientific temper as a key instrument of nation building. They assessed correctly the critical role that science and technology would play in nation building and pursuant to it, they established institutions like BARC. These attract talent; above all, they developed modalities of retaining them and offering them a career span.

Your success raises a question. At a time when the government and public sector have been losing human resources to the private sector and are unable to attract the best talent available, what is that sets apart the atomic energy and space establishments? Is it all a question of monetary incentive or do we respond better to intellectual challenges and a sense of mission and purpose while monetary compensation is maintained at an acceptable level?

The experience of the Department of Atomic Energy seems to confirm the view that within large organisations, there is an intricate synergy between personal fulfillment and individual accomplishment and research-education linkage. Internal human resource development and retention is greatly facilitated by this focus on linking day to day work with academia and research.

Human resources occupy a critical role in the nuclear industry. The life cycle of the nuclear energy sector requires extended time horizon, technological complexity and need for excellence. It is said that on a 'cradle to grave' basis, nuclear activity would exceed 100 years if one were to include monitoring radioactive waste. Human resource development therefore must long precede the nuclear power programme and must continue after 'sunset' even if such a programme were to shutdown.

The nuclear human resource dilemmas of the developed countries are of a totally different dimension. They are facing problems in retaining skilled personnel for facilities that are at the end of the life cycle with no new capacity deployment in the near future. They also have to attract young talent in an ageing population if they wish to revive nuclear power as a green energy option in a world facing climate change scenarios. These problems are accentuated by the volatility in the global energy markets and reduction in government funding for nuclear research.

In October 2007, the OECD (Organisation for Economic Co-operation and Development)/Nuclear Energy Agency member countries came forth with a statement expressing their concern about the difficulties nuclear institutions in many OECD/NEA member countries are experiencing in recruiting qualified specialists. It noted that nuclear education and training have been suffering decline and if no action is taken, the nuclear sector risks facing a shortage of qualified manpower to ensure the appropriate regulation and operation of existing nuclear facilities as well as the construction of new ones.

The recommendations of the OECD/NEA Steering Committee for Nuclear Energy bear repetition here:

1. Governments should assess regularly their requirements for, and availability of, qualified human resources to match identified needs.
2. Governments, academia, industry and research organisations should collaborate nationally and internationally to enhance nuclear education and availability of nuclear expertise, including financial support to universities and scholarships to students.
3. Governments, whether or not they choose to utilise nuclear power, should also encourage large, high-profile, international R&D programmes which attract students and young professionals to become the nuclear experts required for the future.

The policy of our government on human resources in the nuclear field has been on such a course and the BARC Training School deserves our appreciation for successfully fulfilling its mission of training nuclear scientists and technologists for over fifty years. Our satisfaction over this should be tempered with the knowledge that the policy and regulatory landscape is ever changing. We have seen this happen in other sectors such as power, infrastructure and telecom.

This audience is aware of the manner in which the international regulatory environment concerning nuclear commerce has changed since last year opening up new avenues for accelerated deployment of nuclear power in the years to come. This would also bring about a re-adjustment in the internal regulatory environment.

This is spelt out in the Economic Survey for 2008-09. 'The Atomic Energy Act', it states, "needs to be amended to permit private corporate investment in nuclear power, subject to regulation by the Atomic Energy Regulatory Board (AERB) and the Atomic Energy Commission (AEC)." It also calls for framing the rules for private and foreign entry and for allowing up to 49 per cent FDI in the sector.

In the not so distant future, therefore, private utility providers would run nuclear power plants. Such plants would need human resources. While we can import nuclear fuel and technology, human resources would have to be developed and equipped within the country. There are not many academic or professional institutions to train scientists and technologists for the nuclear industry in India. It is here that I foresee one of the most significant challenges for the BARC Training School.

The experience garnered over five decades must be adapted to training and making available nuclear scientists and technologists to the private sector so that the BARC Training School emerges as a world renowned human resource development institution in nuclear science and technology. Successful knowledge management in the nuclear sector at a national level necessitates smooth and orderly transfer of knowledge from research institutions to the industry and from the government and public sector to the private sector and vice versa.

Dr Homi Bhaba, the founder of our atomic energy programme, believed that the sustainability and self-reliance of our nuclear programme is dependent on continuous availability of skilled manpower. The same holds true for the sustainability of accelerated development of nuclear power through private corporate investment.

Our experience in regulation of a hitherto closed sector thrown open to private corporate and foreign investment has been a mixed one. In various areas such as telecom, petroleum and gas, electricity and infrastructure development, public perception of regulatory oversight has been dented as a result of allegations of regulatory bias and conflict of interest in corporate conflicts. We must exercise utmost caution in the regulation of the nuclear power sector so that the public interest and safety is ensured.

To the young graduates who have gathered here today, I would like to say that you are joining a very distinguished family. As you move on with your careers, you would at some stage face questions whether you have made the right choice in life by choosing to study and work in India and have a career in the government. The events of the last one year that have witnessed a global financial and economic meltdown have dimmed the lustre of the temptations of the earlier era. Many Indians are also returning back and the public sector is no longer the employer of last resort at campus placements.

I am confident that your training and work would see all of you emerge as multi-disciplinary specialists spanning multiple technologies and sciences and represent India on the world stage where new opportunities are emerging in nuclear research.

Seventeenth National Children's Science Congress
Science City, Ahmedabad
27 December 2009

I am very happy to be in Gujarat and to address this august gathering today. It is a privilege to meet young scientists and their mentors; together, they demonstrate that persistence in popularising science and stimulating scientific temper yields rich dividends.

The Children's Science Congress has evolved into an unique movement that has a countrywide reach and focuses the energies of the scientists of tomorrow on contemporary and relevant themes. I am glad to learn that there are many child scientists and escort teachers from SAARC countries who are participating in the Congress this year.

The Science Congress is a great leveller; it enables children to immerse themselves in the wonders of science irrespective of their social, family or financial status. It gives an opportunity to children from rural areas and from underprivileged families to pursue their scientific curiosity through voluntary agencies and government organisations that form part of the 'NCSTC (National Council for Science and Technology Communication)– Network'.

It is appropriate that the Seventeenth Congress is being held at Gujarat Science City. As one of the most industrially dynamic and entrepreneurially active state in the country, Gujarat has established new national benchmarks. I am confident that this zeal would extend to promoting and popularising science among children, including through informal and vernacular modes of education.

It is significant that the theme of this year's Congress is focused on planet Earth that is home to all forms of life and the need to explore, share and care for the resources that it provides us with. It has been a week since the issue of climate change was discussed at the global level at Copenhagen. I am sure the young minds gathered here today would debate and better understand natural and human-induced phenomena affecting the stability of our planet and its various ecosystems.

Human history shows that societies that responded to challenges with knowledge, and innovations based on that knowledge, were blessed with success. This will also be true of the world of the future, but with one difference. The residents of the planet Earth are facing more challenges today than at any time in the past.

Their response, therefore, has to be in equal measure.

It is for this reason that popularising science and inculcating a scientific temper among citizens has been a national goal since the time of our freedom movement. The spread of scientific temper was deemed essential for political and economic emancipation of our people. This is encapsulated in Article 51 A of our Constitution and the duty it imposes on every citizen to 'develop the scientific temper, humanism and the spirit of inquiry and reform'.

The challenges of economic development in the modern era of globalisation can only be faced with a strong edifice of science and technological education. The Information Technology revolution and advances in bio-technology and pharmaceutical industries have been made possible by huge public investment in tertiary science and technology education. The public sector nuclear energy, space and defence related industry and the Science and Technology establishment have created the demand for and incubated these science and technology graduates, who thereafter either became entrepreneurs or moved to the private sector.

And yet, it has to be admitted that our scientific output today in terms of researchers in basic sciences is insufficient for our requirements. This has a direct impact on our contribution to innovations and patents. It compares unfavourably with our peers and competitors on the world stage. One reason for this is our lack of focus on the priority that should be accorded to the pursuit of science.

I am aware that prospects for remunerative employment primarily guide the choice of subjects for study and research. Many students in urban and metropolitan areas, I hear, are dropping out of the formal education set-up after secondary schooling to pursue jobs in call centres and other service industries. If true, this is a trend that must be arrested and reversed. We need new investments and incentives from the private sector so that our young people will be encouraged increasingly to pursue and thereafter seek a career in science.

It is accepted the world over today that a continuing supply of high quality scientific and technological manpower is a fundamental requirement for any modern nation to avail of the opportunities of our scientific and technological age.

Making a career in science attractive to our young people is an important goal and the government is making efforts in this regard. Allow me to mention a few steps that have been decided upon:

- Over one million school students are to be given science innovation scholarships and support scholarships for higher education in science over the course of the next five years.
- During the course of the Eleventh Five-Year Plan, the government is committed to expanding the science and technology base of our universities and promoting funding at centres for advanced research.
- The government is also attracting talent at the secondary education stage through discipline-specific education programmes in strategic areas like space and nuclear sciences.
- The prime minister has announced that the annual expenditure on science and technology would be enhanced from less than 1 per cent of GDP to 2 per cent of our GDP in the next five years.

Science and technology is an important instrumentality of the modern state. The purposes to which it can be used have to be defined by the guiding philosophy of a society, polity or state. We in India are committed to a pluralistic society, a composite culture, a democratic way of life with guarantees of fundamental freedoms and human rights to all citizens. Our constitution, and especially its preamble, constitutes our guiding philosophy.

Our challenge is to ensure that every citizen has access to opportunities to develop his/her human potential to the fullest so that they lead purposeful and rewarding lives. This is possible only if we can build and sustain equitable access to the education system, foster science education and research and development that innovate and address developmental problems through effective use of scientific and technological interventions.

To the young scientists assembled here today, I implore them to continue to wonder at the mysteries of nature and use the scientific way of thinking and experimenting to address contemporary problems. They must train their mind to question, to reason, and to accept nothing that does not meet the test of scientific enquiry.

I am sure all the student scientists would go back enriched and inspired to pursue education in science and many would also look for careers in science and technology. It is only then can the national vision of an inclusive society and the national effort to build a truly knowledge based society be achieved.

International Conference on 'Geothermal and Other Energy Resources of Ladakh: Technological and Business Viability'
Hotel Grand Dragon, Leh
5 July 2010

I am happy to be here today to participate in this conference. Over the years I have had many an occasion to attend conferences and seminars pertaining to the subject of energy. To the best of my recollection, however, none of these were focused on geothermal energy. The default, perhaps, can be attributed to our lack of sufficient awareness of this form of energy. Even the Kirit Parikh Report of August 2006 on Integrated Energy Policy did not seem to dwell on the matter.

This gathering of distinguished experts and business personalities is, therefore, only to be welcomed and the University of Jammu's initiative is to be commended.

The subject of energy is compelling, even fascinating. It is a recorded fact of history that all civilisations depended for survival and prosperity on their ability to access energy in sufficient quantities in the form of food and fuel. The advancement of the past two centuries highlights this truism. By the same token, anxiety about continued and continuous access to energy in requisite quantities has resulted in irrational reactions ranging from overt pessimism to undue optimism.

Many years back the Russian Astrophysicist Nicolai Kardashev propounded his theory about stages of civilisations based on their access to three energy sources. He categorised the latter as planetary, stellar and galactic. Others have calculated that our own planet has up to now only reached the 0.72 level in the first, planetary, category and may take a century or two to marshal energy resources on a planet-wide scale.

I personally would lean on the side of optimism and therefore support the view that technology and human ingenuity would lead us to newer sources of energy as also to better utilisation of existing sources and quantities. Hence the relevance of today's gathering.

Exploiting geothermal energy is not new to humankind. Ancient Romans built elaborate complexes in areas where they came across hot water springs. In our own country, hot water springs were traditionally used for religious and medicinal baths. This desire, to harness for use the enormous reservoirs of energy stored underneath the earth's surface, has been strengthened by the advancement of technology in our times.

It is universally accepted that per capita energy consumption in a society is a critical element in its development indices. India lags far behind on this count. Our consumption per head is less than a third of the global average. We also face an acute deficit of electric power. Almost half of all Indian households do not have access to electricity and our average annual per capita consumption of electricity is merely about 30 per cent of the world's average.

This, then, is a measure of the distance to be covered if the pace of development is to be accelerated.

Our reliance on fossil fuels and traditional bio-mass adds a complicating dimension to the situation. A projection of requirements two decades hence indicates that even at present levels of consumption, our annual import of oil would go up to 750 million tons and of coal to 1300 million tons. Add to this the pressing global effort to mitigate emissions of greenhouse gases to address climate change.

The national mission to ensure energy security thus propels us to look seriously at new and renewable energy options with a focus on grid interactive and distributed renewable power, rural and urban applications, and industrial and commercial applications of such renewable power.

Among the various new and renewable energy options, geothermal energy is recognised as the cleanest, without smoke or environmental hazards. If a proper well at adequate temperature is identified, the energy source is limitless, available all through the year and with minimal operating costs, unlike the case of wind or solar power.

India has several geothermal provinces characterised by high heat flow and thermal gradients. Subsequent to the oil crisis of the 1970s, the Geological Survey of India generated data of resource assessment for over 300 hot springs in the country. Subsequently detailed geological, geophysical and tectonic studies on several thermal provinces, geochemical characteristics of the thermal discharges and reservoir temperature estimations were carried out by the National Geophysical Research Institute and the IITs, especially at Puga valley in Ladakh and Tatapani in Chhattisgarh.

Though India has been one of the earliest countries to begin geothermal projects way back in the 1970s, geothermal energy has not emerged as a significant renewable energy option in the country. The preference, instead, is for wind energy and solar energy presumably on account of their easy availability; lower initial investment and proven technology.

Despite this, there is a case for a re-look at geothermal energy. It is estimated that there is a technical potential to produce about ten thousand megawatts of geothermal power in the country. From the point of view of electrification of rural and remote areas, there is even greater potential in terms of the impact of geothermal power where even small projects of five kilowatts can significantly change the economic situation and living standards.

In this context, the experience of some of the Asian countries holds great relevance in developing geothermal energy, overcoming deployment challenges and technical and non-economic barriers.

Geothermal energy accounts for 21 per cent of total primary energy supply in Philippines and 3 per cent in the case of Indonesia. In terms of contribution to electricity generation, geothermal energy constitutes 17 per cent in Philippines and 5 per cent in the case of Indonesia. Both countries have developed geothermal energy as a key element of their energy matrix by targeted policy decisions that included the following:

First: Both countries have adopted specific medium and long-term renewable energy targets, with a separate focus on geothermal energy. Indonesia has enacted Law no. 27 of 2003 that promotes sustainable development of geothermal energy. The country also has set a 5 per cent target for geothermal energy for its energy mix for 2025. The Philippine Energy Plan has articulated a goal for Philippines to become the world leader in geothermal energy. These efforts have led to the evolution of a stable and integrated policy framework to attract investments and private sector participation.

Second: Their policy framework supports renewable energy targets through financial incentives and non-economic support structures. These include feed-in-tariffs where utilities pay a premium for electricity from renewable energy sources that are delivered to the electric grid. Last year, the Indonesian government announced setting of a higher price for electricity produced by new geothermal power plants. The Philippines has also established the National Renewable Energy Board tasked with studying the feed-in-tariff for renewable energy. Both countries also grant income tax and value added tax incentives for geo-thermal projects and exempt geo-thermal exploration equipment from import duties.

Third: The governments in both the countries have made significant efforts in removing economic and non-economic barriers. These include aligning National Energy Policies in favour of renewable energy, reducing the bias in the energy market in favour of conventional fossil fuels, broad-basing energy subsidies provided by the government to include renewable energy, enhancing public awareness of renewables, facilitating electric grid connection and flexible price mechanism for small power producers, encouraging renewable energy for rural focused off-grid applications and improving overall policy and regulatory predictability in the renewable energy market.

The Himalayan region is one of the most promising geothermal areas. It contains about 100 thermal springs and falls in one of the most tectonically active zones. In the 1980s, the first pilot binary five kilowatt power plant was successfully operated by the Geological Survey of India at Manikaran in Himachal Pradesh which proved the power producing capability there.

The Puga Valley geothermal field in Jammu and Kashmir has been estimated to have a temperature of 240 degree centigrade at a depth of 2000 meters. This makes evident its potential and I am confident that this conference would debate ways and means of involving all stakeholders to make this the first viable and operational geothermal power plant.

It is also to be hoped that the regulatory and policy environment governing renewable energy in general and geo-thermal energy in particular would evolve, to enable us to realise the existing potential in Ladakh and deploy it for the public good.

The National Geoscience Awards-2009 Presentation Ceremony

Vigyan Bhawan, New Delhi

4 February 2011

It gives me great pleasure to participate in today's function and give away the National Geoscience Awards for 2009. I would like to congratulate the distinguished scientists and researchers who have been recognised today for their meritorious contributions in the field of fundamental or applied geosciences, mining and allied areas. The government has correctly realised the long term importance of geoscience in its fundamental as well as multidisciplinary forms and has enhanced the scope of the National Mineral Award scheme into the National Geoscience Awards.

Understanding the treasures of planet earth and means to exploit and utilise them in a sustainable manner has been central to human civilisation. Our earth system with its complex inter-linkages between the atmosphere, the hydrosphere, the biosphere and the ecosphere provides us with water and land resources, ecological, water and energy resources. The *Atharvaveda* has an entire hymn of sixty-three verses dedicated to Mother Earth titled 'Bhoomi Sukta'. It says

"Truth, Eternal Order that is great and stern,
Consecration, Austerity, Prayer and Ritual-
these uphold the Earth.
May she, Queen of what has been and will be,
make a wide world for us" ...(1)

"I call to Earth, the purifier,
the patient Earth, growing strong through spiritual might.
May we recline on thee, O Earth,
who bearest power, plenty, our share of food and molten butter" ...(29)

The centrality of geoscience is underappreciated in India among policy makers and educators. There has been an evolution of various geoscientific disciplines into more and more complex areas of study, whether related to geology, geophysics, geochemistry or geo-biology. At the same time, new technologies and tools, many arising out of remote or sophisticated sensing systems and complex computing systems have enabled the creation and manipulation of multi-dimensional multi-disciplinary data encompassing topography, geology, hydrology, biology, hazards, resources and human use, for predictive as well as management applications. The process of specialisation and integration of multiple disciplines is constantly ongoing and remains the test of our geoscientific capabilities and skills.

I would like to raise five issues for the consideration of this learned audience:

First: The existing and developing geoscientific information and knowledge should be harmonised to enable better decision making regarding the exploitation of resources, ensuring environmental sustainability and better risk management, and bringing about the resultant wellbeing of all citizens. We need to develop more sophisticated geoscientific data generation and management systems, create and constantly deepen our pool of S&T manpower, and harness information technology to develop geoinformatic applications capable of integrating multiple disciplines.

Second: Geoscience should be central to our energy and climate change policies. We live in a world which is moving towards reduction of our carbon footprint and leading to increased efficiency of energy production, utilisation and transmission. Geoscientists are critical for data collection, interpretation and policy formulation on mitigation and adaptation and for the larger goal of diversifying our energy portfolio.

Third: We need to enhance public recognition that earth processes need to be better understood for their links to a variety of natural hazards including earthquakes, cyclones, floods, landslides etc. Geoscientists can help us to monitor earth processes, undertake risk assessments and be better prepared for tackling natural, and even man-made, disasters.

Fourth: Rapid development would necessitate increased and efficient use of natural resources. Our demand for minerals and metals would increase alongside an increased demand for agricultural products, leading to greater need for land and water resources. Geoscientists would be required to locate minerals and ores, assess their quality and quantity, and enable their efficient extraction and utilisation. Proper management of this entire chain is indeed crucial for our national security.

Fifth: We need to develop our geoscientific human resources to meet the demand in terms of numbers and breadth of scientific disciplines. For the longer term, we need to integrate geosciences into secondary and tertiary education and make it available as a core academic discipline. We should encourage inter-disciplinary studies and incentivise Public-Private partnerships to expand informal and formal education opportunities in geosciences.

We must make the necessary investment in terms of time, financial and human resources so that our national policies on energy, climate change, water and land resources, agriculture, disaster management, urbanisation, waste management and infrastructure development are informed by the scientific understanding of the geosciences. I hope that the awards given today and the government's steps in creating the Geoscience Advisory Council and the National Geoscience Congress would contribute to this effort.

Inaugural Function of the Eighth J&K Science Congress

Kashmir University, Jammu and Kashmir

17 September 2012

I am delighted to be back in Srinagar and in the midst of so many scientific minds of our country who have gathered here for the Eighth J&K Science Congress. It is commendable that such a state-level conference has been held regularly since 2005.

The theme of the conference–'Science, Technology and Regional Development: Opportunities and Challenges'–is relevant to our times in local, national and global terms.

This audience knows well that modern India's romance with science and technology commenced in the early days of our independence. Its foundations were laid by the Science Policy Resolution of 1958 and the Technology Policy Statement of 1963. While the first aimed at fostering science and scientific research and ensuring adequate availability of research scientists, the second aimed at self reliance and maximum use of indigenous resources.

As a result of these and other initiatives, significant progress was made in higher education in science and technology, in the establishment of industrial research laboratories and in fields like atomic energy, space, agriculture, drugs and pharmaceuticals.

Experience of three decades also revealed, in the words of a competent observer, "the distance between the rhetoric of self reliance and the actual level of technological development and innovation in Indian industry". Further adjustments in policy were therefore made in 1993 and 2003 to respond to new requirements of our economy in the light of changed and changing national and global conditions.

Despite these efforts, and as Prime Minister Manmohan Singh pointed out earlier this year in the ninety-nineth session of the Indian Science

Congress, our relative position in the world of science has declined and our total R&D spending at the current level stands at 0.9 per cent of GDP. The objective, he added, is to take it to 2 per cent by the end of the Twelfth Plan. To pursue this objective, a new science policy is in the offing.

And yet, as Lord Blackett warned a long time back, "science is no a magic wand to wave over a poor country to make it a rich one". He emphasised the importance of the whole innovation chain and the creation of effective networks involving academia, government and business to promote innovation.

It is thus evident that in order to emerge as an effective knowledge power for the welfare of people, stronger capabilities and a more integrated view of science and technology is required. This, besides enhanced financial support, would need more effective mechanisms to catch and encourage talent. Inspiration and creation of role models would be easier if the barriers between teaching and research are lowered if not eliminated altogether by senior and eminent teachers making it a point to teach undergraduate classes.

An essential concomitant would be a new culture of research, greater autonomy and sufficient freedom of dissent. "A successful researcher", said an eminent scientist, "really marches to the tune of his own drum".

The challenge then is three fold: to catch young talent inclined to pursue science studies, to nurture it, and to motivate it sufficiently to remain attached to the domain of science to become the next generation of teachers and researchers.

Research is one aspect of the matter, development leading to technological innovation is another. When the two come together, the objective of socially relevant innovation is achieved. This, in turn, contributes in varying measures to the production of economically relevant public goods. Innovation thus becomes an index of progress and development.

Some institutional push to encourage innovation in our society has emanated from The National Innovation Foundation—India, since its inception in the year 2000. The results remain modest as is evident from the number of patents registered. More therefore needs to be done. This problem was addressed by the National Knowledge Commission and I would like to cite for your consideration a passage from its 2007 Report titled 'Innovation in India' -

> The most important external barrier to Innovation, as perceived by both large firms and SMEs is skill shortage, due to lack of emphasis on creativity, problem-solving, design, experimentation etc in the education curricula. In order to unleash India's Innovation potential, an essential step is systematic reform of the higher education system in India which would act as an enabler for developing the required intellectual capital as well as in laying the foundation for effective collaboration between industry and educational institutions. It could be argued that Innovation, Education (including Vocational Education) and Entrepreneurship are three ends of a triangle, each of which is related to the other.

The report went on to say that another external barrier is the lack of effective collaboration between industry and research conducted in universities and R&D institutions.

The same holds for vocational training and skills development and its potential for employment opportunities. There is room here for huge expansion which should, it is important to remember, be demand-driven and quality-driven. Some of this is underway through various government and private sector schemes. A sharper focus on these would have wider benefits. Given the demographic advantage of a young population, and the ageing population profile of European and East-Asian countries, there is clear case of benefiting from a comparative cost advantage in the foreseeable future.

II

A discourse in conceptual terms on wider national perceptions is one aspect of the matter. This conference has a focus on the state of Jammu and Kashmir and should, rightly, seek a transition from the macrocosm to microcosm and focus on the developmental challenges it faces.

A set of questions readily come to mind:

- What policies and practices would further the development of science and technology in institutions of higher learning in the State?

- How best can the triangle of education (including Vocational Education), Innovation and Entrepreneurship be made operational or given an incentive?
- What steps should be taken to focus initiatives on local conditions and local economy?

The state of Jammu and Kashmir, I am given to understand faces great many challenges in the area of S&T Education and Research infrastructure. Most of these can be addressed by the adoption and implementation of various schemes of Government of India aimed to attract students towards science subjects. Similarly, various doctoral and post doctoral fellowships to promote the interest in research can be availed of. Furthermore, the special packages announced for S&T Sector in Jammu and Kashmir from time to time have to be implemented in letter and spirit to give fillip to the development of scientific temper among youth of this region. This is a moral obligation apart from being a functional one.

Vocational training has to be linked to employability and therefore to different segments of local economy. Acquiring excellence in traditional crafts results in value addition. Similarly, training in service skills needed by the tourism sector could add considerably to employment generation.

Given the geographical contours of the state, the focus of scientific and technological research and innovation should, logically, emanate from the requirements of hydroelectric power generation, rail and road infrastructure, protection of bio-diversity of flora and fauna, Himalayan glaciology, ecological study of lakes and rivers and marine science.

Agricultural research is an area of critical importance. It includes horticulture, forests, sericulture, fisheries, animal husbandry and allied fields. It is pivotal to the economy of J&K as it contributes more than 50 per cent to the net domestic product of the state and is the main source of livelihood for around 80 per cent of the population. Over 80 per cent of net sown area is of food crops and only 42 per cent of the area is under irrigation.

A large number of people are dependent on cattle rearing and sheep breeding. The productivity in this sector, however, is low and the state depends on imports of animal products. Facilities for processing of wool are virtually non-existent.

A good percentage of people are connected directly or indirectly with the horticulture sector in the state. Yet, productivity is low and the sector suffers from low investment, disadvantage of location, poor infrastructure and the presence of many layers of intermediation.

In each of these areas, there are ample opportunities for the scientific community to extend help in realising aspirations of the region in areas like harnessing of hydro electrical potential, better road and rail connectivity, extreme engineering, preservation of biodiversity, issues of health care, food security, accurate weather prediction, agricultural innovation, maintenance of ecology and environment which have a bearing on the regional development.

Food security too is an area of regional concern which needs scientific efforts for improvements. Better weather forecasting is one of the critical aspects for agricultural management. Biotechnology along with information technology has emerged as a core area of economic development particularly on issues relating to food security. There is scope for implementation of the biotechnological techniques and tools for better crop yield for securing improvements in horticulture which is the backbone of the state economy.

Medical institutions in the state have earned a good reputation. Some of this talent should in greater measure be devoted to research related to the health profile of population.

One last thought. While each researcher ploughs the field individually, he or she should also be aware of, and benefit from, what is being done elsewhere in that branch of knowledge. Modern communication techniques have made this much easier. It is said that internationally, one-fifth of research papers are co-authored; this percentage should be higher in national terms. I am sure universities in J&K are conforming to this pattern and encouraging it.

I am confident that this conference will discuss the role of science and technology in developmental process of the state and come up with the measures to respond to challenges that lie ahead. It should identify measures to eradicate the bottlenecks which hamper the application of scientific knowledge and technological support for the betterment of society.

The time has come to give a fresh impetus and dignity to science and technology for catering to the needs and aspirations of this important state of the Union of India. I do hope that the young minds present here will return to their laboratories and class rooms re-energised to do good work in science and to do it for public good.

Inauguration of the Annual Conference of Cardiological Society of India [CSI] and SAARC Cardiac Congress

New Delhi

6 December 2012

I am pleased to be here today to inaugurate the Sixty-Fourth Annual Conference of Cardiological Society of India and the SAARC Cardiac Congress. I extend a warm welcome to all the distinguished delegates from India and other SAARC countries

The Cardiological Society of India was established over six decades ago with the goal of advancement of scientific knowledge and research in relation to the cardiovascular system in all its aspects to improve our basic understanding and to find better preventive measures and treatment of all types of cardiovascular diseases.

The SAARC Cardiac Congress expands the scope of the objectives of CSI to other SAARC countries. It is a welcome development as disease knows no political boundaries. A collective and cooperative effort in combating the killer cardiovascular diseases would be more efficient and effective in tackling this menace which has begun to increasingly impact developing countries, which all SAARC Member States are.

The importance of addressing the challenges related to cardiovascular diseases, which confront the medical fraternity, especially professionals like you, who are working in this field, can be underscored by the following facts:

According to WHO, cardiovascular diseases are the number one cause of death globally as more people die annually from these diseases than from any other cause. It is estimated that 17.3 million people died from cardiovascular diseases in 2008, representing 30 per cent of all global deaths.

Moreover, low-and middle-income countries are disproportionately affected by cardiovascular diseases, with over 80 per cent of deaths in these countries being due to these diseases.

By 2030, it is estimated that almost 25 million people will die from cardiovascular diseases, mainly from heart disease and stroke, which are projected to remain the single leading cause of death.

In India, the situation is no different. Recent studies have shown that heart diseases have emerged as the number one killer in both urban and rural areas of the country. The diseases affect men and women alike. If all age groups are included, heart diseases account for about 19 per cent of all deaths in the country.

According to the consultancy firm, Deloitte, cardiovascular diseases, which were once thought to be impacting the rich and affluent—now, afflict the poor as well. While changing lifestyles, unhealthy eating habits and declining physical activity are the key reasons for high incidence rates in the rich population, the issues of access and affordability account for higher mortality amongst the urban poor and rural population.

These diseases not only impact the physical well being of our people directly, but they can also hold back the economic growth of the country due to increased healthcare expenditure and diminished productivity. According to the same Deloitte study, India is projected to lose approximately US Dollar 236 billion between 2005-2015 due to cardiovascular diseases and diabetes.

The global cost of cardiovascular diseases between 2010-2030 is expected to exceed US Dollar 20 trillion, out of which around 45 per cent would be due to productivity loss from disability, premature death or absenteeism.

The lesson to be drawn from these alarming facts and figures is that the prevention and cure of cardiovascular diseases is not just an important medical necessity but is also a social and economic imperative for sustainable growth and development of countries, especially the developing countries like India.

In this regard, I would urge the medical community to especially look at the challenges in the rural areas. While there is increasing availability and focus on curative care of heart diseases in urban areas, the rural areas and even the poor in urban areas continue to remain deprived of quality diagnostics and interventional cardiac care.

I believe that Indian hospitals conduct over 90,000 heart surgeries a year, which is much less than the 2.5 million required. While we need to continue expanding the availability of high quality curative care of cardiovascular diseases, the age old adage that 'prevention is better than cure' remains equally if not more important in this case.

I am confident that the Sixty-Fourth Annual CSI Conference and the SAARC Congress will deliberate on finding better ways of preventing and curing cardiovascular diseases and also sharing best practises in this field so that the desired objective of providing universal healthcare, especially in the cardiovascular sphere, can be attained for our peoples.

Security and Accountability

"In a fast changing world, the challenges facing intelligence practitioners are enormous. Can they adapt their organisations, policies and practices to a world in which there is a qualitative change in the notion of security and in the nature of threats? Both compel a paradigm shift in procedures and objectives; so does the imperative of accountability in terms of democratic norms of good governance. Each of these needs to be factored into the work patterns of the intelligence operative of tomorrow. A timely synthesis would pave the way for success

Dr Anandswarup Gupta Memorial Lecture
New Delhi
23 March 2009

THE LAW, THE POLICE AND THE PUBLIC–THE IMPERATIVE FOR A BALANCE

It is a privilege to be invited to deliver the Anandswarup Gupta Memorial Lecture this year. Dr Gupta was an unusual police officer. Besides being an outstanding professional and institution builder, he had an introspective bend of mind and developed wide ranging interests. There are good and substantive reasons for recalling his services to the nation.

Anandswarup Gupta's primary focus was on the Indian Police and he devoted most of his life to it. His two books on the history of the Indian Police remain standard works of reference.

Police and policing is admittedly an excitable and contentious subject. Dr Gupta readily conceded the point; for the common citizen, he wrote, the police is "'still the object of public distrust and condemnation, if not hatred". Our Police, he added, was "still in search of a new identity, a new image, a new aim and a new technique".

All societies have needed a law-enforcing authority. The relevance of the subject for the health of the society is thus evident. The critical choice is of methodology; the problem pertaining to it was enunciated by Rousseau. "There will always be", he wrote, "a great difference between subduing a multitude and ruling a society". The police can and has been used for both purposes. The use and abuse of the police, as an integral part of the apparatus of governance, thus becomes central to any debate on proper governance.

A useful starting point of discussion is public imagery. What is the average citizen's perception of the police? In contrast to it, what image does a doctor, a lawyer, a teacher evoke? Why does the contrast persist? How can it be changed?

For analytical purposes and in relation to the police, valid questions pertain to (a) social philosophy and purpose (b) recruitment, training and discipline, and (c) management, control and accountability.

The inherited burden of the past cannot be ignored. The traditional Indian systems were adapted by the British Administration for its colonial requirements. Its public image was commented upon in 1901 by the Governor of Bengal. "In no branch of the Administration in Bengal", he wrote, "is improvement so imperatively required as in the police. There is no part of our system of government of which such universal and bitter complaint is made, and none in which, for the relief of the people and the reputation of the Government, is reform in anything like the same degree so urgently called for." The Indian Police Commission of 1902-03 concurred with this observation, adding that "there is no province in India to which these remarks may not be applied." Despite this candid assessment, the competing imperatives of colonial rule did not induce substantive correctives.

After Independence, public figures and opinion makers talked of the need for police in a democracy to be in tune with the people and obtain their cooperation. In practice, however, no change was discernable nor was any attempt made in the public domain to highlight such change. Two decades later simmering of discontent in the Delhi Police resulting in Calling Attention Notices in the Lok Sabha led to the appointment in 1967 of the Delhi Police Commission. Its findings confirmed that the police establishment continued to be essentially colonial in character. It expressed the view that "the duty of enforcing law and preventing crime is only a by-product of the main function of the police, acting as a peace force, to maintain and uphold the legal and constitutional rights of the people. A police force which understands correctly its position in society and moulds its actions accordingly can easily endear itself to the people, because the latter realise that police work is directed entirely for the good of the society." In a bold observation, it stressed the need for "a revolution in thinking about police is required throughout the country".

The public clamour for change gathered momentum in the seventies and led to the establishment in 1977 of The National Police Commission. It was given wide terms of reference: to examine the role and performance of the Police as a law enforcing agency and as an institution to protect the rights of the citizens enshrined in the Constitution. It made a number of reports. The first of these focused on (i) police accountability mechanisms and (ii) low morale arising out of low wages and poor working conditions. Another report dealt with insulating the police from political and bureaucratic interference. Most of these remained unimplemented. This led to a writ petition in the Supreme Court in 1996. A judgment came a decade later, in 2006.

The Judgment of 22 September 2006 considered the entire background of the matter, took note of the Union Government's move to draft a new Police Act but did not consider it "possible or proper to leave this matter only with an expression of this hope and to await developments further. It is essential to lay down guidelines to be operative till the new legislation is enacted by the State governments." These, it said, "shall be complied with by the Central Government, state governments or union territories, as the case may be, on or before 31 December 2006". The Directions, seven in number, relate to appointment procedures, tenures and the setting up of Police Complaint Authorities at district and state levels.

On 11 January 2007, the date of compliance was extended to 10 April 2007. Failure to comply, partially or fully, by most states led to a contempt petition that was heard in April 2008. Thereafter, a monitoring committee headed by a retired judge of the Supreme Court was set up. There have been comments on its pace of work. A judgment on the contempt petition is yet to come.

The urgency evident in the Judgment of 2006 appears to have waned somewhat.

II

The subject of police reforms also brings in its wake the larger issue of the nature of our State structure and the legislative realm of the Central and State governments. The debate on this is testing the limits of our constitutional framework. It is relevant in this context to recall what Ambedkar said to explain the significance of the term 'Union of States':

"The Drafting Committee wanted to make it clear that though India was to be federation, the federation was not the result of an agreement by the states to join in a federation, and that the federation not being the result of an agreement, no State has the right to secede from it. The federation is a Union because it is indestructible. Though the country and the people may be divided into different states for convenience of administration, the country is one integral whole, its people is a single people living under a single imperium derived from a single source. The Americans had to wage a civil war to establish that the States have no right to secession and that their federation was indestructible. The Drafting Committee thought it was better to make it clear at the outset rather than the leave it to speculation or to dispute."

I happened to read recently the opening statement on the website of the Ministry of Home Affairs. The second sentence reads as follows:

"Though in terms of Entries No. 1 and 2 of List II–'State List'–in the Seventh Schedule to the Constitution of India, 'public order' and 'police' are the responsibilities of States, Article 355 of the Constitution enjoins the Union to protect every State against external aggression and internal disturbance and to ensure that the government of every State is carried on in accordance with the provisions of the Constitution.

It is a pity that the wording, intent, and scope of Article 355 has so far escaped commentary, nor has it been put to use to ensure governance in terms of the Constitution.

Despite Ambedkar's observation and the wording of 355, much of the discussion on impediments to change remains focused on the technicalities and tends to override the imperatives of good governance and public welfare. This could be a case of mistaken perceptions; alternatively, the reason may lie elsewhere. A remark of Machiavelli comes to mind. Men, he wrote, "forget more easily the death of their father than the loss of their patrimony."

May be there are some in our society who consider control over the police as a form of patrimony!

III

Police and policing is not an end in itself. Procedural modalities for the selection of personnel and guidelines for isolating them from political interference is one aspect of the matter; another is the need to make the police force more representative of the diversity of our society. Equally relevant from the citizen's viewpoint is the training of the police in order to induct and nurture a set of values emanating from the Constitution and the principles of the Rule of Law. The avoidance of the colonial mindset of the past has to go hand in hand with imbibing of human rights norms to safeguard the weaker segments of society, minorities, women, children, and the disabled from neglect or excesses emanating from traditional prejudices. The police force needs to render custodial justice, even-handed treatment in communal flare-ups, be fair and gender sensitive in cases involving women. Its handling of cases involving persons from poorer sections of society needs to change demonstrably. Only then would the citizen accept it as people-friendly. Community policing should remain an ideal to strive for. Each of these requires changes in the law as well as in the manner in which the law is actually administered.

In regard to the legal framework the challenge is to establish a just and practical rule of administration "taking men as they are and laws as they can be made." We are fortunate that the element of justice is writ large in the Constitution. Despite it, it took us half a century to accept the need to review and replace the central element of colonial administration. The Sorabjee Committee established in September 2005 has proposed a new Model Police Act for replacing the Police Act of 1861 so as to put in place an appropriate legislative framework to redefine the role of the police, its duties and responsibilities to meet the growing challenges of policing and to fulfill the democratic aspirations of our citizens. It awaits legislative scrutiny and approval.

A new Police Act would be an initial, but by no means final, step in the administration of criminal justice in the country. Today we have a paradoxical situation in which the process is time consuming and yet there is an acquittal ratio of around 90 per cent. A spate of other pieces of legislation would also need to be reviewed if the intent and spirit of the Constitution is to be given the shape of realisable rights of citizens. Many correctives have been suggested by the National Human Rights Commission and by other national commissions and citizen groups. The public expects that as a first step, the procedures of administrative justice could be accelerated.

There is one other matter that needs to be mentioned. No reform process can succeed unless it begins with honest introspection and admits and addresses the question of institutional bias. We have sufficient instances of these in our recent history. I would mention one: the Hashimpura massacre of 1987. As a result of a long period of denial, followed by official complicity to delay scrutiny, justice is yet to be rendered.

The police are an instrument of the State, whose physical attributes are professionalism and efficiency; equally important is the manner in which they are used and the major and minor premises, mostly unstated, that form its operational philosophy. The need to anchor it in the Constitution, its Preamble and the section on Fundamental Rights, cannot be overstated. The people of India are the source of all authority and, in the final analysis, the ultimate accountability of the police is to the people of India. Jawaharlal Nehru underlined this point unambiguously. "Of course", he said, "the police have to function for the maintenance of law and order, for the protection of those who need protection and all that, but they can only successfully do this in a democratic State if they are in tune with the people and they get their cooperation."

Sadly, even after repeated diagnosis and prescription of medicine, the patient is unwilling to be administered the medicine. Every initiative to ensure that Rule of Law be the only point of reference for the police has remained unimplemented by both the executive and the legislature. What is completely lost sight of is the fact that the ultimate victim of this non-implementation is the citizen of India–the common man and woman who is at the receiving end of non-enforcement of rights and discriminatory application of the laws and without the clout to secure either of them.

There is an old saying that unless asked, even a mother does not feed her child. The people of India have waited as various rulers, colonial and national, have come and gone without aligning the police structure to their aspirations. The current situation of the police is attributable as much to state inaction as to the disinterest of citizens. Can the citizens as voters induce political parties to agree to police and criminal justice system reforms as a non-partisan issue outside the realm of competitive politics and use it as a yardstick for assessing commitment to good governance, transparency and accountability?

These and related questions, even if not answered immediately, become the starting point for change that would help bring about the new identity and image that Anandswarup Gupta visualised.

Fourth R.N. Kao Memorial Lecture
CGO Complex, New Delhi
19 January 2010

Intelligence for the World of Tomorrow

I am honoured to be invited today to deliver this lecture to commemorate an iconic personality who dedicated his life to the service of the Republic and created structures deemed essential for the security of the State and the promotion of its essential interests. In another age or another system of governance, he would be honoured suitably in a pantheon of immortals. We as a people, however, are diffident in matters relating to some aspects of the functioning of the State and prefer a discreet veil to a public acclaim. It tantalises imagination but does not add to the compendium of knowledge for succeeding generations.

We remember Rameshwar Nath Kao today for his work and for his engaging personality. In regard to the former, I cannot help recalling a couplet by an Arab poet of the tenth century:

> "These are our works, these works our souls display
> Behold our works when we have passed away."

I personally cannot claim to have known Kao sahib well but do recall an occasion, in early 1980, when I happened to sit next to him on a journey from Bombay to Delhi. He spoke in chaste Urdu, discussed the happening in Iran, and was candid enough to acknowledge that like most other people he had not anticipated the revolutionary changes.

Ramjee Kao created an organisation, negotiated rather than confronted inter-agency contentions and achieved a historic success. He could also be indulgent to a fault. Those who worked closely with him have described Kao as a complex mix of objectivity and subjectivity in matters concerning human relationships. A peer in a position to assess from a distance described him as a fascinating mix of physical and mental elegance, and one who was shy to talk about his accomplishments.

Kao's business in life was intelligence, more specifically external intelligence. Its relevance is in no need of commentary. We can go as far back as Kautilya, or even earlier, to perceive its importance. In fact, the methodological sophistication exhibited in Kautilya's chapters on the secret service and internal security can be read with benefit even today. The same holds good for Sun Tzu's chapter on secret agents. He highlights the relevance of 'foreknowledge' and concludes with the interesting observation that "there is no place where espionage is not used." Over centuries the ambit of intelligence, and the craft itself, expanded and enriched itself in response to requirements. Techniques were refined and technology opened up qualitatively different vistas. In the twentieth century individual agents on specific assignments gave way to regular agencies. Fascination with the unknown also brought forth a vast amount of literary output that combined fact and fiction, working powerfully on public imagination and even lending respectability to questionable acts. There is merit in C.P. Snow's observation that "the euphoria of secrecy does go to the head."

Intelligence, by definition, is primarily directed at anticipating happenings. Intelligence information, by its very nature, is a glimpse of reality. It is often inconclusive because the methods of acquisition are at times surreptitious. On the other hand, the probabilities of reality that can be established by intelligence information are necessary and sufficient to enable national decision-makers to make reasonable judgments about courses of action. While intelligence information is at times incomplete, good intelligence often has made the difference between victory and defeat, life and death. By the same token, faulty intelligence leads to failures of varying degrees. Over time, reasons for failure are analysed and classified. These range from overestimation to underestimation, lack of communication, unavailability of information, received opinion, mirror-imaging, over-confidence, complacency, failure to connect dots and subordination of intelligence to policy. Case studies on each of these abound; they are a sobering reminder of Karl Popper's observation that "the more we learn about the world, and the deeper our learning, the more conscious, specific and articulate will be our knowledge of what we do not know."

The qualities that go to make a good intelligence operative have been defined in all systems of governance. A medieval classic called it "delicate business involving some unpleasantness" to be "entrusted to the hands and tongues and pens of men who are completely above suspicion and without self-interest, for the weal or woe of the country depends on them." In an interesting passage in his book, the formidable Mr Allen Dulles observed that "a good intelligence officer must have an understanding of other points of view, other ways of thinking and behaving, even if they are quite foreign to his own." Record shows that this is easier said than done even in normal times. The ability to assess what Troksky called "changes in mass consciousness in a revolutionary epoch" is rarely acquired by those who collect and analyse intelligence. The reason for this would seem to lie in insufficient comprehension of the nuances of a changing situation, inadequacy of coverage and inability to challenge working assumptions.

Other problems emerge as occupational hazards. Compulsive secrecy tends to become obsessive and impacts the personality of the individual. An intelligence organisation, one observer has noted, tends to be a self-sufficient society to which "the outside world becomes more and more remote and its realities less and less important." Rob Johnston, who conducted an ethnographic study of the U.S. intelligence community in 2005, observed that "within the intelligence community, more organisational emphasis is placed on secrecy than on effectiveness." Making a judgment about open source versus secret information, a professional concluded that ninety per cent information comes from the former and only ten per cent from the latter. "The real intelligence hero", he wrote, "is Sherlock Holmes, not James Bond."

The need to strike a balance between secrecy, openness and efficacy on a continuous basis is thus essential. Much greater coordination is required to maximise results in complex situations. The time-honoured formula of 'need to know' has to be modified by the requirement of the 'need to share'. The point was driven home by an eminent leader very recently: "I'll never fault anybody for not having full intelligence, what I will fault is when we have full intelligence that's not shared."

II

Beyond the confines of professional competence, the question of intelligence is intrinsically linked to the nature of challenge perceived by a society. It tends to be based on past experience and on assumptions that seem logical. This is essential but not sufficient and its relevance now is increasingly open to question. The resulting dilemma was aptly expressed a few years back by the historian and jurist Philip Bobbitt:

> Now it happens that we are living in one of those relatively rare periods in which the future is unlikely to be very much like the past. Indeed the three certainties ...about national security – that it is national (not international), that it is public (not private), and that it seeks victory (not stalemate) – these three lessons of the past are all about to be turned upside down by the new age of indeterminancy into which we are plunging.

Bobbitt went on to assert the need to appreciate "the essential ambiguity" of attacks to which societies may be subjected to and as a result of which strategies of retaliation and deterrence may become less useful. In such a world, he added:

> We must move our thinking from threat-based strategies that rely on knowing precisely who our enemy is and where he lives, to vulnerability-based strategies that try to make our infrastructure more slippery, more redundant, more versatile, and more difficult to attack.

This conceptual shift, from threat-based to vulnerability-based strategies, would necessitate a comprehensive reorientation of the work of the State and therefore of its intelligence apparatus, its objectives and its work methods. Some of this is already underway in the light of the experience of the first decade of the twenty-first century; this, however, have been pragmatic and halting since the requisite paradigm shift in thinking is yet to be put in place. The extent and speed with which it is done may well determine success or failure in the foreseeable future.

To develop the argument further, I would like to borrow the definition of the term vulnerability from the meaning given to it in the terminology of computer security. There it is referred to as a weakness which allows an attacker to reduce a system's Information Assurance. This happens at the intersection of three elements: a system susceptibility or flaw, an attacker's access to the flaw, and an attacker's capability to exploit the flaw. In societal terms, this would read as (1) flaw or susceptibility (2) existence of an enemy or a threat (3) ability of the threat to exploit the flaw. Such a framework would necessitate going beyond the traditional approach to a comprehensive assessment of both the susceptibility of the target and the capability of the opposing force.

A complicating factor of increasing relevance is the changing nature of the actors on the global stage. In addition to nation states, it now includes a mix of non-State entities, benign and malignant. In the absence of effective multilateralism, the relative power of these non-State actors has increased to reflect the fragmentation of interests.

The conclusion is inescapable that in the world of tomorrow, the nature of intelligence required for comprehensive security would be qualitatively different. This would have implications for the methodology of acquiring and analysing it. As a first step, it would necessitate a wider understanding of target areas. Much too often, governmental intelligence efforts have focused on politico-military and economic intelligence. While its relevance cannot be questioned, its sufficiency can be. The reason is obvious. Most often, the standard check list does not go beyond or behind the super-structure, does not look at societal realities, pays inadequate attention to other people's ways of thinking and behaving. Intelligence services, as David Kay of the Iraq Survey Group put it, "don't do a very good job of trying to understand the soft side of societies."

Nor does the check list take a good look at the national security implications of non-traditional threats including cyber-attacks, attacks on food and water security, bio-terrorism, pandemics or worst case apocalyptic visions of the future. It has, for instance, been assessed that in a post-pandemic world dangerous patterns of inter-state behaviour may emerge and seriously endanger security of states.

The ambit of intelligence, consequently, has to be comprehensive. It is to be assessed simultaneously on three planes: State-centric, society-centric and environment-centric. The dynamics of these may be different and may require different tools of analysis. The resulting conclusions may be fluid, complex and contradictory and thereby challenge the analytical skills of the operative to bring forth options that can be comprehended and acted upon. Access to these skills, if not available in-house, would necessitate review of security rules that generally govern the functioning of intelligence organisations.

III

A particularly serious problem relates to the misuse of intelligence. The classic instance in recent times is the process leading to the invasion of Iraq in March 2003. The July 2004 Report of the US Senate Select Committee on Pre-War Intelligence Assessment of Iraq revealed that "group think dynamics" led the intelligence community to interpret ambiguous evidence as conclusive and ignore in the process established mechanisms to challenge assumptions and group think. Closer to the mark was the secret Downing Street Memo of 23 July 2002 in which the head of British intelligence reported after discussions in Washington that "intelligence and facts were being fixed around policy" of regime change. The Iraq Enquiry now in progress in London is shedding more light on this.

These instances can be multiplied. They are not the monopoly of one nation or set of nations. They are revealed earlier in open societies and less so in closed ones. They have led to follies and catastrophes. Failures propel thinking in the direction of correctives and reforms. They focus analysis on the political or economic pressures at work in individual societies. These, together, propel thinking in the direction of accountability and necessitate oversight. Both are considered unwanted and bothersome by intelligence communities for reasons that range from secrecy and operational efficiency to downright contempt for any individual, body or arrangement that endeavours to assess their functioning. The problem nevertheless exists and was posed by an expert in precise terms:

"How shall a democracy insure its secret intelligence apparatus becomes neither a vehicle for conspiracy nor a suppressor of the traditional liberties of democratic self-government?"

It is hardly necessary to remind an Indian audience that ministerial responsibility to the legislature, and eventually to the electorate, is an essential element of democratic governance to which we are committed by the Constitution. The methodology of this is in place for most aspects of governmental activity; the exceptions to it pertain to the intelligence and security structure of the state.

How then is oversight and accountability ensured?

The traditional answer and prevailing practice, of oversight by the concerned minister and prime minister and general accountability of the latter to parliament, was accepted as adequate in an earlier period but is now considered amorphous and does not meet the requirements of good governance in an open society. Concerns in the matter have primarily arisen on two counts: (a) the nature and extent of supervision over intelligence services exercised by the political executive and (b) the possibility and scope of misuse of these services by the political executive. Both concerns emanate from the absence of specific accountability, on these matters, to the legislature.

The problem is not a new one and has been faced by other democratic societies. In late 1970s opinion in the United States reached the conclusion that "oversight of the Intelligence Community is essential because of the critical importance of ensuring the nation's security, as well as checking the potential for abuse of power." As a result, two congressional committees were established in 1976 and 1977. Despite this, the 9/11 Commission Report of 2004 found the congressional oversight of intelligence "dysfunctional" and recommended structural changes. A similar exercise was conducted in the United Kingdom through the Intelligence Services Act 1994 that established the Intelligence and Security Committee of Parliament to examine the expenditure, administration and policy of the intelligence services. Other countries like Canada, Australia, South Africa, Norway, Germany, Argentina, the Netherlands, Poland and Romania have also put in place similar mechanisms of public accountability.

It has been argued that the scope of the mandate of the parliamentary intelligence oversight committee is crucial for its success. Three models of the mandate can be identified: (a) comprehensive to include both policy and operations, as in the U.S. and Germany (b) limited to matters of policy and finance, as in UK (c) focused on human rights and rule of law, as in Norway. The basic purpose of all three is to ensure that government policy in a given field is carried out effectively within the boundaries of the law. For this reason, it is felt that without access to some operational detail, an oversight body can have or give no assurance about the efficacy or the legality of the intelligence services.

Given these models of calibrated openness to ensure oversight and accountability, there is no reason why a democratic system like ours should not have a Standing Committee of Parliament on intelligence that could function at least on the pattern of other Standing Committees. Since internal and external intelligence do not in our system report to the same minister, the possibility of entrusting this work to the Standing Committee on Home Affairs may not meet the requirement.

In the same spirit, and keeping with the practice of other democracies such as the United States of America and the United Kingdom, the concerned agencies should make public their mission statement outlining periodically their strategic intent, vision, mission, core values and their goals. Existing models range from periodic executive review of the mission statement to statutory definition of the function of these agencies. Furthermore, and in step with the globalised information architecture, there is a case for greater openness with regard to the history of intelligence institutions. We need to study initiatives taken elsewhere and determine the extent to which we can proceed in the matter.

The shortcomings of the traditional argument, of leaving intelligence to the oversight of the executive, became evident in the Report of the Kargil Review Committee and its sections on Intelligence in its Findings and Recommendations. It identified flaws, acknowledged the absence of coordination and of 'checks and balances', and noted the absence of governmental correctives. The Report referred to relevant systems in major countries but did not include in it their systems of oversight and accountability.

Some correctives were introduced pursuant to the establishment of the National Security System and the report of the Group of Ministers on the reform of the national security system in its entirety. These improvements enhanced internal accountability and coordination but did not go far enough and did not put in place a more open system of public accountability. In the discussions that followed the publication of the Kargil Review Committee Report, and apart from inter-agency spats and the blame game, one informed commentator described it as a "substantive contribution in educating our Parliament and public opinion" aimed at "introducing transparency in this sensitive sector."

Arguments of this nature tend to be condescending. They ignore the time-honoured formula which is the bedrock of democracy: that "instead of looking on discussion as a stumbling block in the way of action, we think it an indispensable preliminary to any wise action." They belittle the capacity of elected representatives to be responsible in matters of national security. Also overlooked is the fact that depending on the fall of the electoral dice, these same representatives are transformed into the political executive entrusted with the responsibility of supervising the work of intelligence agencies.

The contention that openness and public discussion would compromise the secrecy essential for intelligence needs to be examined carefully. Operational secrecy is one aspect of the matter and has to be maintained. The legislature, nevertheless, is the organ of the state that allocates funds and is therefore entitled to insist on financial and performance accountability. The practice of subsuming allocations is not conducive to transparency; it may even encourage misuse. The proposed Standing Committee could fill this void; it could also function as a surrogate for public opinion and thus facilitate wider acceptance of the imperatives of a situation. Given the nature of emerging threats to human security, a wider sampling of opinion would in fact facilitate better comprehension of the issues and of possible remedies to attain total national power and comprehensive defence.

IV

Let me conclude by saying that in a fast changing world, the challenges facing intelligence practitioners are enormous. Can they adapt their organisations, policies and practices to a world in which there is a qualitative change in the notion of security and in the nature of threats? Both compel a paradigm shift in procedures and objectives; so does the imperative of accountability in terms of democratic norms of good governance. Each of these needs to be factored into the work patterns of the intelligence operative of tomorrow. A timely synthesis would pave the way for success.

Social Justice

❝... to secure to all its citizens: **Justice**, social economic and political ...

—Preamble of the Constitution of India

❝Justice is the first virtue of social institutions. Therefore in a just society the liberties of equal citizenship are taken as settled; the rights secured by justice are not subject to political bargaining or to the calculus of social interests

—John Rawls

Fifth *India Today* 'State of States' Conclave
The Taj Mahal Hotel, New Delhi
14 September 2007

It gives me great pleasure to address the Fifth *India Today* 'State of States' Conclave. I particularly commend the *India Today* Group for systematically building up quantitative reference points for debate and policy making on a range of social and economic development themes.

The focus of the State of States Report this year, 'Inclusive Growth', is timely. One cannot but be struck by the fact this issue has continued to dominate every critique of governance in India for over a century. It was at the Nineth Session of the Indian National Congress at Lahore in 1893, that Dadabhai Naoroji commented, and I quote: "The greatest question before you, the question of all questions, is the poverty of India. This will be, I am much afraid, the great future trouble both of the Indian people and of the British rulers. It is the rock ahead."

The situation was no different five decades later, as is evident from Palme Dutt's observation in 1946: "India is a country of poor people. But it is not a poor country. Between these two lies the problem of the existing social and political order in India."

Thus a century after Dadabhai Naoroji, "the rock" continues to exist and portends "the great future trouble". The poverty of Indian people is still the "question of all questions".

The macro-economic figures of the Indian economy appear good. We have had a real GDP growth of 9.4 per cent for 2006-07 and an exchange rate per capita GDP of $880; in Purchasing Power Parity terms, the per capita GDP climbed to around $4000. Our savings and investment rates have increased, there was a gross FDI inflow of $19.5 billion in 2006-07 and good reasons exist to believe that there have been productivity and efficiency improvements.

The evident contradiction perplexes observers and leads to two questions:

- What does this mean for a large segment of our population?
- What is the true wealth of our nation? Is it national income or material wealth? Or are the people of India, our true wealth?

If the latter, the only measure of national progress should be the quality of life of our people.

The recently published report of the National Commission for Enterprises in the Unorganised Sector vividly portrays the extent of poverty and vulnerability of a vast section of our people. The sense of satisfaction at the macro-economic situation stands diminished with the realisation that 77 per cent of our population, totaling 836 million people, have an income of around Rs 20; half a dollar in exchange rate terms, and two dollars in PPP terms. This poor and vulnerable segment of the Indian population represents the broad category within which the dynamics of poverty alleviation plays out.

The poor are not homogenous. There are movements across sub-categories. Thus, the sub-category of extremely poor and poor, whose expenditure per day is less than Rs.12, have reduced by one third from 30.7 per cent of the population in 1993-94 to around 22 per cent of the population in 2004-05. But those who moved out of such grinding poverty have graduated to the next sub-category of those who are marginally poor and vulnerable and whose daily expenditures constitute less than Rs 20 per day. Indeed, this is poverty alleviation, but in a technical sense. We must ask as to how the well being of a person changed on a rise in expenditure from Rs 12 to Rs 20 per day? At the other end, the middle and high-income categories have also roughly increased by about one third, from 18 per cent of the population in 1993-94 to around 23 per cent of the population in 2004-05.

While all citizens contribute to the national effort, in public perception, there are two Indias–an India focused on wealth accumulation and another India focused on poverty reduction. We have a situation where the richest 10 per cent of the population account for slightly less than 30 per cent of the share of expenditure and the poorest 10 per cent of the population account for less than 5 per cent. Thus overall economic growth of the country has not yet translated itself into fair distribution of the fruits of development. Wealth accumulation at the top has been more impressive than poverty reduction at the bottom. The challenge is to accept that wealth accumulation and poverty reduction are two sides of the same coin and need to be addressed together.

The debate so far has been mainly concentrated on income poverty and inequality. It is held that economic development leads to poverty reduction and eventually to human development. While the broad causality of this is true, the extent of impact is dependent on the income distribution pattern of a country. If as in India, the richest segment of the population captures a larger share of the economic development, the extent of poverty reduction would be lower for the same quantum of economic development.

More than income inequalities, what are particularly worrisome are the stark human development inequalities that adversely impact upon life chances and capabilities of our people. These can be grouped under four heads:

1. Ability to survive: the life expectancy and child mortality issues;
2. Access to basic health care, especially for the most vulnerable;
3. Access to education and human resource development initiatives;
4. Gender issues and the empowerment of women.

We have many examples from around the world and within the country where public policy choices have ensured that human development outcomes have far exceeded the potential embedded in the economic development that was achieved by nations and states. This was done through a conscious focus on income distribution patterns and ensuring that public spending on basic health and education remained high.

How does India rank on these parametres? Public expenditure on education in India is around 3.3 per cent of GDP and on health is around 1.2 per cent of GDP. This is low by any standards, and especially for the extent of poverty that exists in India. Much more needs to be done.

Inequalities in our society have other markers too. These pertain to disadvantaged groups and minorities, to the place of residence such as the urban-rural divide, to regional disparities in development. Each of these acts as inequality multipliers by negating substantive freedoms and life chances for individuals. Some of these were analysed in depth in the India: Social Development Report published last year by the Council for Social Development, New Delhi. The report also sought to develop a Social Development Index and classify twenty of the larger states of the country on the basis of six component indices – demography, healthcare, basic amenities, education, unemployment and poverty, and social deprivation.

These are not esoteric philosophical or economic issues. They are vital political themes that find a strong resonance in the basic principles of our polity. Article 37 of the Constitution defines the application of the Directive Principles of State Policy as 'fundamental in the governance of the country'. Article 38(2) states that: 'The state shall, in particular, strive to minimise the inequalities in income, and endeavour to eliminate inequalities in status, facilities and opportunities, not only amongst individuals but also amongst groups of people residing in different areas or engaged in different vocations.' Article 39 also calls on the State to direct its policy towards securing that "the citizens, men and women equally, have the right to an adequate means of livelihood" and that "children are given opportunities and facilities to develop in a healthy manner and in conditions of freedom and dignity".

Mahatma Gandhi accepted that his ideal of equal distribution is not realisable and advocated equitable distribution as an achievable goal. This could be one parameter for assessing the 'State of States'. Inclusive growth could thus be the subtext of all of our developmental efforts.

Ernst & Young's Entrepreneur of the Year Award Programme
Taj Palace Hotel, New Delhi
20 November 2007

I deem it a privilege to address this distinguished gathering today on the occasion of the presentation of the Entrepreneur of the Year Awards.

Entrepreneurship and wealth creation are indeed ancient themes in Indian history. Kautilya wrote in the *Arthashastra*: "The king shall ever be active and discharge his duties; the root of wealth is activity, and of evil its reverse." Over the years, wealth creation was an act of reverence, an instrument of influence and even considered worthy of worship. Yet, entrepreneurship is also a very recent theme. A young India today sees opportunity all around.

Never before in our history have so many entrepreneurs in India become as successful and demonstrated such an extent of wealth creation as in the past decade. We are told that the aggregate net worth of the four richest Indians, all entrepreneurs, stands at US$ 180 billion; the net worth of India's 40 richest stands at US$ 351 billion, more than double their net worth last year. For perspective, this amount is roughly over a third of our GDP at current prices!

Any economic or social process to be sustainable in the long term has to find broad-based and multiple sources of sustenance in the economy, polity and the society at large; it should represent an aspirational matrix for people and there must be a reasonable consensus that such a phenomenon adds to the public good. Entrepreneurship development and wealth creation are no exception. What then are the core elements that must be taken into account if the tremendous successes of our entrepreneurs of the last decade are to be sustainable?

Firstly: A much under-discussed issue of entrepreneurship in India is that of 'Social Capital'. It has been said that 'social capital is not what you know, but who you know'. In India, existing facts substantiate that social capital plays a crucial role in human capital formation, economic performance of firms and superior performance of some social groups and geographic regions. What are the affiliations that produce bonds and networks of trust and reciprocity that aid in economic performance of firms and individuals?

Recent research by Harish Damodaran has indicated the importance of caste affiliations in India in promoting 'Particularistic Exchange Networks based on Mutual Trust' as opposed to 'Impersonal Exchange Networks based on Contract Law'. Over time, this has been the basis in India for the emergence of business communities and large business familial networks. It has also promoted particular business and investment cultures that have been successful in Indian and other cultures.

The flip side to this story is self-evident. While there has been a relatively wider access to opportunities for entrepreneurship facilitated by education, there are no Dalit industrialists or business houses. Likewise, those from other under-privileged, minority and marginalised communities have been confronted with what could be called the 'glass ceiling of entrepreneurship and capitalism'.

In the West, one has heard of the tremendous incubation and entrepreneuring impact of affiliations to premier Indian technical and management institutes such as IITs and IIMs. Unless social capital is based on such impersonal affiliations, lack of access to it would continue to hinder what I consider an absolute necessity–of broad basing entrepreneurship in India. Indian business and industry must ponder on this if the current economic dynamism and entrepreneurial enthusiasm is to remain sustainable.

II

Secondly: Entrepreneurship in India is associated with the manufacturing industry and services. While the current share of agriculture in GDP is around 18.5 per cent, that of services is 55 per cent and of industry around 26 per cent. The growth rate in the agriculture sector has been a mere 2.7 per cent in the last financial year. Yet, more than half of the population directly depends on this sector. The adverse impact of the low growth in agriculture is more than the sectoral contribution to the GDP. The Economic Survey of 2006-07 notes that poor agricultural performance has implications for 'the inclusiveness of growth'. The potential for entrepreneurship and innovation in agriculture is enormous and it has a multiplier payback effect on the society.

Sustainable and inclusive growth and enduring employment generation demand new initiatives in the agriculture sector. The government has emphasised the need for another big push to agriculture through a 'Second Green Revolution'. Issues of low investment, unbalanced fertiliser use, a distorted incentive structure, low crop yields and low seed replacement rates need innovative and technological redressal. I look forward to the day when one of the 'Entrepreneur of the Year' awards would be dedicated to agriculture.

III

Thirdly: The vital causation between governance and entrepreneurship is often overlooked. Besides individual drive and motivation, the enabling environment to promote entrepreneurship and aid wealth creation is a direct result of good governance. It is through the prism of good governance that innovation and entrepreneurship are rewarded and recognised for their ability to generate employment and help in the percolation of the wealth created. We are currently in a sweet spot where macro economic conditions in India, global factors, the current stage in the evolution of our industry and corporate and national governance have converged and led to the unprecedented growth and success of entrepreneurship in India in the past decade.

As a generation, the India of today looks at the future with immense optimism–in fact, the whole nation seems to be imbued with an entrepreneurial zeal. The motto seems to be–if they can, so can we! May this infectious enthusiasm prevail at all levels.

Book release: NREGA Published by the Lal Bahadur Shastri Institute of Management

Conference Hall, 6 Maulana Azad Road, New Delhi

3 February 2010

It gives me great pleasure to release the report published by the Lal Bahadur Shastri Institute of Management on the Mahatma Gandhi National Rural Employment Guarantee Act 2005 and its implementation in six states. Professional feedback of this nature would be useful to the government for appraisal, diagnosis, remedial action and capacity building for the NREGA.

The Act itself has been a game-changer in the governance of the country. It has for the first time, both nationally and internationally, articulated a rights-based approach to guaranteeing wage employment at such a vast scale. Let us consider the numbers:

In 2008-09, around 45 million households have been provided with wage employment and 2160 million person days of employment have been generated;

Average wage paid in 2008-09 has increased to Rs 84, an increase of around a third as compared to 2006-07;

In 2008-09, participation of SCs and STs has been 55 per cent and women workforce participation has surpassed the statutory minimum requirement of one third and has increased to 48 per cent.

The primary objective of improving wage employment is being achieved with some success. Equally important are the auxiliary objectives of improving natural resource management, promoting equity and gender equality across communities, bringing about financial inclusion and insurance coverage and using technology at the rural level for improved governance. The government is committed to ensure the success of these objectives and any assessment of performance has to cover them.

As a nation, we have to redeem the pledge of the founding fathers to eliminate divides–urban-rural, male-female, divides of caste, tribe, community and religion. The vision is of every citizen having every opportunity to improve his/her human capacities and leading a fulfilling and dignified life. The NREGA is a step in empowering rural citizens to steer their own destiny and ensuring that development processes are not only sustainable but also in consonance with the aspirations and desires of citizens.

Like all programmes, the implementation of the Mahatma Gandhi National Rural Employment Guarantee Act 2005 is a work-in-progress. Suggestions for correctives have come from individuals and organisations supportive of the programme. Every such contribution towards better implementation and operationalisation of the Act would contribute to national prosperity and individual well being of a large number of Indians. It is my hope that the report published by the Lal Bahadur Shastri Institute of Management would also do so.

The Ninety-Seventh Birthday of Shri Justice V.R. Krishna Iyer

High Court Auditorium, Ernakulam, Kerala

12 November 2011

I was commanded by the Legend to be here today and little choice did I have but to comply!

I candidly admit that I am happy and truly privileged to participate in today's function to celebrate the ninety-seventh birthday of Justice V.R. Krishna Iyer.

"Sublimely mild, a spirit without a spot" is what can be said of Vaidyanathapura Ramakrishna Iyer, a man who made it his life's mission to resist injustice, secure justice and take up just and compassionate causes– within the realm of law and beyond it.

Few would know of his passion for animal welfare or his early career in politics as a member of the Legislative Assembly.

It was indeed fortuitous that Justice Iyer came back to the Bar. He was a visionary in championing human rights jurisprudence with a focus on women, dalits and the marginalised, much before it emerged on the international or national scene. The vision and morality of our Constitution was his guide all through. His stint in the High Court and the Law Commission was focused on delivery of justice to the common citizen.

In a span of seven years as a Judge of the Supreme Court during 1973-1980, when the nation was in a political and legal tumult, Justice Iyer put the citizens and the values of the Constitution at the centre of his focus. The guarantees given to us by our Founding Fathers through the Constitution were reinterpreted for a new age, and new instruments fashioned to deliver justice. Thus, judicial remedies were sought through the instrumentalities of Public Interest Litigation, broader concepts of locus standi, and the Constitution was seen for what it could deliver to people.

His activism continued after retirement with renewed vigour, and is visible to this day. Justice Krishna Iyer can justifiably lay claim to be a Karma Yogi all his life. In an opinion piece on 'Justice, Justices and Justicing' a few years back, he made some pithy observations. Allow me to cite one of these:

> There are three great pathologies that alienate the judiciary from the people. The curative pharmacopoeia of fundamental judicial reform to counter these comprises forensic democratization, a process of social justice delivery and structural transformation of the judicial system through innovative facilities for the have-not humanity. This trinity of recipes demands institutional creativity, procedural humanism, and joint action by the executive, the legislature and the judiciary, inspired by the radical values inscribed in the Constitution

Prof. Upendra Baxi has rightly observed that Justice Iyer is "an embodiment of secular saintliness". He deserves the nation's appreciation and gratitude for his contribution.

Change, great change, has characterised the decades since Independence. The past two decades have accentuated the trend. The success of our polity is to be measured by the dexterity with which we have negotiated the rapids of this transformation.

As we survey the recent past, we notice a fundamental shift in the debate from development of economy and industry to human development. This has propelled the discourse with greater vigour to questions of sustainability and equity, to the quest for fairness and social justice, and for ensuring the right of every citizen to have equal access to opportunities for personal growth and development of one's capacities to the fullest, and for leading fulfilling and meaningful lives.

There is also recognition that there can be no sustainable improvement in public welfare without good and institutionalised processes of governance and unflinching commitment to democratic norms, constitutionally-anchored fundamental rights and universally-accepted human rights.

At the global level over the past few decades a state of gross prosperity has been achieved; it remains unprecedented when looked at as an aggregate. The advances in terms of scientific and technological knowledge and applications far outstrip the combined achievement of humanity to date. We have produced ever more, consumed ever more, and wasted ever more than in history. Yet, we also know that these are aggregates, and averages always hide the condition of those below the average.

All over the world one hears today the cry of the common man protesting against the exclusion of the majority from accessing the benefits of economic growth and prosperity engendered by globalisation of financial markets, economies, investment flows and processes. Real incomes of the top percentile across developed and emerging countries have grown disproportionately higher, exacerbating income inequalities. It is now clear that the system that has worked so well for the top percentile has delivered far lesser returns to others.

It is even more surprising that income distribution has worsened despite the great strides in narrowing the gaps in health and educational achievement across population groups. It is now globally recognised that human development is adversely affected under conditions of inequality, and that this can be quantified across indicators of health, education and income.

The Human Development Report 2011 of the UNDP published last week has demonstrated that around a quarter of the human development at the global level is lost due to inequality. The South-Asian region suffers the second largest human development losses due to inequality, after Sub-Saharan Africa.

In the case of India, there is an overall human development loss of over 28 per cent due to inequality. The loss due to inequality of human development achievements in education are the highest in the case of India and amount to over 40 per cent. While the Report does not cover overlapping inequalities, we know from our experience that certain groups of marginalised such as women, scheduled castes and scheduled tribes, linguistic and religious minorities and those below the poverty line, experience multiple deprivations and exclusions.

Inequality is a problem in the long run, especially when it kills aspiration for personal and societal betterment. In India, the matrix of inequality spans gender, the rural-urban divide, class, caste, tribe, linguistic and cultural groups. While growth is a necessary condition for societal welfare, it is not sufficient and does not automatically lead to equality in accessing development and opportunities for growth.

Indeed, securing to all citizens equality of status and opportunity is a solemn resolve that finds mention in the Preamble of our Constitution. The State has a constitutional and moral duty to expand opportunities for those being left behind. Thus, the State has on the one hand focused on affirmative action and provision of a social safety net for those marginalised, while on the other moved to improving the capabilities of citizens to be more productive through skills and improved infrastructure.

Here, once again, I find of relevance what Justice Krishna Iyer has written:

> If Indian democracy is to redeem its tryst with destiny, a creative protocol and code of ethics must become the vogue in public life. Consensus must be the rule of life, contentment of the lowliest the testament and participative process the habit of governance.

As I conclude, I am reminded of the words of Dr Rajendra Prasad on his election as the first President of Independent India. "I have always held that the time for congratulation", he remarked, "is not when a man is appointed to an office, but when he retires".

I feel honoured to take part in the birthday celebrations of Justice Krishna Iyer and, in all humility, congratulate him for all his multifarious contributions to the nation, in and out of office.

Social Philosophy

"The way out of the serious distemper between social institutions and the world purpose of bringing about a cooperative commonwealth resulting in dignity, noble living and prosperity for all, (is) the restoration of the lost relationship between the individual and the eternal

—Dr Sarvepalli Radhakrishnan

Inauguration of the National Conference on 'The Interfaith Movement–Where do we go from here?'
Indira Gandhi National Centre for the Arts, New Delhi
31 October 2008

By inviting me to this gathering today, Dr Karan Singh sahib propelled me to do focused thinking on a subject that is more is more often than not taken for granted and therefore inadequately understood.

It is a truism that nature is endowed with diversity. One dimension of it is human diversity that takes the shape, amidst other manifestation, of varieties of experiences, faiths and belief systems.

Faith has been defined as belief in the trustworthiness of an idea. The basis of this belief may be physical or metaphysical. Either way, it leads to a conviction that something is, secondly to a determination to accomplish objectives associated with this conviction and thirdly to a sense of satisfaction linked to the achievement of the preceding two

Given the richness of human experience in space and time, the manifestations of faith have been equally diverse. In most of these, the endeavour is to relate human existence to an ultimate point of reference that is an infinite or absolute essentiality existing by the necessity of its own nature.

One consequence of this is the emergence of similarities as well as divergences of perceptions.

The human being is a social animal and normally lives in a society of fellow humans. Bertrand Russell had once noted that "the misfortune of human beings may be divided into two classes: those inflicted by non-human environment and those inflicted by other people", adding that "the evil that men inflict on each other have their main source in evil passions rather than ideas or beliefs".

This leads us to a set of questions. How do ideas pertaining to faith take shape in relation to society? What is perceived to be the result of interaction of faith per se with the sum total of societal values?

Social life also has a political dimension. A sociologist who studied the impact of religion upon the political sphere concluded that the impact of politics on religion or faith could take the shape of (i) religiously relevant political action, or (ii) politically conditioned religious action. In such a framework, the potential of contestation becomes unavailable.

This has practical implications. One aspect pertains to the State. Speaking of religion in imperial Rome, Edward Gibbon had noted that "the various modes of worship, which prevailed in the Roman world, were all considered by the people, as equally true; by the philosopher, as equally false; and by the magistrate, as equally useful. And thus toleration produced not only mutual indulgence, but even religious concord.

Instances of a somewhat similar approach are to be found in India history and in the state practice of modern India. "The Indian Constitution", writes Professor Gurpreet Mahajan, "dealt with the issue of religion by endorsing the principle of non-establishment of religion by but without advocating the separation of religion from politics"

Experience leads us to conclude that such an approach is insufficient in the context of the civil society. It suggests that diversity of faiths necessitates proactive initiatives aimed at expanding the areas of comprehension and reducing misunderstandings. This creates the need for communication and dialogue, for what is known in contemporary parlance as interfaith dialogue.

An essential pre-requisite is the acceptance of the validity of spiritual experience of all. Delhi's own fourteenth century sufi saint, Hazrat Nizamuddin Aulia, put it succinctly:

"Har quam raast rahe, deen e wa qilba gaahe"

Every people know the right path, the faith and place of worship.

The next logical step is an empirical one and takes us to locate points of convergence. A small booklet *Unity in Diversity*, sent to me by Dr Karan Singh, is a good example.

The world we live in is characterised by the shrinking of spaces. Isolation and exclusivity are matters of the past. Ignorance of the other is no longer bliss. In fact, the 'Other' has increasingly and unavoidably become a part of the Self. This larger Self, therefore, needs to be understood and accommodated in our perception and practice.

It is here that the Interfaith Movement has a role to play. This is being understood globally. The 2002 Millennium World Peace Summit of Religious and Spiritual Leaders spelt out its basic principles. These need to be furthered. A critical role in this will be played by inculcating its values in the educational system. Only this can provide the right type of nourishment to the mind

A global movement is a good thing. It is, however, no substitution for national efforts. Nowhere is this more relevant than in our society. Amartya Sen has written about the long history of the argumentative tradition in India, and, as he put it, "its relative neglect in ongoing cultural discussions". I can do no better than to cite his argument:

"The contemporary relevance of the dialogic tradition and of acceptance of heterodoxy is hard to exaggerate. Discussions and arguments are critically important for democracy and public reasoning. They are central to the practice of secularism and for even-handed treatment of adherents of different religious faiths".

The Interfaith dialogue is critical to our health as a society. Its success would lie in widening the ambit of its adherence, and their acceptance of it as an imperative necessity.

I may, in the end, add a corrective and a caution. Indian history is full of instances of dialogues initiated by rulers. Good examples of these are Emperors Asoka and Akbar. In the seventeenth century Prince Dara Shikoh undertook a remarkable exercise of putting together communalities and convergences of two major faiths but added that his work had "no concern for the common folk of the either community".

While the intellectuals have a role in initiating such a dialogue, its practical relevance in a democratic polity would lie in its dissemination among the common folk who, at least in India, have some experience of interactive co-existence and can, therefore, build upon it and should consciously be assisted to do so. This process of assistance begins in schools but cannot succeed unless it is imbibed by the society as a whole.

Thirteenth Radhakrishnan Memorial Lecture
Indian Institute of Advanced Study, Shimla
16 April 2009

The Intellectual and Society: Role and Responsibility

I do have happy memories of some years of schooling spent in this city and this is reason enough to relish the opportunity to return. This feeling is accentuated manifold by the honour bestowed by you today in inviting me to deliver the annual Radhakrishnan Memorial Lecture.

Sarvepalli Radhakrishnan was unquestionably one of the great Indians of the twentieth century. As a philosopher he interpreted Indian thought to the world in what has been called the 'battle of consciousness.' The Republic bestowed on him the highest offices of the State and he in turn added lustre to them. A constitutional head of state in a modern democracy cannot, with justice, lay claim to Plato's ideal of a "perfect guardian"; despite it, the philosopher in Radhakrishnan did inject a deeper perspective, draw attention to values and help the system, as he put it, "do the right thing". Inaugurating this very Institute in 1965, he cautioned against the deification of error and becoming 'prisoners of the status quo'.

Three centuries earlier another man of philosophy, Baruch Spinoza, had prescribed for himself a rule of communication: "to speak in a manner intelligible to the multitude, and to comply with every general custom that does not hinder the attainment of our purpose." Radhakrishnan would have readily endorsed this. Less reverential is Bertrand Russell's observation that philosophers are for the most part constitutionally timid, dislike the unexpected and therefore invent systems which make the future calculable!

Given Radhakrishnan's intellectual stature, it would be beneficial to explore his views on the role of the intellectual in public life. These make interesting reading and retain a contemporary relevance.

He addressed the question in his 1942 lectures delivered at the University of Calcutta and at the BHU; these were published in 1947 as *Religion and Politics*. The imperative, spelt out in the first lecture, was the 'very rapid' pace of change:

"Everywhere round about us we hear the sound of things breaking, of changes in the social, in the political and economic institutions, in the dominant beliefs and ideas, in the fundamental categories of human thought. Men of intelligence, sensitiveness and enterprise are convinced that there is something radically wrong with the present arrangements and institution ..."

He traced the cause to "the serious distemper" between social institutions and the world purpose of bringing about a cooperative commonwealth resulting in dignity, noble living and prosperity for all. The way out, he suggested, was "the restoration of the lost relationship between the individual and the eternal"; hence the relevance of religion. Established religions, however, cannot meet the world's need for a soul.

Having sought to establish a balance between the ideal and the practical, Radhakrishnan spelt out a role for the intellectual in the final lecture. The relevant passages are noteworthy:

"The final ends of political action are to be considered by the thinker and the writer. In them society becomes conscious and critical of itself. They are the character of a society. Their business is to educate us to a consciousness of the real self of society, and to save guardians of the values of a society, the values which are the real life and us from spiritual callousness and mental vulgarity ...

"The intellectual need not take an active part in politics or in the actual affairs of administration. It is their primary function to serve society with intellectual integrity. They must create social consciousness and sense of responsibility which transcends the limits of the political community. Those who can serve society in this way have a duty not to engage in politics. For every society there will be a few for whom participation in political activity would be a perversion of genius, a disloyalty to themselves ...

"If the intellectuals abandon the interests of culture, and repudiate the primacy of spiritual values, we cannot blame the politicians who are responsible for the safety of the state".

Two and a half decades later, and while replying to a Farewell Address by the Members of Parliament, he put forth a more benign perception of men of politics:

"Politicians do not mean people of twisted tongues or cold hearts. They are men with warmth of feeling, who have compassion for the suffering of humanity. We should, as politicians, exert our utmost to alleviate the sufferings of humanity. Politics should not absorb all our life; it is indispensable, but not the whole life".

Embedded here are perceptions of intellectual activity and the role of intellectuals, as also of politics and the purpose of political activity. Each has a bearing on life in society and on the meaning of citizenship. For this reason, it remains relevant.

II

The debate on the linkage between thought and action, and the moral imperative for action, is a perennial one. Neither exists in isolation. It has been argued that the notion of pursuit of knowledge for its own sake, in contrast with knowledge pursued explicitly for some particular end, is misleading. The intellectual's responsibility, admittedly, is to think; but thinking in itself is an activity and as such is linked to the activity which is the implementation of thinking; a refusal to see it so is to be morally culpable. The intellectual thus becomes a critical element in the value system of a society.

A definition of the intellectual and his role was provided by the sociologist Edward Shills:

"In every society there are some persons with an unusual sensitivity to the sacred, an uncommon reflective-ness about the nature of their universe, and the rules that govern their society. There is in every society a minority of persons who, more than the ordinary run of their fellow men, are enquiring, and desirous of being in frequent communion with the symbols which are more general than the immediate concrete situations of everyday life, and remote in their reference in both time and space. In this minority, there is a need to externalise the quest ... This interior needs to penetrate beyond the screen of immediate concrete experience marks the existence of the intellectual in every society".

The intellectual is thus entrusted with a special responsibility. It necessitates corresponding action. Such an approach would lend credence to Marx's observation that "philosophers have only interpreted the world, in various ways; the point is to change it." Nor was Marx alone in urging a linkage. "The intellectual", wrote Vaclav Havel in 1986, "should constantly disturb, should bear witness to the misery of the world, should be provocative by being independent, should rebel against all hidden and open pressure and manipulations, should be the chief doubter of systems of power and its incantations, should be a witness to their mendacity". By doing so the intelligentsia risks, in Toynbee's telling phrase, becoming an outcaste, born to be unhappy because its very existence is a reproach to the society concerned.

In a celebrated essay in 1967, Chomsky had asserted that in considering the responsibility of intellectuals "our basic concern must be their role in the creation and analysis of ideology" and to see events in their historical perspective. The same point was made by Edward Said in his Reith Lectures in 1993 when he urged the contemporary intellectual "to speak the truth to power", and do so by "carefully weighing the alternatives, picking the right one, and then intelligently representing it where it can do the most good and cause the right change".

At the other end of the spectrum, the intellectual is viewed as a dangerous creature capable of poisoning minds, destabilising order and creating chaos. Paul Johnson, in a selective survey, has questioned the "moral and judgmental credentials of intellectuals" and cautioned about "the heartless tyranny of ideas" emanating from them. Such perceptions have been used to create or sustain closed societies, including some masquerading as open ones. We have enough examples in our own times of dictatorships of the right or the left, and of societies imposing a monopoly of control anchored on race, religion or atavistic claims.

The debate on what the intellectual can and should do, and in what manner, has taken place in most societies. The impulses and imperatives vary, so do the constraints. It is of particular relevance in a society like ours where, to echo Edward Said's caution, "easy certainties provided us by our background, language, nationality … so often shield us from the reality of others".

On the basis of the role played by intellectuals in different societies, it is possible to develop a typology. They can be academics, writers, artists or activists. Creativity and courage are the two essential conditions for their public role. There is also a symbiotic relationship between the ideas generated within a society and its institutions of social sciences. Nor can external influences or linkages be overlooked; researchers have spoken of the impact on national perceptions of international 'epistemic communities' defined as network of professionals and experts who share normative beliefs, lay claim to policy-relevant knowledge and impact policy perceptions.

III

Where then do we locate the role and responsibility of the intellectual in contemporary India?

India, it has been said, is a political and economic paradox: a rich-poor nation with a weak-strong state. Persistent centrism, and continuous realignment, is one of its striking features. This has accommodated a wide spectrum of interests, classes, status groups, regions and communities in the political process and development structures. This accommodation has not always been equitable. The Constitution provides the point of reference; its Preamble is the key to its social, political and economic philosophy and to its core value system. It has been described as a moral document embodying an ethical vision; this compels attention to Ambedkar's observation that constitutional morality is not a natural sentiment and has to be cultivated.

On Radhakrishnan's parametres, therefore, amongst the primary responsibilities of the intellectual would be to educate the society on these values and to assess the extent to which they are being adhered to. An unavoidable concomitant of this would be the necessity of 'speaking the truth to power'. The challenge before the intelligentsia, wrote Rajni Kothari six decades after Radhakrishnan's lectures, is "to keep alive the flame of hope and resurgence, and to continue offering ideological alternatives to the struggling segments of the mass public." The role of the intellectual thus becomes integral to the healthy functioning of a society.

The nature of the society in question, and the relationships secreted in its interstices, provides the starting point of analysis. Any critique of the Indian polity would thus involve scrutiny on multiple axes and require threefold examination of the relationship of the state and society, the state and democracy and the polity and the economy. Our quest would focus on the role of the intellectual in the furtherance of this critique.

Since time constraints come in the way of a comprehensive analysis, I shall endeavour to confine my remarks to five specific areas, namely institutions, economic amelioration, corruption, rights and environment.

Institutions: The structure of our polity took shape through intensive debates during the freedom struggle and in the Constituent Assembly. The Constitution bestowed centrality on the state and impacted on the relationship between it and the society. A good deal of social activity came to be focused on ways and means of impacting state perceptions and activity. Interest groups in society thus came to focus on elections as the first and logical step in this endeavour; the excellent work in this field done by Lokniti has been widely acknowledged. In the process, however, the democratic functioning of the society came to be considered by most as synonymous with the electoral process. Ashis Nandy has termed it 'psephocracy'. The study of the actual functioning of the institutions received inadequate attention and the wider implications of this for public debate and discussion were, exceptions apart, insufficiently scrutinised by the intellectuals. Its impression on public perceptions is all too evident today and raises questions about the health of our institutions and the state of governance. There are some exceptions to an otherwise pervasive neglect; Pratab Bhanu Mehta and Rajni Kothari, amongst others, are illustrative of these.

Mehta's critique is on the failure of the State in the removal of inequality. There is, he asserts in an eloquent passage, a deepening of democracy on the one side and its corruption on the other: "It would be a rare citizen who has not felt the force of both narratives directly. The difficult question is how to bring the two together". Democratic practice has in effect meant advancement of group interests through competitive negotiations rather than through the diffusion of democratic norms. This has led to 'a profound disenchantment with the state". The Indian State, in its day to day transactions, is often "neither feared nor loved: incapable of having the rule of law secured either through an effective set of institutions, nor the eliciting of allegiance to its dictates by inspiring a sense of obligation". One reason for this disenchantment with the state, he concludes, "is the perceived failure of the instruments of accountability since democracy has become non-deliberative." The deliberative capacities and oversight functions of the Parliament are in decline and elections are rarely fought on policy issues. Political parties are in disarray. Mehta's solution lies in correctives to statism through a new politics of redistribution arising out of the policy of economic liberalisation: "What Indian democracy needs is a new sense of the relationship between the public and the private". He accepts that this will require an extraordinary effort. No blue print, however, is put forth except the suggestion that the proceeds of disinvestments should be earmarked for poverty alleviation and human resource development.

To Rajni Kothari, democracy "as a system has not been realised in practice" and remains an aspiration. The turbulence in India compels attention to the "deeper psycho-spiritual dimensions of Indian reality", to societal perspectives rather than political ones. The Indian scene is characterised by a tradition of tolerance of pluralism, dissent and opposition. An unwelcome consequence of it is tolerance of "ambiguity, deprivation and humiliation". The consensual polity that emerged in the early decades of the Republic was supported by "charismatic power and pliable tradition". The strength of the consensus was unavoidably contingent on the organisational skills of the elites and on the levels of discovery. When both faltered, new sets of actors emerged to redefine the contents of politics in terms of new agenda of aspirations. These new movements are "no longer limited to economic or even political demands, but seek to cover women's issues and questions of public health as well as ecological and cultural issues. They include a sustained attack on sources of internal decay and degeneration". They demand new instruments of political action, non-party and party-like. This necessitates a review of ideological positions on the nature and content of democracy.

One aspect of the institutions of democracy pertains to Rule of Law. A few years back a senior law officer of the government posed a candid question: have the three organs of the State discharged their constitutional obligations and functioned within the limits set forth by the constitution? His own answer was that the Rule of Law is "under serious threat" arising out of 'cancerous developments eating into the fabric of each institution' and with "each is destroying itself from within". Others too have spoken of the under-reach of some institutions and over-reach of others, both resulting in disturbing the balance visualised in the Constitution.

There is little or no evidence to suggest that the requisite correctives are underway; nor has any concerted effort been made by public intellectuals to turn the grievance into a movement.

"Sixty years after Independence", writes the historian Ramachandra Guha, "India remains a democracy. But the events of the last two decades call for a new qualifying adjective. India is no longer a constitutional democracy but a populist one". A Report published by the CSDS last year on the 'State of Democracy in South Asia' calls for a new political imagination to build democracy that would 'meaningfully accommodate minority and marginal groupings'. It calls for a reworking of political institutions to free democracy from the stranglehold of dominant caste and class elites.

Economic amelioration: These views on institutions, reflective on one plane of a widespread frustration over their demonstrated shortcomings, have not prevented civil society movements led or supported by intellectuals advocating correctives in some areas of social life, and putting some of them in place through changes in the institutional framework. I refer in particular to the processes leading to the enactment of the Right to Information Act and the National Rural Employment Guarantee Act, both in 2005. The first has led to the empowerment of the citizen vis-à-vis the state and is unquestionably the first major step towards transparency. We have, as Aruna Roy put it, "an obligation to those who are denied access to shrinking public spaces" adding that "campaigns have repeatedly demonstrated the power of collective participation to change the direction of governance". The origins of NREGA go back to the Right to Food campaign initiated in 2001 with the writ petition in the Supreme Court and developed into a movement thanks to what Jean Dreze has called "skilful activism". Despite uneven implementation by state governments, and some criticism by the World Bank lately, NREGA's uniqueness as an instrument of ameliorating the condition of the rural poor by helping them avoid hunger and distress migration by providing opportunity to earn a living wage in a dignified manner cannot be questioned. The process is assisted by the monitoring mechanism established by the Supreme Court; the Eighth Report by Commissioners N.C. Saxena and Harsh Mander in August 2008 is indicative of the scope of the initiative and the extent of intellectual-activist involvement in it.

Public opposition to specific instances of acquisition of agricultural land for SEZs, and the related discussions on approaches to industrialisation, continues to propel the debate about alternate models of development strategy. This has received an impetus in the wake of the global financial crisis. The need for financial stimulus and the re-emergence of the public sector as the engine of the economy has reinvigorated many intellectuals to question the premises of 'neo-liberalism' and the policies arising out of it. Prabhat Patnaik is a case in point.

On a wider canvass, Amartya Sen has stressed the need for "ideas about changing the organisation of society in the long run". Do we, he enquires, "really need some kind of "new capitalism" rather than an economic system that is not monolithic, draws on a variety of institutions chosen pragmatically, and is based on social values that we can defend ethically? Should we search for a new capitalism or for a "new world" that would take a different form?"

Corruption: In a paper written in 2004, Peter deSouza called corruption "Democracy's inconvenient fact". The Approach Paper to the Eleventh Five-Year Plan considered corruption "endemic in all spheres". Former central vigilance commissioner Vittal characterised it as "financial terrorism", as anti-national, anti-poor and anti-development, and as "the root cause of very poor governance in India." More disturbing is the perception that "as crass individualism makes its way, the social attitude towards corruption is more forgiving." Corrective movements like Parivartan have based their effort on effective use of the RTI and the mechanism of social audit and Jansunwai have received support of intellectuals and civil society groups; they have produced results in specific cases. This is acknowledged in the Report of the Administrative Reform Commission on 'Ethics in Governance.' ARC's specific recommendations would need for implementation political will and focused public support in much greater measure than is forthcoming at present.

Rights: The doctrine of rights has evolved in recent years. A conscious effort, as yet uneven, has been made to give content to concepts of equality and justice. The role of the judiciary, and of the Public Interest Litigation, has contributed substantially to it. The ambit of rights has been amplified by the 1997 judgement of the Supreme Court in Vishaka v State of Rajasthan ruling that 'provisions in the international covenants pertaining to human rights can be read into the domestic law in the absence of any inconsistency between the two, as a canon of construction'.

The position taken by a wide cross section of intellectuals on communal, economic or regional issues like the Babri Masjid demolition, the 2002 Gujarat riots, or the more recent happenings in West Bengal on land acquisition, in Orissa and Karnataka on security of minorities and on regional chauvinism and communalism in Maharashtra, are indicative of an awareness that is to be welcomed.

In regard to actualisation of group rights, intellectual, public and governmental initiatives have been taken to ascertain the factual situation on deprivation and discrimination "in production, distribution and social sectors." The problem has been summed up by Amitabh Kundu: "Unequal economic opportunities lead to unequal outcomes which in turn lead to unequal access to political power. This creates a vicious circle since unequal power structure determines the nature and functioning of the institutions and their policies. All these result in persistence of initial conditions". Exploratory efforts have been initiated by the government to put in place a Diversity Index and create an Equal Opportunity Commission. Intellectuals have contributed to both in good measure. Both would need a wider degree of public support to allow these to pass the test of legislative approval.

Environment: Movements to protect and safeguard the environment have an older vintage and fall into two broad categories: micro movements based on result oriented efforts on specific issues and with wide public participation, and macro movements to influence policy. The most famous in the first category is the Chipko movement of the early 1970s. Others movements have related to opposition to the construction of major dams and hydel projects and to instances of environmental disasters; examples of these are the Silent Valley, Tehri Dam and Narmada River Valley projects and the Bhopal gas tragedy. Despite the involvement of eminent activists, large scale public support on a sustained basis was often lacking and only the movement to oppose the Silent Valley project was fully successful. On the other hand, grass-root levels efforts in Maharashtra, like the Pani Panchayat and Ralegan Sidhi, associated with Anna Hazare, have been more successful.

At the level of activist intellectuals, and despite the good work done by environmentalists like Sunita Narain and Vandana Shiva, public awareness of environment issues is still in its infancy and there is merit in Vandana Shiva's observation that "the environmental movement can only survive if it becomes a justice movement."

The instances cited in this very brief survey present a varied picture ranging from frustration to success and to a mix of both. The latter may induce the optimist to advocate, as a hard-nosed realist put it in another context, patient accumulation of partial successes. The intellectual, admittedly, must speak truth to power; the manner of speech, however, cannot be that of the angry poet expressed so eloquently by the Majaz:

"Barh ke is Inder sabha ka saaz o saaman phoonk doon
Is ka gulshan phoonk doon, uska shabistaan phoonk doon
Takht-e-sultan kya, main saara qasr-esultan phoonk doon."

IV

It is now time to revert to the role and responsibility question in regard to intellectuals. Most would accept the need to speak truth to power and do so by advocating the correct alternative. In doing so awareness and analysis of the major and minor premises of proposed approaches becomes unavoidable. T.K. Oommen has taken the argument a stage further and, in the context of our constitutional values, developed the "perspective from below" that helps "institutionalisation of equality and justice" in contrast to the view from above that assists 'perpetuation of hegemony.' The response of the state to social movements, he adds, "does not fall into unilinear patterns; (it) is dictated by the nature of the mobilisation attempted by a movement. Conversely, the character of the party in power is critical variable in determining state response." This could range from facilitation to toleration and discreditation, even repression.

Where then do we conclude? The answer is neither easy nor simple. A position nevertheless needs to be taken. The journey, of necessity, is a lonely one. I cannot help recalling a passage from that most indomitable of intellectuals, Edward Said:

"Nothing in my view is more reprehensible than those habits of mind in the intellectual that induce avoidance, that characteristic turning away from a difficult and principled position which you know to be the right one, but which you decide not to take. You do not appear too political; you are afraid of seeming controversial; you need the approval of a boss or an authority figure; you want to keep a reputation for being balanced, objective, moderate; your hope is to be asked back, to consult, to be on a board or prestigious committee, and so remain within the responsible mainstream; some day you hope to get an honorary degree, a big prize, perhaps even an ambassadorship. For an intellectual these habits of mind are corrupting par excellence. If anything can denature, neutralise, and finally kill a passionate intellectual life it is the internalisation of such habits."

Gandhi*ji* would have put the point across in his own way. "I know the path", he said. "It is straight and narrow. It is like the edge of a sword. I rejoice to walk on it. I weep when I slip."

Inauguration of the Diamond Jubilee Conference of Indian Sociological Society
Jawaharlal Nehru University, New Delhi
11 December 2011

It is hazardous to venture into a realm that everybody claims to know but few actually do! The pitfalls for the uninitiated are evident. Nevertheless, I would be audacious and admit that it is a privilege to be invited to inaugurate the Diamond Jubilee Conference of the Indian Sociological Society.

As a discipline and despite its impeccable European pedigree, Sociology as an independent discipline evolved in the face of considerable skepticism. Early in the last century, Henry Ford of Yale University cautioned that "those who yield to its plausible pretensions go astray". Two decades later Read Bain of Miami University denounced sociology for its inaccuracy, indefiniteness, and terminological confusion and called sociologists as "scientific charlatans." Similar views were expressed elsewhere too.

That phase is now over. Sociology is today seen as a vital tool in understanding societies and the ongoing social changes.

Indian sociology is distinguished by its grounding in Indian reality and the diversity in its scope of research. Great names like G.S. Ghurye and M.N. Srinivas have been associated with it. Today, it is a subject of study and research in over fifty universities and in many research institutes.

The Diamond Jubilee Conference of the Indian Sociological Society is thus timely, with its focus on the social transformation in India and issues emanating from it. The sociologist, in a word, has become indispensable to the process of governance and management.

The world has been transformed in the past two decades. The changes span global and national, political, economic and social order resulting in decreased salience of national sovereignty, of traditional social institutions and established patterns of political and economic activity. This period has witnessed significant advancement in scientific and technical knowledge and achievement of gross prosperity unparalleled in human history. This prosperity co-exists with unprecedented inequalities. The resulting tensions between and within nations in terms of material advancement and prosperity is all too evident.

As societies struggle to respond to these challenges, they call upon sociologists to decipher what Emile Durkheim called material and nonmaterial social facts and the related issues of social stratification and problems emanating from it.

The Greek historian Plutarch had observed that "an imbalance between rich and poor is the oldest and most fatal ailment of all republics". All over the world one hears today the cry of the common man protesting against the exclusion of the majority from accessing the benefits of economic growth and prosperity engendered by globalization of financial markets, economies, investment flows and processes. Real incomes of the top percentile across developed and emerging countries have grown disproportionately higher, exacerbating income inequalities.

It is now clear that the system that has worked so well for the top percentile has delivered far lesser returns to others.

This is not merely an economic phenomenon, related to income distribution and disparity of wealth. Social inequality is a reality, with differences in status, opportunity and power, and the absence of an overarching framework of social justice. It has its own impact on levels of human development.

It is known that social disparities are not always congruent with economic inequality and that difference in power and status can chart through non-economic realms. Social and occupational stratification work as much to constrain opportunities and life chances of individuals as economic factors. Inequality is a problem in the long run, especially when it kills aspiration for personal and societal betterment.

II

In our own country, the matrix of inequality spans gender, the rural-urban divide, class, caste, tribe, linguistic and cultural groups. While growth is a necessary condition for societal welfare, it is not sufficient and does not automatically lead to equality in accessing development and opportunities for growth.

Our Founding Fathers focused on this reality and brought to bear a unique and insightful sociological bearing into the framing of the Constitution of our Republic. Indeed, securing to all citizens equality of status and opportunity is a solemn resolve that finds mention in the Preamble of our Constitution.

The problem was addressed by Dr B.R. Ambedkar who conceded the existing social reality and noted that the new institution of democracy was only "top dressing on Indian soil that was essentially undemocratic". He emphasised that an essential ingredient of constitutional morality was ensuring that political democracy is followed by social democracy, a way of life which recognises liberty, equality and fraternity as the principles of life forming 'a union of trinity' where to divorce one from the other is to defeat the very purpose of democracy.

Thus the Indian State has on the one hand focused on affirmative action and provision of a social safety net for those marginalised, while on the other moved to improving the capabilities of citizens to be more productive through skills and improved infrastructure.

Six decades later, it would be valid to raise two questions:

- To what extent have we succeeded in ushering in social democracy and nurturing the seed of social equality and social justice?
- How far has the state progressed in meeting its constitutional and moral duty to expand opportunities for those left behind?

The answer to both demands a sociological enquiry, and is a subject matter for this Conference.

III

The second issue that I would like to deal with is the increasing salience of urban sociology. Social evolution in today's world is closely related to urbanisation and economic progress, a linkage that is under-appreciated.

Over half of humanity lives in urban spaces today. Today, there are twenty-one mega-cities with three in India–Delhi, Mumbai and Kolkata. As a matter of fact, Delhi and Mumbai are two of the world's four cities with population of over 20 million. The twenty-first century would indeed be an urban century.

Urbanisation and urban migration has transformed social space and social time, and left its imprint on the spatialisation of social order. It is an arena demanding sociological study of the pulls and pressures of individual citizenship and community living in cities, dichotomy of gated communities and sprawling slums, of conflicts centred on domicile and migration, culture and language, religion and profession.

While our cities propel economic growth, prompt economic and social change, and spark widespread innovation and entrepreneurship, our urban spaces and governance mechanisms have also become the theatres for political conflicts and economic struggles. While some critics speak of "elite capture" of our urban spaces and indeed of all 'urban commons'; others bemoan that 'exclusionary' urbanisation is benefiting certain social groups to the detriment of others.

Urbanisation has also led to unique forms of identity assertion and political mobilisation amidst competing claims. These emerge from diverse social, political and linguistic groups seeking to appropriate urban spaces and opportunities for social and economic advancement. How society manages and addresses these claims is critical to keeping our urban spaces inclusive, and preventing the metropolitan cities from becoming exclusionary and exclusivist.

We do need a public debate to ensure that our urban spaces remain 'national' in their character, that there is transparency and inclusiveness in urban governance and so that our cities do not succumb to narrow or sectarian monopolies. It is here that urban sociology can help us understand the latent social and political stimuli and tectonic movements before pent-up subterranean social pressures erupt in an earthquake!

IV

Finally, I would like to note the emerging influence of public sociology, of this trend of a triple public dialogue among sociologists, between sociologists and the general public, and within the general public in the country. The professional sociologist has moved beyond being a catalyst of public debate, and has in some instances moved to take on the mantle of a civil society activist, with a view to inform publics and governments and bring about changes in policy.

The sociologist has in such instances also taken the mantle of mediating between the citizen and the State, and as a result empowering the former and bestowing greater legitimacy to the latter.

Though this phenomenon is welcome, it has its critics who feel that public sociology delegitimises the discipline and could politicise, corporatise or even dumb-down the subject.

Yet, one must welcome this trend of Public Sociology that has resulted in a better informed, rational and vibrant public space going beyond regional and national confines. It is also the correct response especially when the common citizen feels disempowered and dehumanised while facing the relentless onslaught of technology, globalisation and the might of the market and the State.

I hope that the post-conference seminar in Kerala later this month would debate this aspect in some detail.

Sixty-First Annual Convocation of Panjab University
Panjab University Gymnasium, Chandigarh
16 December 2011

The Challenge of Change

Convocations are occasions to honour intellectual achievement and celebrate life in academia. The pursuit of knowledge however does not end with the acquisition of a university decree. The young people leaving the portals of academia today to venture into the world beyond it would value the training and counsel received here.

I congratulate the graduating students and the distinguished personalities who have been awarded the Honoris Causa. Their achievements are a source of joy and pride to the University and the nation.

Today's universities are no ivory towers where knowledge is pursued only for its own sake. It is accepted that teaching and research in a university, and the advances in knowledge it produces, should in considerable measure also related to the demands of change and transition in our society, polity and economy.

This duality of academic purpose, with a sharper focus on the imperatives of change, stands emphasised.

Those familiar with the history of philosophy would know of a group of thinkers known as Stoics. Amongst them Marcus Aurelius, a Roman Emperor of the first century AD who, following the Greek philosopher Heraclitus, dwelt on the concept of change. Three of his dicta are of perennial relevance and I would like to recall them:

- "We shrink from change; yet is there anything that comes into being without it?"

- "Observe how all things are continually born of change; teach yourself to see that Nature's highest happiness lies in changing the things that are, and forming new things after their kind."
- "To be in the process of change is not evil, anymore than to be the product of change is a good."

Today, in the second decade of the twenty-first century, we cannot but realize that progress is not possible without change and that we are indeed living in a period of great change touching societies, polities and economies and transforming them in fundamental ways as part of a calculus of significant historical movement.

And yet, there is ambiguity about the meaning of change. Questions about its causes, nature, dimensions and desirability do arise. Many a time, the nature of change is a part of the process of change itself.

A vivid instance of change of global dimensions was witnessed in the closing decade of the twentieth century. The century itself, characterised by innovation and great technological advancement as well as unprecedented levels of conflict and bloodshed, was brought by the weight of its internal contradictions to the point where, in the words of an eminent historian "it risked both explosion and implosion." Change had become inevitable; change did happen, albeit unevenly.

We witnessed it, firstly, in the dramatic shift in the international system emanated from the winding down of the politico-military conflict between the superpowers and their respective blocs. The concept of power changed, and highlighted the new role of hard and soft power.

This was followed, secondly, by globalisation wherein scientific and technological revolution, enhanced movement of people, goods, services and peoples tended to erode the boundaries between nation-states, and over-shadowed traditional concepts of sovereignty.

A third aspect was global cultural interactions resulting in what Immanuel Wallerstein called "universalism through particularism and particularism through universalism."

Each of these posed new challenges and compelled us to revisit our categories of thought and the value systems emanating from them.

Globalisation has led to the emergence of aspiration, comparison, competition and dissatisfaction as drivers of change. People today have comparative yardsticks to assess their situation, the performance of their governments and societies, and to see what alternatives exist, or can be fashioned. They demand that they be given choices and chances in their social, economic and political lives so that they can actively determine their destinies.

The information and communications revolution and the proliferation of social media has led to the flow and control of information becoming unpredictable and non-linear, flowing in many directions at the same time.

As a result, change today is increasingly more disruptive, more difficult to manage, more complicated to harness for achieving desirable political and social outcomes. It is, nevertheless, far reaching.

II

Such are the dimensions and implications of change at the macro-level. How does it operate at the micro-level, at the level of individuals? How prepared are we for it?

For an individual, change assumes significance only when each one decides to change or make changes. When we move beyond observing changes, we exercise choices to secure desirable outcomes from processes of change. These outcomes bring about transitions.

Sometimes, we are so fixated with changes as they occur that we miss the transition and the change may not lead to any meaningful outcomes for us. Such changes without meaningful personal transitions are not transformative.

Fear of the unknown is a psychological reality and, as Bertrand Russell once said, "to conquer fear is the beginning of wisdom." Resistance is very often to the process of transition rather to the change itself. People resist changes to their defined identities, the sense of their group or community at work and at home, the chaos and uncertainty they come across, the risks of a new beginning, and of what they have never done and been before.

The impetus for change and transition presents us with an opportunity and a threat. It interrupts our lives in unpredictable ways and disrupts our patterns of work and thought. It affects social relations and equations. Yet, it also gives us an opportunity to review what is right and wrong with our current modes of working and thinking. It allows us to introspect, and choose differently to better our lives. It leads to improved and informed decision making.

Issues of change and transition are central to understanding the social and political processes in any country. It is useful to look at some of the socio-political factors that impact on how people engage with and adapt to change:

First: Crises are important signposts of significant change that receive wide public acceptance due to the immediacy of the extraordinary situation facing a country or a community. It establishes a sense of urgency for change and thus reduces the threshold of resistance. It is far easier to push through systemic changes after major economic or political crises.

Second: The temperament of a people, both at the individual and community levels, determines how they view and engage with the world. While it would not be accurate to reduce communities or nations to set stereotypes, we do acquire our temperament through socialisation and are influenced by the thoughts, attitudes, and behaviour of our parents and significant others. These processes influence individual and group attitudes. By the same token, experiences of being marginalised, deprived or disempowered could seriously impact levels of tolerance, acceptance, and optimism and discourage trust and erode hope. It is more likely to breed cynicism, criticism, pessimism, and even abuse.

Third: Our values, belief systems and life experiences determine attitudes to change and taking of risks. Some groups are inherently more risk taking and adapt to changes in the socio-economic environment at a faster rate than others. This is not limited to social groups but also extends to professional groupings. For example, those in the IT industry are more used to change and adapt faster to changes in their work environment brought about by rapidly changing technology or external economic factors. Our past learning curve and adaptation experiences to change also provide us with tools, skills and acquired wisdom to tackle change and transition in our lives.

Fourth: Our engagement with change is influenced by our ability to deal with diversity and heterogeneity, accept non-conformist behaviour that may stamp on sensitive social and political ground, and mode of tackling with vested interests and groups, especially elite behaviour. Nations and communities that are inclusive, heterogeneous, outward looking and have a high tolerance for difference and dissidence are better in managing and implementing sustainable change.

III

The foregoing is not all a theoretical discussion of change and transition. They have practical and immediate implications for students graduating today and for those still in the portals of academia. The young citizens of this Republic are indeed seen as change agents by the State and our society.

You are privileged to be born in an era that abounds in new hopes and possibilities, extraordinary opportunities and means to realise them. This scale of change within the span of two decades is unprecedented in our history. As a consequence, our yardsticks of what constitutes success, the aspirational goals of our society, have also substantially changed.

As you leave the portals of the university, each one of you has aspirations and dreams of success and social acclamation. Some of these relate to pecuniary success and status attainment. At the same time, you are also bound by the laws of the land and the values of our nation and society in terms of legally and socially acceptable means of achieving these goals.

The sociologist Robert Merton had pointed out that effective equilibrium between *culturally defined aspirational goals* and *socially structured means to achieve them* is maintained only so long as those that conform to both the goals and the means achieve satisfaction. Where symbols of achievement across classes remain unchanged but are coupled with limited opportunity for segments of the population to achieve them, social anomie or cultural chaos prevails with the disappearance of predictability or regularity of behaviour.

A word of caution here would not be out of place. A product is easier to adopt than a process. Thus, technological change is easier to adopt and absorb than social or societal change. Yet, unless there is harmony between the two, the absorption would be less than total and the resultant gap would leave room for, perhaps generate, tensions. This is evident in our society and needs to be attended to diligently.

As youth, you have the option of setting your own goals without being pressured. You could choose to either conform or go against the flow of your peers. Yet remember Gandhi*ji's* dictum that the means matter as much as the ends. Achieving goals at any cost will impose unacceptable costs on you, your family, your community and the nation in the long run.

At the same time, there is a responsibility on the State and the society to provide you with all opportunity to develop your capabilities to the fullest and to facilitate achievement of your goals within the framework of law and our Constitution.

I wish the graduating students all success in their future academic and professional endeavours. I congratulate the distinguished personalities who have been awarded the Honoris Causa today.

Golden Jubilee Celebrations of India International Centre
International Centre, New Delhi
22 January 2012

A MEADOW OF THE MIND

Anniversaries are occasions to celebrate, and there is much to celebrate on a fiftieth anniversary. I am happy, indeed honoured, to be here today, doubly so because it was a very distinguished predecessor of mine, Dr Sarvepalli Radhakrishnan of revered memory, who presided over the inaugural ceremony of the Centre on 22 January 1962.

The stated purpose of the venture, emanating from a pooling of ideas and models from different lands, was for 'the quickening and deepening of the true and thoughtful understanding between peoples of nations.' Jawaharlal Nehru, present on the occasion, was realistic enough to accept that "the Centre will, of course, not change the nature of the world but will help in the process, which is very essential today."

Half a century on, the impulse to look back is irresistible.

A perceptive historian at the turn of the century had sought to gaze into the world of tomorrow. He used the symbolism of *meadow*, *park* and *garden* and went on to describe the characteristics of each:

> In a meadow all is profusion, randomness, variety. A park is for the most part publicly maintained, highly regulated with different sectors for different uses. A garden is smaller and more inwardly turned; it aims for the sublime, not the efficient or the just.

My own experience of the Centre suggests the presence of all three, in proportions that vary from individual to individual, occasion to occasion, pursuit to pursuit. Here lies its multi-dimensional character, a trait that allows diversity, even eccentricity, to flourish.

And, of course, we have our share of uni-dimensionality – from the sublime to the mundane. The ambiance permits sufficient space, perhaps in actualisation of the poet Ghalib's perception:

"Dair nahin, haram nahin, der nahin, aastan nahin
Baithe hain reh-guzer pe hum, ghair hamain uthae kyun"

Personally speaking, I would like to characterise this *reh-guzer* or pathway as a meadow of the mind, a location and an ambience that allows for pursuits ranging from philosophical speculation to artistic creativity and to what Disraeli called "the hair-brained chatter of irresponsible frivolity."

Some years back, the Centre published a book *Birds of the IIC*. These include the spotted owl. For us here, therefore, Hegel's owl of Minerva is a resident entity ever ready to demonstrate the capacity to understand existing realities or even go beyond Hegel and prognosticate on emerging ones. Talks, lectures, discussions, seminars, exhibitions all contribute to the process.

The peripatetic amongst us finds welcome refuge in the Lodi Gardens, only to return and quench the thirst with reviving liquids on offer! And, of course, a good and wholesome cuisine does help since a full stomach usually leads to moderation of approach and eschewal of radical deviations!!

II

A question may well be posed. How does this contribute to a deepening of understanding among peoples and nations?

I submit for consideration a general preposition. Since human behaviour is often shaped by apprehensions or misunderstandings, the removal of these should have a primacy in the promotion of welfare of humankind.

The twentieth century, it has been said, was characterised by mega-myths and mega-deaths. It saw the end of colonialism and apartheid but not of disparities between and within nations. It witnessed great ideas of social transformation succumbing to their own contradictions. Writing in the last decade of the century, a historian said the world risked both explosion and implosion and needed change.

And change did come, in ample measure but accompanied by its own limitations. On one side, converging technologies and emerging social trends changed the landscape in societies and in their functioning; on the other, the new actuality is yet to mature in thought processes.

Both enhance the scope for non-understanding and misunderstanding.

Some years back Professor Rajni Kothari had urged his audience, in its quest to better comprehend the fast-changing Indian reality, "to think beyond the merely political and tap the deeper psycho-spiritual dimensions of the Indian reality."

I would venture to suggest that the IIC's intellectual charter was and remains this, but riveted on a wider, global, scale where a perceptive observer would note rapid emergence of new situations and patterns of behaviour. Both result in fresh perspectives in culture, economics and politics. The difficulty is that the tools of analysis, and the vocabulary of discourse, is often embedded in a past that was qualitatively different.

In a period of nation states, national sovereignty, economic autarky and exclusive cultural identity, the founders of the IIC spoke of *peoples of nations*. In the past five decades, however, the import of these concepts stands modulated.

Globalisation—economic and cultural, has done much good and some harm and has led to calls for a re-erection of dykes. The same holds good for universalisation of political values. Justice, democracy, human rights, good governance–nationally and globally–are impeccable in themselves but often stand diluted or abandoned for other considerations. Butros Ghali's aspiration, "to maintain the integrity of each while finding a balanced design for all," is yet to be achieved.

Each of these propels us towards a quest for greater understanding amongst peoples premised on closer scrutiny of values and institutions. Prescription would not work. The challenge would be to eschew hegemonic or homogenising models and contribute towards the promotion of justice, equity and diversity reflective of the ground reality of the world we live in.

In a cynical essay, Bertrand Russell once wrote that philosophers are constitutionally timid, dislike the unexpected and that "few of them would be genuinely happy as pirates or burglars."

But have we not had enough of pirates, burglars and adventurers–some in present-day incarnations–who have destroyed societies, systems and peace for misperceived gains? Would we not be better served if those among us who care to introspect, devote energies to locating the sources of misunderstanding and promotion of common good?

The imperative of patience and understanding, in a period of great change and crumbling certitudes, is evident. It requires cultivation of tolerance as a virtue, acceptance of diversity as a necessity, imbibing a spirit of enquiry as imperative and adoption of scientific temper as desirable.

I am confident the IIC fraternity, each in his or her own perception, would continue to contribute to this noble venture and make our shrinking world a better place for coming generations.

Youth and Sports

> Olympism is a life philosophy which draws together sport, culture and education in the aim of creating a harmonious balance between body, will and mind. ... Olympism is constructed around three core values: excellence, friendship and respect
>
> —Objectives of the Olympic Movement

Fifth Convocation

Lakshmibai National Institute of Physical Education, Gwalior

26 October 2007

I am greatly honoured to be the Chief Guest at the Fifth convocation of this prestigious and unique institution and to deliver the Convocation Address today. I am grateful to minister Aiyar for inviting me to participate in this Convocation. I am greatly honoured by the Institute's decision to confer the Degree of Doctor of Letters (Honoris Causa) on me. It imposes a responsibility on me to further the cause of sports, a cause close to my heart.

The Institute was established in 1957, the centenary year of the First War of Independence, and located at Gwalior, where Rani Lakshmibai had laid her life for the cause of freedom. This year marks the 150th anniversary of 1857, and I feel privileged to be here in Gwalior today.

The importance of physical education in the rise and fall of nations is an underestimated fact of history. In ancient Greece, Plato and Aristotle agreed that the right kind of person could be shaped through public education that stressed gymnastics to discipline the body and music to discipline the mind and soul. Indeed, ancient civilisations that could harness and impart physical education training on a systemic and institutional scale among their population could survive and thrive. The grammar and idiom of physical education has changed over the centuries–its essential role in human resource development, promotion of good health, recreation and social bonding remains unchanged.

In India, the archaeological excavations of Mohenjo-Daro and Harappa, references in Vedic literature, *Ramayana* and *Mahabharata* and ancient Indian literary works attest the vital role of sports and games in our social and cultural life. The primacy of physical education and sports was best articulated by Swami Vivekananda who said: "Be strong my young friends, that is my advice to you. You will be nearer to heaven through football than through the study of the Gita."

We have all heard the dictum of 'a healthy mind in a healthy body'. But indicators of national health are not very encouraging. The Third National Family Health Survey reveals that around 80 per cent of children in the age group of 6-35 months are anaemic. Over 50 per cent of married women and around 25 per cent of married men are anaemic. Around 20 per cent of children under three years of age suffer from acute under-nutrition or wasting. Around 38 per cent of all children under three years face stunted growth, indicating chronic long-term under-nutrition. Public expenditure on health is around 1.2 per cent of GDP and is low by any standards.

At the outset, I wish to discuss the legal framework that guides sports and physical education in India. In the Constitution of India, in the Seventh Schedule, 'sports' comes under the State List clubbed with 'theatres and dramatic performances, cinemas, entertainments and amusements'. It is a supreme irony that while the Indian cinema and entertainment industry emerged as a global leader and is much feted and admired, sports in the country did not develop and prosper to the same extent.

Under the Constitution, broad basing and increasing the popularity of sports and games is primarily the responsibility of states. In actual practice, allocation of resources to sports by state governments has been minimal. The question of inclusion of 'Sports' in the Concurrent List needs to be pursued for effective involvement of all stakeholders in the development and promotion of sports in the country.

The link between policies on sports and physical education, human resource development and youth affairs in the country was also weak for a long period. Until 1982, sports was seen as a secondary activity under the HRD Ministry. It was after India hosted the IX Asian Games that a new Department of Sports was created under the HRD Ministry. This was expanded to a Department of Youth Affairs and Sports in 1985 and became a Ministry only as late as May 2000. Polices on physical education, sports and youth affairs were synchronised through the National Sports Policy 2001, National Youth Policy 2003 and the National Policy on Education 1992.

On the international plane, the view that "access to physical education and sport should be assured and guaranteed for all human beings" finds expression in the UNESCO International Charter of Physical Education and Sport of 1978. Article 1 of the Charter emphatically states: "The practice of physical education and sport is a fundamental right for all". The right to play and to participate in sports has been embodied in United Nations instruments like the Convention on the Rights of the Child and The Convention on the Elimination of Discrimination against Women. It is increasingly accepted that the opportunity to develop and preserve physical powers and capabilities is an essential condition for the effective exercise of fundamental human rights.

What a statistical anomaly it is that a billion people could only win one medal during the last three Olympics! An analysis of the number of Olympic medals per million population done for the past three Olympics puts India as the last country of the list. The same is the result when the Olympic medal tally is standardised by GDP. Why have not the human and material resources of the country found adequate expression in terms of national performance in sports and games? Are the reasons systemic to our polity and structure of government?

A few elements stand out:

1. Competitive electoral politics has meant that the political class has primarily focused on games and sports that have caught the imagination of the people and of the market. Thus, political and market interest in cricket has distorted the time, attention and effort that should have gone to other sports and games.
2. Increasingly, sports and games are becoming commercialised. Sponsorships, endorsements and prize moneys are becoming important motivating criteria. Likewise, media coverage that is the oxygen for popularising and broad-basing most games and sports, tends to gravitate towards games with mass appeal such as cricket.
3. In today's day and age, scientific and professional back-up is essential for development of and excellence in sports. Requisite support in terms of nutrition, psychology, medicine, physiology

and biomechanics is vital if our sportspersons are to achieve global standards. Our sports management and administration did not give adequate emphasis to this issue.

4. The value of sports and games in promoting the spirit of unity and brotherhood and as a voice for public good is under appreciated in the country. If the example of cricket is taken, the game brings together the entire nation in the true sporting spirit and further has played an important role in bringing together the peoples of cricket playing nations. The United Nations had adopted the theme of 'Sport for Development and Peace' in its Agenda in 2001, recognising the 'convening power' of sports. National and International organisations have enlisted star sportsmen and major sporting events in campaigns to promote immunisation and other public health measures, to support the fight against racism and apartheid, and for human rights.

To the young men and women who have been awarded degrees and distinctions today, I offer my warm felicitations and best wishes for a successful career and a happy life. This youth of the country are our most precious asset, and it is up to the nation how best their energy and enthusiasm is harnessed for the development and progress of our nation. To the young students here, I wish to say that they should not be deterred by the systemic and institutional constraints that afflict our sports and games. Your presence, knowledge and skills are urgently required in educational and sports institutes across the length and breadth of our country. You will carry with you the values and the spirit that you have imbibed at this institution–healthy competition, respect for opponents and for rules, teamwork and fair play. You will symbolise the unity and diversity of India.

The Inauguration of 'Statistics Day-2010'

Vigyan Bhawan, New Delhi
29 June 2010

It gives me great pleasure to participate in today's inaugural session of the Fourth Statistics Day that is being celebrated to commemorate the birth anniversary of Late Professor Prasanta Chandra Mahalanobis, a recognised global leader in the discipline of statistics. As an architect of development planning in the nascent republic, he had guided the evolution of statistical studies as an important instrumentality for policy planning and implementation. He was also a great builder of institutions through which he laid the foundation for promoting teaching and research in statistics and for developing the official statistical system in the country as the first Statistical Adviser to the Union Cabinet.

It is befitting that we celebrate the Statistics Day in honour of the memory of Professor Mahalanobis. This function also brings together the statistics fraternity of the country and creates awareness about their contribution to the nation. I also congratulate Professor Aloke Dey who has been conferred the National Award in Statistics that had been instituted in honour of Professor P.V. Sukhatme.

We have come a long way since the first Statistical Abstract of British India was published over a century and a half ago. As a growing and diverse economy with a host of complex variables affecting human and economic development in the country, the importance of collection and analysis of statistical data alongside enhanced coverage, timeliness and reliability of such data can hardly be overemphasised. It is a subject on the Concurrent List, and in keeping with the emphasis on decentralisation, the statistical system brings together the central and state governments in the collection and generation of data.

The central government remains committed to strengthen the credibility and the transparency of the official statistical system and has in 2005 set up the National Statistical Commission with the mandate to serve as the nodal and empowered body for all core statistical activities, to evolve and lay down national quality standards and exercise statistical coordination between the Centre and the States. The government is also in the process of implementing the various recommendations of the Commission.

It is also very appropriate that Statistics Day 2010 has the theme of 'Child Statistics'. India is home to one-fifth of the world's children. Around 440 million people in the country are children and they constitute 42 per cent of our population. These young citizens of the country constitute a potential demographic resource that could propel the nation to higher orbits of economic progress and human development. Realising the potential, however, is neither a given nor automatic.

The reality is in stark contrast. Every third malnourished child in the world lives in India; every second Indian child is under weight; three out of four children in India are anaemic; and every second new born has reduced learning capacity due to iodine deficiency. The Working Group on Development of Children for the Eleventh Five-Year Plan has highlighted the following critical concerns regarding the status and condition of children:

> High mortality and morbidity, poor outcome achievement in education and development; chronic imbalances in access to services and opportunities; high risks of neglect and lack of protection; fragmented and sectoralised service outreach to address cross-sectoral needs, unequal distribution of development benefits, and low levels of investment and attention.

The need to put in place a framework for assuring our children their right to survival, protection and development is well-recognised. The Constitution of India accords a special status to children as deserving of special provisions of protection to secure and safeguard the entitlements of "those of tender age". We have recently enacted legislation to operationalise the Fundamental Right to Education for our children aged six to fourteen years. Our accession to the UN Convention on the Rights of the Child imposes additional obligations and commitments. The National Policy for Children 1974 had declared children as a 'supreme national asset'. The National Plan of Action for Children 2005 regards the child as 'an asset and a person with human rights'.

The commitment to make children a priority of our development agenda thus exists. The outcomes of such a commitment, however, are yet to materialise. It is here that systematic compilation of comprehensive statistical information on children can guide our policy makers and planners engaged in bettering the situation of our children.

It is also heartening that various ministries and departments of the government have agreed to set up an 'India Forum on Child Statistics' as an institutional mechanism comprising all major stakeholders dealing with child related issues. I congratulate the Chief Statistician of India for setting up this Forum and hope that it would foster coordination and collaboration and improve the credibility and transparency in the collection and reporting of statistical data on our children and the families they come from. This should enable compilation and tracking of national indicators on the well-being of our children across all population segments and presentation of data in terms understood by non-technical audiences.

While policy makers and national leaders have always appreciated the contribution of our statisticians, their public profile has declined since the time of Prof. Mahalanobis and other great statisticians of his ilk. We must do everything we can to improve the working conditions and status of our statistics fraternity in the government. We must also encourage our youth to choose statistics as an academic pursuit and as a profession.

ہیں اور وہ تجارتی اعتبار سے کامیاب بھی ہیں۔ موسیقی کی صنعت اردو غزلوں، نغموں اور قوالیوں کی بدولت ترقی کر رہی ہے۔

اس ضمن میں ایک اور بات قابلِ ذکر ہے۔ اردو اب ایک بین الاقوامی زبان بن گئی ہے اور برصغیر ہند کے باہر بھی اس کا مطالعہ اور فروغ جاری ہے۔ انٹرنیٹ بھی اس سلسلے میں کافی مددگار ثابت ہو رہا ہے۔ اس میں شک نہیں کہ اگر اردو مراجعت کے عمل سے گزر کے اسی سرزمین سے ناپید ہو جائے جہاں وہ پیدا ہوئی ہے تو یہ ایک بہت بڑا المیہ ہوگا۔

آخری تجزیے میں اُس سوال کا تعلق ہندوستانی تکثیریت کے ہمارے تصور اور ہندوستانی تہذیب کے دائرے سے ہے۔ کیا اس میں سب کو شامل ہونا چاہئے یا یہ استثنائی ہو؟ آیا اسے وسیع المشرب ہونا چاہئے یا اس کے برعکس؟ کیا ہم اُن عناصر کو برقرار رکھیں جنھوں نے ماضی میں اسے تنوع بخشا ہے اور آج بھی بخش رہے ہیں یا ایک متعصبانہ رویہ اپناتے ہوئے اسے ترک کر دیں؟

کسی بھی شمع سے بیزار ہو کیوں کوئی پروانہ
یہ کیا اس دور کا دیوانہ پن ہے ہم نہیں سمجھے

میں یونیورسٹی کے شعبۂ اردو کا شکر گزار ہوں وائس چانسلر صاحب اور توقیر احمد خاں صاحب کا کہ آج انہوں نے مجھے یہاں مدعو کیا۔ جے ہند۔

اشاعت وغیرہ میں سستی کی وجہ سے ایسا نہیں ہو پارہا ہے۔ جون ۲۰۰۷ء میں ختم ہونے والی میعاد کے لئے لسانی اقلیتوں کے کمشنر کی پینتالیسویں رپورٹ میں مختلف ریاستوں میں لسانی اقلیتوں کے لئے تحفظات پر عمل درآمد میں خامیوں کا ذکر کیا گیا ہے۔ اس میں کہا گیا ہے کہ ''لسانی اقلیتوں کو فراہم کئے گئے آئینی تحفظات اسی وقت حقیقت کا روپ لے سکتے ہیں جب ان کے نفاذ کے لئے ضروری قانون بھی موجود ہو۔''

اس لئے، جب تک سرکاری سطح پر زیادہ کارگر اقدامات نہیں کئے جاتے اس کے علاوہ کوئی چارہ نہیں کہ کنبے اور اردو بولنے والے فرقے کی سطح پر منظم کوشش کی جائے۔ اس موقع پر دنیا کے دیگر مقامات پر زوال آمادہ زبان بولنے والے فرقوں کے تجربے کا ذکر بے محل نہ ہوگا۔ امریکہ میں مقیم یہودی فرقے نے ہفتے کے آخر میں عبرانی زبان کی تدریس کا انتظام کر کے ایک اچھی مثال قائم کی ہے۔ اسپین میں کیٹالان اور کناڈا میں فرانسیسی زبان کامیابی کے ساتھ زبان کے احیاء کی اچھی مثالیں ہیں۔

اس کے ساتھ ساتھ اردو کو اپنی مادری زبان کہنے والوں کے لئے ضروری ہے کہ وہ ریاست کو اپنی آئینی ذمہ داریوں کو پورا کرنے کے لئے آمادہ کی جانی والی کوششوں کو زندہ رکھیں۔ اس میں شک نہیں کہ رائے عامہ اور انتخابی دباؤ سے بھی نتائج برآمد ہوتے ہیں اور ایسا ہندوستان کی کئی ریاستوں میں ہوا بھی ہے۔ ہمیں ہر وقت یہ بات یاد رکھنی چاہئے کہ ہمارے آئین کے دیباچے میں شامل چار اصولوں میں سب سے پہلا اصول انصاف ہے اور جیسا کہ فلسفی جان رالس (John Rawls) نے کہا ہے۔ ''انصاف کی بناء پر حاصل ہونے والے حقوق پر سیاسی سودے بازی نہیں ہوسکتی اور نہ ہی انھیں سماجی مفادات کی جمع تفریق کے عمل سے گزارا جاسکتا۔''

تاہم اس تاریکی میں افق پر روشنی کی کرنیں بھی نظر آتی ہیں۔ اس انحطاط کے باوجود اردو اخبارات اور رسائل نے اپنا وجود قائم رکھا ہے اور ان میں نئی زندگی کے آثار بھی نمایاں ہوئے ہیں۔ کارپوریٹ میڈیا نے اردو پریس میں دلچسپی کا اظہار کیا ہے۔ اردو میں کتابوں کی اشاعت کا سلسلہ جاری ہے اور ان کی قیمتیں بھی زیادہ نہیں ہیں۔ دوردرشن اردو کے علاوہ کئی اردو چینل وجود میں آئے

مادری زبان کے تعلق سے یہ صورت حال مختلف ہے۔ دفعہ ۲۹ کے تحت اپنی مخصوص زبان اور رسم الخط کا بنیادی حق ہے۔ دفعہ ۳۵۰ الف کا یہ مقصد ہے کہ "ہر ریاست اور اس ریاست کے اندر ہر مقامی حاکم کی کوشش ہوگی کہ لسانی اقلیتی زمروں سے تعلق رکھنے والے بچوں کو تعلیم کے ابتدائی درجے میں مادری زبان میں تعلیم دینے کی کافی سہولتیں مہیا کرے۔" اردو بولنے والے بچوں کی کثیر تعداد کے لئے نا قابل حصول ہے۔ بعض حالات میں ان کی لسانی شناخت کو نظر انداز کر دیا جاتا ہے۔ جب کہ بعض صورتوں میں اردو زبان کے اساتذہ اور نصابی کتابوں کی عدم دستیابی کی وجہ سے پرائمری اسکول کی سطح پر انتظامات نا کارہ رہ جاتے ہیں۔ ان مسلسل کوتاہیوں سے شک ہوتا ہے کہ اس سلسلے میں کی جارہی کوششوں میں اخلاص نیت کا فقدان ہے۔ ناگزیر طور پر نتیجہ یہی برآمد ہوتا ہے کہ کئی محاذوں پر ناکامی کی داستان ہے۔

ریاست اپنے آئینی فرائض کی انجام دہی میں، اردو بولنے والے طبقہ اس زبان کو سیکھنے اور اس کی بقا کا حق حاصل کرنے میں اور کنبے انفرادی طور پر اس کے لئے خاطر خواہ اضافی کوششیں کرنے میں ناکام رہے ہیں۔ سوال یہ اٹھتا ہے کہ اب کیا کیا جائے۔ سینگال کے ایک شاعر کی بات اس بحث کے سیاق میں برمحل معلوم ہوتی ہے اور میں اسے آپ کے ملاحظے میں لانا چاہتا ہوں:

> "انجام کار ہم اسی چیز کو محفوظ رکھیں گے جس سے ہمیں محبت ہے۔ ہمیں اسی سے محبت ہوتی ہے جو ہماری سمجھ میں آئے اور ہماری سمجھ میں وہی آتا ہے جو ہمیں سکھایا جاتا ہے۔"

سب سے زیادہ ضرورت اس بات کی ہے کہ جو لوگ اردو کو اپنی مادری زبان قرار دیتے ہیں انھیں اردو سکھانے کی تدبیریں کی جائیں۔ یہ کام پرائمری اسکول کی سطح سے شروع کیا جانا چاہئے اور اسے کم از کم ثانوی سطح کے کسی حصے تک جاری رہنا چاہئے۔ اگر قومی لسانی پالیسی کے تحت تشکیل شدہ اور تسلیم شدہ لسانی فارمولے میں اردو کو وہی مقام دے دیا جائے جو اس کی ساتھی ہندوستانی زبانوں کو حاصل ہے تو یہ مسئلہ حل ہو جائے گا۔ افسوس کی بات ہے کہ کچھ ریاستوں میں سرکاری اسکولوں میں ایسا نہیں ہو رہا ہے اور دوسری ریاستوں میں اساتذہ کی بھرتی اور نصابی کتابوں کی

مدارس کا کردار بھی قابل ذکر ہے۔ مدارس کے نصابات تعلیم کے سیاق میں کہا جاسکتا ہے کہ انہوں نے مشکل دور میں اردو کی بقا کا کام انجام دیا ہے اور اسے نوجوان نسل کے ایک طبقے تک پہنچانے میں مدد کی ہے۔ تاہم انہیں اسباب سے ان کی یہ کوشش ایک مخصوص طبقہ کے ان افراد تک محدود رہی ہے جنہوں نے معاشی یا دیگر وجوہات کی بنا پر نارمل سرکاری اسکولوں پر مدرسوں کو ترجیح دی ہے۔ ساتھ ہی اردو کو مدارس تک محدود کر دینے سے اس کا مزاج بھی متاثر ہوتا ہے جو بنیادی طور پر سیکولر اور بعض اوقات آزادہ رو بھی ہے۔

دھڑکنیں صدیوں کی جس میں، کیف بے باکانہ ہے

زبانیں سیکھنے اور انہیں زندہ رکھنے کی کئی وجوہات ہیں۔ سب سے پہلے تو گھر میں مادری زبان کی حیثیت سے ان کے انجذاب کا عمل ہوتا ہے اور بعد ازاں بنیادی (اور ثانوی) سطح تک تعلیم کے ذریعے انہیں تقویت دی جاتی ہے۔ اس کے لئے اسکولوں، نصابی کتابوں اور اساتذہ کی ضرورت ہوتی ہے جن کا انتظام ریاستی یا مقامی حکومت کرتی ہے یا انھیں سماجی کوششوں سے مہیا کرایا جاتا ہے۔ دوسرے یہ کہ زبانوں کو سیکھنے کے لئے معاشی مجبوریاں اور معاشی مواقع کی تلاش محرک کا کام کرتی ہیں۔ اس کا مطلب ہے سماج میں رائج تعلیم اور ملازمت کی اہلیت کے وسیع تر سانچوں میں شرکت اور تعلیمی اداروں اور اساتذہ کی فراہمی کے لئے سماج کی مطلوبہ کوشش۔ تیسرے یہ کہ کسی زبان کو سماجی یا مذہبی وقار یا علمی کمال کے لئے ترجیحی اور اختیاری طور پر سیکھا جائے۔

اس طرح ایک زوال آمادہ زبان کو دو سطحوں پر چیلنج کا سامنا ہوتا ہے۔ مادری زبان کا موروثی شعور ایک بچے کی ذاتی، سماجی اور ثقافتی شناخت کا حصہ ہوتا ہے اور باقاعدہ تعلیم کے ذریعے اس کی تشکیل و استحکام ہونا چاہئے تاکہ وہ ناخواندگی سے خواندگی کی جانب ترقی کر سکے۔ بعد ازاں زبان کے احیاء کی تحریک اور اس کے خط و خال کی تشکیل لازمی طور پر معاشی عوامل کے ذریعے ہونا چاہئے۔ ہندوستان سمیت بیشتر کثیر لسانی سماجوں میں آخر الذکر کام وہ زبان انجام دیتی ہے جو انتظامیہ تجارت اور بین علاقائی اور بین الاقوامی مواصلات میں استعمال کی جاتی ہے۔ یہاں یہ تصویر بہت واضح اور کلیتاً قابل قبول ہے۔

حال اور مستقبل سے سروکار چاہئے۔ جن اعداد وشمار کا ابھی کچھ دیر پہلے حوالہ دیا گیا ان کی بنیاد پر اردو اس وقت کس مقام پر کھڑی ہے؟ ہماری سماجی اور ثقافتی زندگی میں اور ہماری سیاسی اور معاشی زندگی میں اردو کا کیا مقام ہے؟ ایک مخصوص فرقے سے اس کی نسبت اور اس کے تمام ان کہے مضمرات کو کیسے ختم کیا جائے تا کہ اردو کو زبانوں کے رنگا رنگ منظر نامے اور ہندوستان کی ثقافتی تنظیم میں اس کا جائز مقام مل سکے؟ اسے کس طرح تقویت دی جا سکتی ہے اور اس کے مستقبل کو کیسے تابناک بنایا جا سکتا ہے؟

ایک جانب تو اردو کی حیثیت کا سرکاری اعتراف بڑی پابندی اور باقاعدگی کے ساتھ کیا جاتا ہے۔ سالانہ جلسے کیے جاتے ہیں۔ مشاعروں کی سرپرستی کی جاتی ہے لیکن اس کے اپنی واضح حدود ہیں۔ ''اس سے زبان کی یاد تو قائم رہتی ہے۔ اس کی ترقی نہیں ہوتی۔'' اس دوہرے رویے پر تبصرہ کرتے ہوئے ساحر لدھیانوی نے برسوں پہلے کہا تھا۔

غالبؔ جسے کہتے ہیں اردو کا ہی شاعر تھا
اردو پہ ستم کر کے غالبؔ پہ کرم کیوں ہے

گذشتہ سال ایک مبصر نے ایک اخبار میں تبصرہ کرتے ہوئے لکھا تھا کہ ''اردو کو ہندی سنیما، ایف۔ایم، ریڈیو، مدارس اور پارلیمنٹ میں گاہ گاہ شعر خوانی نے زندہ رکھا ہوا ہے۔'' انہوں نے پروفیسر گوپی چند نارنگ کے اس تبصرے کی جانب توجہ مبذول کرائی کہ ''اردو ایک ایسے مریض کی مانند ہے جو اپنی زندگی کے آخری ایام میں آکسیجن پر زندہ ہے۔ یہ اردو والوں کی آخری نسل ہے۔''

بلاشبہ 'بالی وڈ' کی فلموں نے اردو کو زندہ رکھنے میں ایک اہم کردار ادا کیا ہے۔ تاریخ داں رام چندر گوہا نے India after Gandhi میں شامل ایک بصیرت افروز باب میں اس کا جواز پیش کیا ہے۔ ایک دیگر زاویہ نظر سے، ایرا بھاسکر اور رچرڈ ایلین نے Islamicate Cultures of Bombay Cinema پر کافی روشنی ڈالی ہے جس کا مقصد تاریخ، ثقافت، زبان، فرقے اور معاصر دباؤ کے نقطہ ہائے اتصال کو اجاگر کرنا اور انہیں کے الفاظ میں ''ہندوستان کے تکثیری اور کثیر ثقافتی تخیل میں اس کی ثقافتی اور سیاسی قدر کو دکھانا ہے۔''

نے اس معاملے میں اپنے نظریات کو دہرایا۔

جولائی ۱۹۵۸ء میں جاری مرکزی وزات داخلہ کے ایک سرکلر میں چند دیگر متعلقہ سہولیات کے ساتھ ساتھ، ان بچوں کو پرائمری سطح پر اردو زبان کی تدریس کی سہولت فراہم کرنے کی بات کی گئی تھی جن کی مادری زبان اردو ہے۔ اس سرکلر میں نہ تو آئین کی دفعہ ۳۵۰الف کا حوالہ دیا گیا تھا اور نہ ہی دفعہ ۳۴۷ کے نفاذ کی بات کی گئی تھی۔

امریکی اسکالر پال براس (Paul Brass) نے ۱۹۷۴ء میں شائع اپنی کتاب Language, Religion and Politics in North India. میں ان پالیسیوں اور طریقہ ہائے کار پر خاصی روشنی ڈالی ہے۔ جنھیں اپنا کر بعض ریاستوں نے ''اردو بولنے والوں کی بڑی تعداد کو' اپنی مادری زبان میں حصولِ تعلیم کی' راہ سے بھٹکانے میں کامیابی حاصل کی۔''

اس طرح سیاسی تنگ نظری اور زبان کو غلط فہمی کی بناء پر ایک فرقہ کے ساتھ منسوب کرنے کے نتیجے میں یک لسانی رویہ معرض وجود میں آیا اور تکثیری سماج کے لسانی تنوع اور آئین کے مزاج پر غالب آگیا۔

۱۹۷۲ء میں حکومت ہند کی قرارداد کے ذریعے اردو کے فروغ اور ترقی کے لئے گجرال کمیشن قائم کیا گیا۔ اس قرارداد میں کہا گیا تھا کہ ''اردو کسی ایک ریاستی حکومت یا فرقے کا معاملہ نہیں ہے۔ اس کی ترقی کی ذمہ داری مرکزی حکومت پر بھی عائد ہوتی ہے''۔ ۱۹۷۵ء میں کی گئیں گجرال کمیشن کی سفارشات اور ۱۹۹۰ء میں علی سردار جعفری کمیٹی کی سفارشات پر جو بھی عمل درآمد ہوا ہے، اس سے صورت حال میں کوئی بامعنی تبدیلی واقع نہیں ہوئی ہے۔ نہ ہی ۱۹۹۰ء میں قائم کردہ قومی کونسل برائے فروغ اردو زبان نے اپنے بنیادی مقصد کے حصول میں کوئی اہم کامیابی حاصل کی ہے۔ یہ پشیمانی اصلاح کن ہونے کے بجائے رسمی ہی رہی۔

میری زباں پہ شکوۂ اہلِ ستم نہیں
مجھ کو جگا دیا یہی احسان کم نہیں

ماضی کا نوحہ اسی وقت بامعنی ہوسکتا ہے جب اس سے سبق حاصل کیا جائے۔ آج ہمیں

کی راہ آسان کی جارہی ہے یا اس میں اڑچنیں ڈالی جارہی ہیں؟

☆ مختلف ریاستوں میں اردو خواندگی کی سطحوں میں ناہمواری کی کیا وجہ ہو سکتی ہے؟

☆ ریاست کے ذریعے چلائے جارہے اسکولوں کے علاوہ اور کون سے ادارے ہیں جو اردو خواندگی کو فروغ دینے کا کام کررہے ہیں؟

دستیاب سرکاری اعداد و شمار کی بنیاد پر پہلے دو سوالوں کے تعلق سے خالدی نے جو نتائج برآمد کیے، ان سے ظاہر ہوتا ہے کہ پرائمری اور سیکنڈری اسکولوں میں اردو میڈیم میں داخلے کے اعتبار سے اردو خواندگی مہاراشٹر اور بہار میں سب سے زیادہ ہے۔ کرناٹک اور آندھرا پردیش میں کچھ کم ہے اور دہلی اور اتر پردیش میں سب سے کم ہے۔ ۲۰۰۸ء — ۲۰۰۷ء میں کل داخلوں کی فیصد کے اعتبار سے۔ یہ مہاراشٹر میں ۶٫۵۳، بہار میں ۵٫۲، آندھرا پردیش میں ۲٫۸، دہلی میں ۱٫۰ اور اتر پردیش میں ۰٫۴۰ فیصد ہے۔

تیسرے اور چوتھے سوالات کے جواب کے لئے ہمیں حالیہ تاریخ کا مطالعہ کرنے کی ضرورت پڑے گی۔ یہاں میں جواہر لعل نہرو کے اپنے جائزے کا حوالہ دے سکتا ہوں۔ ۱۶؍ جولائی ۱۹۵۳ء کو وزرائے اعلیٰ کو بصیغۂ راز لکھے گئے اپنے مکتوب میں انہوں نے ''ذہنی کم مائیگی، تنگ نظری اور ناپختگی کا'' ذکر کیا تھا جو ''کثیر آبادی کے ذریعے بولی اور لکھی جانے والی اردو زبان کو راندۂ درگاہ کرنے کی دانستہ سازش'' کی خاصیت تھی۔ دو ہفتہ بعد یکم اگست کے مکتوب میں یہ بات ایک وسیع تر تناظر میں دہرائی گئی ہے:

> ''ہم چھوٹی سے چھوٹی قبائلی زبان کی اس کے علاقے میں ہمت افزائی کرتے ہیں لیکن اردو کا نام زبان پر آتے ہی ہم میں سے کئی لوگوں کی پیشانی پر شکن آجاتی ہے، جب کہ اردو اسی ملک کی زائیدہ اور ہماری ہشت پہلو ثقافت کا ایک جاندار اور شاندار حصہ ہے۔ مجھے اس تنگ نظری سے بہت دکھ ہوتا ہے جو اکثر و بیشتر ہمارے راستے کی رکاوٹ بن جاتی ہے۔''

اُسی سال اکتوبر میں حیدر آباد میں منعقد آل انڈیا کانگریس کمیٹی کے اجلاس میں نہرو جی

تو پھر ہم اردو بولنے والوں کی تعداد میں کمی کی توجیح کہاں تلاش کریں؟ چونکہ زبان کا معاملہ خاص کر نسبت قلبی اور استعمال سے تعلق رکھتا ہے، اس لئے اس بات کا امکان نہیں ہے کہ کوئی اسے رضا کارانہ طور پر یا روشن خیالی سمجھ کر چھوڑ دے گا۔ اس کی وجہ لازمی طور پر کسی قسم کی مجبوری یا ضرورت ہی ہوسکتی ہے۔ اس لئے ہمارے بنیادی سوال کی کلید اُن عوامل میں تلاش کی جانی چاہئے۔ جن کا ذکر پروفیسر ڈی سوان نے کیا ہے اور ان تین قسم کے ممکنہ حالات میں جن کا انہوں نے تصور پیش کیا ہے۔ ہمارے سوال کا جواب دوسری صورت حال میں نظر آتا ہے۔ یعنی اسکولی سطح پر یا سرکاری حکام کے ذریعے استعمال کی جانے والی زبان۔

یہاں میں سرکاری اعداد و شمار یا اعلانات سے ظاہر ہونے والے دو قسم کے حقائق کا ذکر کرنا چاہتا ہوں۔

۱۔ ۲۱ راگست ۲۰۱۱ء کو راجیہ سبھا میں ایک سوال کے جواب میں وزارت برائے انسانی وسائل نے بتایا کہ مختلف ریاستوں میں واقع کیندریہ ودیالیوں میں اردو اس لئے نہیں پڑھائی جارہی ہے کیونکہ ان میں سے کسی اسکول میں بھی بیس یا اس سے زیادہ طلبہ نے اردو کو اختیاری مضمون کی حیثیت سے نہیں لیا۔ اسی وجہ سے اردو ٹیچر کی کوئی اسامی منظور نہیں کی گئی۔ اس سے یہ نتیجہ نکالنا آسان ہے کہ کم سے کم مجوزہ تعداد میں اردو داں طلبہ کیندریہ ودیالیوں میں داخلہ حاصل نہیں کر پاتے۔ ان اعداد و شمار کے دیگر مضمرات بھی ہیں کیونکہ یہ اسکول بنیادی طور پر مرکزی سرکار کے ایسے ملازمین کے بچوں کے لئے ہوتے ہیں جن کا تبادلہ ہندوستان میں کہیں بھی ہوسکتا ہے۔

۲۔ میساچوسیٹس انسٹی ٹیوٹ آف ٹیکنالوجی (MIT) سے وابستہ مرحوم ڈاکٹر عمر خالدی نے گزشتہ سال اپنے انتقال سے کچھ عرصہ قبل کئے گئے ایک مطالعے میں اسکولی تعلیم کے پیمانے سے ہندوستان میں اردو خواندگی کی صورت حال کا جائزہ لیا تھا اور پانچ سوال اٹھائے تھے۔

☆ پرائمری اسکولوں میں کتنے طلبہ کے پاس اردو زبان بہ حیثیت ذریعۂ تعلیم تھی؟

☆ سہ (یا چہار) لسانی فارمولے کے تحت کتنے طلبہ اردو کو بہ حیثیت ایک مضمون پڑھ رہے ہیں؟

☆ آیا مختلف ریاستوں میں حکومت کی مرکزی، ریاستی اور مقامی سطحوں پر اردو تعلیم و تدریس

والے تھے۔ اگر آپ ان میں جھارکھنڈ، مغربی بنگال، مدھیہ پردیش، تامل ناڈو اور دہلی کو بھی شامل کرلیں تو یہ تعداد ۴ کروڑ ۸۵ لاکھ ۵۰ ہزار ہو جاتی ہے۔ اعدادوشمار سے یہ بھی پتہ چلتا ہے کہ ۱۹۸۱ء اور ۱۹۹۱ء کی مردم شماری میں اردو بولنے والوں کا فی صد علی الترتیب ۵.۲۵ اور ۵.۱۸ تھا۔

آبادی میں مجموعی اضافے اور آبادی سے متعلق مزید واضح اعدادوشمار کے تناظر میں اس گراوٹ سے ایک سوال پیدا ہوتا ہے۔ اردو زبان سے عام طور پر منسوب علاقوں اور گروہوں کی آبادی میں حسب معمول اضافوں کے باوجود اردو بولنے والوں کی تعداد کیوں گھٹ رہی ہے؟ کیا اس سے یہ اشارہ ملتا ہے کہ اردو بولنے والے ایک مخصوص انداز میں اردو سے کنارہ کشی کررہے ہیں؟ ایسا کیوں ہوتا ہے؟ ایک وسیع تر تناظر میں اس بات کی وضاحت پروفیسر ابرام ڈی سوان (Abram De Swan) نے اپنے ایک مقالے میں کی ہے جو اکتوبر ۲۰۰۴ء میں یوروپین ریویو میں شائع ہوا تھا:

> ''اپنی مادری زبان ترک کرنے والے ایسا یا تو نقل مکانی کی وجہ سے کرتے ہیں یا اس لئے کہ انہوں نے کسی اور چیز کو اختیار کرلیا ہے اور اس نئی زندگی میں کسی دیگر زبان سے ان کی توقعات زیادہ وابستہ ہوجاتی ہیں۔ یا وہ اسے اس لئے نظرانداز کرتے ہیں کہ اسکول میں، سرکاری حکام میں، یا عدالتوں میں کسی دیگر زبان کو ترجیحی حیثیت حاصل ہوتی ہے اور ان کی اپنی زبان کو حقارت کی نظر سے دیکھا جاتا ہے۔ یا انہیں اس کا استعمال اس لئے ترک کرنا پڑتا ہے کہ ان پر کسی دوسری قوم کی حکمرانی ہوتی ہے جو اپنی زبان ان پر تھوپ دیتی ہے، اور دل برداشتہ ہوکر، وہ اپنی زبان کے تحفظ کی فکر کرنا چھوڑ دیتے ہیں۔''

وہ مزید لکھتے ہیں کہ چونکہ ''ہر زبان لوگوں کی اجتماعی تخلیقیت کی پیداوار ہوتی ہے جس کا اظہار سیکڑوں یا ہزاروں برس پر محیط ہوتا ہے، اس لئے اس زبان کی موت تہذیب وثقافت کا ایسا نقصان ہے جسے کبھی پورا نہیں کیا جاسکتا۔''

سے پیدا شدہ ہندوستانی محرکات اور ردِعمل کی وضاحت کرنے کی کوشش کی ہے۔ اس کا ایک پہلو زبانوں کا تنوع تھا۔ ایسے مواقع پر جب بھی میں نے ان سے ہندوستانی روپے پر نظر ڈالنے اور ان زبانوں کو گننے کے لئے کہا جن میں اس روپے کی قیمت لکھی ہوئی ہے، میرا پیغام حتمی طور پر ان کی سمجھ میں آ گیا ہے!

آپ کو معلوم ہے کہ مجلسِ قانون ساز میں زبان کے معاملے پر ہونے والی پُر زور بحثوں کے بارے میں تاریخ دانوں اور ماہرینِ سیاسیات نے بہت کچھ لکھا ہے۔ ان مباحث کے نتائج آئین کے حصہ ۱۷ اور اس کے آٹھویں فہرست بند میں منعکس ہوتے ہیں۔ مگر اس سے مسئلہ حل نہیں ہوا۔ کچھ سال بعد علاقائی شناخت کے اظہار کے لئے لسانی یکسانیت کی تحریک ظہور پذیر ہوئی۔ ان توقعات کی تکمیل کی غرض سے ریاستوں کی تنظیم جدید کے لئے کمیشن قائم کیا گیا جس کی رپورٹ ۱۹۵۵ء میں پارلیمنٹ میں پیش کی گئی۔

یہ بات قابل ذکر ہے کہ آٹھویں فہرست بند میں شامل موجودہ بائیس زبانوں میں سے بیش تر کو علاقائی نسبت کی بنا پر کسی نہ کسی ریاست میں ایک گھر ملا ہوا ہے۔ اردو اس سے مستثنٰی ہے کیوں کہ کئی ریاستوں میں بکھری ہوئی ہونے کے باوجود یہ اپنے آپ کو بے خانماں پاتی ہے اور اسے اس بے گھری کے تمام نتائج سے نبرد آزما ہونا پڑتا ہے۔ سندھی کے ساتھ بھی یہی صورت حال ہے، یہ بات دیگر ہے کہ سندھی بولنے والوں کی تعداد ۲۵ لاکھ ۷۰ ہزار ہی ہے۔

آج میں اردو کی بے گھری کے بعض پہلوؤں کی جانب توجہ دلانا چاہتا ہوں۔ سرکاری طور پر تسلیم شدہ زبان ہونے کے ساتھ ساتھ اردو کو آندھرا پردیش، بہار، دہلی، جموں و کشمیر، جھارکھنڈ اور اتر پردیش میں بعض خصوصی مقاصد کے لئے سرکاری زبان کا درجہ بھی حاصل ہے۔ (ان مقاصد کی تفصیلات مختلف النوع ہیں اور یہ اثرات کو اساسی طور پر محدود کرتی ہیں۔)

۲۰۰۱ء کی مردم شماری کے مطابق، ملک میں ۵ کروڑ ۱۵ لاکھ اردو بولنے والے تھے جو کل آبادی کا ۵٫۰۱ فیصد ہوتا ہے۔ کسی زبان کو بولنے والوں کا یہ چھٹا سب سے بڑا گروپ تھا۔ پانچ ریاستوں یعنی اتر پردیش، بہار، مہاراشٹر، آندھرا پردیش اور کرناٹک میں ۴ کروڑ ۱۵ لاکھ اردو بولنے

Annexure

ایک بے خانماں زبان کو درپیش چیلنج:
عصری ہندوستان میں اردو

وائس چانسلر پروفیسر دنیش سنگھ صاحب

پروفیسر سدھیش پچوری صاحب

پروفیسر توقیر احمد خاں صاحب

یہ میخانہ ہے، بزم جم نہیں ہے
یہاں کوئی کسی سے کم نہیں ہے

کہا جاتا ہے کہ کسی یونیورسٹی کے چانسلر کی شکل کبھی کبھار ہی نظر آنی چاہئے اور اس کی آواز شاذ و نادر ہی سنی جانی چاہئے۔ اس وجہ سے اور کچھ دیگر اسباب کی بنا پر، میں اس بات کو اپنے لئے باعث افتخار سمجھتا ہوں کہ مجھے دہلی یونیورسٹی کا انتیس واں نظام لیکچر دینے کے لئے مدعو کیا گیا۔ اس اعزاز کے لئے میں وائس چانسلر جناب دنیش سنگھ صاحب اور شعبۂ اردو کے صدر پروفیسر توقیر احمد خاں صاحب کا شکر گزار ہوں۔

حاضرین میں سے بعض کو یہ علم ہوگا کہ میں تقریباً چالیس برس تک سفارت کار رہا ہوں اور اس دوران میں نے غیر ملکی حکومتوں اور سامعین کو اپنے ملک کے تنوع اور بے مثل سماجی وثقافتی رنگا رنگی

Note: Refer to page no. 434 to 451 for English translation of Urdu speech